BIOPHILIA

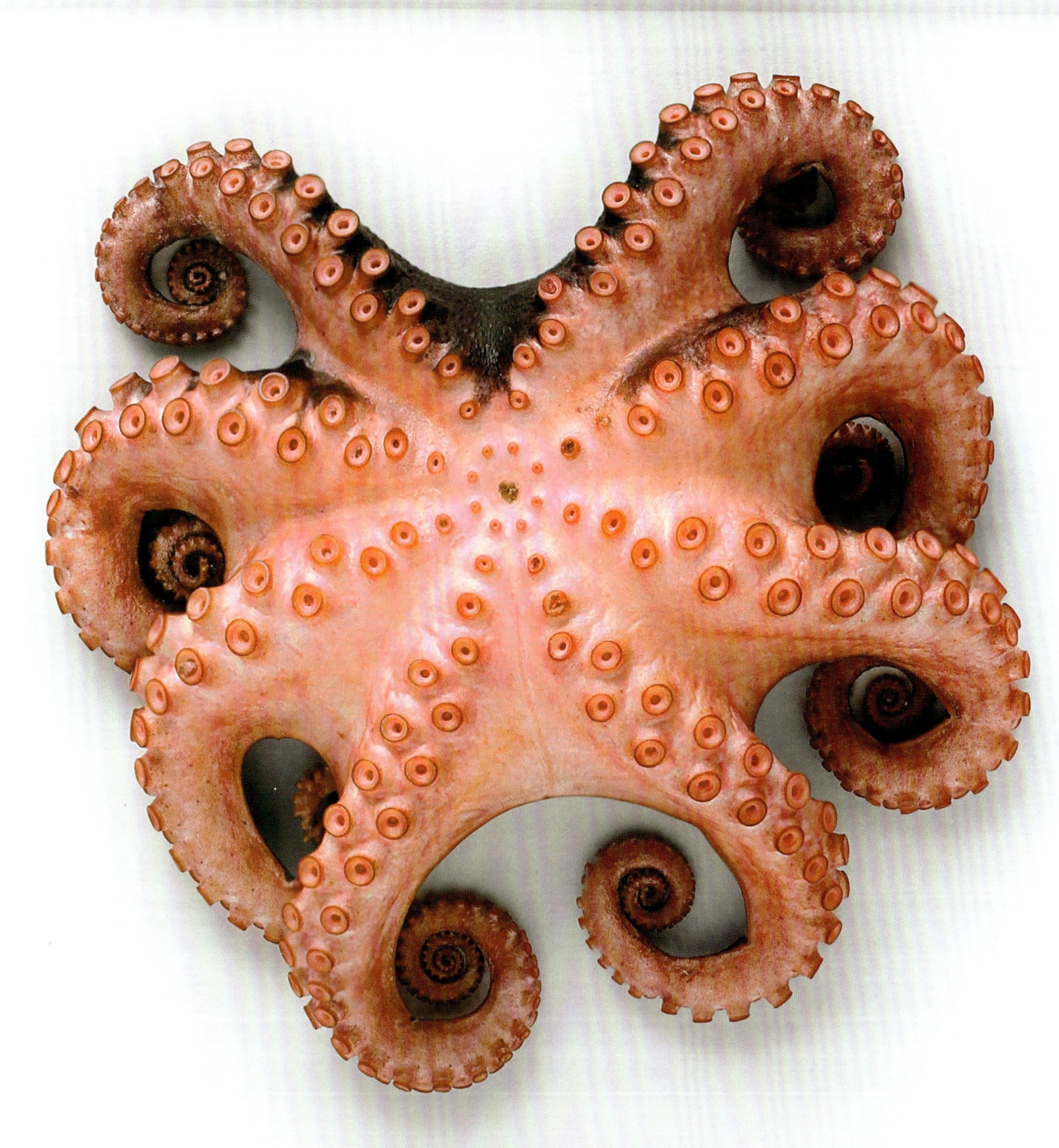

BIOPHILIA

CHRISTOPHER MARLEY

Abrams, New York

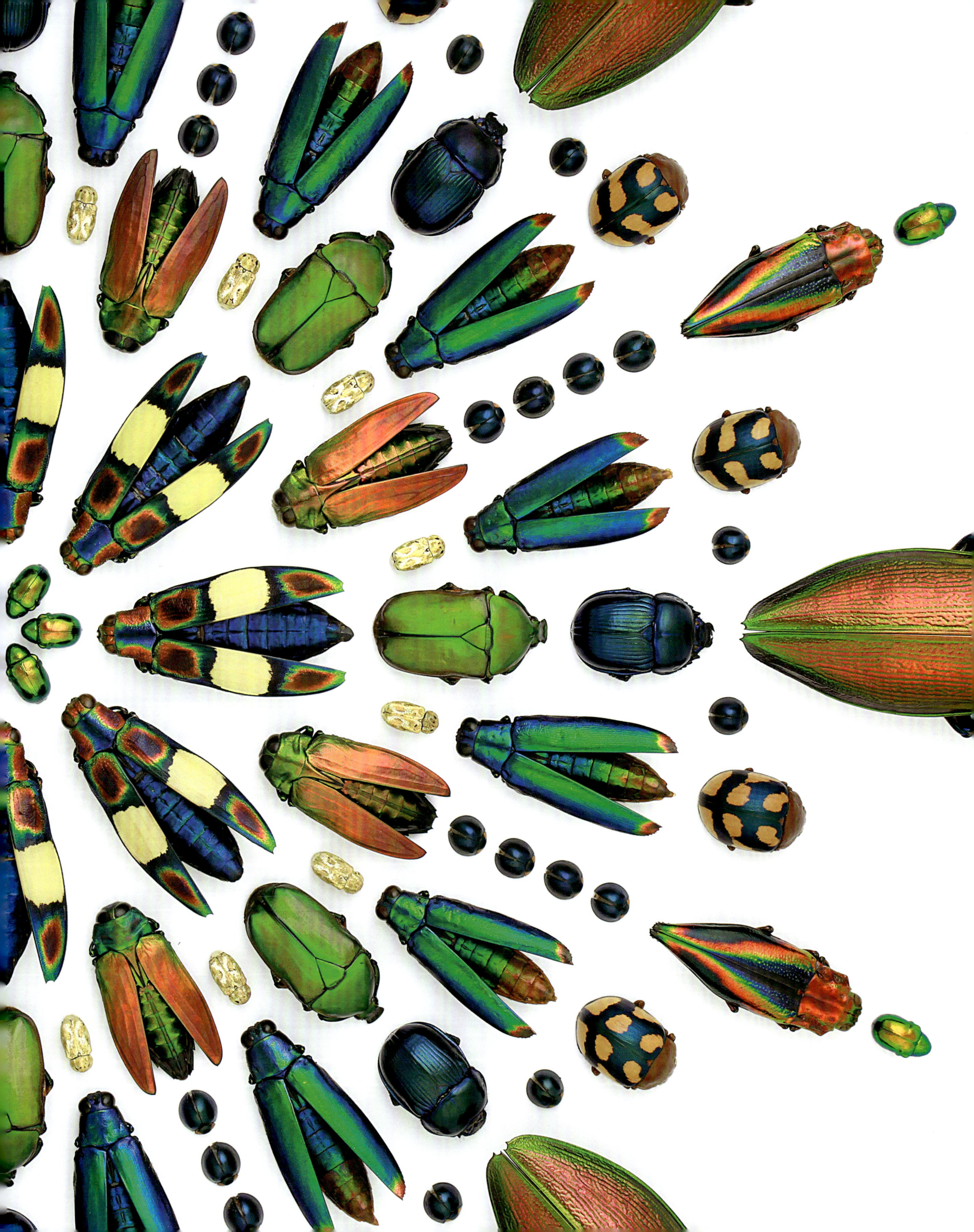

CONTENTS

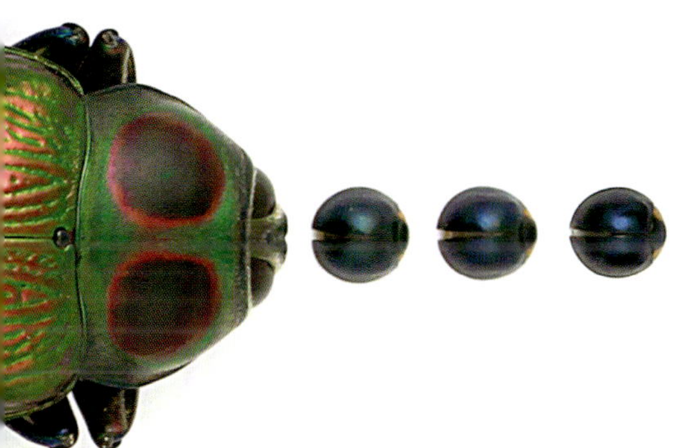

VIRAL AFFECTION

WE'RE ALL INFECTED

Biophilia is a condition that, to one degree or another, affects all of humanity. It is not a disease (though if it were, I'd have a raging case of it) but an instinctive sense of kinship with the rest of the living, breathing world. It is, literally translated, "love of life." The word is attributed to psychoanalyst and philosopher Erich Fromm, who defined it as, "the passionate love of life and of all that is alive," in his *Anatomy of Human Destructiveness.* Biophilia is pervasive, impellent, and very likely the reason you are reading this book.

As human beings, we are at the top of the food chain in every ecosystem that we inhabit, yet we retain an innate affection for the rest of creation. I have never met—indeed, I cannot imagine—a person who does not derive stimulation and fulfillment from some form of life apart from our own species, one who cannot and does not appreciate a single plant or single nonhuman animal species. I suspect that if such a person exists, he or she must be abjectly miserable or purely evil.

It is our biophilia that causes us to find so much beauty and satisfaction in nature. We do not love nature because it is beautiful; we find beauty in nature because we are a part of it, and it is a part of us. And, as with our own bodies, we are programmed to care for it, to cherish it, and to be good stewards of it. Honest arguments as to the most effective methods to fulfill these obligations, and how best to balance the needs of nature with the needs of humankind, are legion (don't I know it), but it goes against our instincts to be disdainful of the natural world or to wish it harm, just as it goes against our nature to disdain ourselves and do ourselves harm.

Theories abound regarding the origins of our biophilia. Famed biologist E. O. Wilson hypothesizes that it is an inevitable result of our evolutionary genealogy; that our long history of dependence on nature for survival has produced in us an instinctive bond that persists even as our cultures become increasingly urbanized. Others hold that biophilia is a component of our divine DNA—an abiding reverence and appreciation for the creations with which we share our planet. For my part, I hold to the latter, but whether our biophilia evolved with us or was placed in us, the fact remains indisputable that we as a species are burdened with a stewardship over this planet. To aid us in fulfilling that obligation, we have within us an appreciation, an empathy, and an affection for the life systems around us. Thankfully, it is a symbiotic relationship. The more we grow in understanding and appreciation of the natural world and the more we invest in it, the greater the peace, satisfaction, and joy we receive from our association in return, just as we involuntarily develop love for those people we truly understand and serve. As with all ordained goodness, the more we give, the more we receive.

As an artist and a chronically afflicted biophiliac, I have scoured the globe exploring, studying, and seeking exquisite natural specimens to incorporate into my work and share with an increasingly digitized populace. I began with insects, and they remain my area of expertise, but I thoroughly relish being immersed in the beauty of every aspect of the natural world—animal, vegetable, and mineral.

WHERE'S THE LOVE?

When I began, fifteen years ago, to create artwork that used arthropods as my medium, I was uncertain if people would welcome such creatures into their homes, even in the form of works of art. When I opened an art gallery in Hermosa Beach, California, to showcase my work, I found that nearly every visitor was eager to recount his or her own visceral memory of an unexpected encounter with a bug—and the vast majority of these were negative. So common were the conversations that I wondered at the time if my little gallery might have been a unique healing place where people could cathartically confess their insect phobias. But after thousands of exchanges and years of appearances at book signings and speaking engagements, I've come to realize just how common and indelible human-bug interactions are.

At least on the surface, our innate need to interact with the nonhuman life-forms that surround us appears to be a love-hate relationship. Surely there is nothing more quintessentially natural than erratic, ever-present insects; however, there does not seem to be an overabundance of adoration aimed at them nor a lot of healing therapy that incorporates them. If we are supposedly possessed with an unalterable need to associate with nonhuman organisms, how can we collectively loathe the most common among them?

I am no exception. As I related in my book *Pheromone*, I spent the first thirty years of my life with a stifling phobia of insects. When I began to experiment with utilizing insects in artwork, my fear dramatically reversed polarity, and I became just as emphatically infatuated with them. However, even my transformation from bug-phobe to bug-phile has been embarrassingly schizophrenic.

For example, a few years ago I was working in Costa Rica with Jimmy Flott, a Central American jewel scarab expert and dear friend. At the time, there was some interest in turning my odd occupation into a reality TV series (apparently it was too odd even for reality TV), and we wanted to collect and film in an unexplored area. Jimmy secured permission for us to work on tribal lands in his country, where foreigners are not often permitted. We hiked in with portable generators and mercury vapor lights to attract a sampling of nocturnal species, and we spent many hours covered in insects of every stripe—some huge, some scary, and some dangerous. As we jockeyed for the biggest, most outrageous catches through the night, I fearlessly came away with the winner. It was the largest *Acrocinus longimanus* I'd ever seen, a ferocious longhorn beetle with a powerful bite. My primal phobia of insects had obviously been vanquished—that is, until we shut off the generator and tried to get a few hours of sleep. It was then, in the pitch-blackness, that I lay awake for most of the night, scared sleepless by the thought of what might crawl across my face should I doze off. In spite of my having spent the preceding decade exploring jungles the world over hunting insects, I couldn't escape my childhood fears. I felt like an idiot.

It has become abundantly clear to me that where arthropods are concerned, there is very little middle ground. They are otherworldly enough to fit only awkwardly into the loosest interpretation of our nature-love. There is a pervasive, uneasy familiarity—an unrequested intimacy that has tainted the human race against them—yet we cannot ignore their presence. Like an embarrassing uncle or delinquent stepbrother; we don't necessarily want to have anything to do with them, but they're still family. This emotional dichotomy seems to stick in our collective craw.

SCIENCE IS NOT IMMUNE

As I've come to the realization that insects are, in the psyche of most of the human population, in a class of nature by themselves, I've also noticed that entomology, the scientific study of insects, is distinct from other branches of zoology in at least one overarching way.

It seems that other branches of zoology are chiefly concerned with their respective subjects for their own sake, for the purpose of better understanding their behavior, establishing their taxonomic hierarchy, and, especially, conserving them. The herpetologist observing monitor lizards, the ornithologist who spends years with wrens or turacos or cockatoos, the cetologist studying baleen whales—all are chiefly concerned with the animals in their own right and with trying to protect *them* from *us*.

With arthropods, however, it is usually the other way around. The vast majority of entomologists are more concerned with how the insect world is affecting some aspect of human life. We want to know why insects do what they do for *our* sake. Why do they eat our homes? How do they transmit diseases to us? What does their life cycle tell us about a death or crime? How do they destroy our crops or decimate our forests? In the world of entomology, perhaps more than in any other branch of zoology, it's all about us. And yet precious little attention is focused on studying the emotional and spiritual effects insects have on humanity. These deep-seated feelings are not simply innate fears or inherited prejudices. In my experience, the man-bug emotional construct is surprisingly abstruse.

ENTOMOLOGICAL PSYCHOLOGY OR PSYCHOLOGICAL ENTOMOLOGY?

I have been moved by the myriad communications I've had with collectors of my work—as well as detractors—that illustrate the fact that some of mankind's most affecting interactions with nature revolve around arthropods.

I have a client who is a therapist specializing in the treatment of severely traumatized children, and she regularly incorporates insect specimens in her therapy sessions. She role-plays with her patients, using the ugly bugs as the bad guys and the pretty ones as the good guys, and has found that insects are a more effective vicarious role-playing medium for her patients than the more traditional ones used to help hurting children tell their stories.

A woman found me at a book signing in San Francisco to tearfully express her appreciation for being given a beautiful way to remember her young daughter, who had recently passed from leukemia. The child had been crazy about bugs, and one of the defining joys they had shared was chasing after butterflies together.

A lovely actress recounted to me an experience she had while performing onstage at the Sundance Theatre. A large tiger swallowtail butterfly landed on her hand and stayed there for more than a minute while she carried on her soliloquy. She earnestly related that it took everything in her power not to stop in the middle of her performance and just relish the experience.

It is important to note that these poignant interactions are not relegated to the uninitiated. Scientists from Charles Darwin to Wilson and Bernard d'Abrera tell of their most deeply held beliefs being confirmed, if not formed, by their experiences with insects. It is apparent to me that a study of the emotional and psychological effects that insects have on us, and how they fit in the biophilic scheme of things, is in order.

BEAUTY CLEARS THE FOG

The phylum Arthropoda presents a dizzying diversity of millions of species, which is both an impetus for our instinctive, emotional reactions and a hindrance to processing them. The need that drove Carl Linnaeus to create a comprehensible system for ordering the world's organisms almost three hundred years ago is present in all of us. But arthropods are so incomprehensibly diverse that even today there is no complete catalog of them. Entomologists can't even agree on how many species have been described, let alone guess at how many might remain to be discovered. They range in color, size, shape, texture, and behavior like no other creatures. This unknowable quality simultaneously fuels people's imaginations and arouses their suspicions. It keeps us wary yet (even if only subconsciously) intrigued.

We need a coherent frame of reference to process this pervasive, chaotic realm and reconcile largely negative feelings about bugs with the love we are programmed to feel for the organisms that share our world. In my experience, the most effective way to help open our collective arms and welcome even the most maligned creatures into our embrace is to heighten our appreciation for their aesthetics. This is one of the most valuable purposes my work serves. I have found that when my subjects are meticulously composed, it makes the translation more intelligible for the public at large, just as random musical notes, once properly orchestrated, can enter the heart and sway it almost against our volition. Once an appreciation for the aesthetics of insects is born, it is amazing how quickly old prejudices and stereotypes fall away. When people begin to see beauty where they had previously known only a mundane, distasteful, or even frightening world of arcane organisms, positive changes in their perceptions of arthropods as a whole are sure to follow.

I *almost* completely agree with the well-known quote of the Senegalese environmentalist Baba Dioum, "In the end, we will conserve only what we love, we will love only what we understand, and we will understand only what we are taught." But the final line rubs me the wrong way. I believe that we will only truly understand what we experience. The general populace does not need to be told what to think and feel about the mysterious world of insects. The emotional investment is already there in spades. People do, however, need the opportunity to have comprehensible experiences with them. I am confident that these types of experiences will result in understanding, and that this understanding will lead to awe, even love.

If the work I do provides no other benefit than to kindle a new appreciation of insects (and any other creatures that evoke trepidation in the human heart), that is enough for me. It is the primary reason why I do what I do: because it brings people—myself and others—joy.

So here's to biophilia infecting us all just a little more acutely. In my experience, it is a contagion with uniquely healing properties.

RECLAMATION

and the Pursuit of the Karma-Friendly Taxidermic Experience

I hate killing things. I grew up in a family of hunters and went a few times myself. I have every respect for responsible hunters, who are among the most effective practical environmentalists, not to mention our original conservationists. And there were some aspects of hunting that I loved: getting outdoors, witnessing wild habitats mingled with even wilder animal life, and experiencing these enigmatic creatures up close. But the actual killing of an animal—I just couldn't get past the acute sense of loss I always experienced. It was a heavy, poignant feeling. Not a valueless one, but for me not an enjoyable one either.

I don't even like to kill insects. I am embarrassed to admit that to this day, I usually hand the specimens I net to one of my local catchers to dispatch. So when my particular form of artwork incorporating insect specimens began to take shape about a decade and a half ago, it was born with a congenital incongruity. Though I thrilled at the experience of colliding the unappreciated world of insects with the neoteric world of precision design, this inner conflict remained. The natural artifact itself cannot be improved upon by any artistic interpretation; of that I was certain. So to use the specimen itself in my work was and is the ultimate medium of design. But to take a life, even that of an insect, is burdensome and weighty—there is no avoiding it.

However, as I studied insect ecology, I came to understand that it is virtually impossible to over-collect an insect species using accepted collection methods in a healthy environment. As the bottom of the food chain, insects' prolific breeding enables them to feed entire forests. Consequently, a collector, or even several collectors, running around the jungle with a butterfly net can't hope to make an appreciable impact on insect populations. The real threat to insect populations all over the world is habitat destruction. If an insect species' habitat or host plant is destroyed, the entire population can be (and some have been) decimated in a single season. Insofar as insect collecting can provide economic benefits to local people by providing employment, it helps to reduce the pressure to turn habitats into farmland, thereby preserving the species that inhabit them. As self-serving as it may sound, the fact remains: Insect collecting is a boon to wild insect populations and their habitats. I find great satisfaction in knowing that the communities of insect aficionados I am helping to build are, in fact, aiding in the preservation of the very species being collected.

Unfortunately, the ecological benefits of responsible insect collecting don't usually apply to vertebrates. With very few exceptions, vertebrates do not breed like insects and do not rely on the presence of a single plant species to survive. In ecological terms, the value of the life of a single vertebrate animal is almost always higher than that of an insect, because it is so much more difficult to replace. And so it seemed that if I were to stay true to my conscience, my orderly vision for the natural world would necessarily be expressed solely in the realm of arthropods.

Then, a few years ago as I was wandering through my father's aviaries, I had an epiphany. Dad has been an avid breeder of midsize Australian parrots with rare color mutations since long before I came onto the scene. I don't know how or why he developed such an intense and specific passion, but he has perfected his husbandry and aviaries to a level that very few in his field could match. On this occasion, I reflexively opened one of the refrigerators where he stored the fresh fruits and vegetables that made up a part of the royal diet his birds enjoyed, and I noticed, as though for the first time, that his freezer contained some gorgeous dead birds: a plum-headed parakeet, some finches, and a couple of rosella parrots. When I was growing up, dead birds in the freezer were as typical a sight as pot roast, but now I wondered why my dad was saving them.

Everything dies, and when you have as many birds as my father does, you come to accept this as a matter of course. But for him, the passing of each bird is a true loss and, in some cases, a rather acute one. My father does not breed pets; his goal is to provide each bird with a healthy, undisturbed, and happy life, so the loss that he feels is not exactly intimate nor is it largely financial. I believe it is simply because it is a life, and to him, life is dear. That is why this hobby has been such an ardent passion for him and why, when one of his animals dies, it can't just be thrown in the garbage. There must be some time for emotional separation before that final disposal can take place. Hence, growing up, my siblings and I always dug past dead birds to get to our Popsicles and never thought anything of it.

I suddenly realized that my dilemma of wanting desperately to work with organisms of all kinds but not being willing to kill them had found a limited solution. In the case of my father's birds, at least, I could work with the specimens that died of natural causes. It may have been an extremely sparse and sporadic supply, but it was a start. It was a type of reclamation that I could feel good about. I might not be doing anything to help preserve a species, but I was certainly preserving the splendid beauty of an organism that would otherwise become worm food.

After months of methodically working through all of my years of accumulated contacts, I was overjoyed to find that there were other individuals and institutions, breeders, aviaries, aquariums, sanctuaries, and zoos that had similar practices. The opportunity to preserve rare and exotic birds, reptiles, and other vertebrates was suddenly becoming a reality. I was ecstatic.

Like my father, many of the people I work with really have no explanation for why they keep their dead creatures (except for the oft-claimed, "I was going to have them necropsied, but never got around to it"). However, I suspect the reason is always the same. All of these institutions and individuals are in the business of preserving, sustaining, and relishing life—the life of the creatures they feel the greatest fascination for and kinship with. This life has value that goes far beyond the merely financial or anthropomorphic, and the body that was a vessel for that life does not instantly become trash simply because it ceases animation. It is difficult to accept death, and so, in an attempt to moderate feelings of loss, there are individuals as well as institutions that keep their former treasures on ice. And for some of them, my work is exactly the alternative to worm food that they were hoping for.

INSECTS

I was nineteen when I received a letter advising me that my two-year missionary assignment would be to the Atacama Desert in Chile. Tellingly, my very first thought was, "Oh no! What kinds of bugs live there?"

My baptism of fire began in the border town of Arica. I was renting a room from a family that had two small boys. On the night of my arrival, I was getting ready for bed when a creature out of Middle-earth stomped across my wall and through a hole into the children's room next door. I jumped off my bed and ran through the house, screaming for everyone to get out.

As the alarmed family members were all running into each other and trying to understand my panicked Spanglish, the four-year-old approached me holding what appeared to be a mutant cockroach by the antennae. "You don't mean this?" he asked incredulously, as he held the struggling behemoth up to my face. Shockingly, I never regained their respect. I started finding roaches in impossible places—in my zipped-up toilet bag or tucked in tightly at the bottom of my bedcovers—and for some reason their carcasses always seemed to find their way into my shoes. It was extraordinarily not funny.

After I was transferred to the bustling city of Antofagasta, my situation deteriorated further when I moved into a pension that had seven particularly unhygienic dogs living on the roof. I would wake up each night covered in fleas, and as it turns out, you can't squish a flea. I would run outside to the bathroom, switch on the light, and then hop back and forth, giving the giant roaches that covered the walls and ceiling a few seconds to scatter. Entering the bathroom, I had to try to keep my eyes on the dozen or more beasts that remained, watching me hungrily as I ripped off my clothes and picked off fleas to throw into the toilet.

A few more years of exotic travel and similar bug interactions were like healthy doses of steroids to keep my phobia big and strong. In Hong Kong I went to a midnight showing of *Mimic*, a passable movie about sewer-dwelling roach things that ate people. After the movie I was walking down into the subway when a giant roach flew at me and landed on my cheek. If I could only package those moves. I'm pretty convinced that if not for roaches, my phobia might have subsided a couple of decades earlier than it did.

In the following pages you'll see what I have come to love about the world of arthropods. I now find their sleek design, outrageous colors, and diverse forms as enchanting as those of any other organisms in nature.

You'll notice a conspicuously glaring absence of roaches.

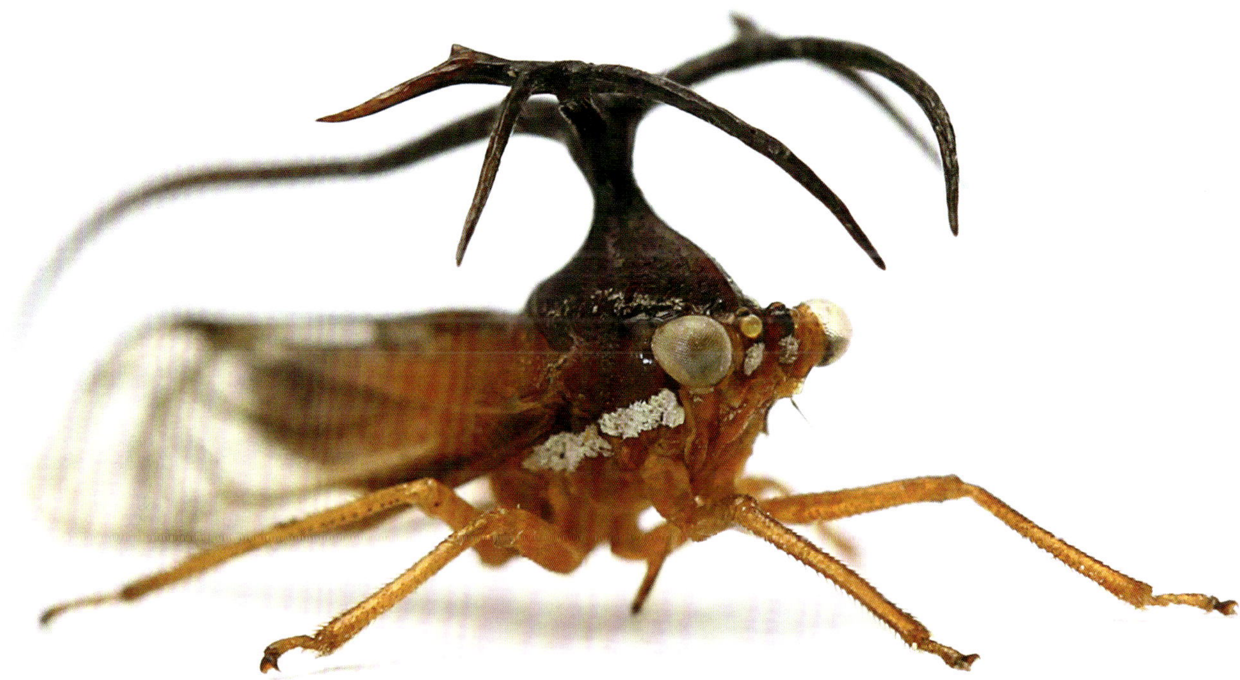

Treehopper

Venezuela

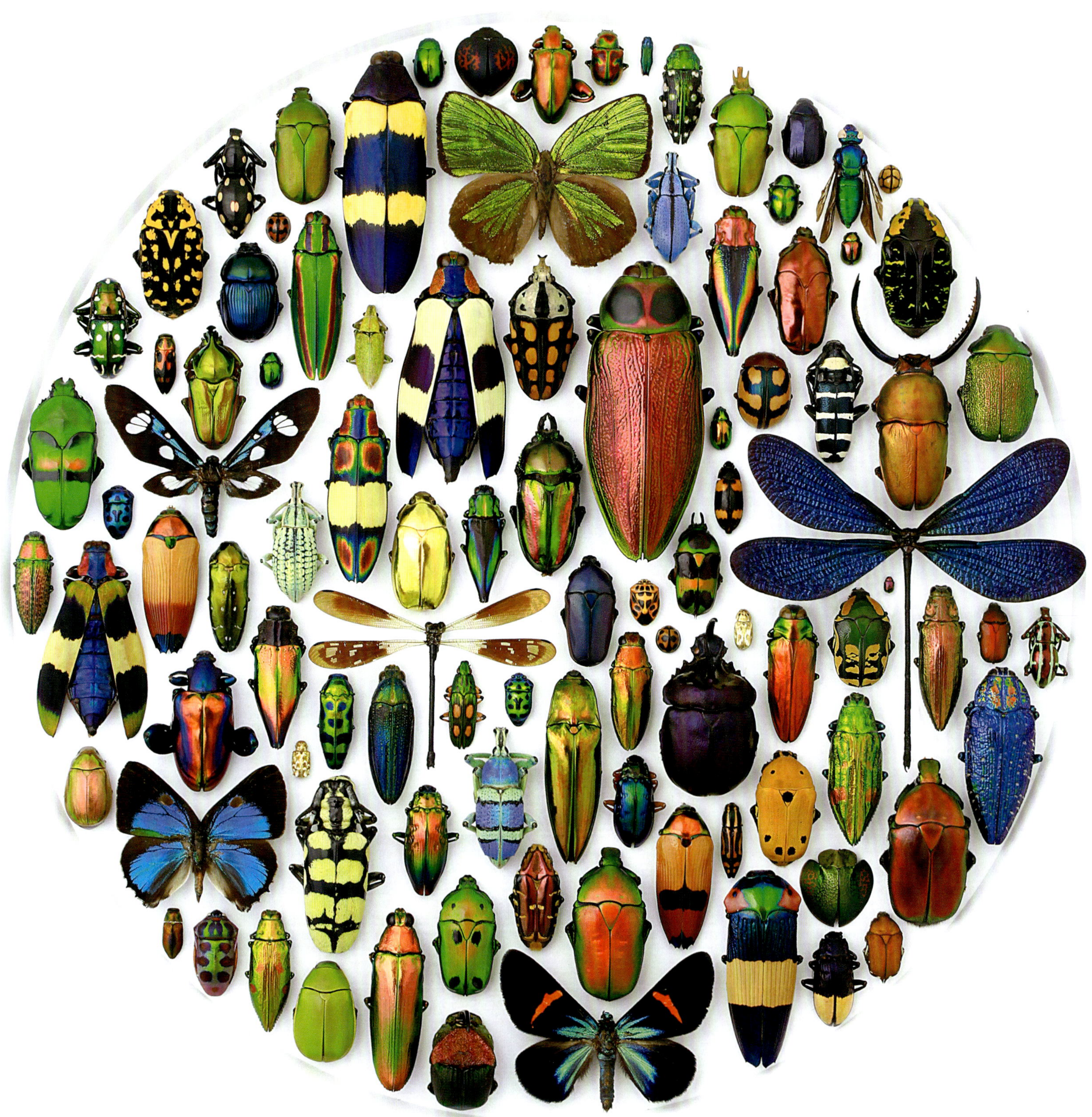

Aesthetica Sphere

Worldwide

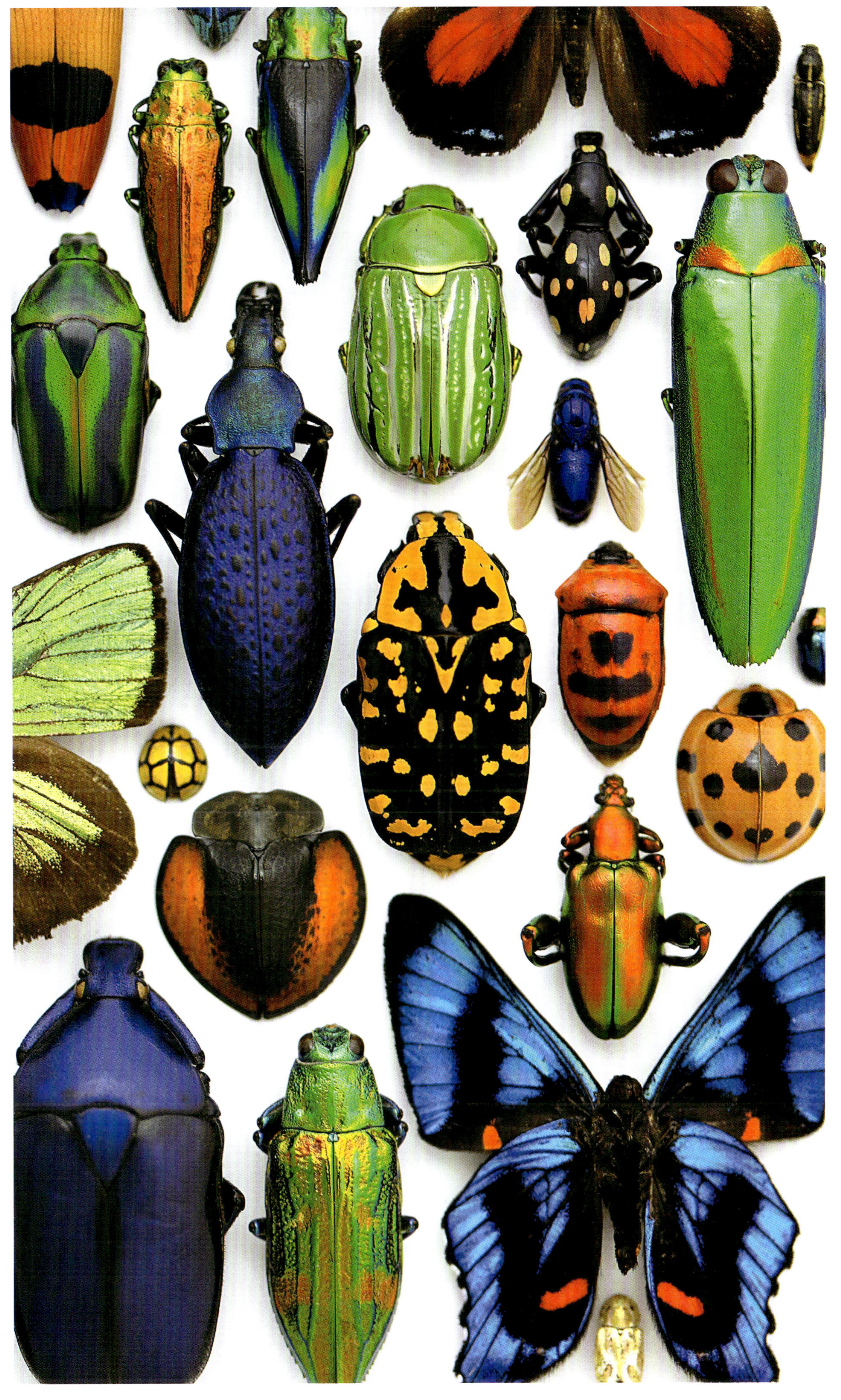

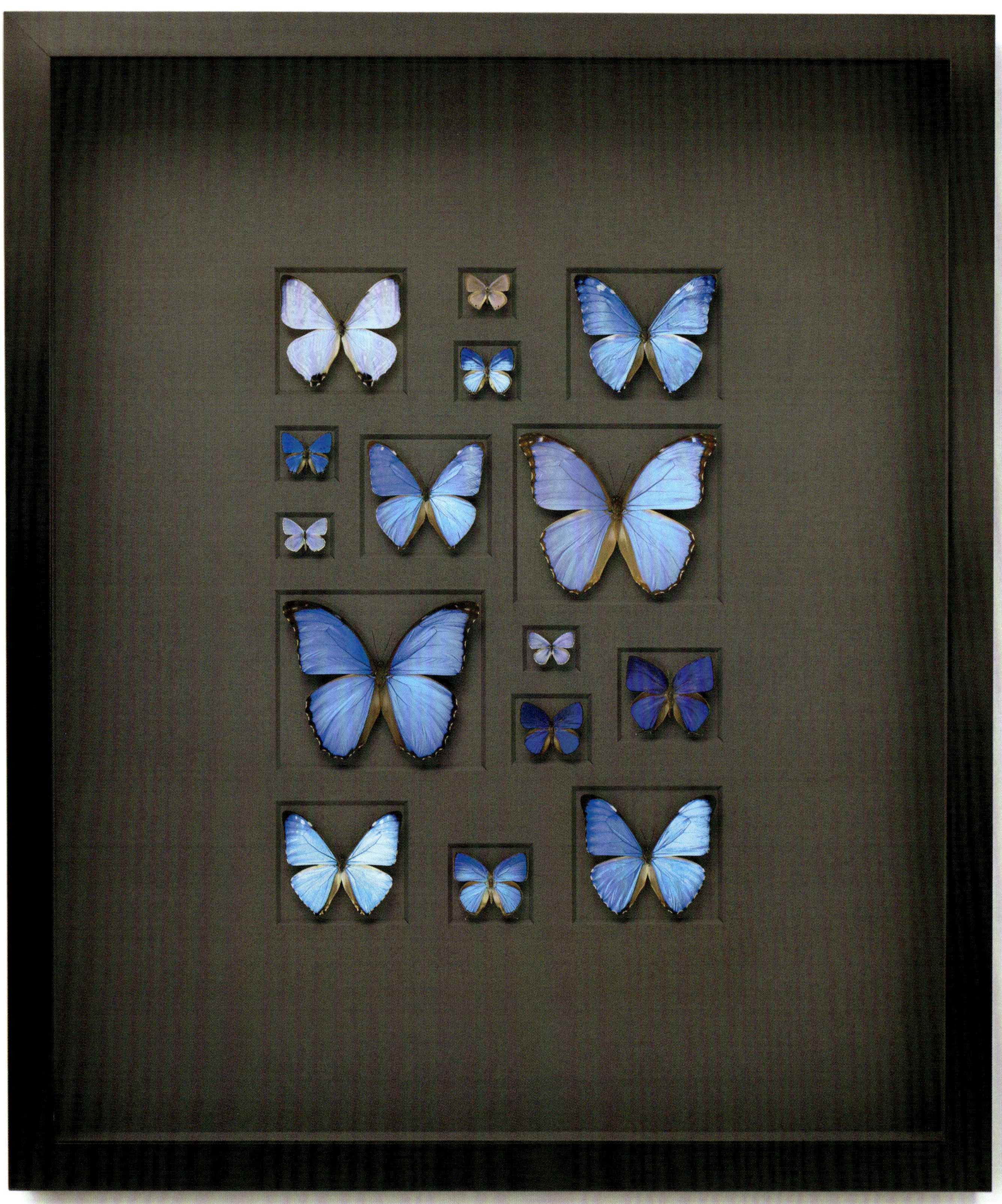

Cerulean Butterflies

Peru, Argentina, Brazil, Irian, Sulawesi, France

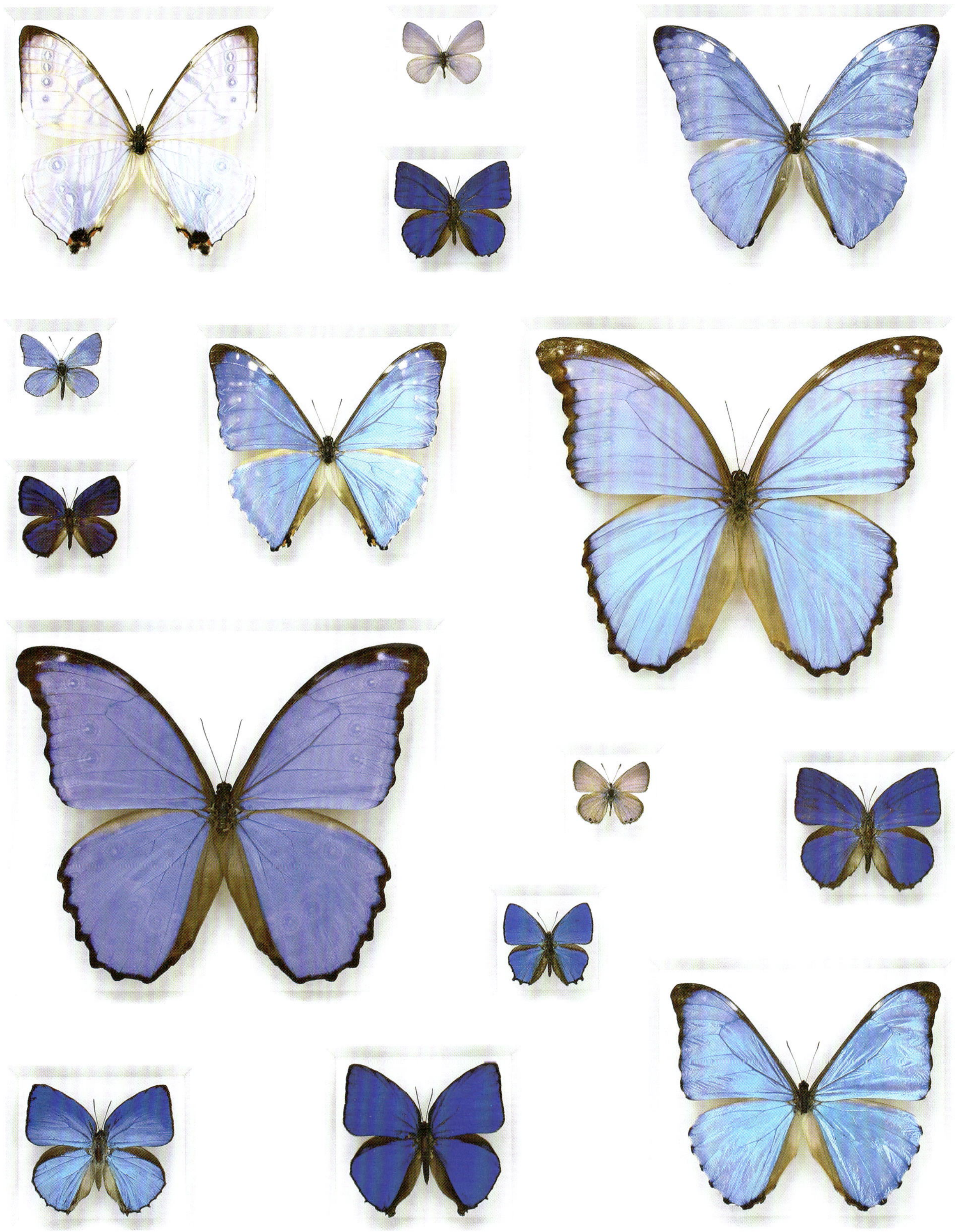

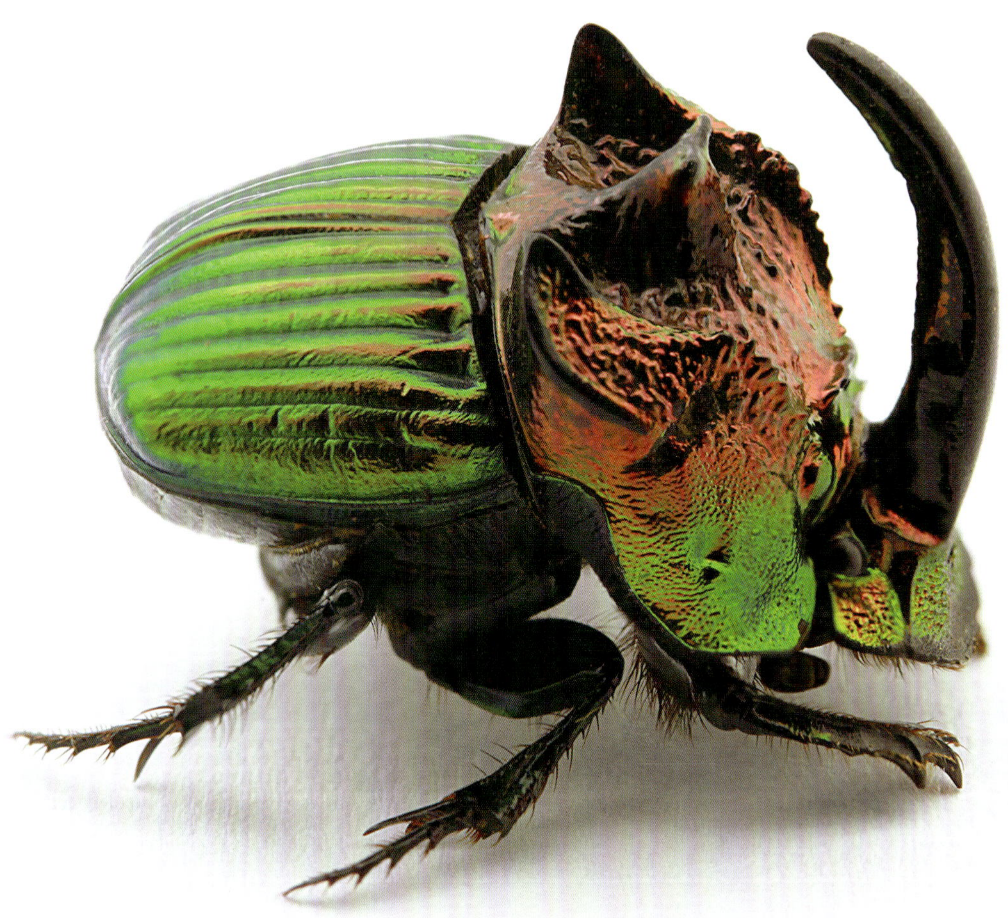

Rainbow Dung Beetle

United States

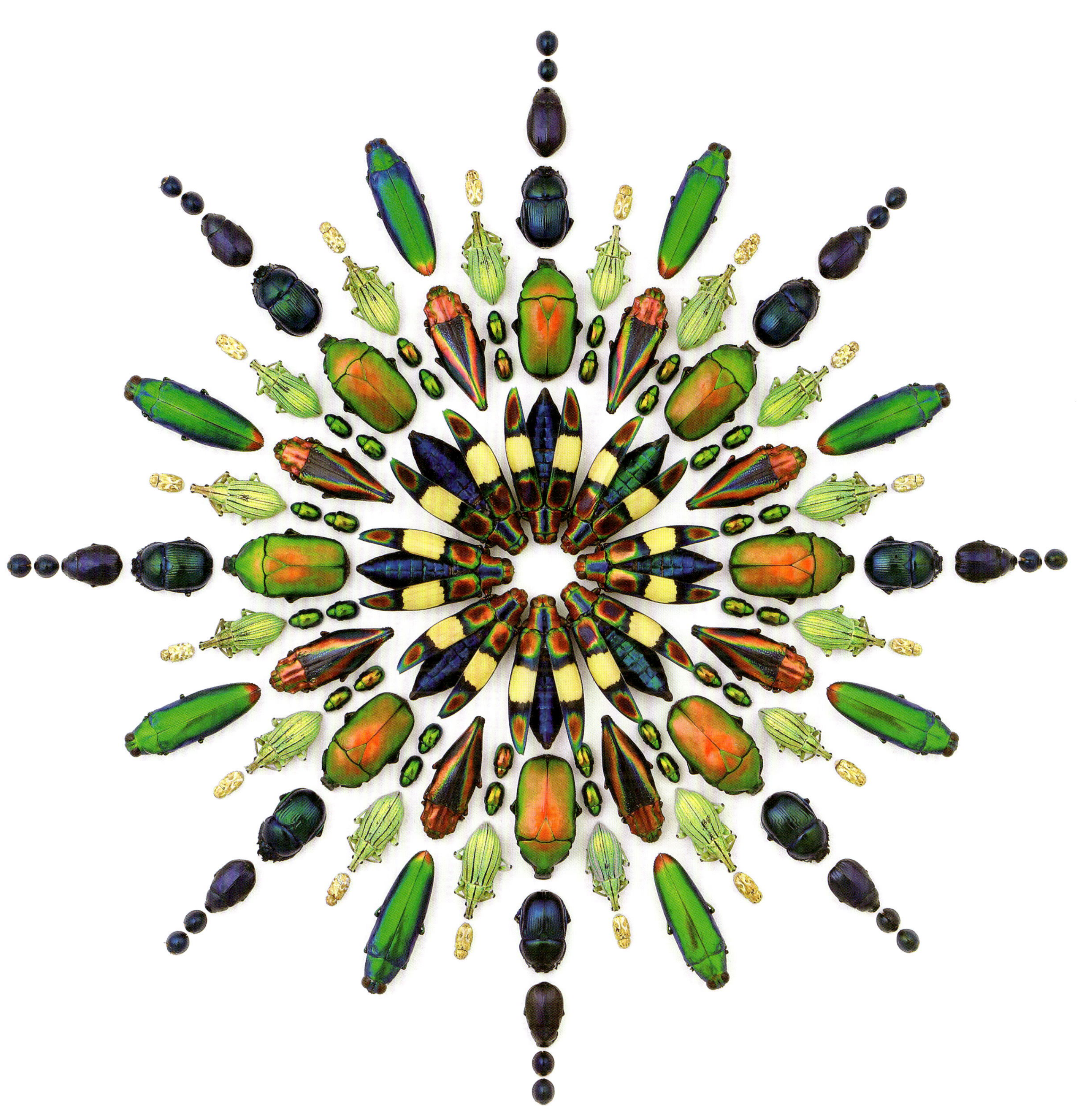

Fulgens Prism

Malaysia, Indonesia, Thailand, Japan

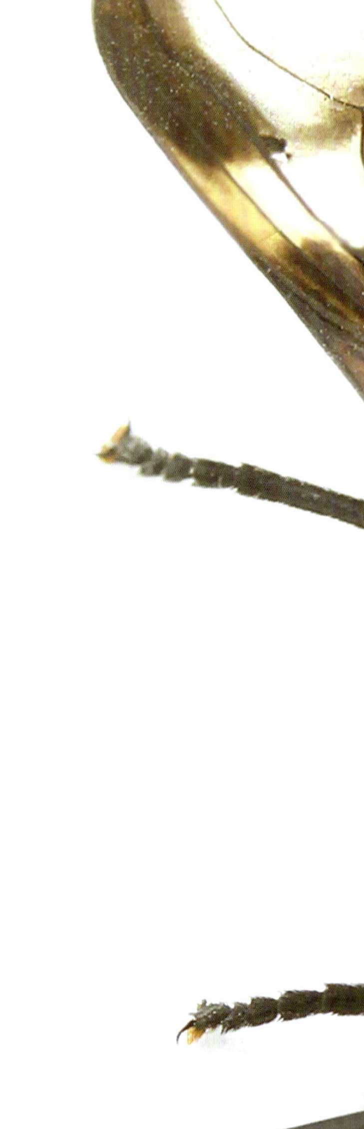

Stalk-Eyed Fly

Indonesia

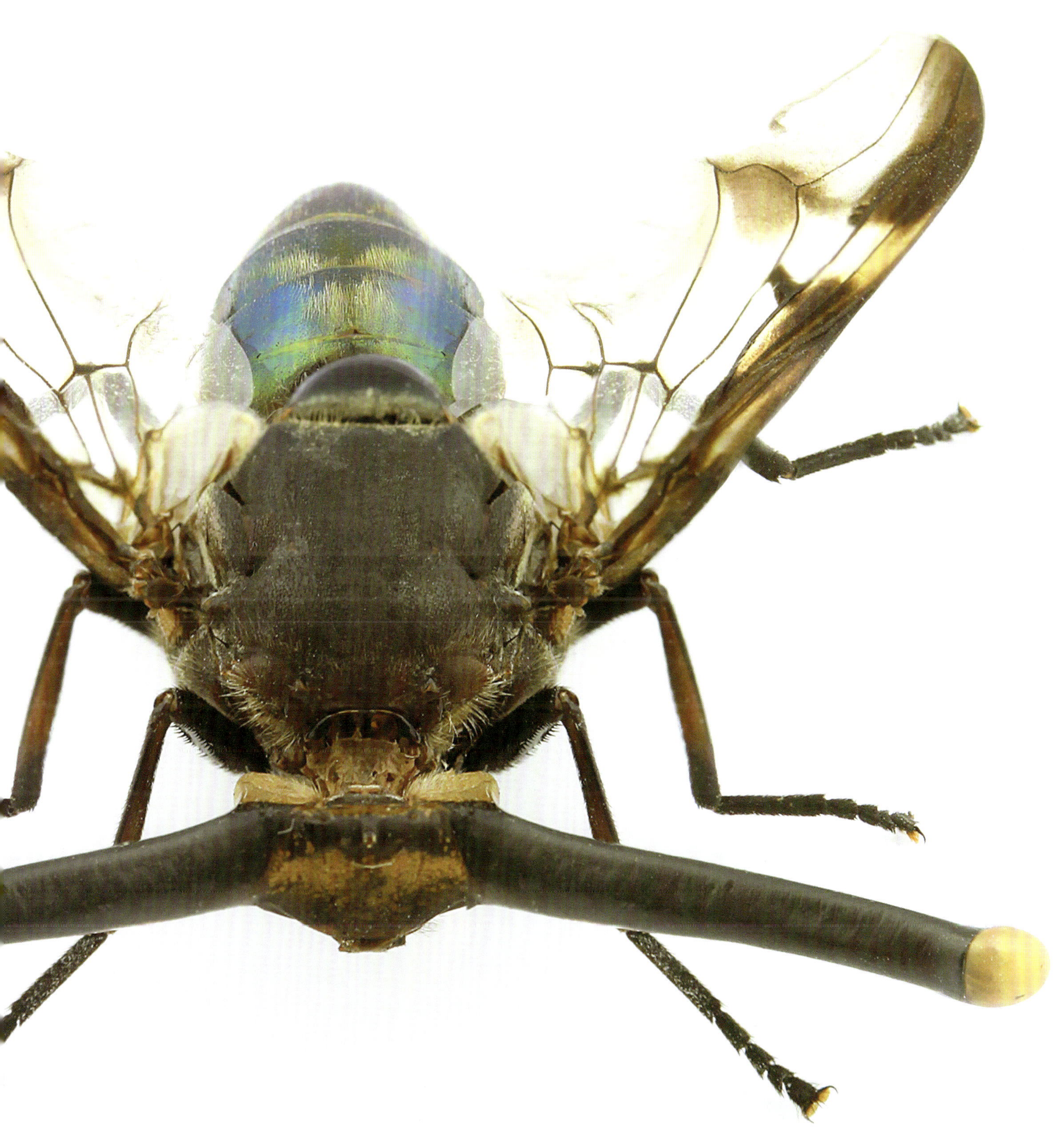

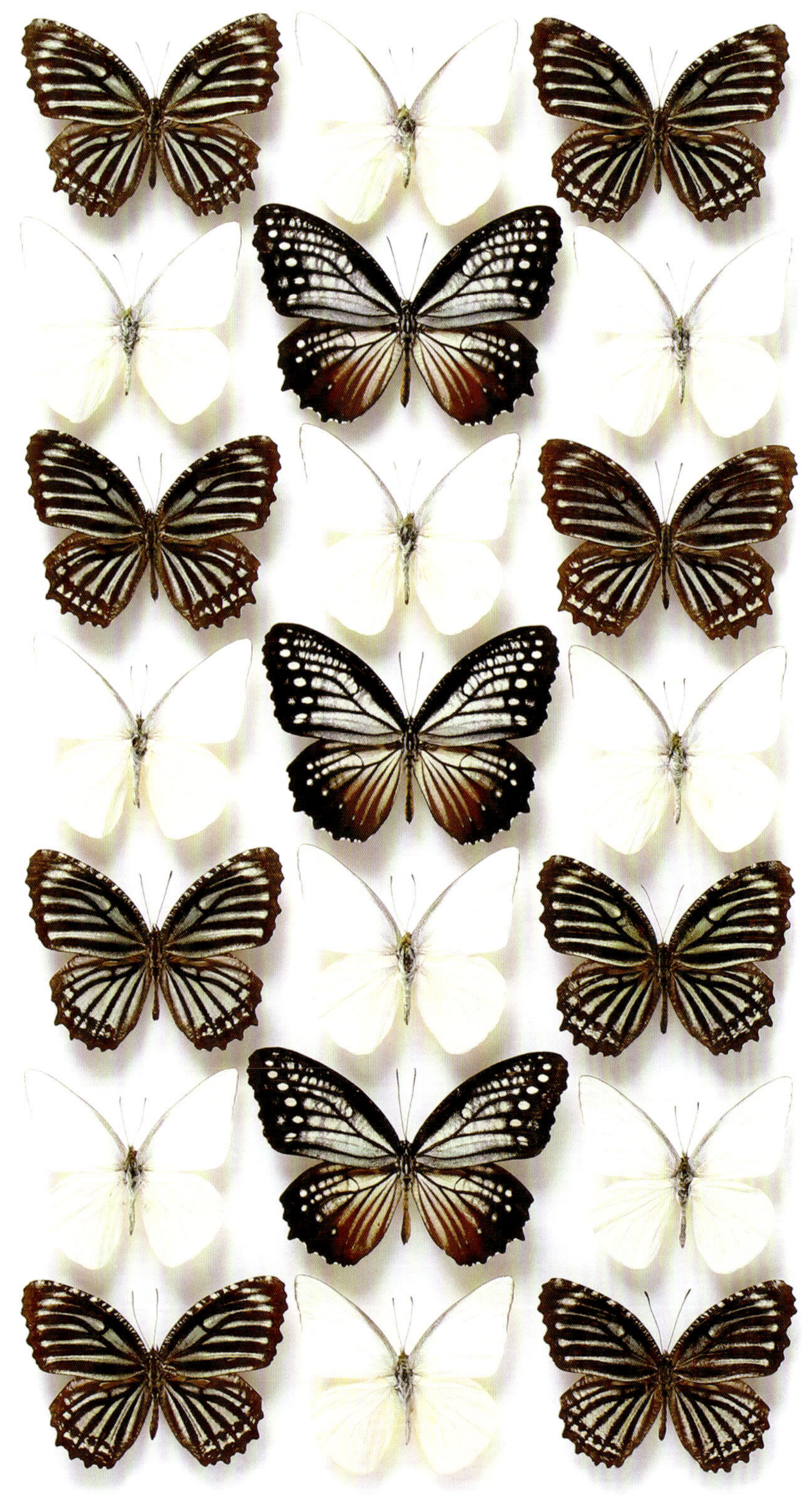

Elymnias

Bali, Mindoro

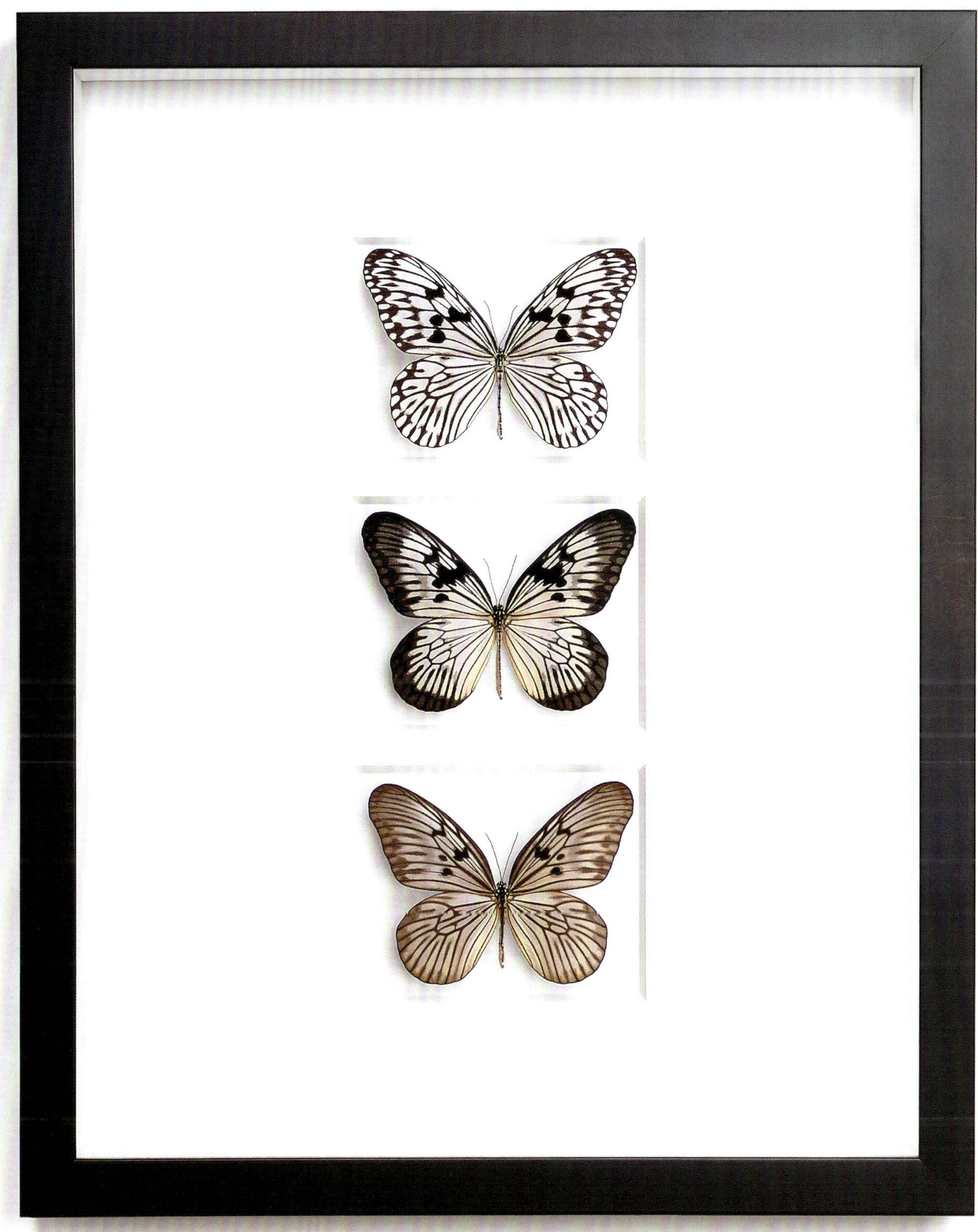

Rice Paper Butterfly Study

Indonesia

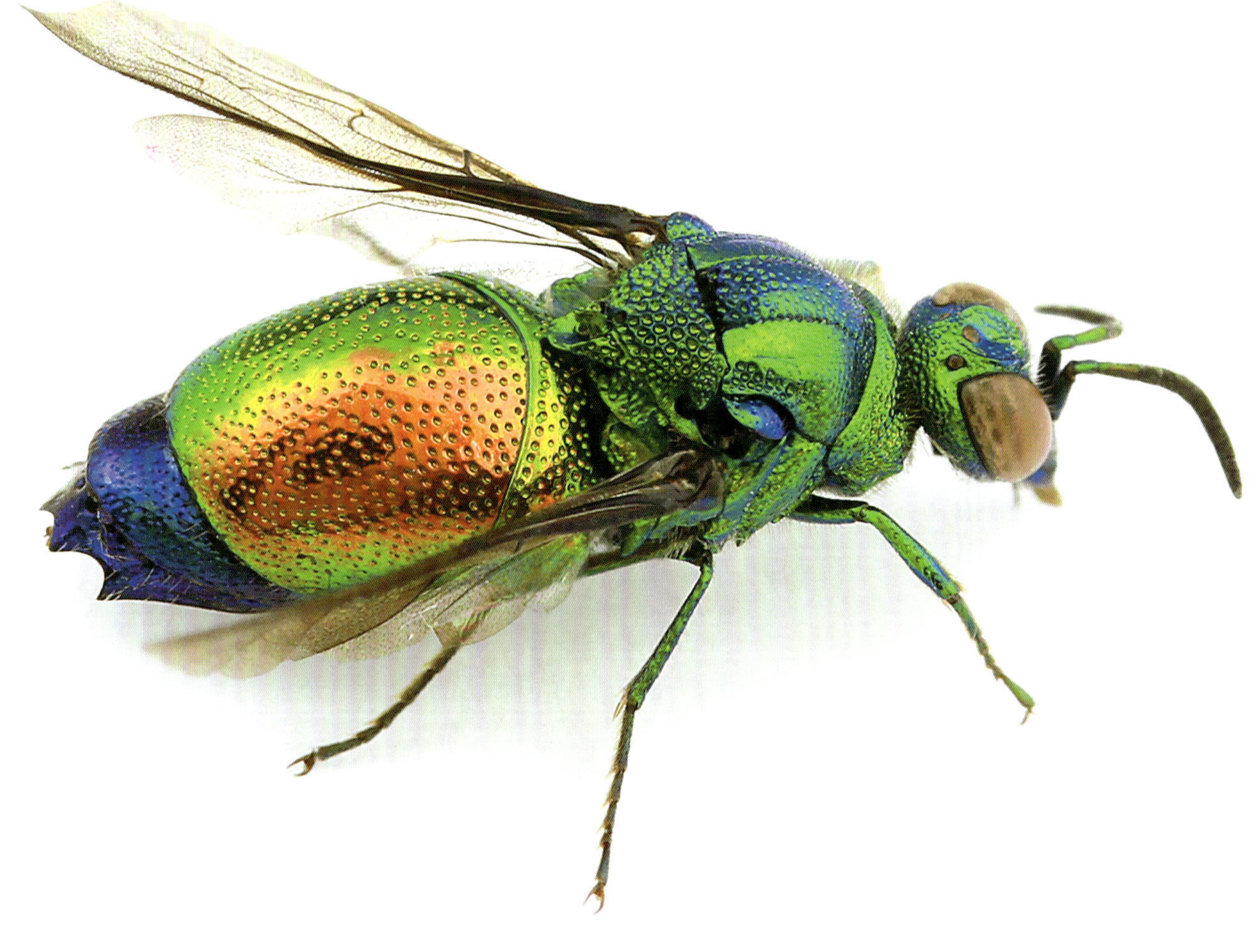

Cuckoo Wasp

Cyprus

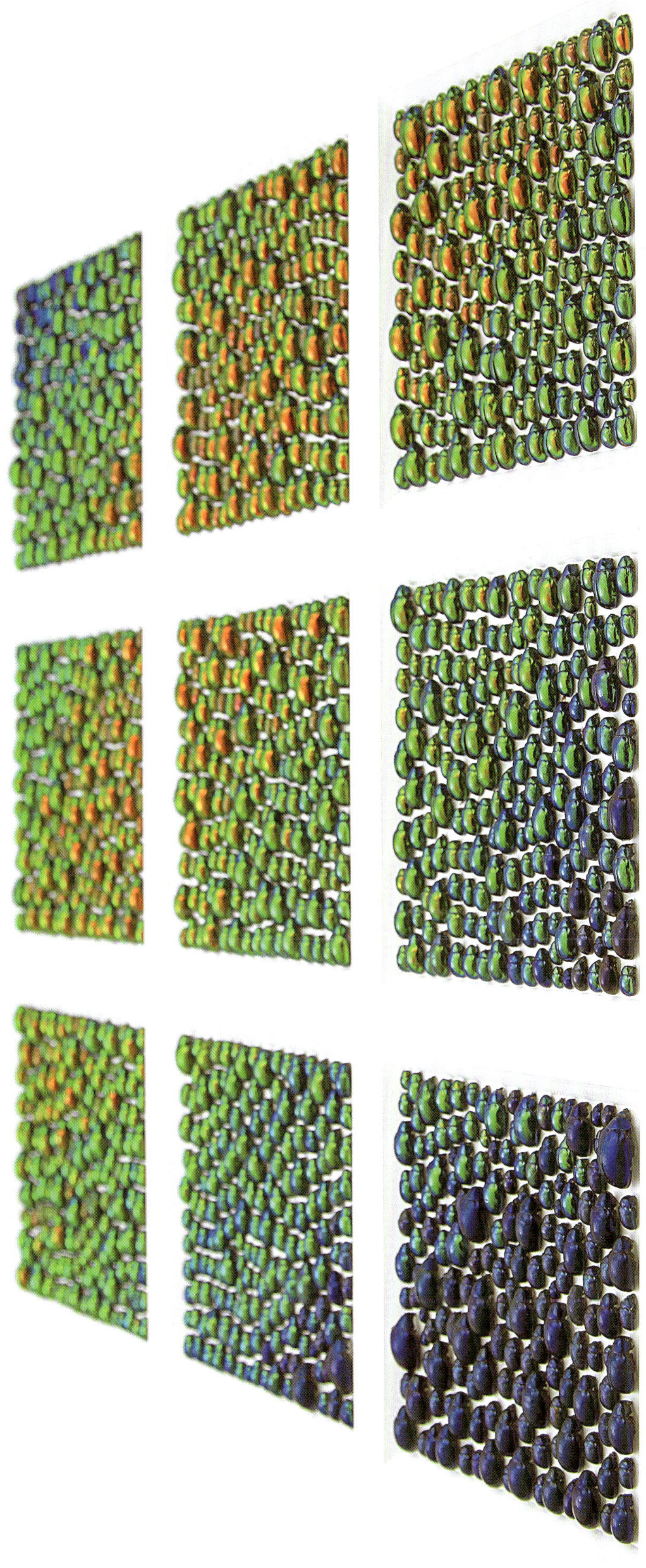

Chrysomelid Arrayal No. 1

Java, Peru

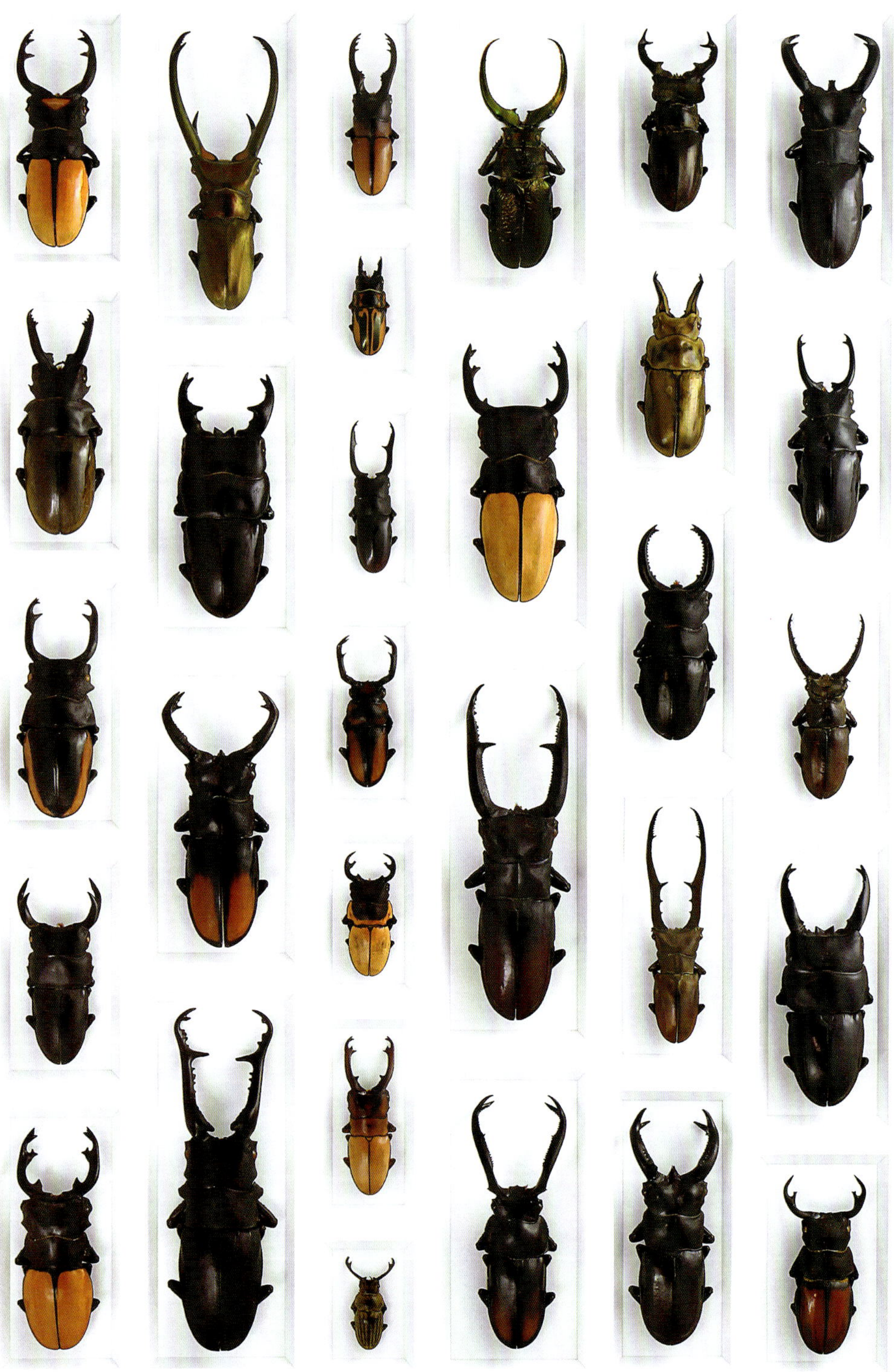

Limited Stag Beetle Mosaic

Indonesia, Thailand, Borneo, Chile

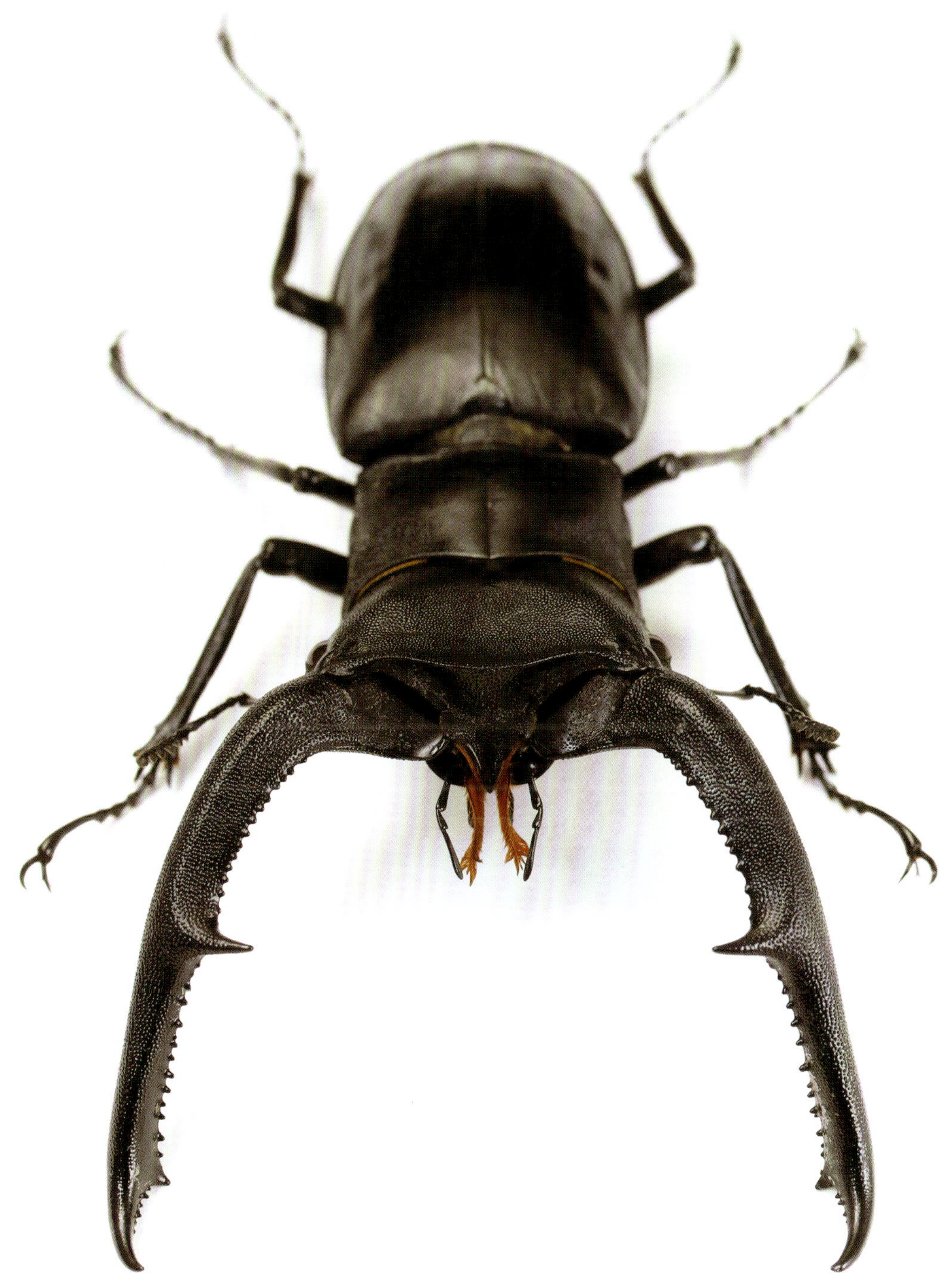

Stag Beetle

Indonesia

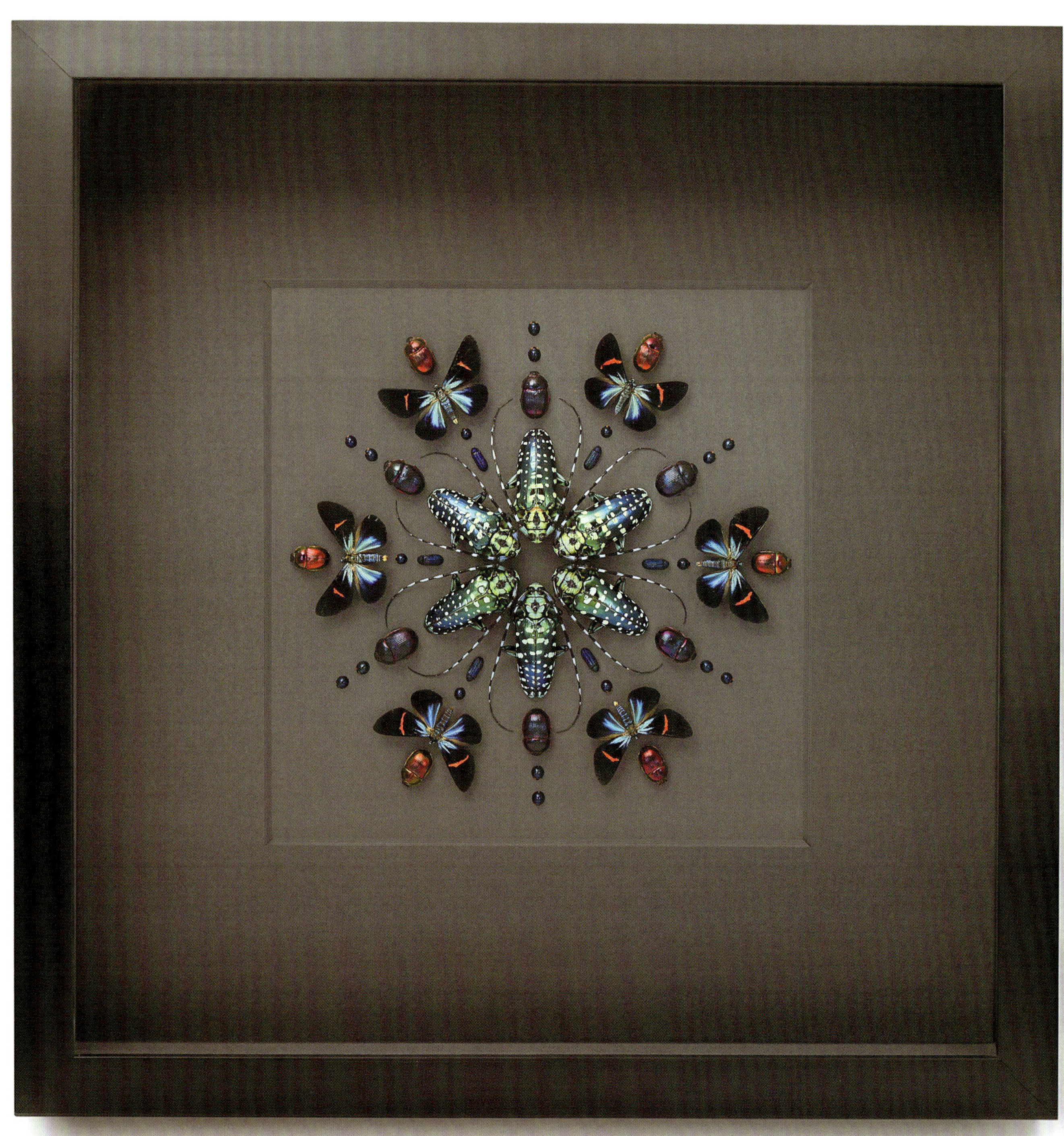

Solli Prism

Thailand, Cameroon, Japan, Indonesia, Bali

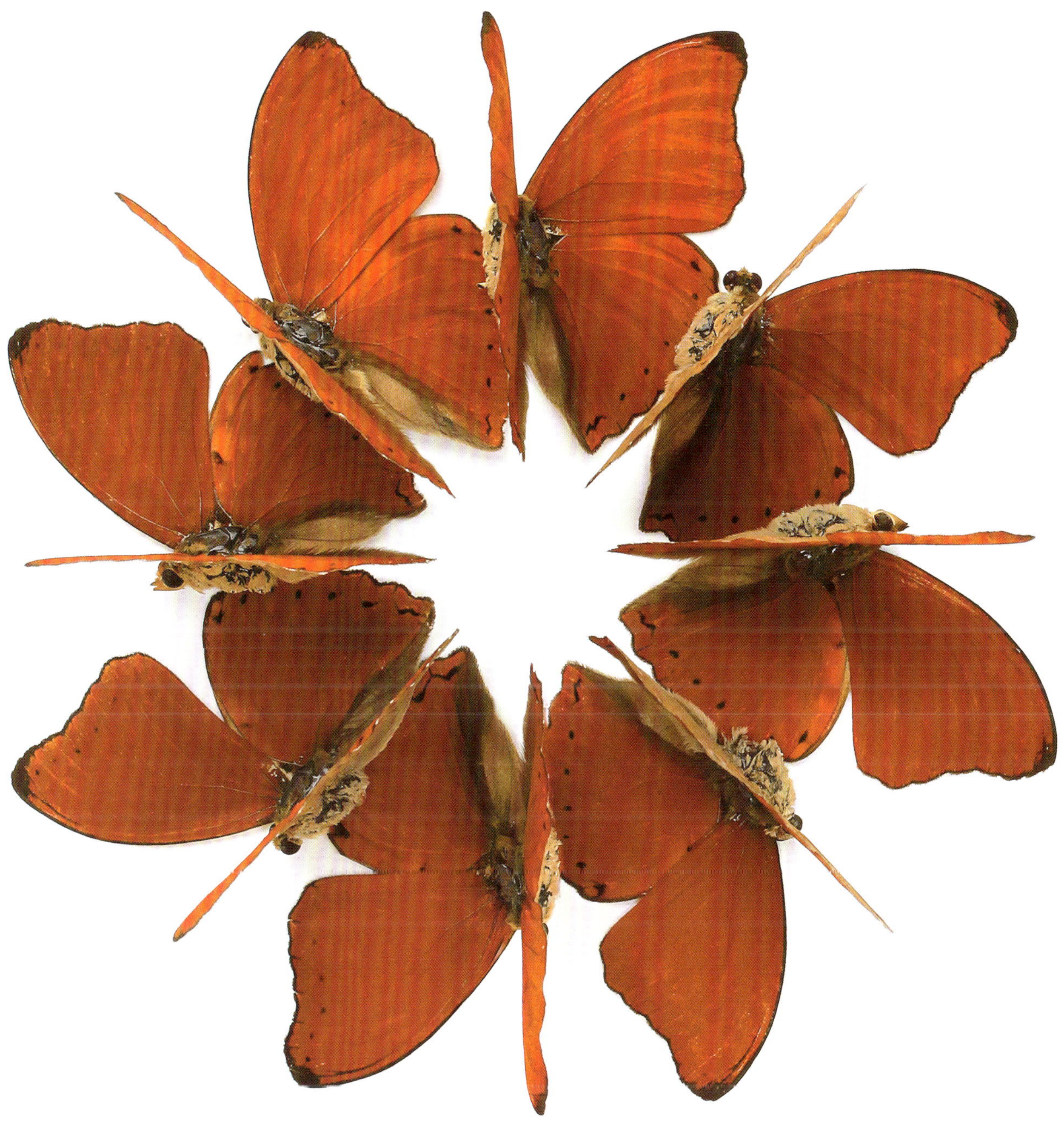

Sangaris Ellipse

Central African Republic

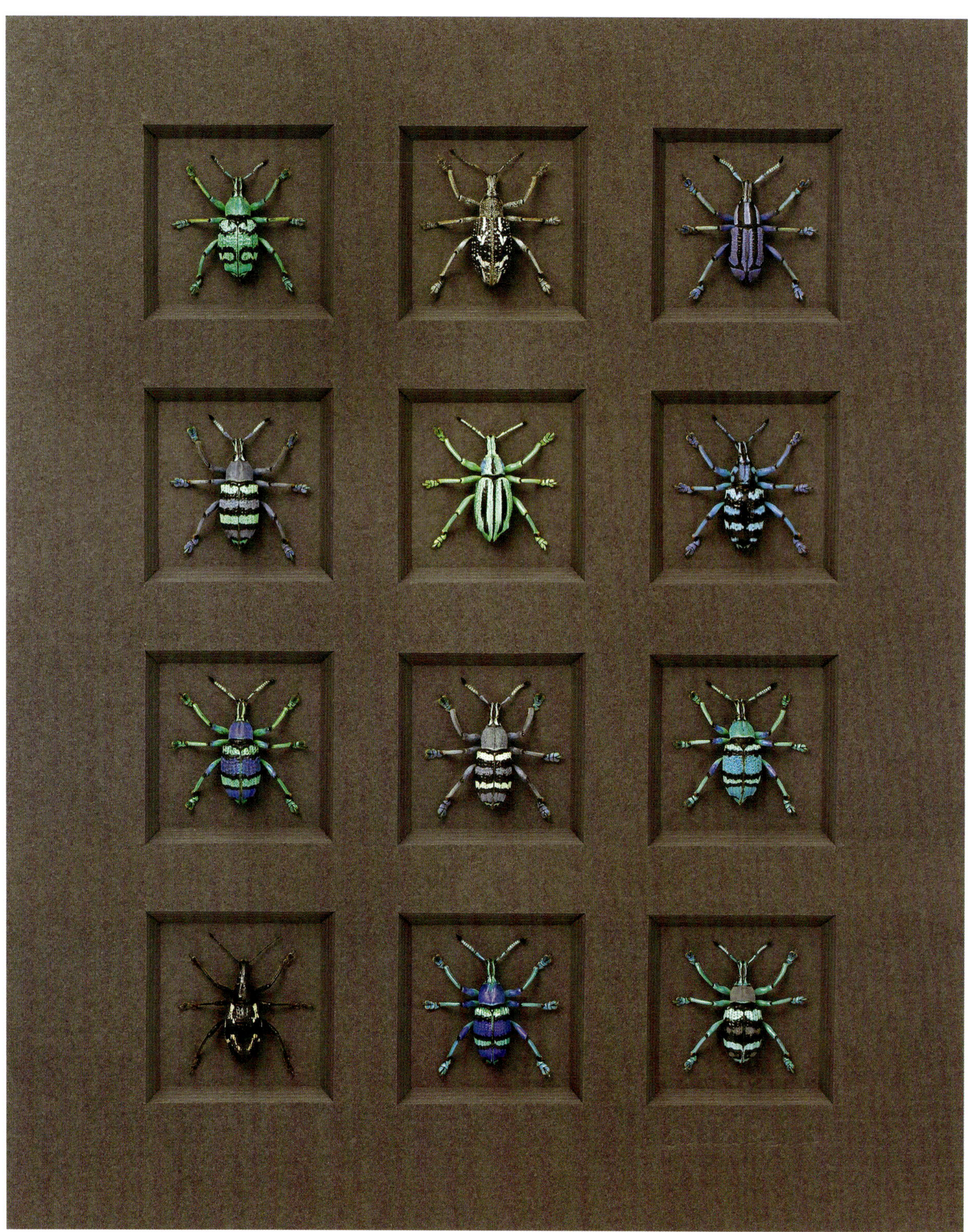

Eupholus Deviation

Indonesia, Papua New Guinea

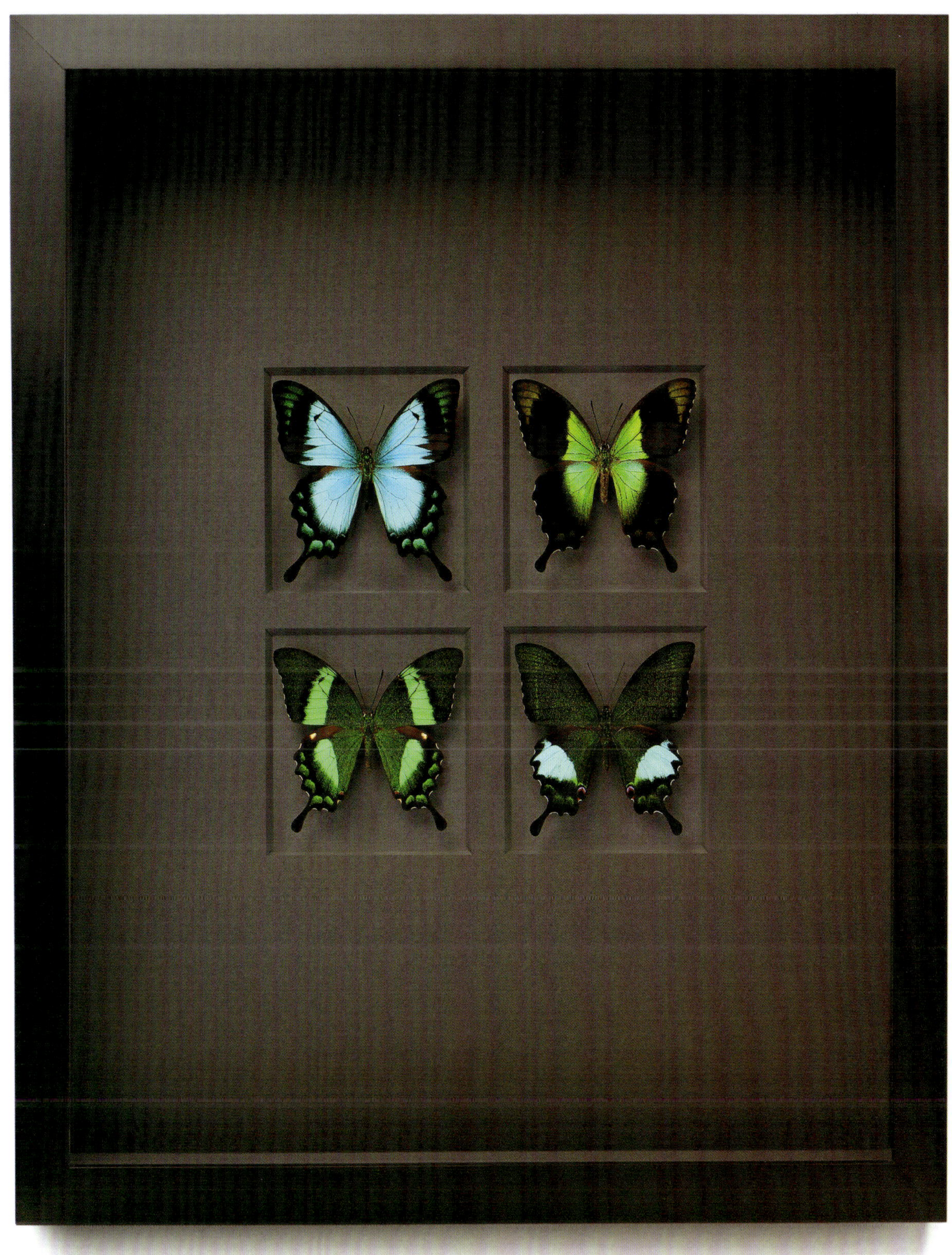

Gloss Swallowtails

Indonesia, Malaysia

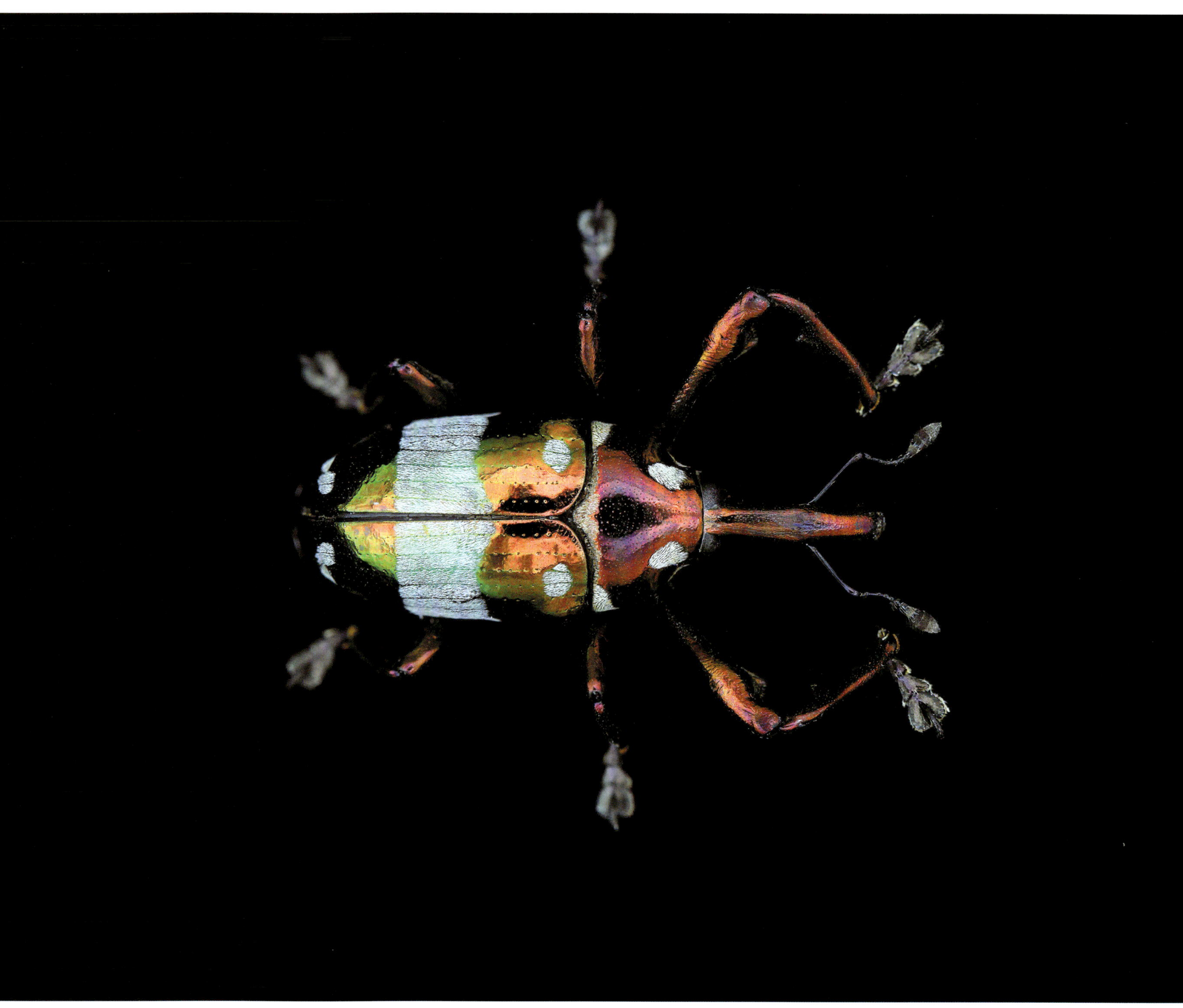

Tropical Weevil

Philippines

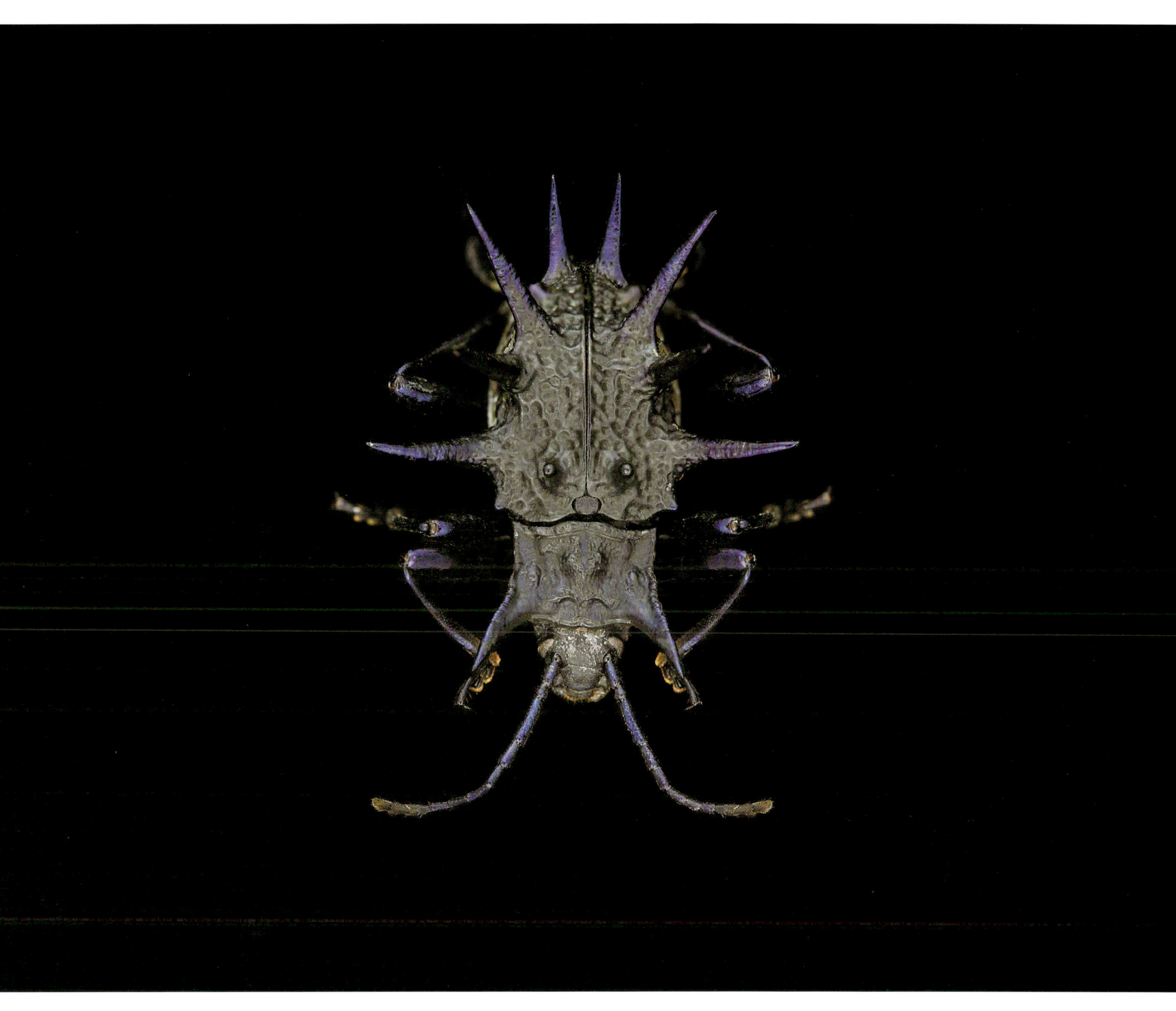

Spiny Leaf Beetle

Borneo

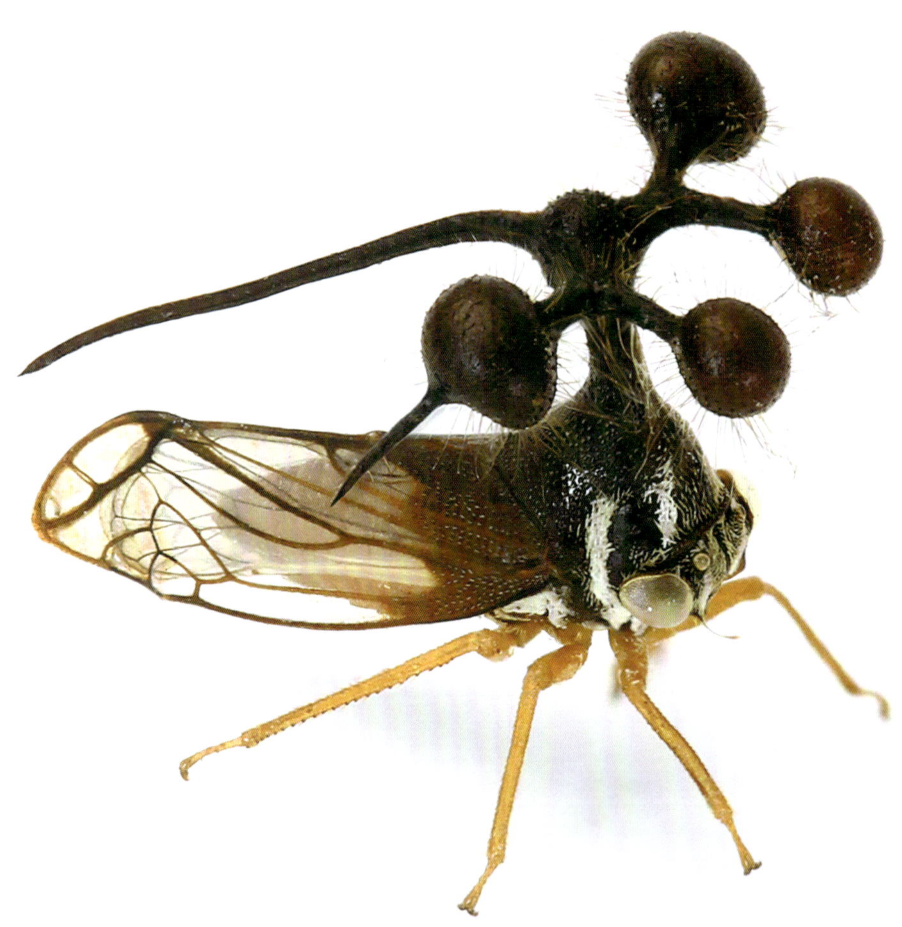

Globe-Bearing Treehopper

Brazil

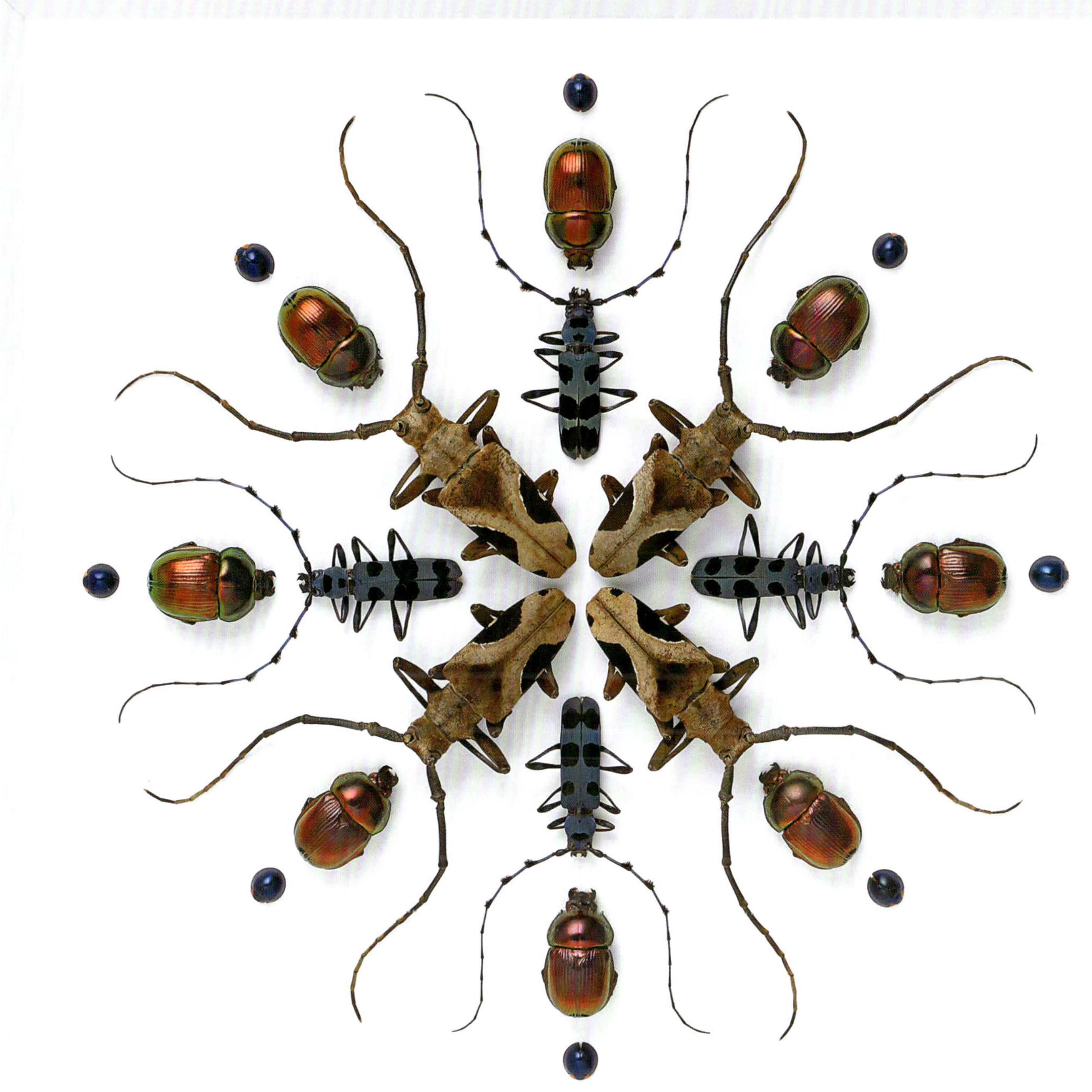

Crucifera Prism

Thailand, Slovenia, Japan, Indonesia

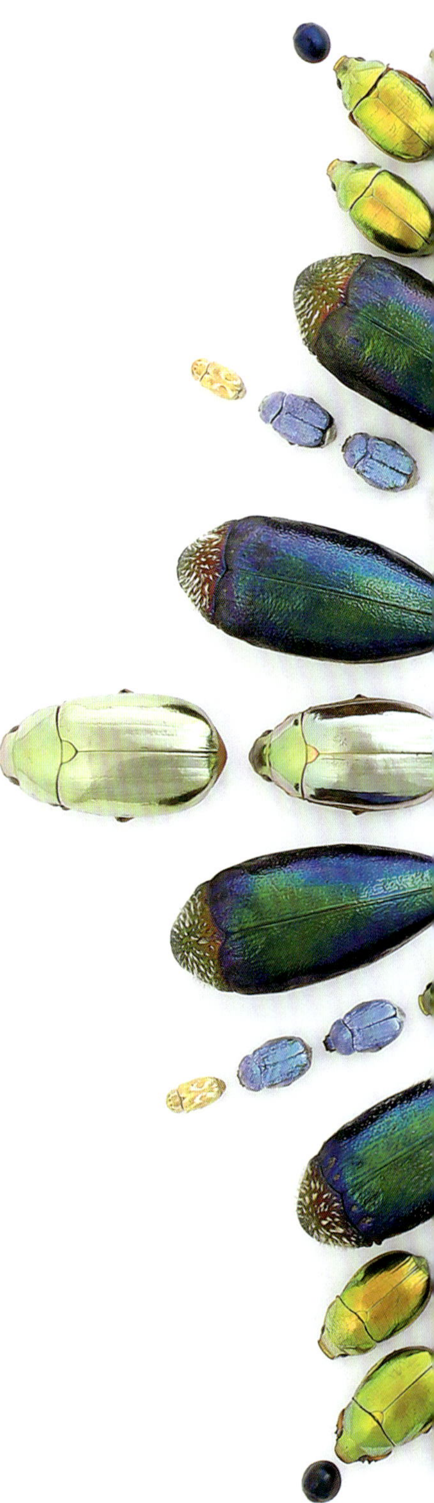

Chrysina Prism

France, Costa Rica, Indonesia, Honduras, Australia, Tanzania, Borneo

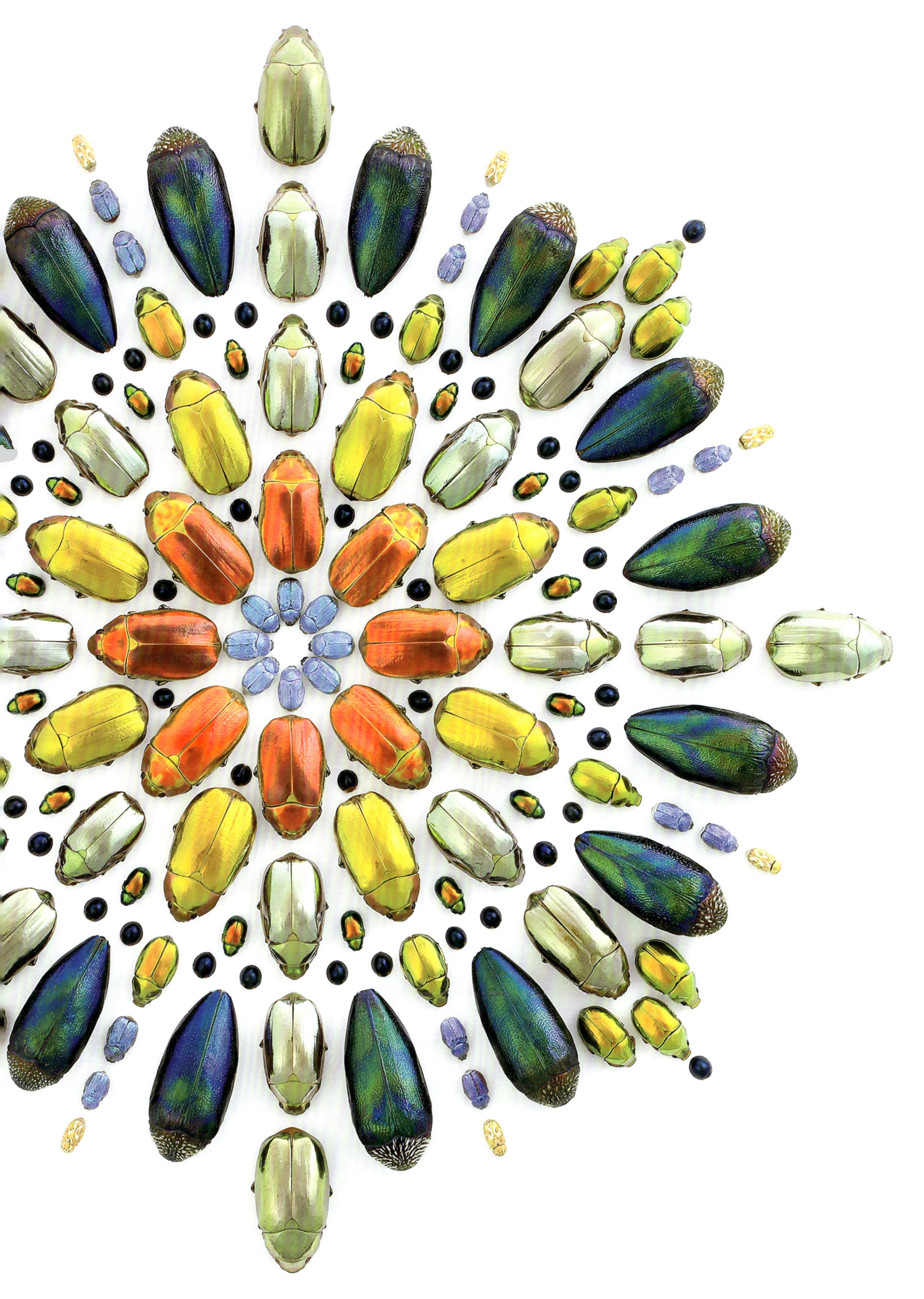

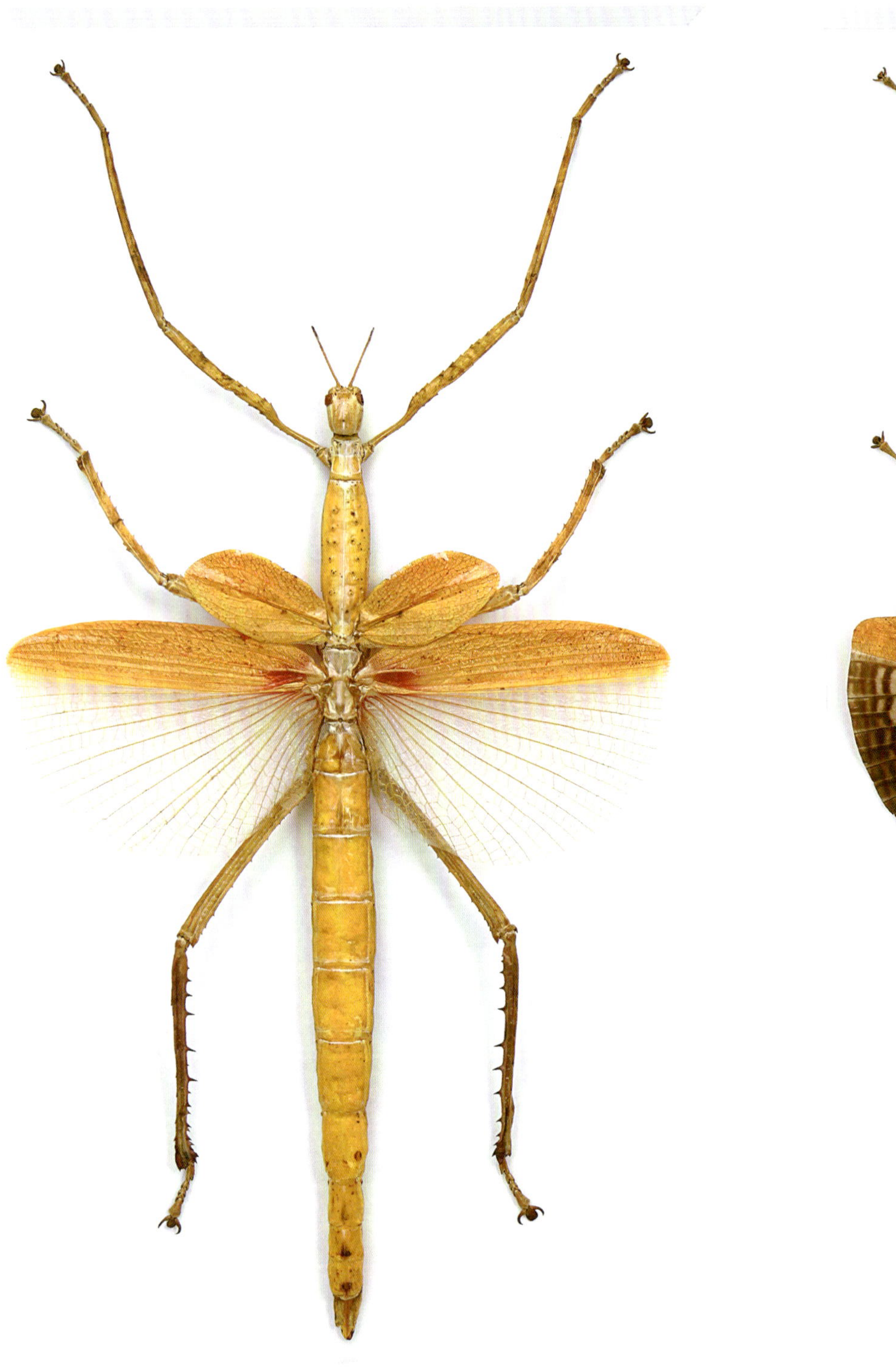

Versi Walking Sticks

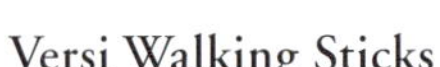

Java, Halmahera Island

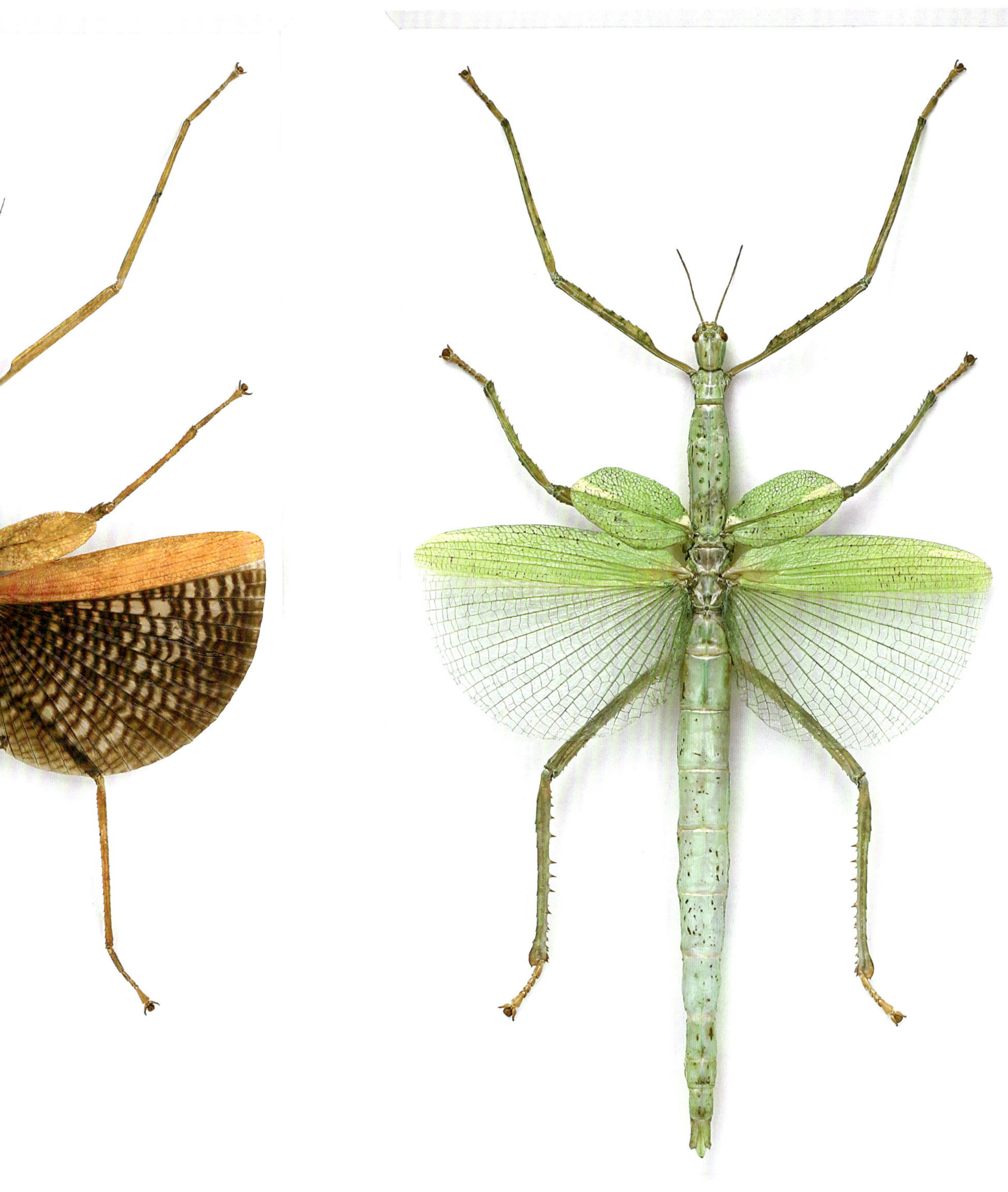

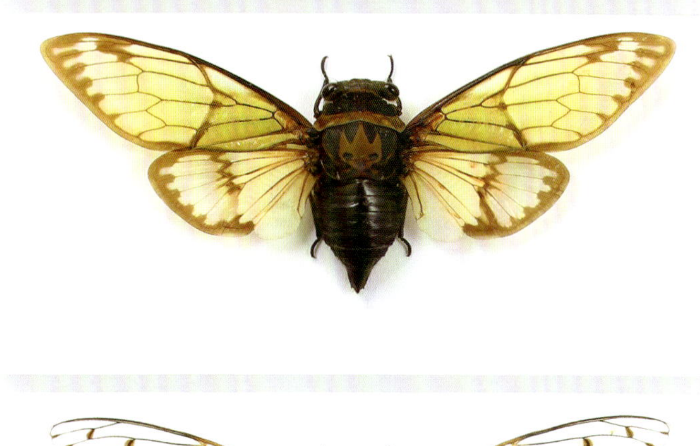

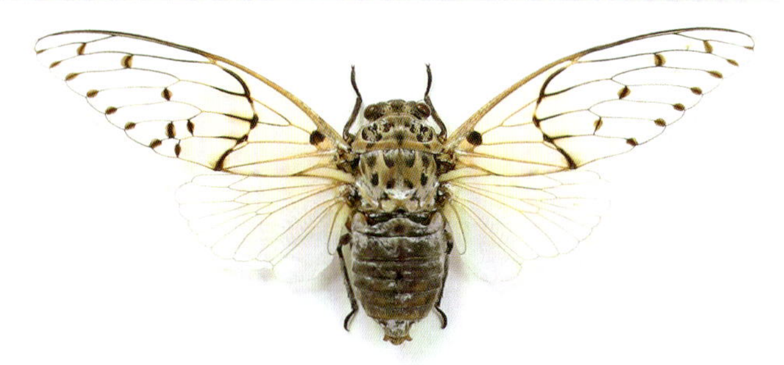

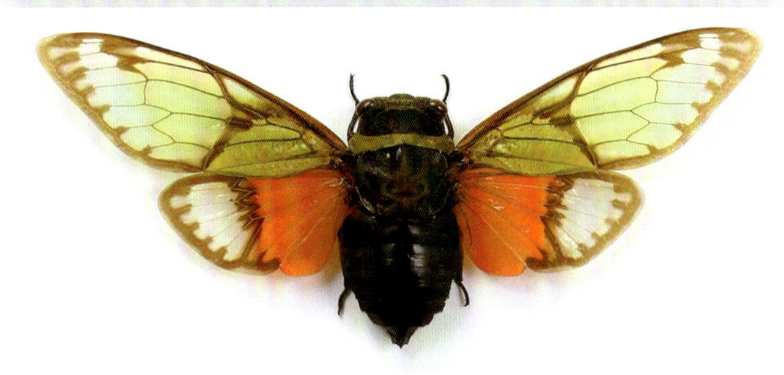

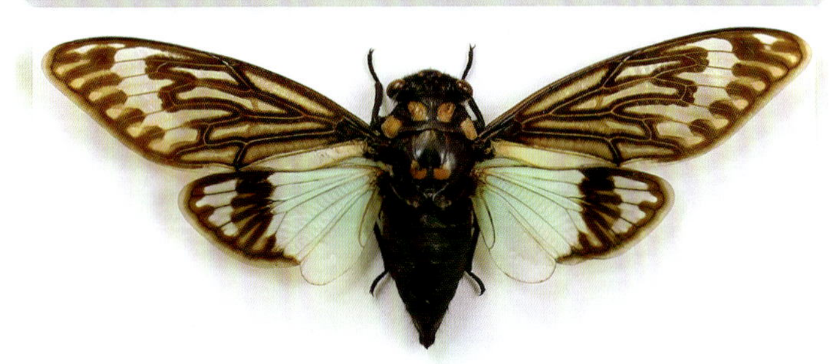

Tropical Cicadas

Thailand

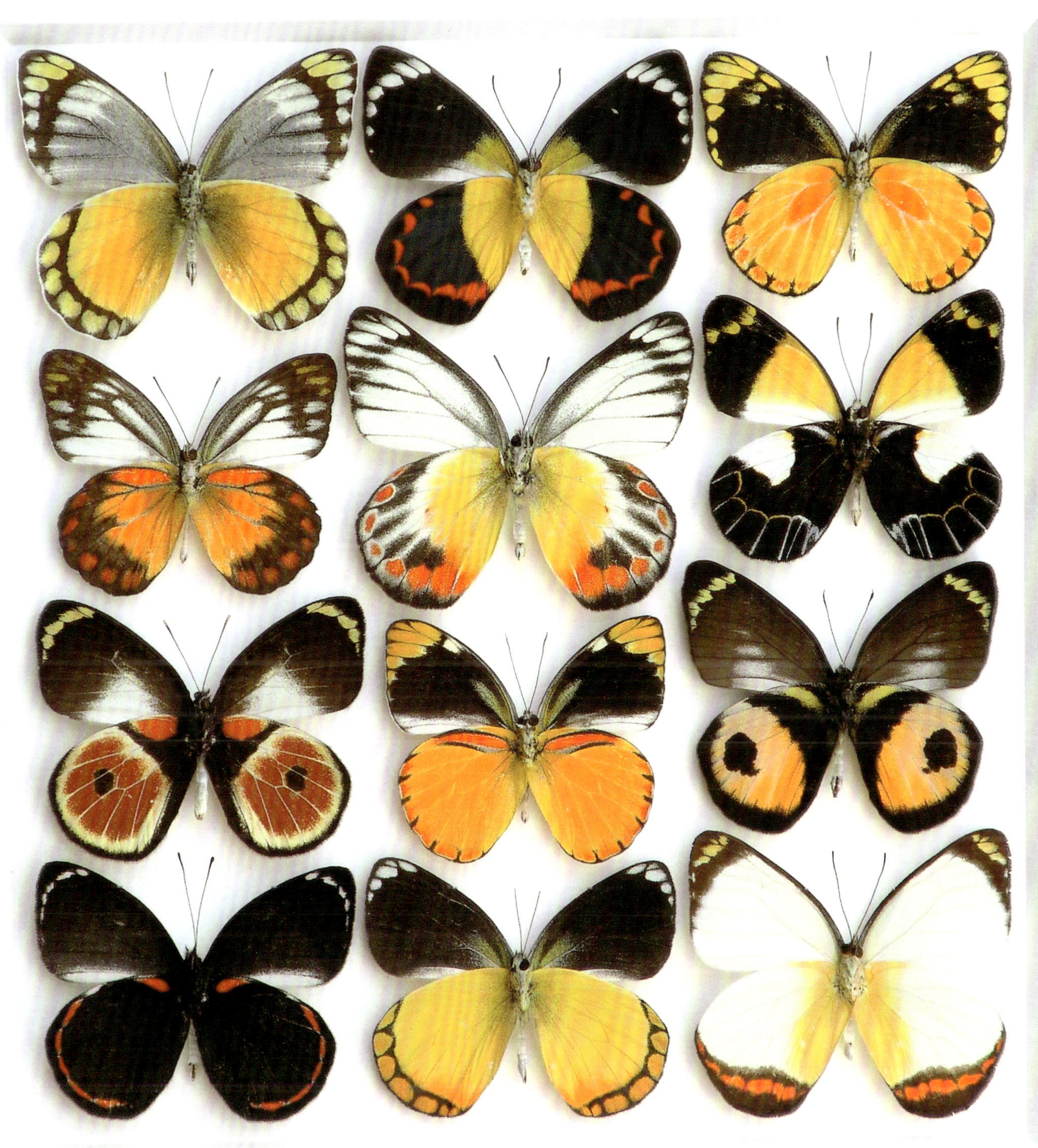

Delias

Indonesia, New Guinea

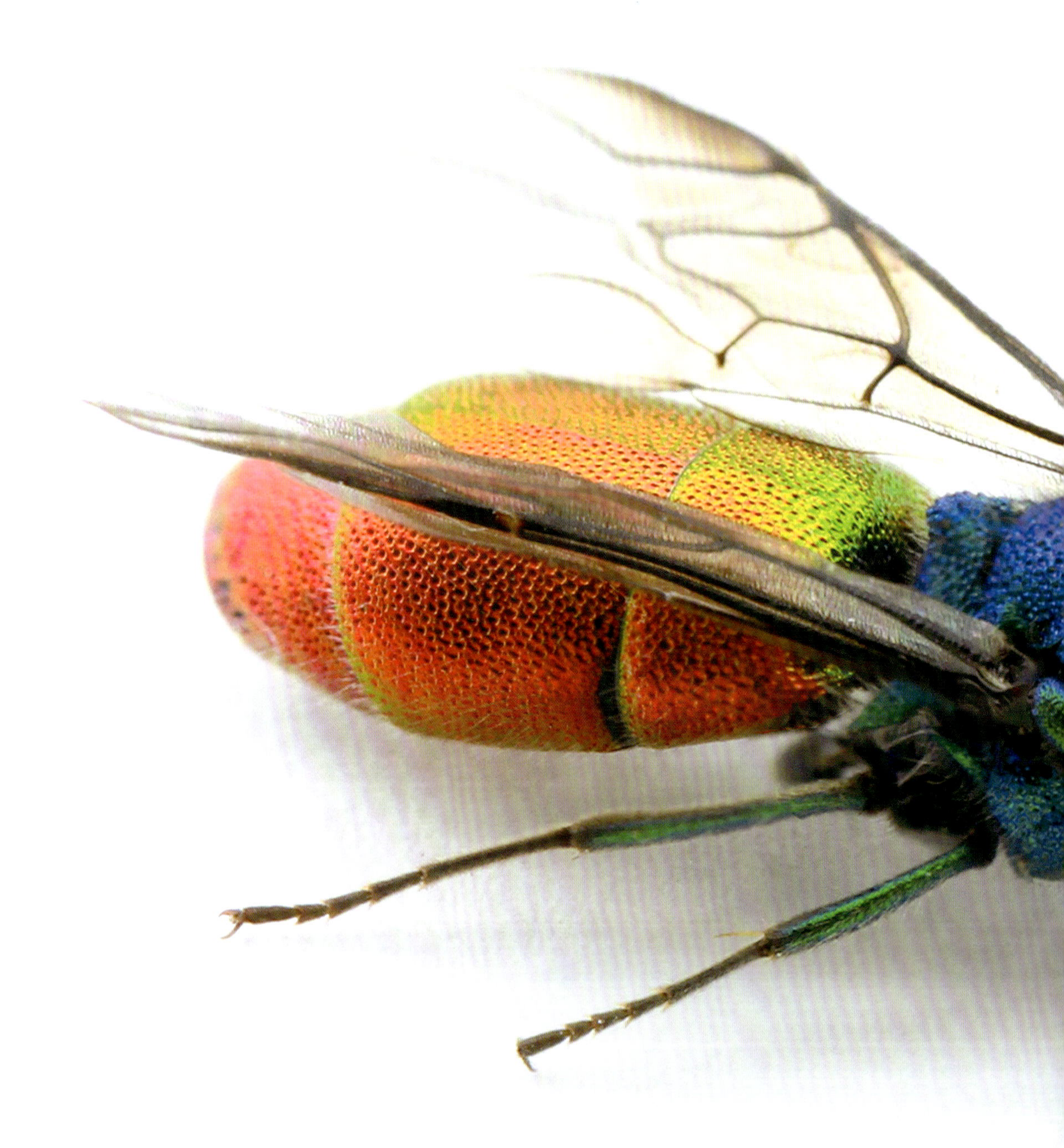

Cuckoo Wasp

Macedonia

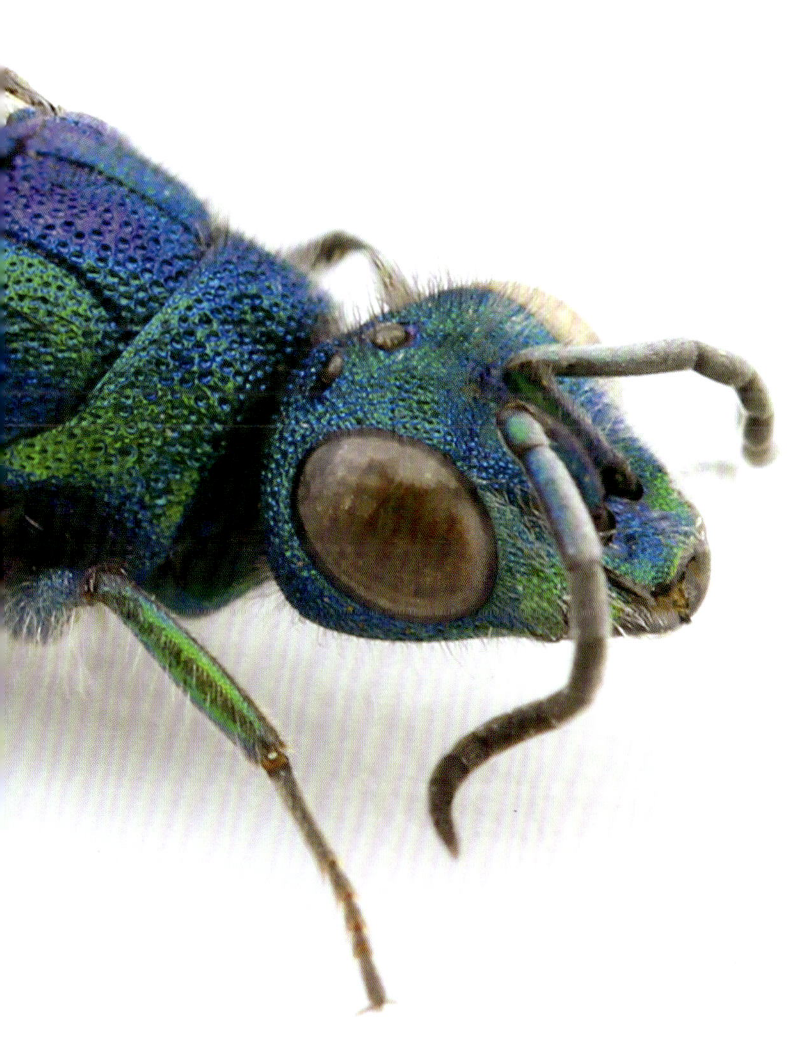

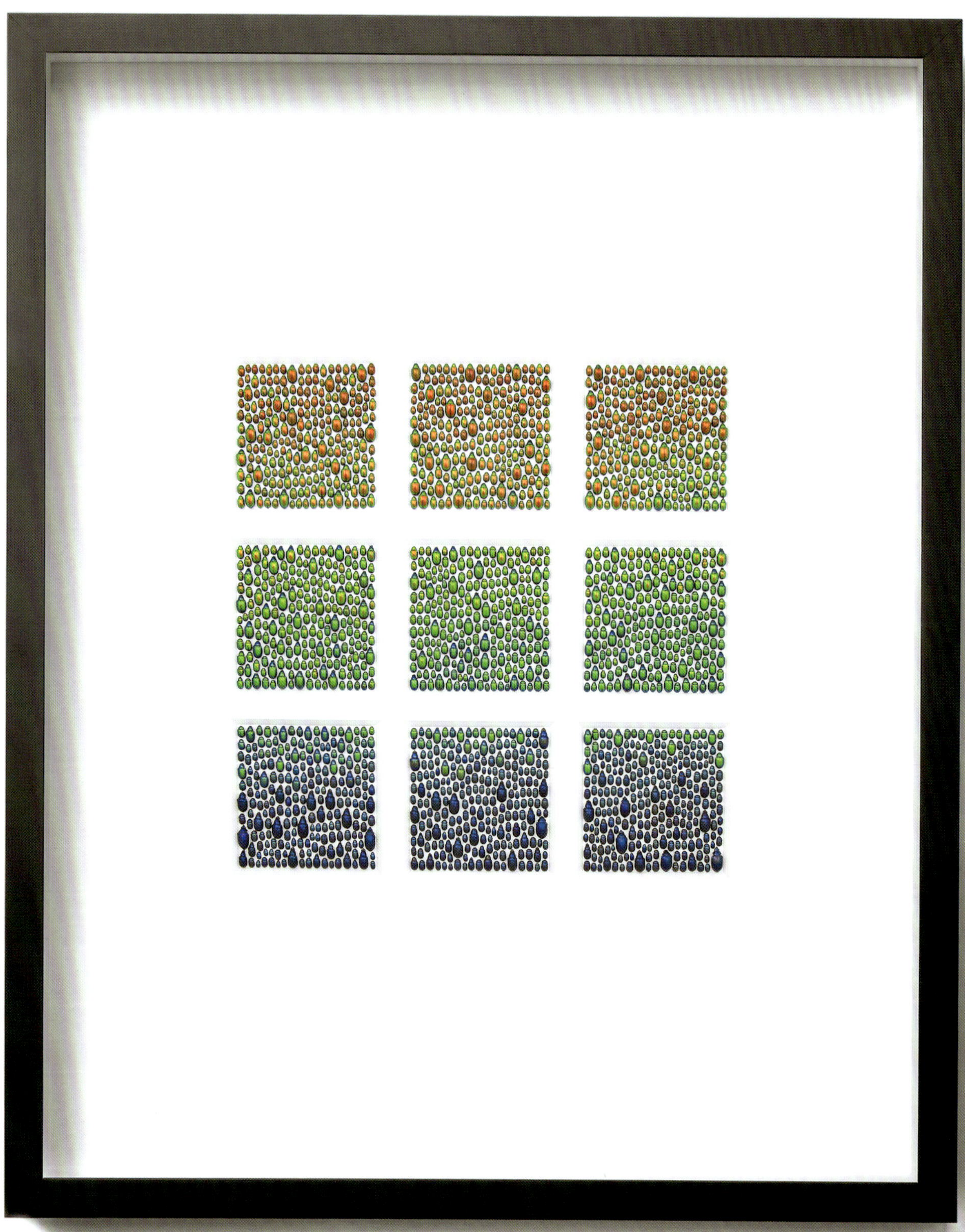

Chrysomelid Arrayal No. 3, Chrysomelid Arrayal No. 2

Java, Peru

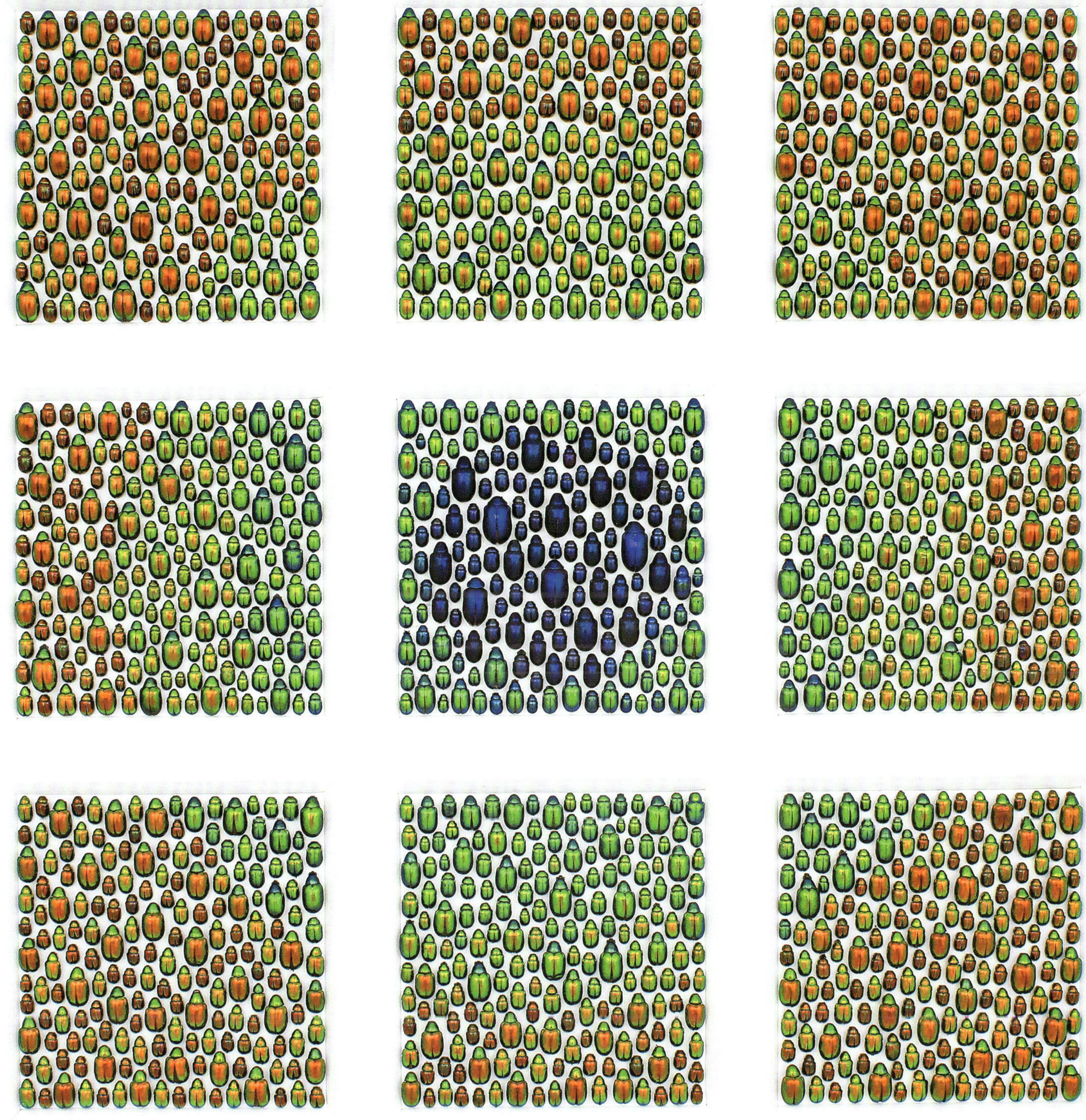

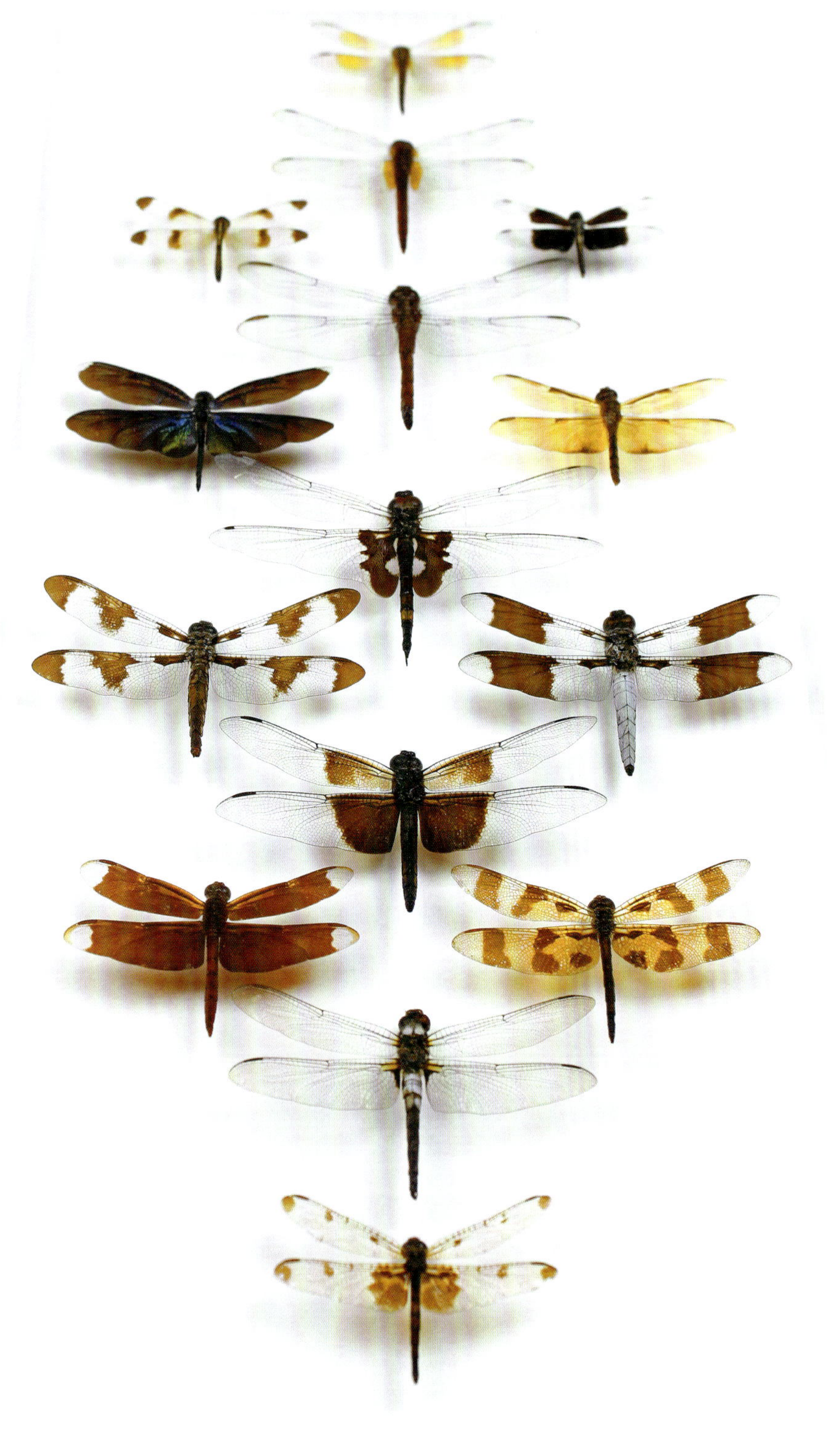

Dragonfly Formation

Thailand, Malaysia, Indonesia, United States

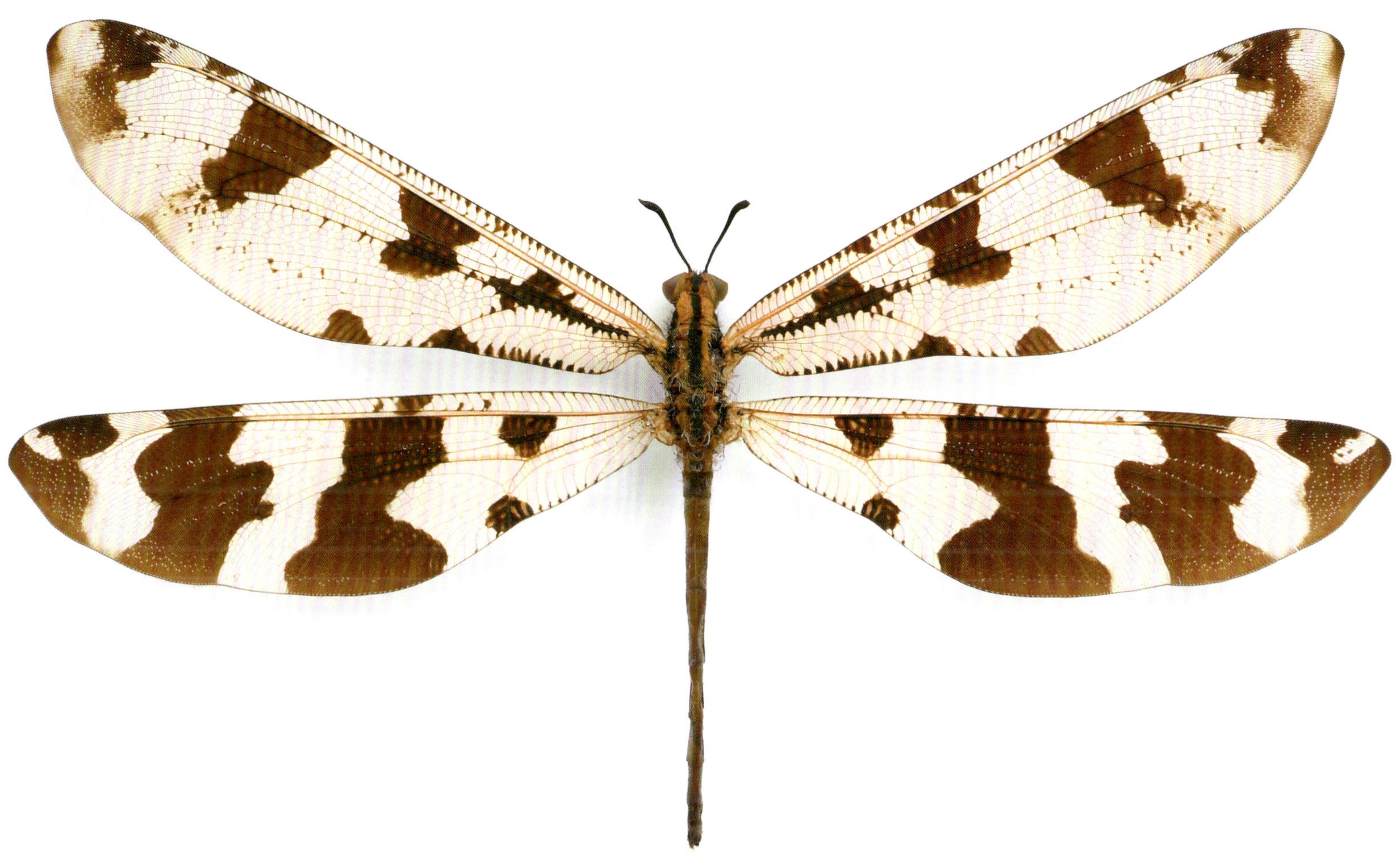

Regal Ant Lion

Thailand

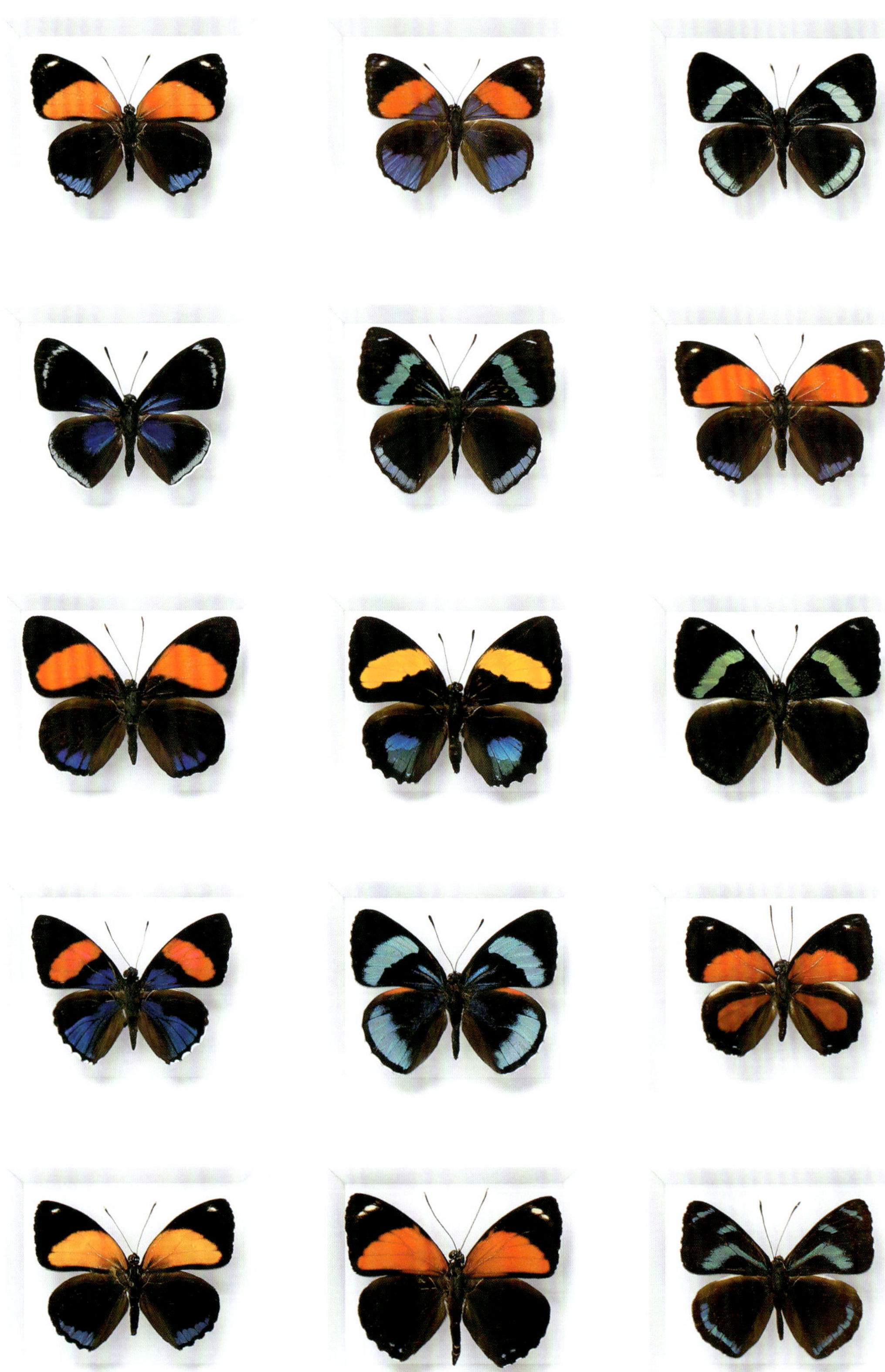

Callicore Butterflies

Peru

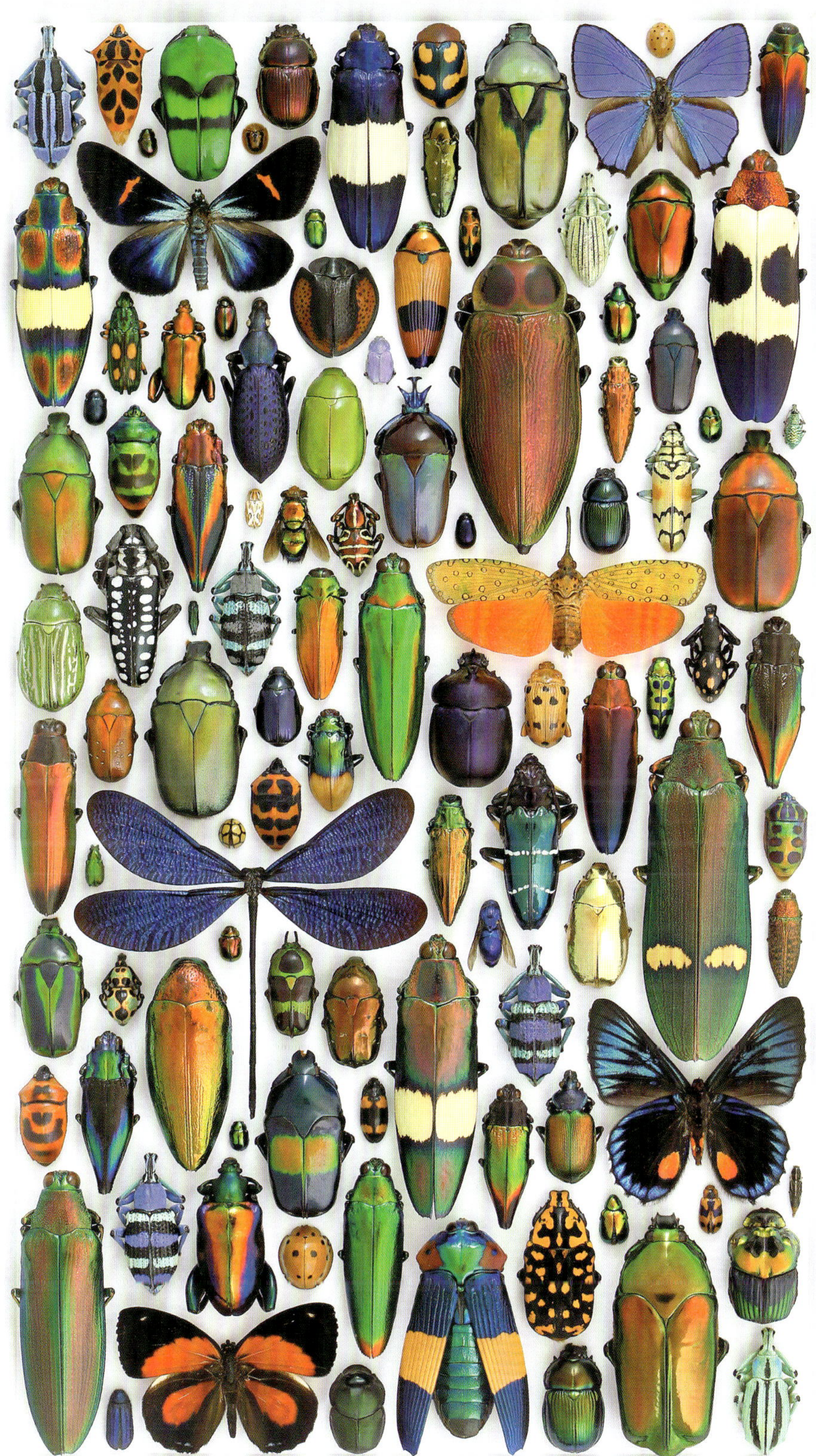

Aesthetica Mosaic

Worldwide

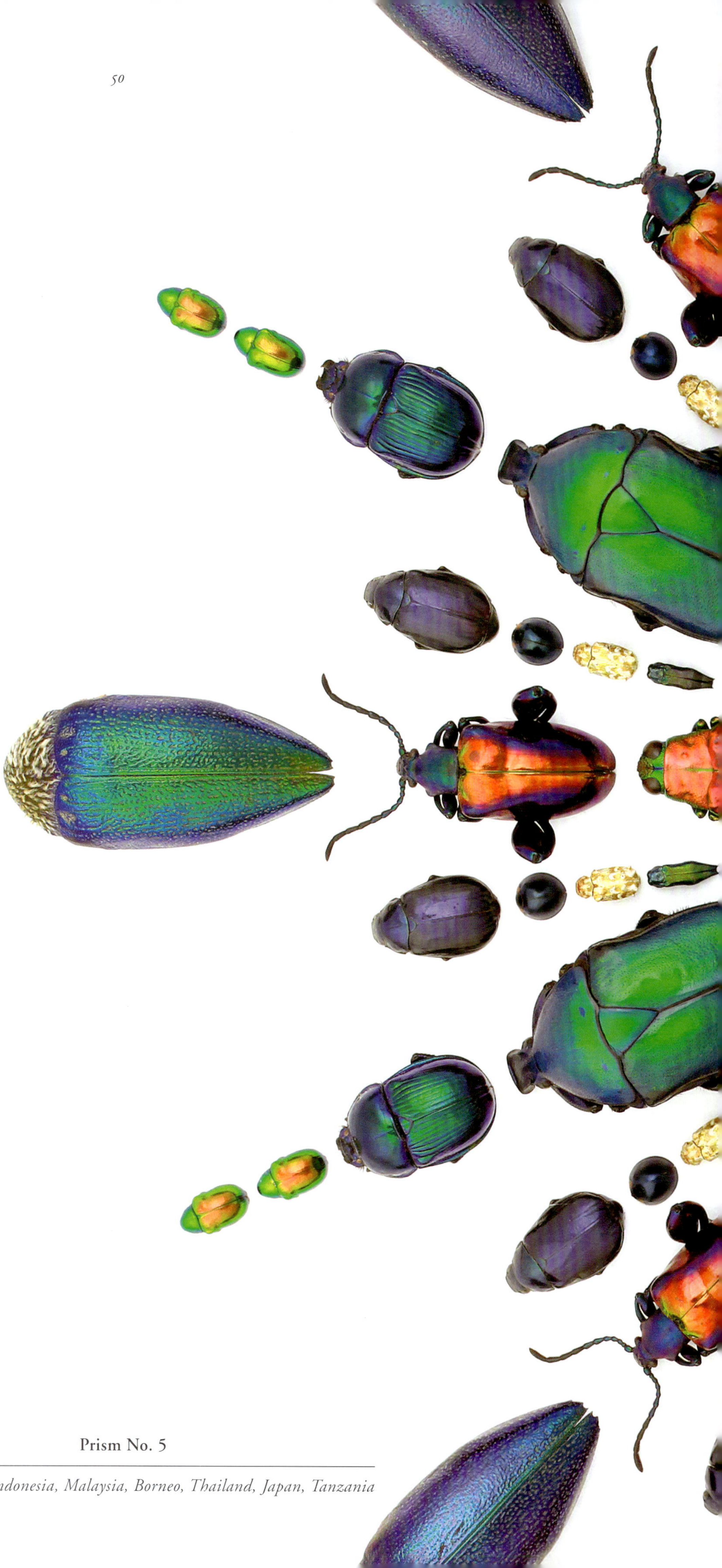

Prism No. 5

Romblon Island, Indonesia, Malaysia, Borneo, Thailand, Japan, Tanzania

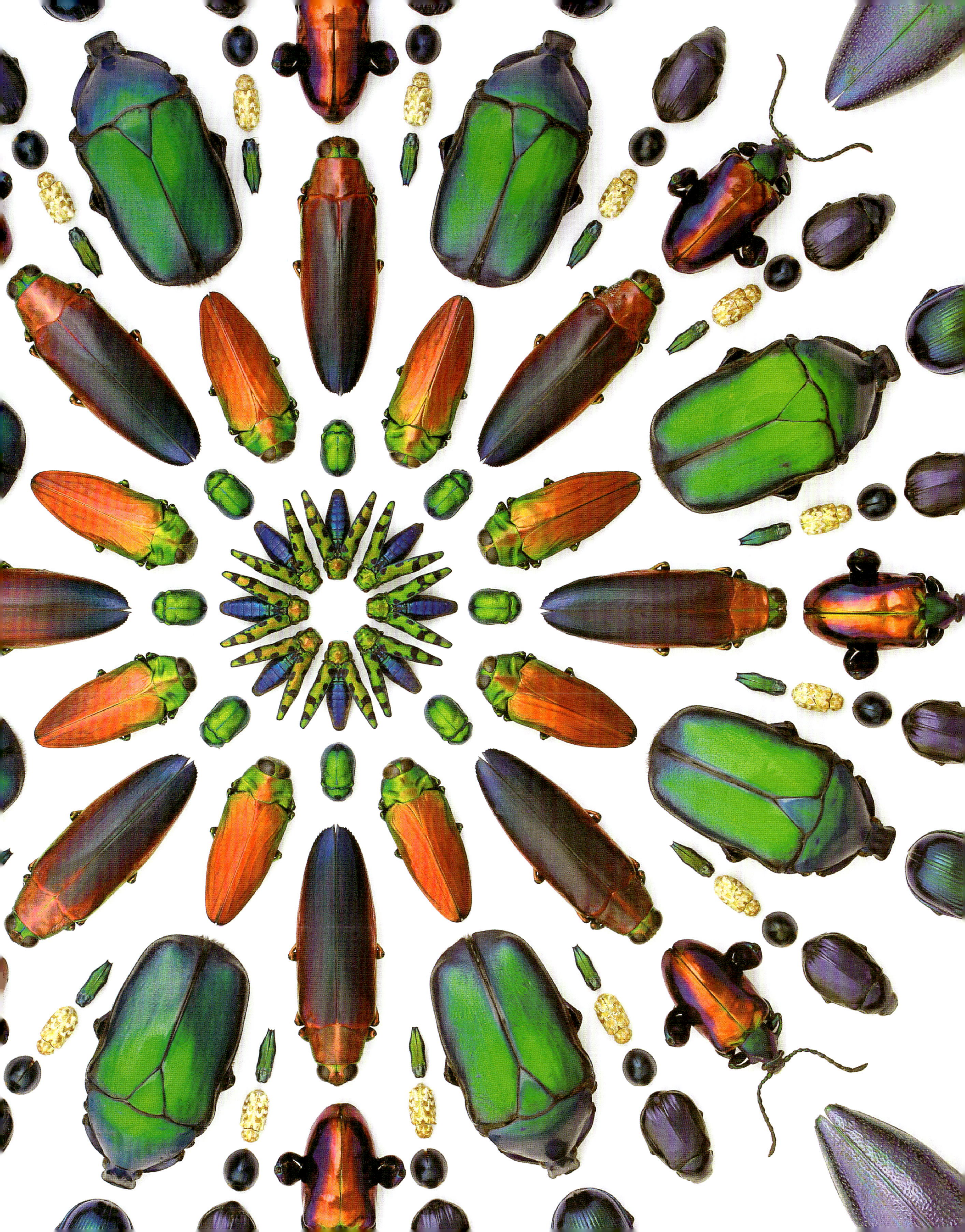

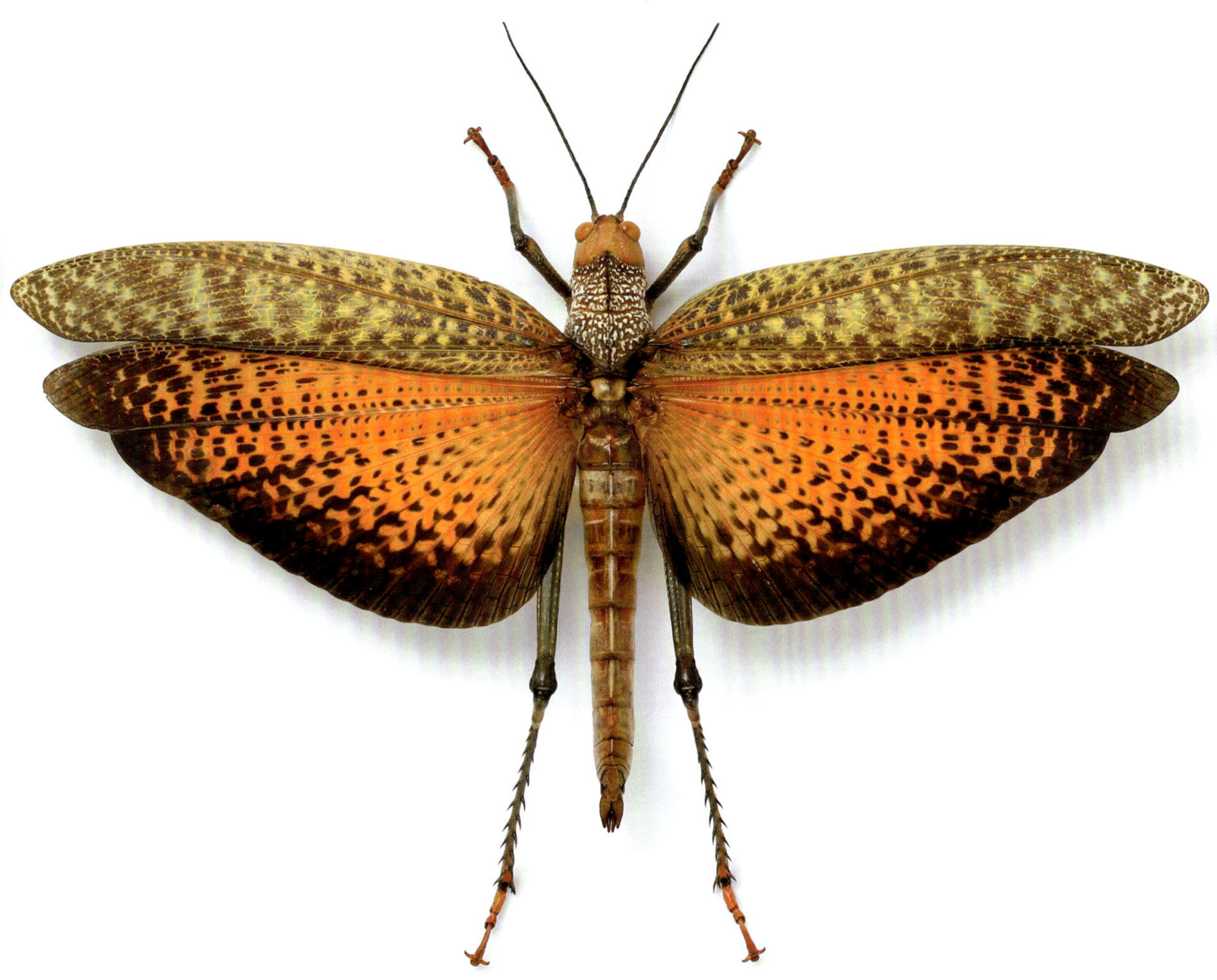

Tropical Locust

Guatemala

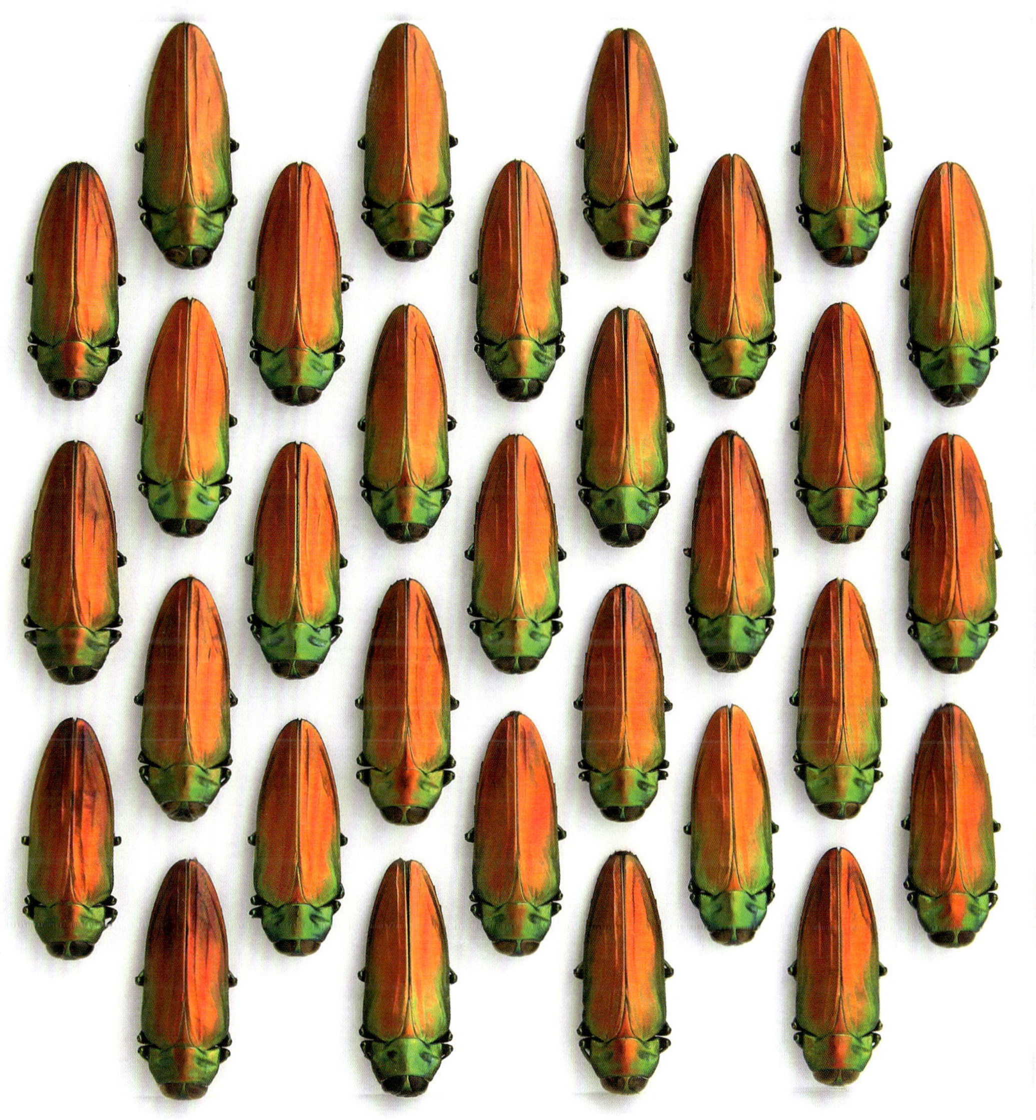

Sumptuosa

Morotai Island

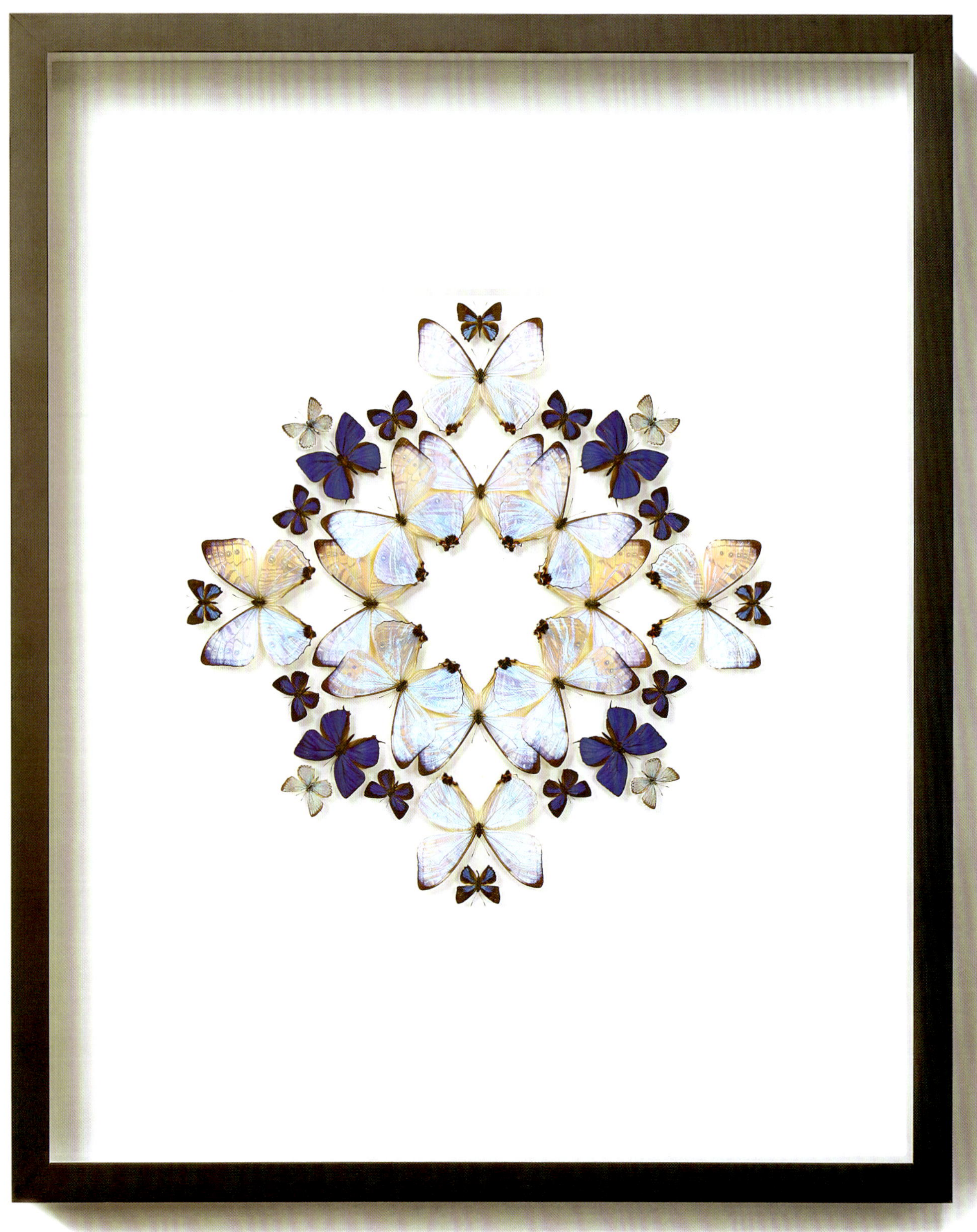

Lumens Prism

Peru, Indonesia, France

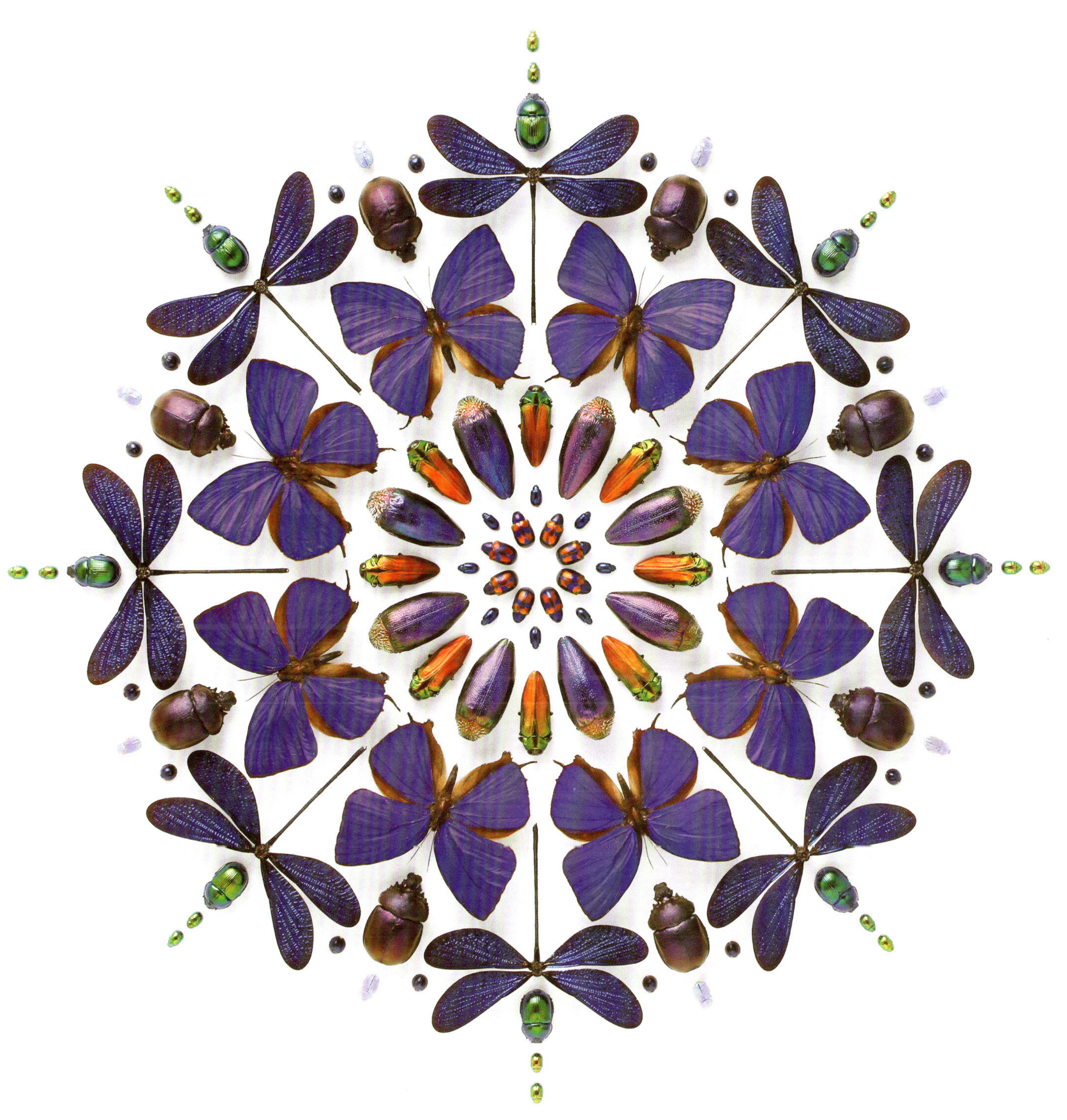

Sumptuosa Prism

Laos, Indonesia, Tanzania, Philippines, Thailand, Japan, France

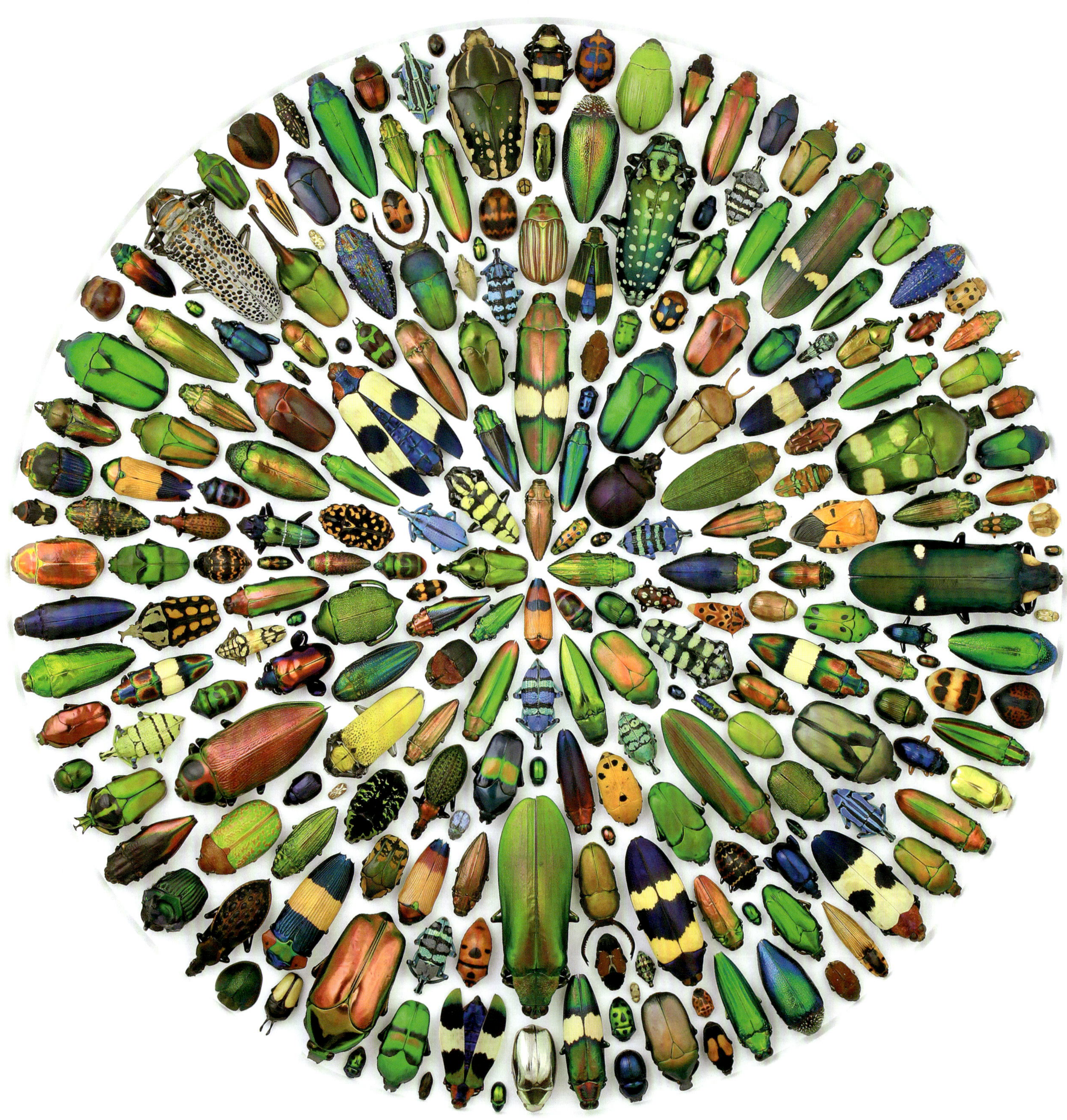

Limited Mosaic Prism

Worldwide

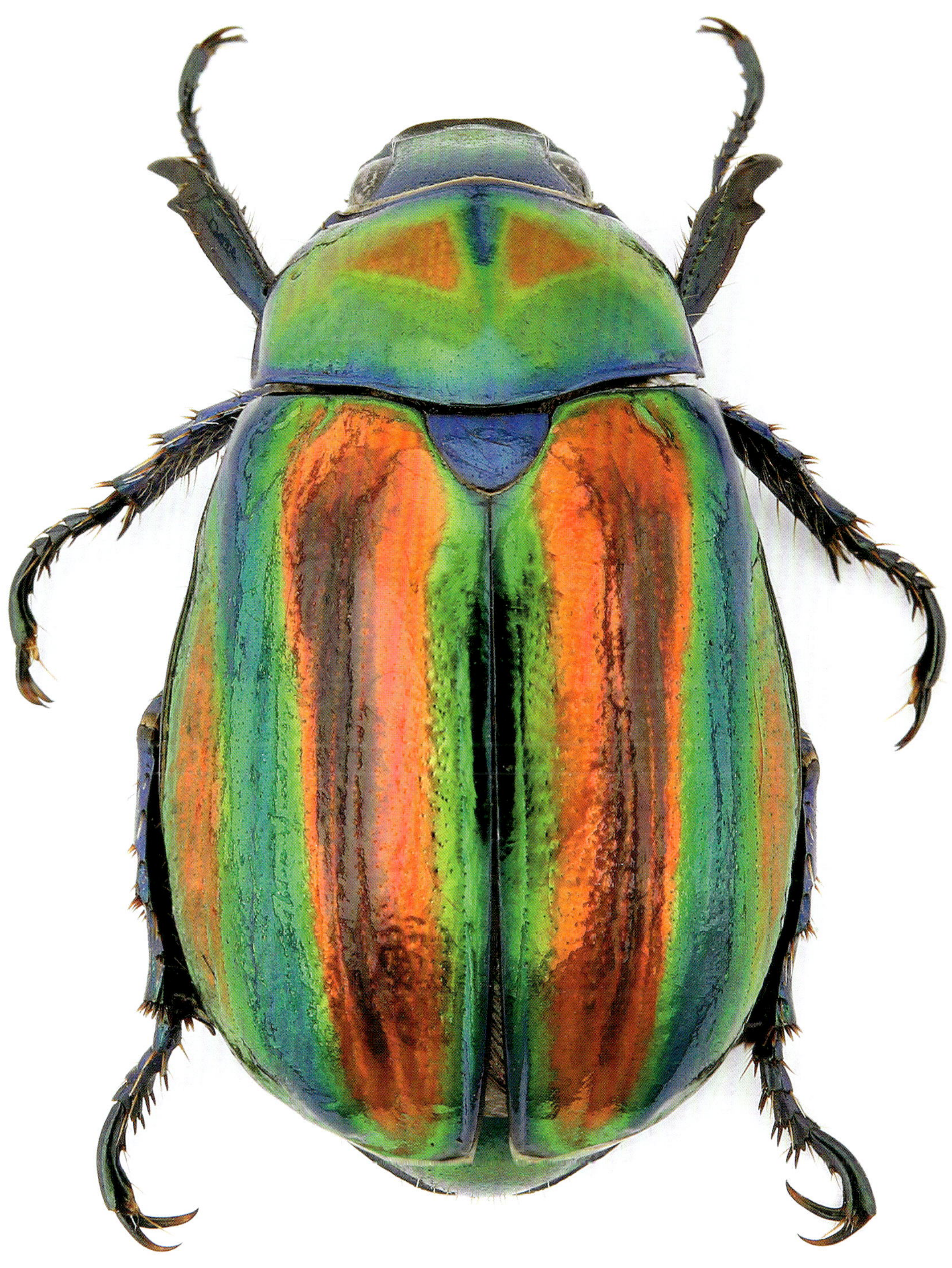

Rainbow Scarab

Laos

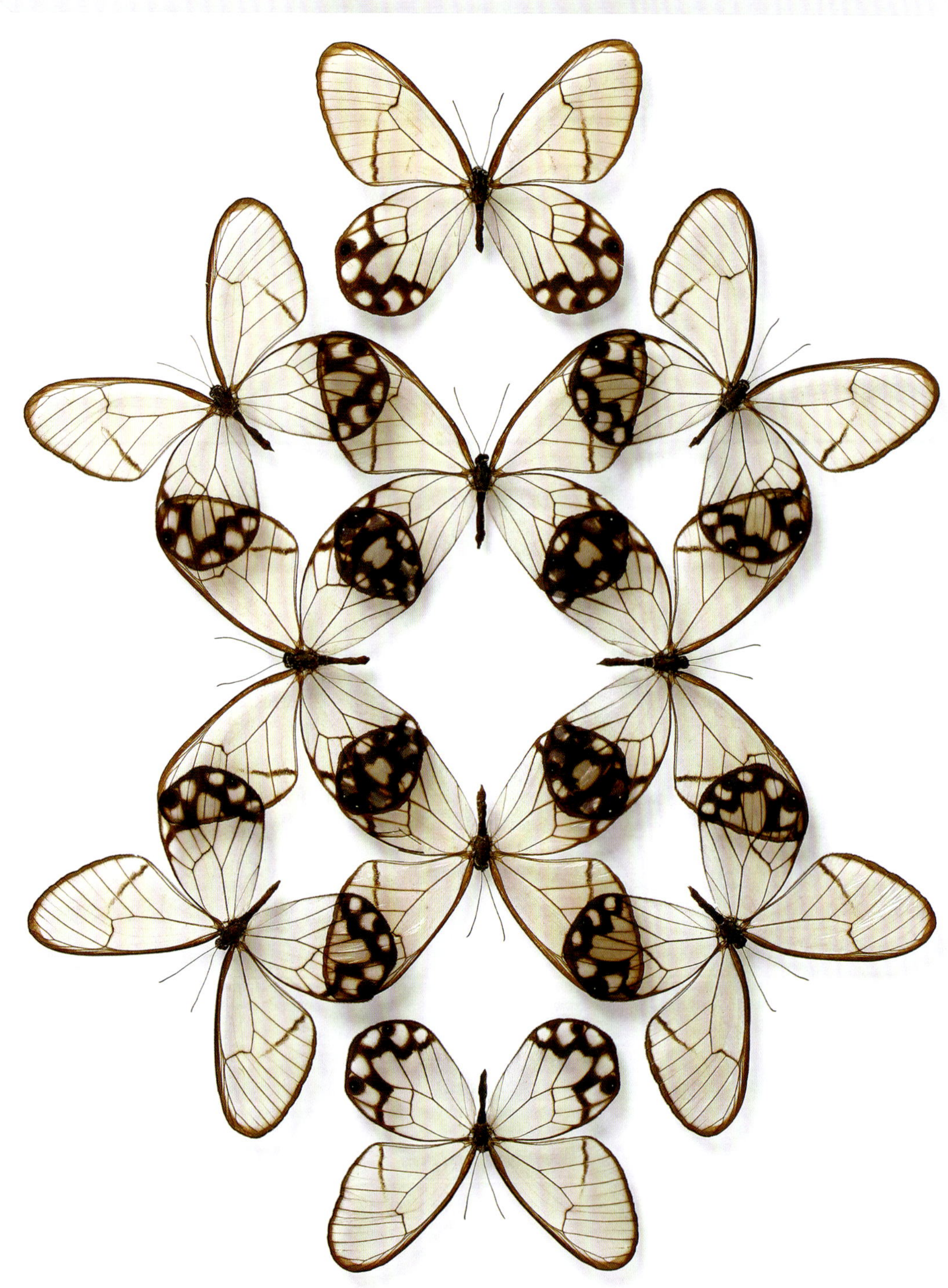

Clearwing Butterflies

Peru

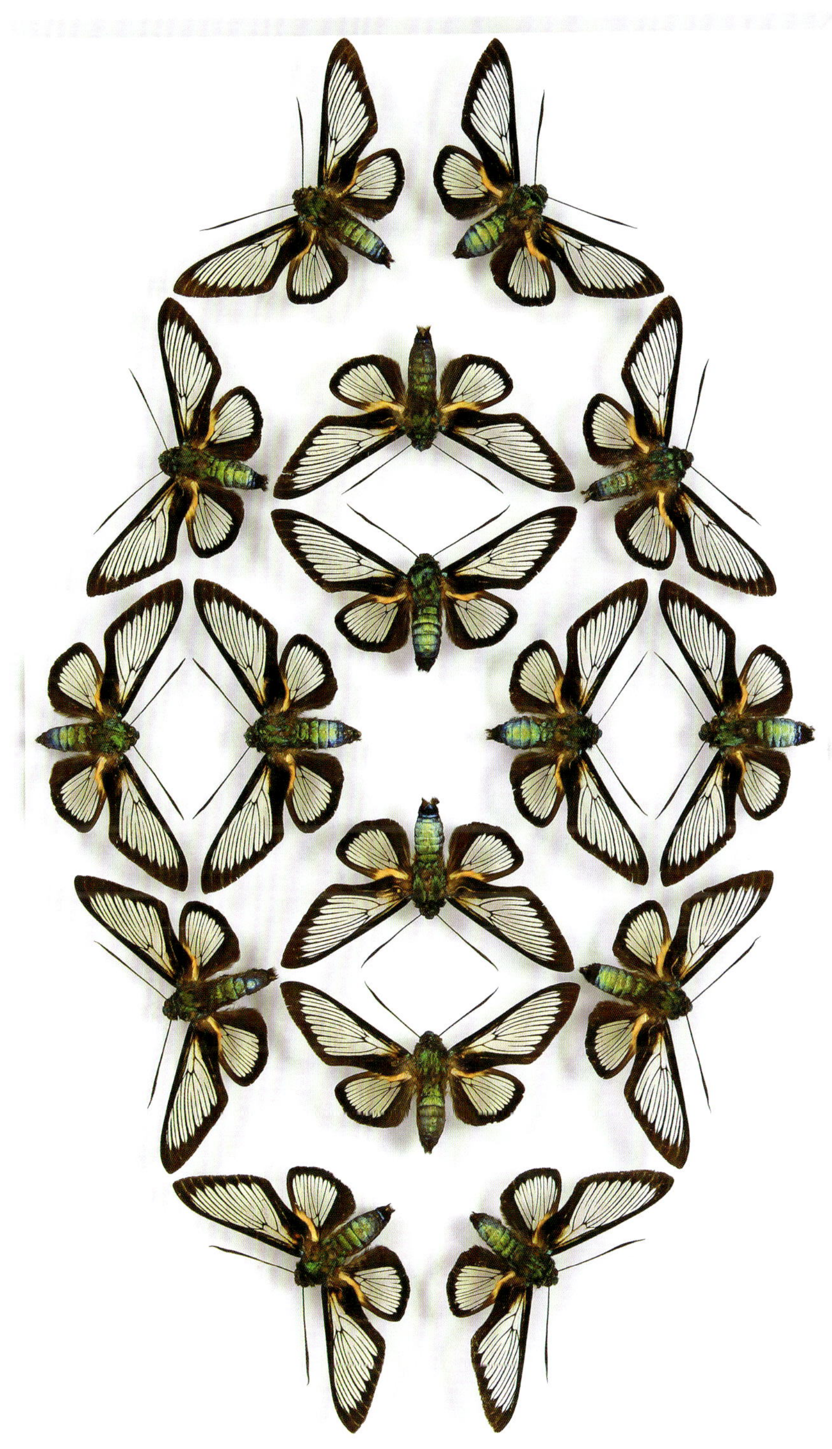

Clearwing Moths

Aru Islands

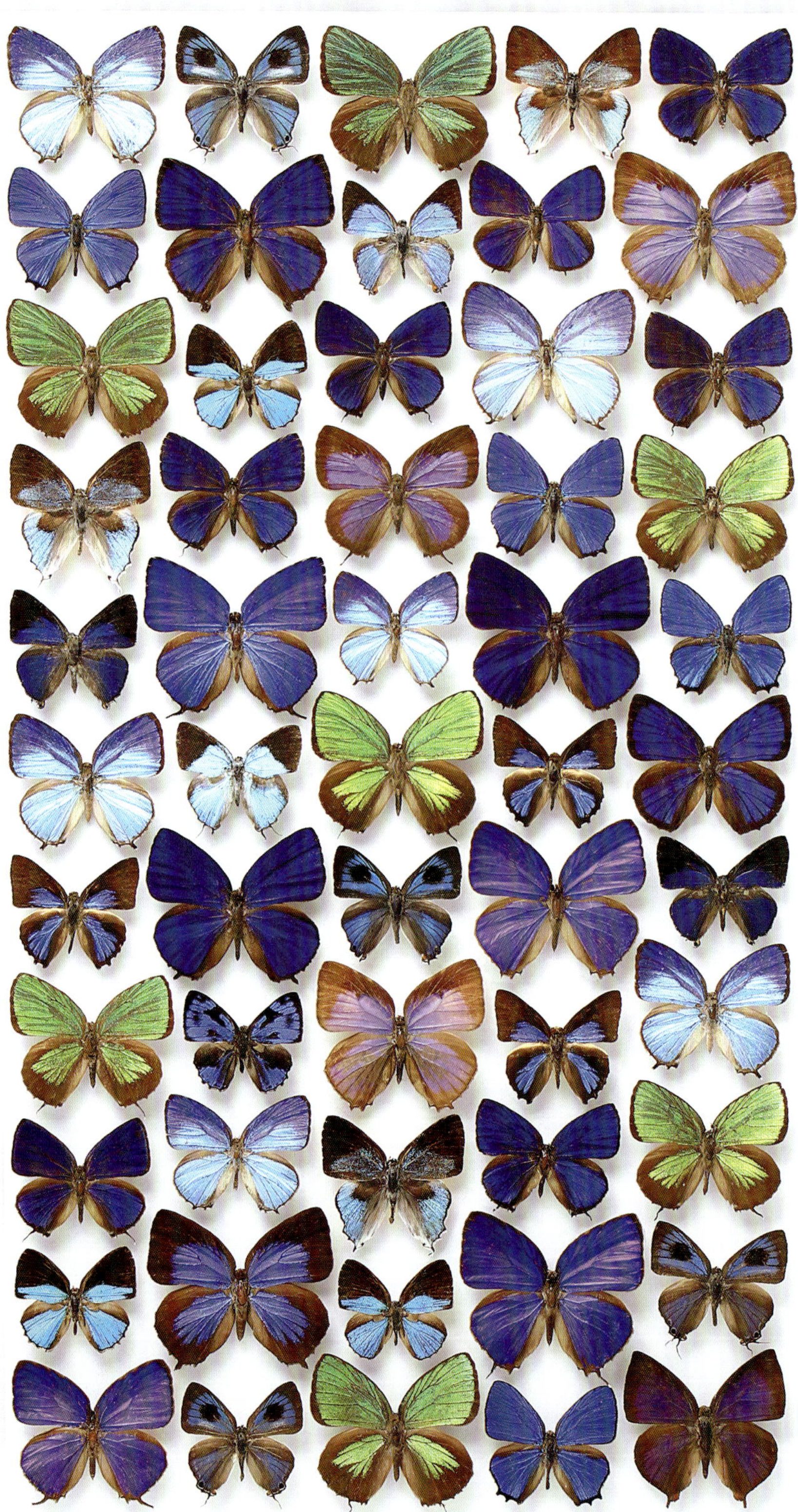

Limited Lycaenidae Mosaic

Southeast Asia

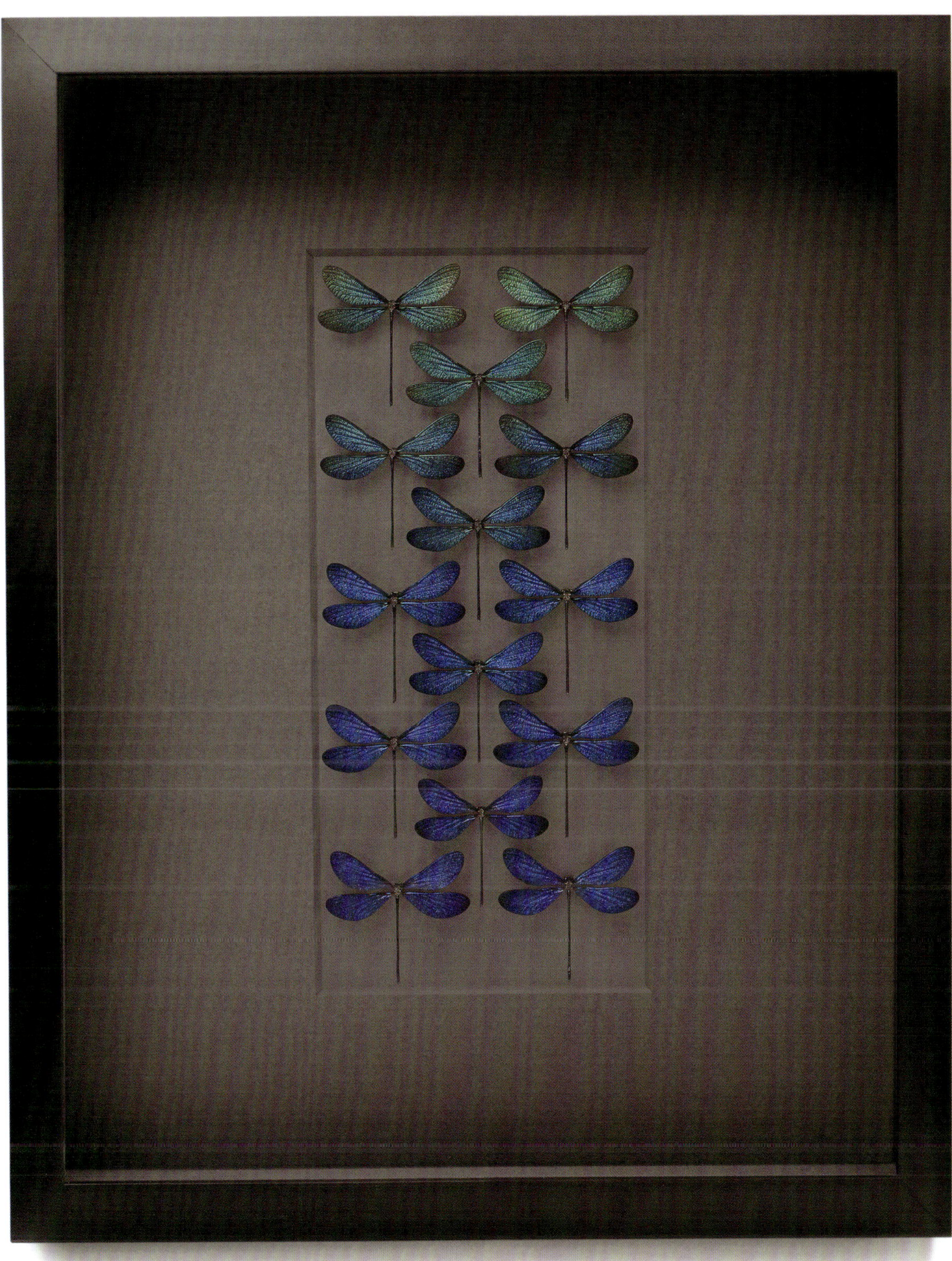

Damselfly Wash

Philippines

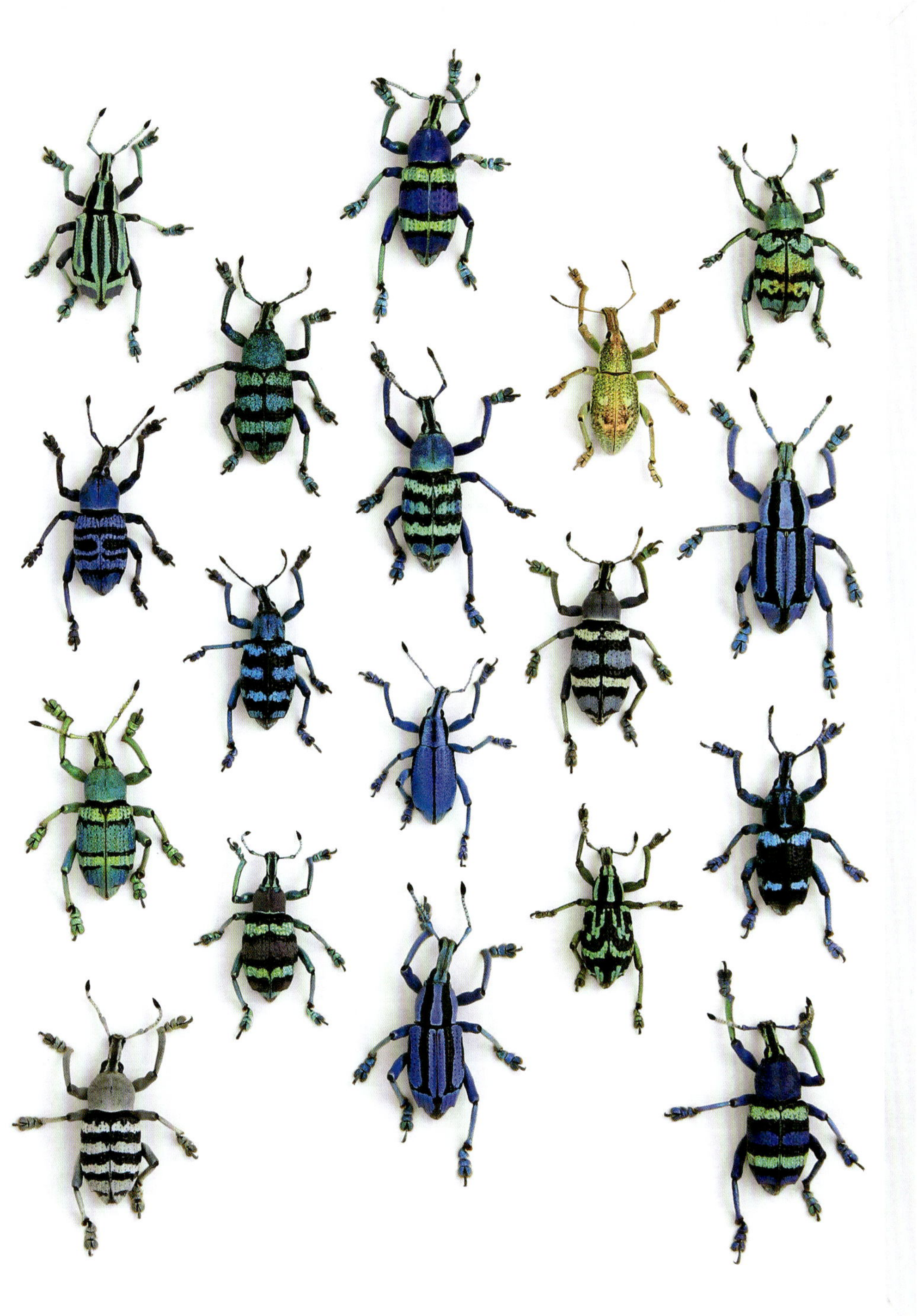

Walking Weevils

Indonesia, Papua New Guinea

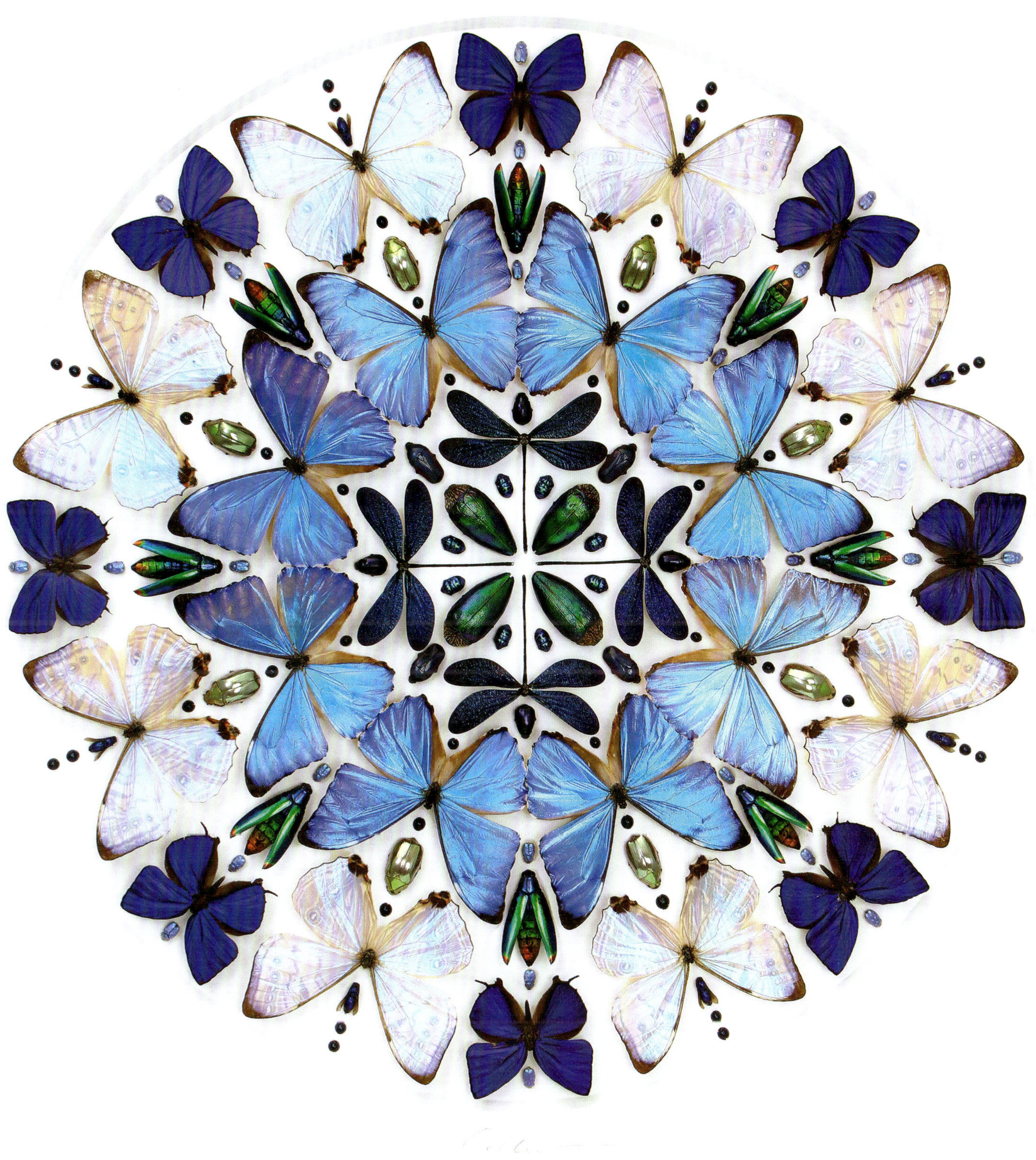

Limited Aesthetica Prism

Tanzania, Philippines, Indonesia, Thailand, Peru, Costa Rica, France

SEA CREATURES

I hate obvious solutions to visual problems. As a designer, I am driven toward efficient and precise visual results, but as an artist, my objective is to inspire people to see natural artifacts with fresh eyes. So when I started looking beyond the world of insects for subject matter and found a plentiful supply of sea creatures, I was at once inspired and skeptical. Unlike insects, seashells are as ubiquitous in home decor as doilies and Thomas Kinkade prints. I needed to break through the roadside-souvenir-shop aura of seashells without distracting from their already perfect (if a little overexposed) geometry. The temptation to overcompensate for the mindless and simplistic treatment shells have received was strong, but after wrestling back many a frantic and gaudy instinct, I settled on my motif. I hope it bridges the divide between the trite and the overwrought.

Another concern I faced in turning to sea creatures was that the positive environmental effects accompanying my work with insects could not be claimed for shell collecting. Though many of the species I use are simply found objects, as anyone who has roamed a Caribbean beach after a storm can attest, still, the best my work could hope for was an environmentally neutral effect. And while shell collecting is heavily regulated—especially in the Philippines, where the majority of my specimens originate—the fact remains that some seashell specimens are indeed the result of targeted dives to collect living mollusks.

However, as I began to explore using specimens from the sea, I started seeing reclamation possibilities in every aspect of humanity's interaction with the oceans. From the animals that die of natural causes in fisheries to bycatch to food supply lines, it seemed that fascinating, even if sometimes common, creatures were already present in established industry. I was thrilled to realize that I could create beauty out of waste without adding to the pressure on wild populations. Some of the specimen preservation lengths I have had to resort to, especially with the soft-bodied invertebrates, are both convoluted and costly, but the results have more than compensated for the headache.

So while my work with sea creatures is not as strictly environmentally advantageous as it is in my reclamation and insect series, I think it does indeed showcase some innovative uses for what might otherwise end up in a landfill or a sushi platter. Who would have guessed that seafood could be so *visually* delicious?

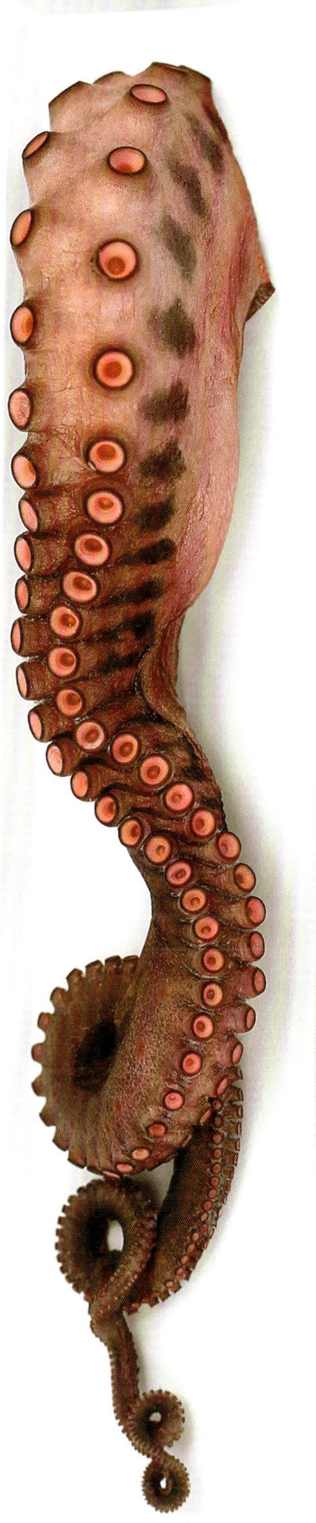

Octopus Tentacle

Atlantic Ocean

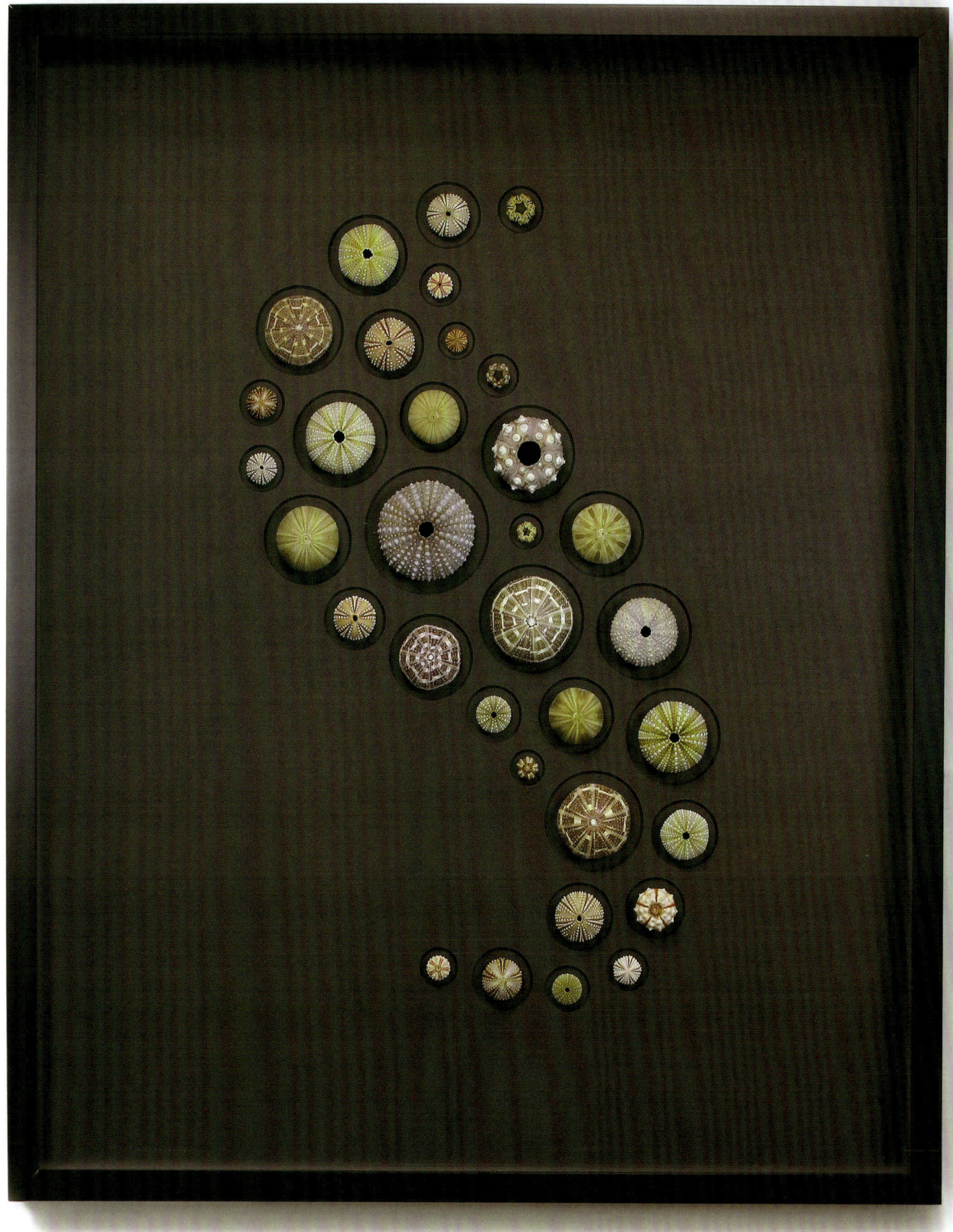

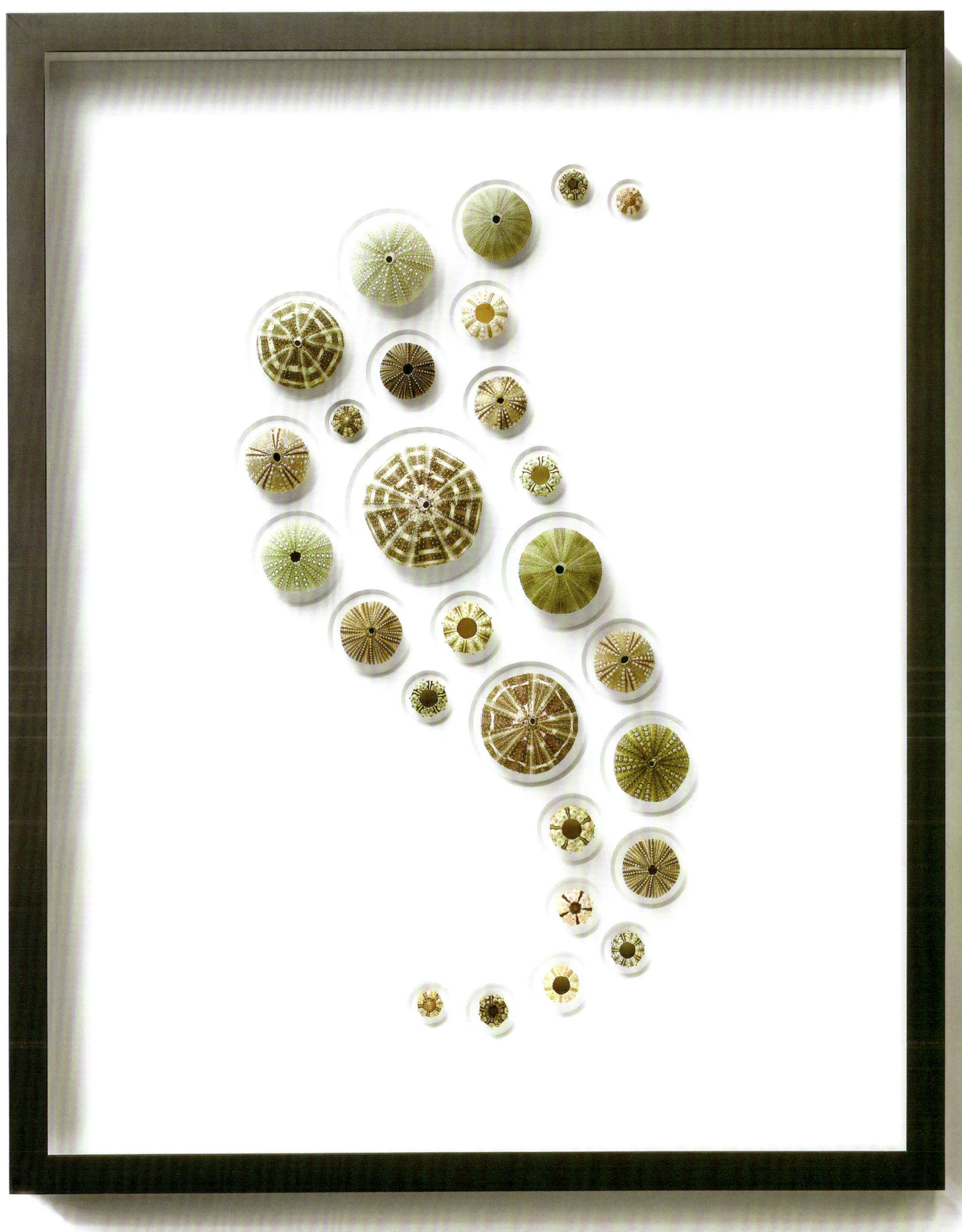

Urchin Spheres

Thailand, Philippines, Mexico, United States

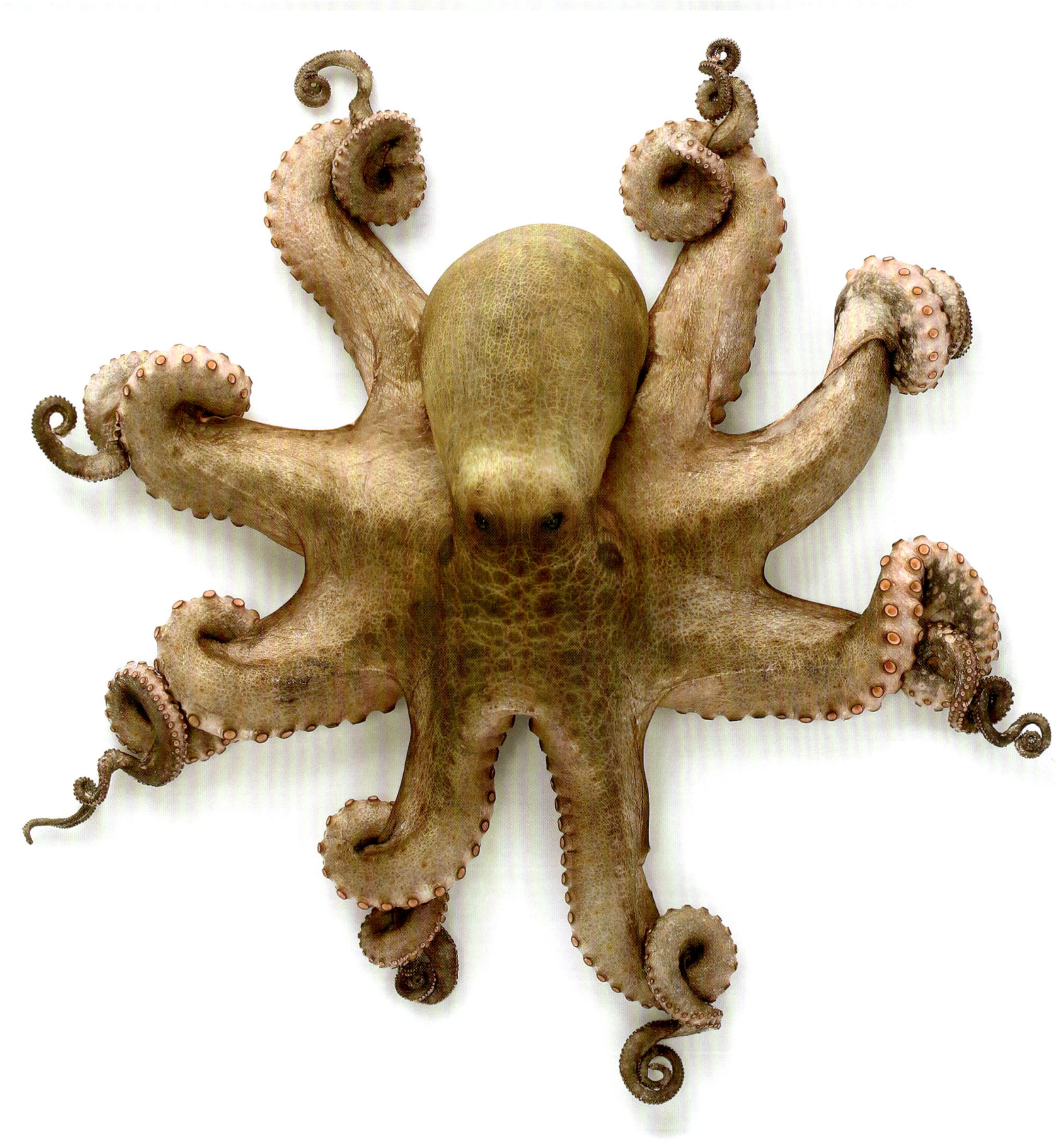

Preserved Octopus

Atlantic Ocean

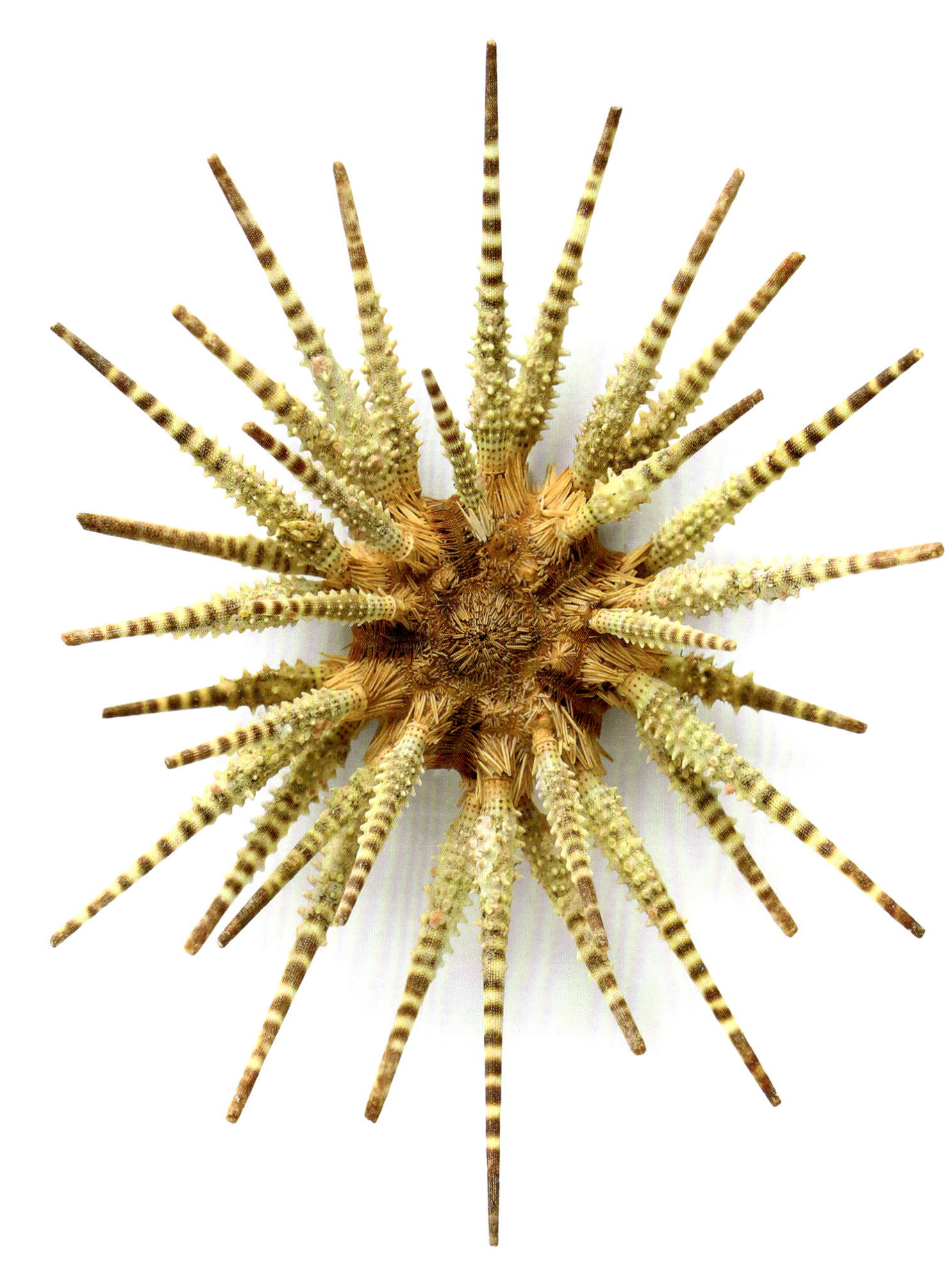

Barnacled Sea Urchin

Philippines

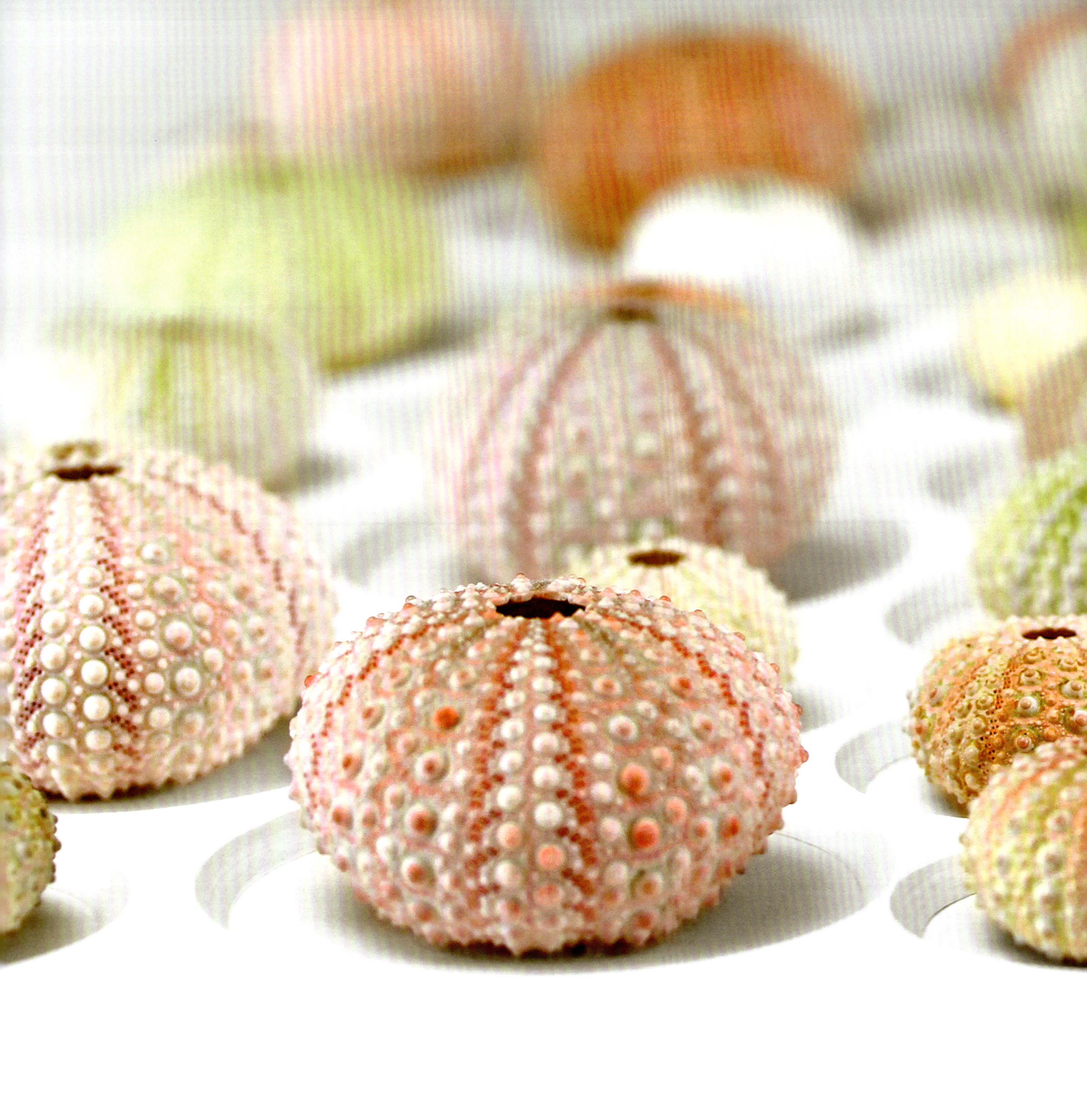

Pastel Urchin Mosaic

Philippines

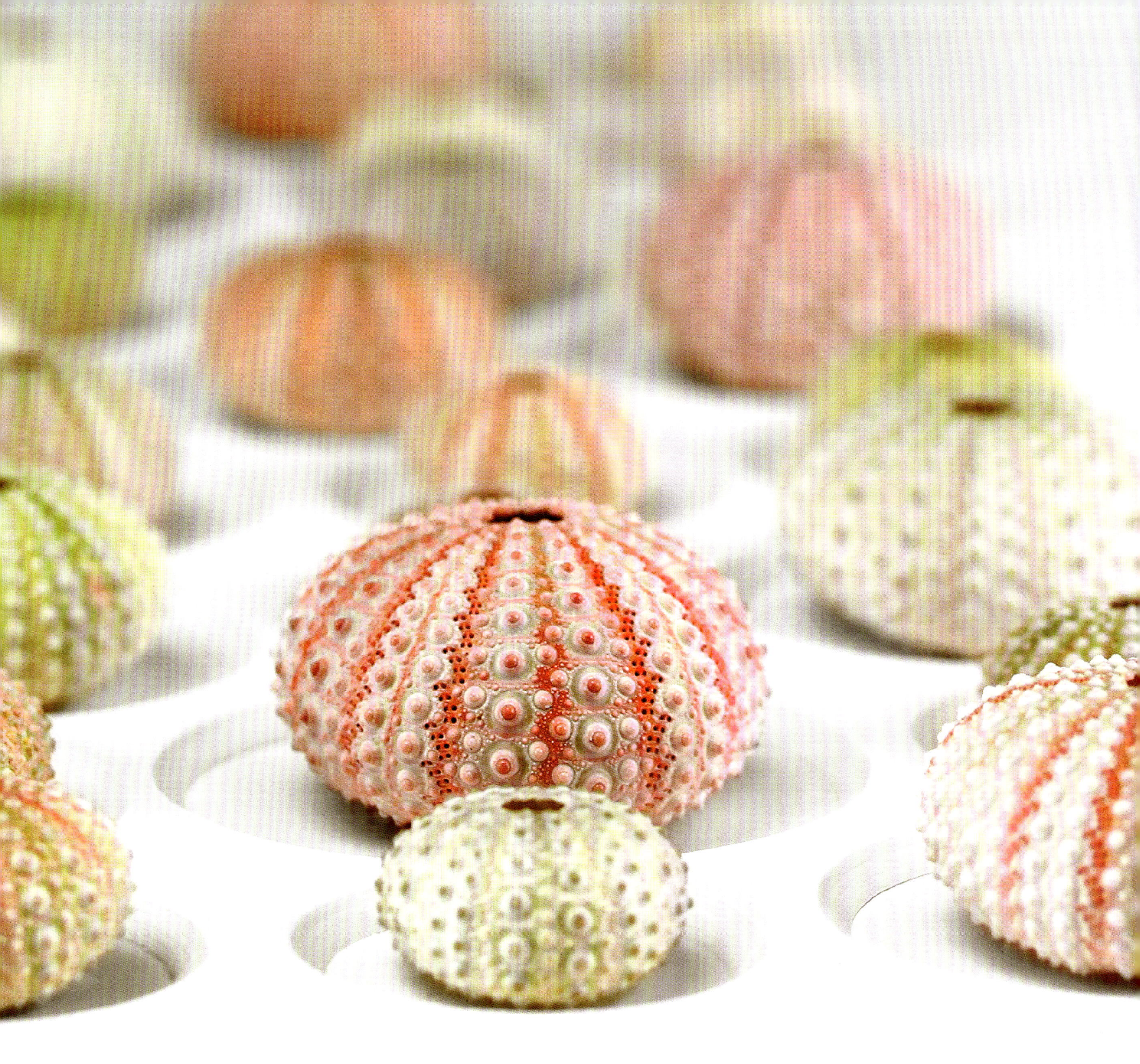

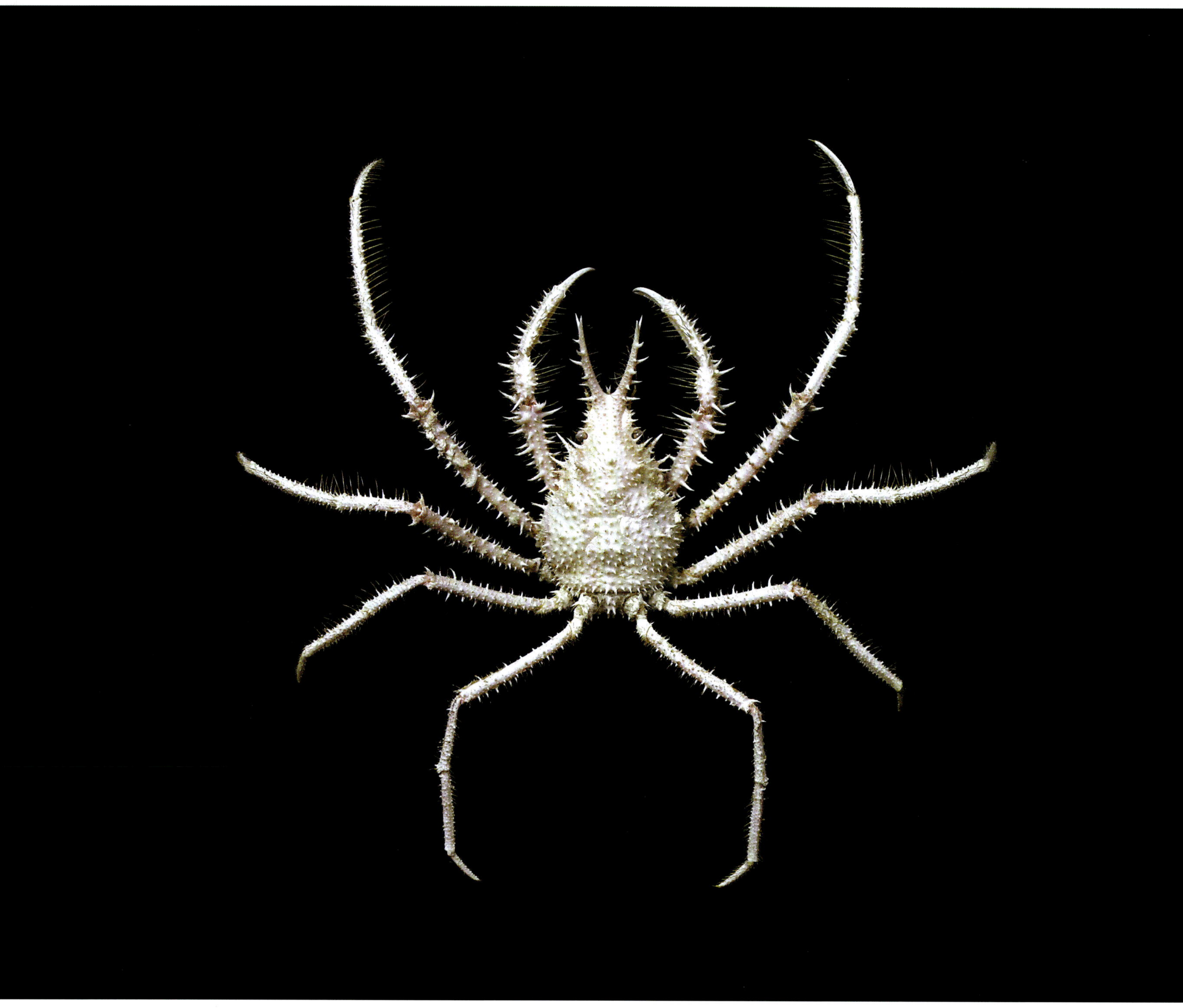

Spider Crab

Philippines

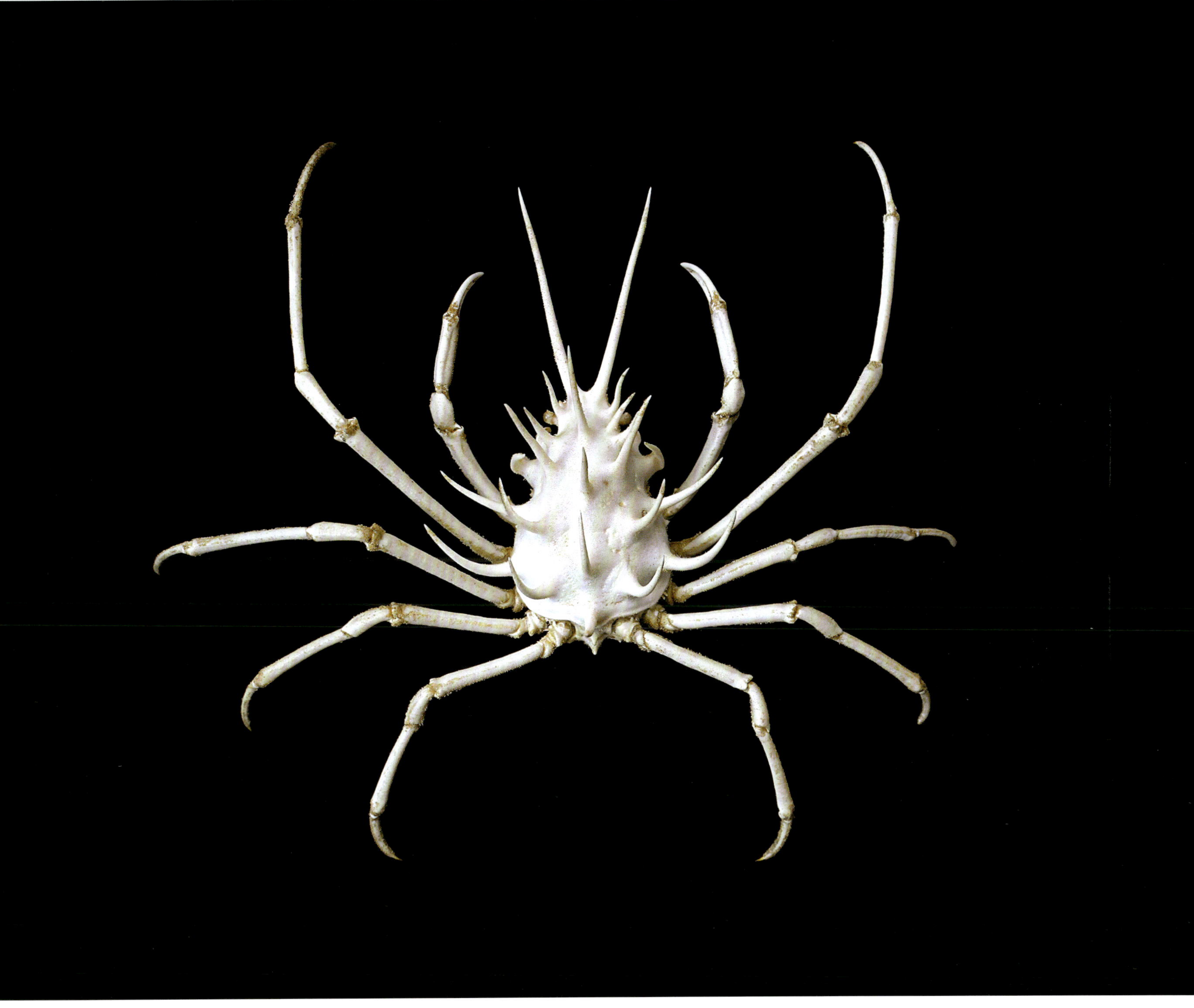

Thorn Crab

Philippines

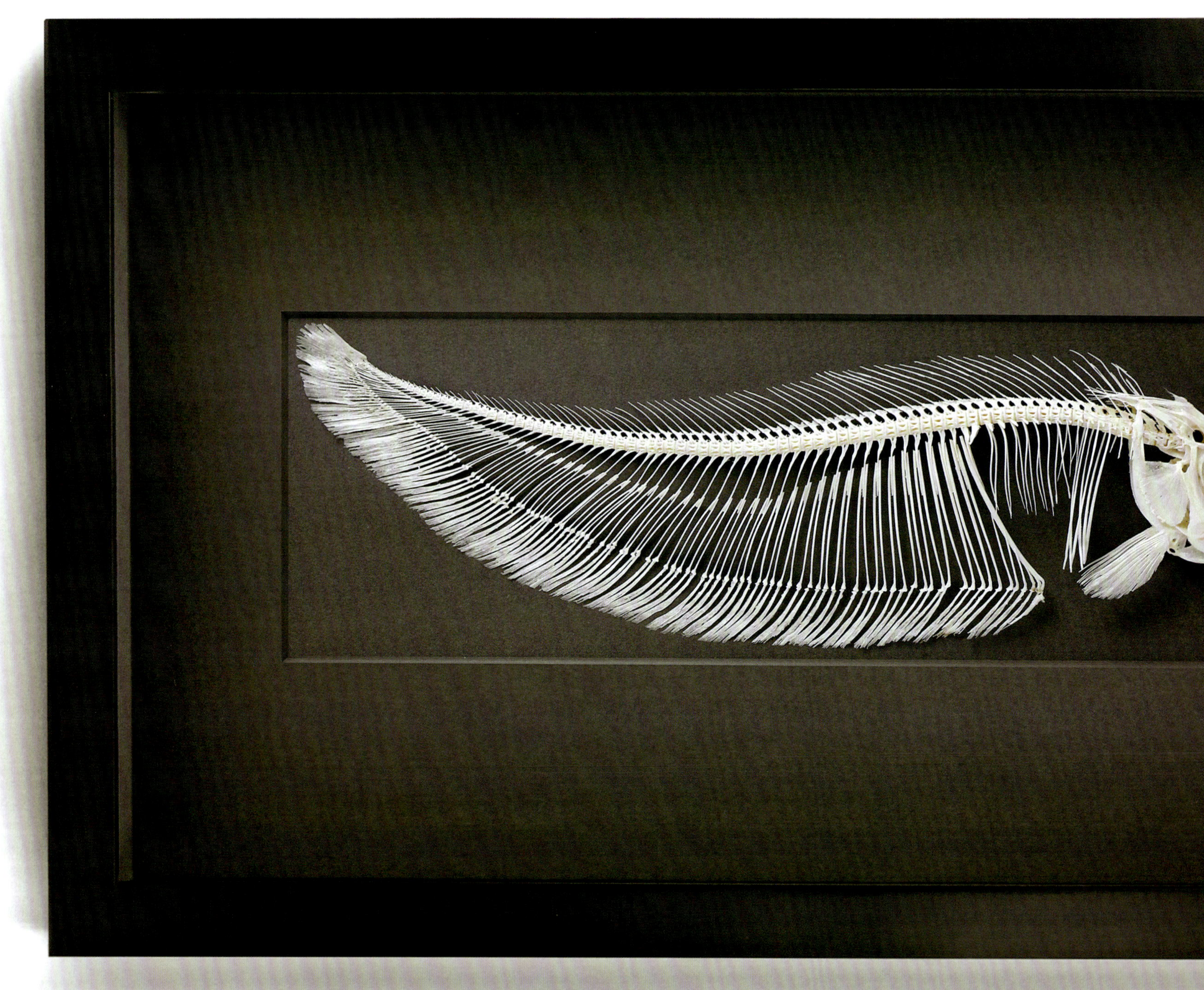

Knife Fish

Thailand

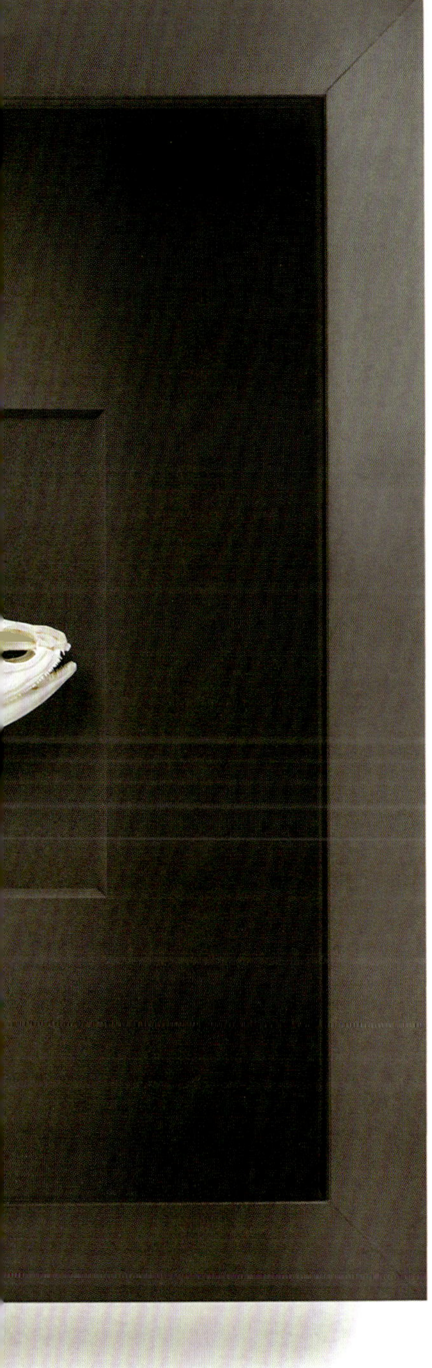

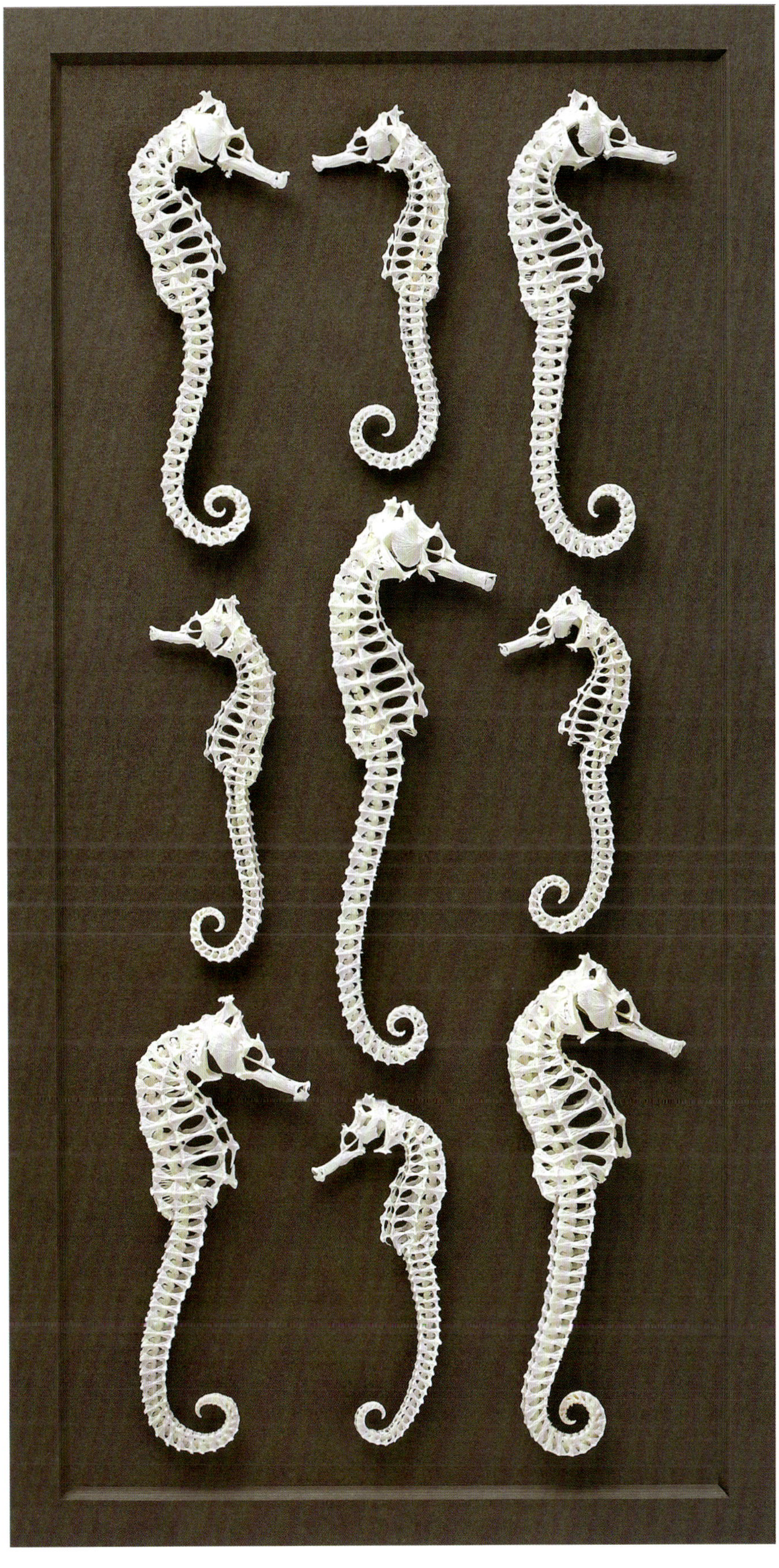

Sea Horse Skeletons

Philippines

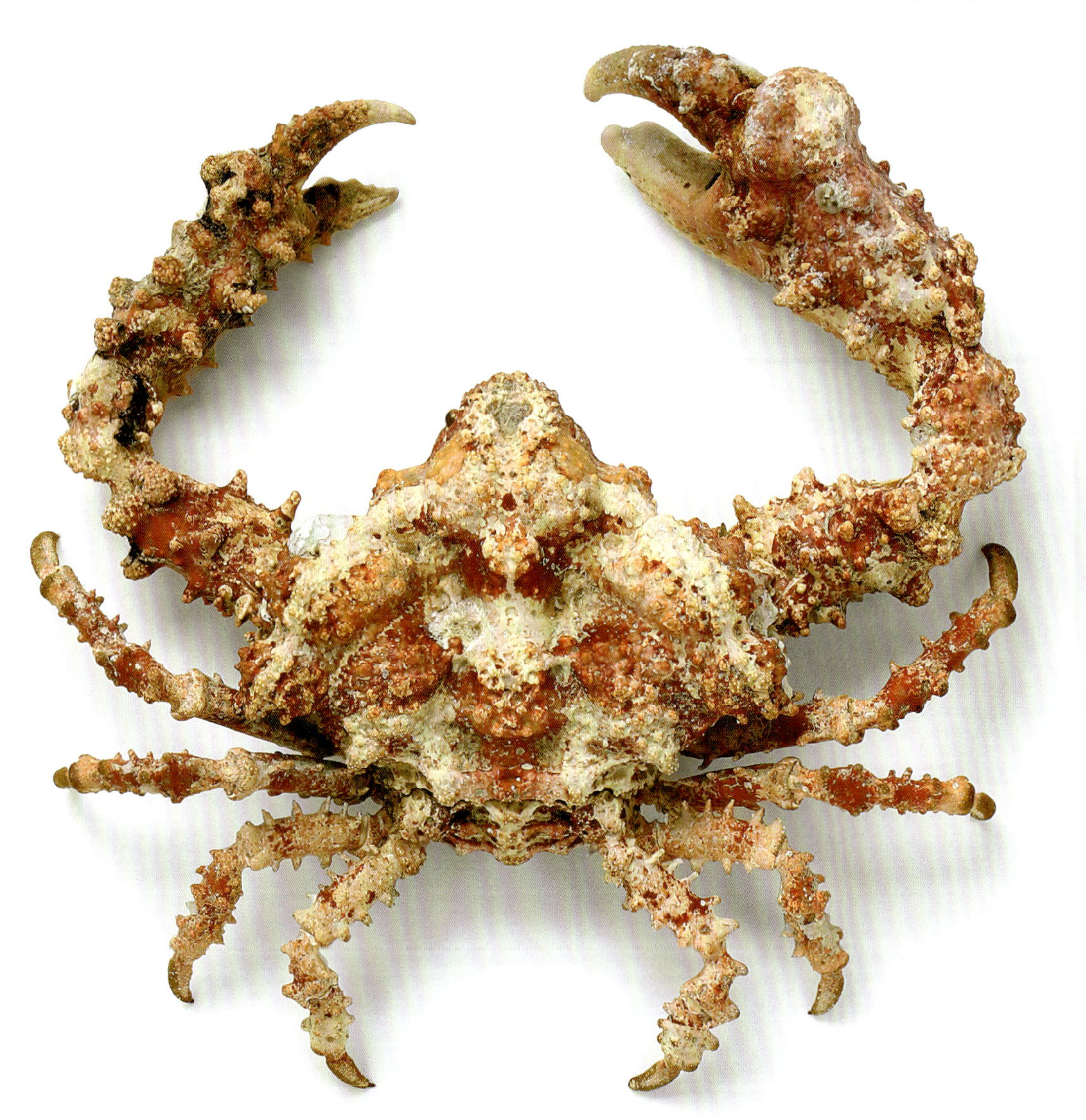

Horrid Elbow Crab

Philippines

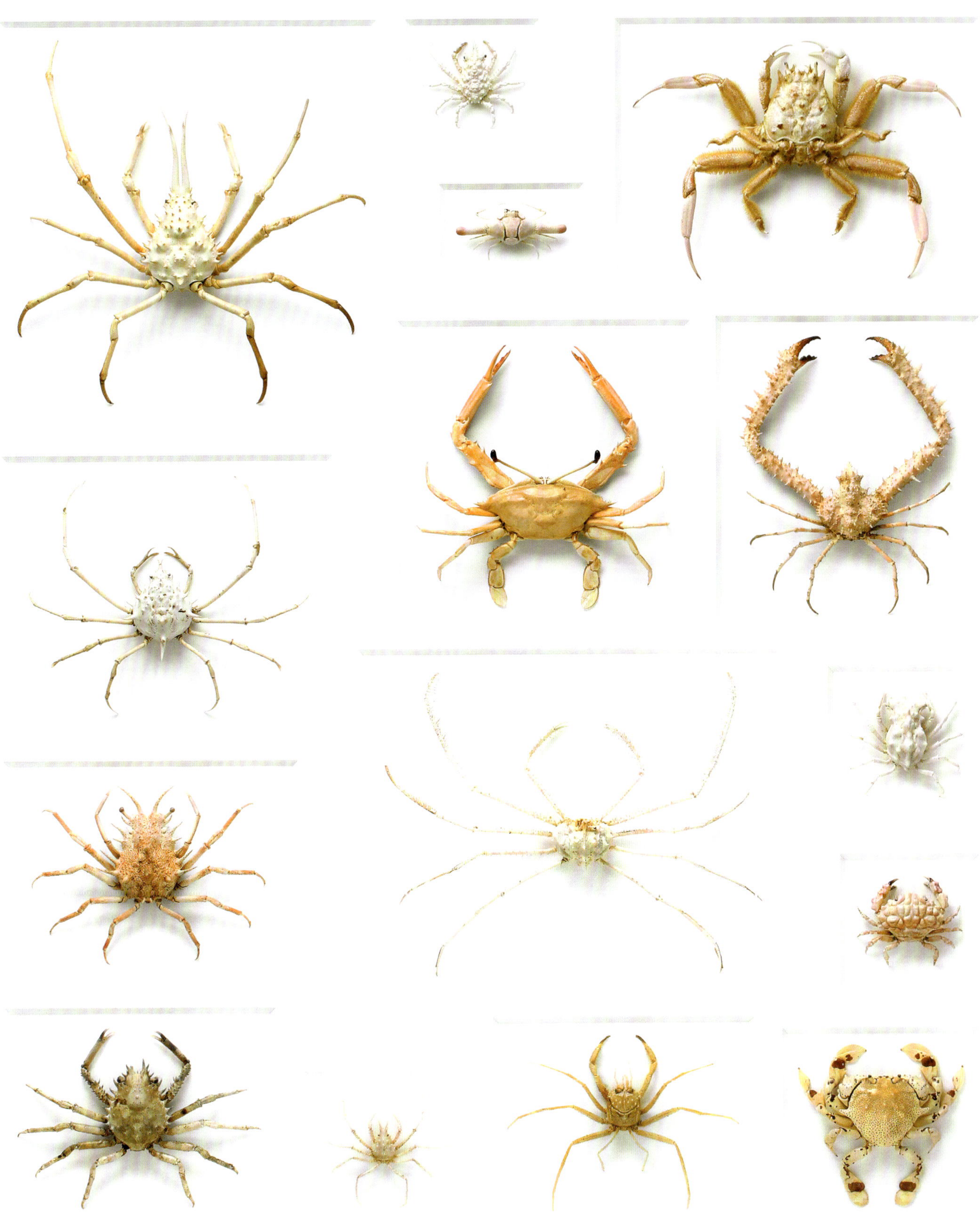

Decapod Mosaic

Philippines

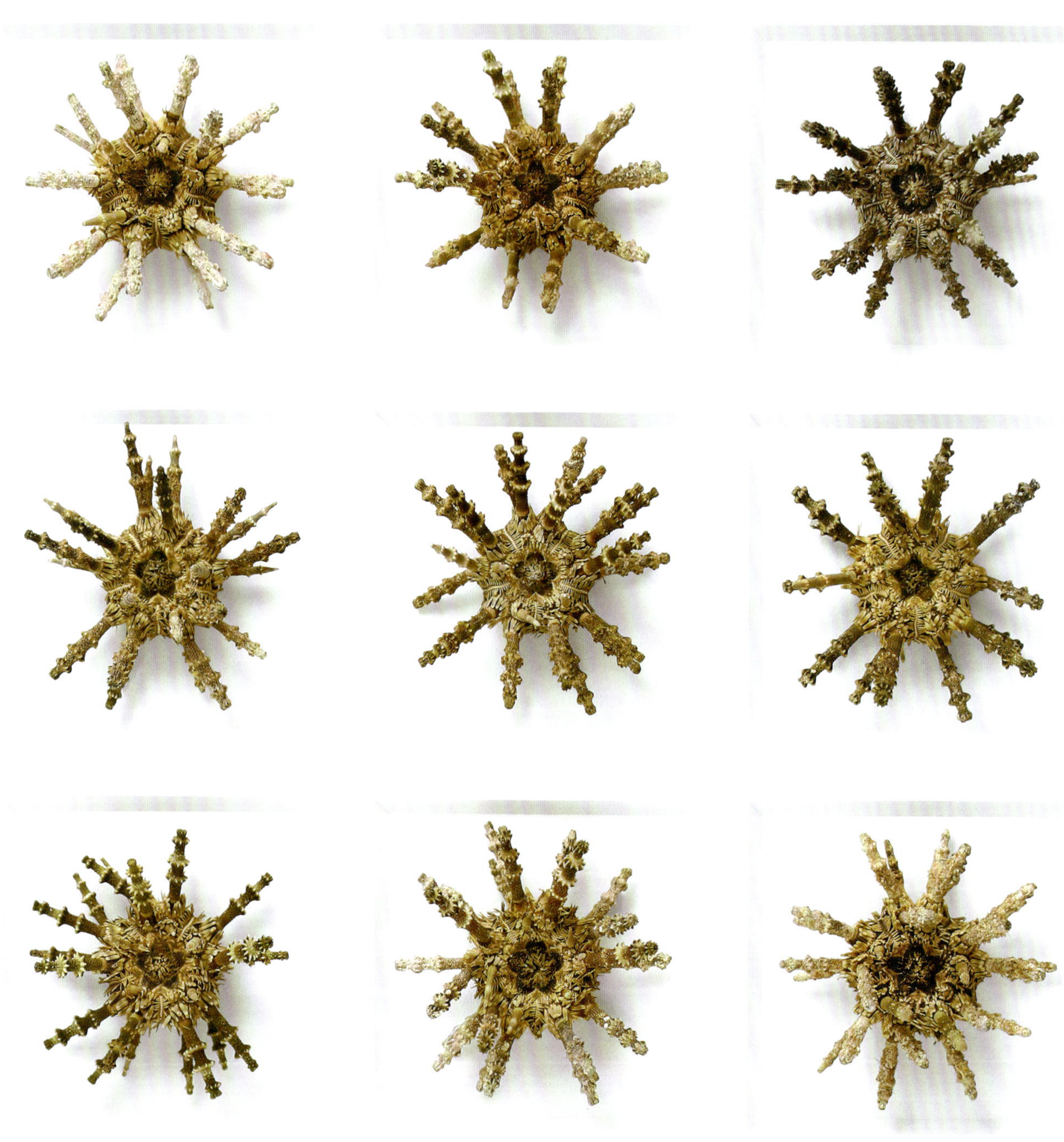

Sputnik Urchins

Philippines

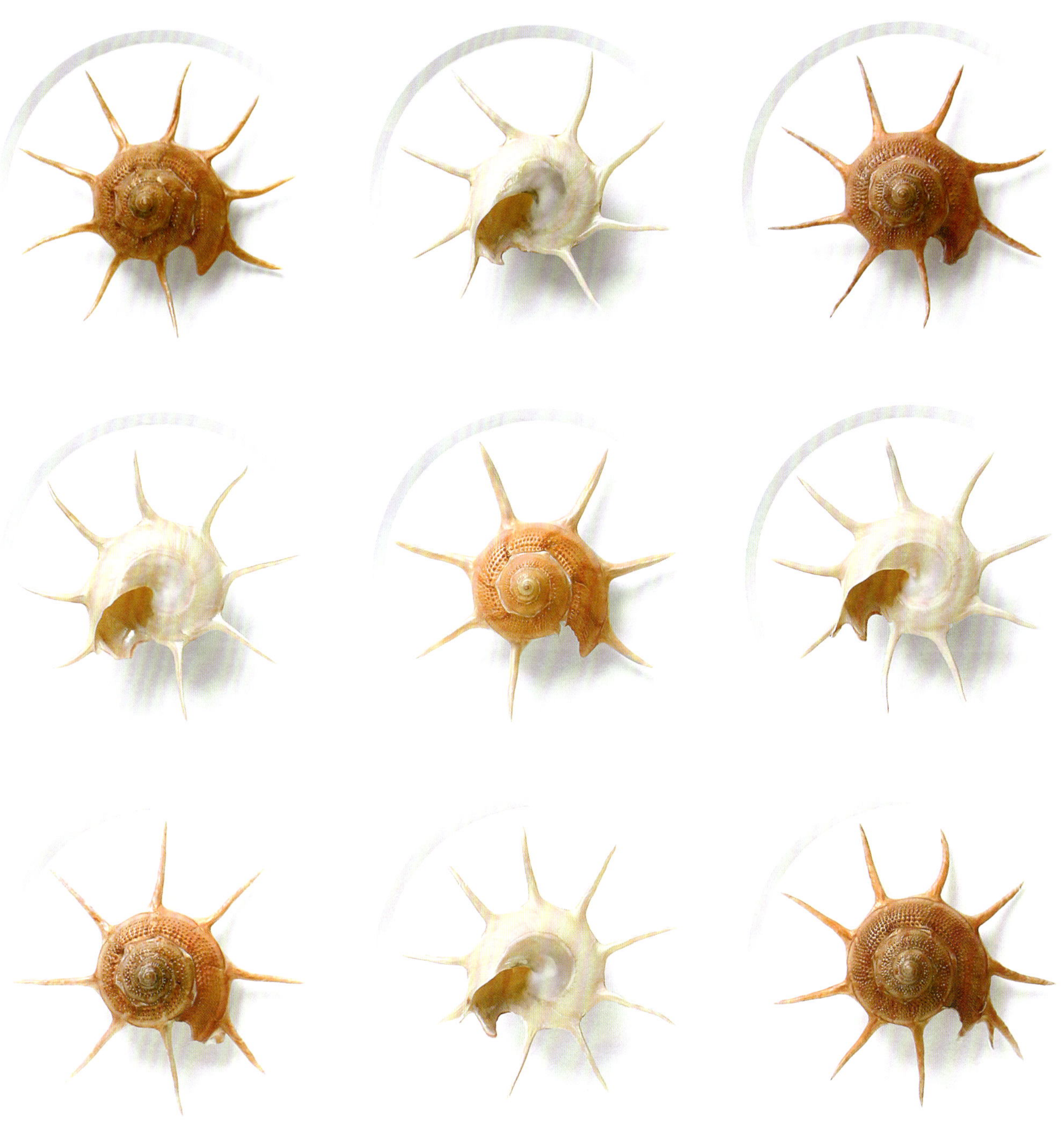

Gilded Starshells

Philippines

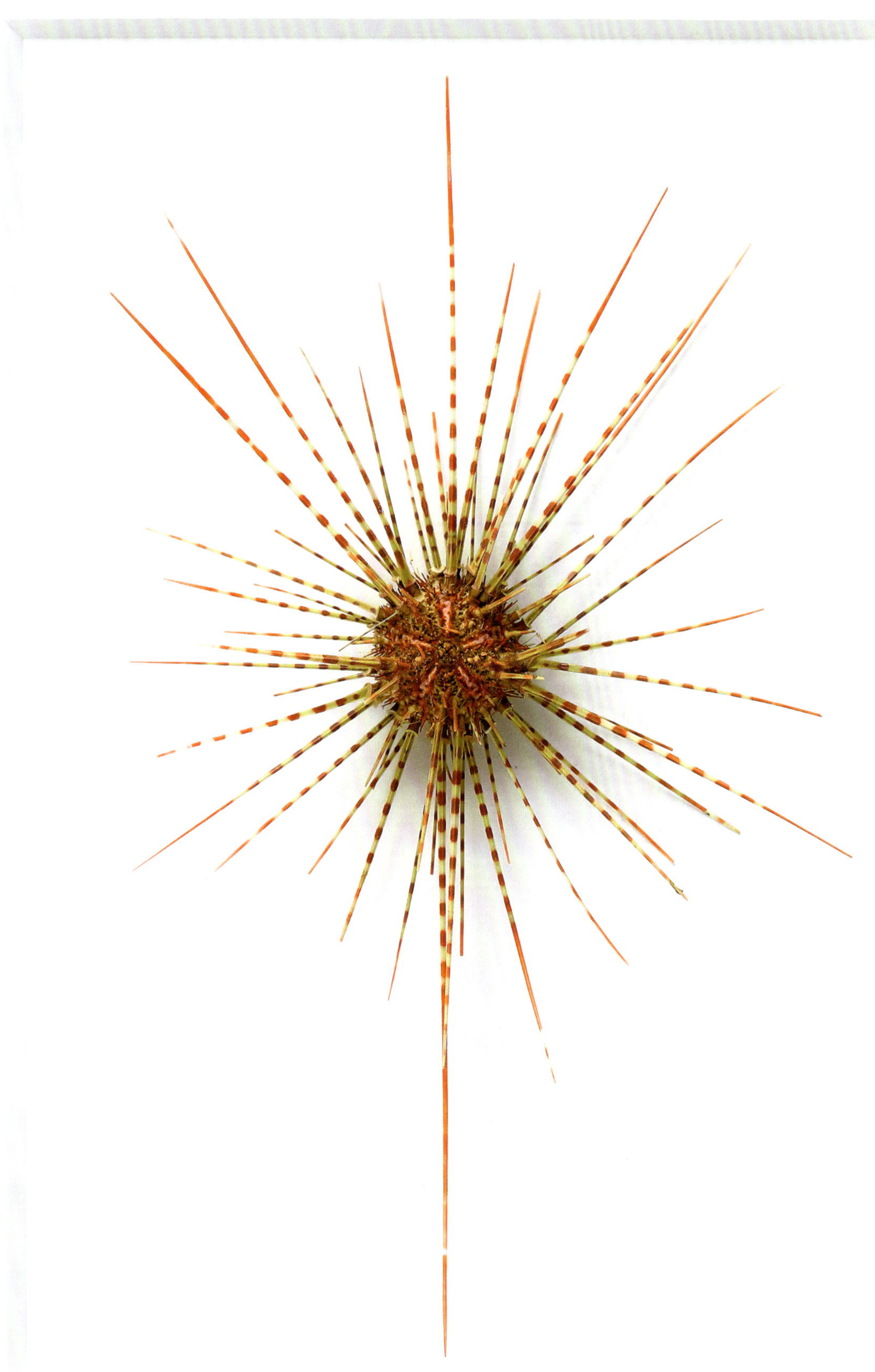

Maillardi Urchin

Philippines

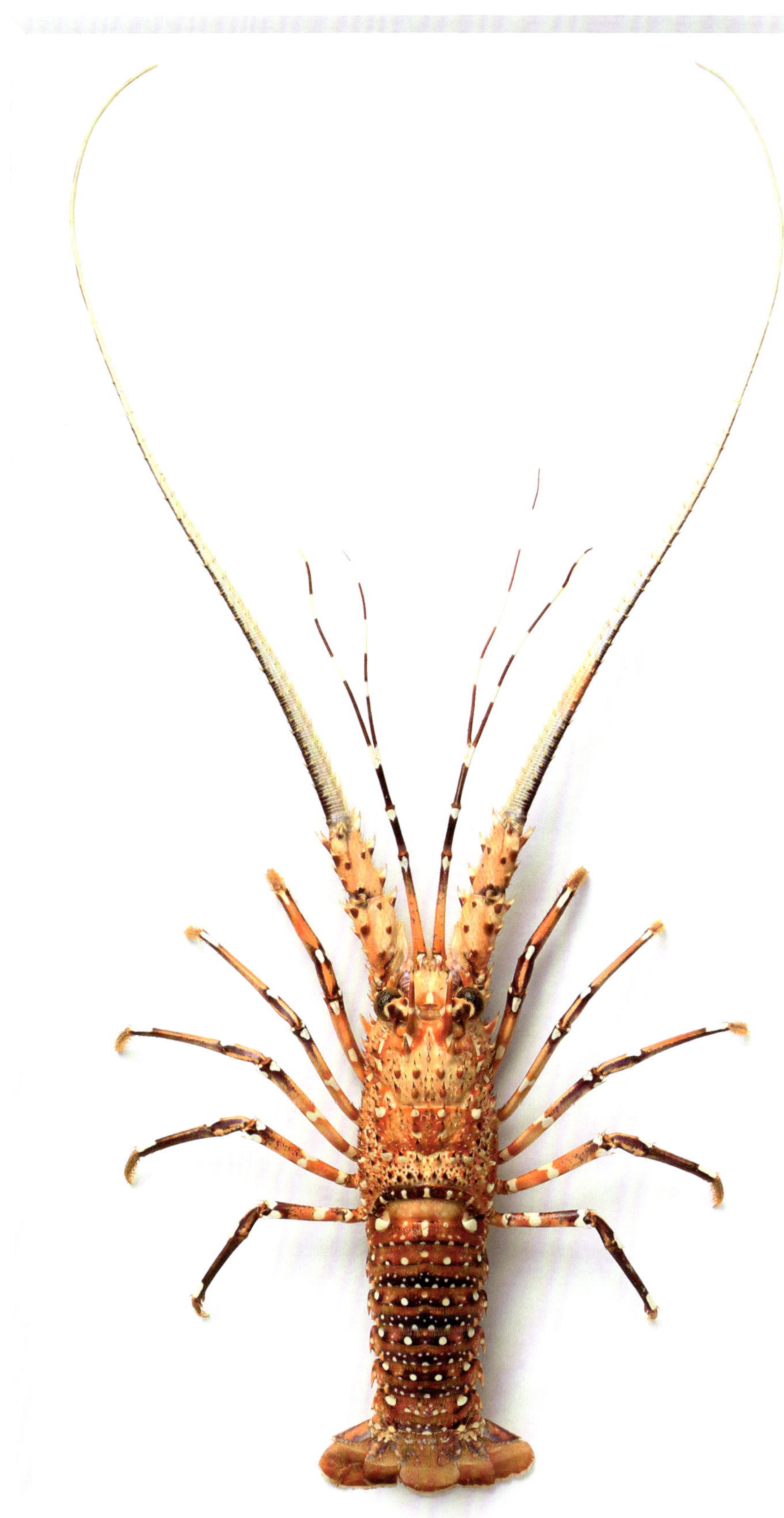

Painted Lobster

Indonesia

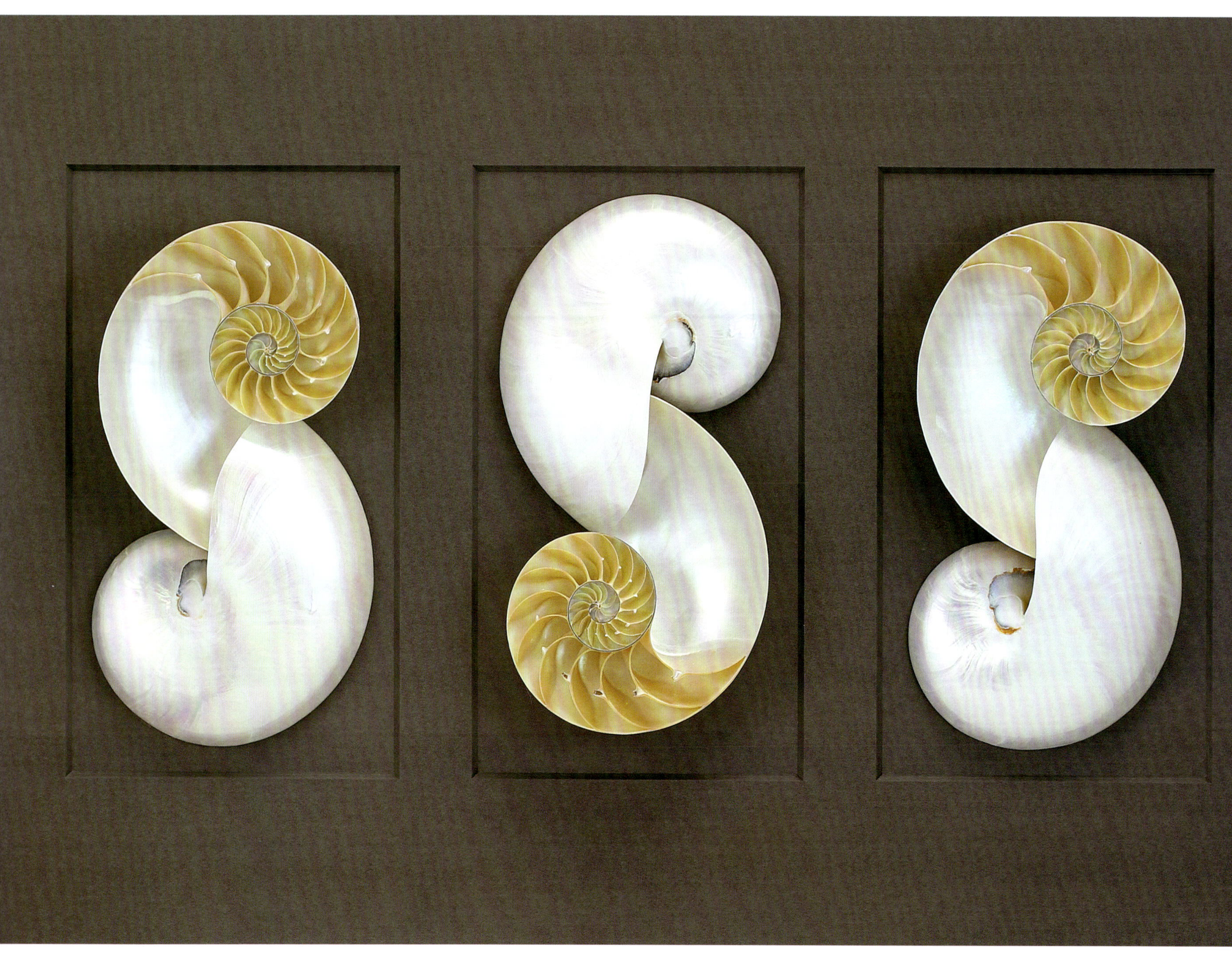

Nautilus Trio

Philippines

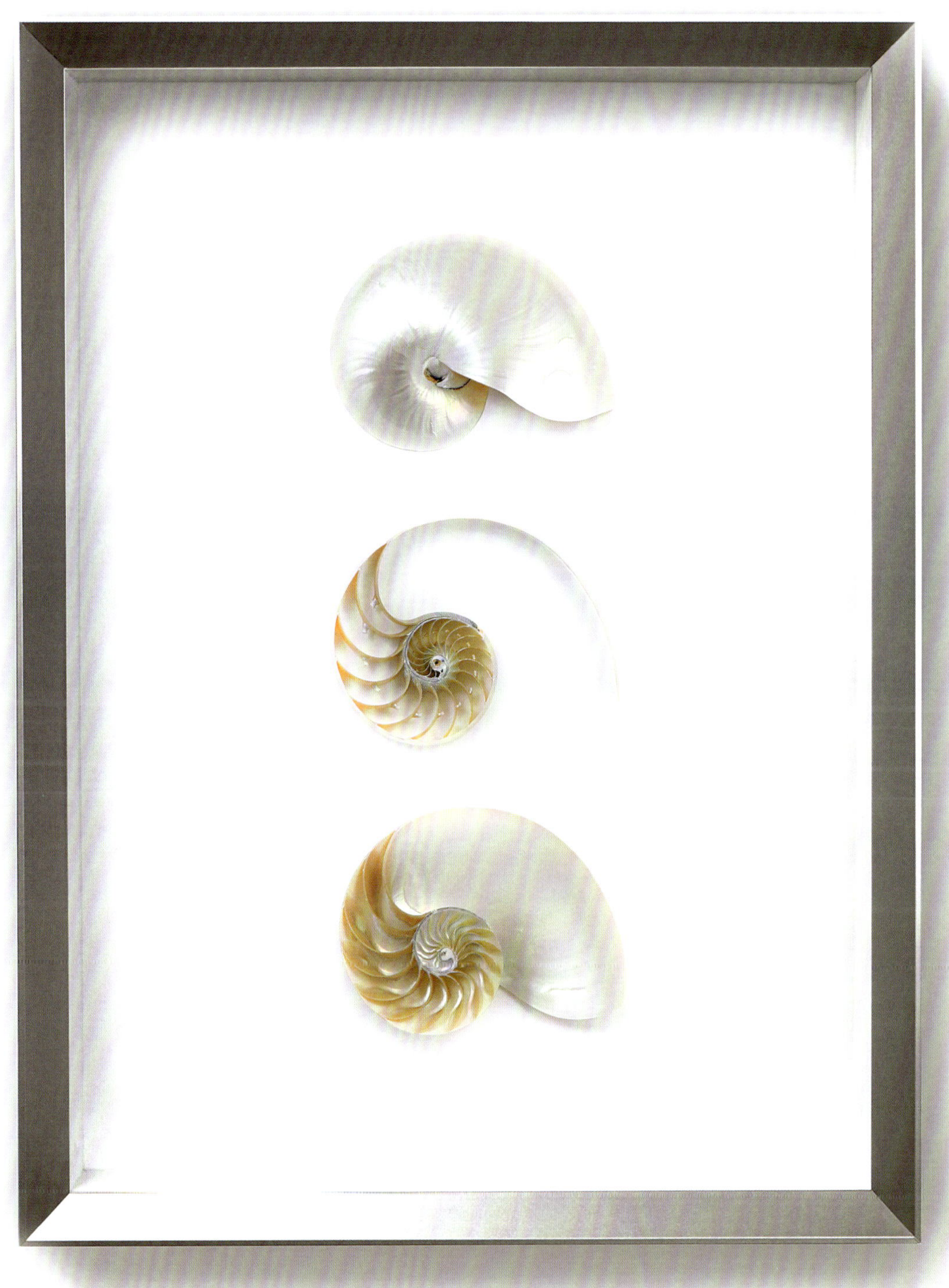

Nautilus Triptych

Philippines

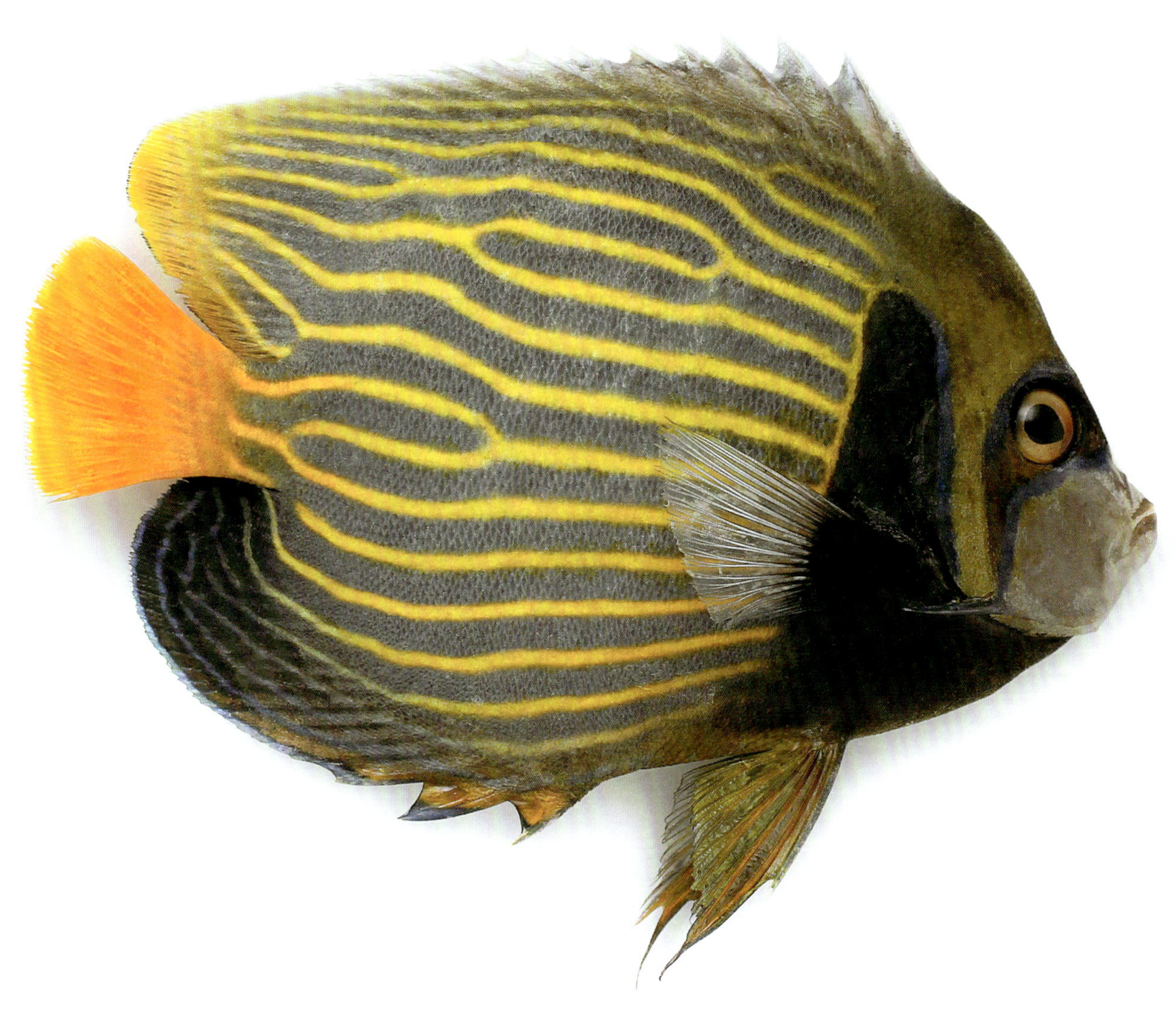

Emperor Angelfish

Red Sea

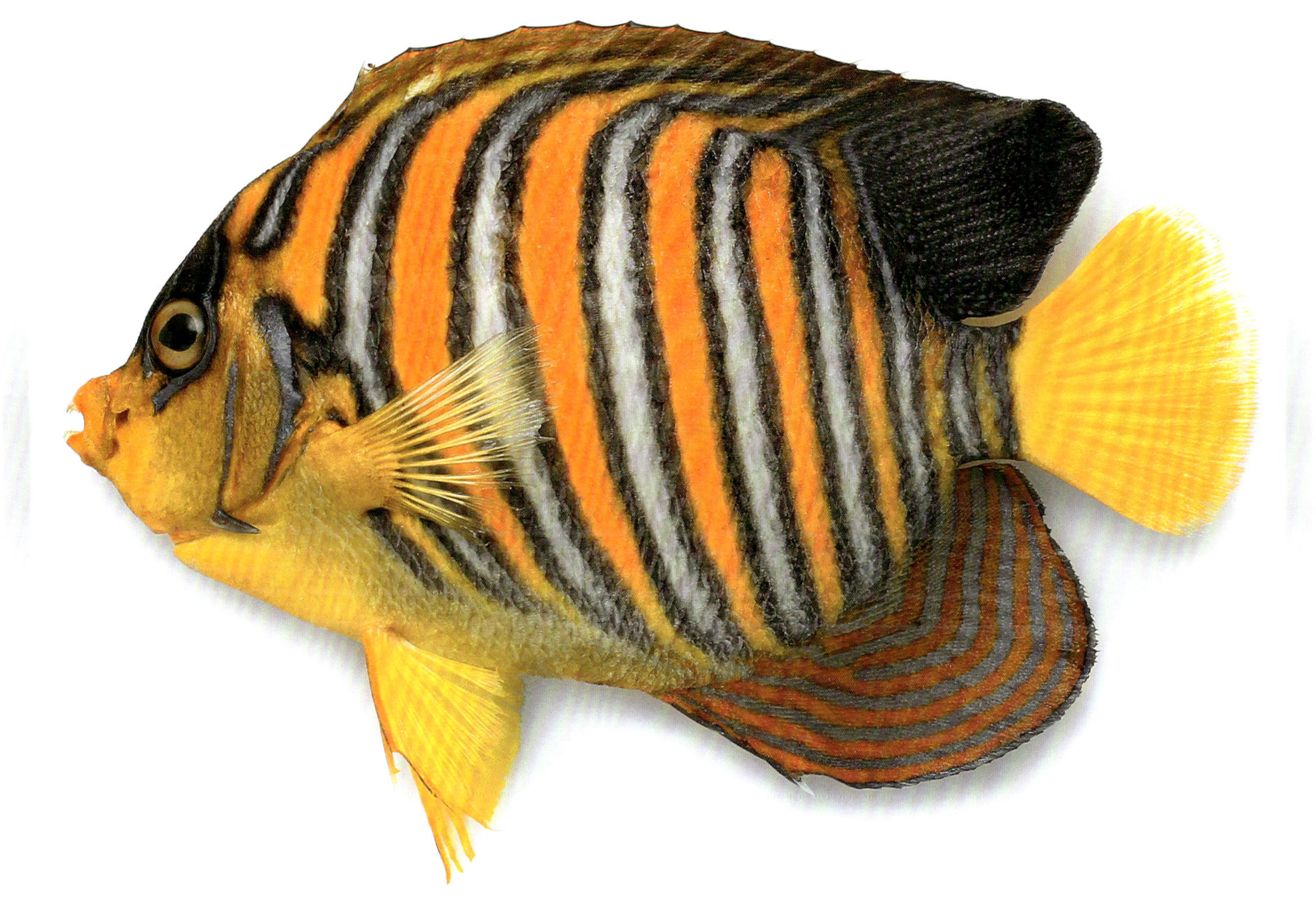

Regal Angelfish

Indian Ocean

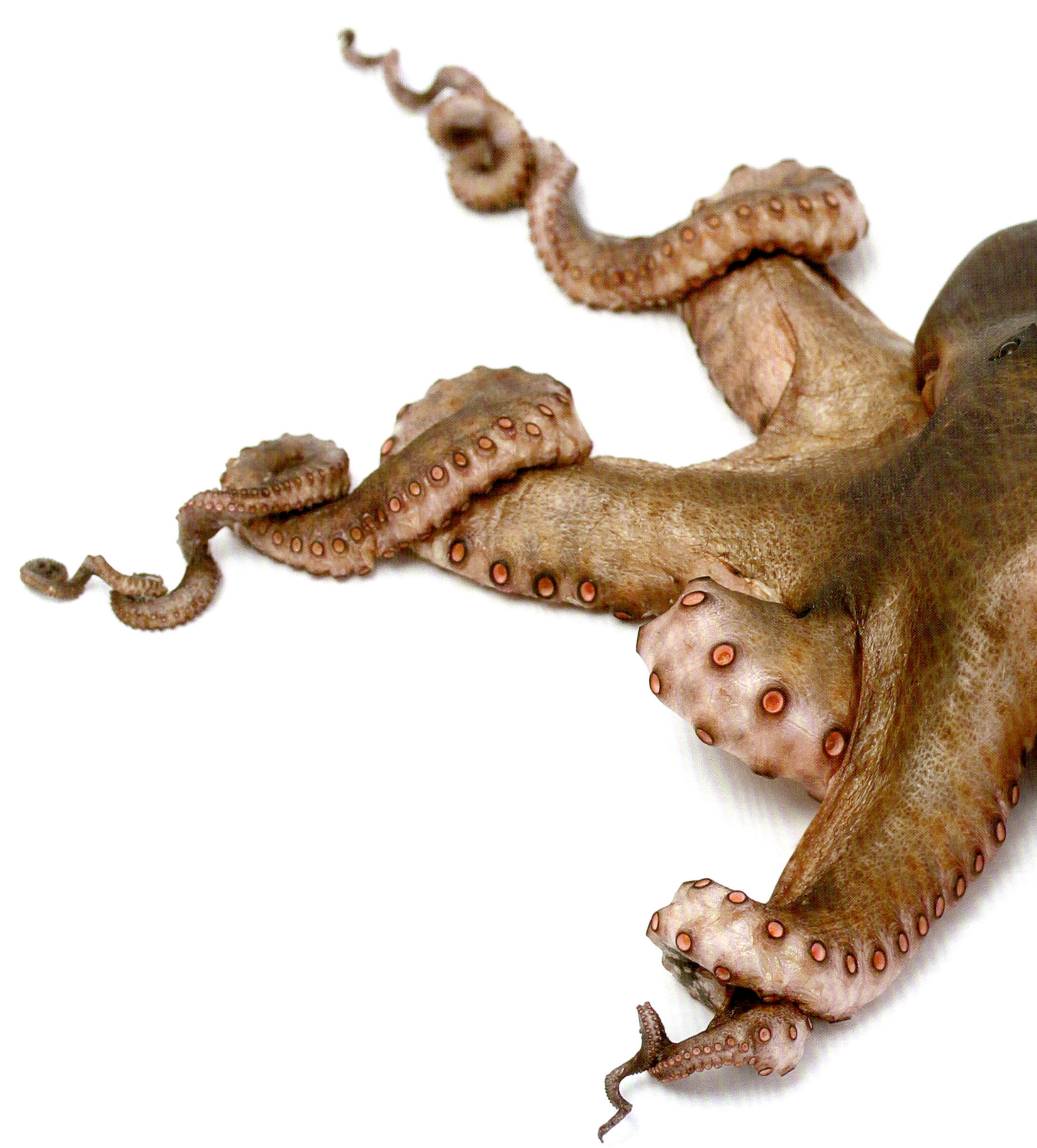

Octopus

Atlantic Ocean

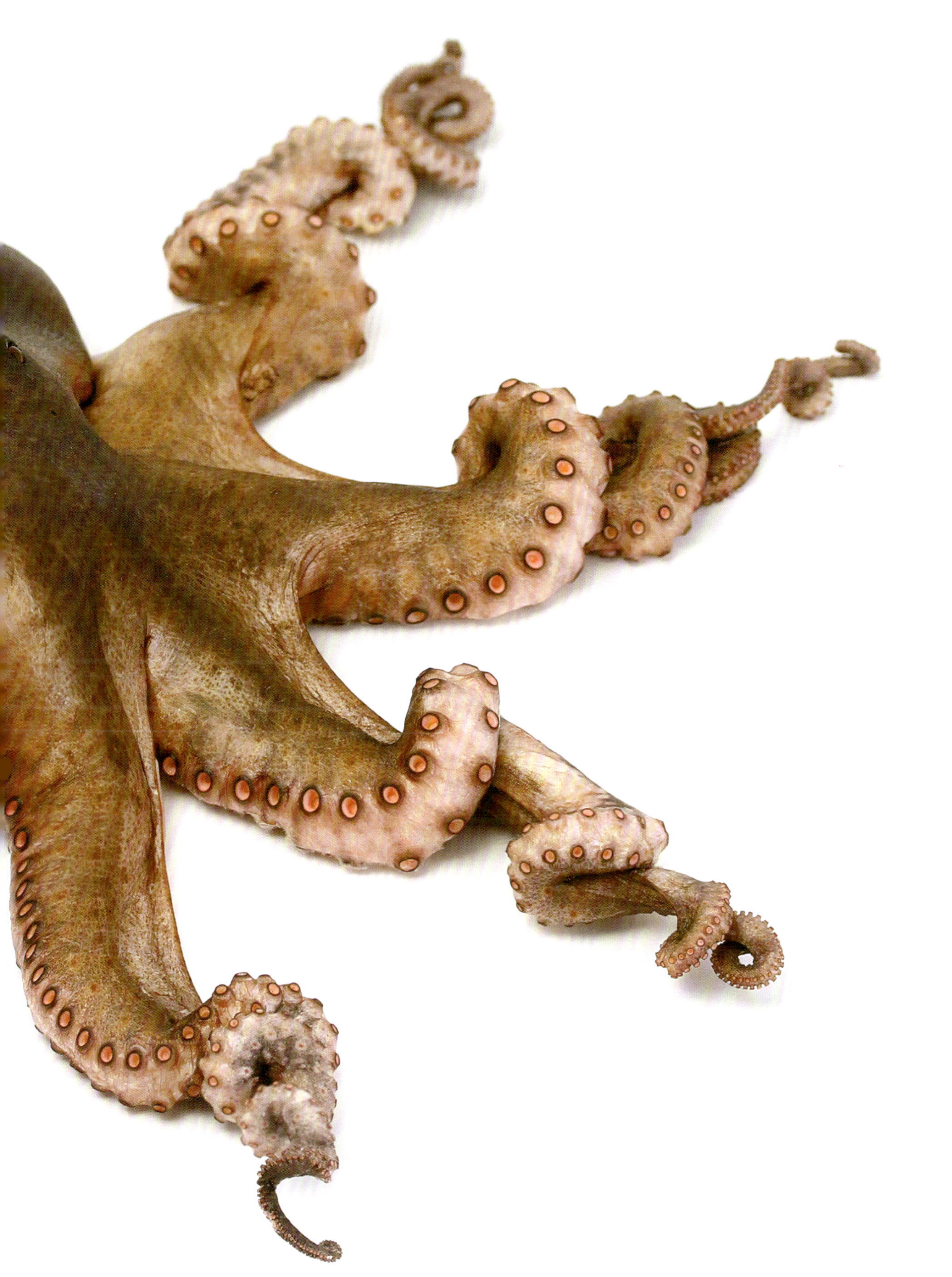

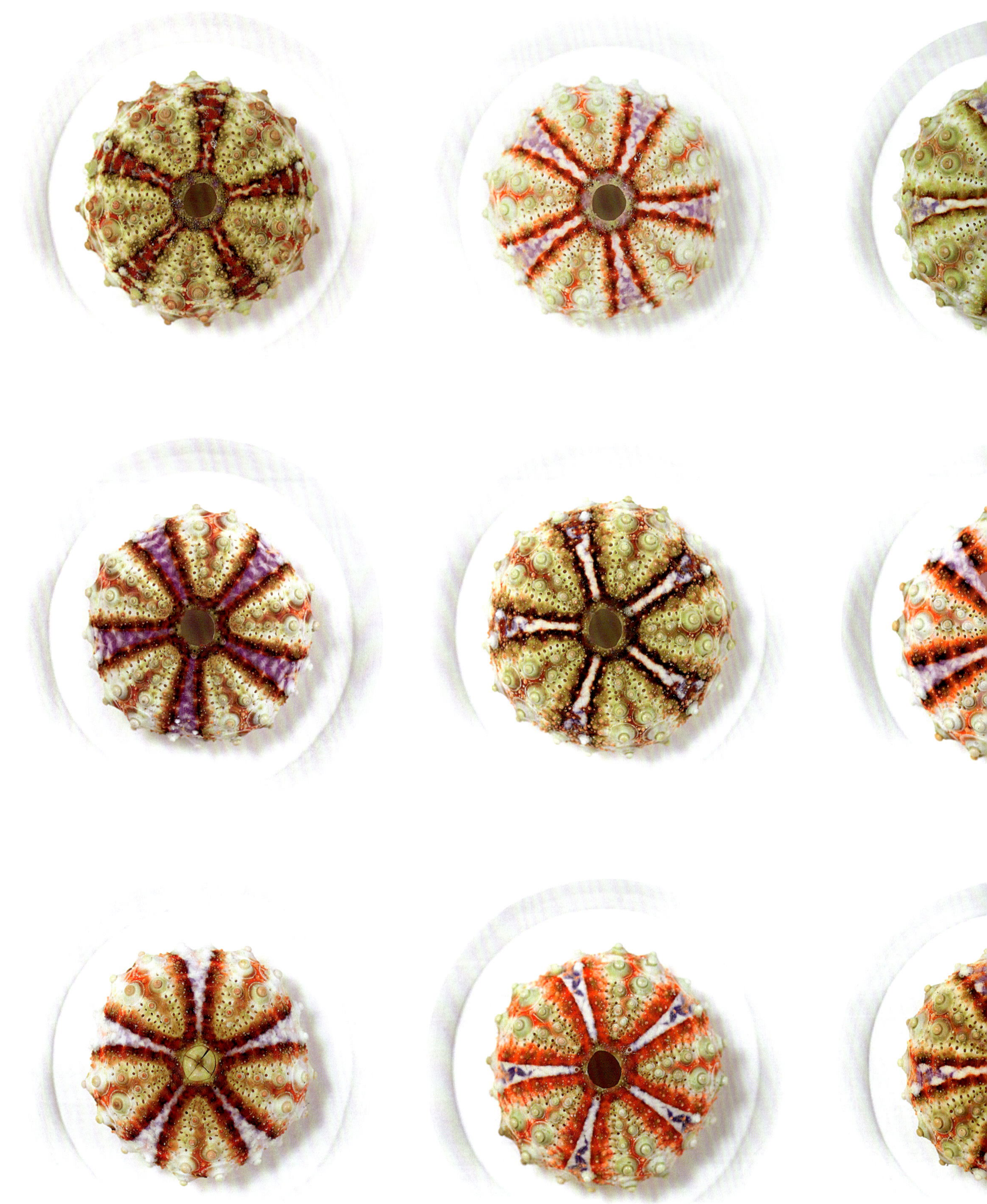

Variegated Urchins

Philippines

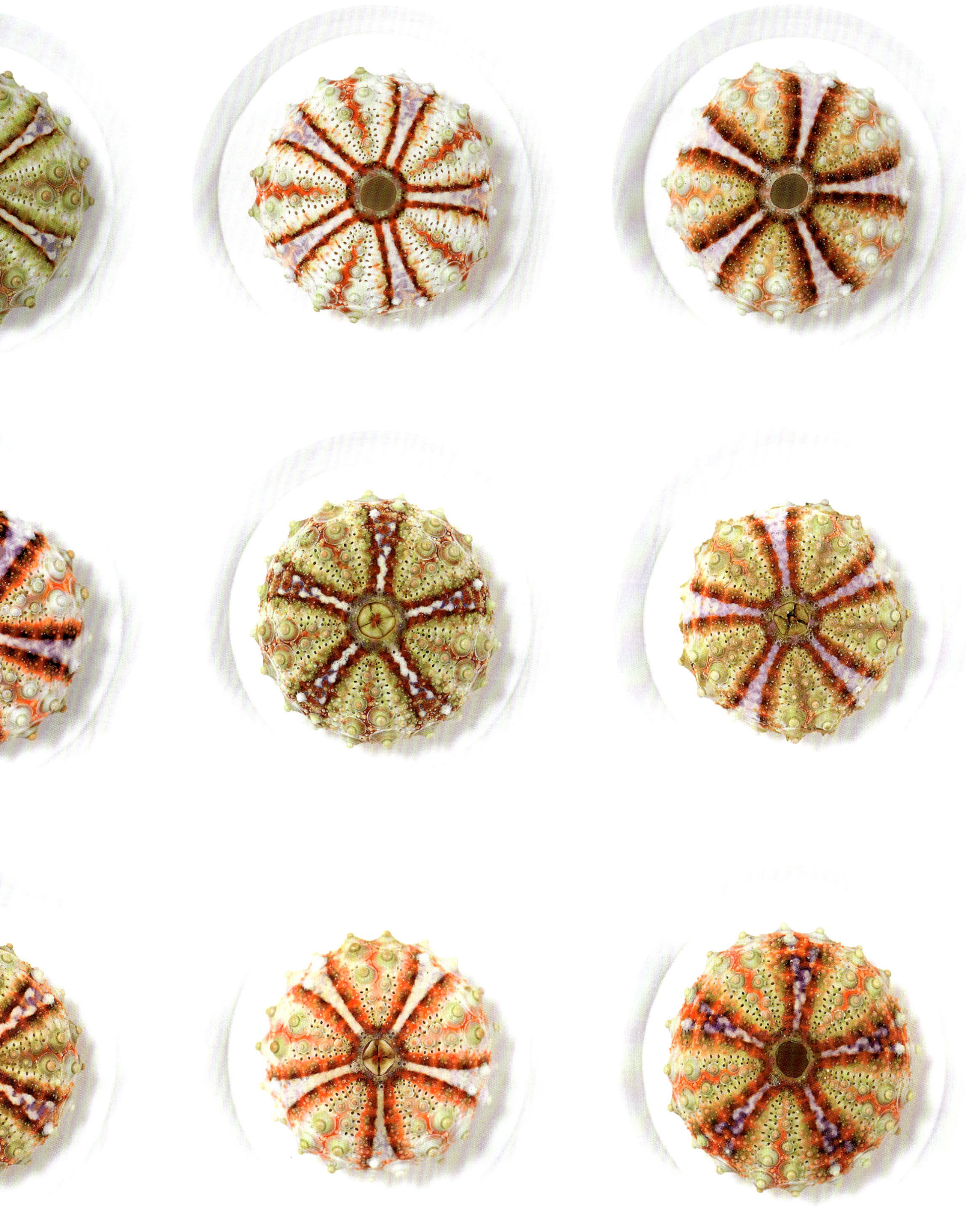

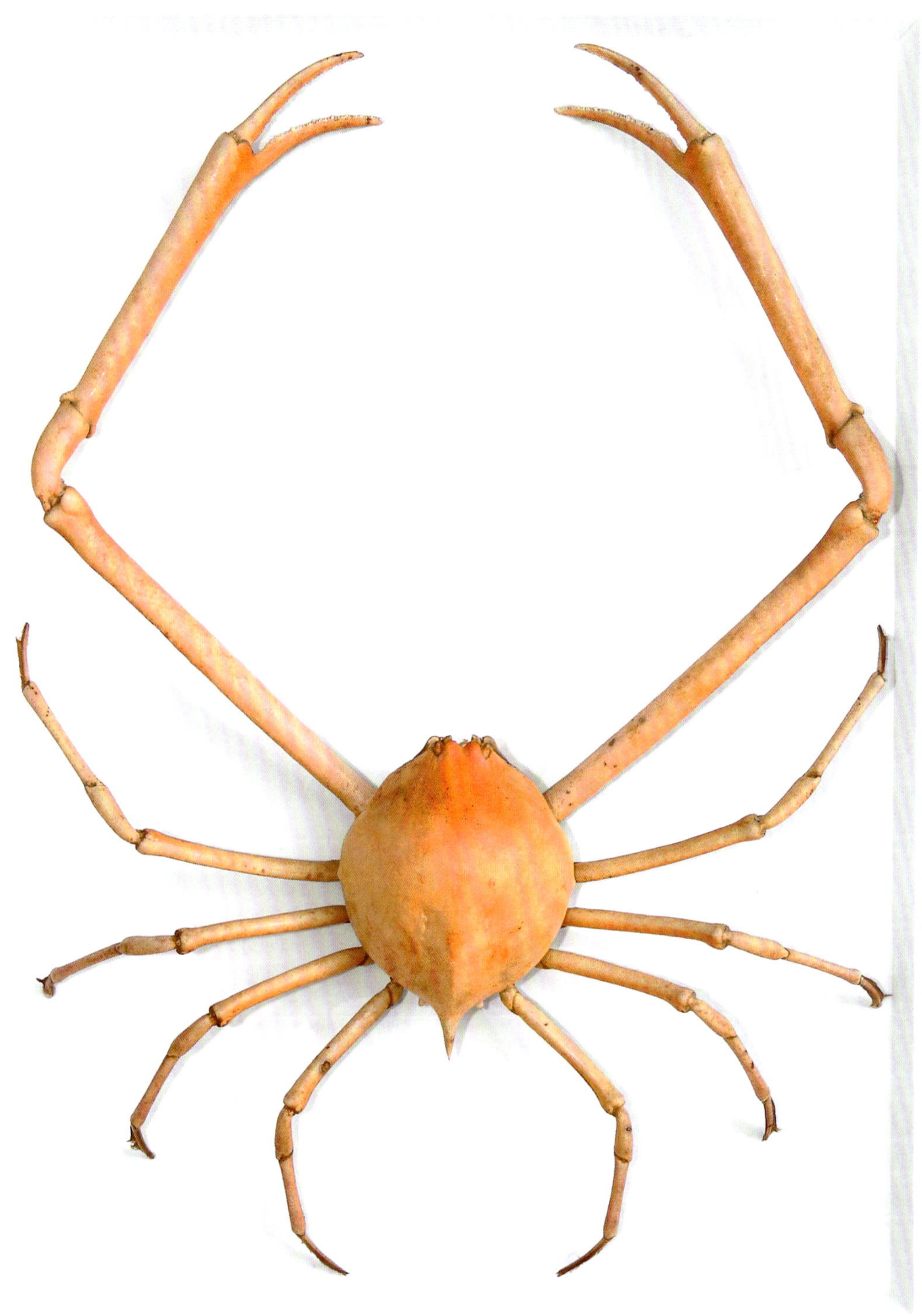

Pebble Crab

Philippines

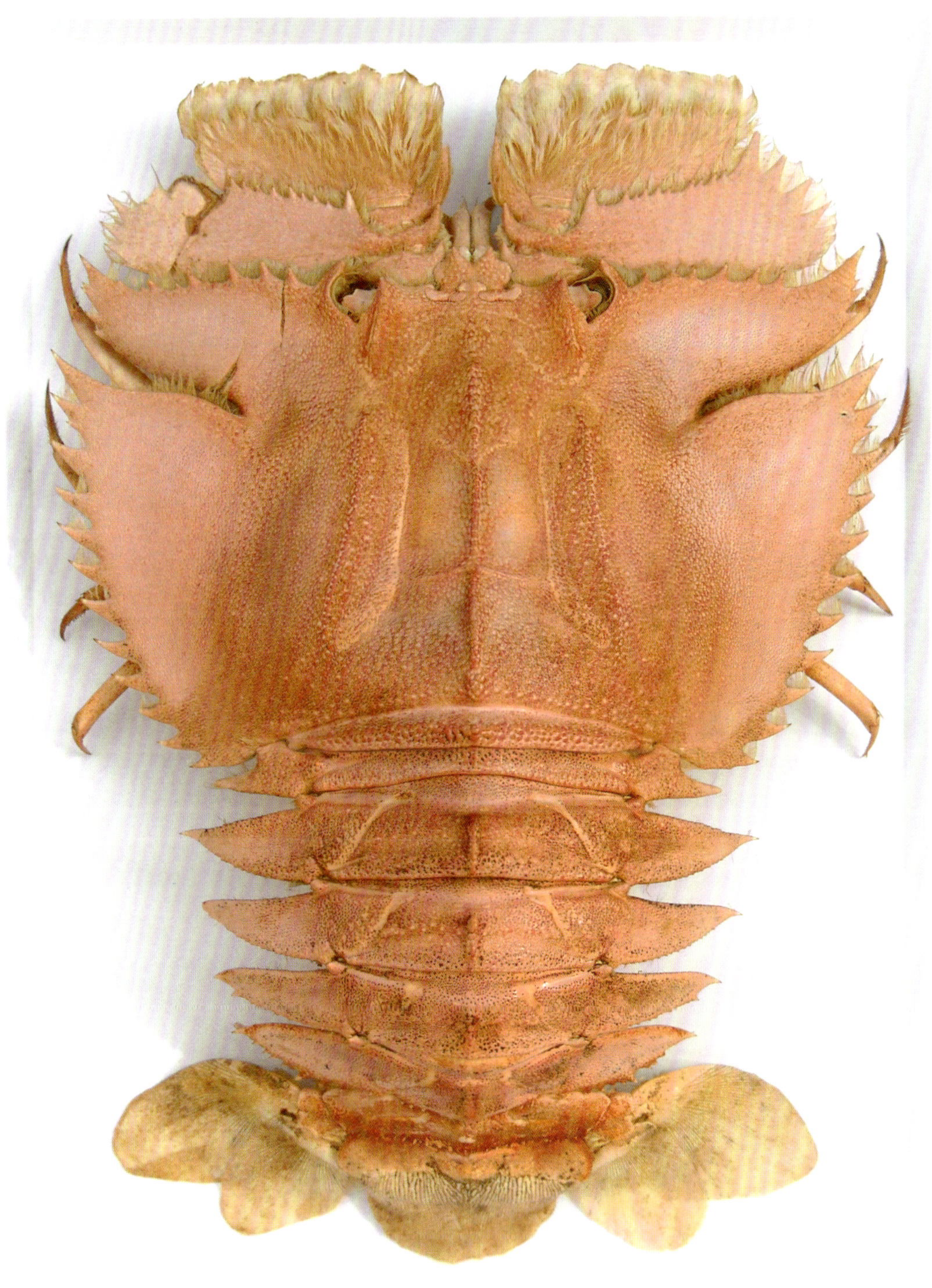

Slipper Lobster

Philippines

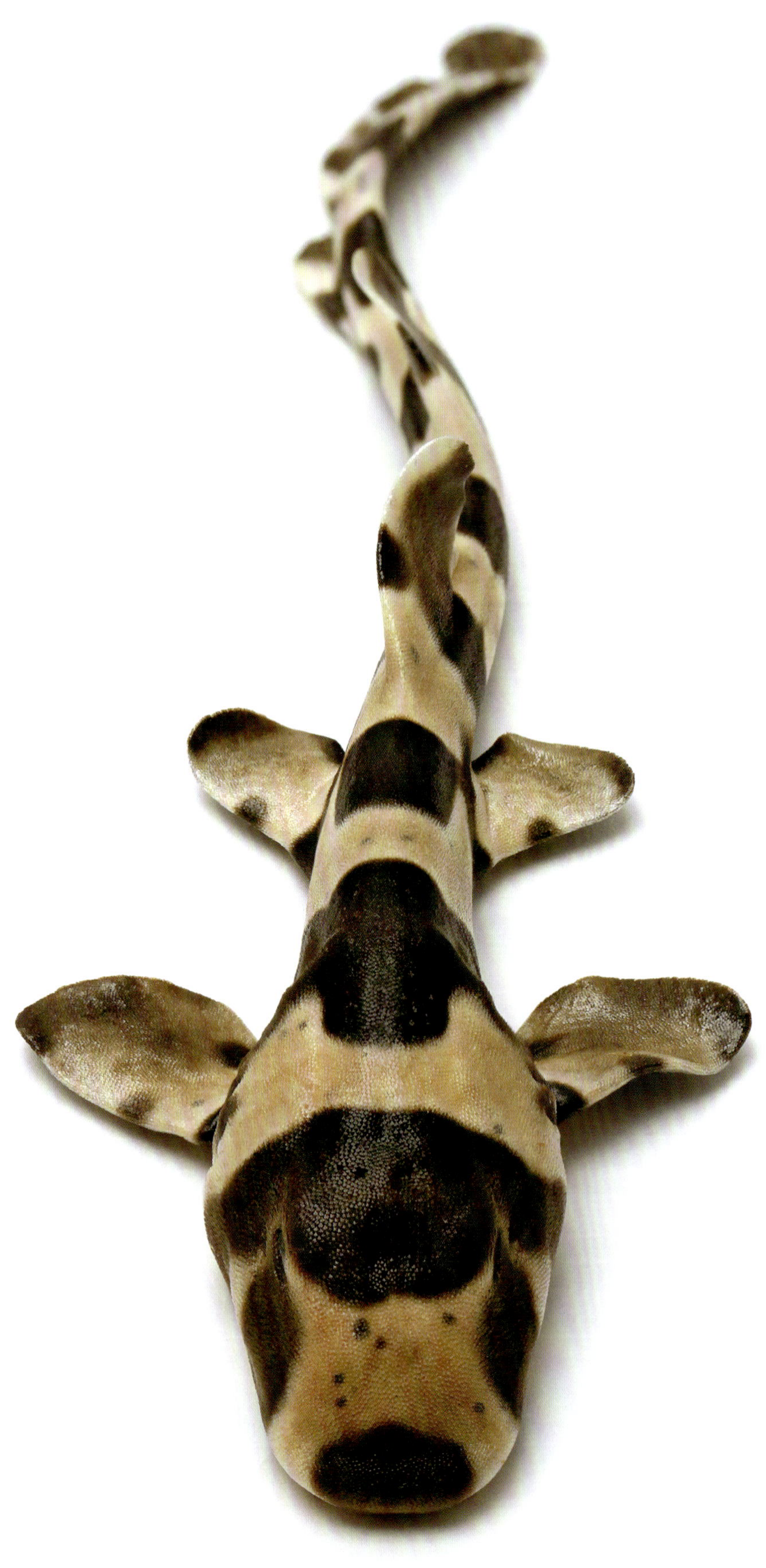

Banded Cat Shark

Japan

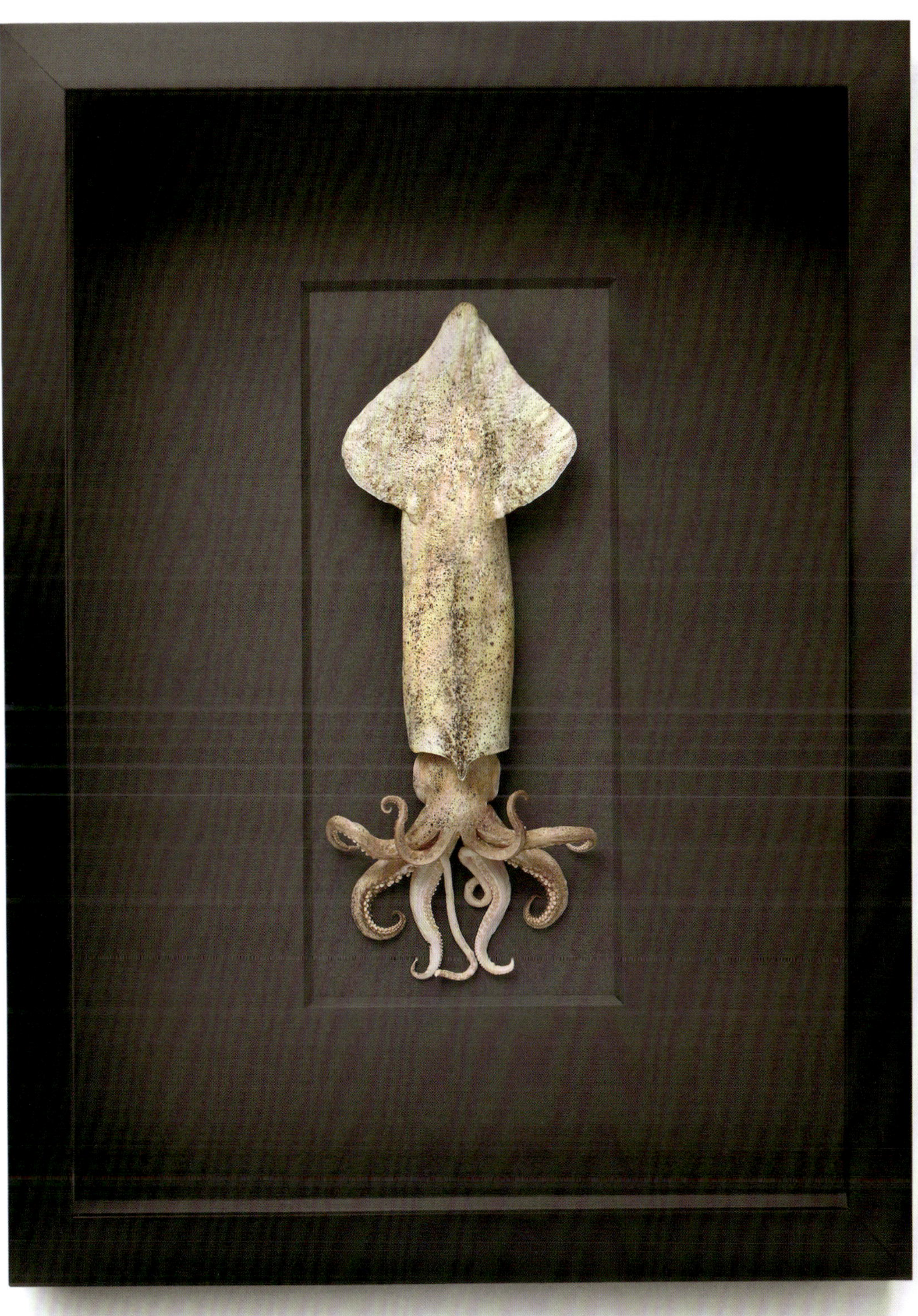

European Squid

Atlantic Ocean

REPTILES

Many years ago, a phrase to the effect of "beauty is in the eye of the beholder" came into vogue. I don't know of a group of people more acutely aware of the theory of beauty's relativity than artists—as our livelihood depends entirely upon the eyeballs of you beholders. Even so, I have to concede that I am bewildered by those who can find no beauty in reptiles. I understand there are phobias, and I admit that a healthy fear of something that can kill you is reasonable. But how can anyone see the lithe elegance of a serpent and not wonder at The Designer's purpose in creating a living line? They are an artist's ultimate medium, able to convey any feeling through pure form. Perhaps this is why snakes are silent; vocal communication is redundant in an organism that can express all through an unlimited variety of body language.

And of course, snakes are only the beginning of the unappreciated wonders in the reptile world. There are chameleons that articulate their feelings through colors whose vibrancy is only eclipsed by those of their next mood. Monitor lizards—the only true dragons the world has ever known. Crocodiles that have remained virtually unchanged since the days of the dinosaurs. Geckos, the barking, playful puppies of the lizard realm. Tortoises as stately and innocuous as a tree—and nearly as old and slow.

That a pervasive antipathy toward reptiles exists in the world is nonsensical to me, though I admit I came into this world with a preprogrammed affinity for them. My earliest and most vivid interactions with nature all revolved around snakes and lizards. Whether as pets, objects of study, or thrilling encounters in the wild, they ignited my love for both nature and art.

So when opportunities first presented themselves for me to attempt reclaiming specimens that had died in captivity, it seemed almost too good to be true. Not only have I been able to rekindle my love for species I have been familiar with for decades, but I have also been given others that are so deadly, rare, or obscure that I would never have had the chance to work with them on such a tactile level in any other way. It has been the realization of a boyhood dream.

I hope my work in this chapter will help to create a few more admirers of reptiles by focusing attention on the elegant form, structure, color, and texture of these preserved specimens. But to those of you who emerge from these pages unwavering in your aversion to reptiles, still unable to appreciate even the purely aesthetic elements of these intriguing creatures—you might want to consider getting those beholders checked.

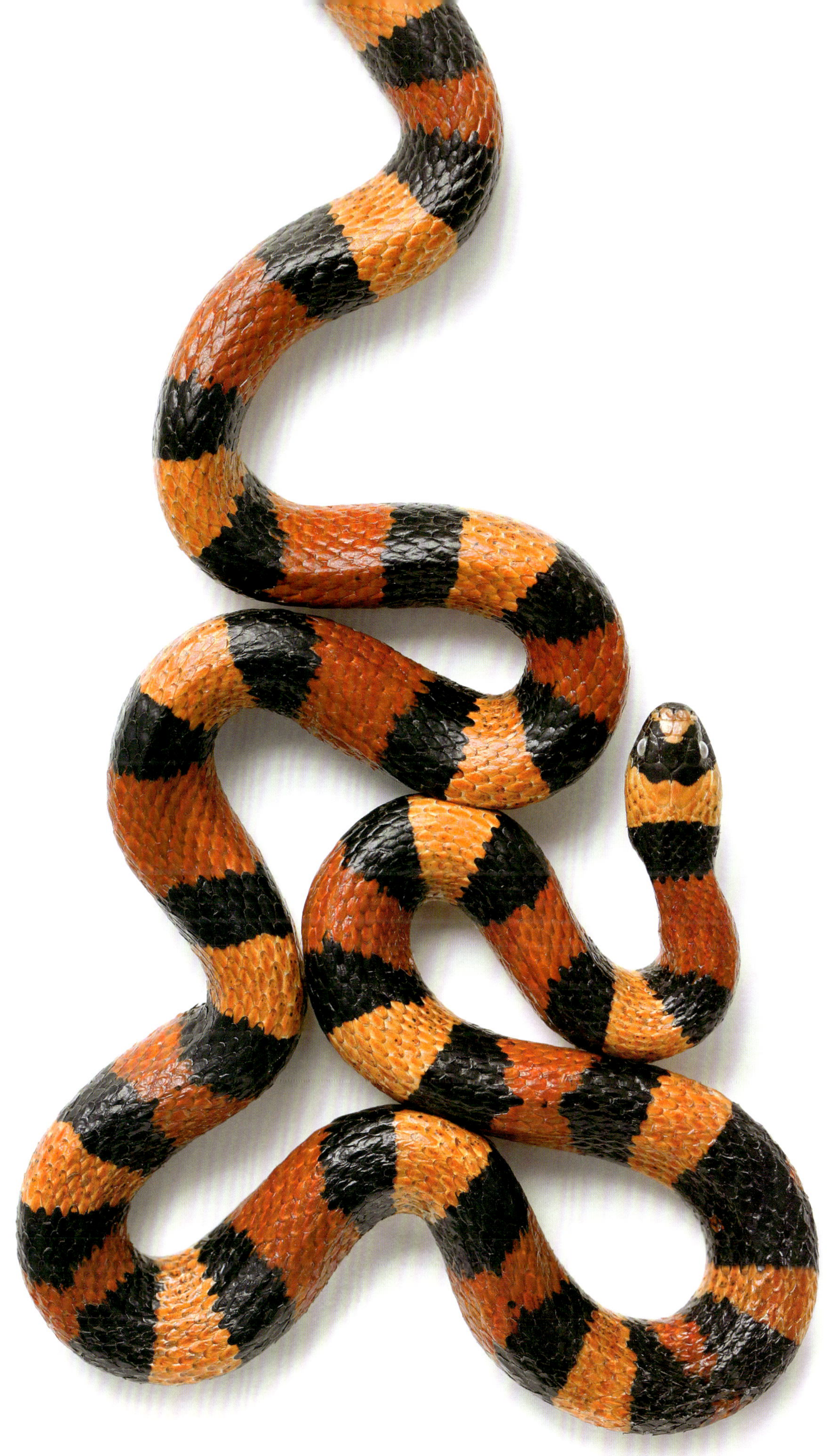

Apricot Pueblan Milk Snake

Mexico

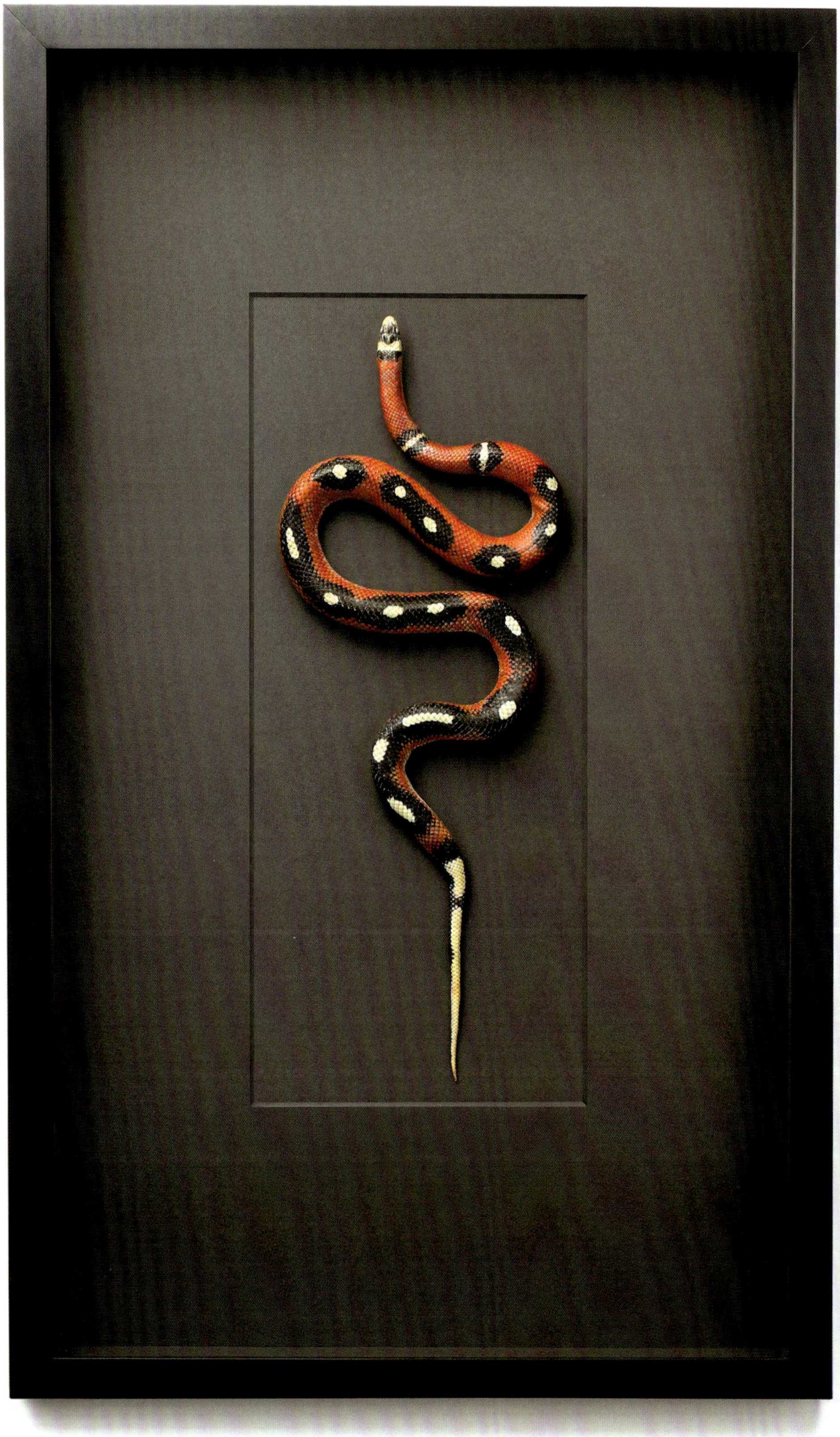

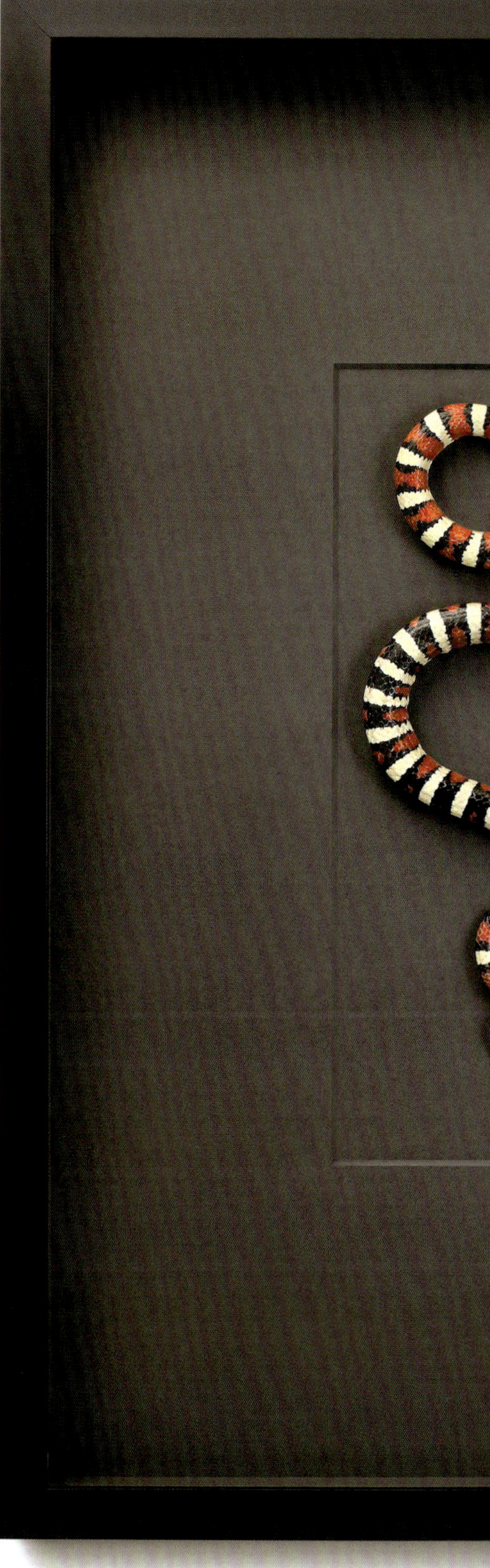

Splotched Sinaloan Milk Snake

Mexico

Mountain King Snake

Western United States, Mexico

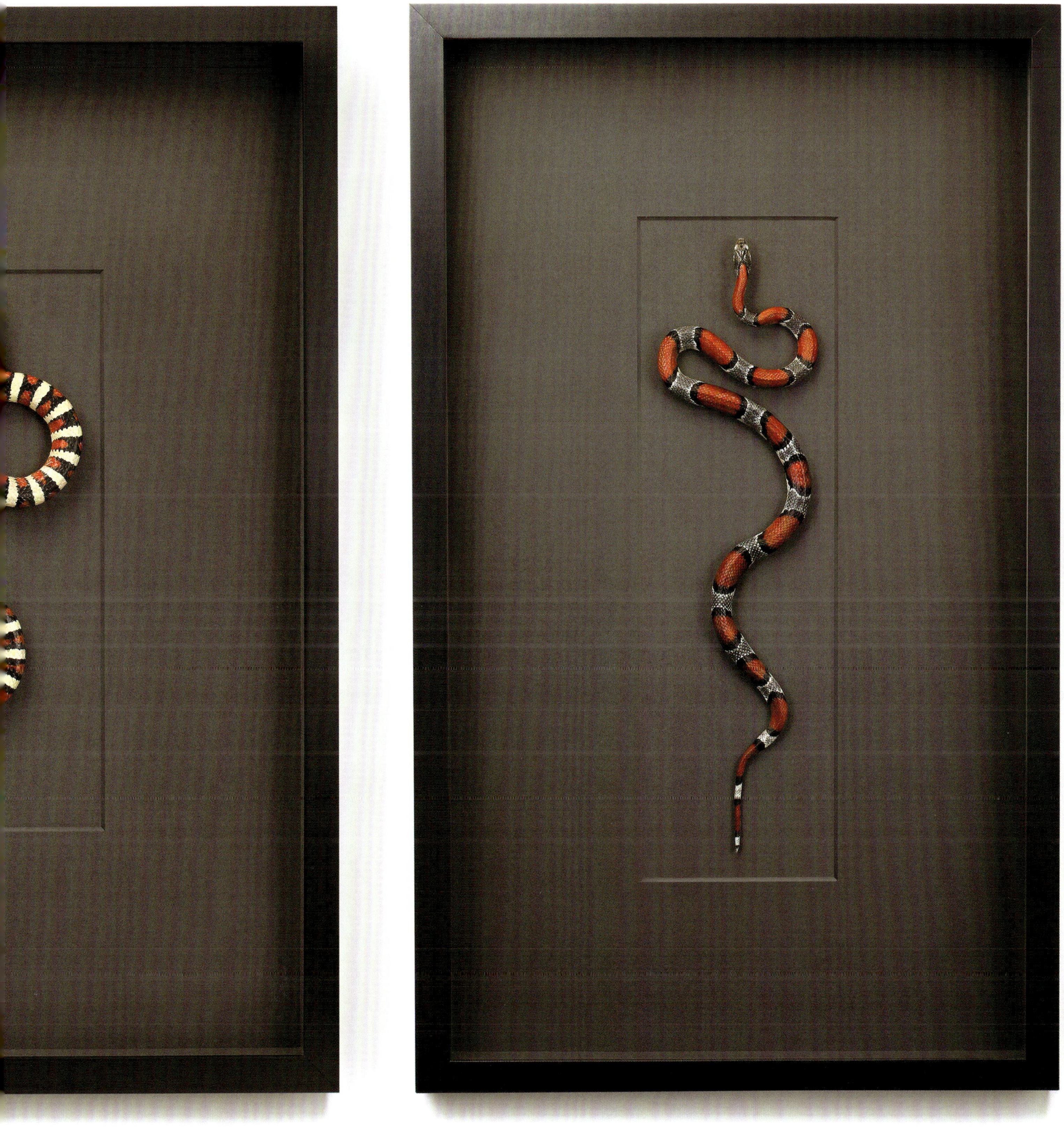

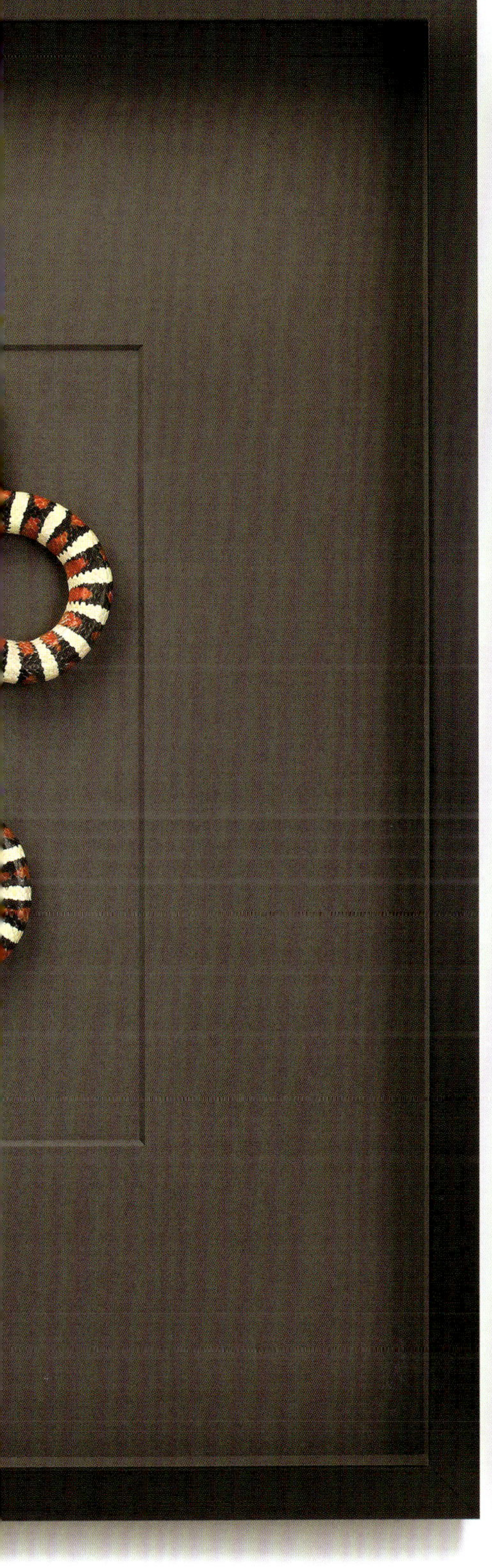

Gray-Banded King Snake

Southern United States, Mexico

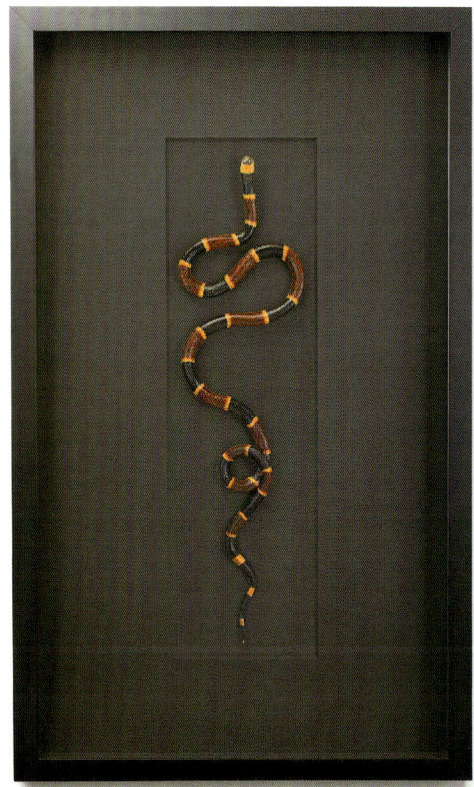

Coral Snake

Eastern United States

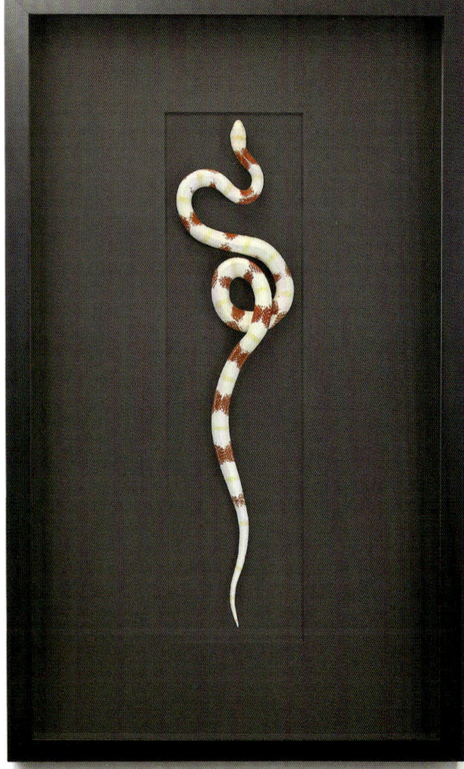

Albino Nelson's Milk Snake

Mexico

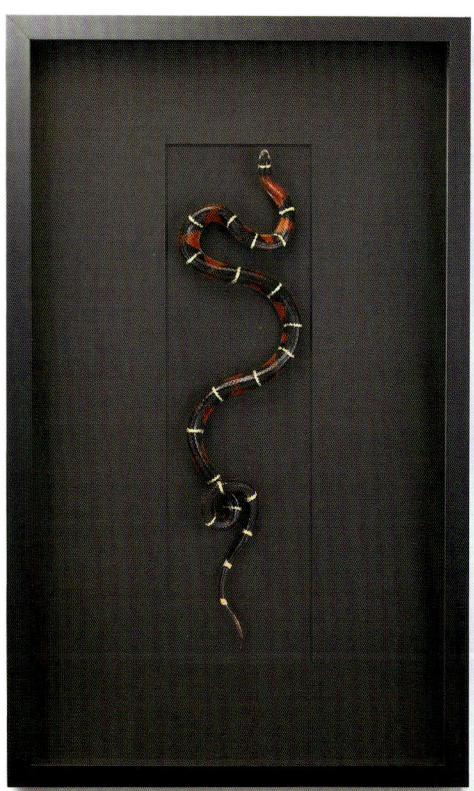

Aberrant Nelson's Milk Snake

Mexico

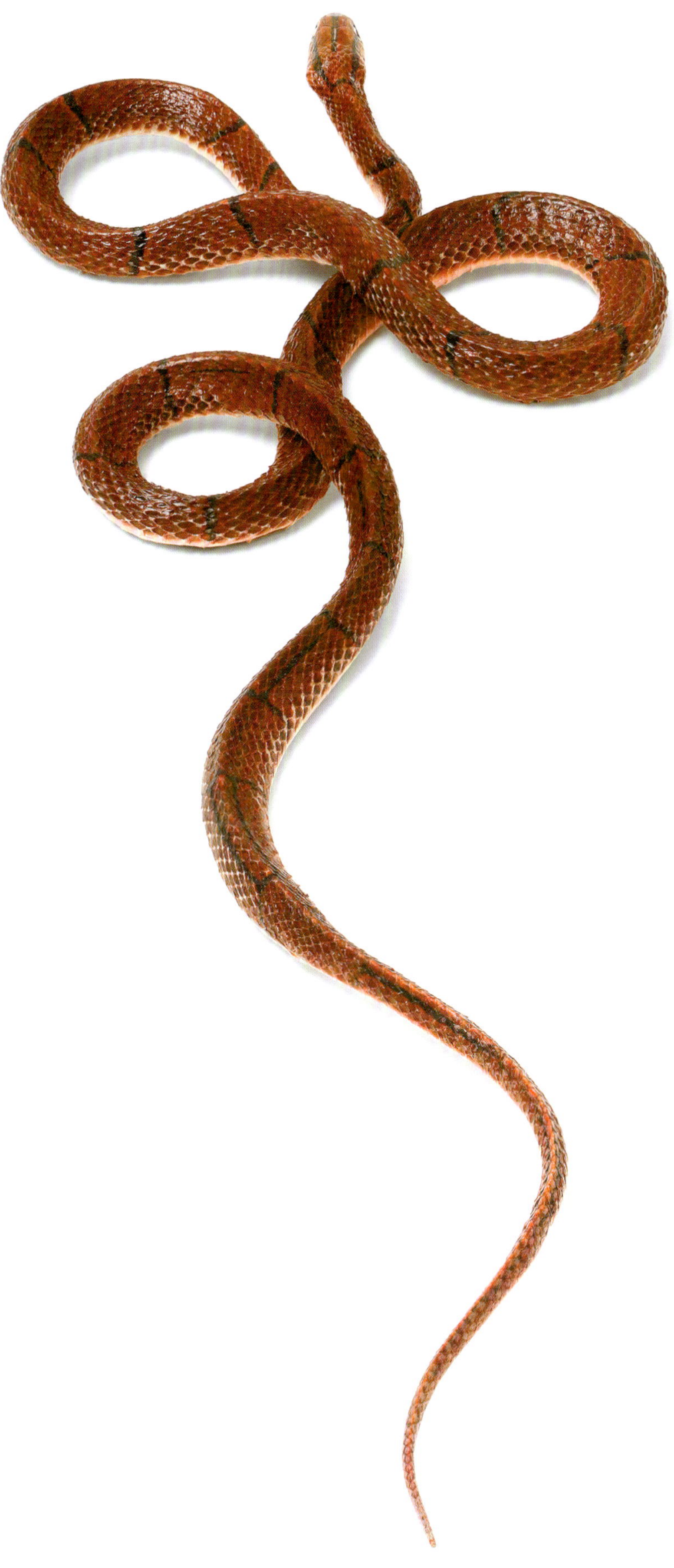

Bamboo Rat Snake

Thailand

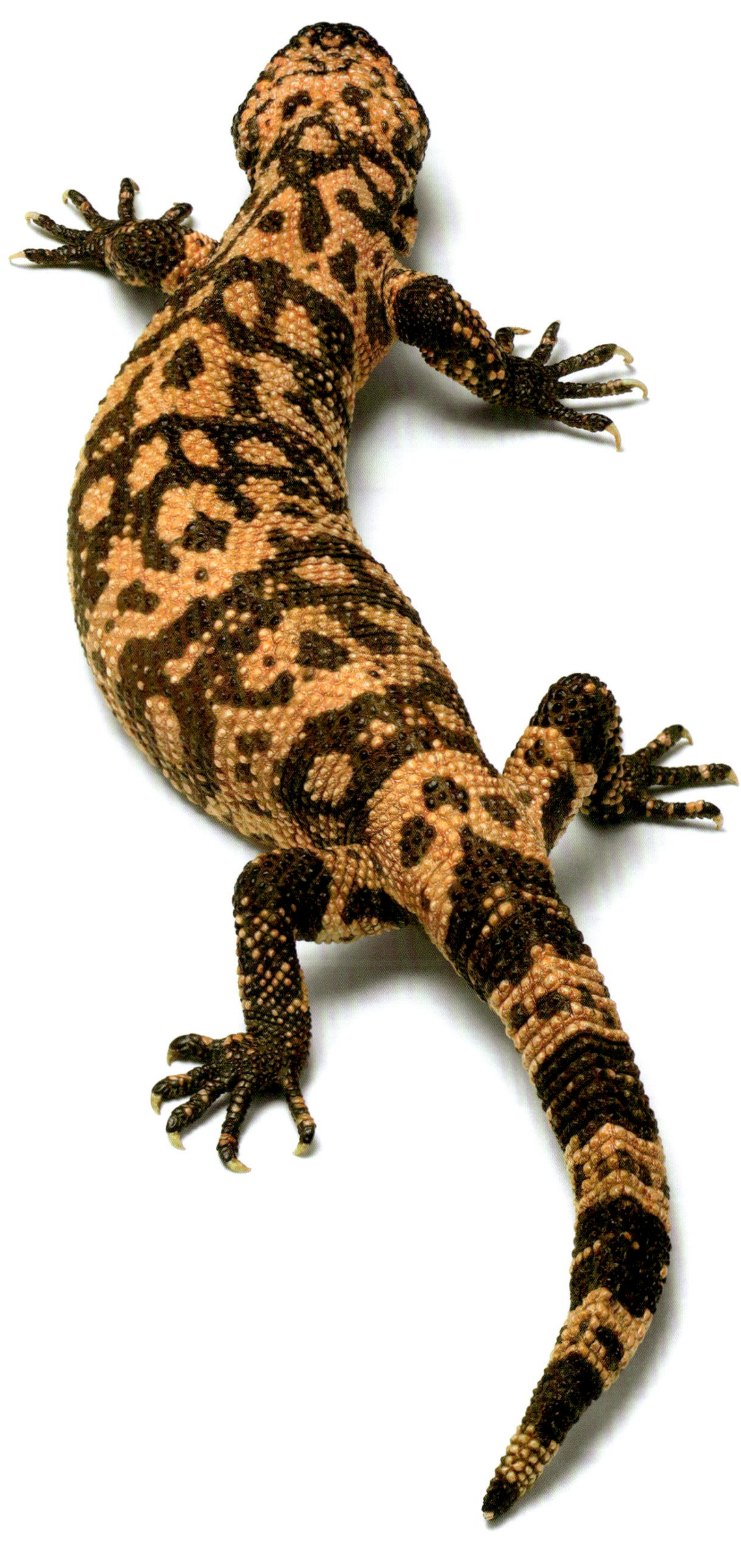

Gila Monster

United States

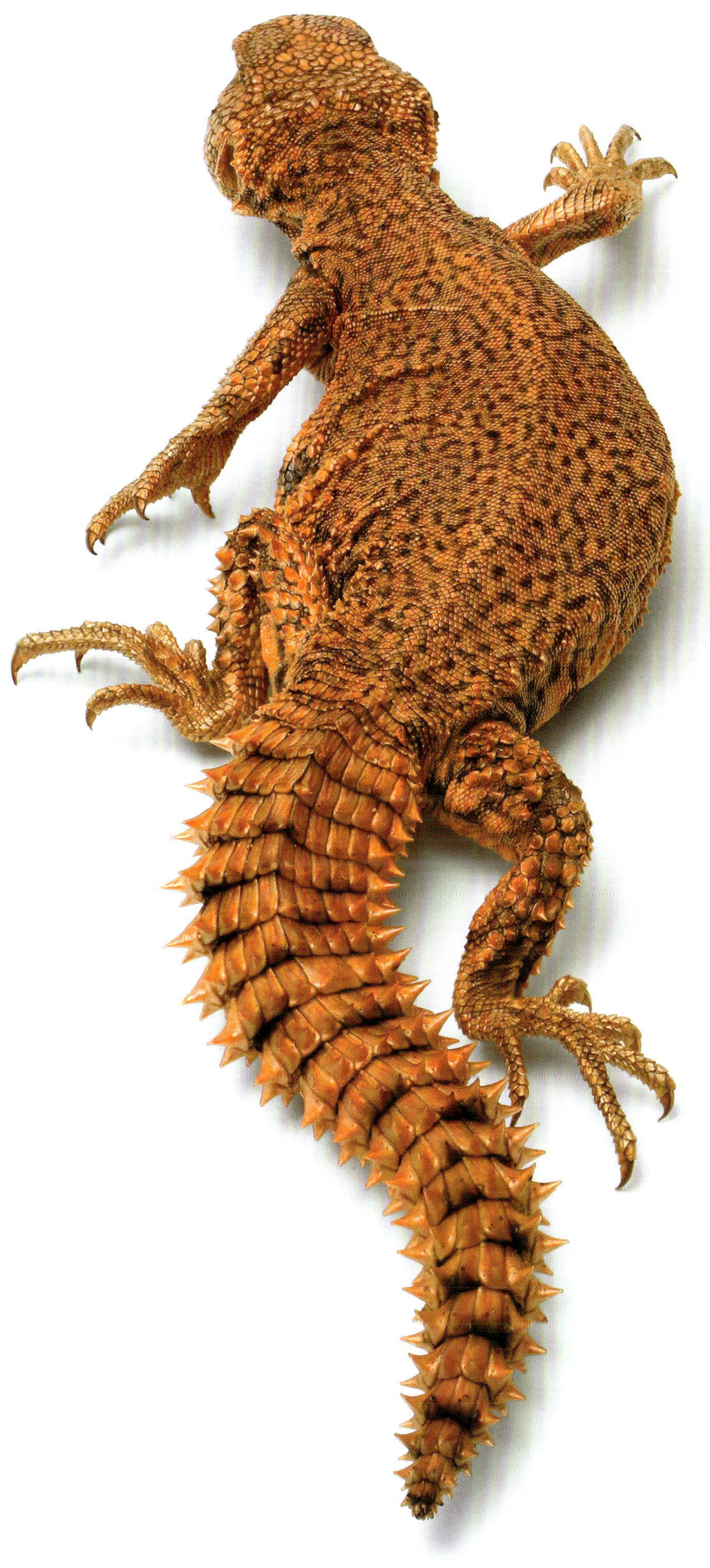

Saharan Uromastyx

Algeria

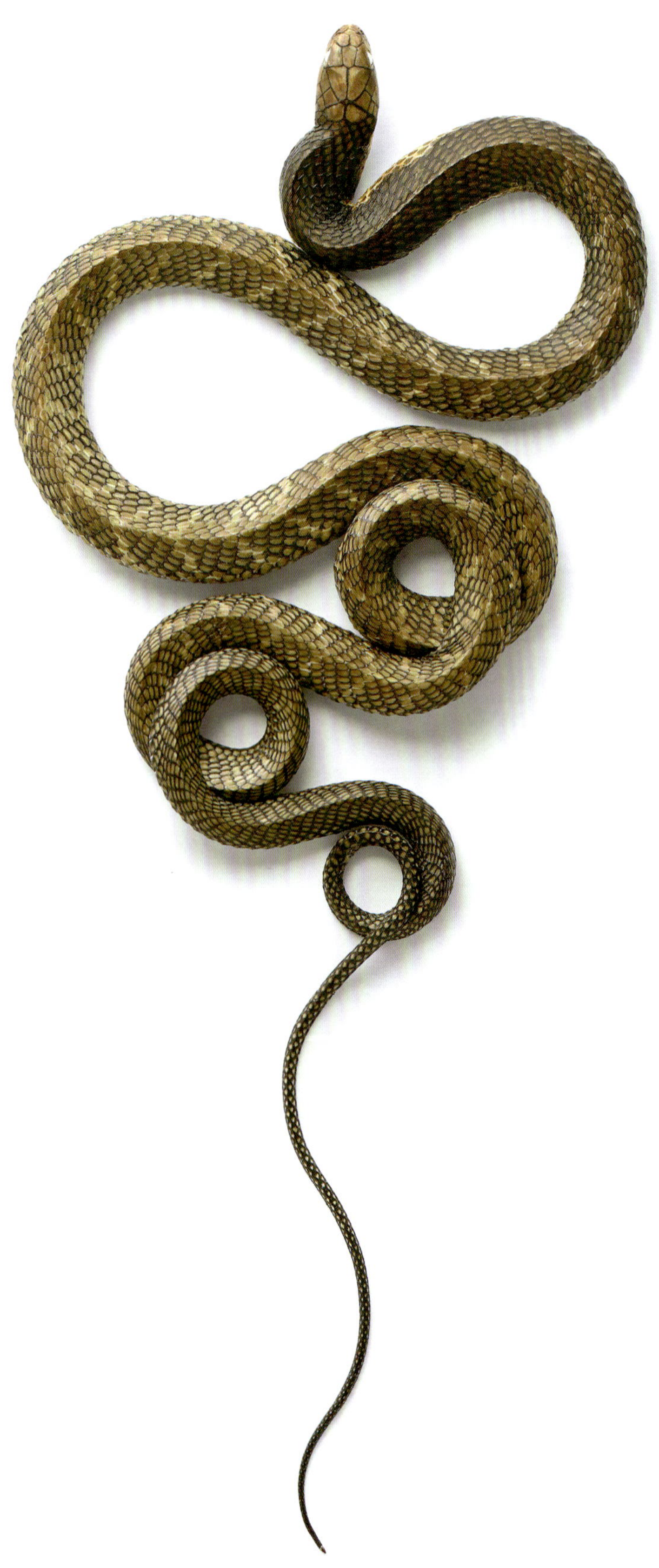

King Cobra

Myanmar

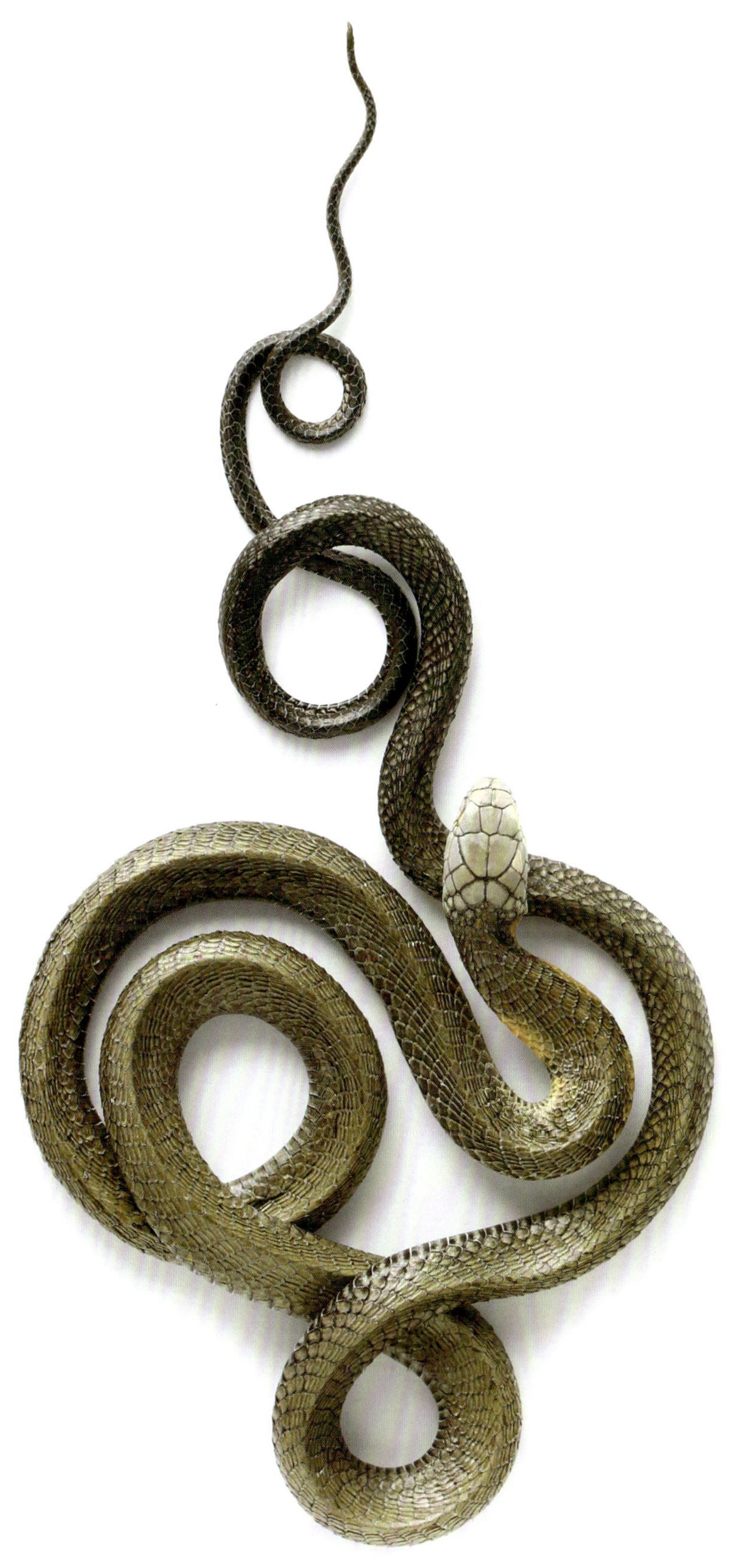

Asian Cobra

Sri Lanka

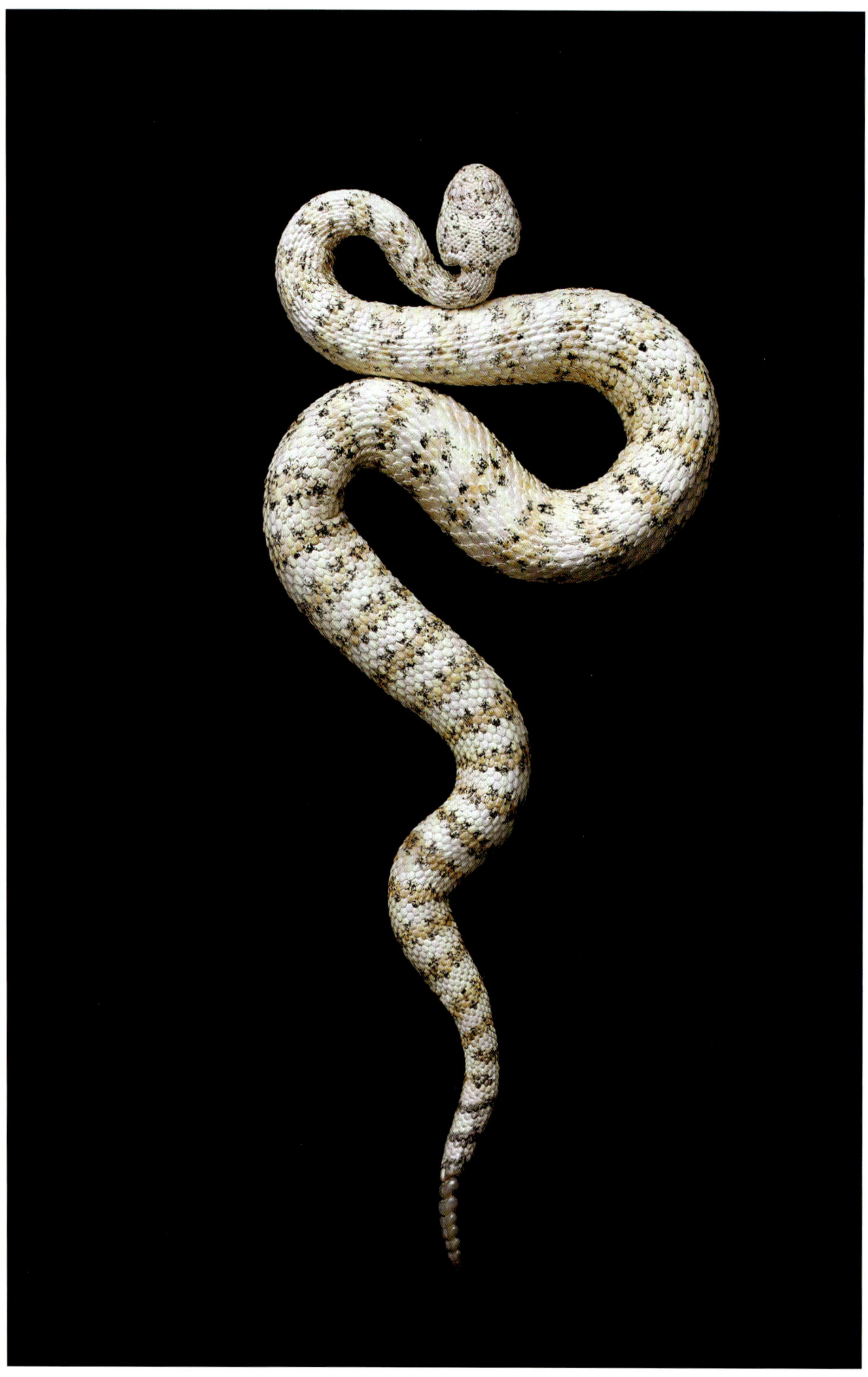

Speckled Rattlesnake

United States, Mexico

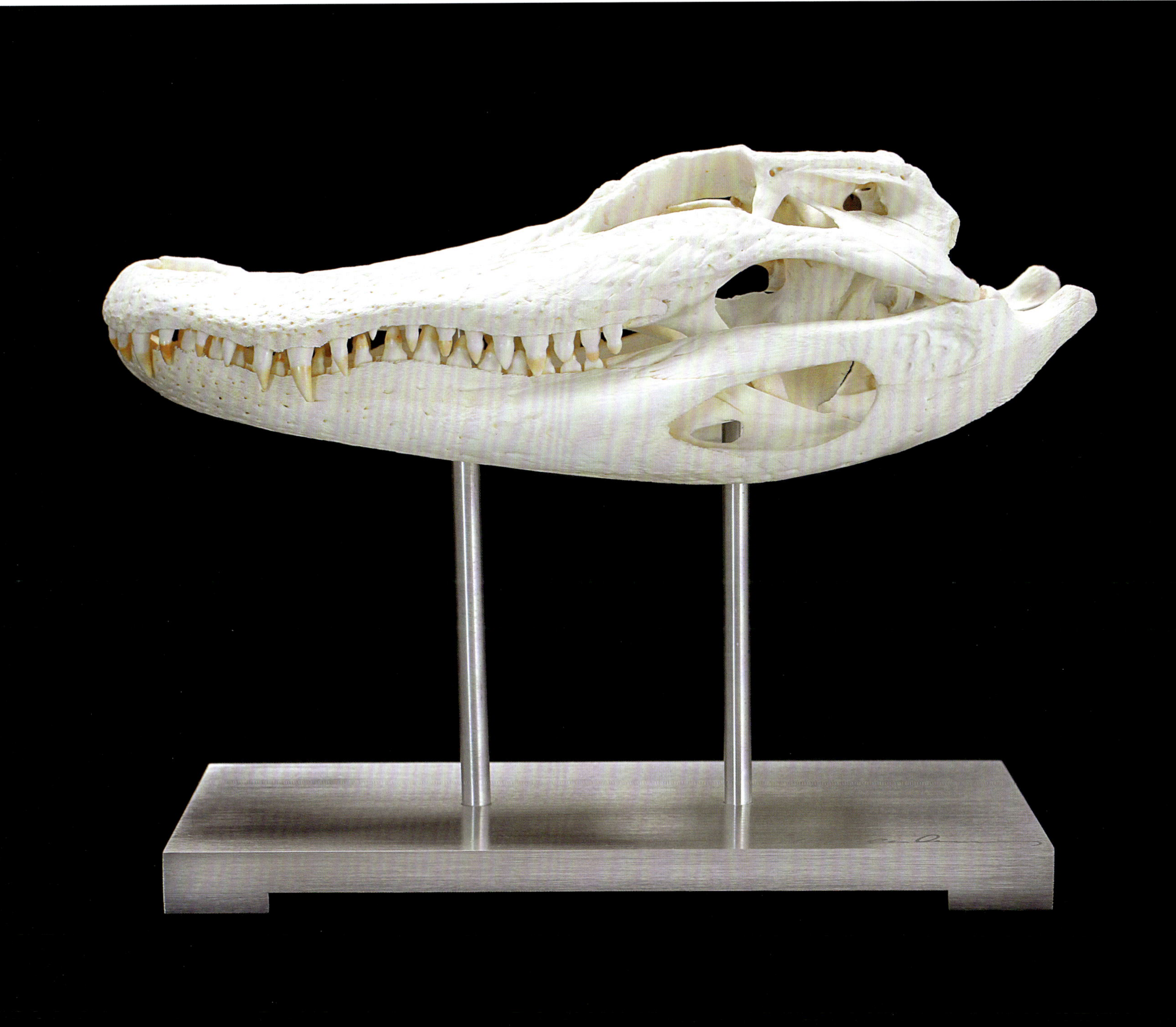

Reclaimed American Alligator

Southern United States

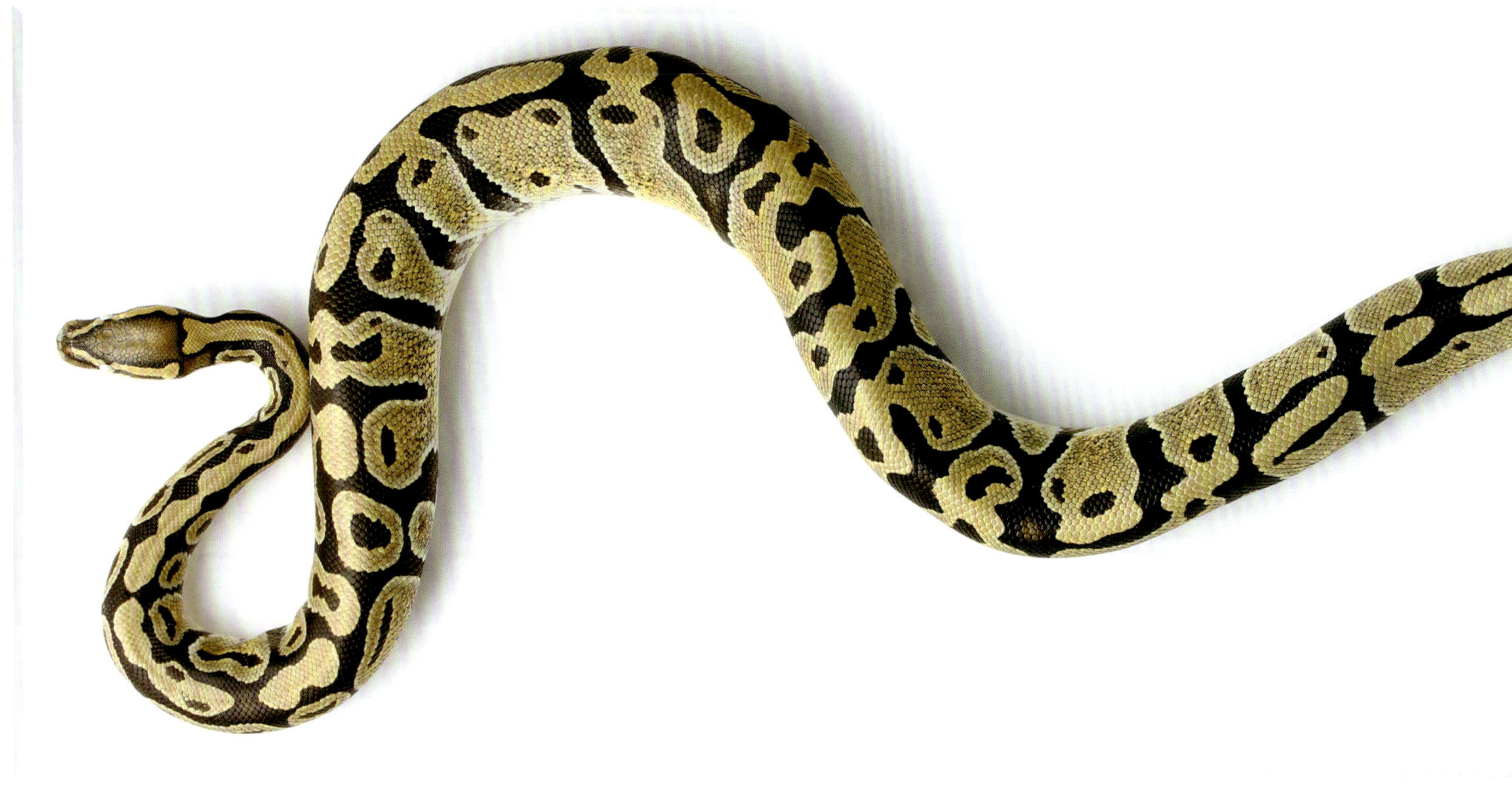

Royal Python, Mojave Form

Ivory Coast

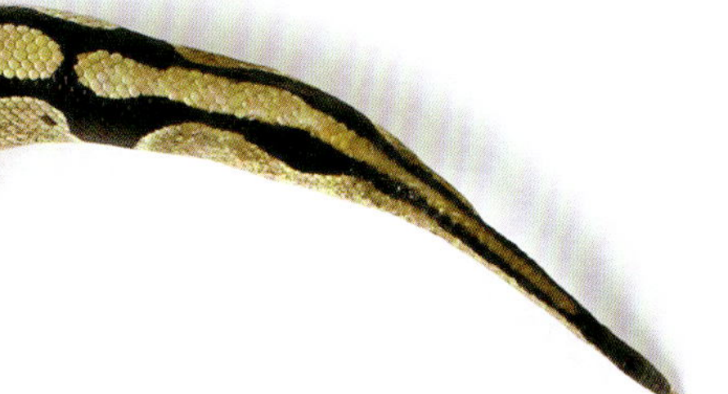

Royal Python, Vanilla Form

Ghana

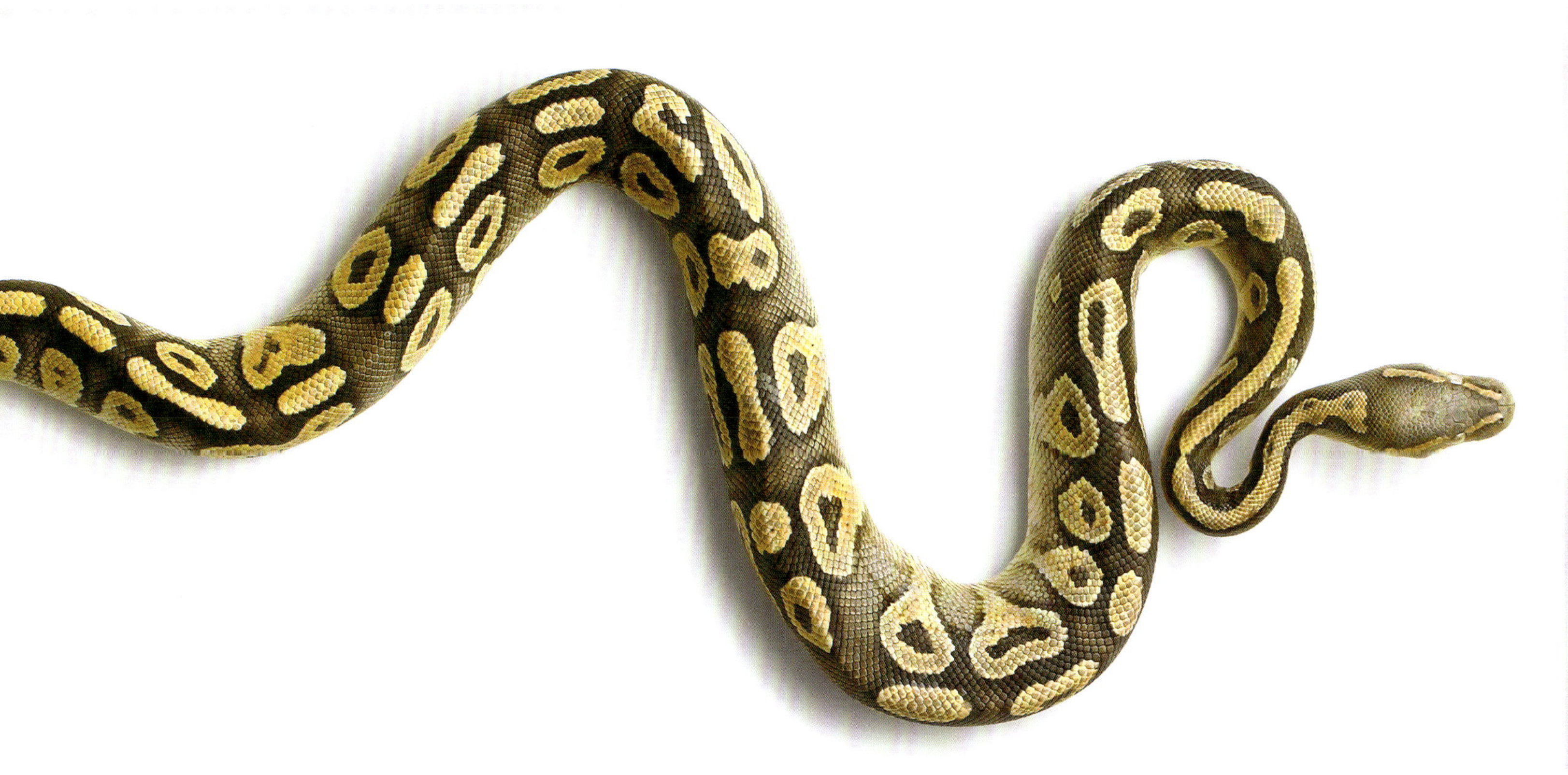

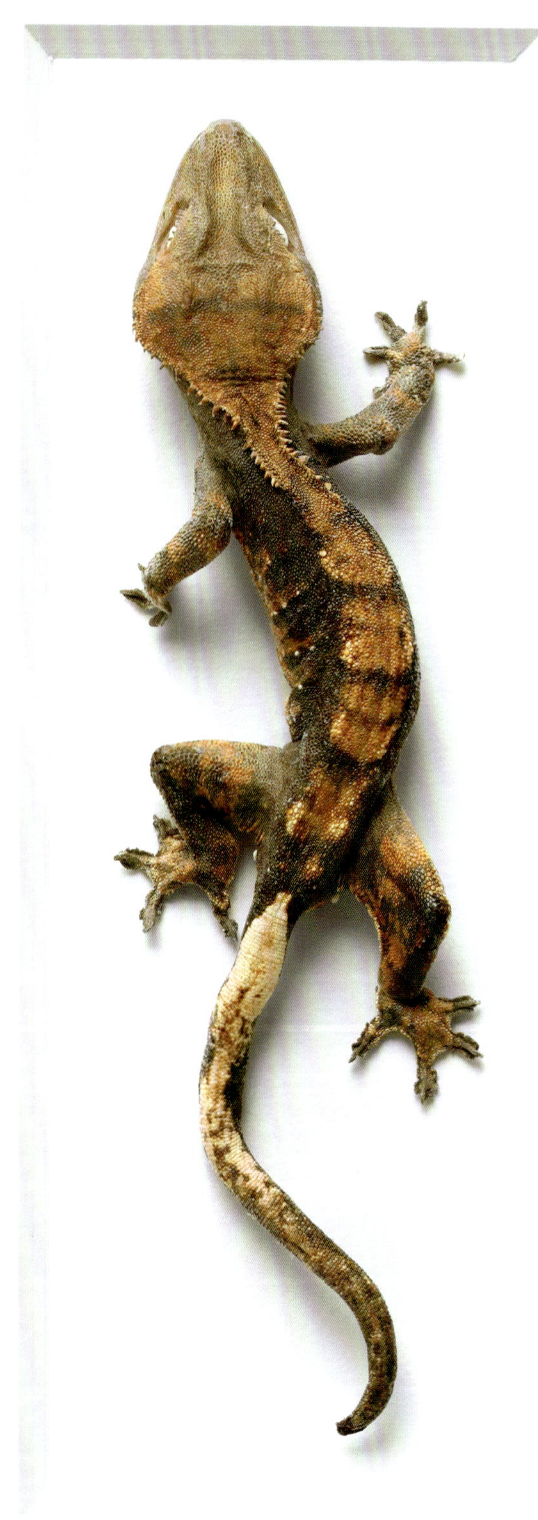

Crested Gecko

New Caledonia

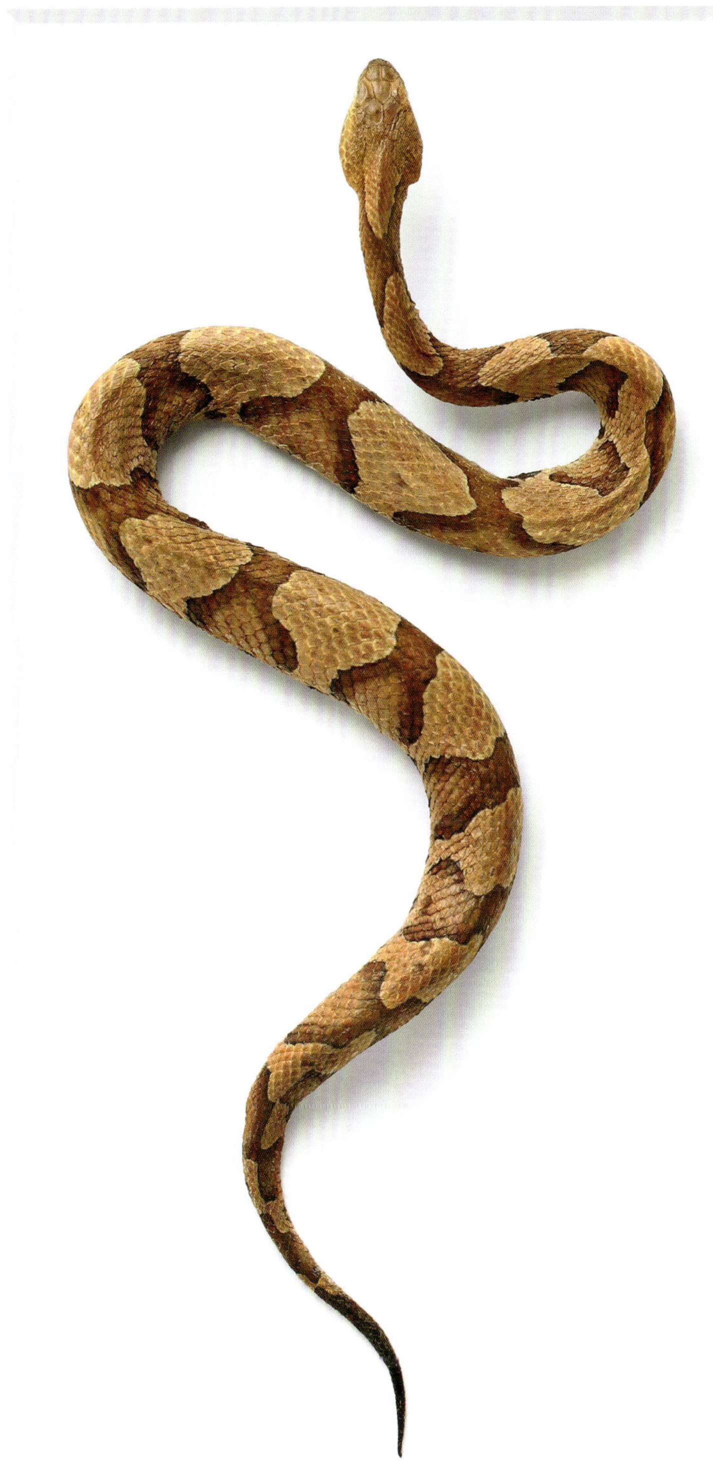

Copperhead Viper

United States

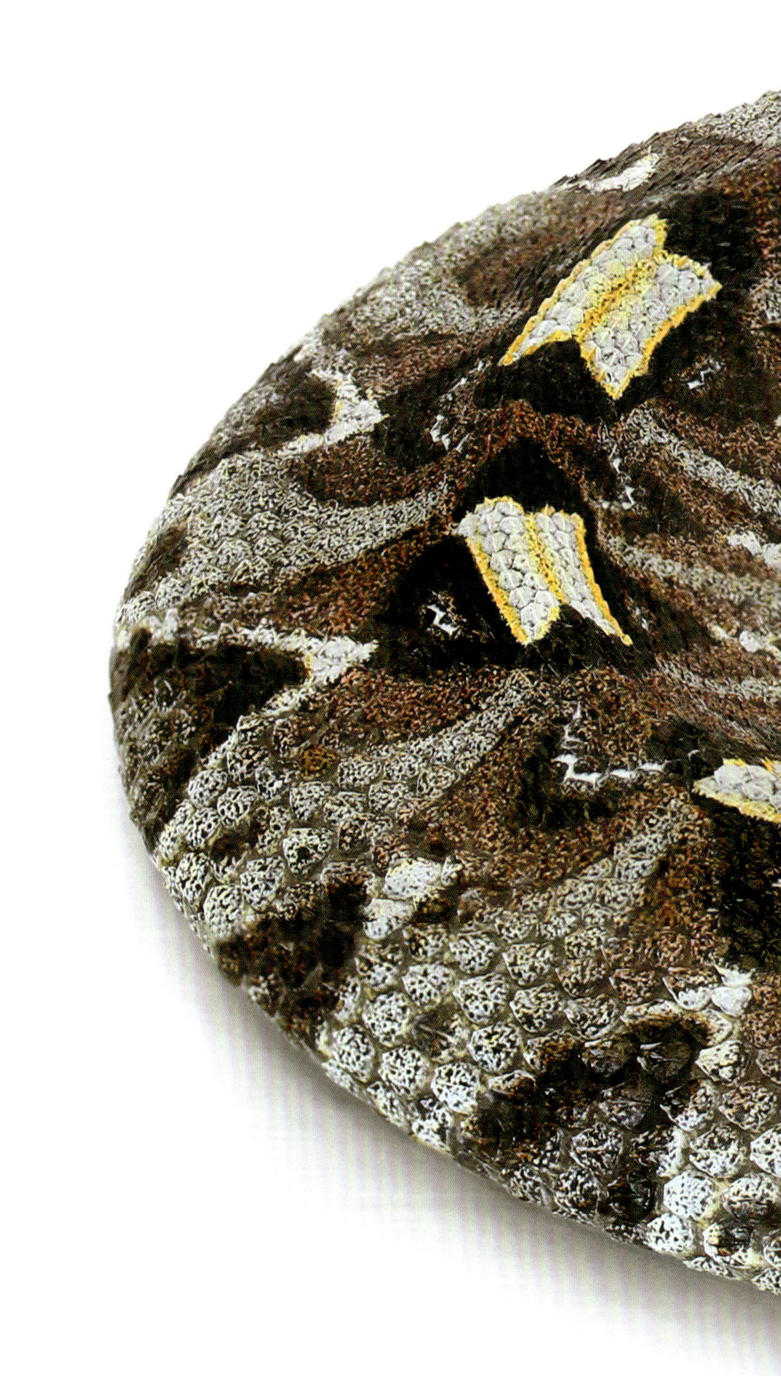

Rhinoceros Viper

Central African Republic

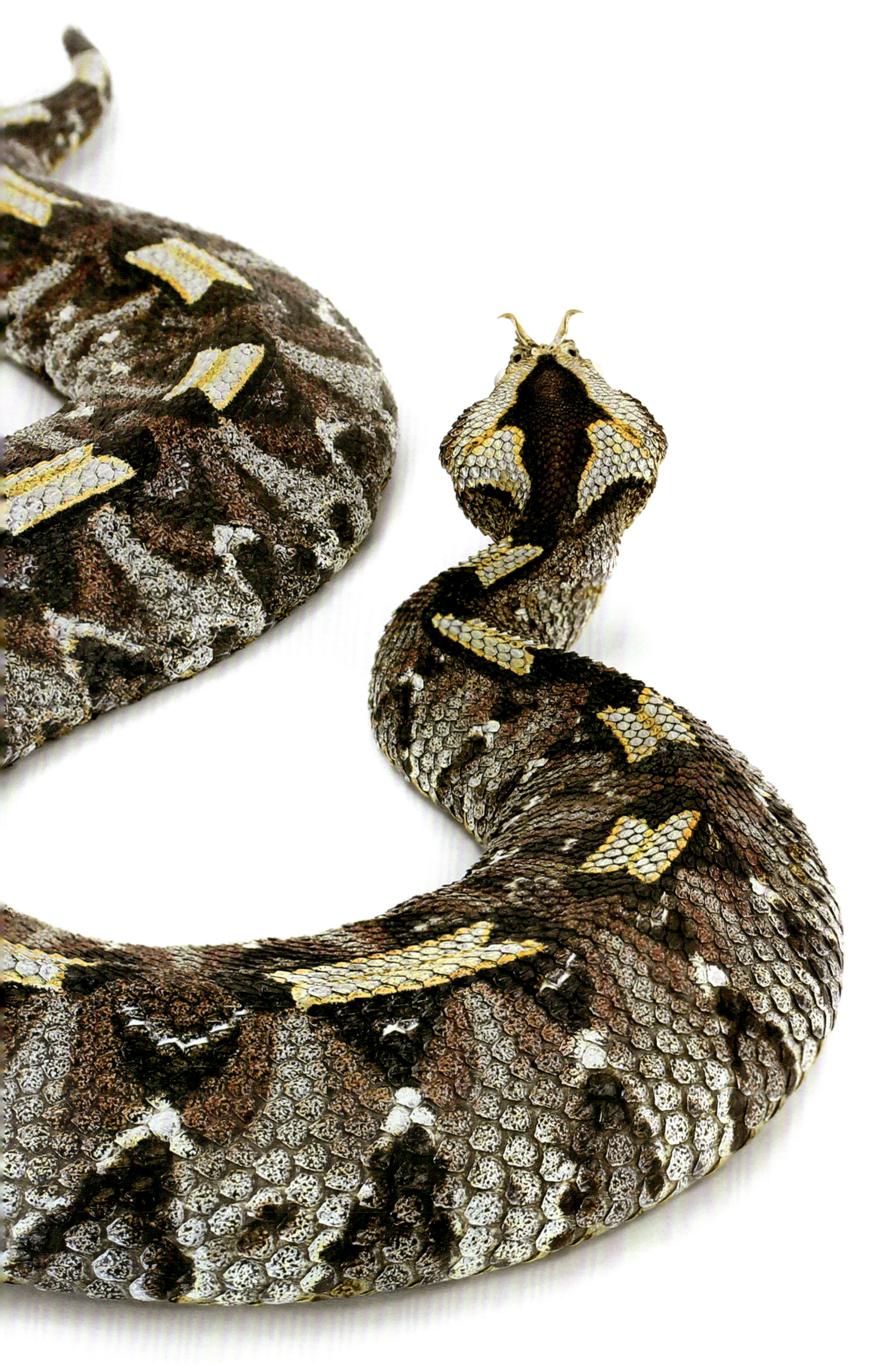

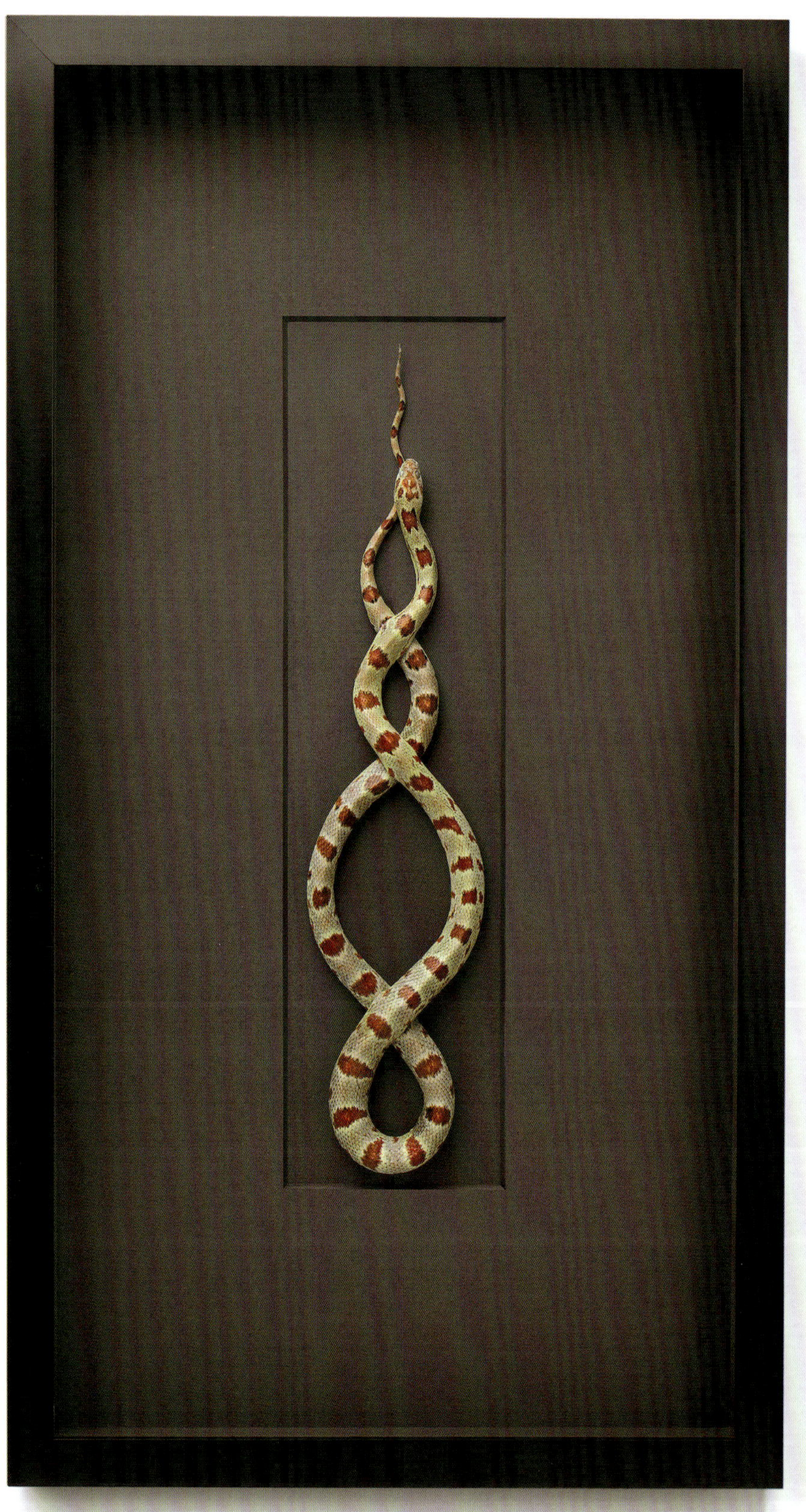

King/Corn Snake Hybrid

United States

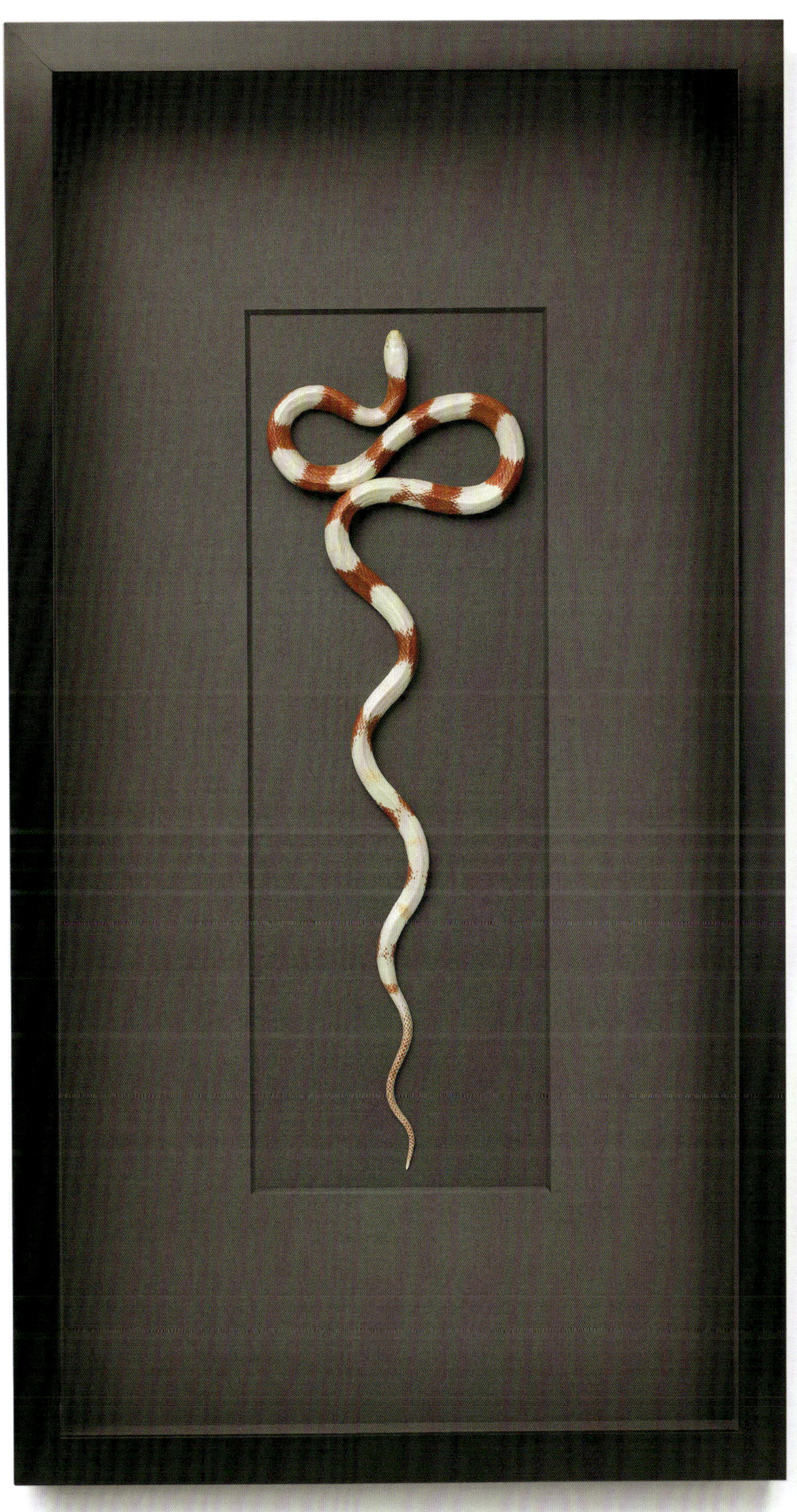

Albino Nelson's Milk Snake

Mexico

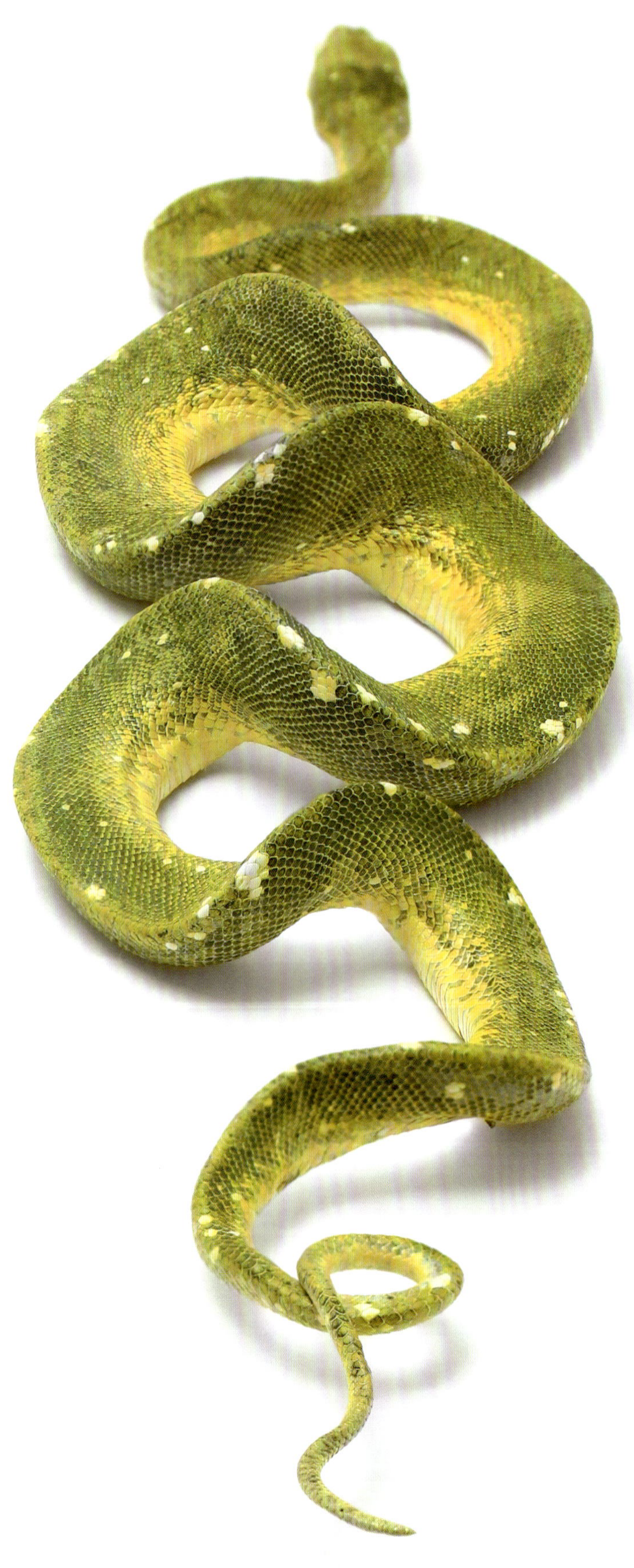

Green Tree Python

Australia

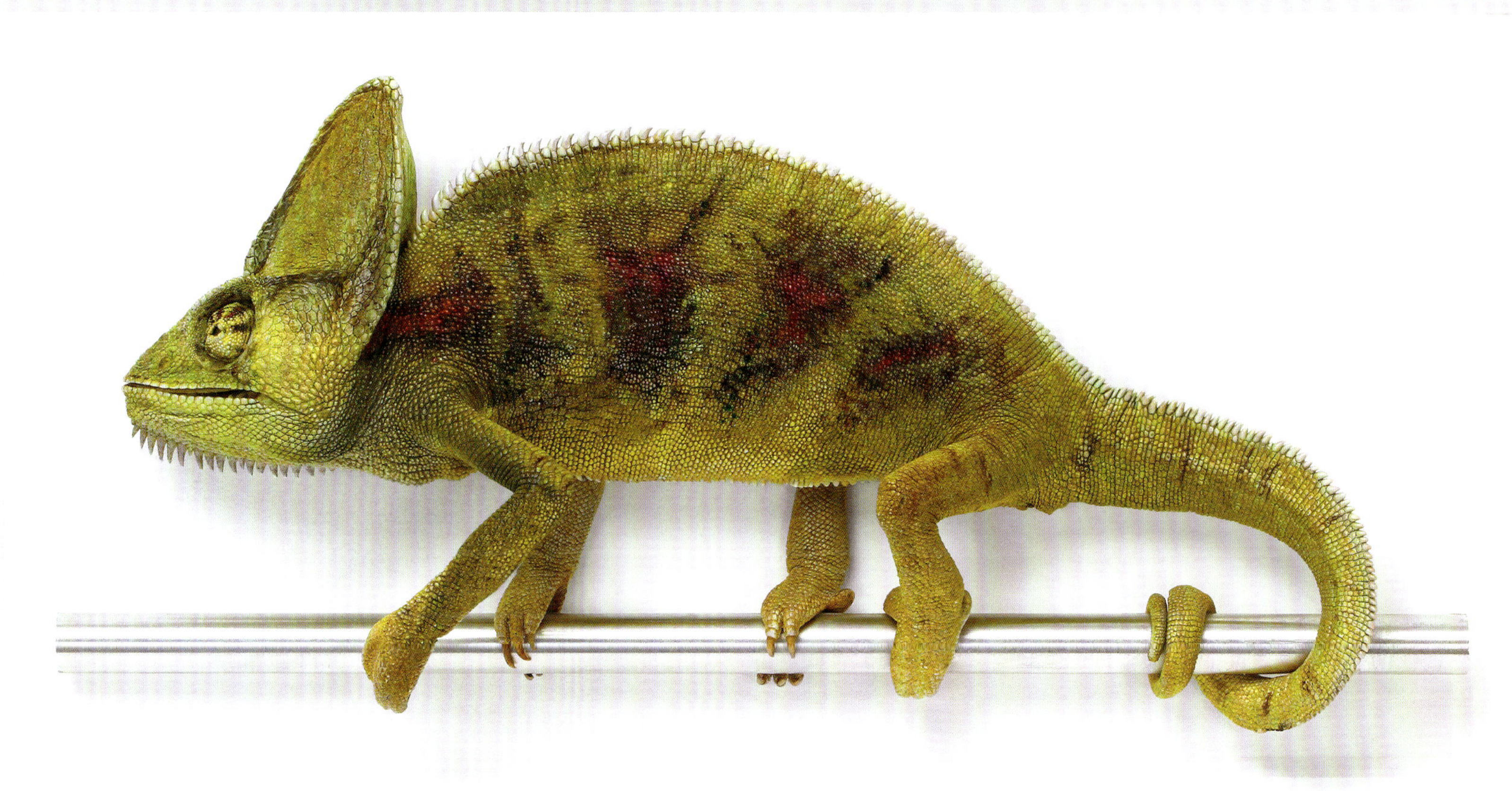

Veiled Chameleon

Madagascar

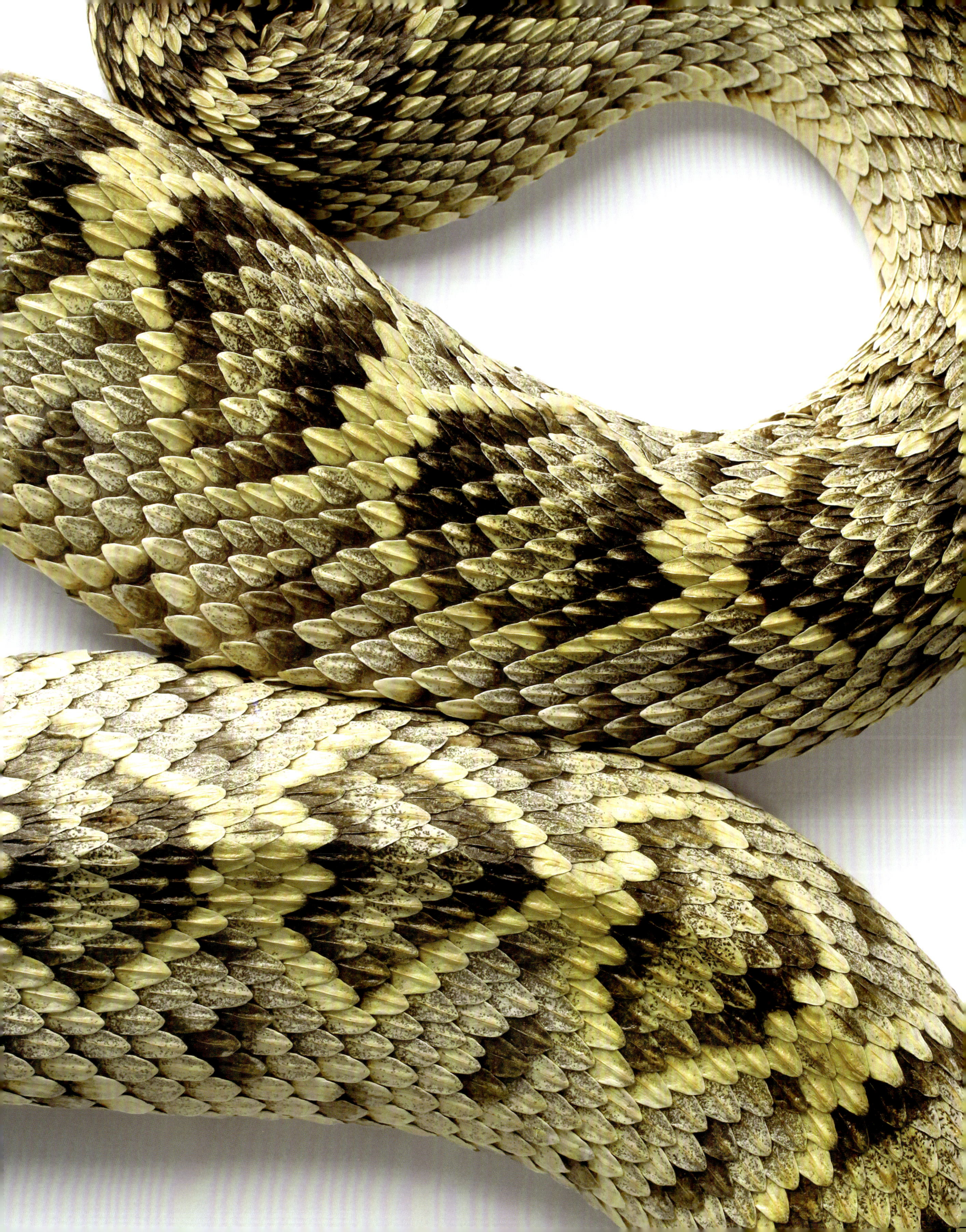

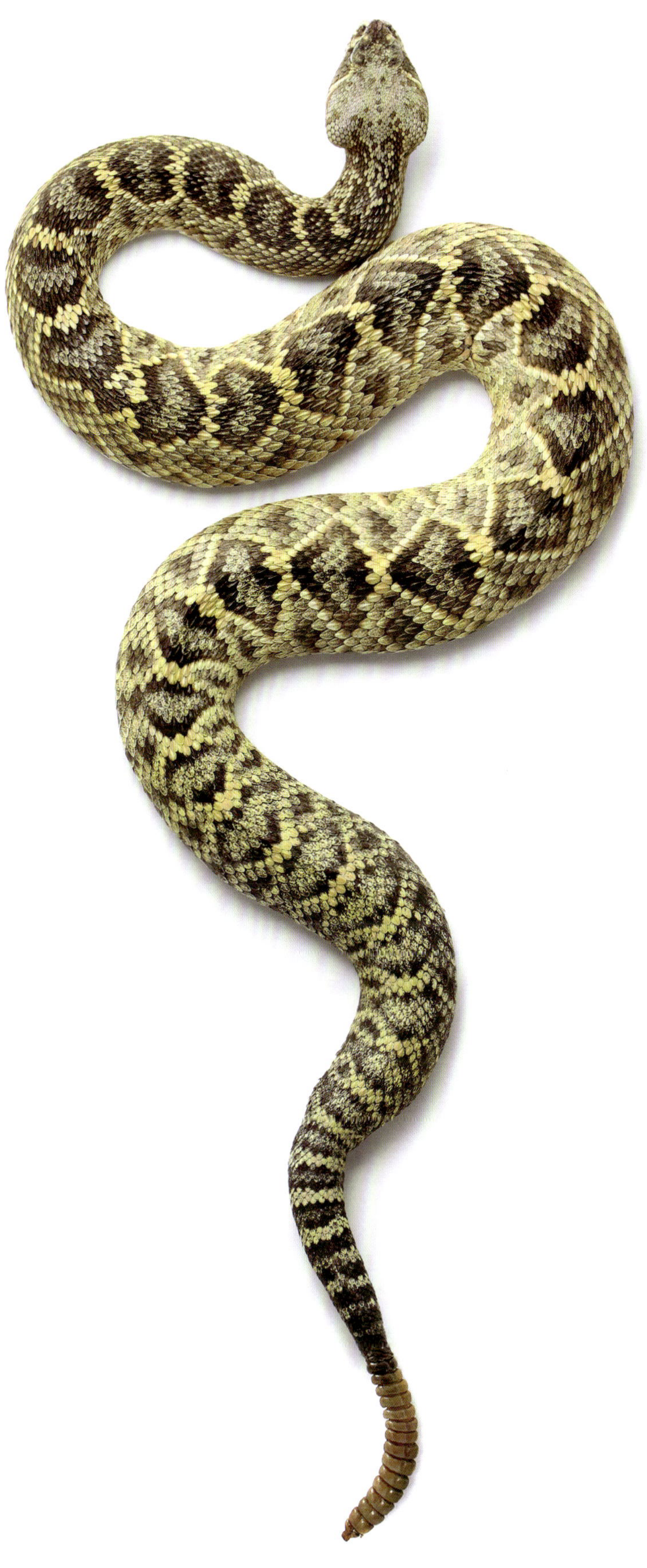

Eastern Diamondback Rattlesnake

United States

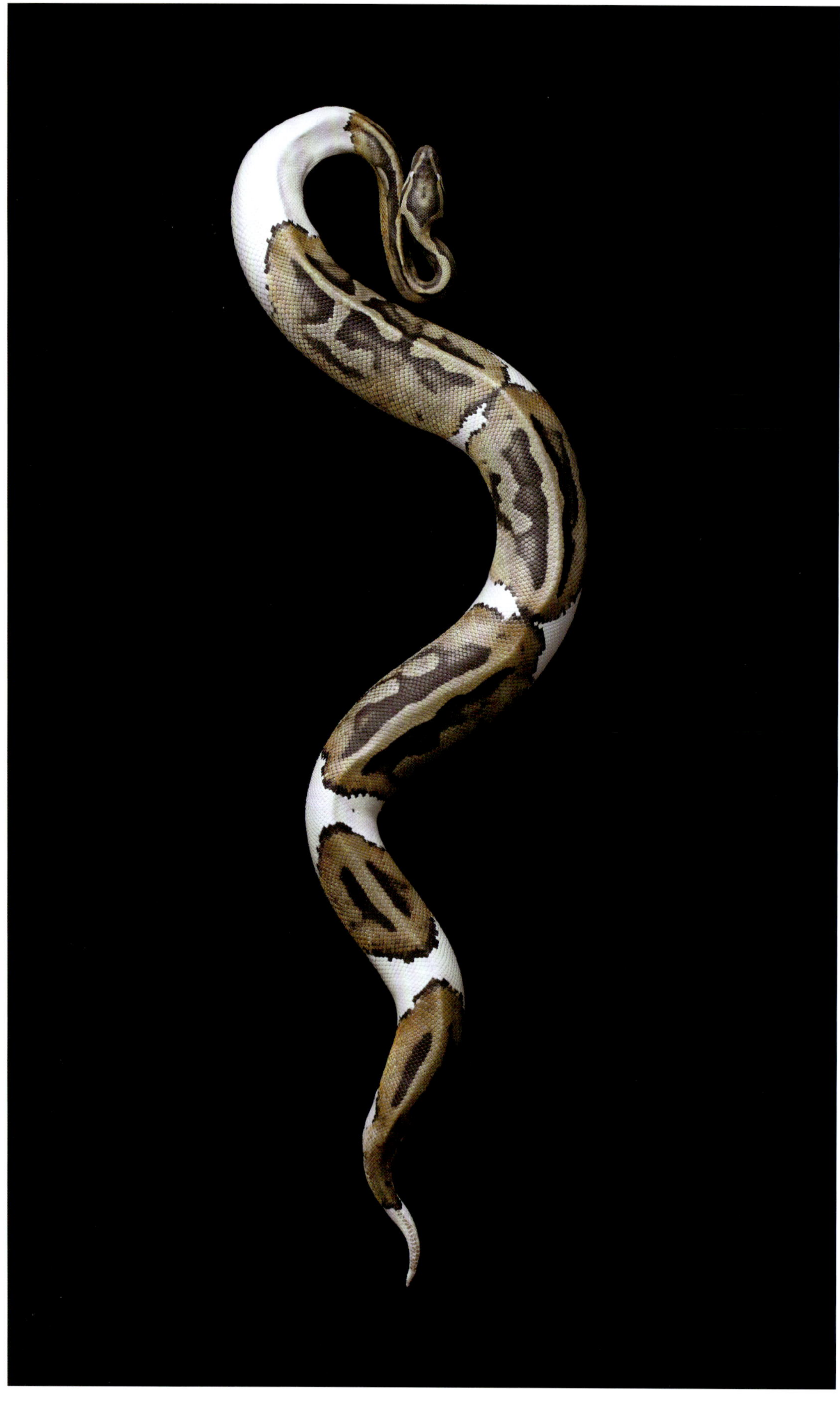

Piebald Royal Python

Nigeria

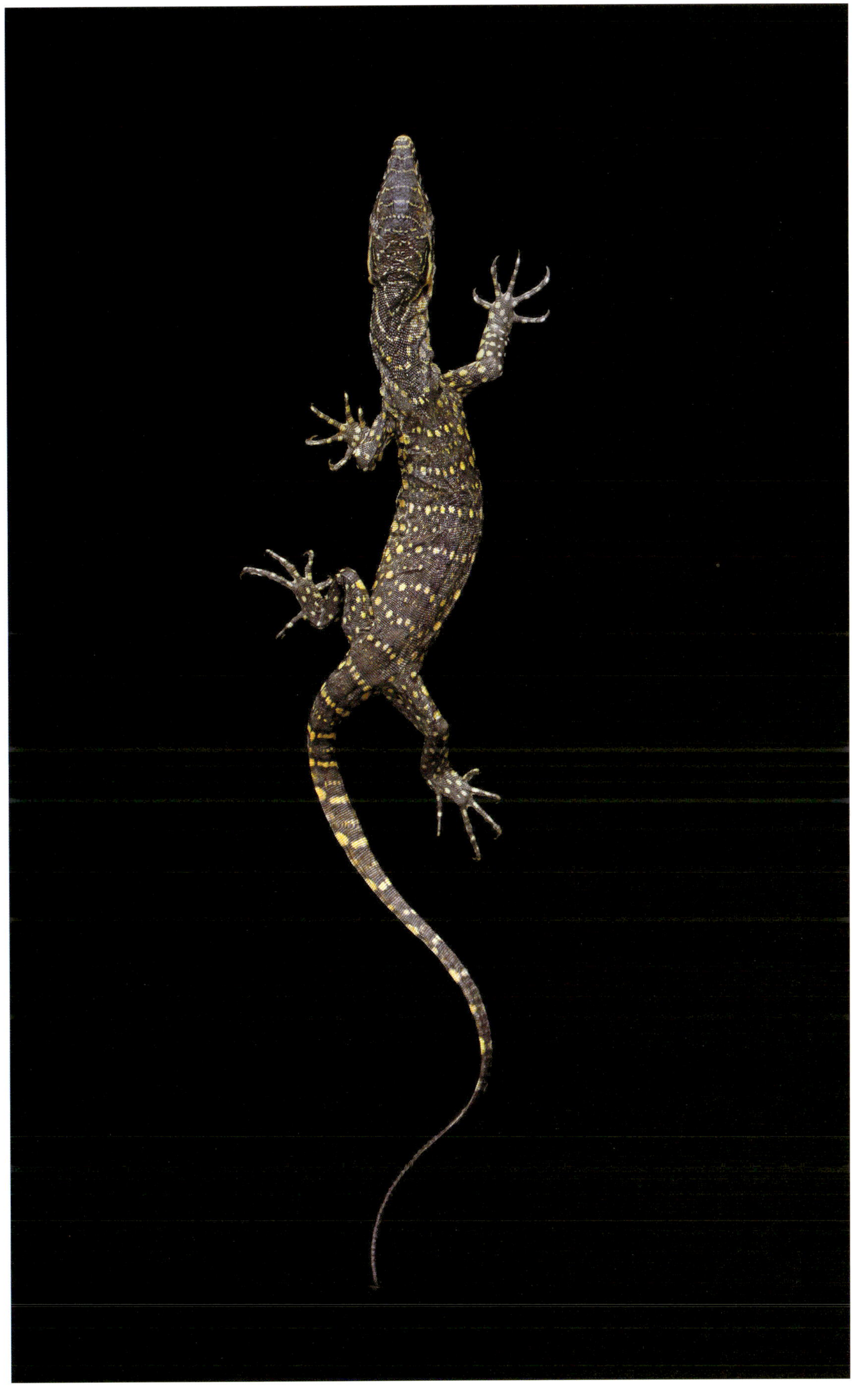

Asian Water Monitor

Indonesia

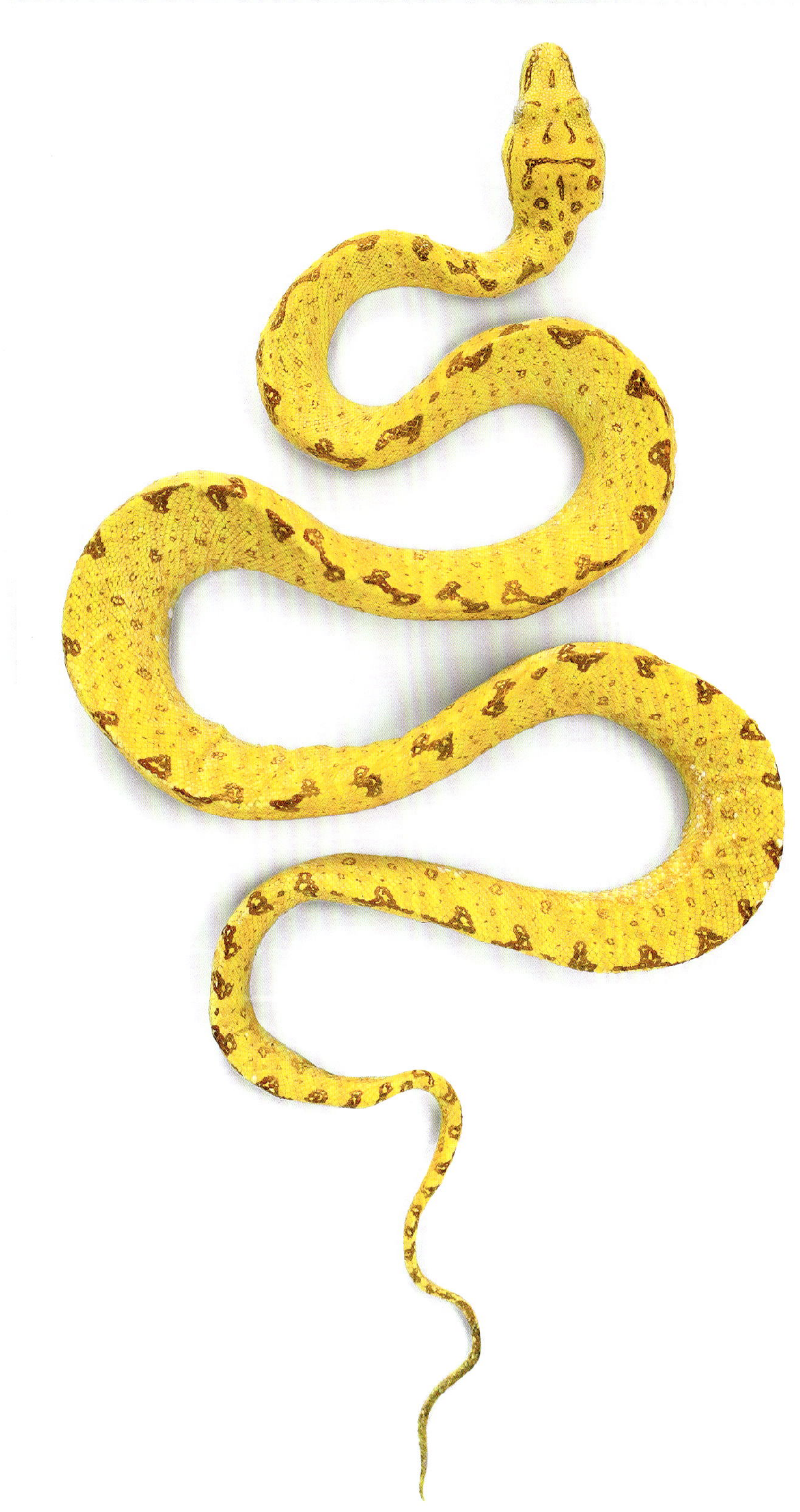

Green Tree Python

Australia

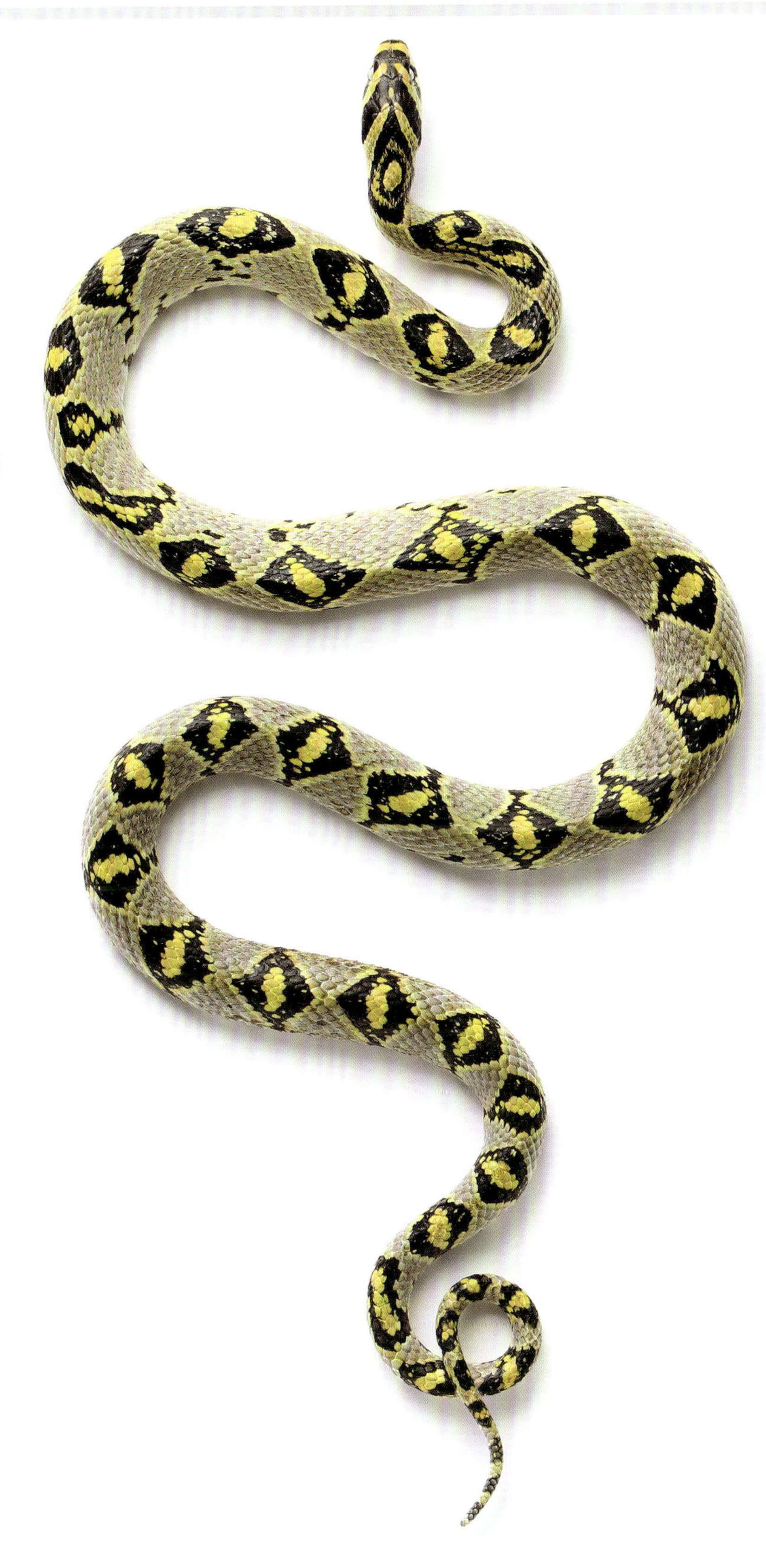

Mandarin Rat Snake

China

BIRDS

My father has been committed to raising birds his entire life. Whenever we moved, the first project to be undertaken, long before we unpacked, was to start building aviaries. Of all of his children, I think Dad's birds ate the highest-quality, most varied diet. He would feed, tend, and watch them for hours at a time. And to be honest, I never understood it.

I mean, to me, birds were always a bit, I don't know… vanilla. My young passion for nature was inextricably comingled with my particular penchant for monsters. Art (well, what passed for art in my prepubescent mind) and nature were inseparable entities. For me, that part of the natural world that most approximated the demonic beasts of my imagination—or at least featured body parts that could be incorporated therein—was where the rubber met the road. Birds, especially my dad's birds, with all their docility, softness, and elegant grace, were kind of the sissy side of nature. When he would drag me out to his aviaries to gaze at some newly feathered color mutation or rave about a new clutch of impossible-to-breed whatevers, I could only politely feign interest long enough for him to become reabsorbed in his triumph so I could make my escape.

No, birds were not for me. Real men loved reptiles. Big cats. Wolverines. Admittedly, we might still be a little (a lot) freaked out by bugs, but we didn't spend our time fawning over little birdies. It didn't seem to fit the persona of my dad either—the toughest guy I knew.

Then, at ten years old, I found a dead finch in the garbage in one of Dad's aviaries. I remember being a bit shocked that it was there. I don't know what else I thought he might do with a bird that passed on after it spent its obligatory time in the freezer. I picked it up and examined it. The tiny beak, only strong enough to crush the most tender grains. The claws that were quickly drying out, but that could still be flexed and unflexed (kind of like a monster's!). But the wings were what captivated me most. When extended fully, each feather was perfectly arranged, and when folded, each retracted to its rightful place. The wings were so much more ordered and purposeful than they appeared to be when the birds were erratically flitting across their enclosures.

I determined that this treasure could not be wasted. I took it into the house and rummaged through my mom's sewing things until I found the materials I thought I would need to preserve it forever. I fully extended the wings, and with straight pins I strategically fastened them in place. I secured the sagging head in an erect and more lifelike position, and voila—a bird in flight! I went outside, tied a string around it, and spun around and around, letting more and more string play out like a kite as my bird "flew." I was just beginning to think I might be able to understand what my dad saw in these creatures when he came up to me and asked what I was up to. I explained that I was preserving that which he had so callously discarded; that I wanted to be one of those guys who make something beautiful out of dead stuff—at which point my father explained what I would actually need to do if I really wanted to preserve the bird forever. I was thoroughly grossed out and quickly gave it back to him.

Though my first attempt to salvage a dead bird was short-lived, it planted a seed. Granted, it was a seed that would not bloom for another three and a half decades, but like the rare corpse flower, when it finally bloomed, it did so with a stinking vengeance.

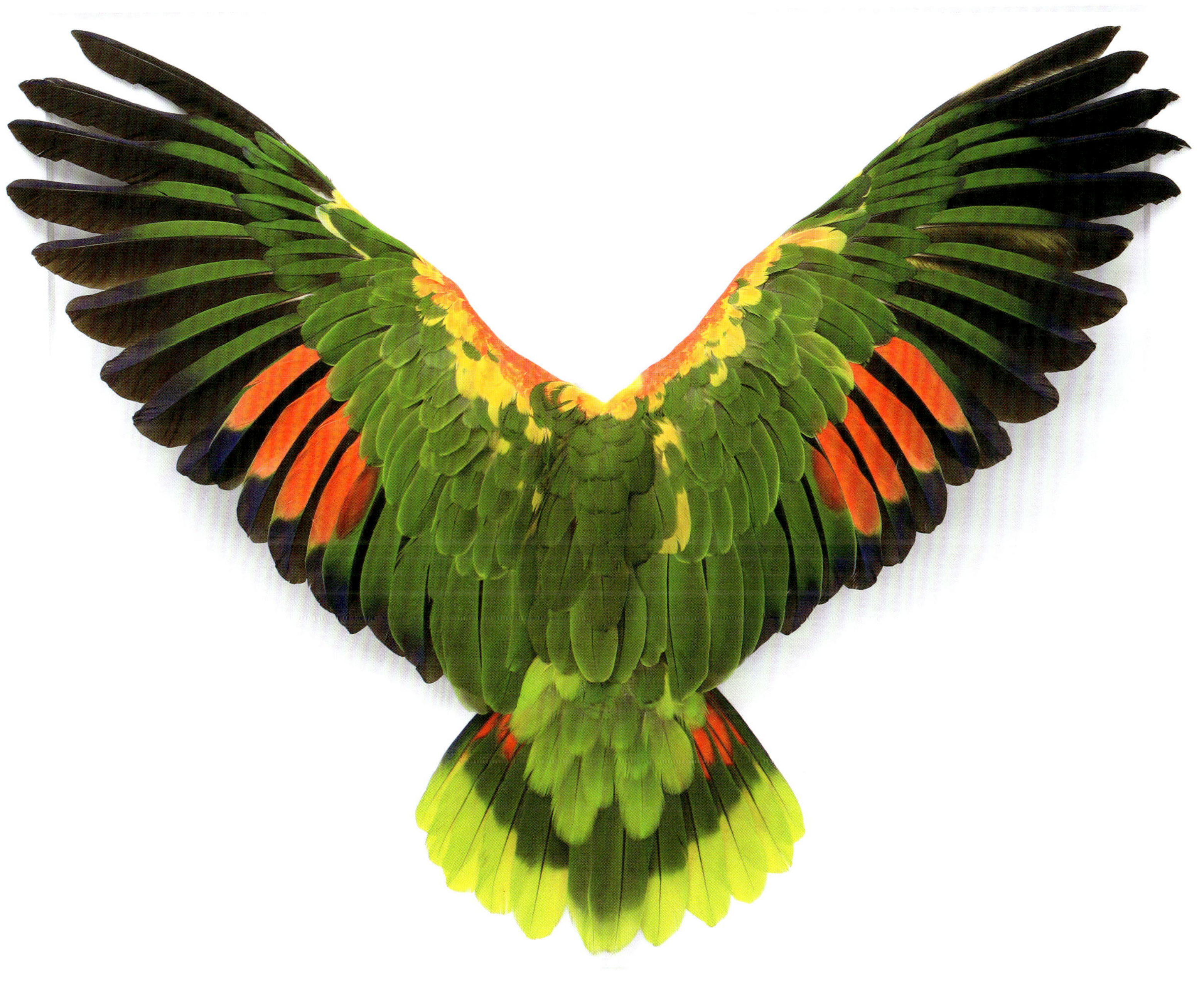

Double Yellow-Headed Amazon

Guatemala

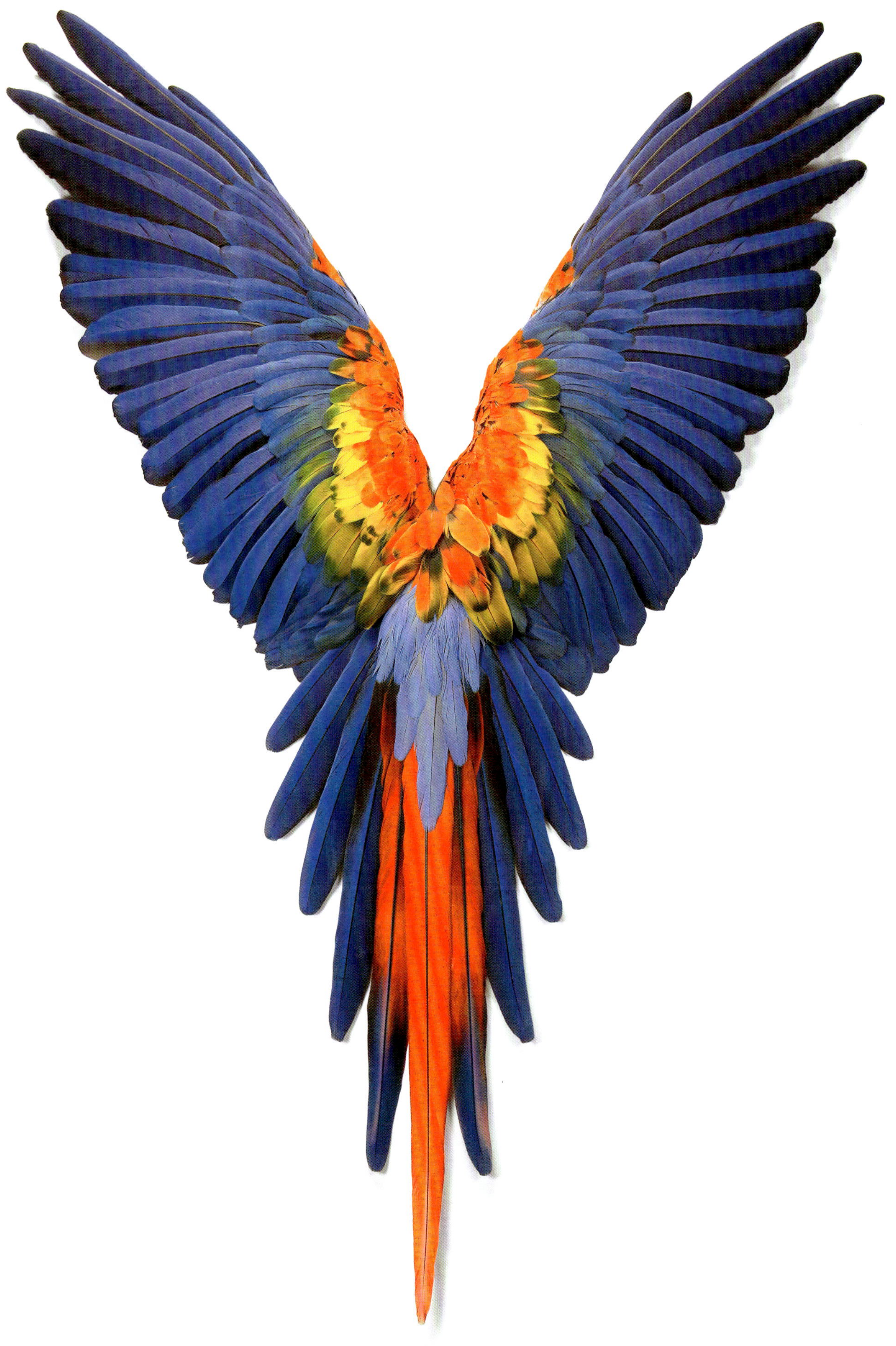

Scarlet Macaw

Brazil

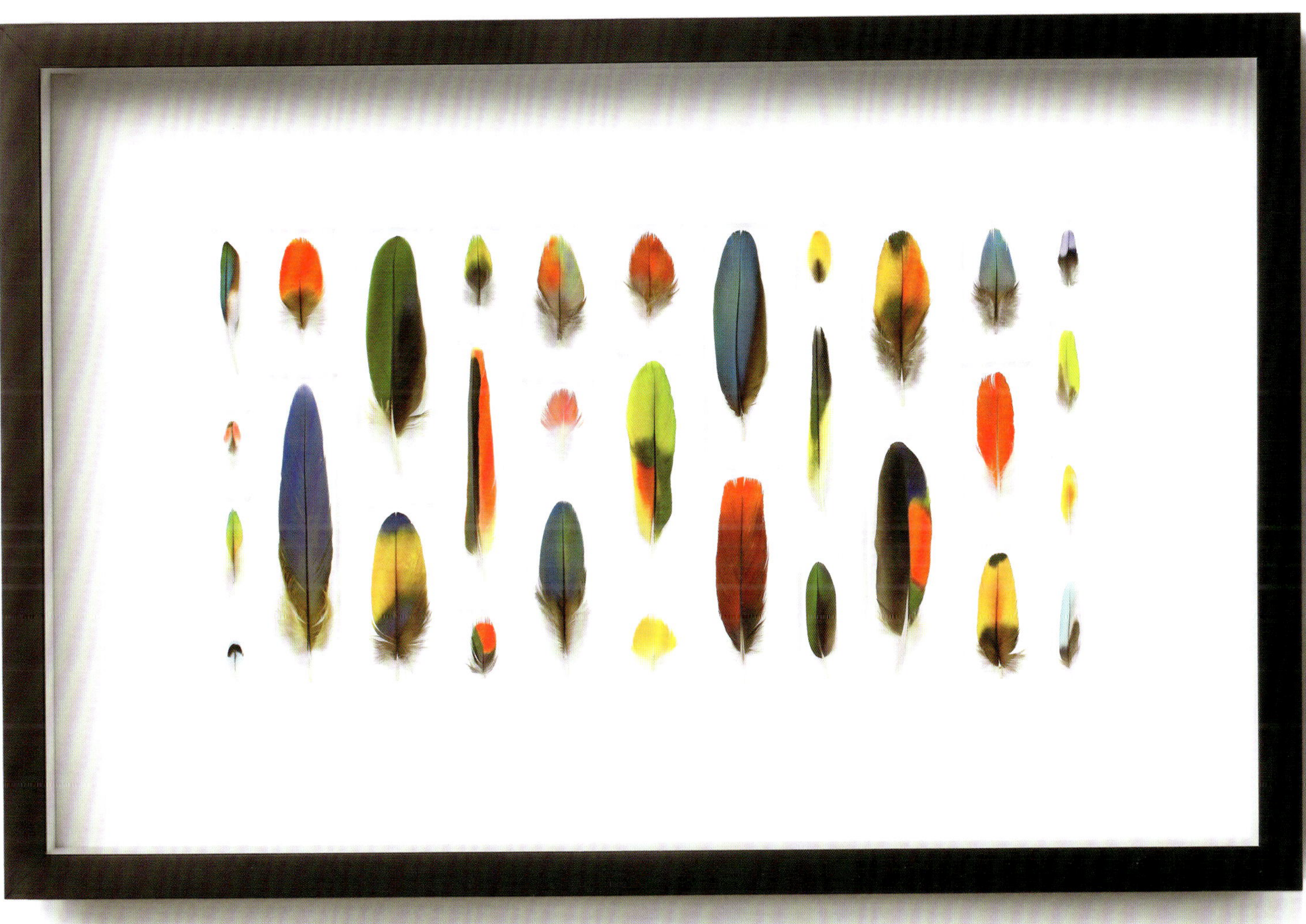

Feather Mosaic

Worldwide

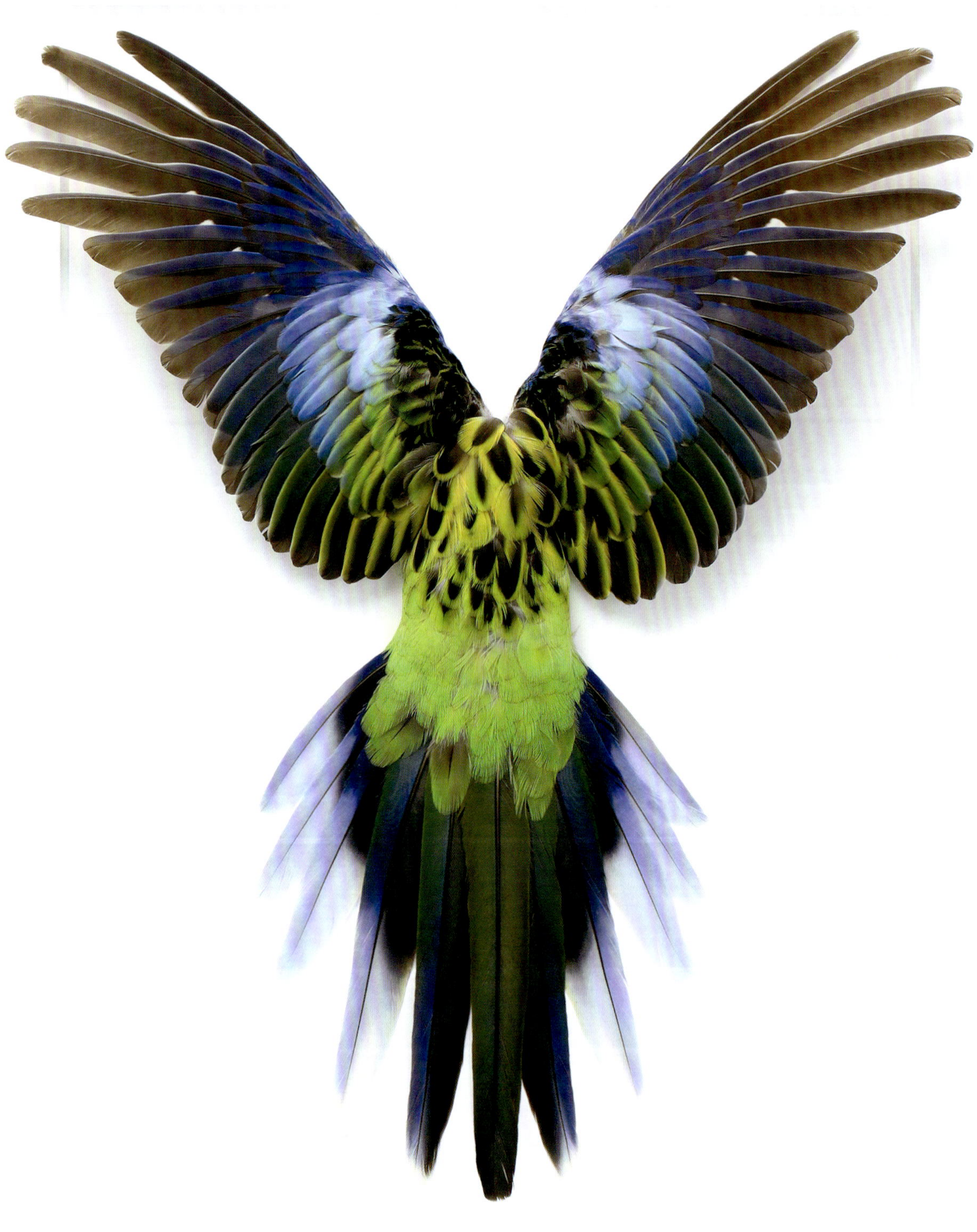

Pale-Headed Rosella

Australia

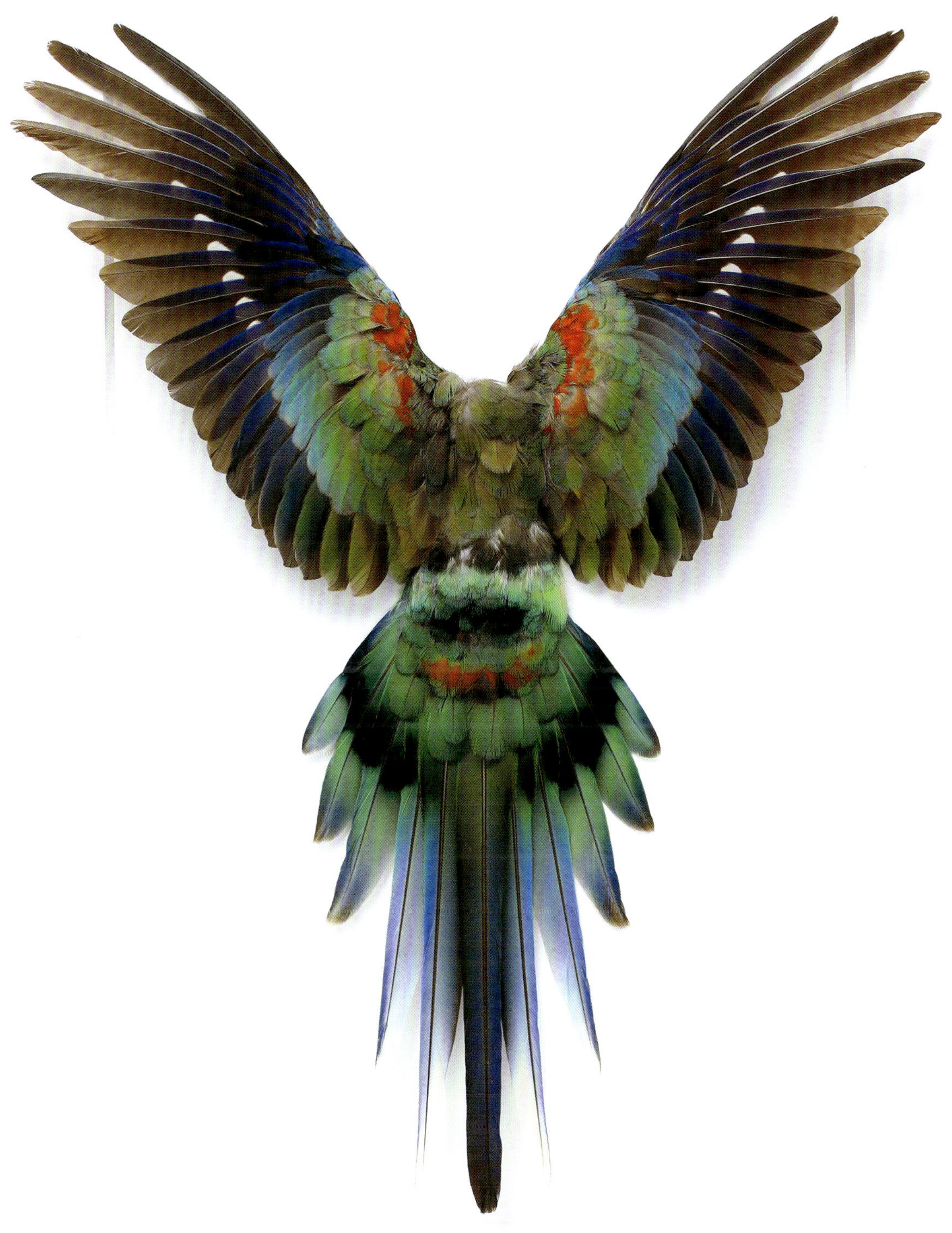

Red-Rumped Parrot

Australia

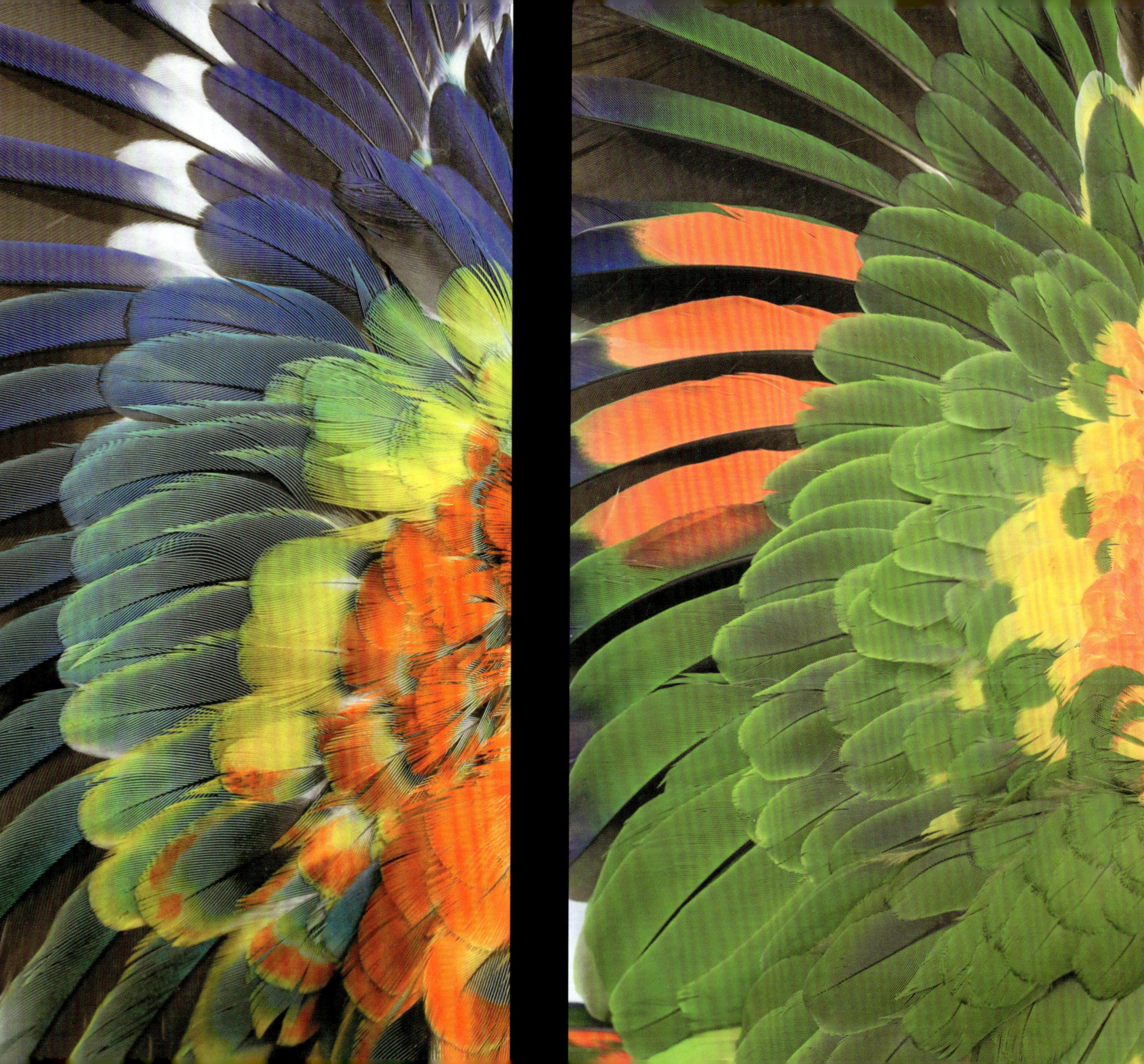

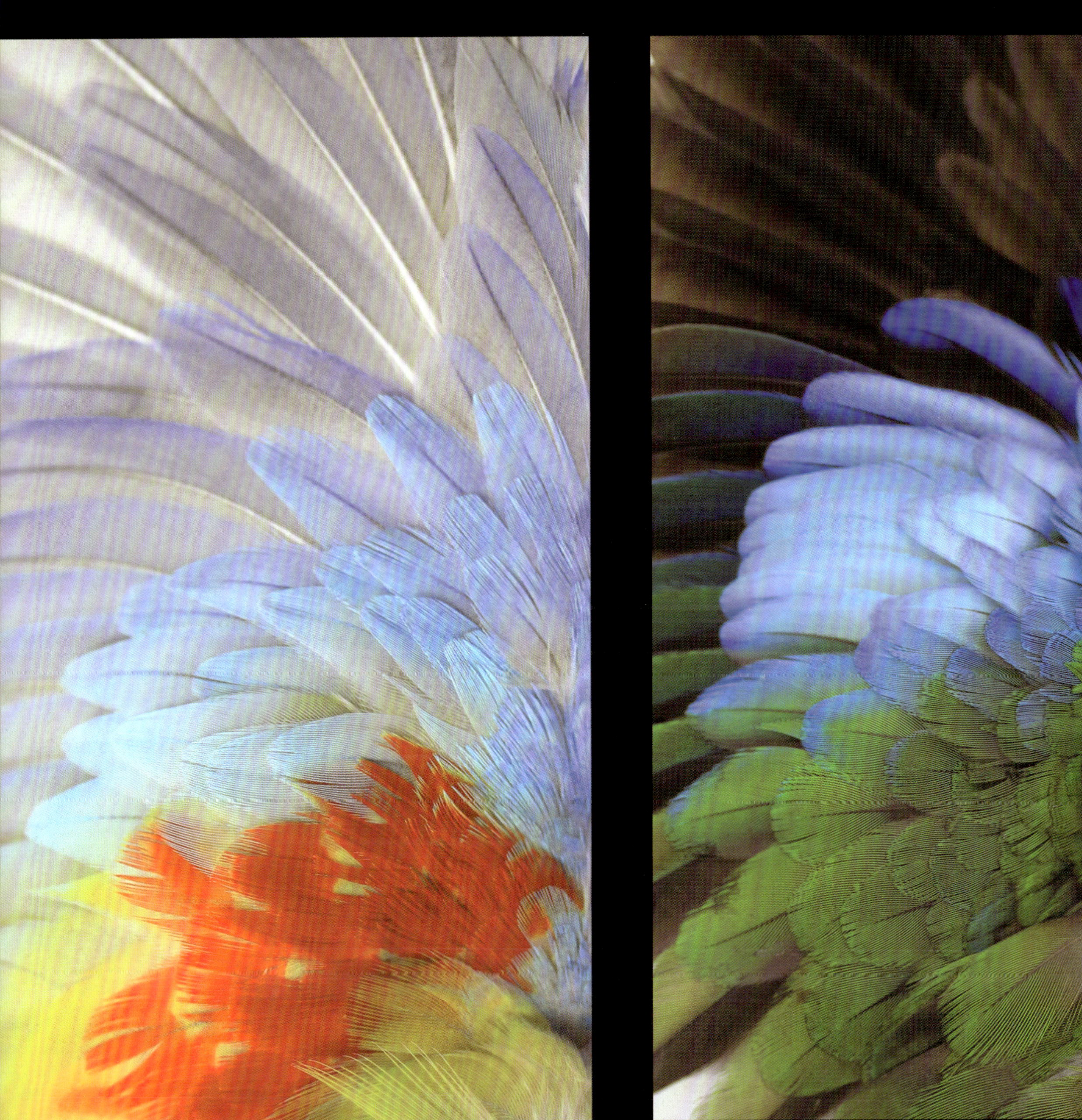

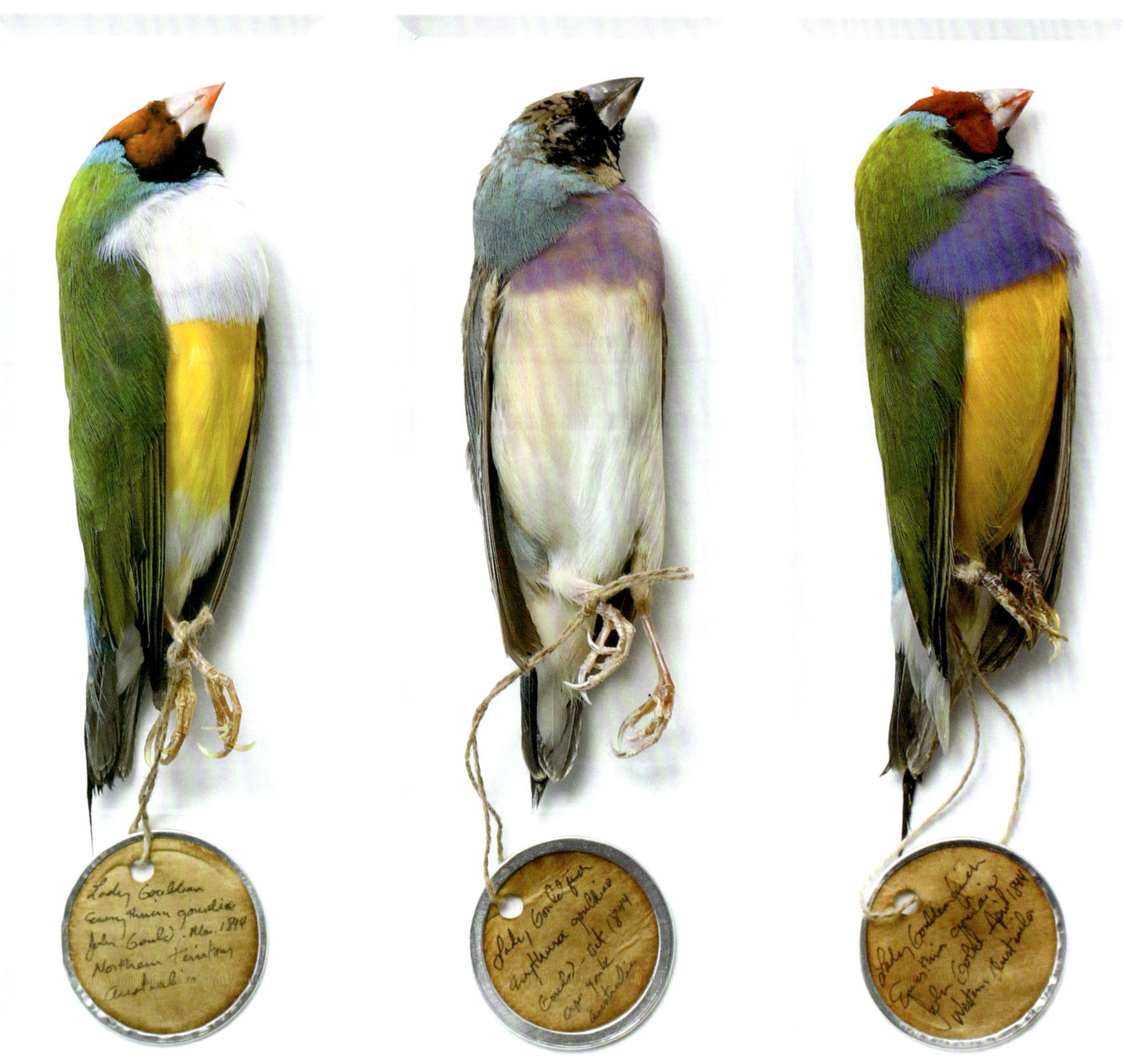

Gouldian Finches, Museum Collection

Australia

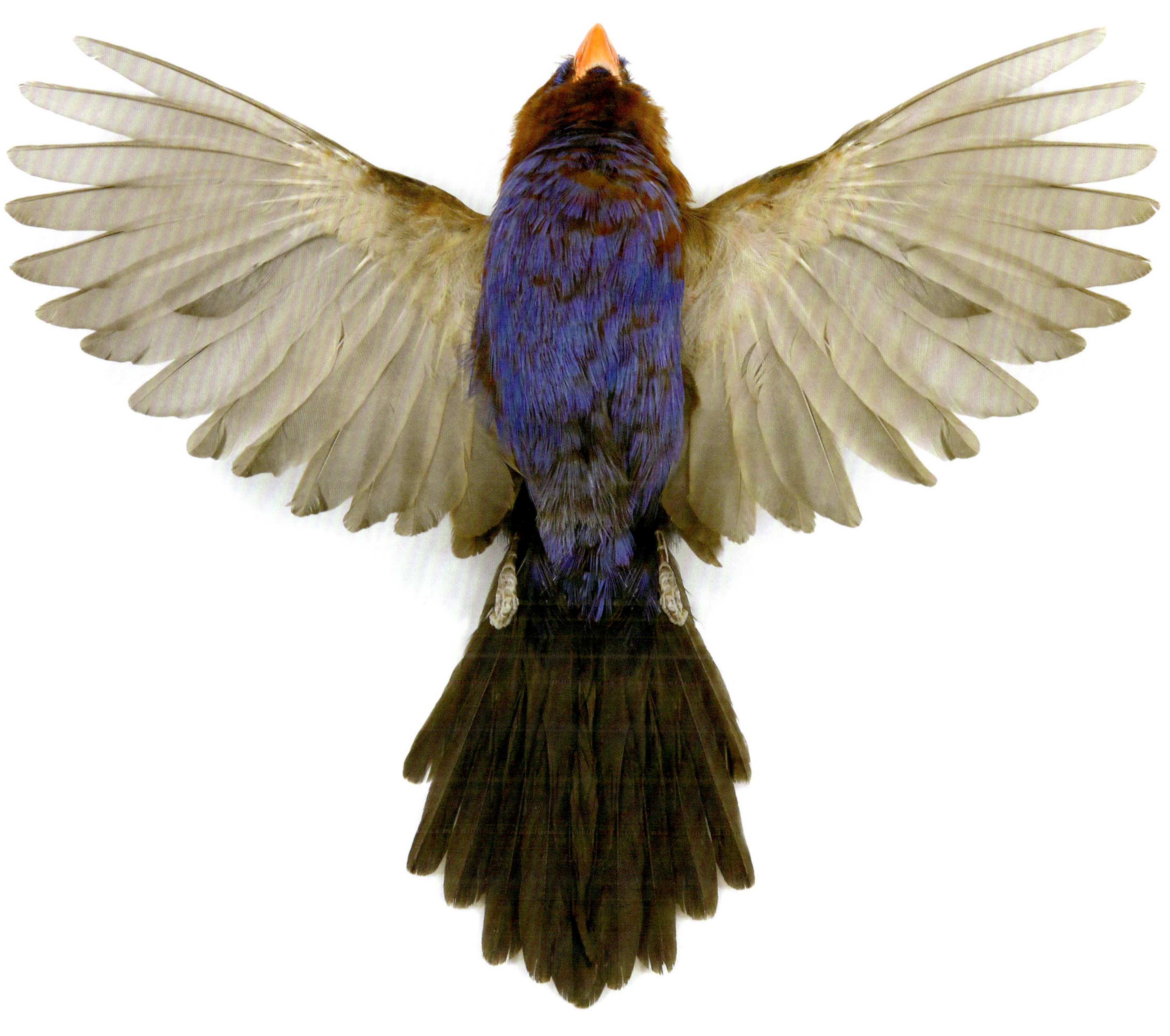

Purple Grenadier Finch

Uganda

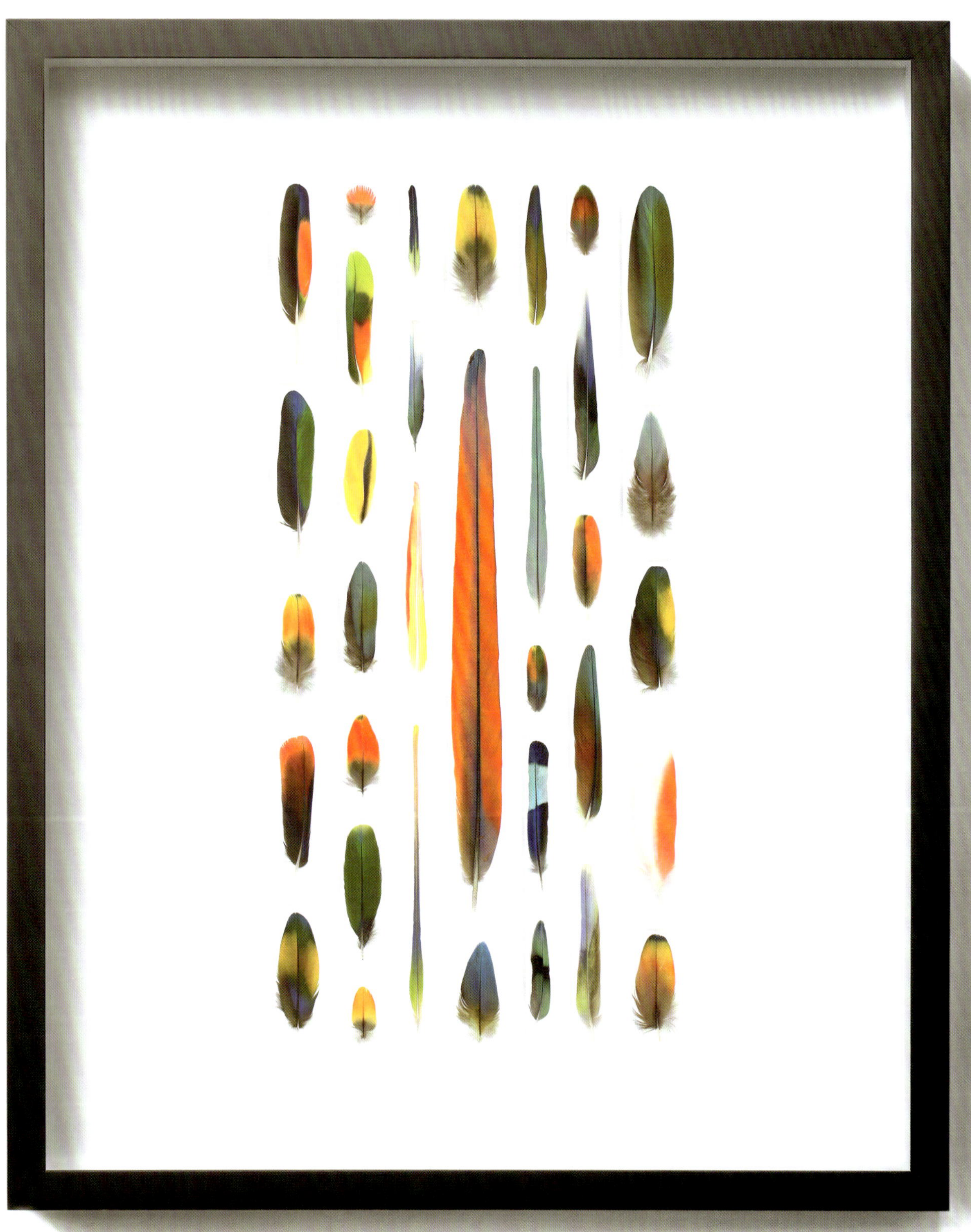

Feather Mosaic

Worldwide

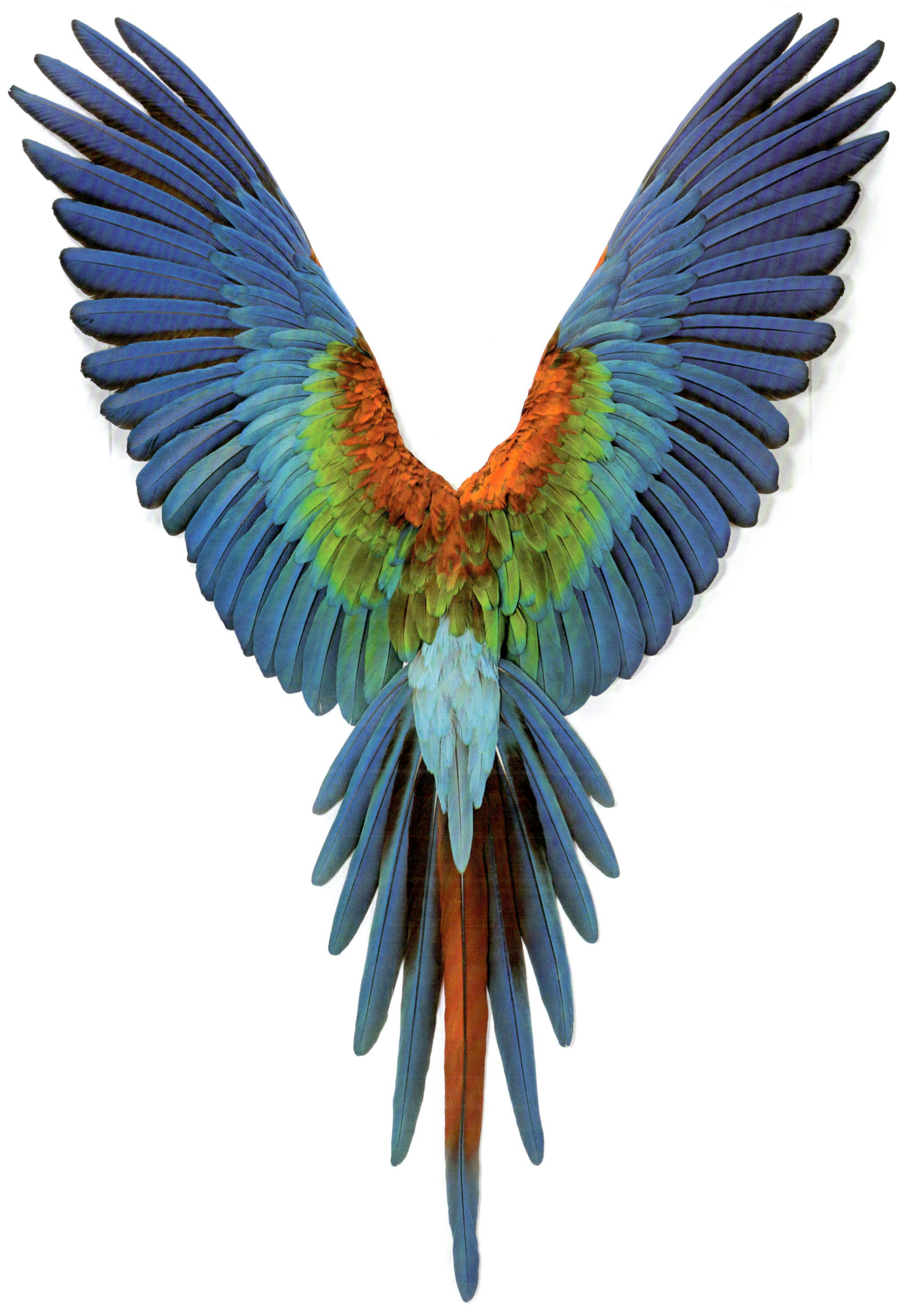

Green-Winged Macaw

Venezuela

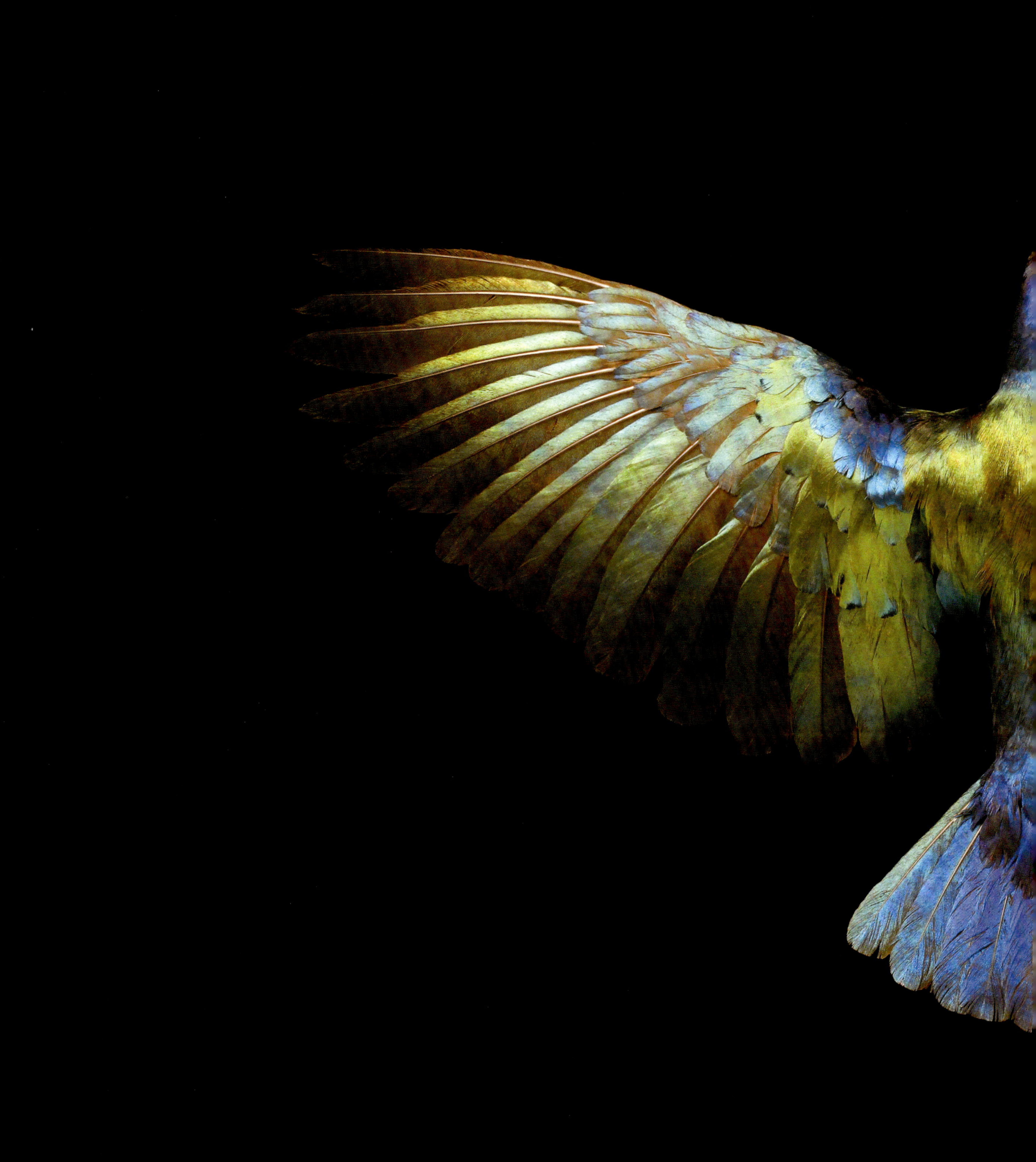

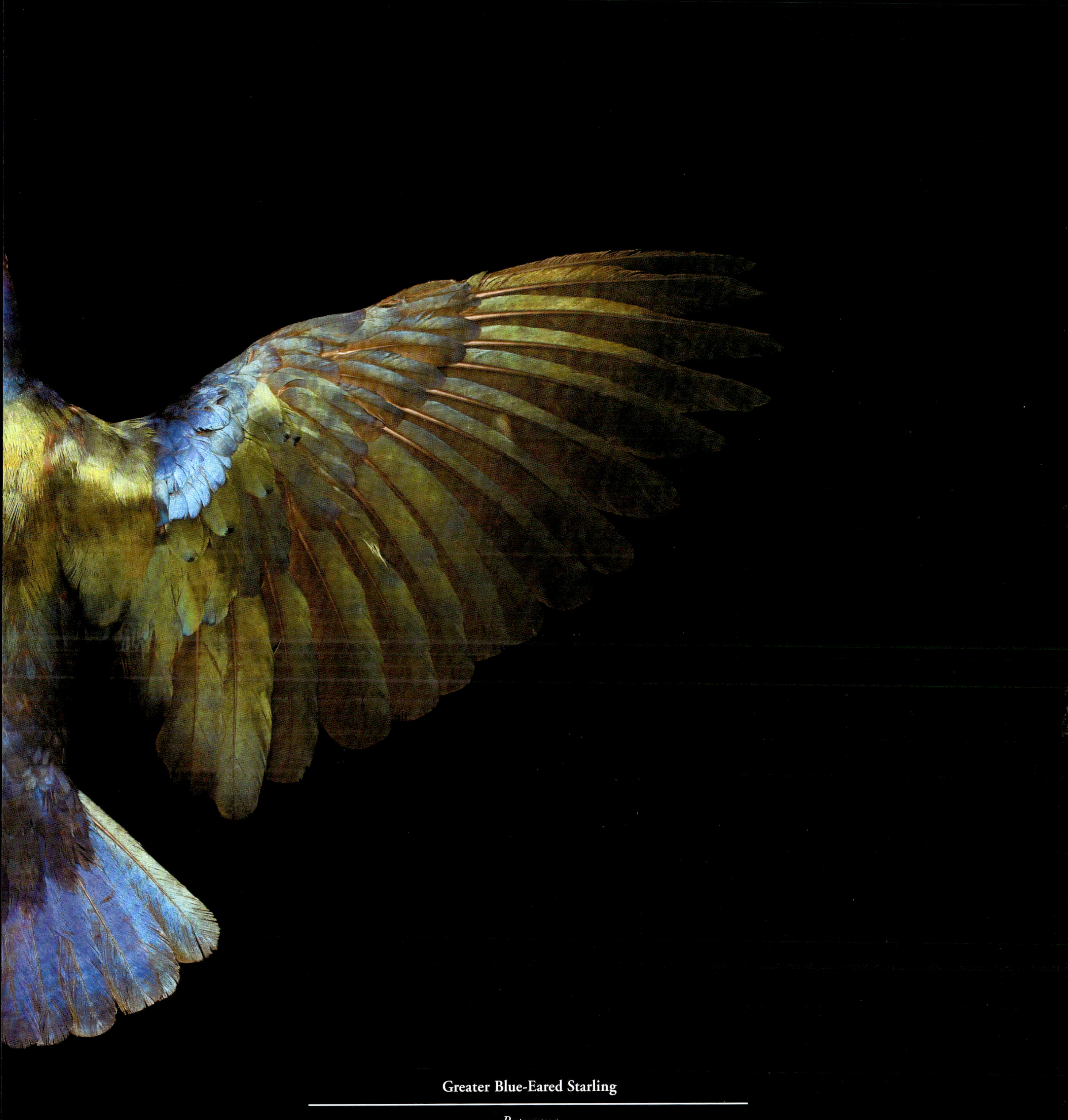

Greater Blue-Eared Starling

Botswana

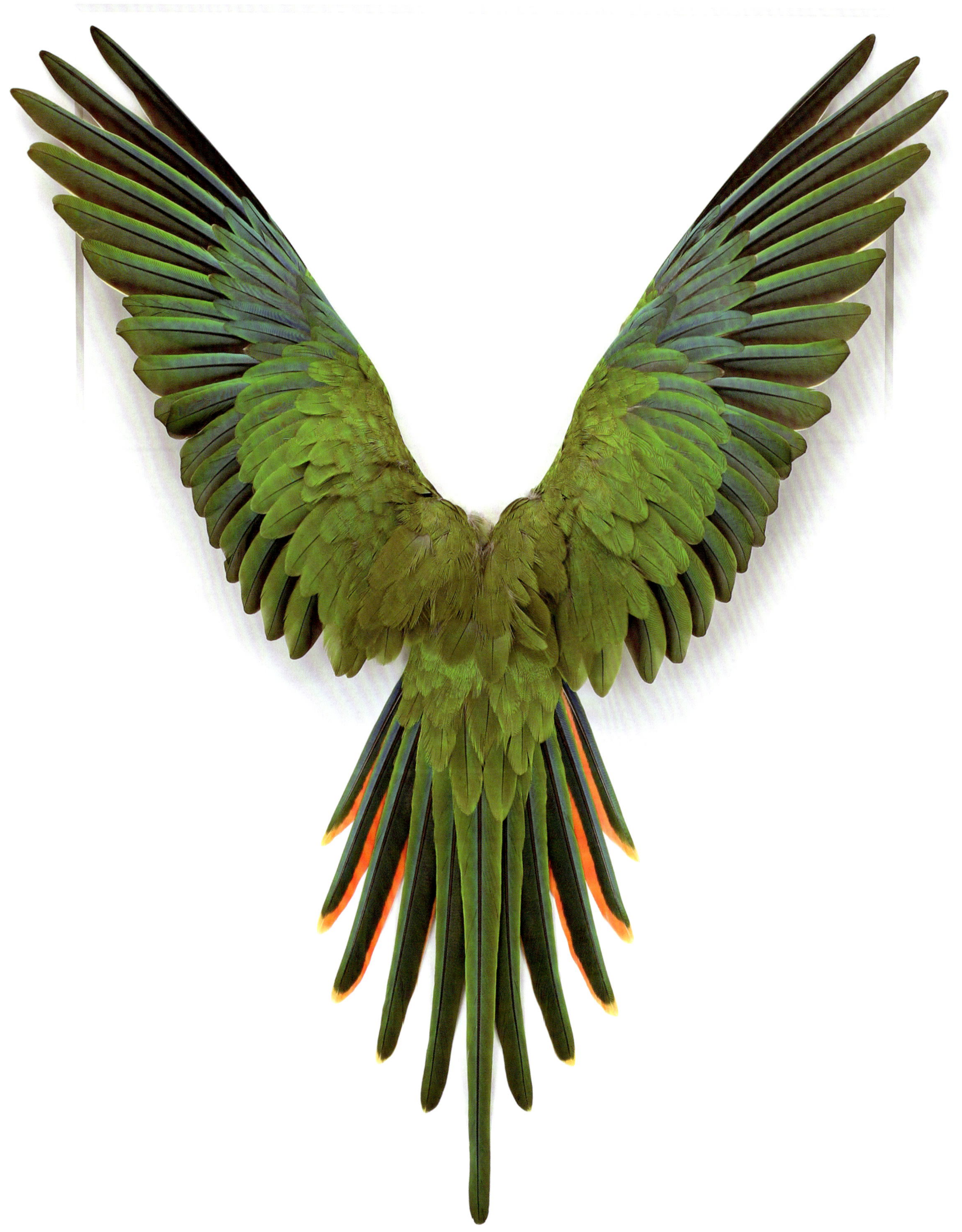

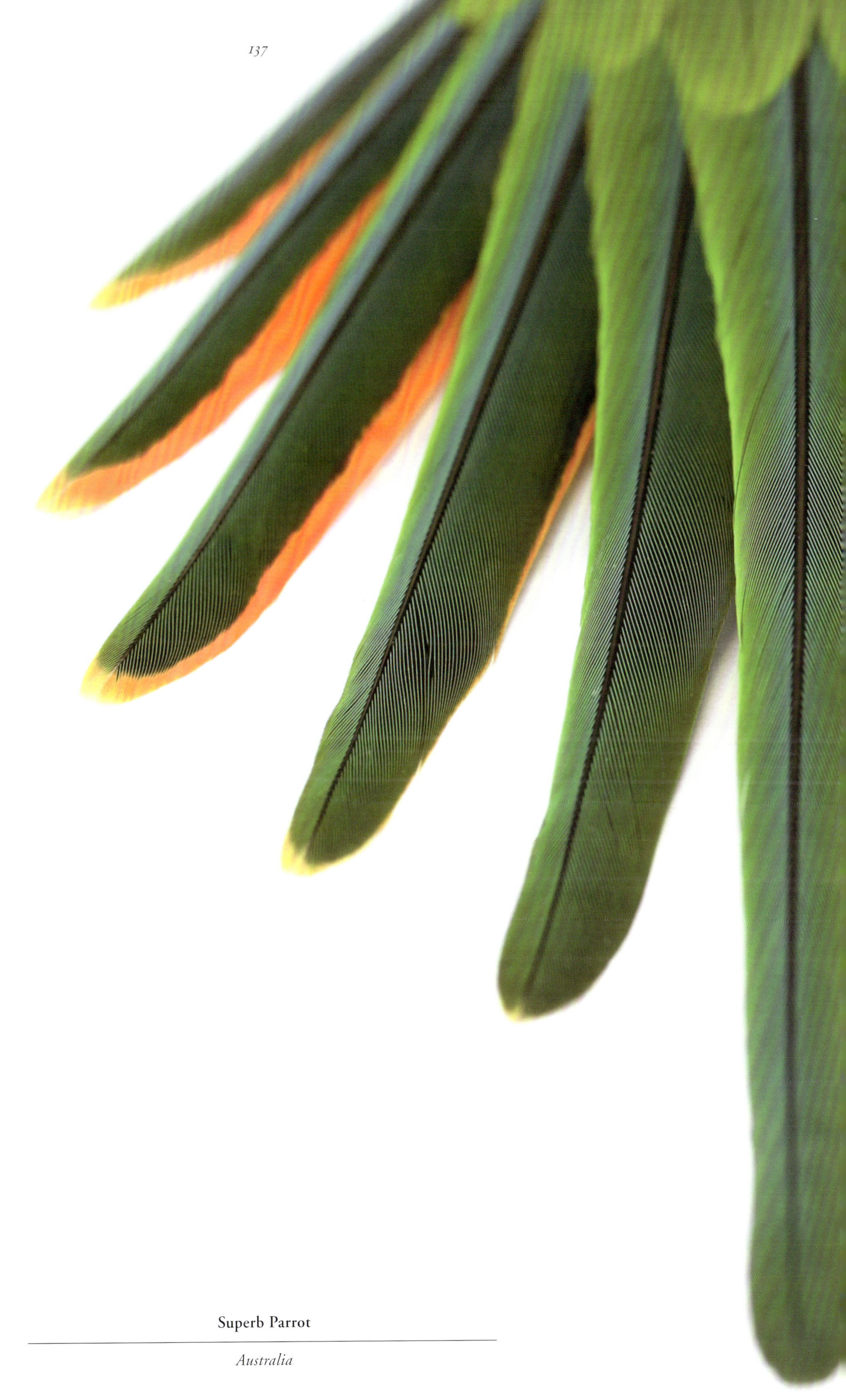

Superb Parrot

Australia

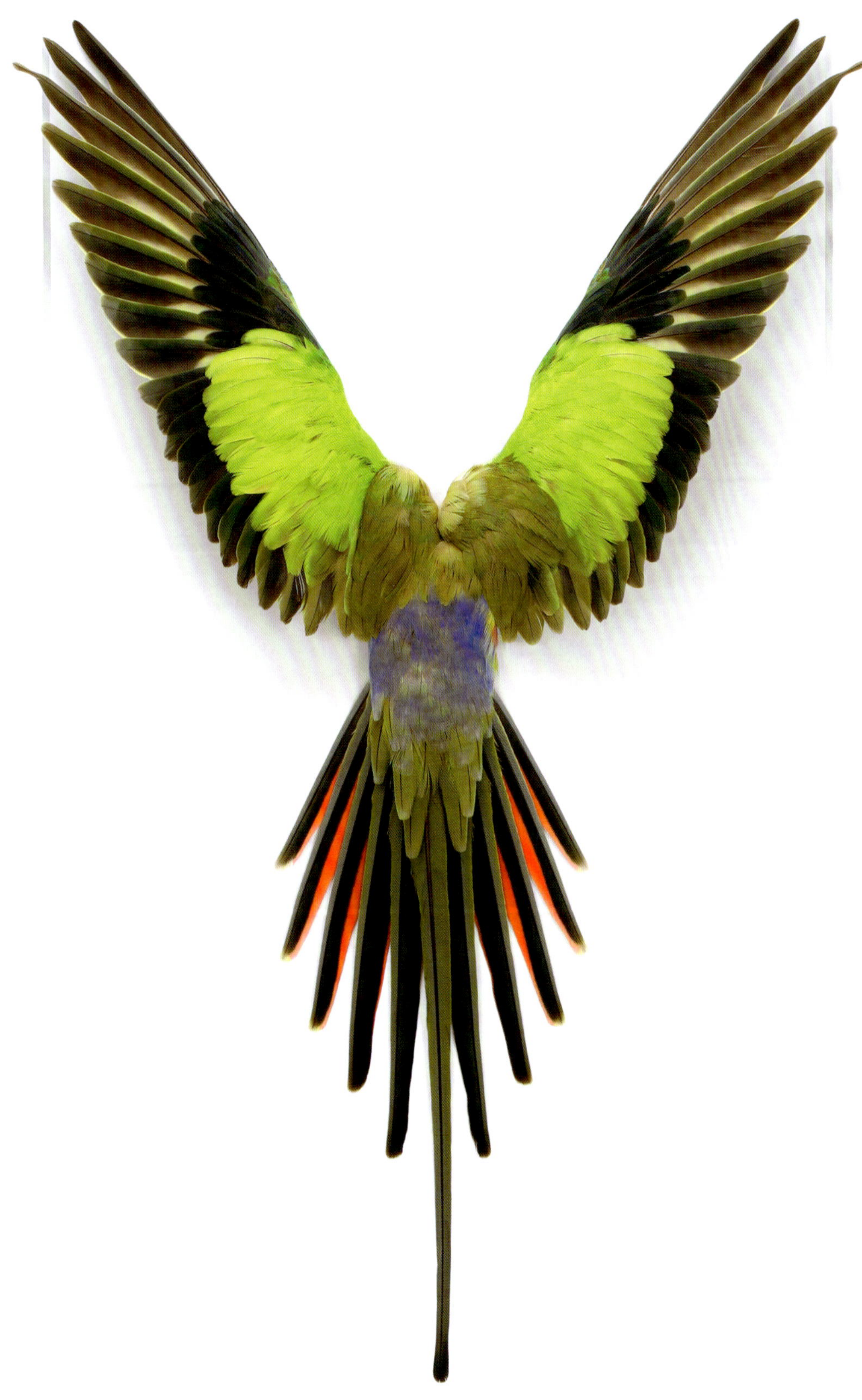

Princess of Wales Parakeet

Australia

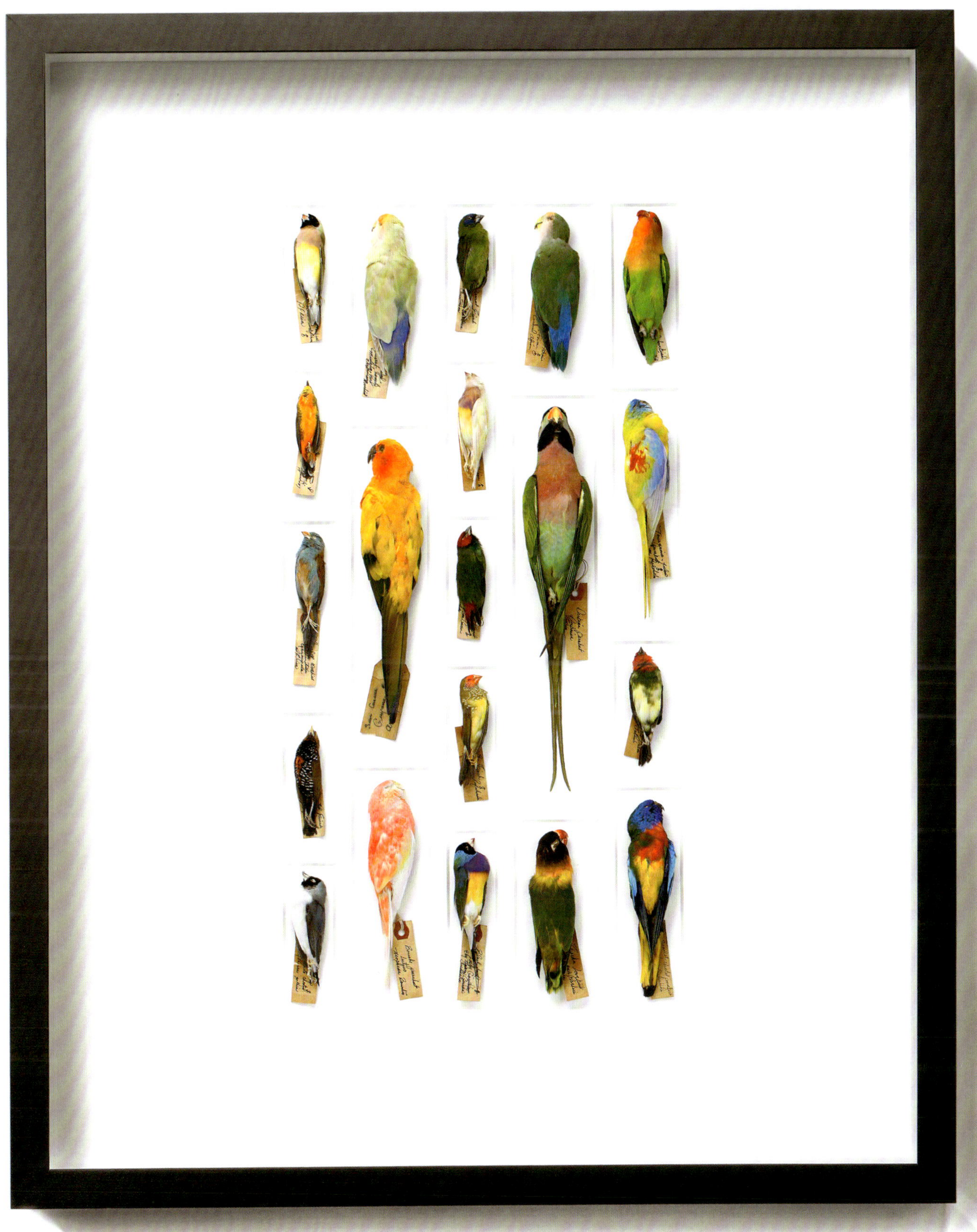

Ave Museum Collection

Worldwide

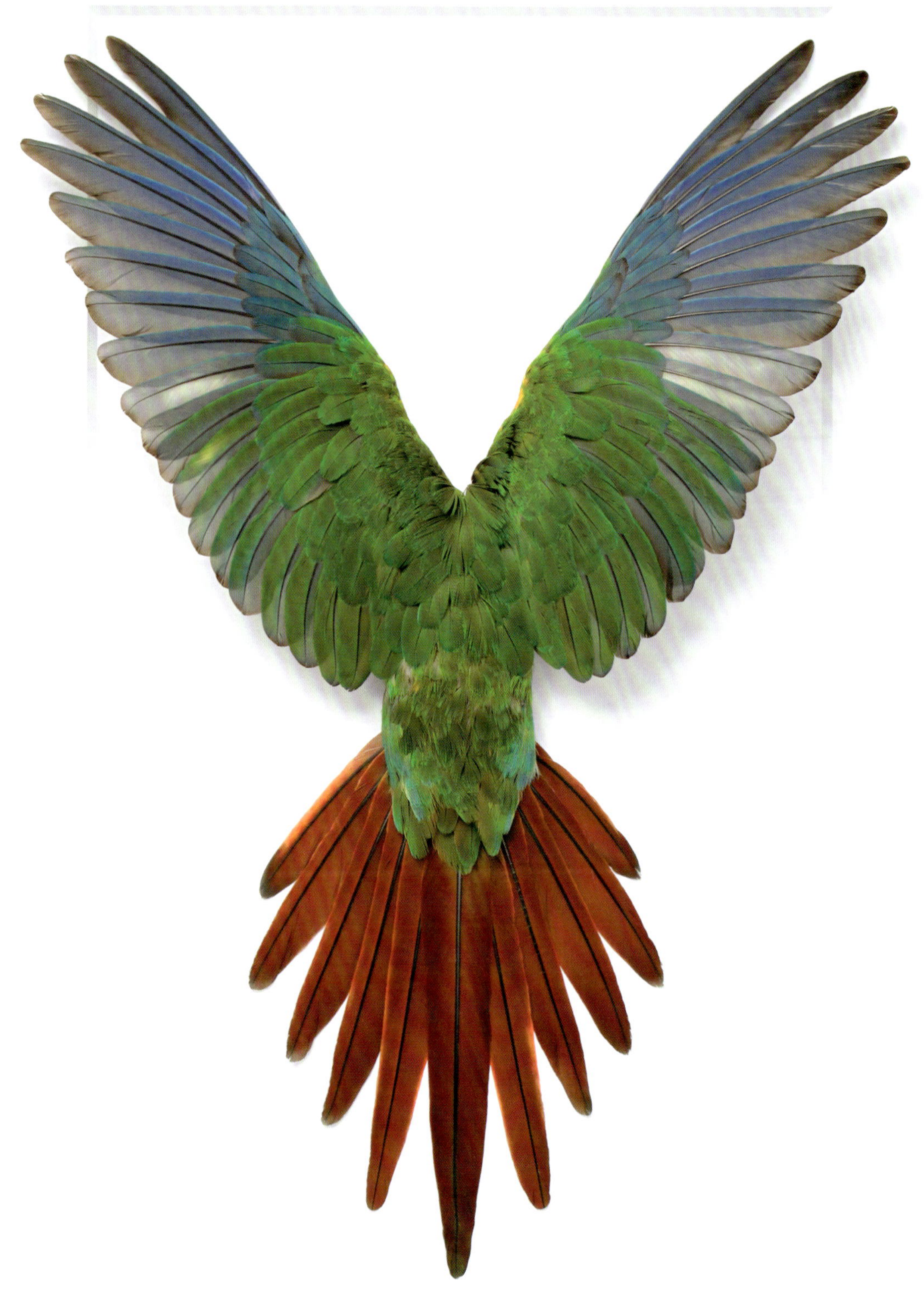

Green-Cheeked Conure

Bolivia

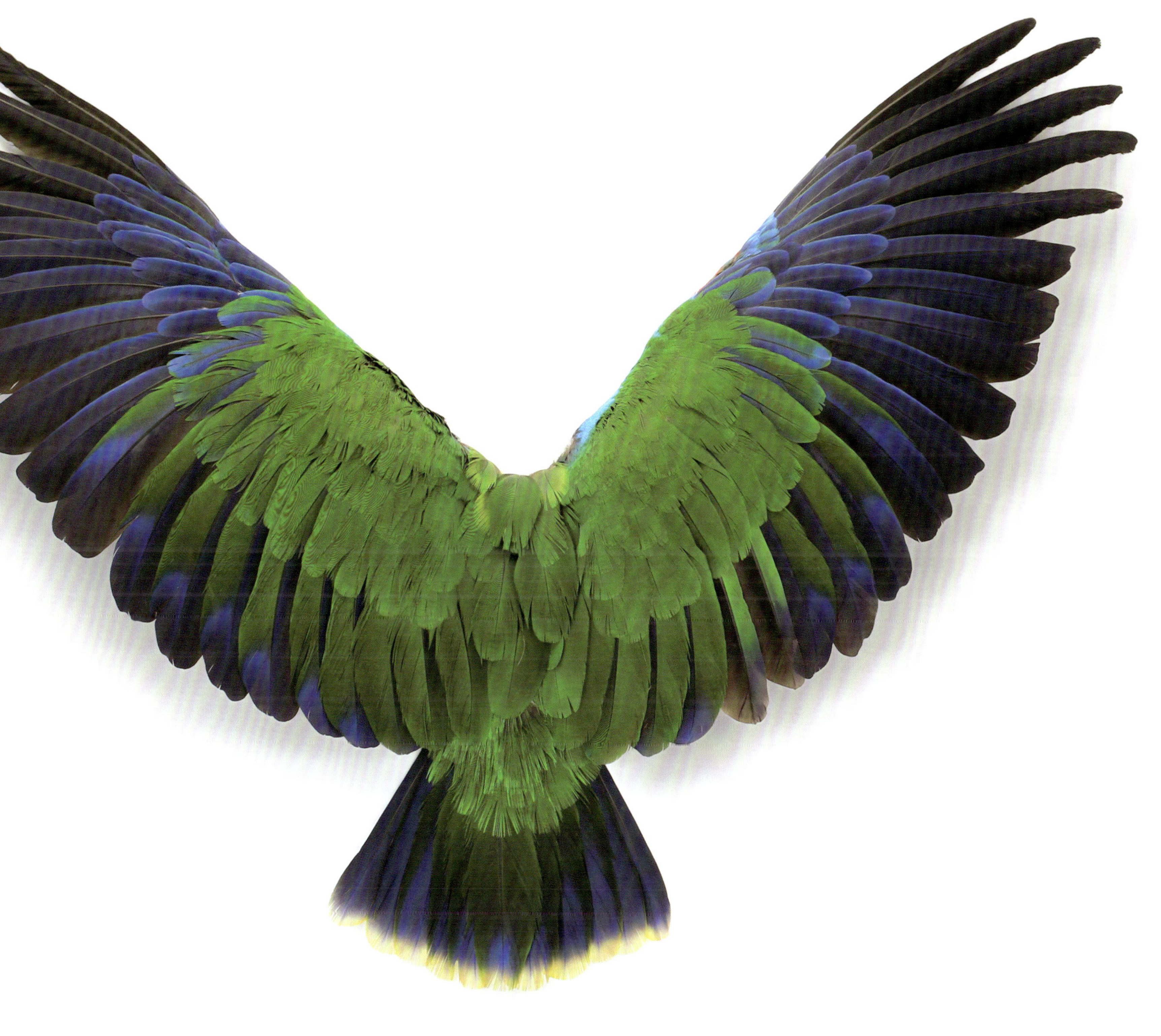

Vos Eclectus

New Guinea

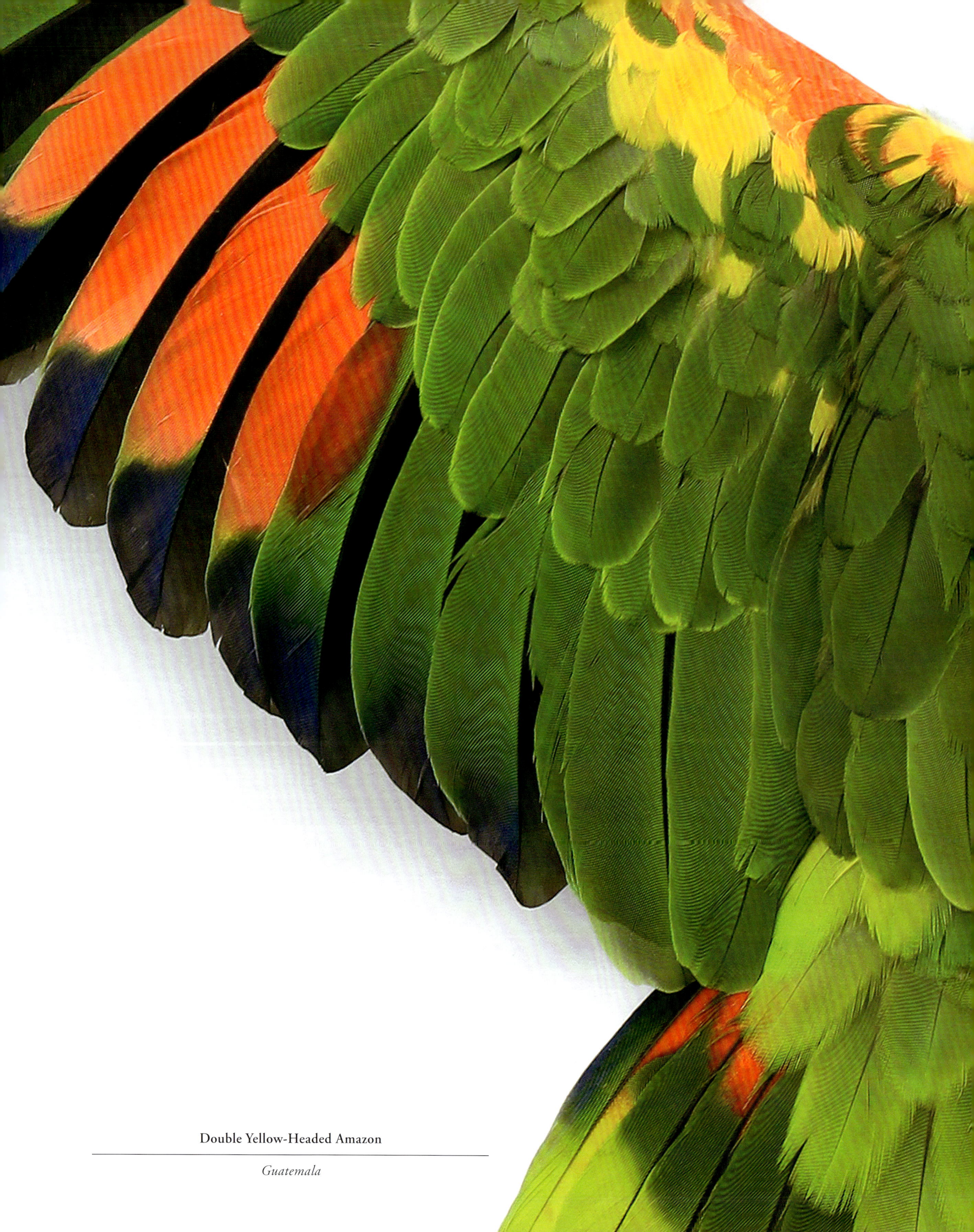

Double Yellow-Headed Amazon

Guatemala

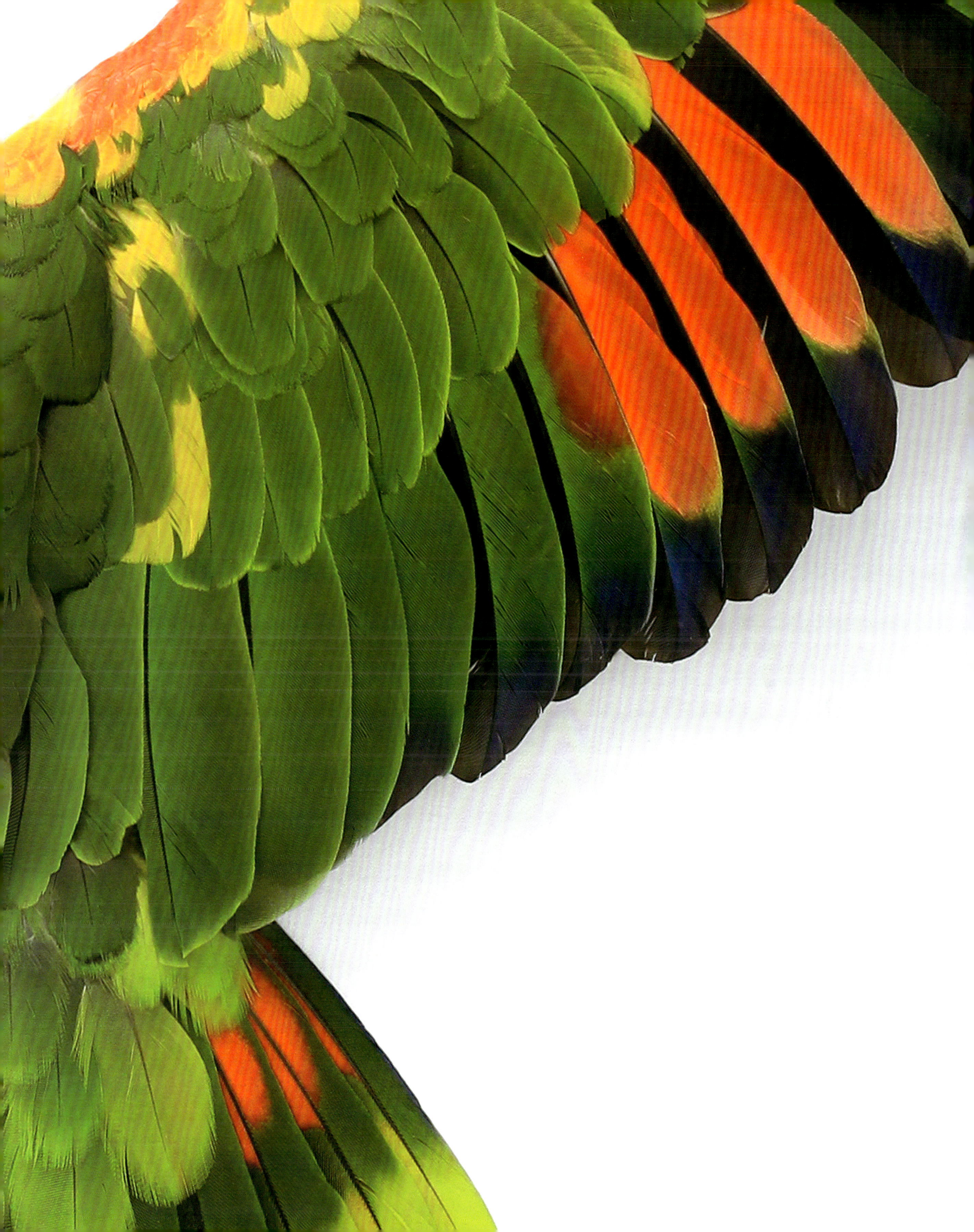

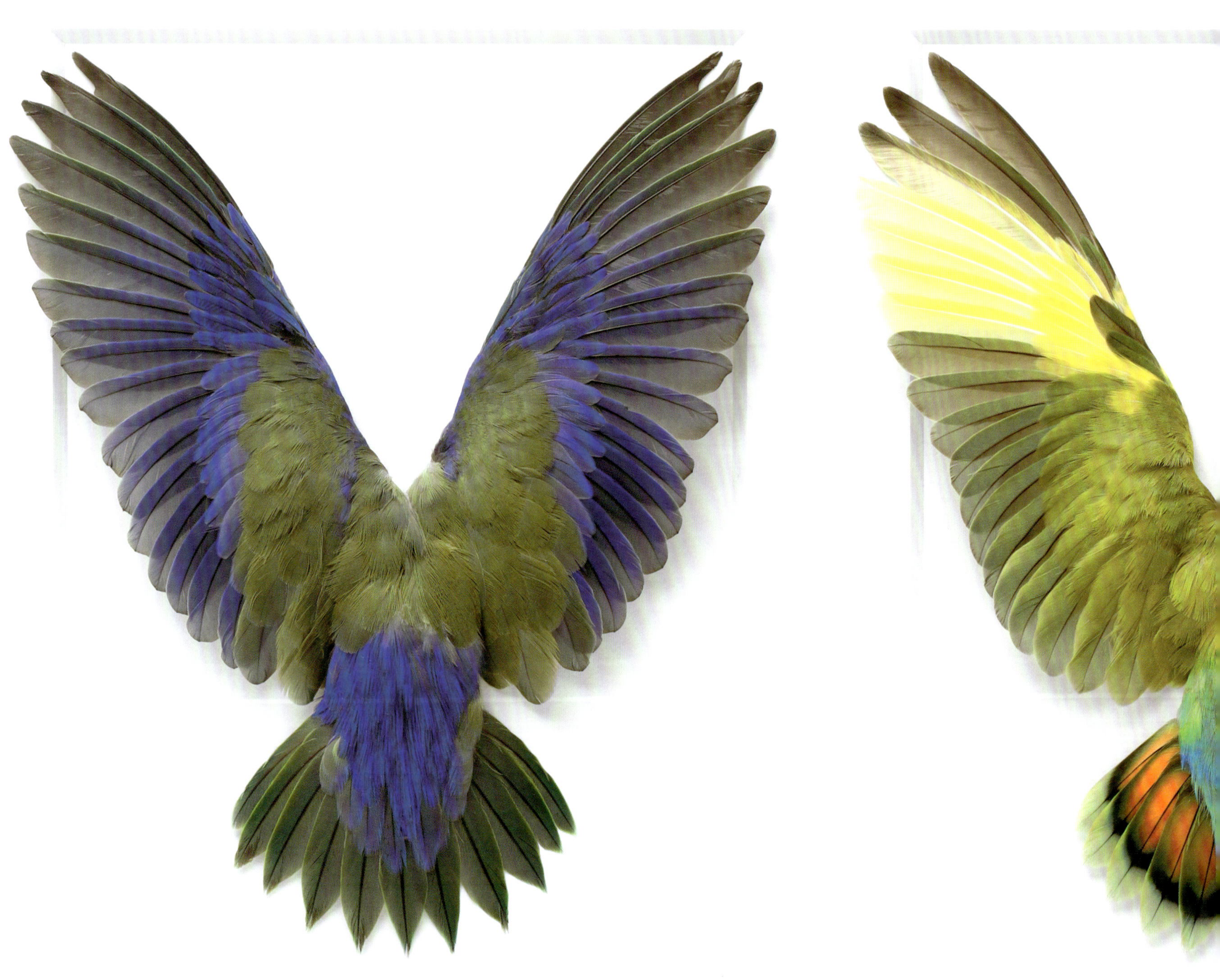

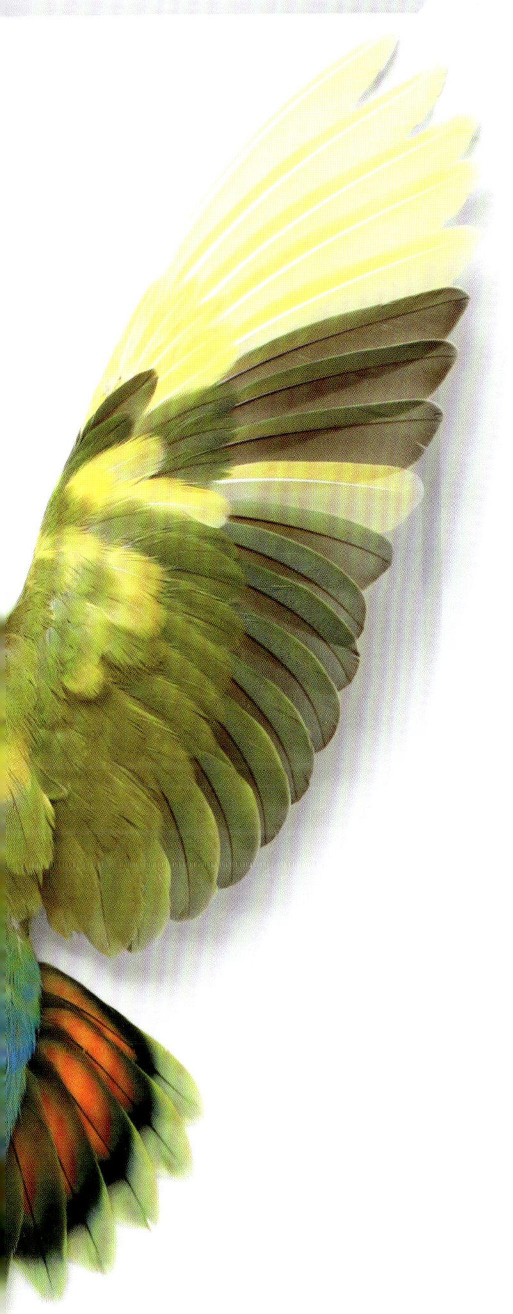

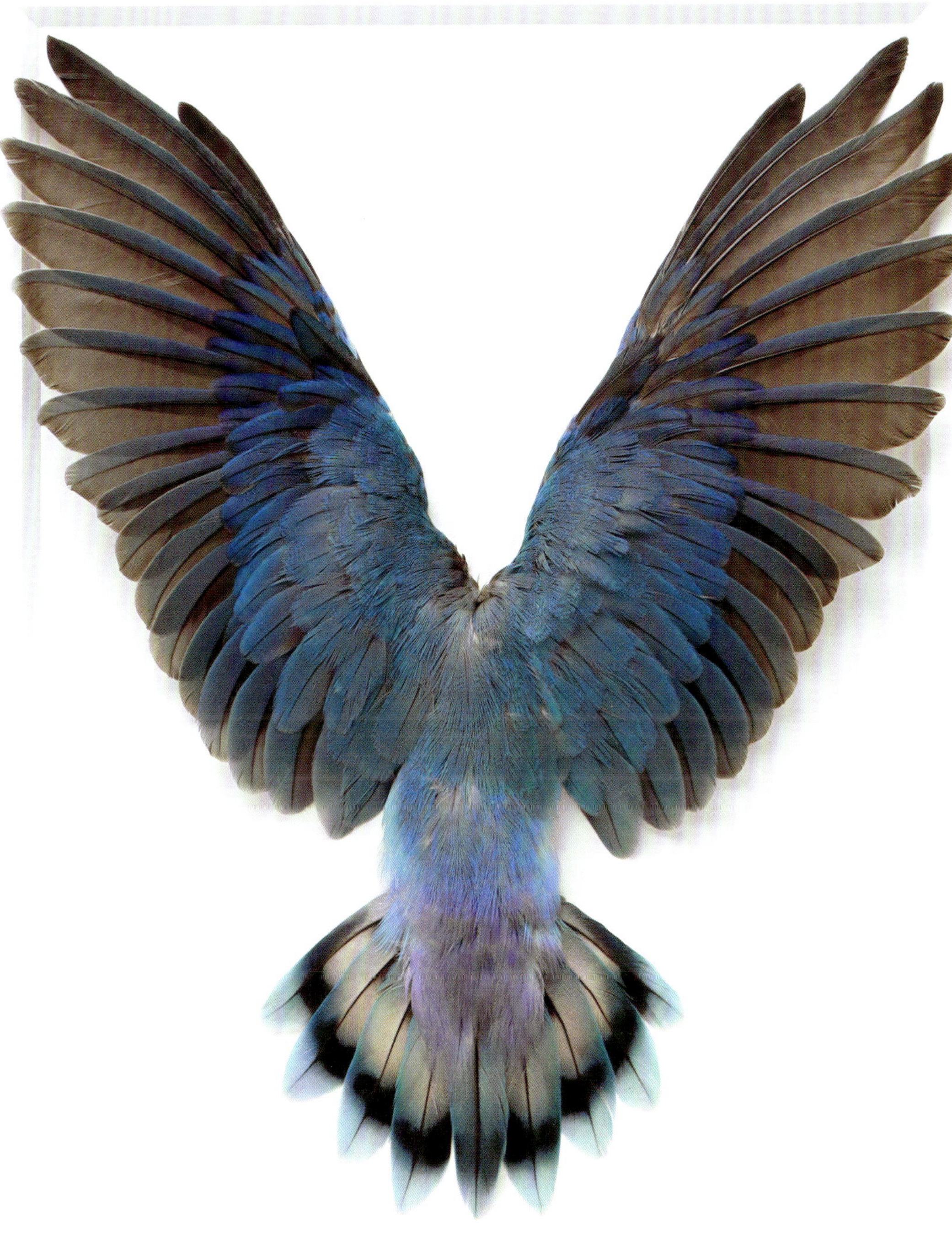

Agapornis Parrot Color Forms

Tanzania, Namibia

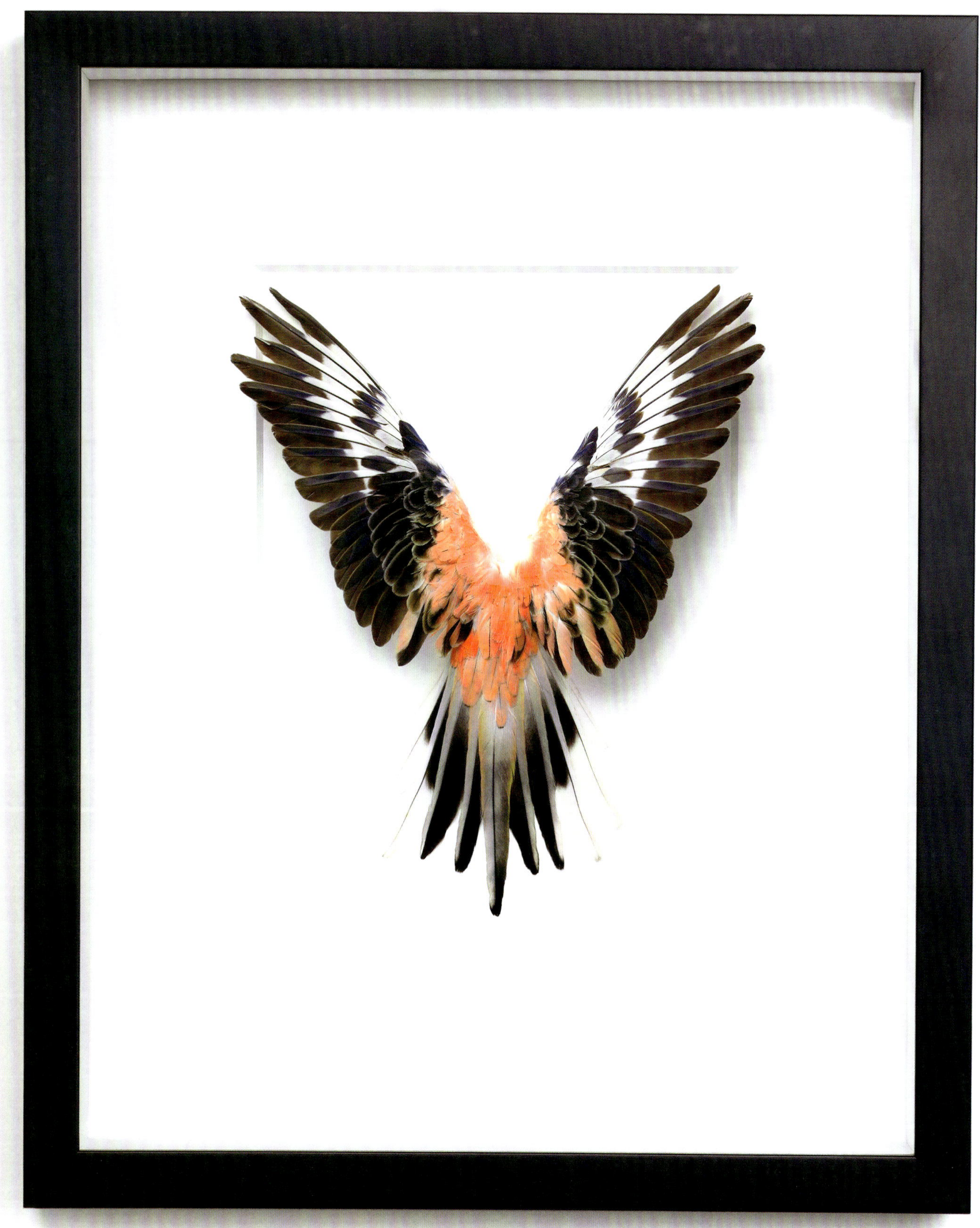

Bourke's Parakeet

Australia

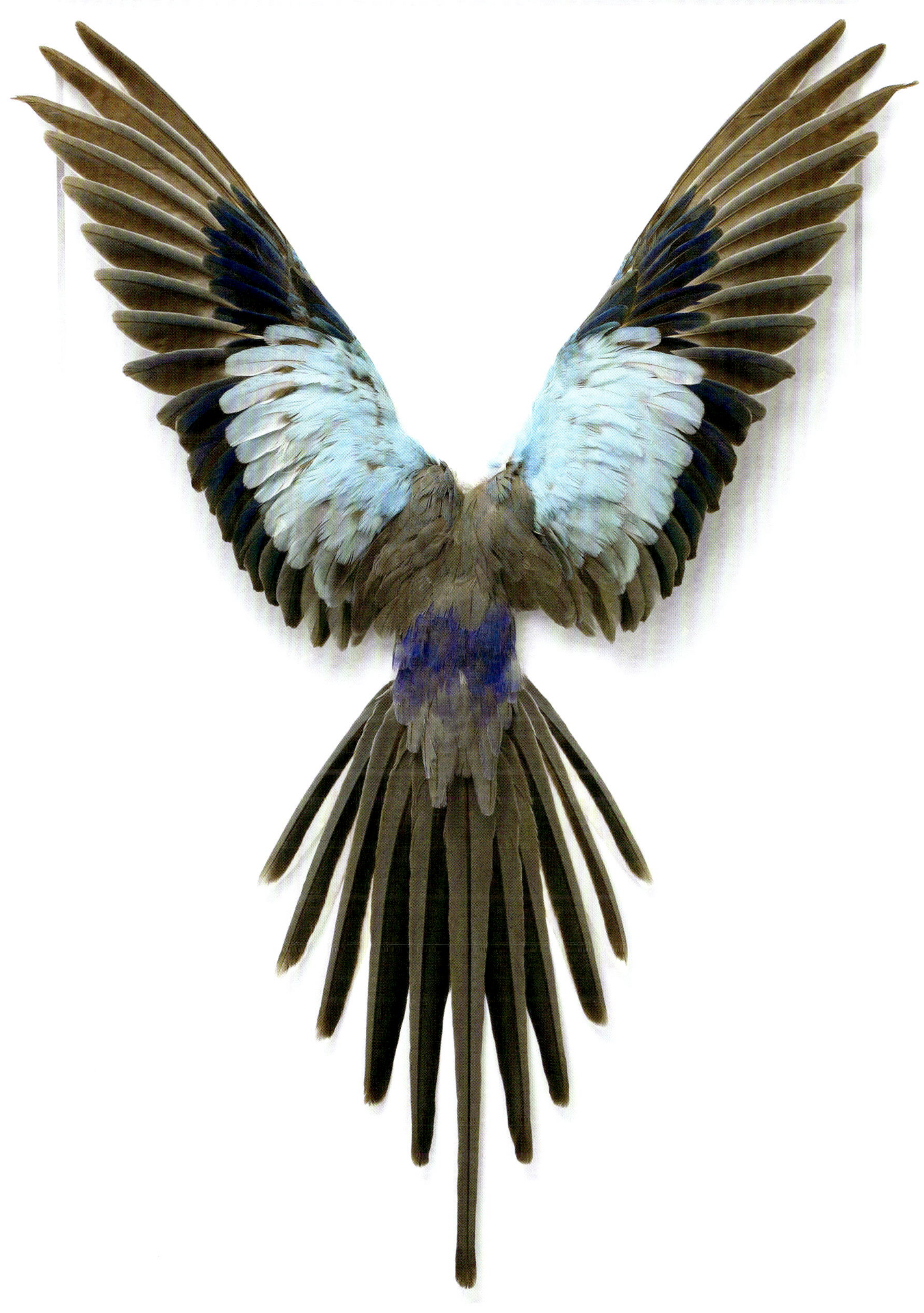

Princess of Wales Parakeet

Australia

MINERALS

Minerals are the most common, accessible, and utilized of all natural artifacts. We walk and ride on them, define our spaces with them, and base our currencies on them, all while relying on their distinct properties for a myriad of practical purposes, from telling time to computing. We have also been blessed with their finer properties: crystals of such fire and rarity that the whole world seems consumed with their discovery and acquisition, and fossils that tell incredible stories of creatures and epochs that we could never have dreamed of otherwise. Our passions as well as our societies are forged in the realm of minerals.

However, the same quiet, eternal properties that make them literally foundational to our civilization also facilitate our apathy toward the stony bulk of our planet. I have done my share of preaching about the dangers of our society careening into an increasingly virtual world. The damaging effects of living in two dimensions can easily be seen in both the macro and the micro, from a generation of youth with rising levels of apathy and isolation to the marriages of friends that have ended due to gaming addictions or online second lives. It is clear to me that we are designed to experience as much of the natural world as possible with all five of our senses. There is a grounding, satisfying, and nourishing effect when we do.

This needed interaction between humans and nature almost always begins with minerals. For my sons, their earliest formative experiences were all about throwing rocks into a pond or toddling up a gentle mountain trail. Searching for agates at the beach and playing in (and eating) sand. Pockets, bottom drawers, and sippy cups constantly filled with little mineral treasures.

Then, children discover moving images on screens, and all too often, the solid, substantial realm of minerals is forgotten in favor of flash. Five-second clips and five-word texts take the place of the observation, study, and contemplation of the timeless elements of our earth. We permit it at our peril.

Perhaps the answer is a return to the basics: unplugging and going outside. I couldn't recommend throwing rocks into a pond more highly. And if you can drag a child along, all the better. That is, after all, how revolutions have often begun: with a single rock throw.

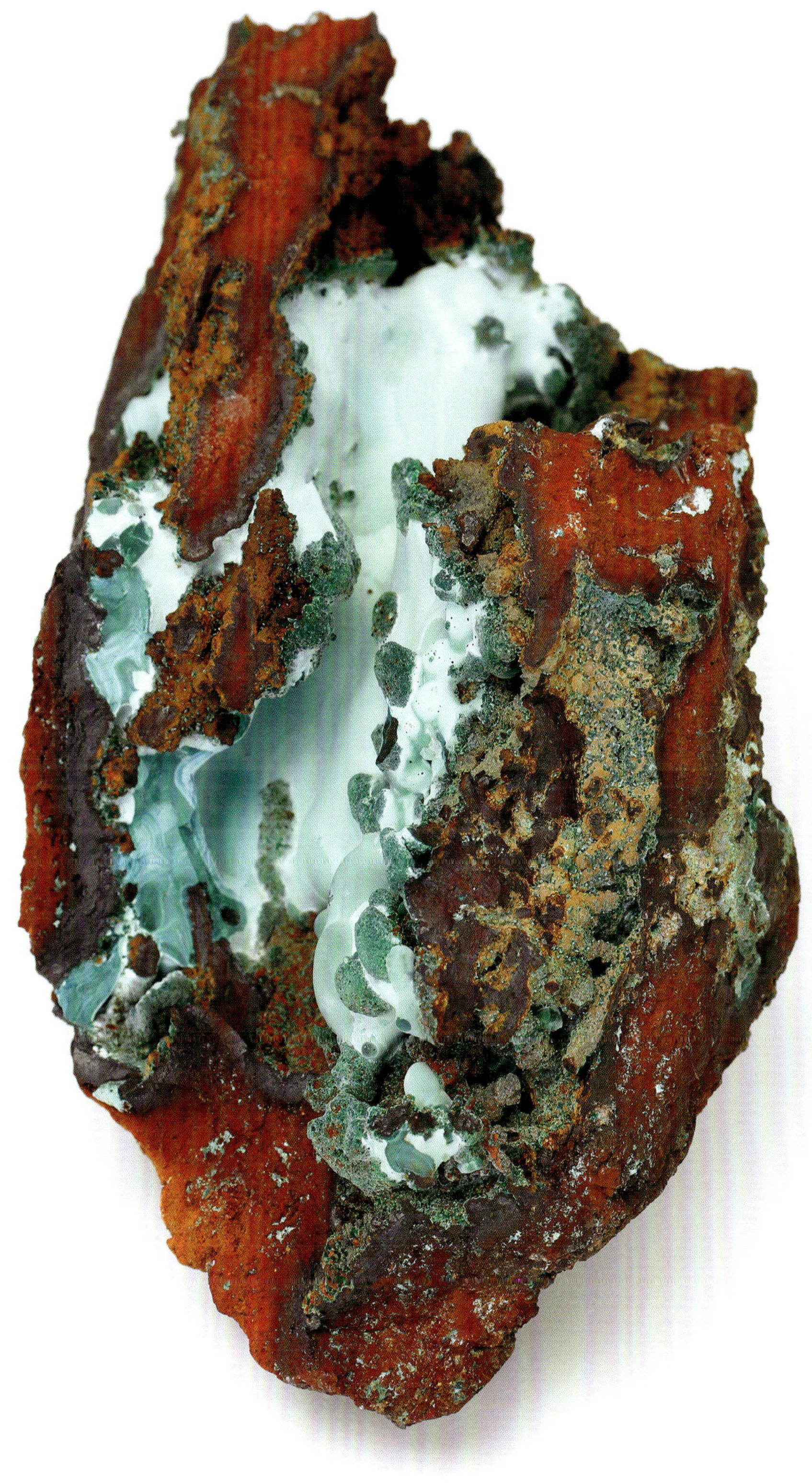

Rosasite

Mexico

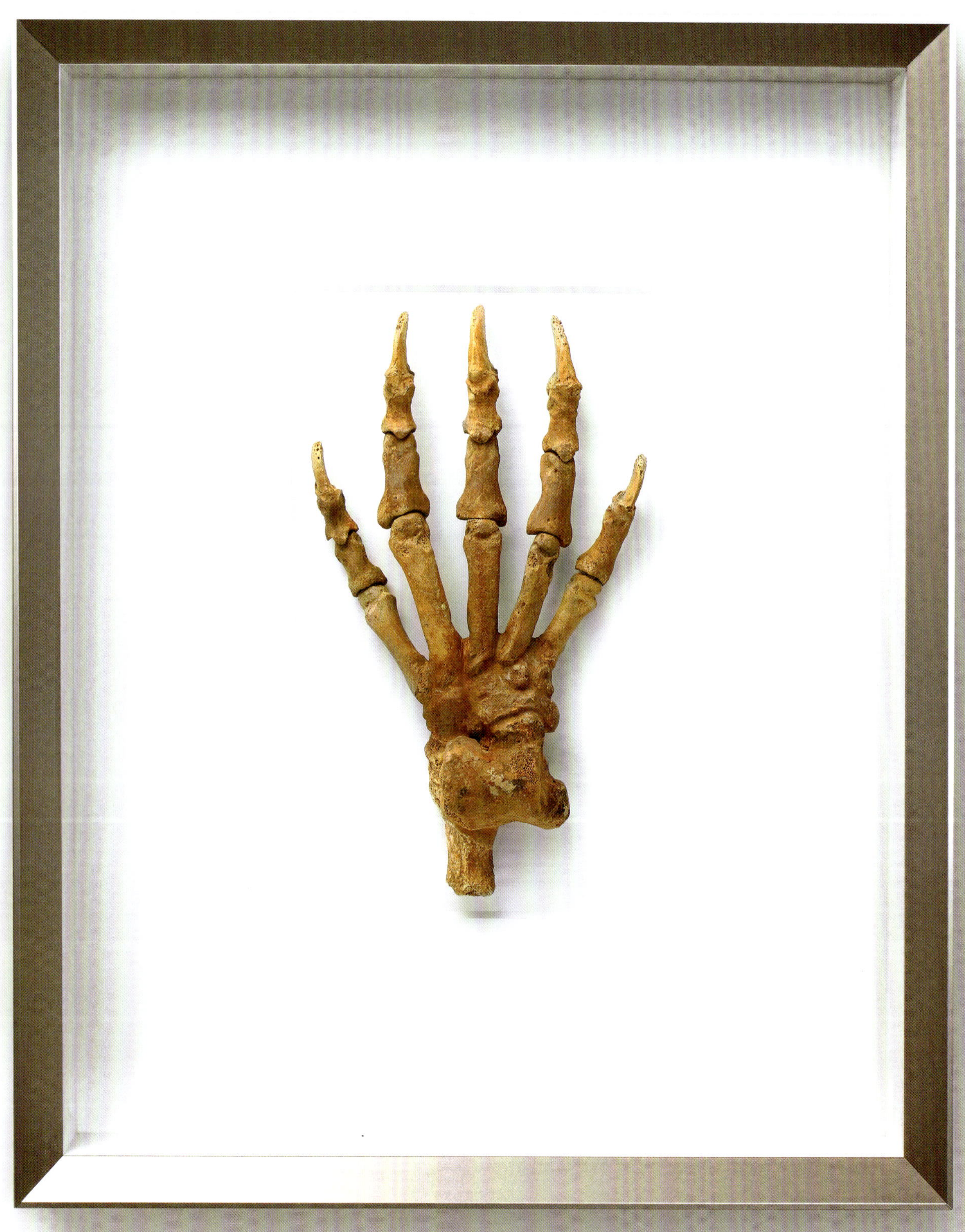

Pleistocene Cave Bear Paw

Russia

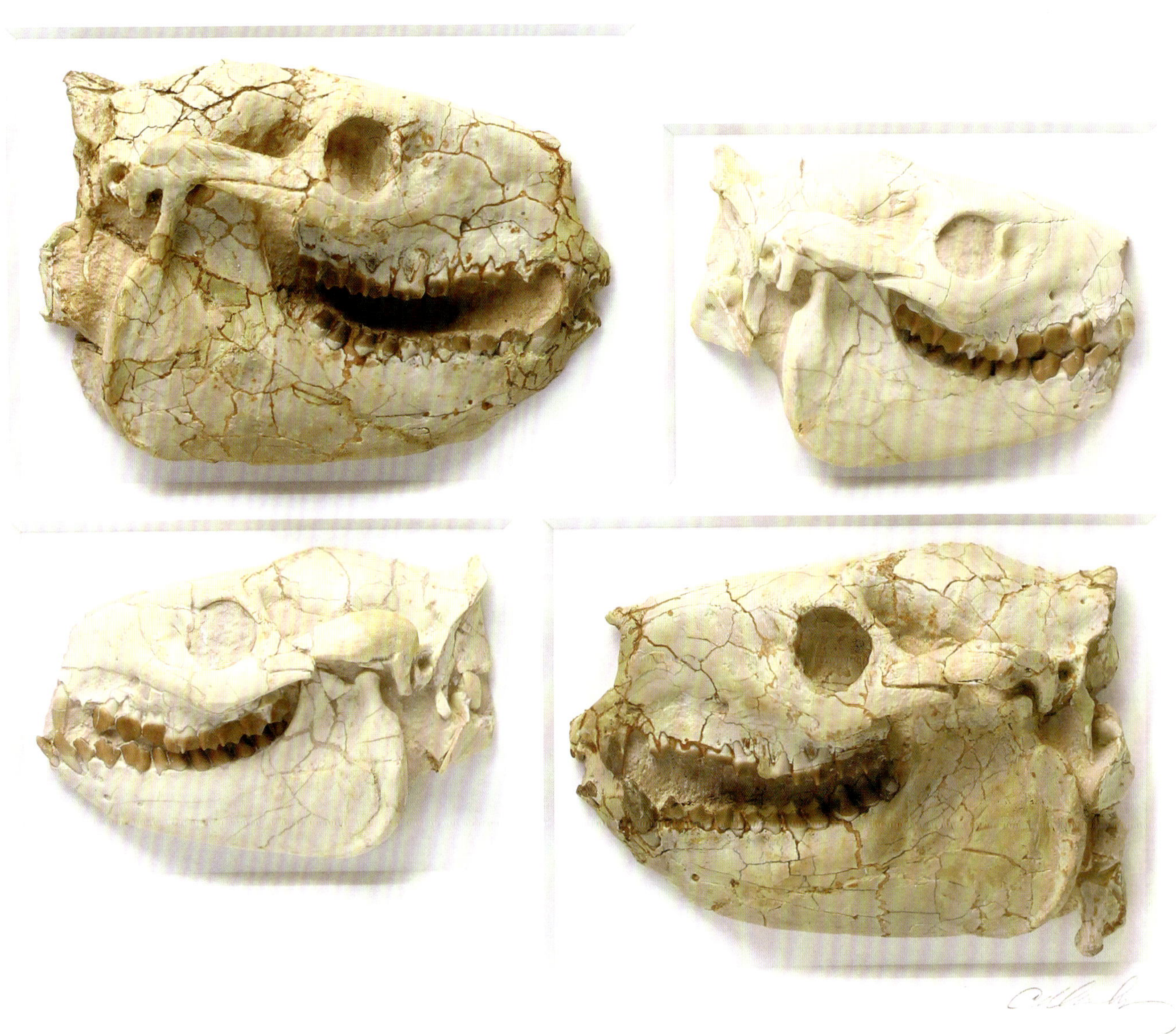

Miocene Oreodont Skulls

United States

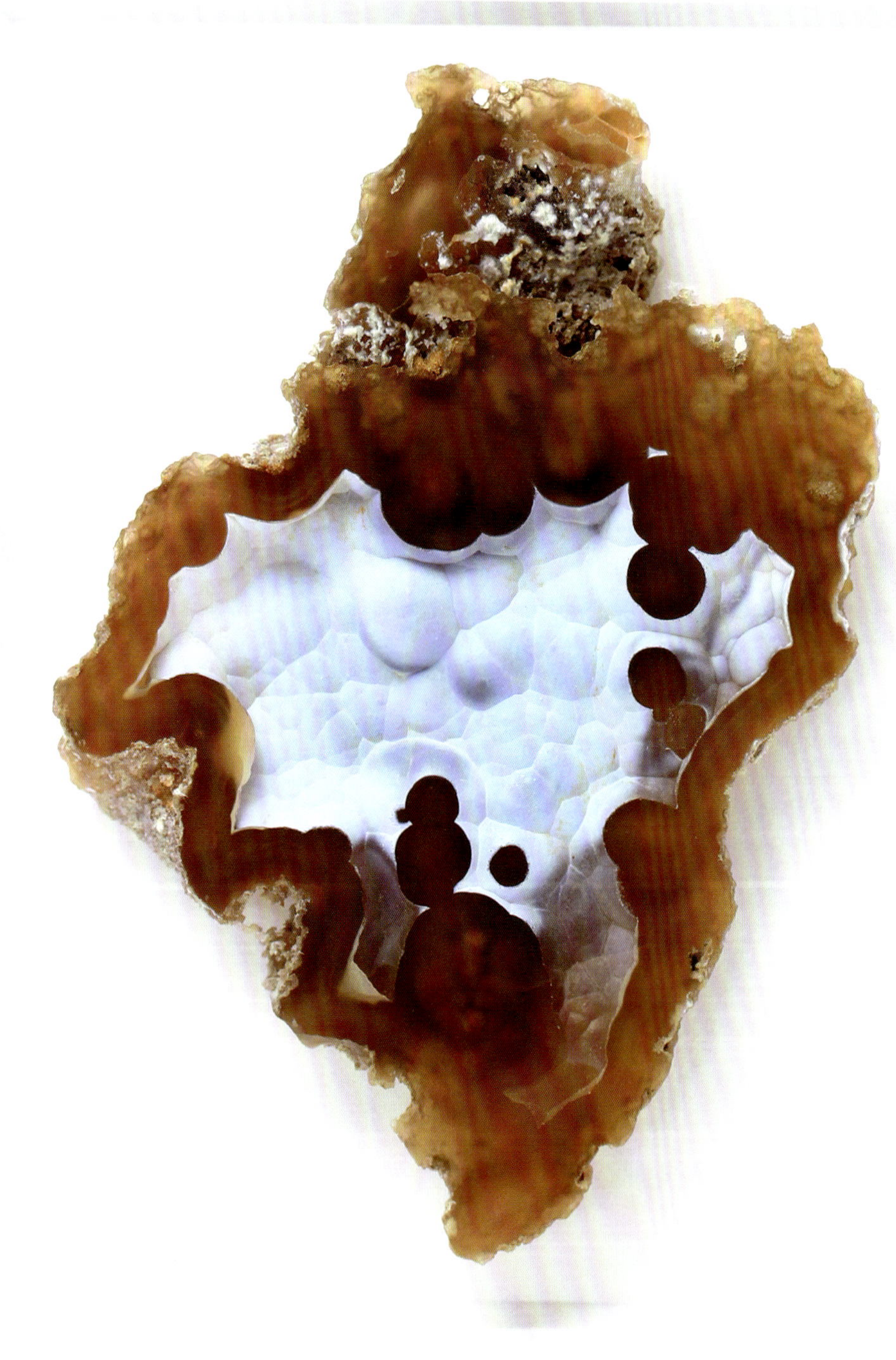

Miocene Agatized Coral

United States

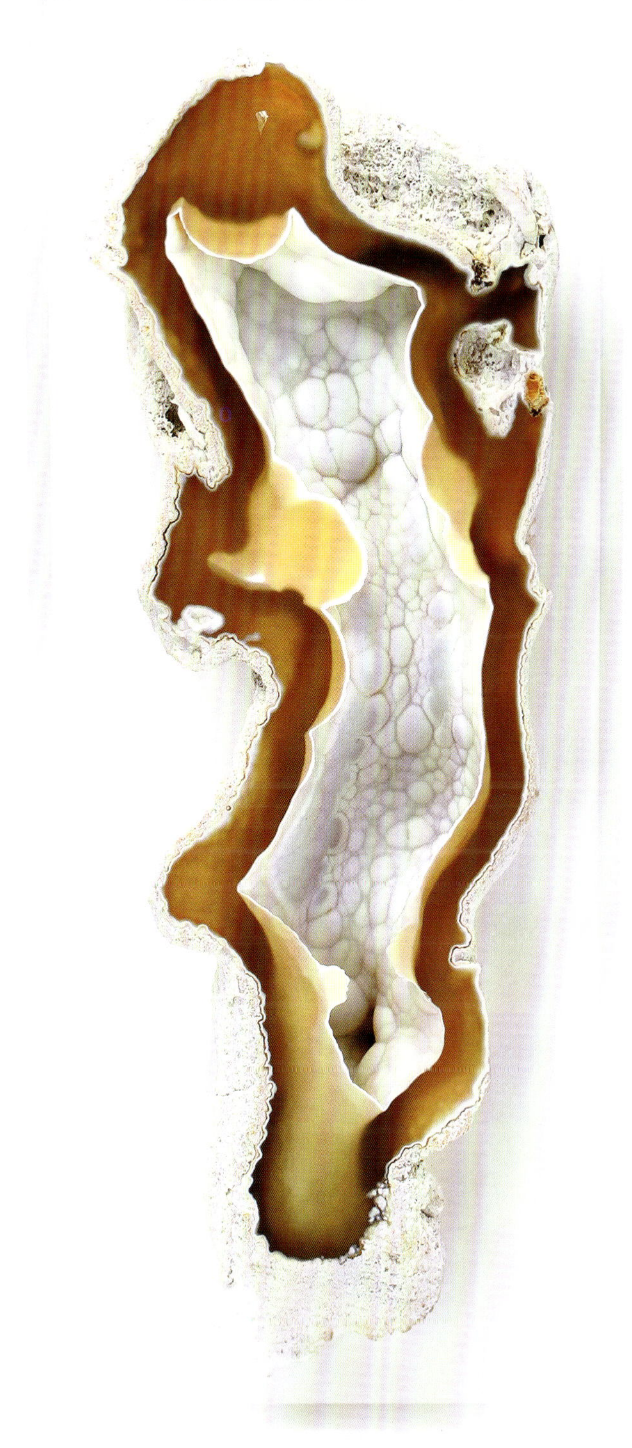

Miocene Agatized Coral

United States

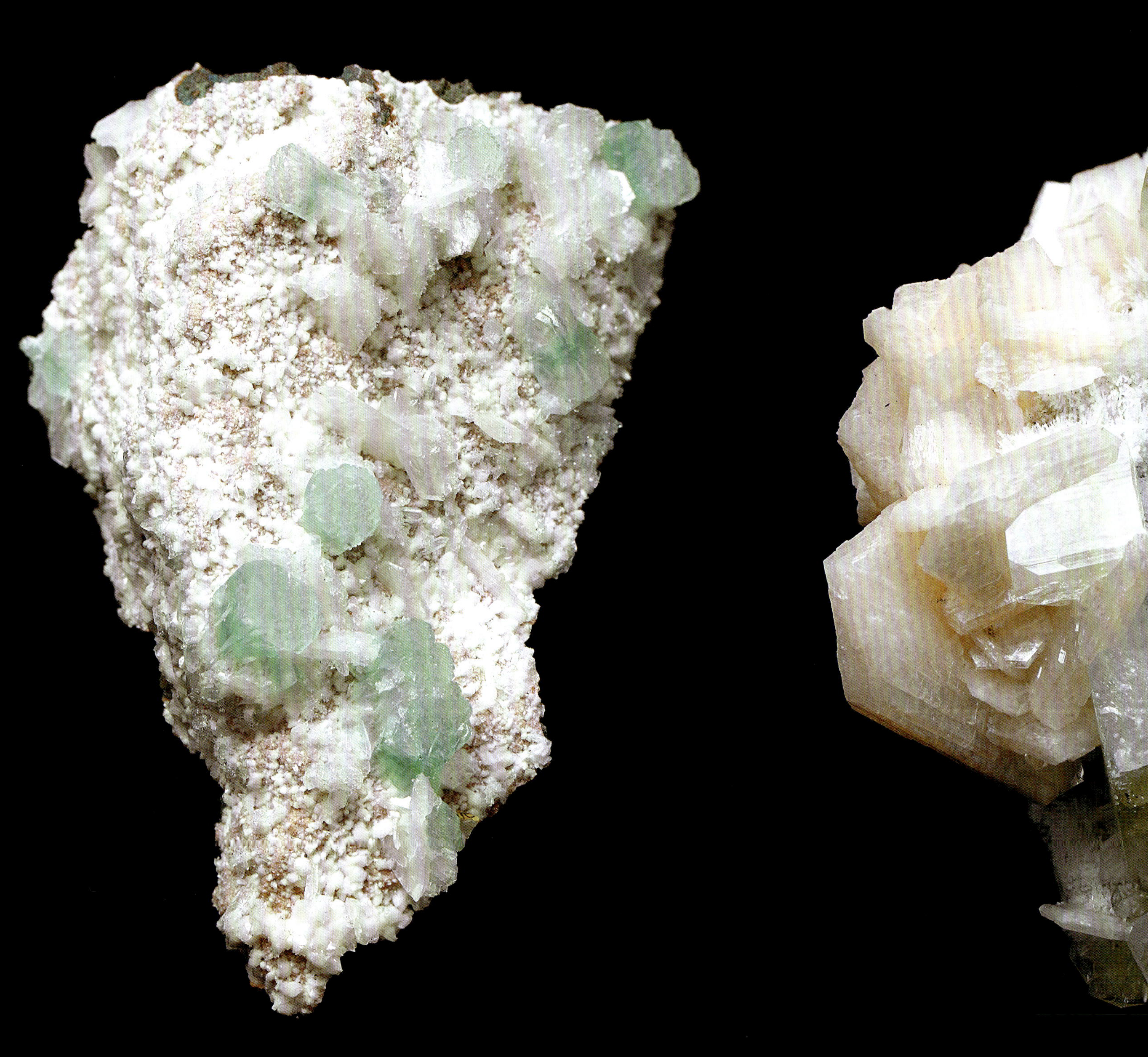

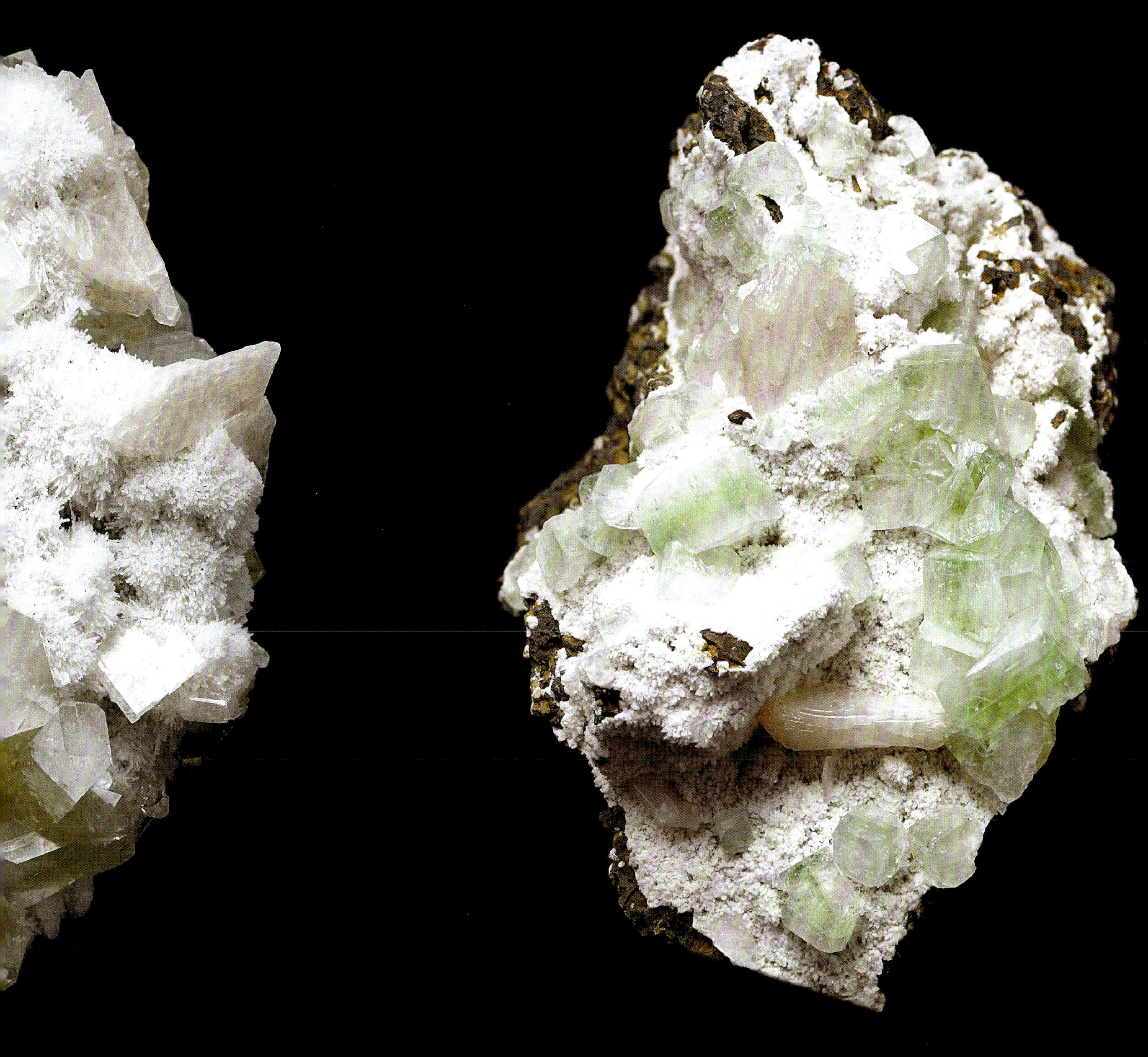

Three Indian Zeolites

India

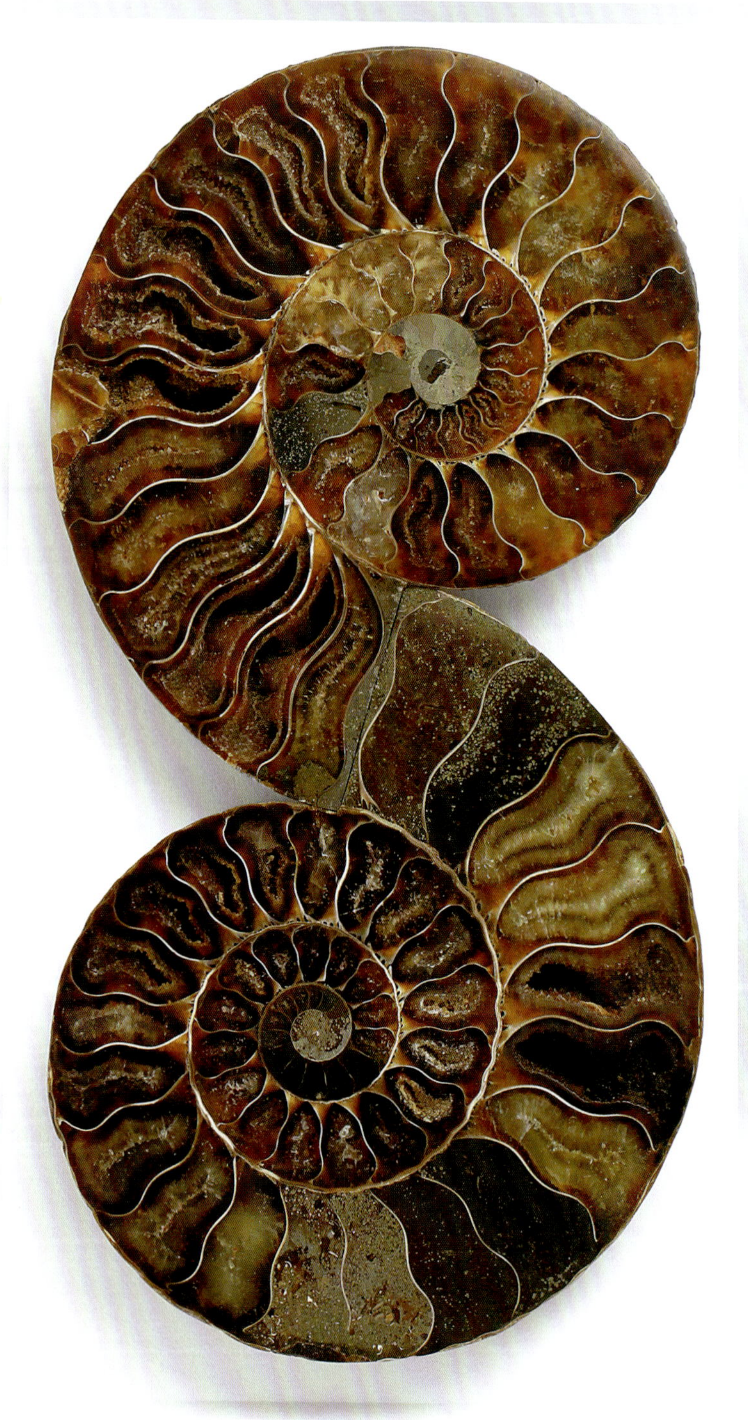

Cretaceous Ammonite Duo

Madagascar

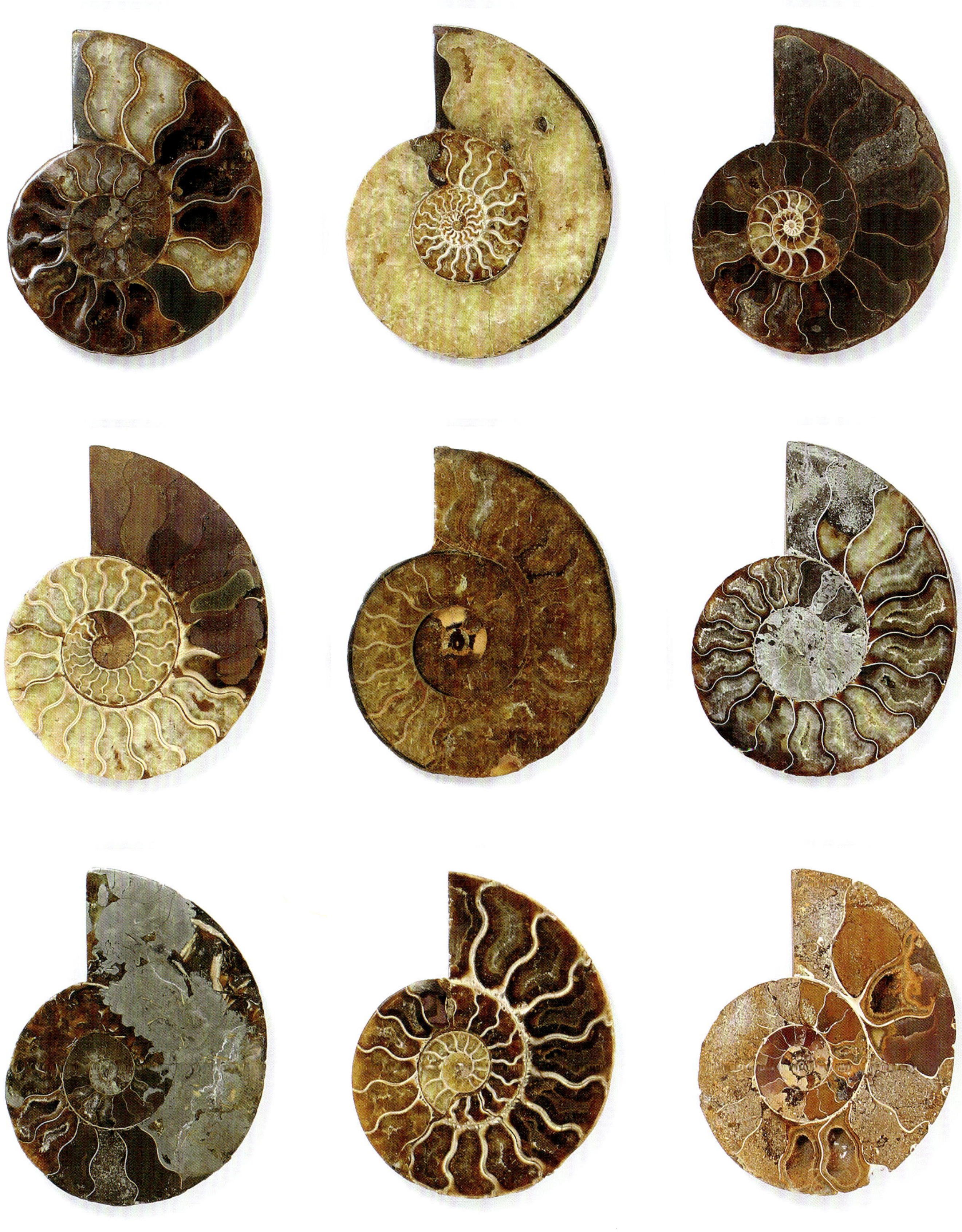

Cretaceous Ammonite Study

Madagascar

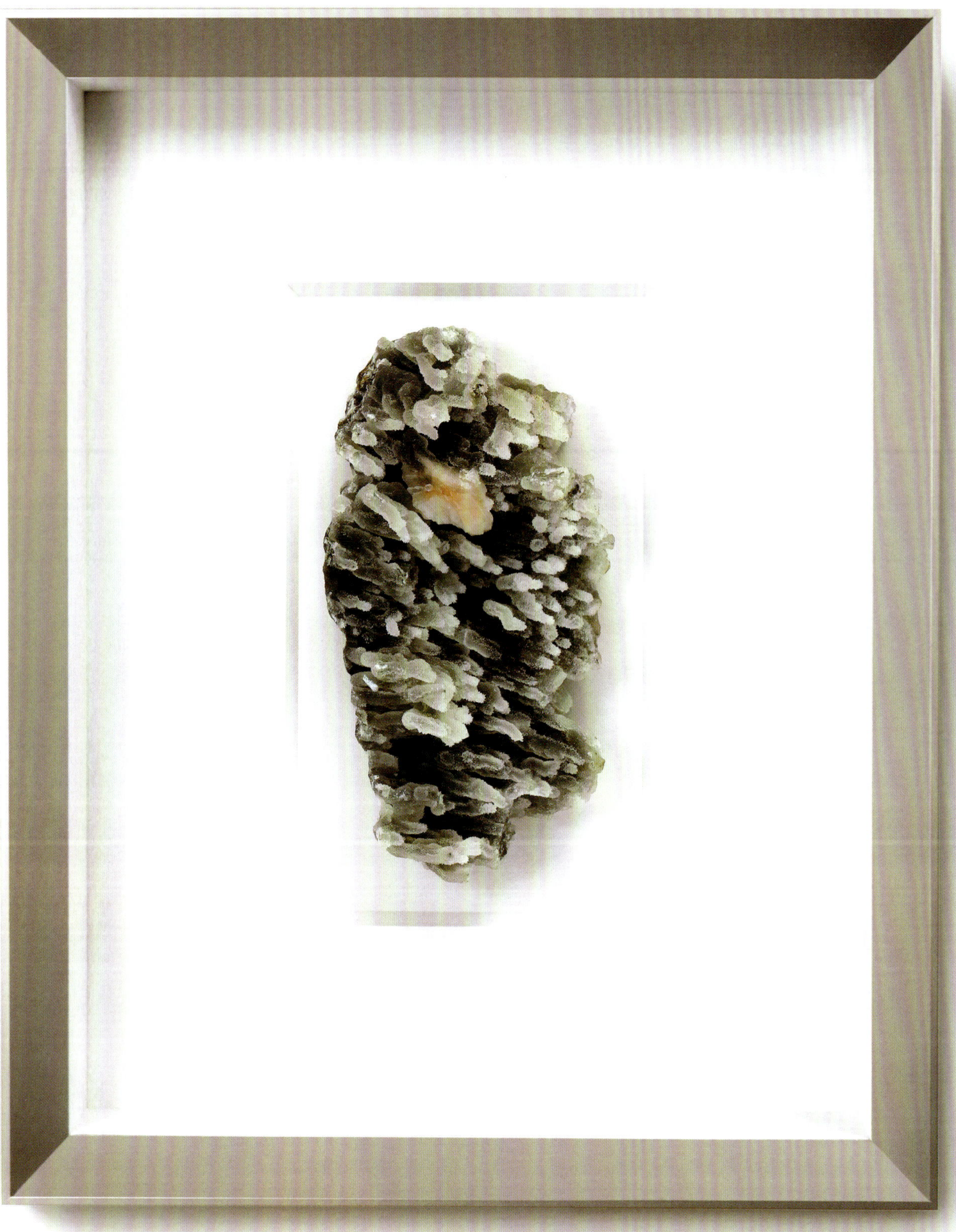

Chalcedony

India

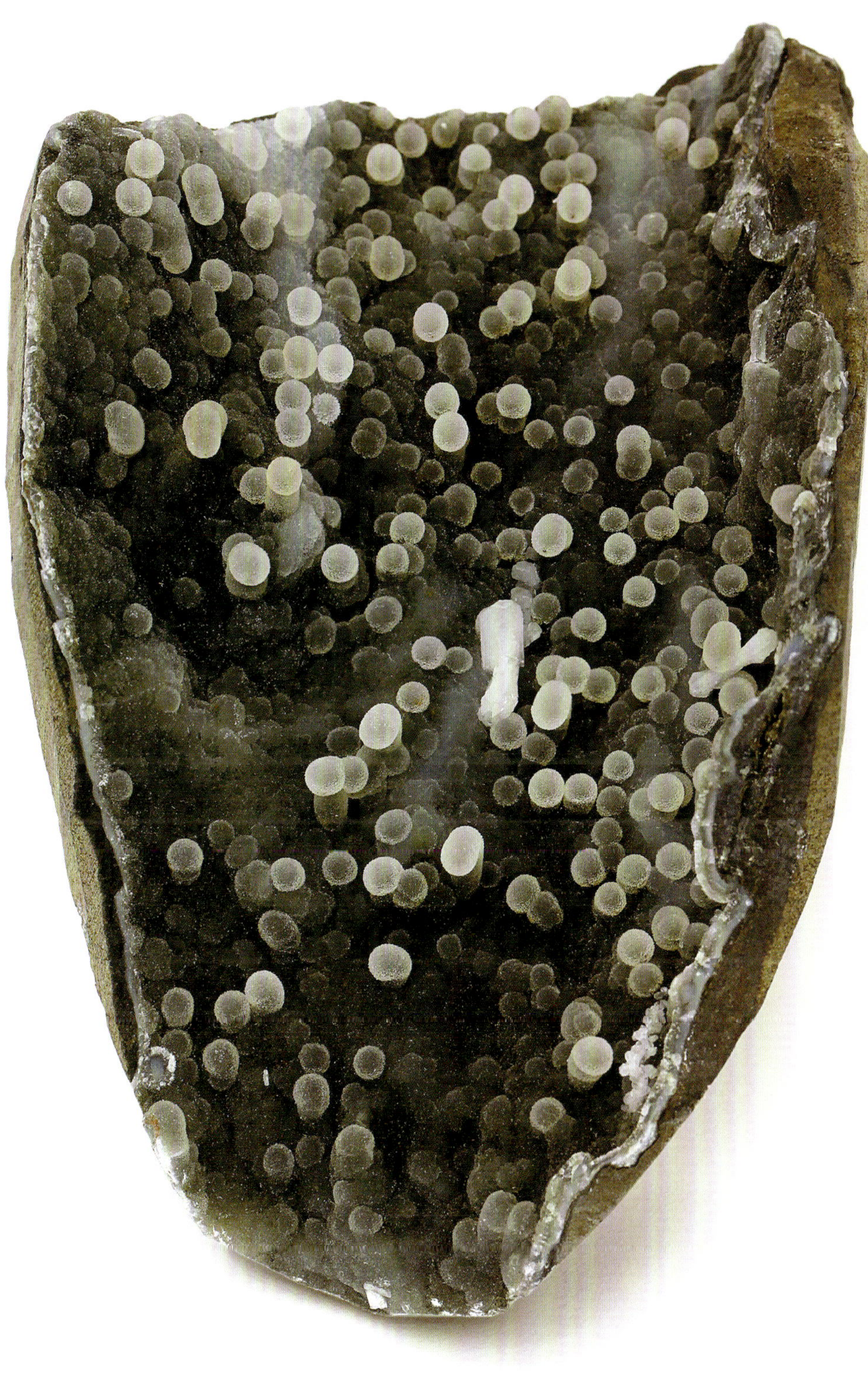

Chalcedony

India

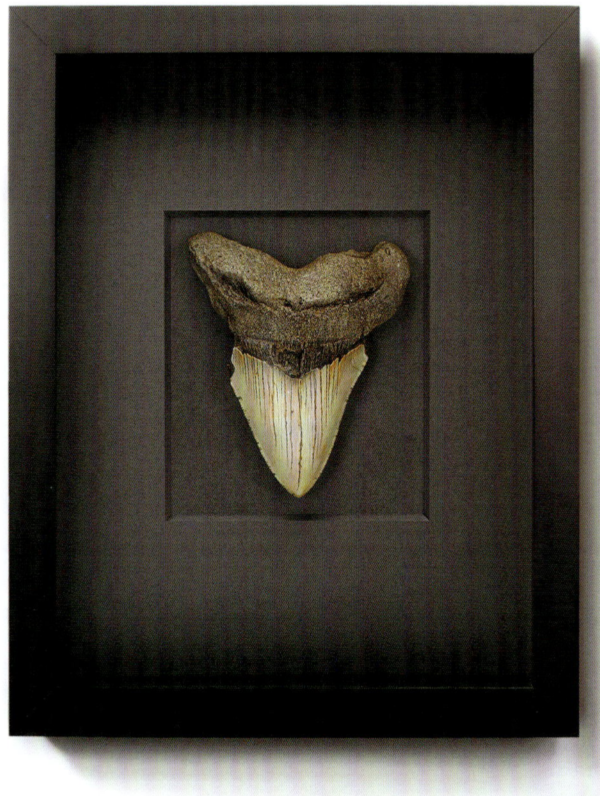

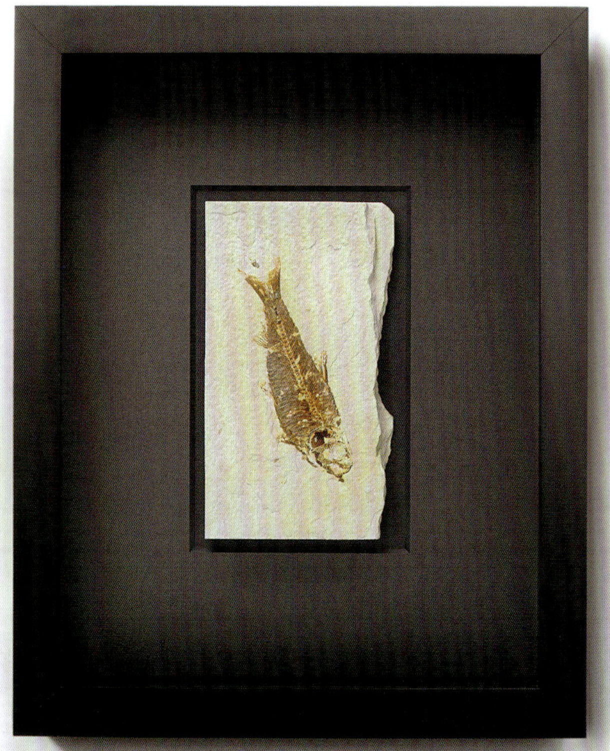

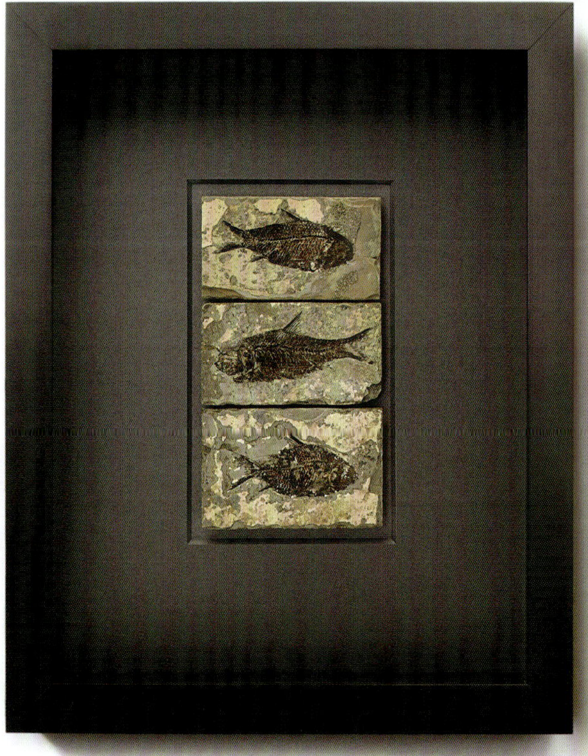

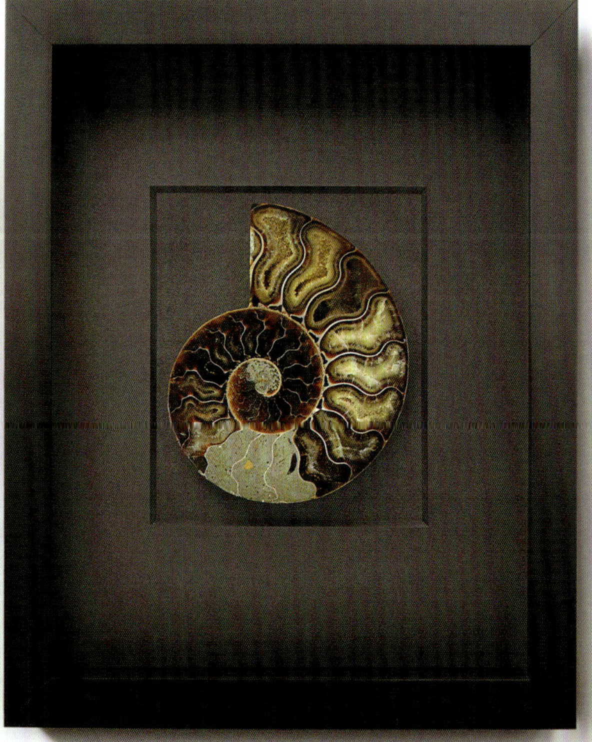

Megalodon Tooth

United States

Fossilized Knightia

United States

Jianghanichthys

China

Ammonite

Madagascar

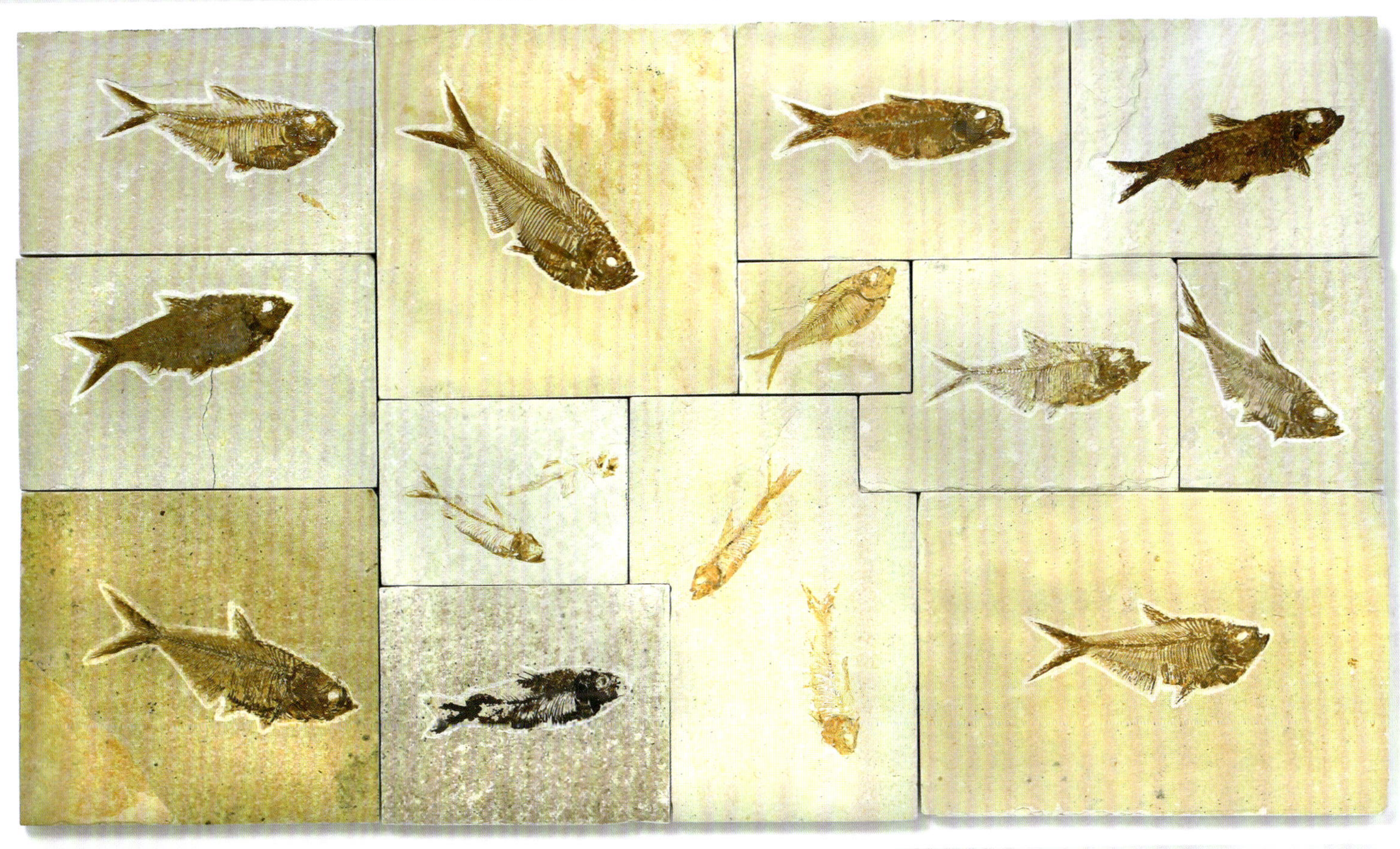

Eocene Fossil Fish Mosaic

United States

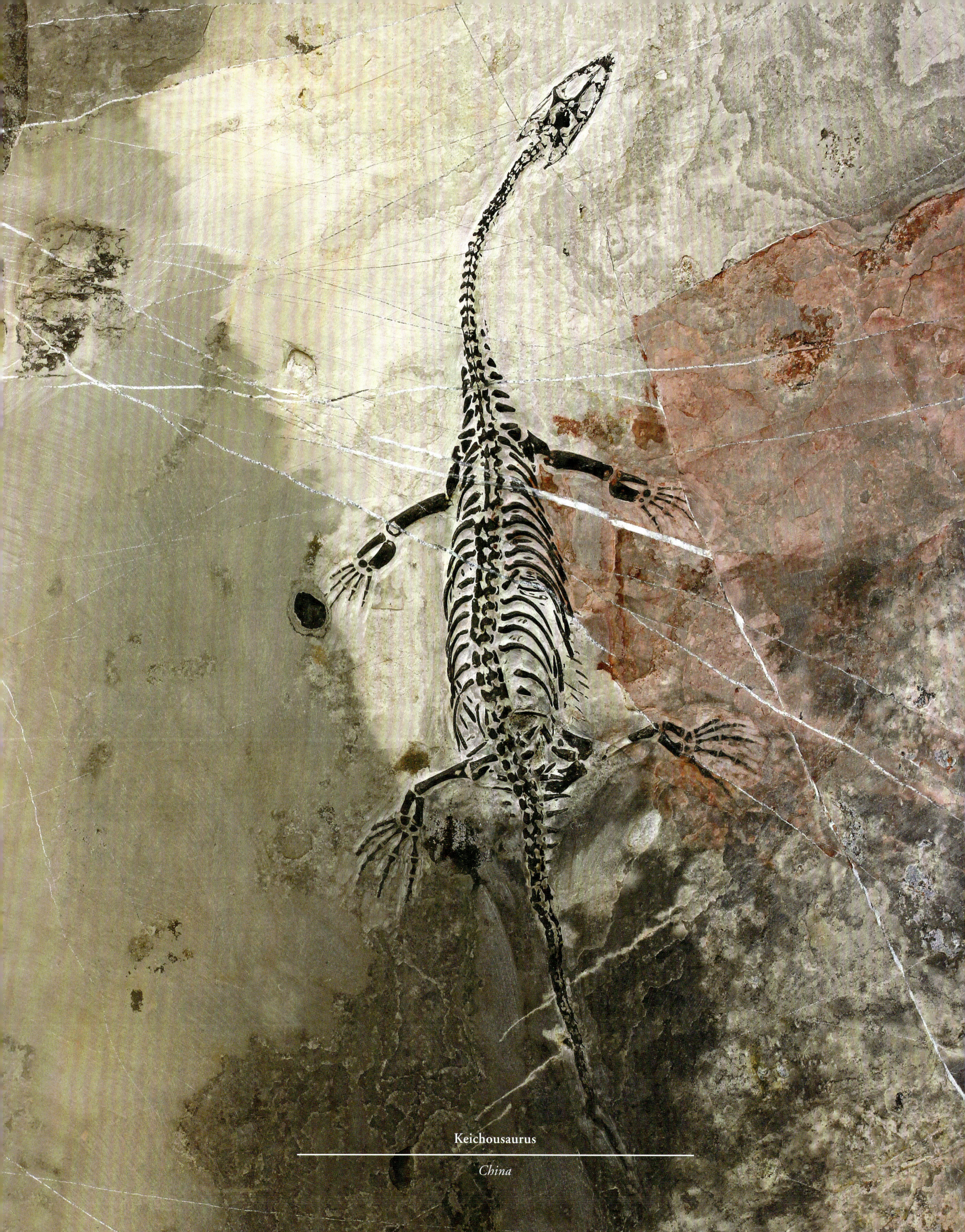

Keichousaurus

China

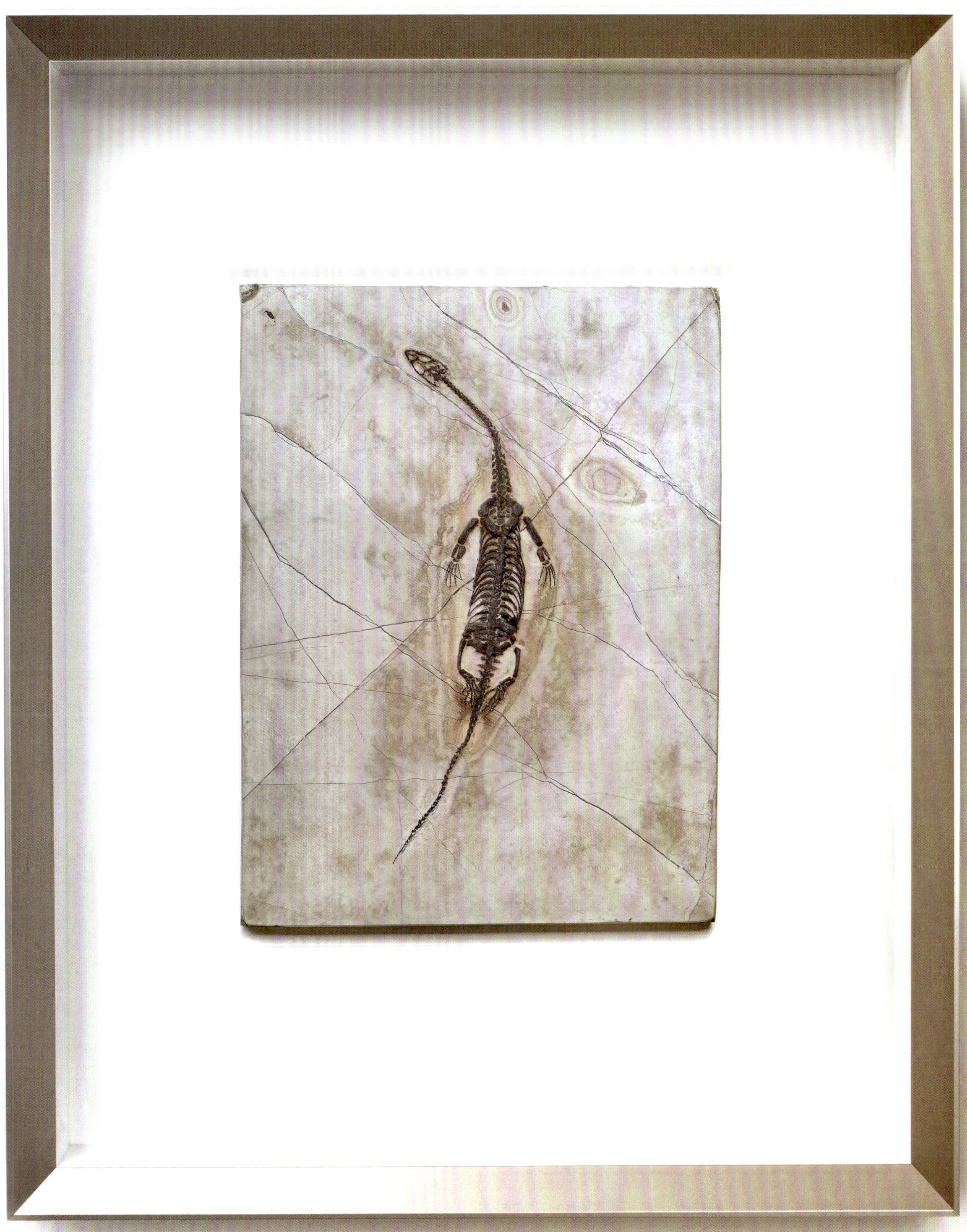

Keichousaurus

China

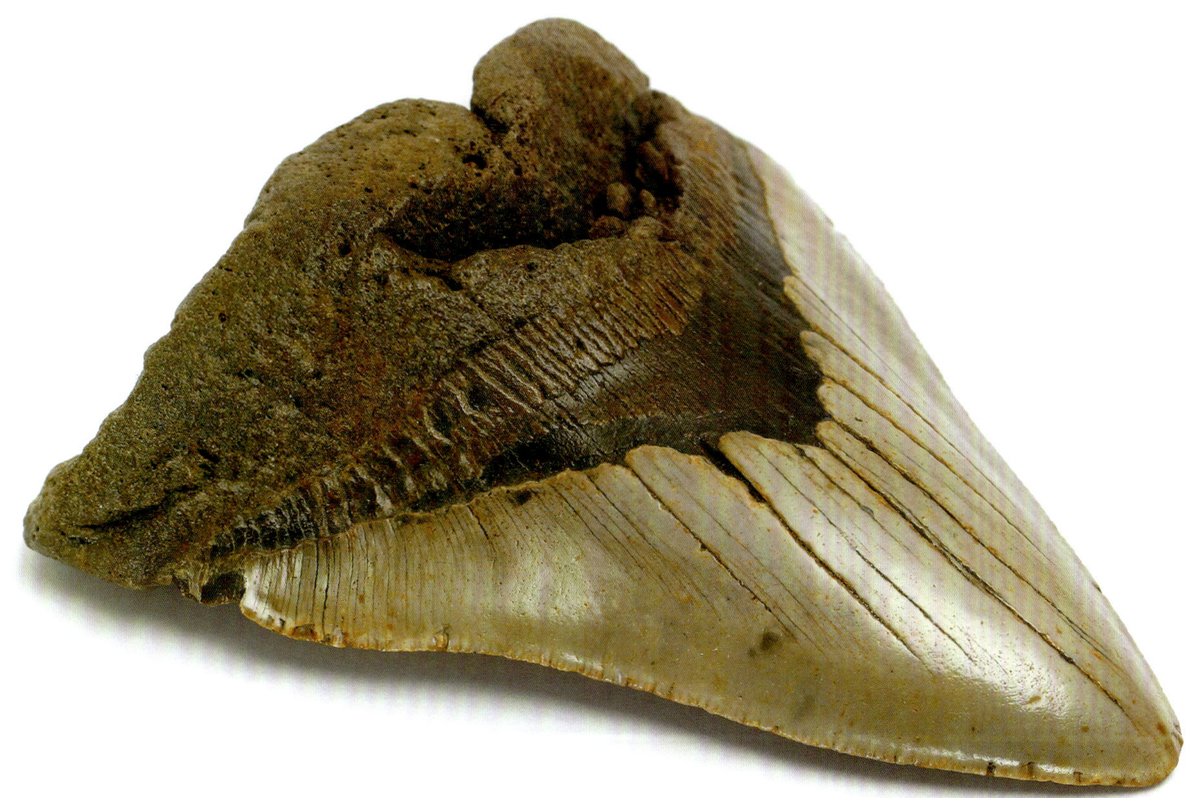

Megalodon Tooth

United States

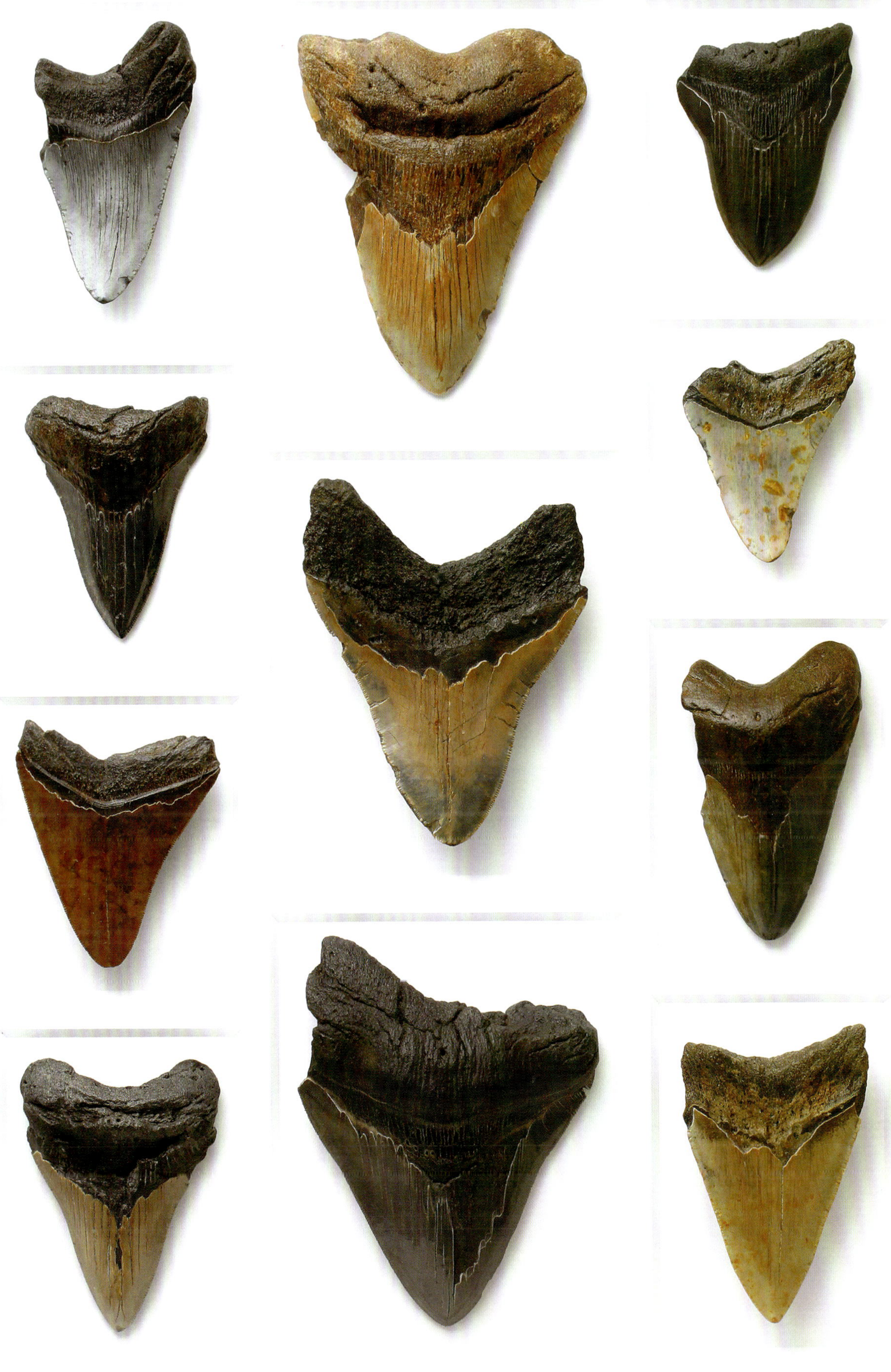

Megalodon Tooth Mosaic

United States

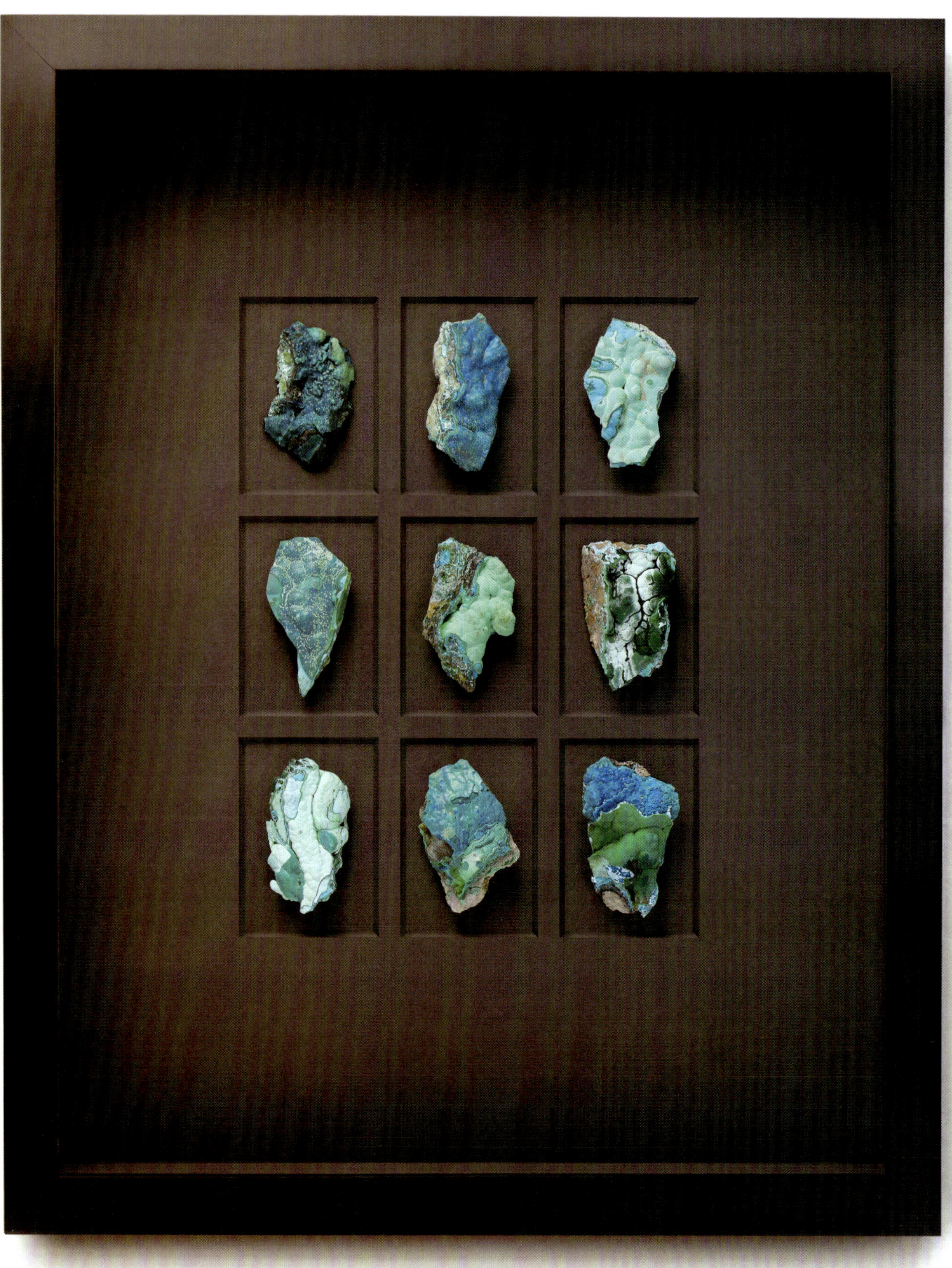

Malachite and Azurite

Democratic Republic of the Congo

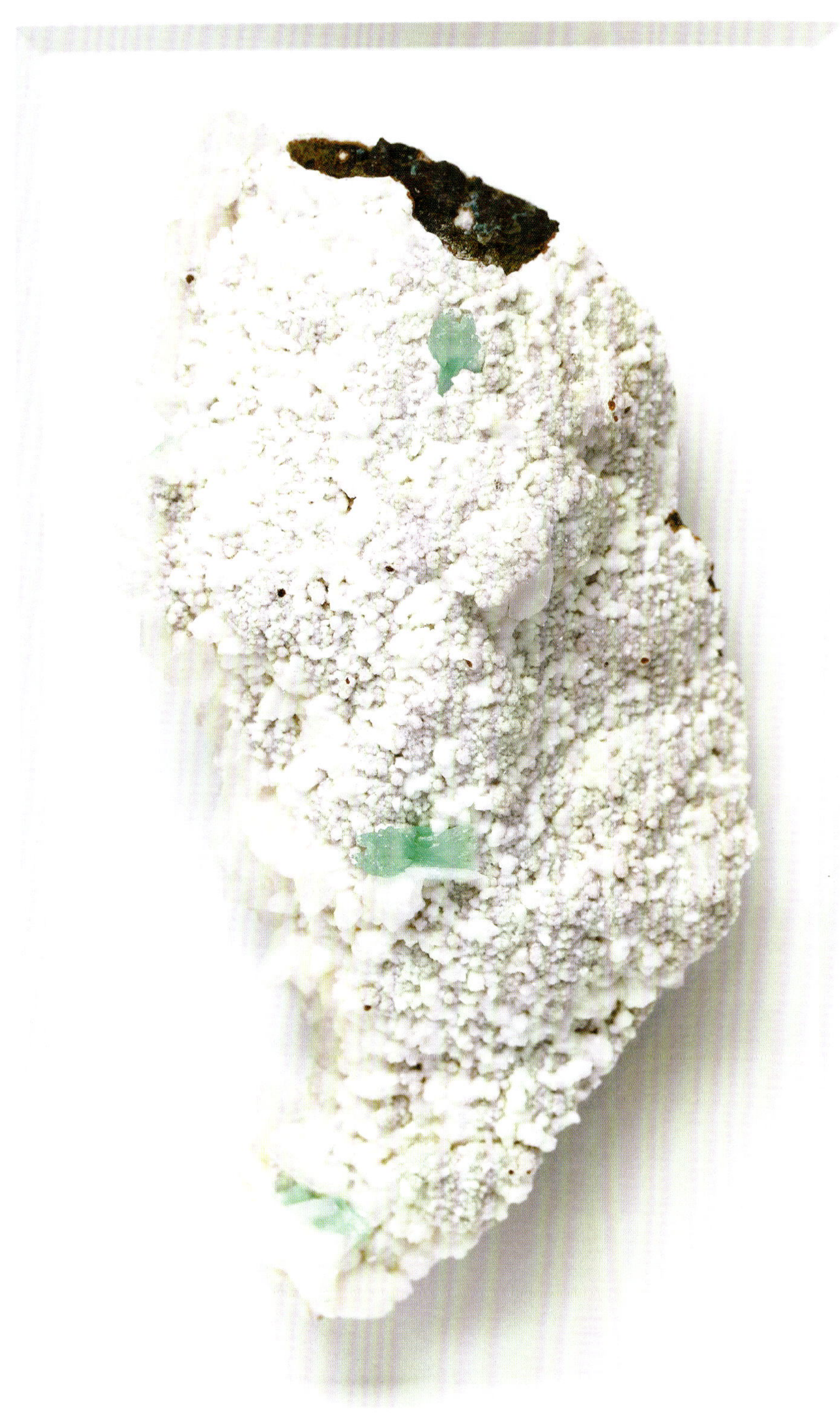

Heulandite and Apophyllite

India

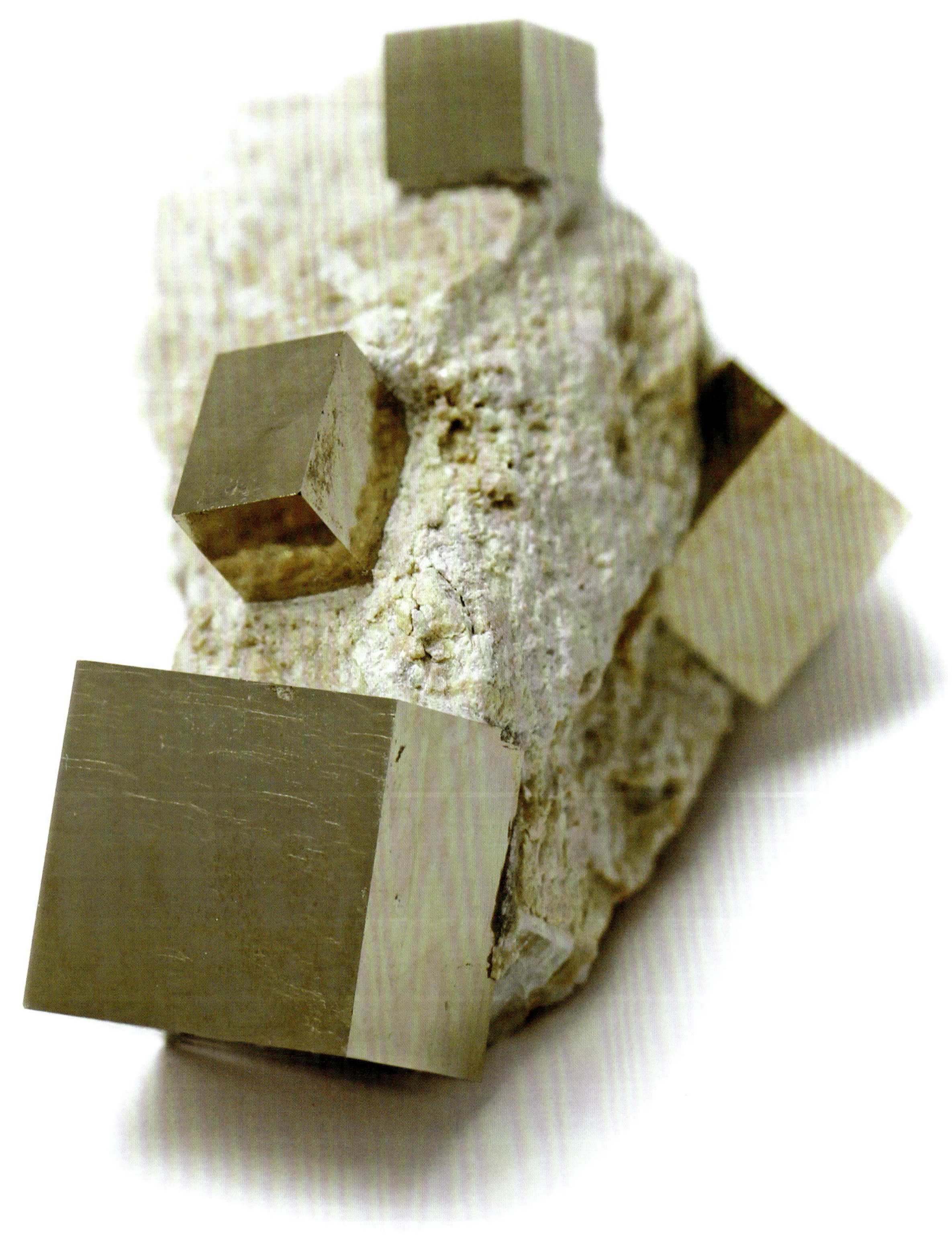

Pyrite, Cube Formation

Spain

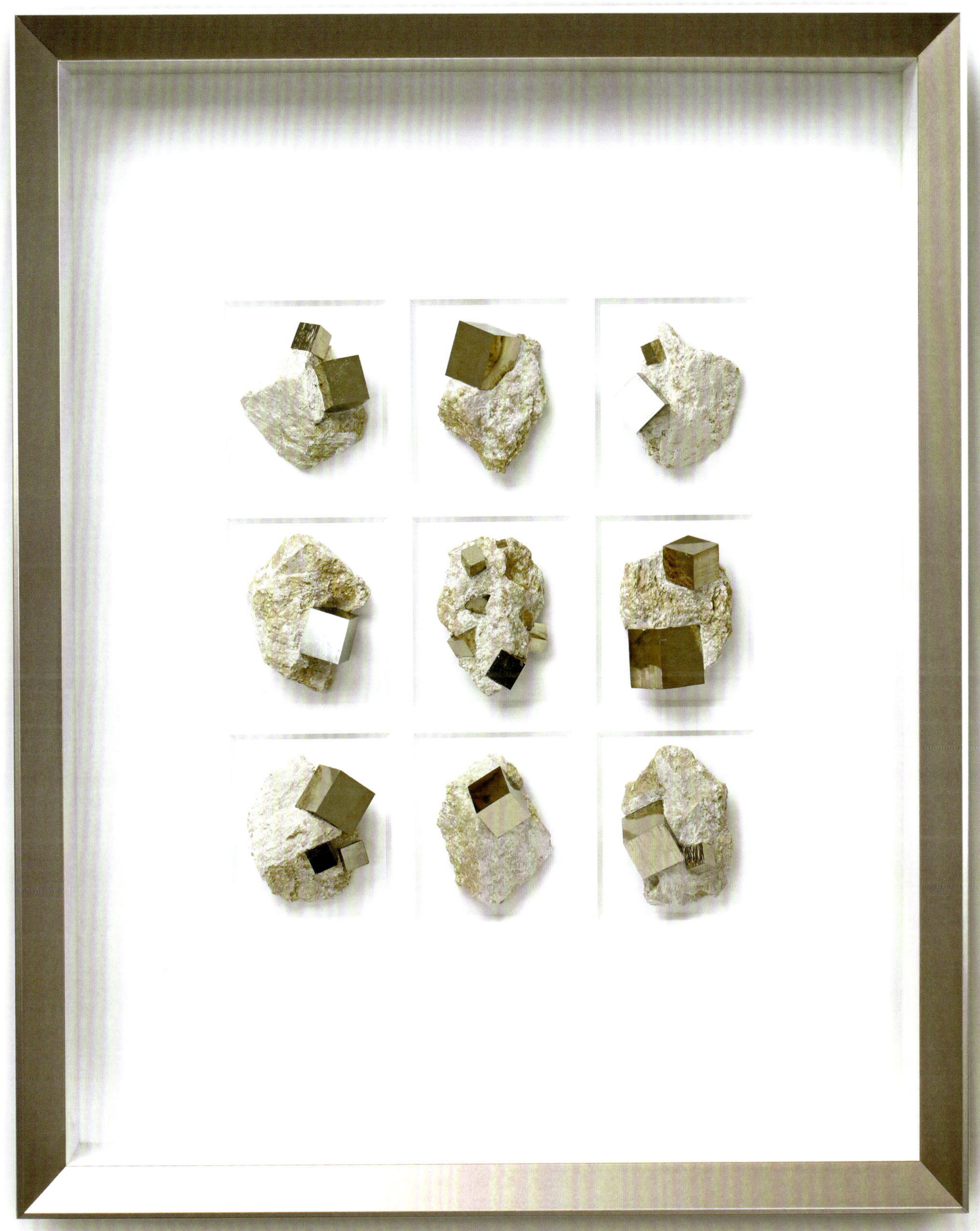

UNITY

Crystals, insects, birds. Animal, vegetable, mineral. What is the through line? What is the humming energy that permeates the entire natural world and makes each element, each organism, however divergent, however obscure, equally enthralling when viewed in the light of design? What is it that draws us to affiliate with them, to experience them, to make them a part of our consciousness?

It is Unity. Unity is the backbone of the biophilia theory. It is because we are a part of nature that we innately love it. And when we begin to see natural elements that relate to one another visually, as disparate as they may be, it is enthralling precisely because it reinforces the fact that we also belong. Our love of nature is not just a starstruck crush or a hopelessly unrequited pursuit. If minerals and insects can match, if birds and fish can go together, if fossils and serpents can form a perfect ensemble, then surely humankind belongs as well. When nature is unified, humankind cannot help but be included in the group hug.

At some point in the last half century, biophilia, or love of nature, became synonymous with the conservation of nature. And somehow, in the past few decades, that conservation has increasingly taken the form of extricating humankind from nature. Obviously, conservation is an element of biophilia that is of great importance, but it does not begin to encompass the myriad aspects of our love for the forms of life around us. Unless we can kindle an appreciation for the aesthetics of nature, there is little hope for exciting much enthusiasm for its preservation. Without meaningful interactions with nature, we begin to deteriorate emotionally and spiritually. A wholly digitized, two-dimensional, and materialist society is one that we should conscientiously fight to avoid.

I have four sons. I know firsthand the healing, invigorating effects of immersion in nature, and I know how vacuous lives can become when they are deprived of it. So lest I be mistaken for another in the cacophony of voices attesting that all aspects of nature-love only serve the greater purpose of heightening our awareness of its fragility—to justify isolating humankind from it—let me be clear. My passion and purpose in writing this book, in building my business, in preserving the elements of this earth that I find alluring, is precisely to bring happiness to my patrons and to myself. I never tire of it. That my focus on the structural and aesthetic aspects of nature's elements fosters a greater appreciation for them and thereby adds to the inspiration to protect them is, I hope, one of the positive results of my work. But if it is the only one, then I have failed indeed. For great is the value of our love of nature and its creatures and elements on its own merits. Nature feeds, liberates, inspires, and blesses us. It has blessed and enriched my life more than I can calculate.

Truly, what is needed in humanity's relationship with nature is not extrication or isolation or separation. It is Unity.

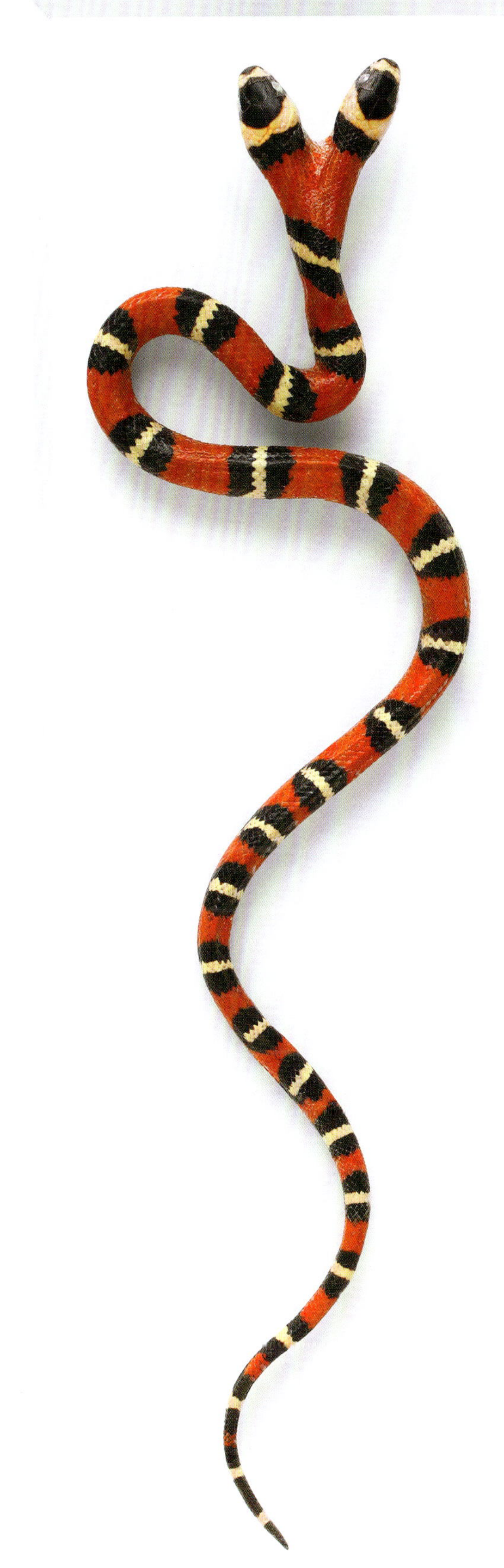

Two-Headed Scarlet King Snake

United States

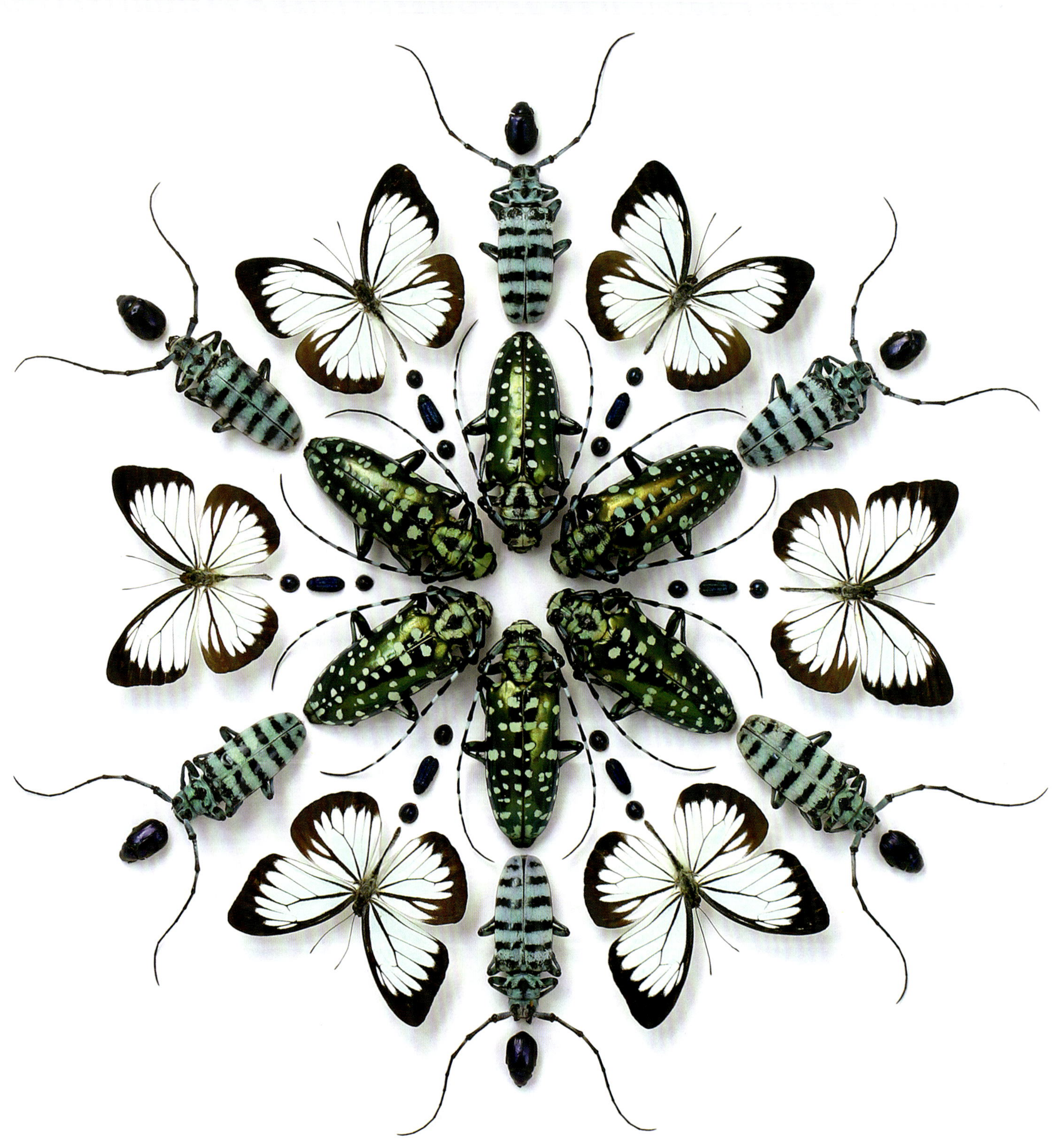

Elegans Prism

Thailand, Indonesia, Cameroon, Malaysia

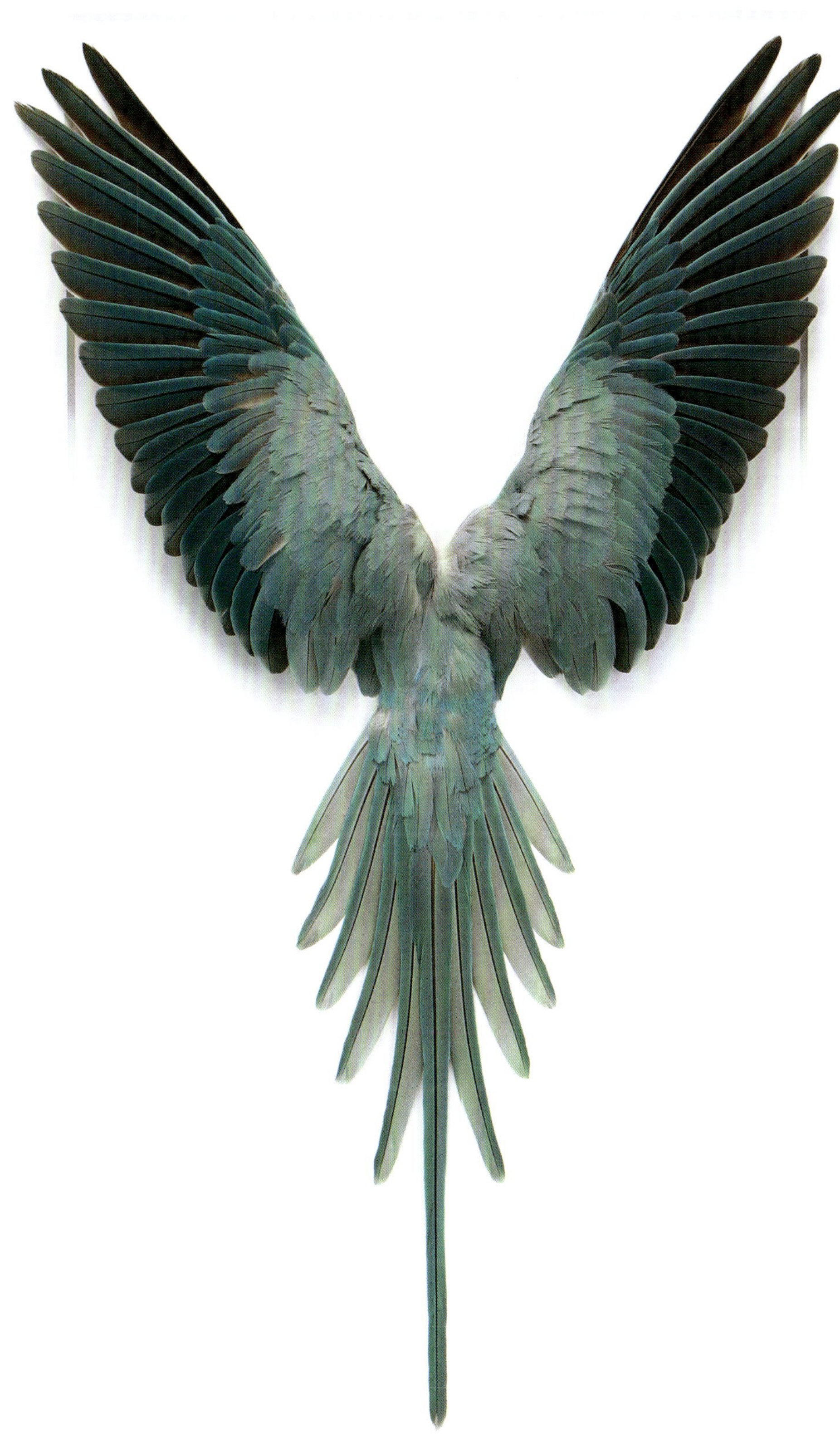

Indian Ring-Necked Parrot, Blue Form

Myanmar

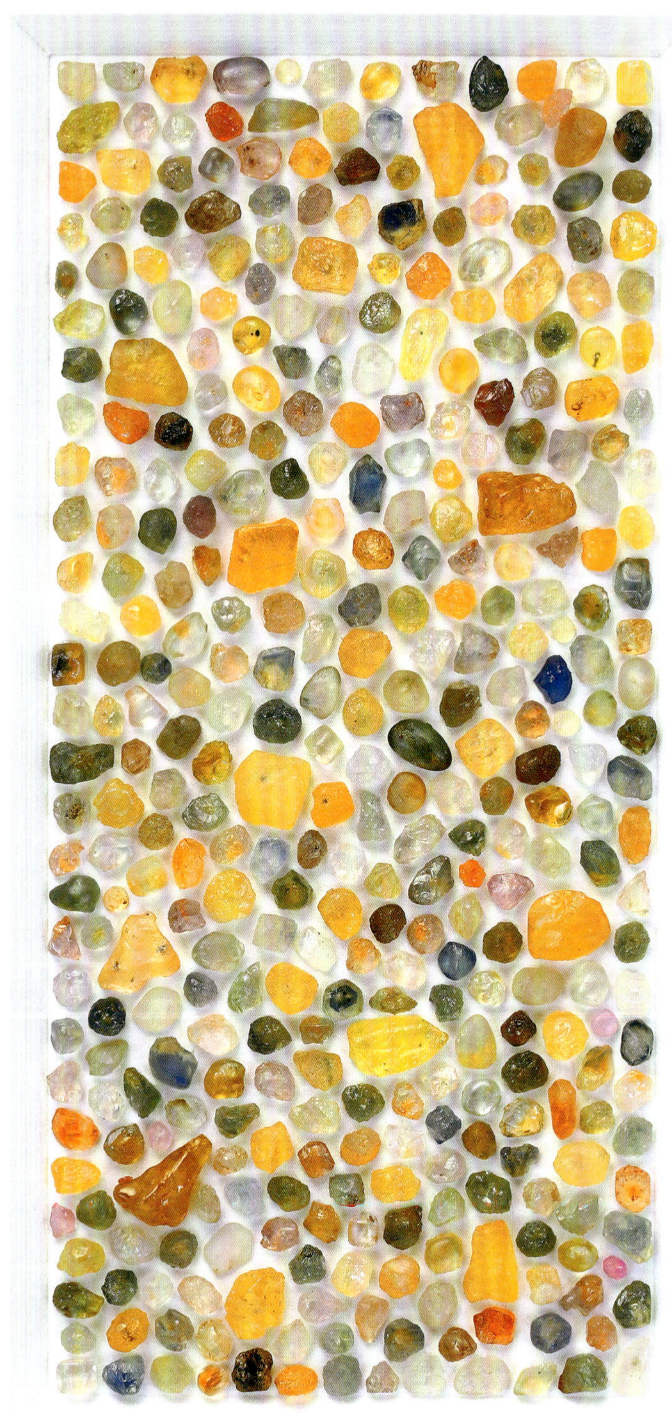

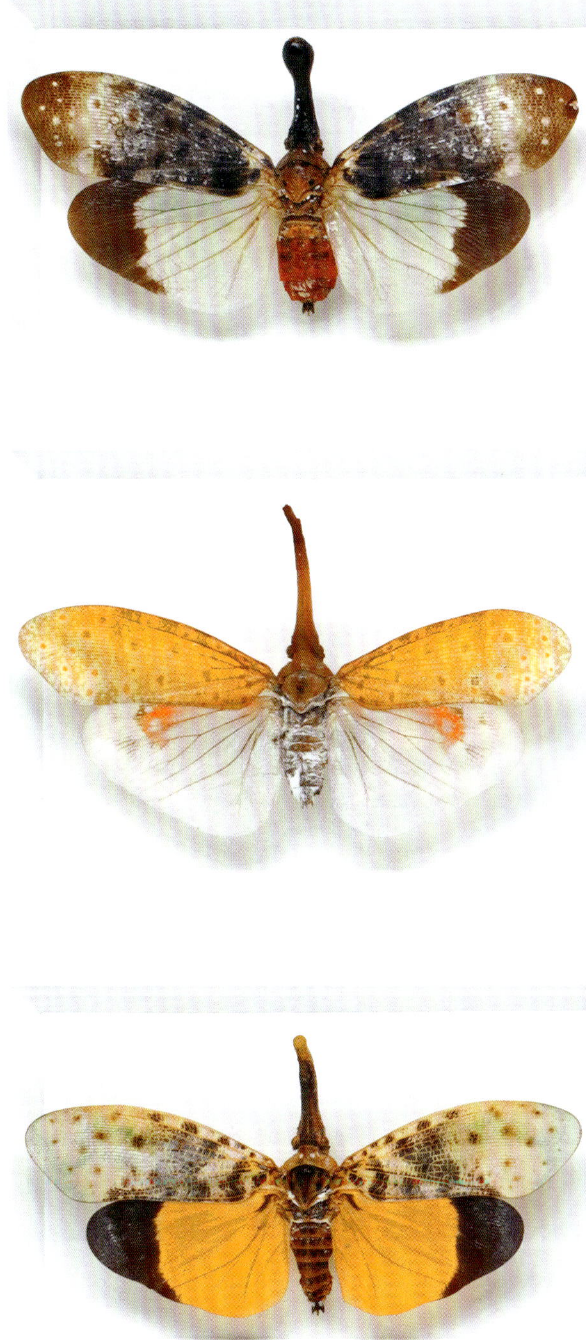

Rough Sapphires

Madagascar

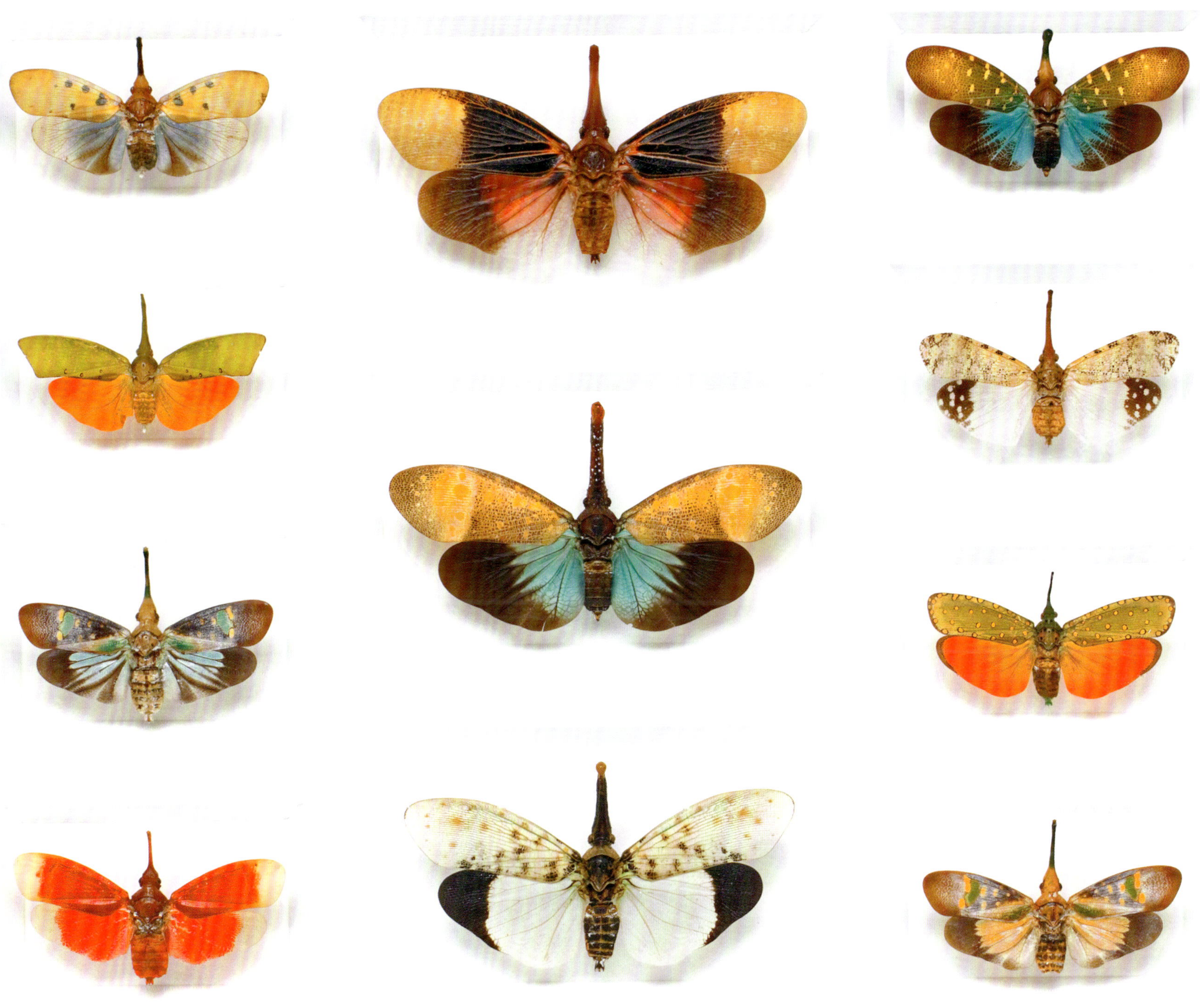

Lantern Fly Mosaic

Thailand, Indonesia, Malaysia, Peru

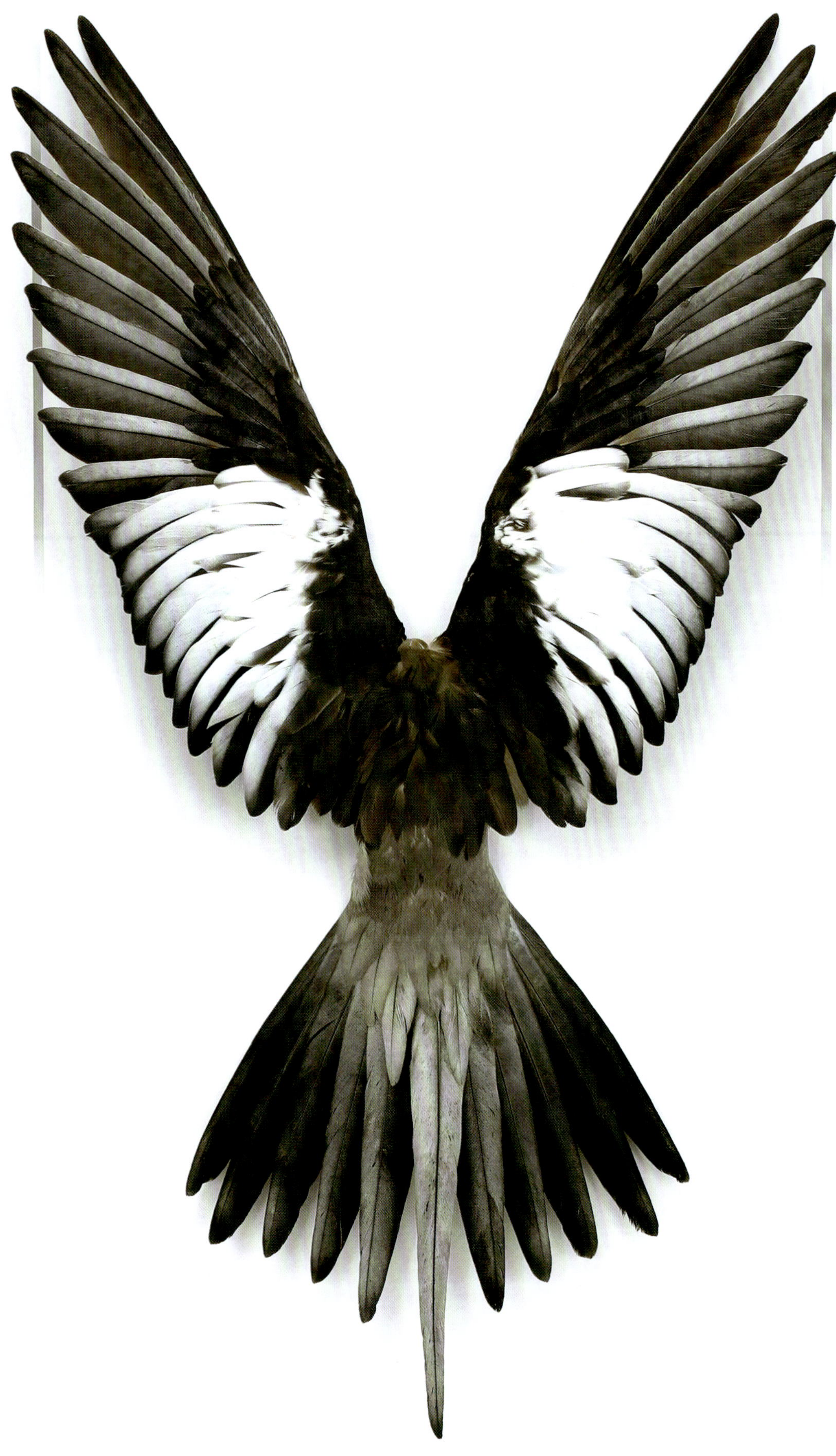

Black Quarrion

Australia

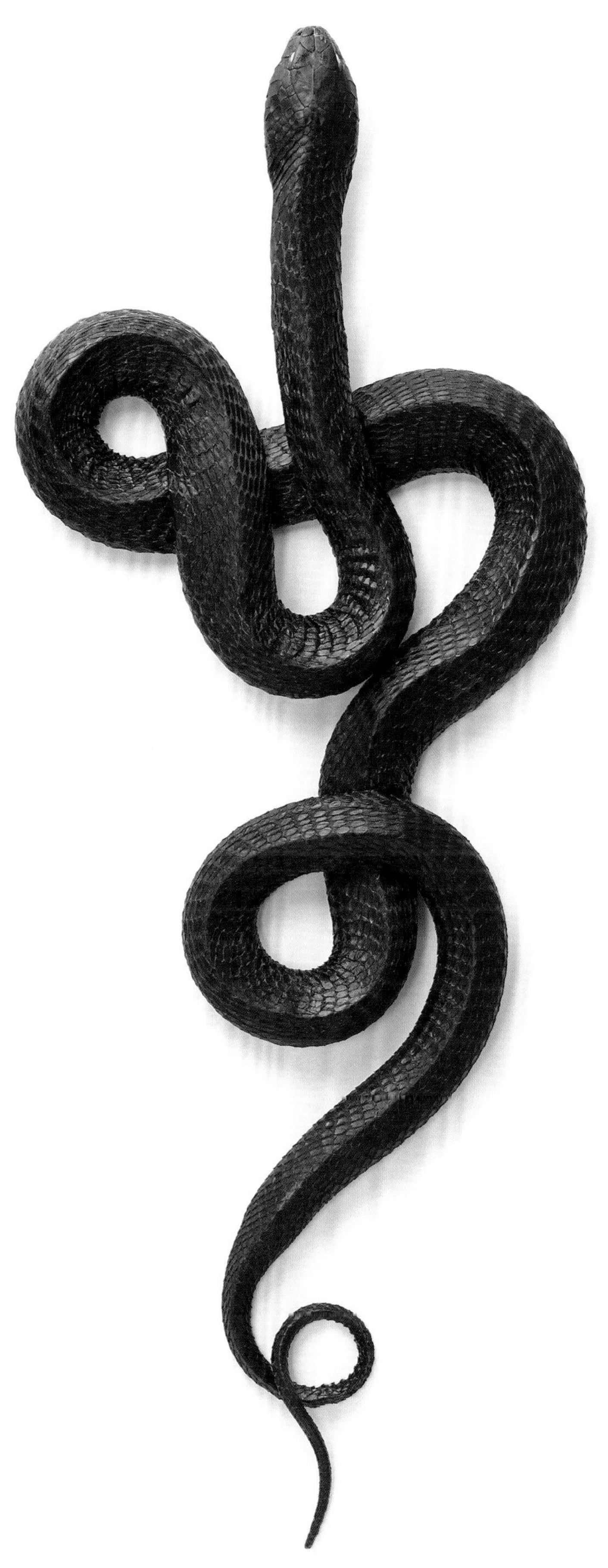

Black Cobra

Pakistan

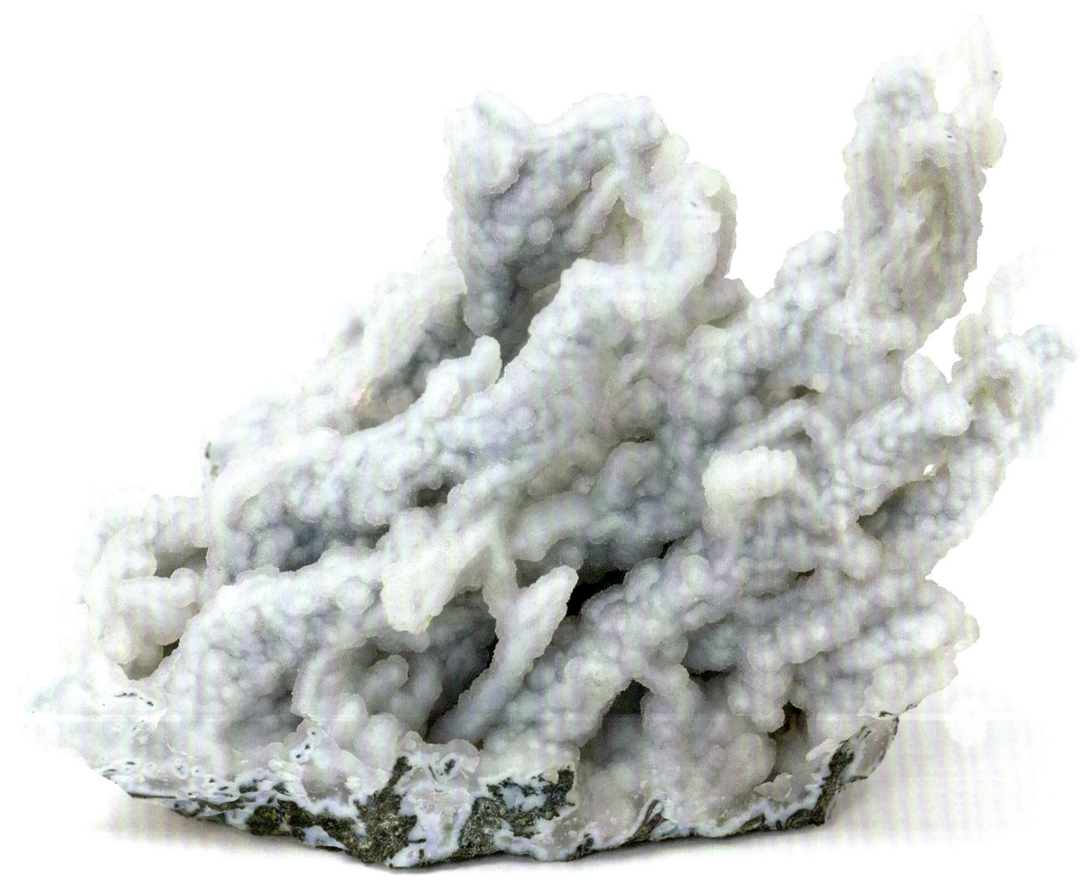

Blue Chalcedony

India

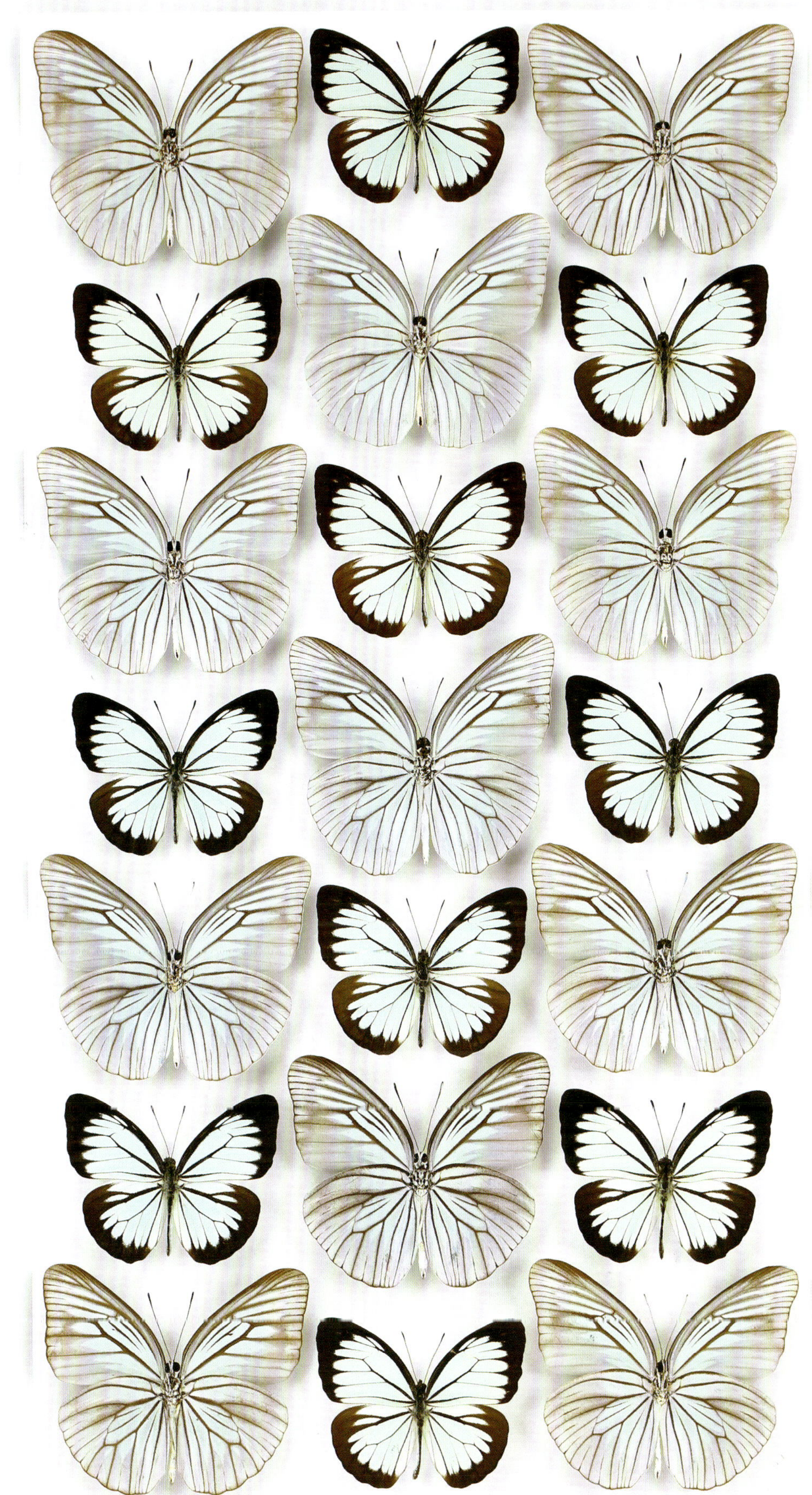

Silver Celestina

Malaysia, Indonesia

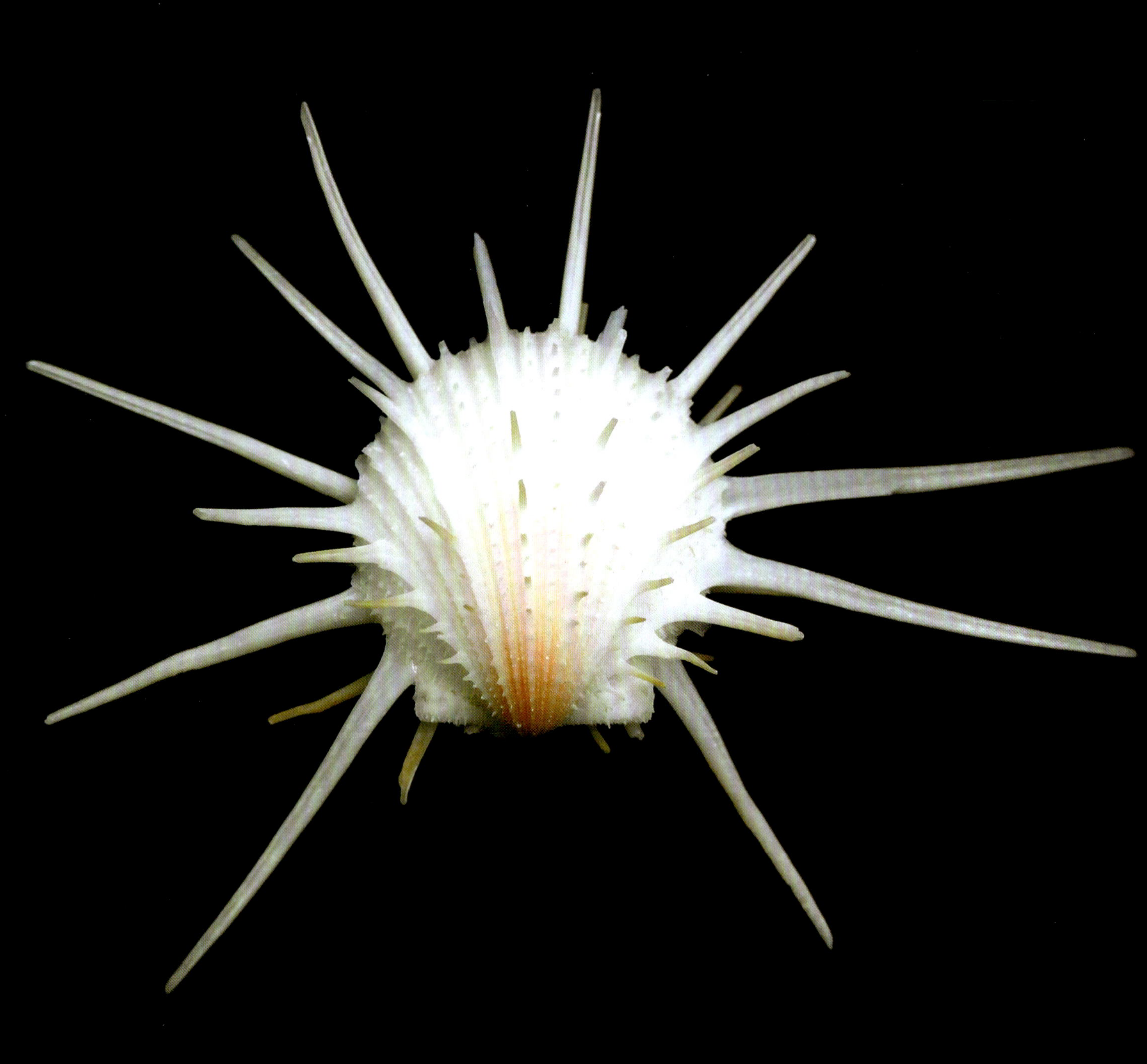

Imperial Spiny Oyster

Philippines

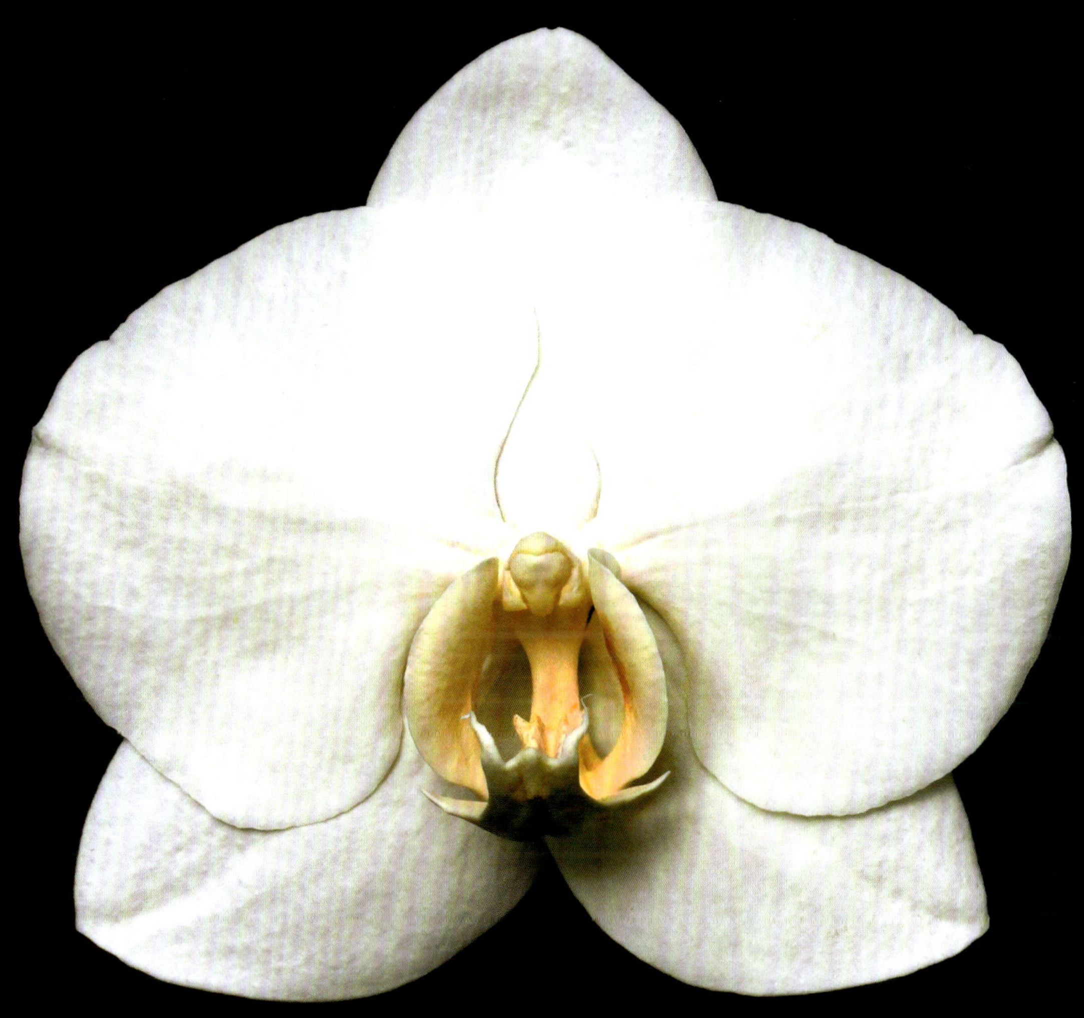

Preserved Phalaenopsis

Borneo

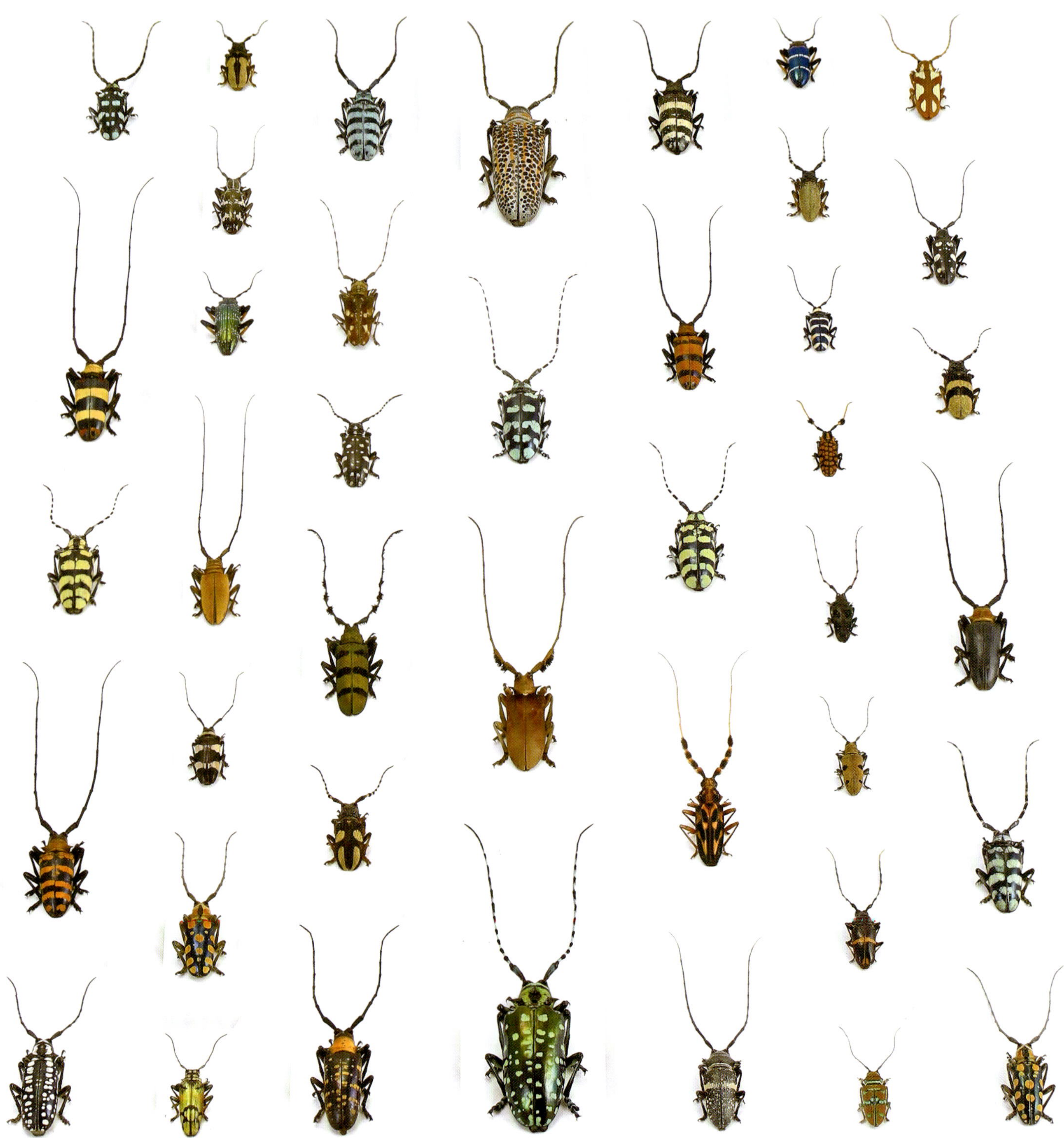

Limited Longhorn Mosaic

Asia, Africa

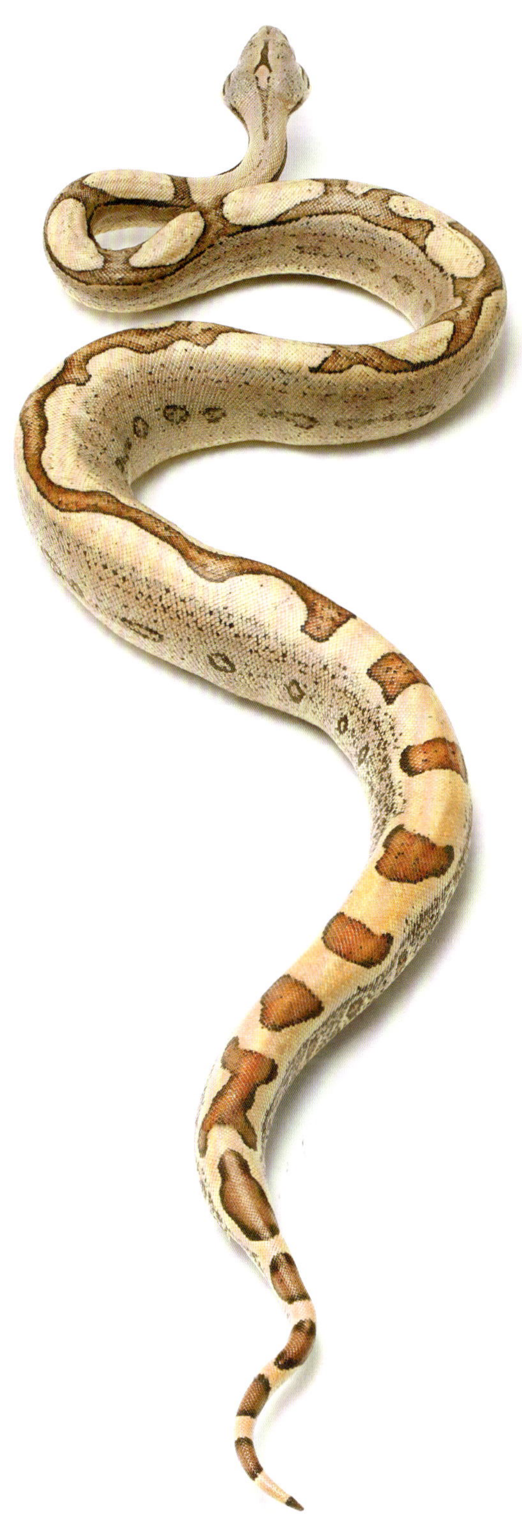

Red-Tailed Boa

Suriname

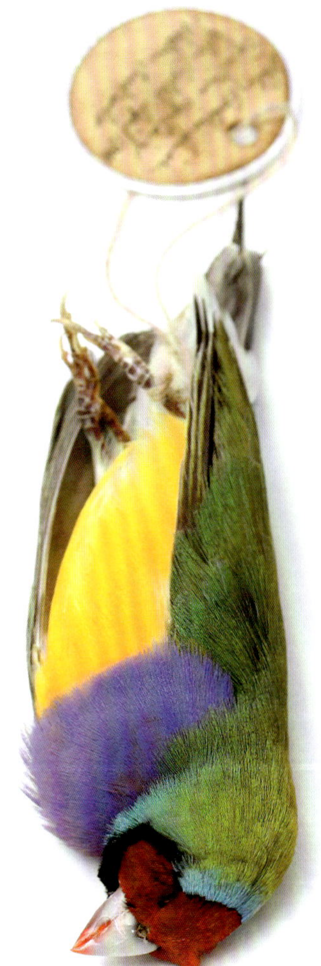

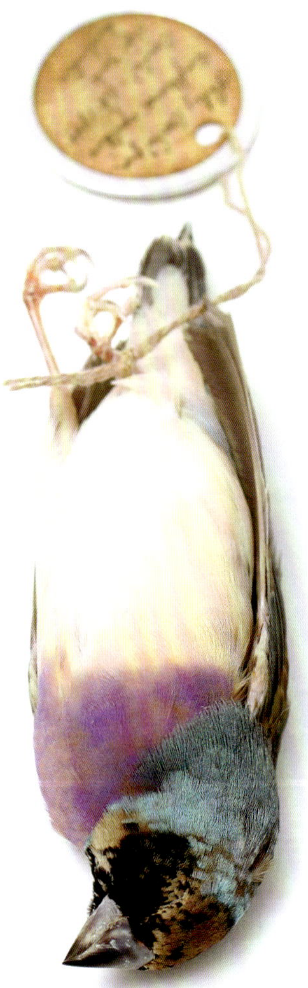

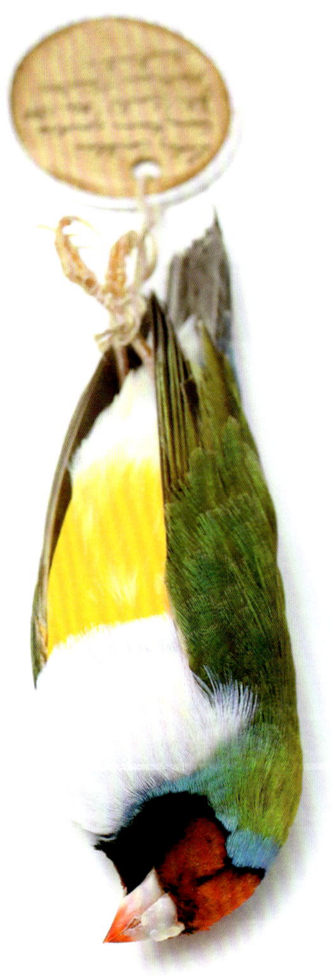

Gouldian Finches

Australia

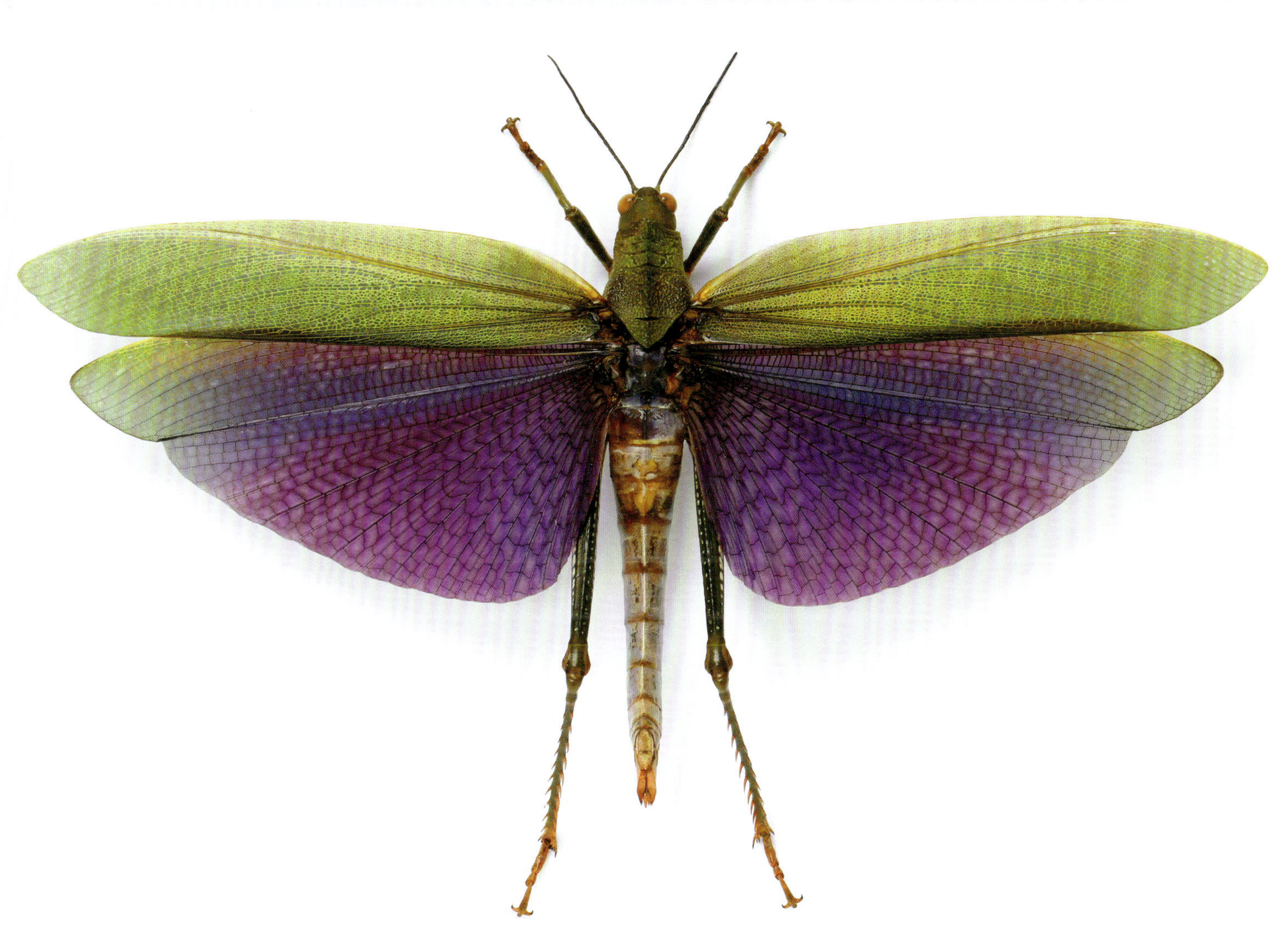

Amazon Grasshopper

Ecuador

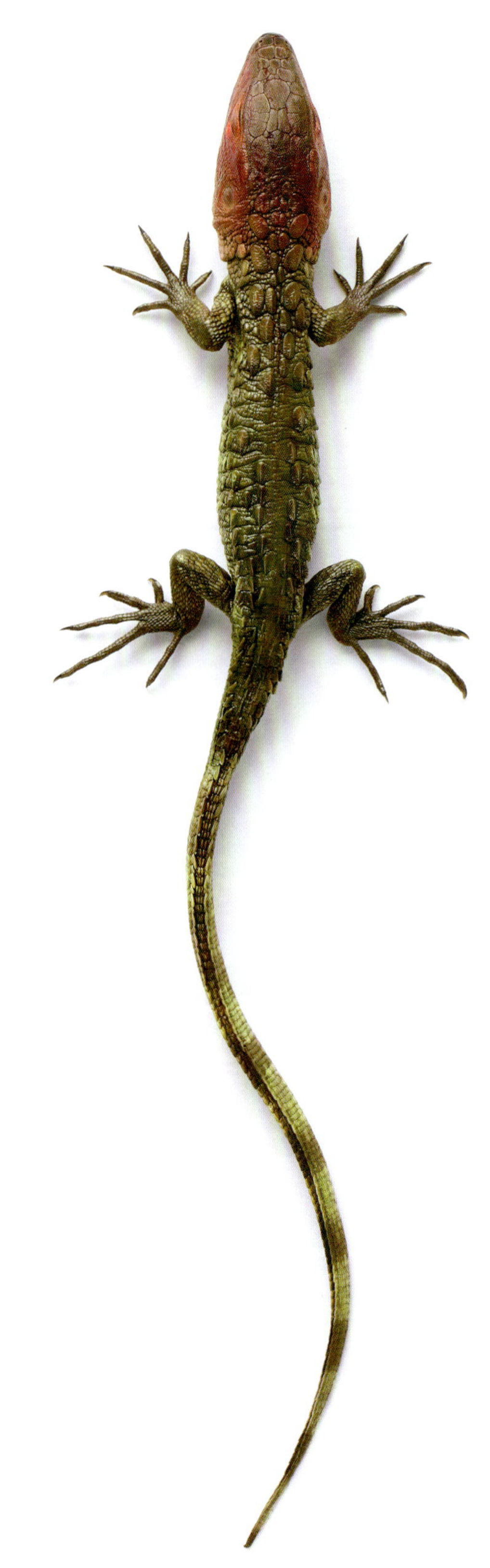

Caiman Lizard

Colombia

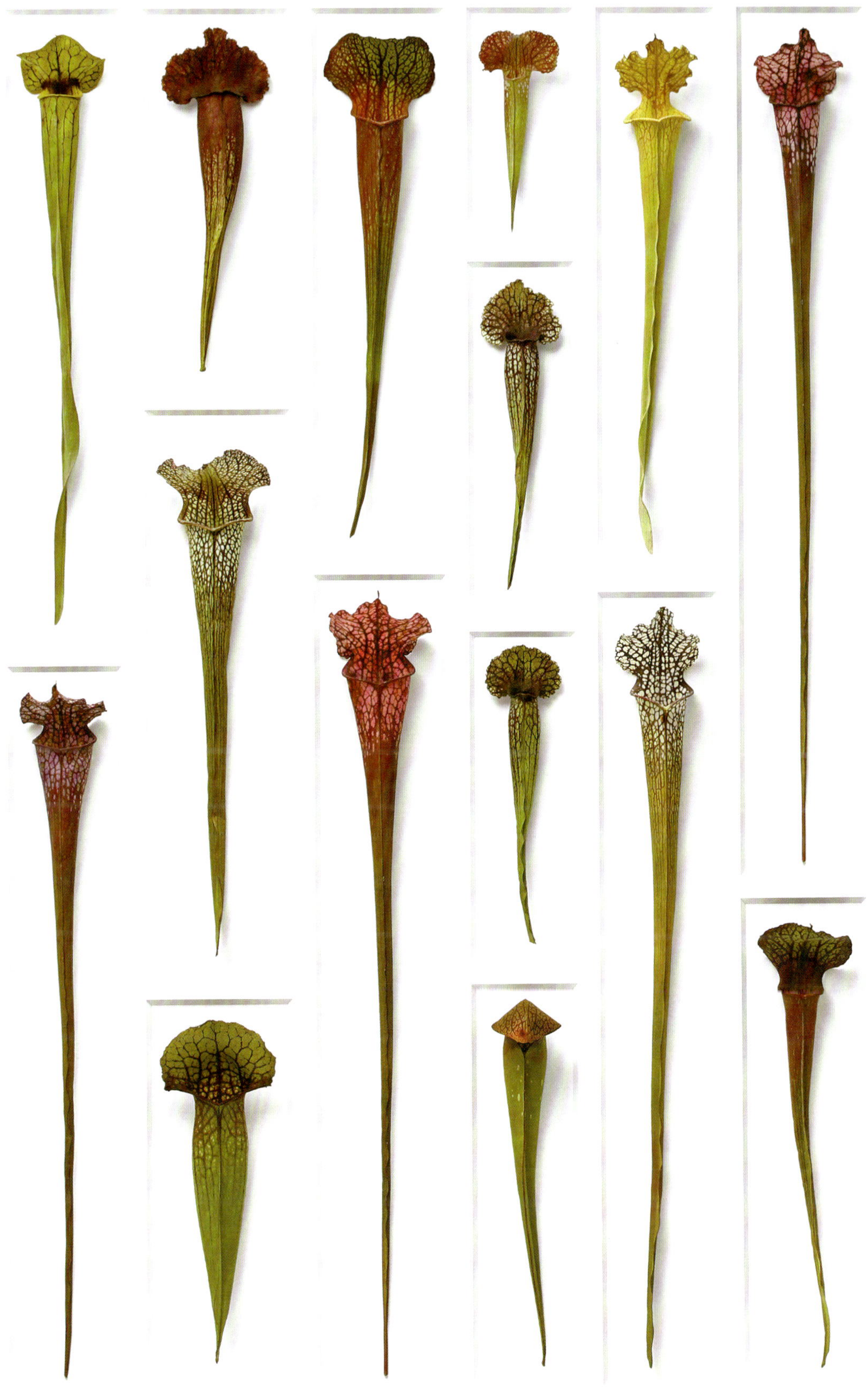

Pitcher Plant Mosaic

United States

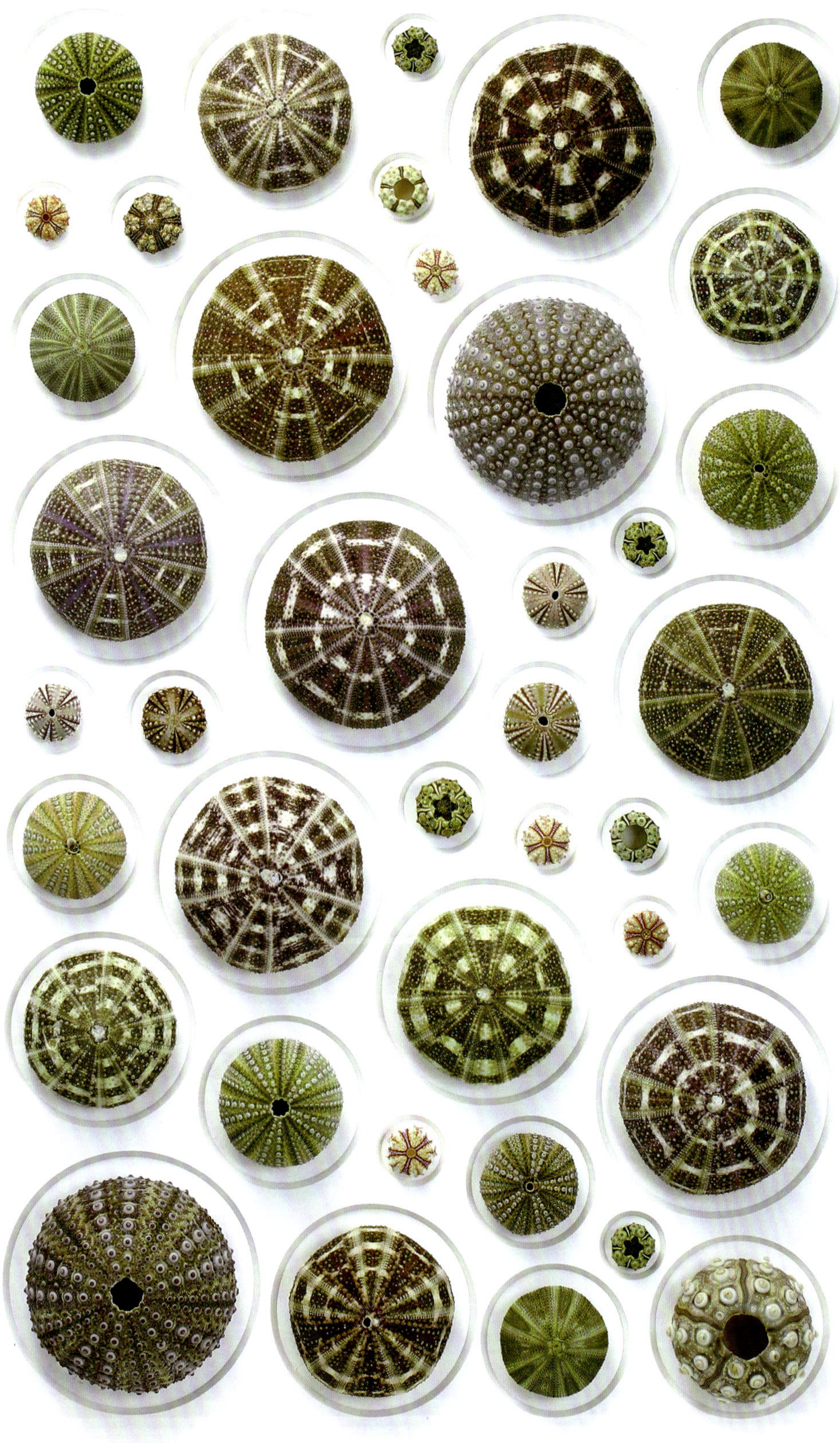

Urchin Spheres Mosaic

Philippines, Thailand, Mexico, United States

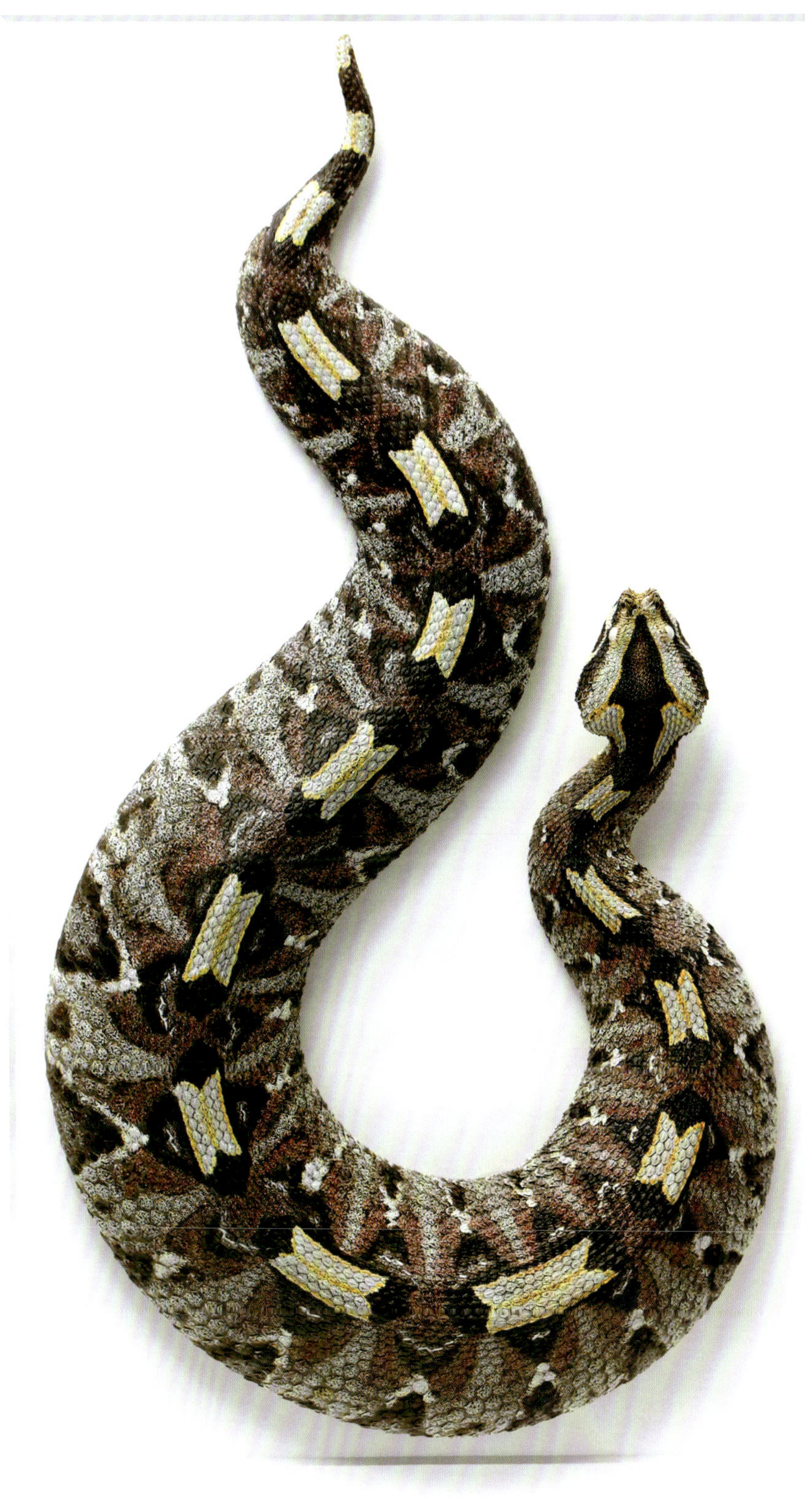

Rhinoceros Viper

Central African Republic

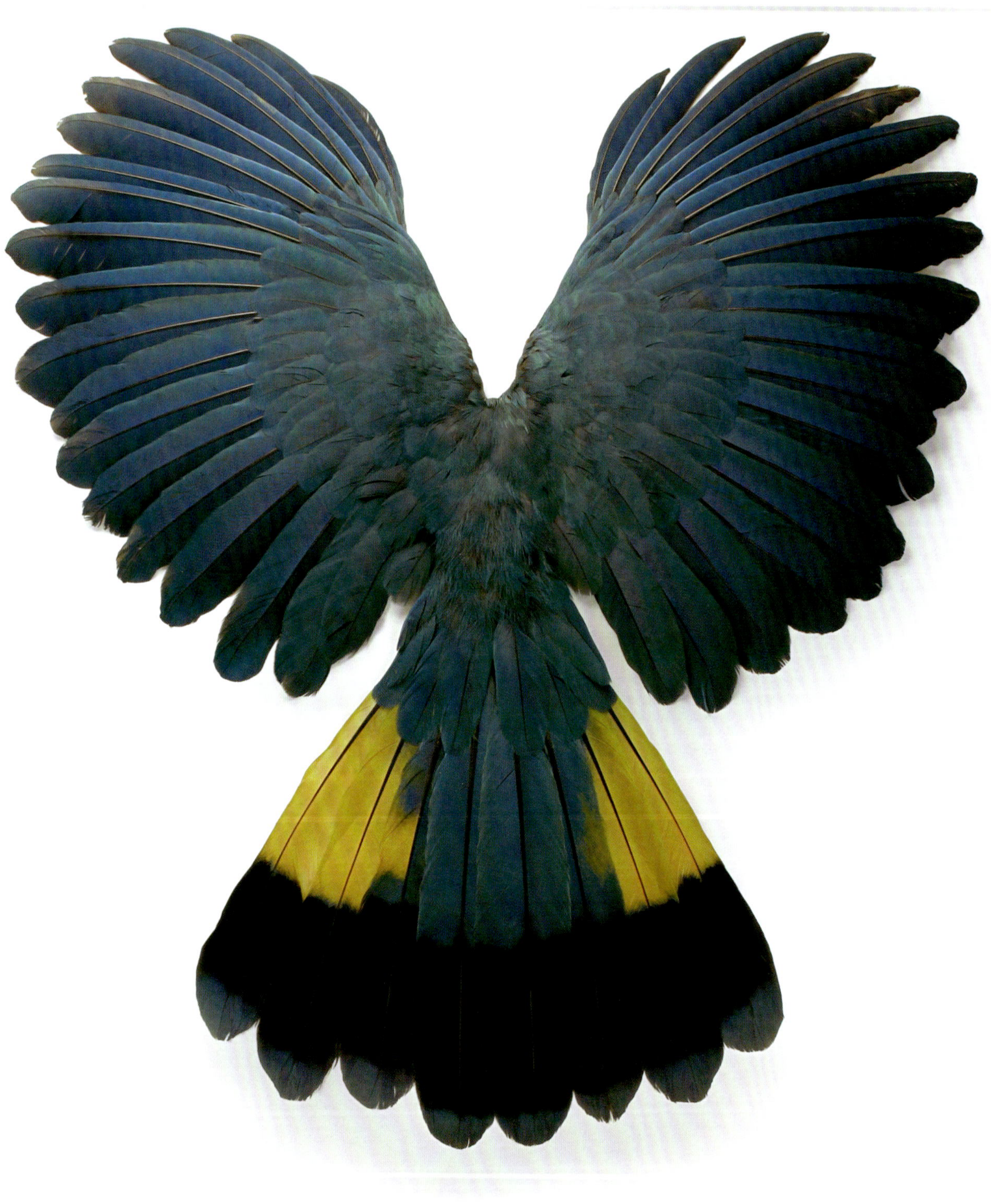

Great Blue Turaco

Democratic Republic of the Congo

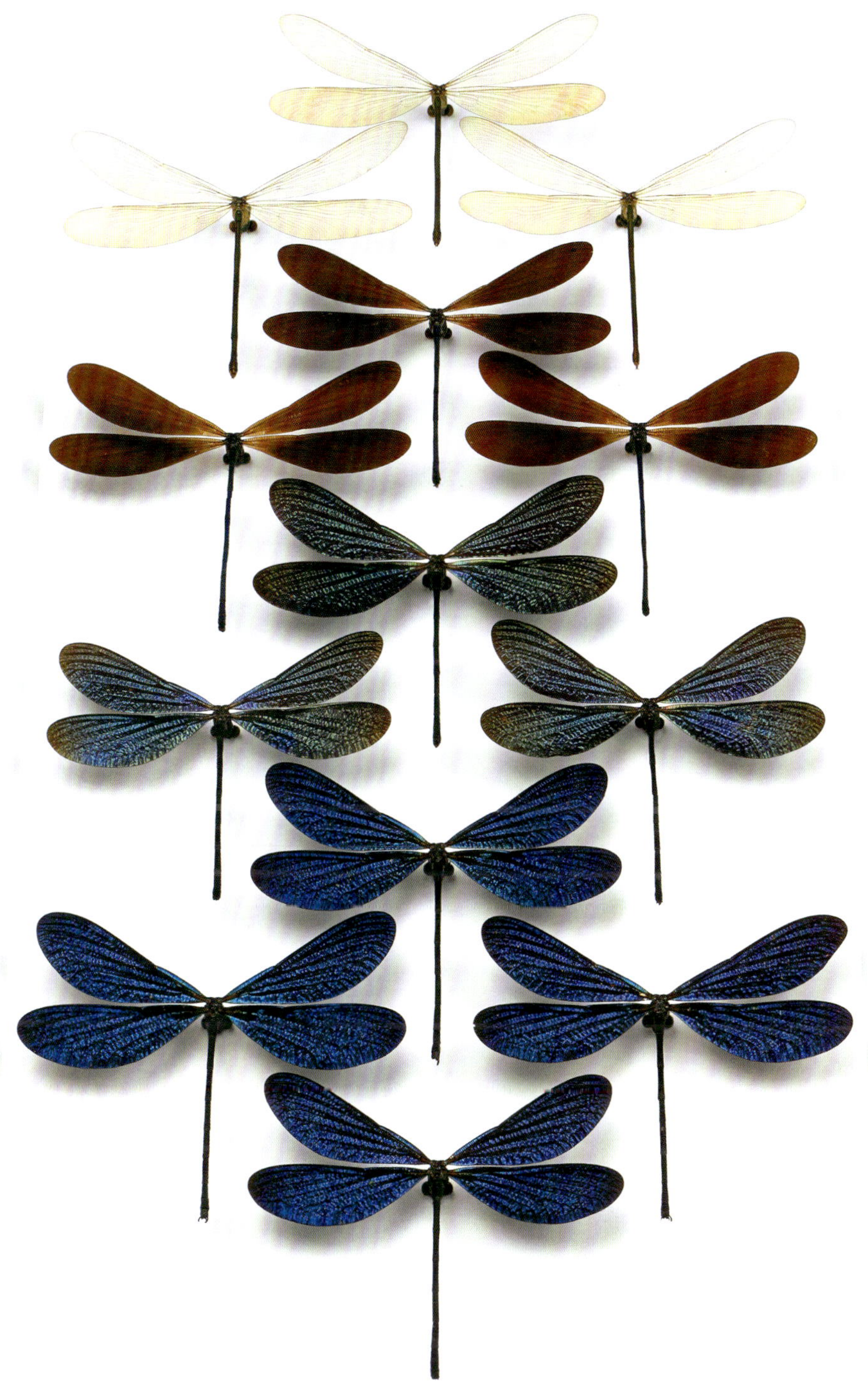

Damselfly Wash

Malaysia, Indonesia, Philippines

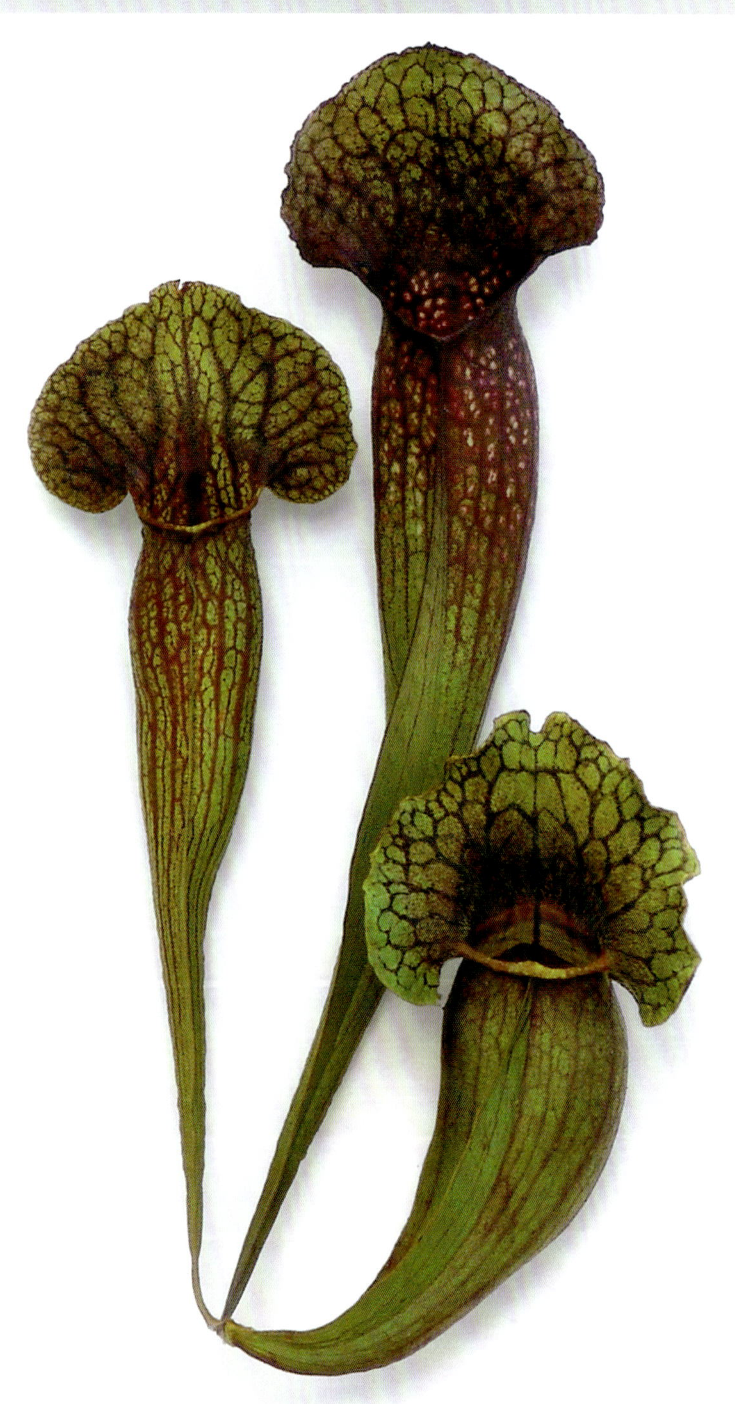

Carnivorous Pitcher Plants

United States

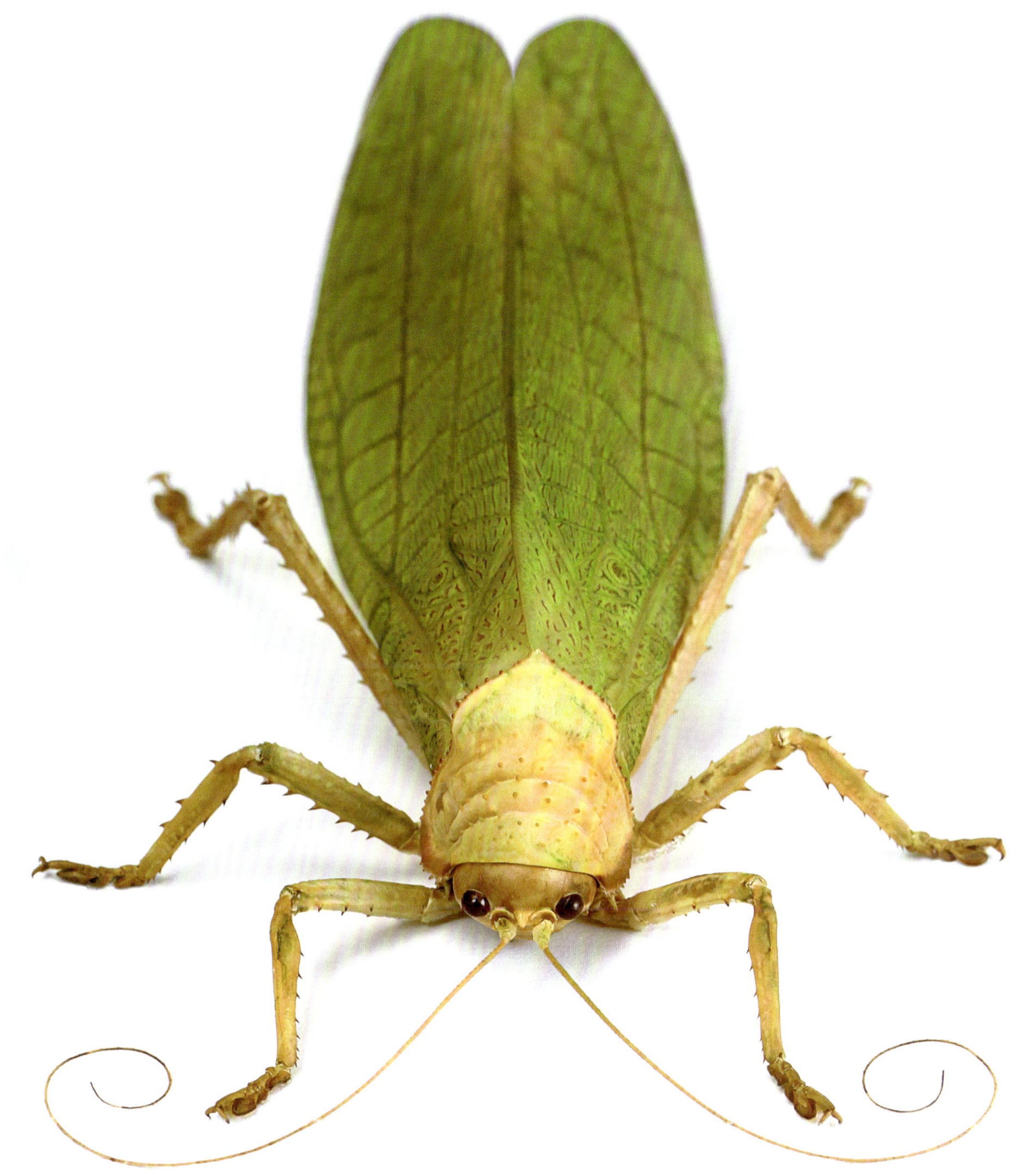

Leaf Mimic Katydid

Thailand

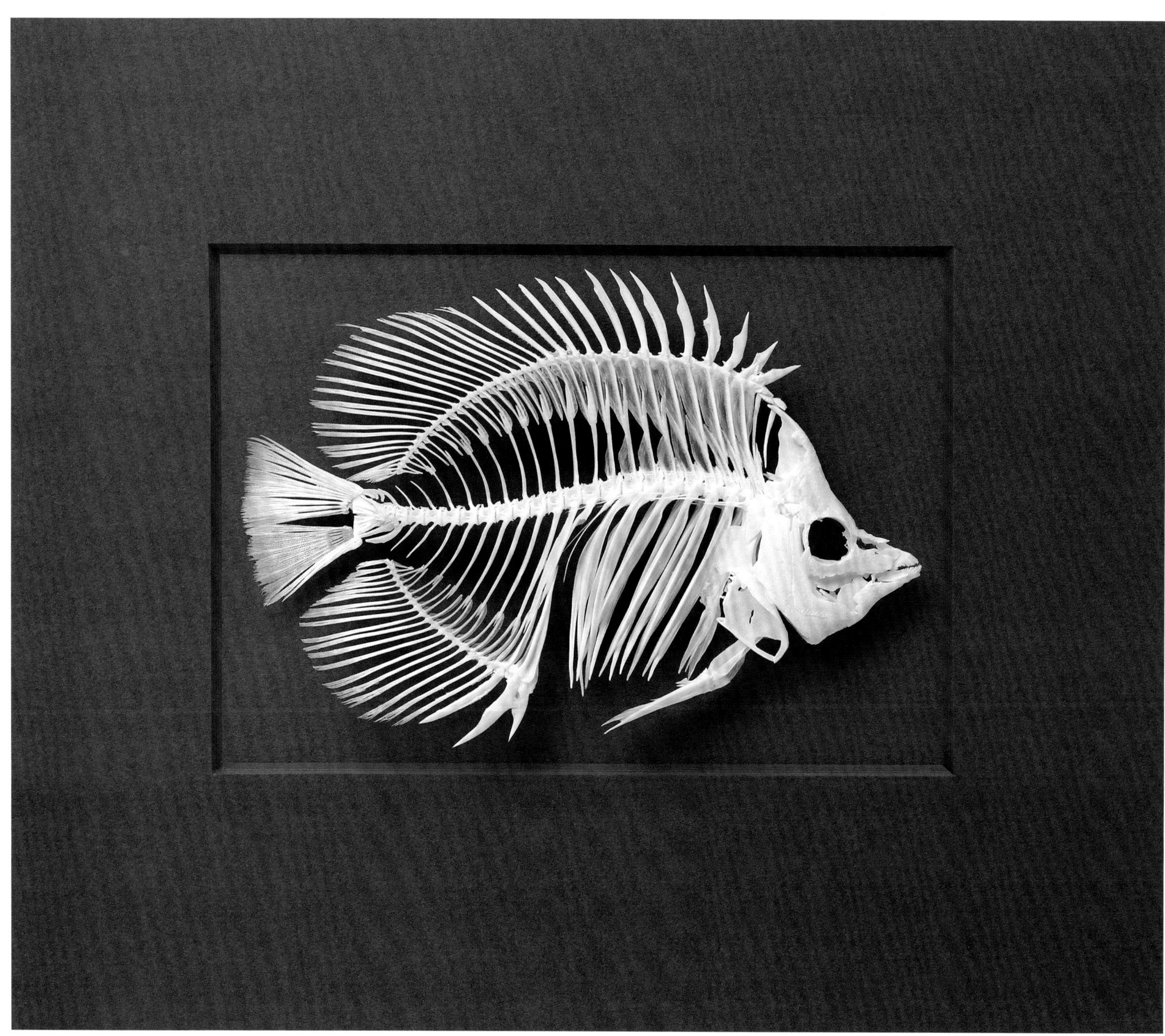

Butterfly Fish

Hawaii

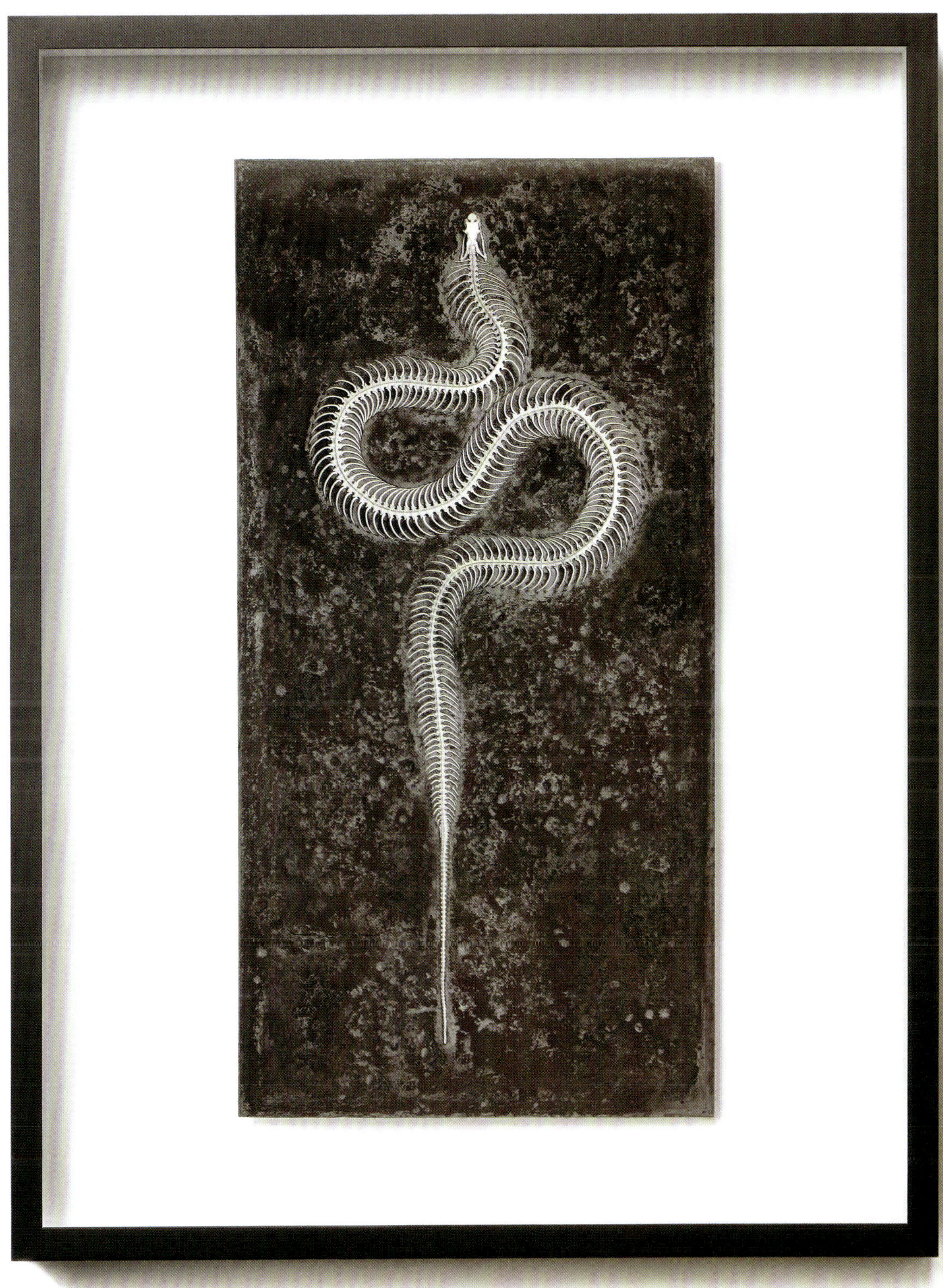

Cobra NeoFossil

Malaysia

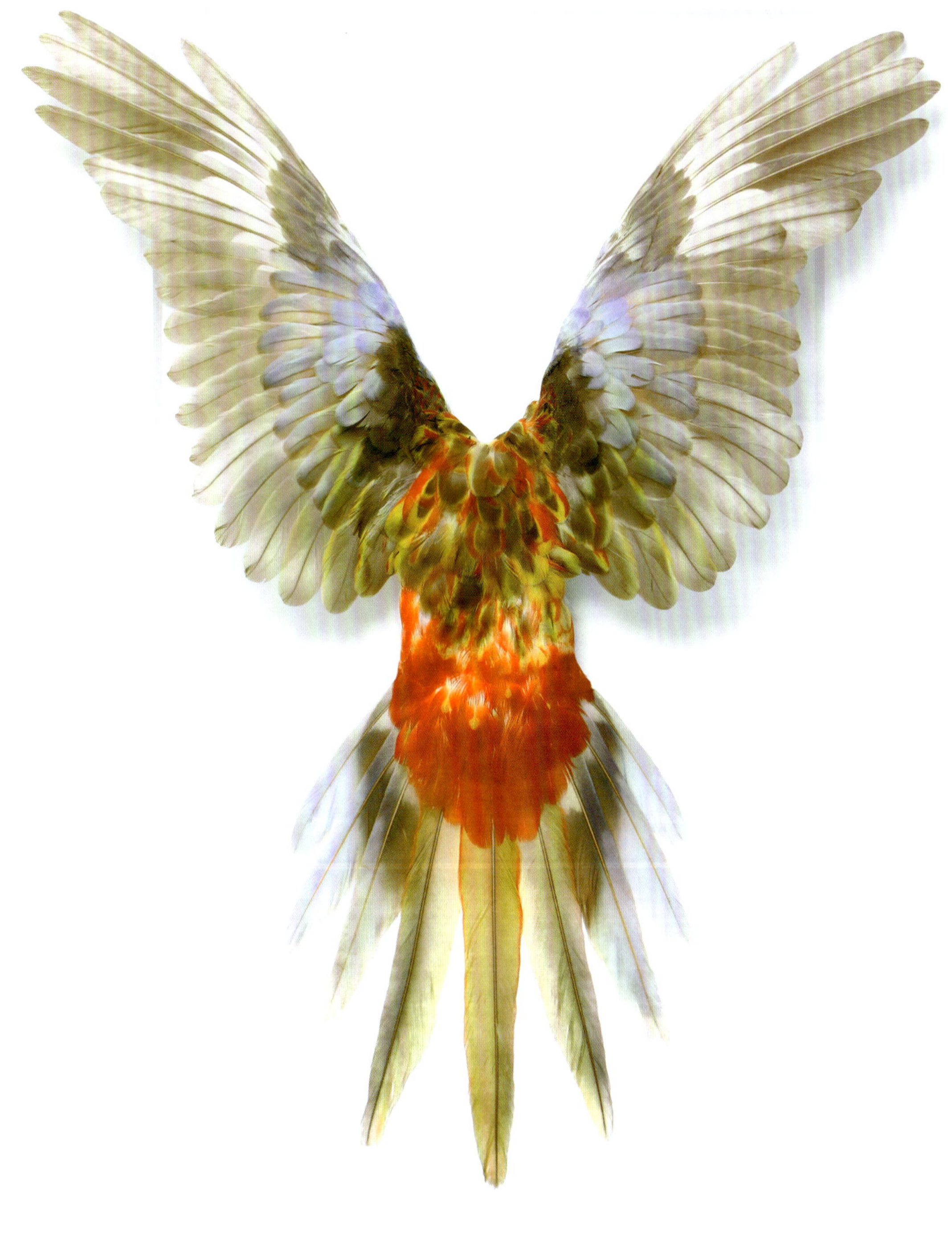

Opaline Eastern Rosella

Australia

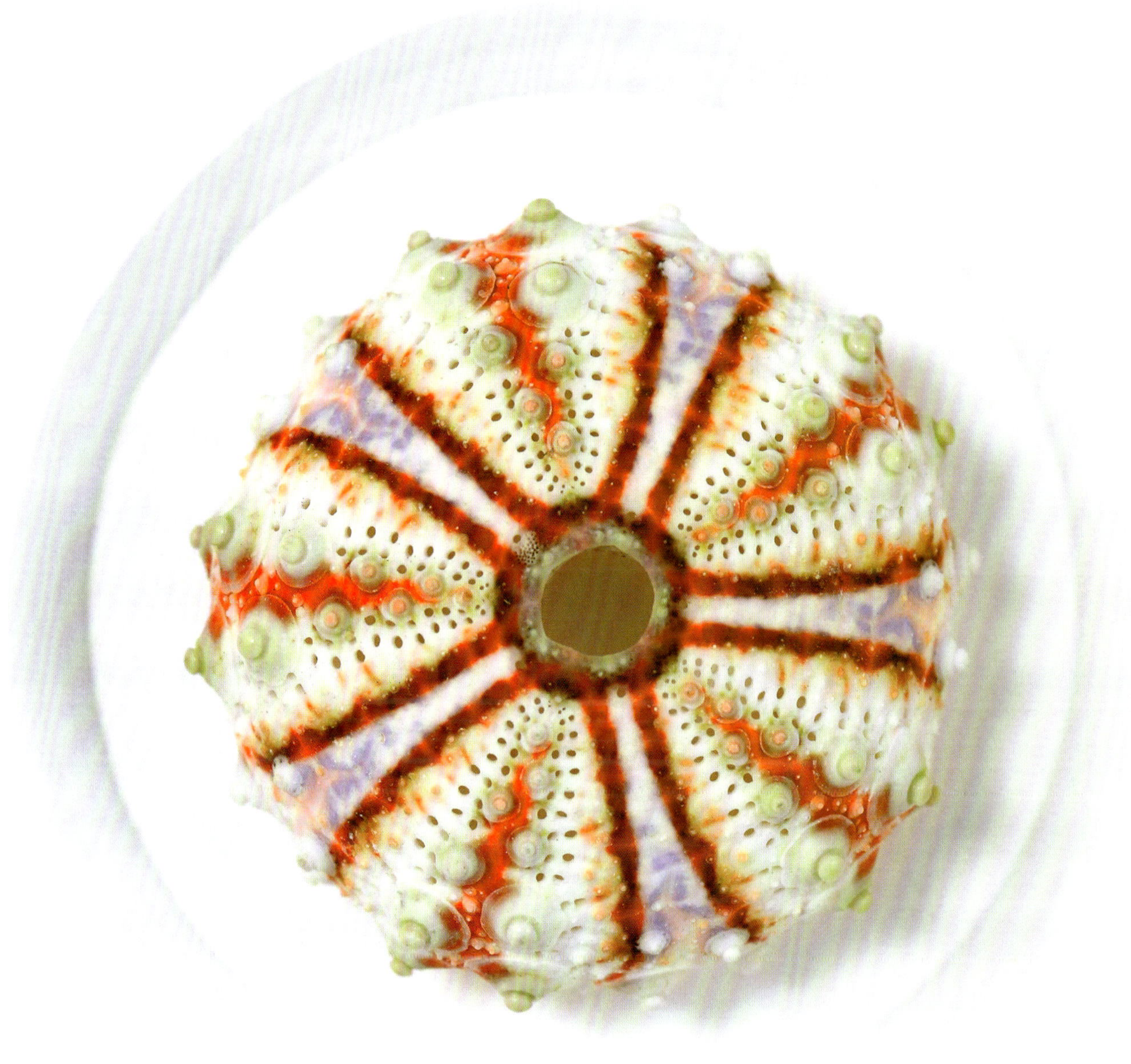

Variegated Urchin Test

Philippines

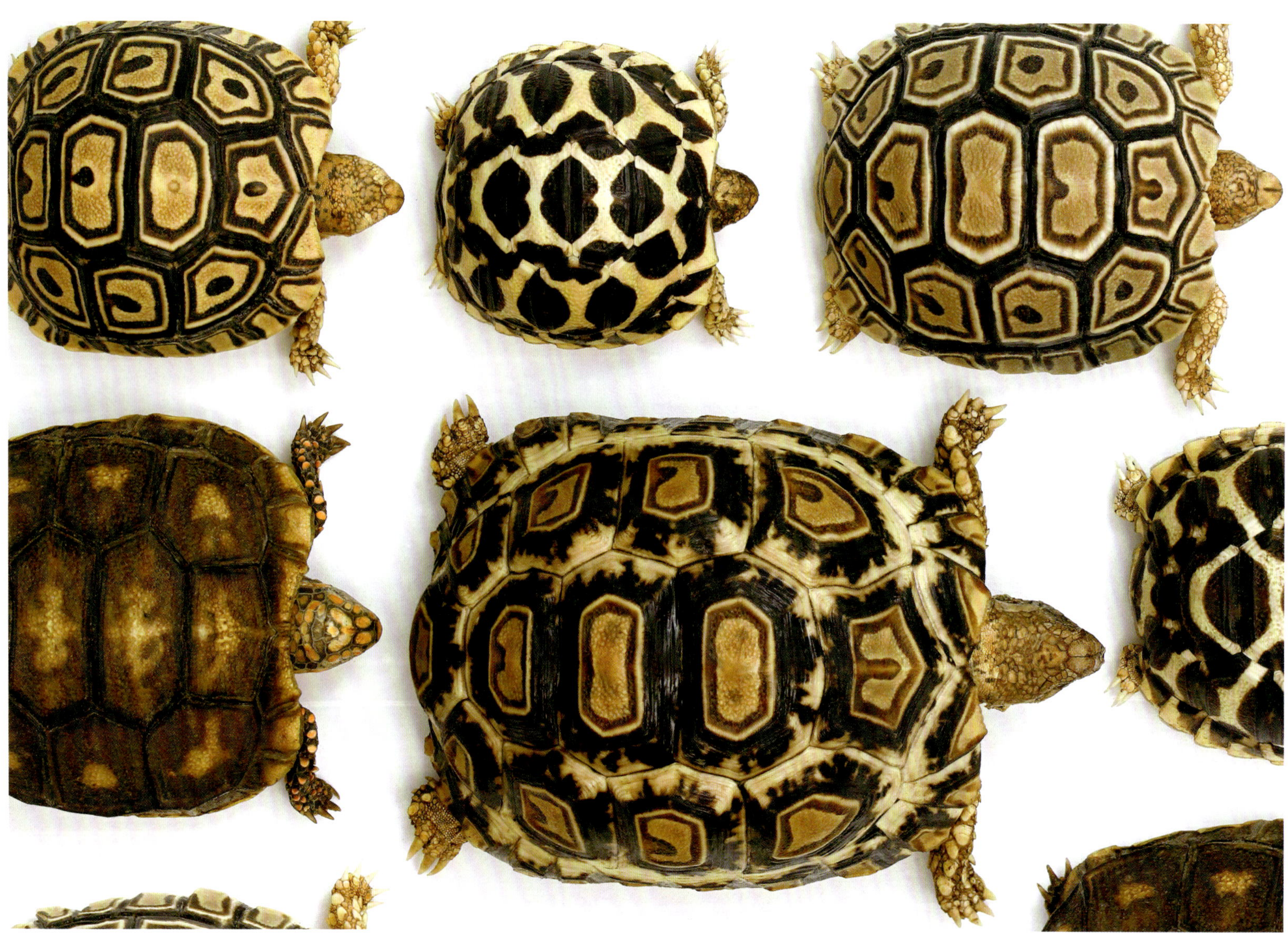

Tortoise Mosaic

Africa, Venezuela, India

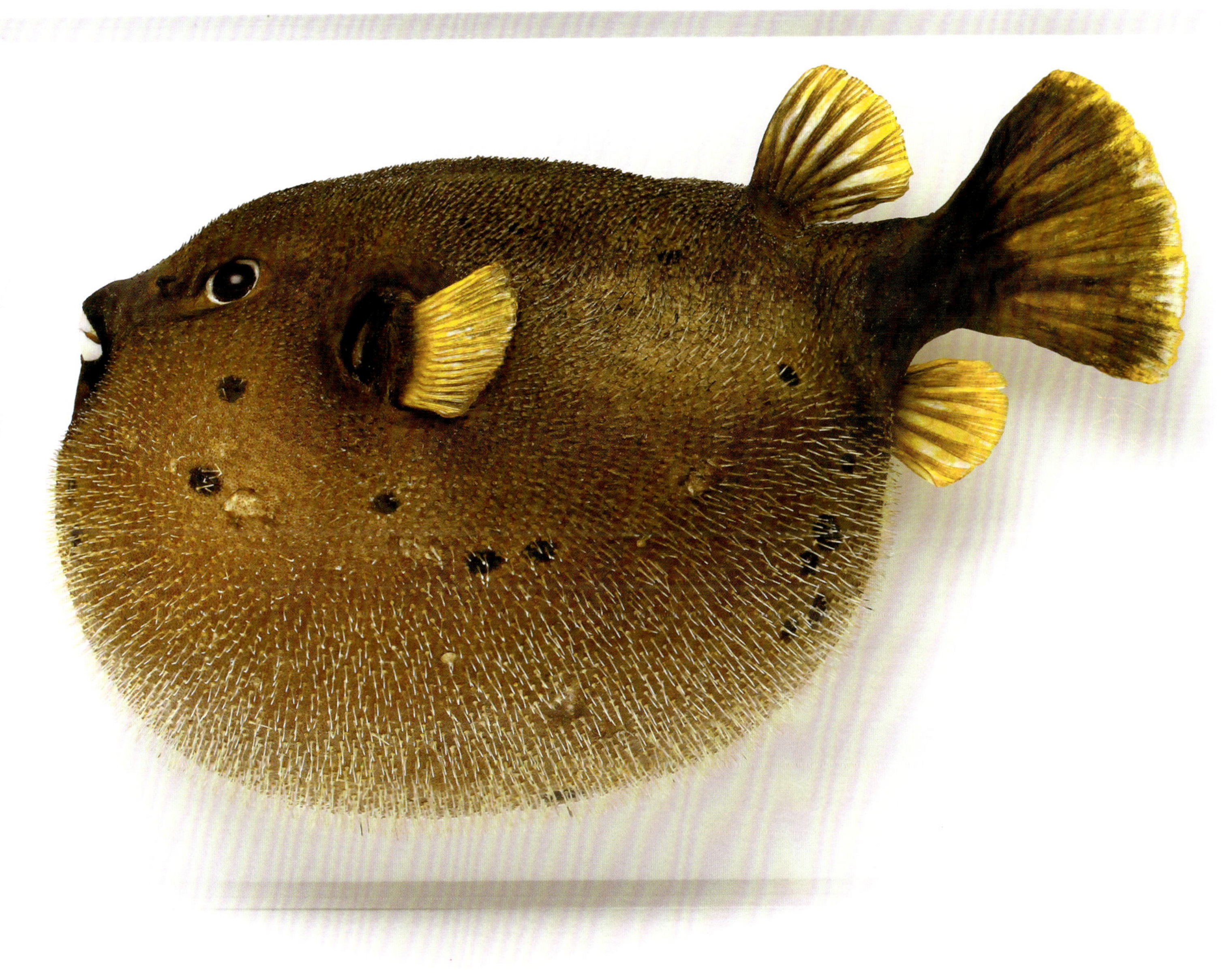

Puffer Fish

Indonesia

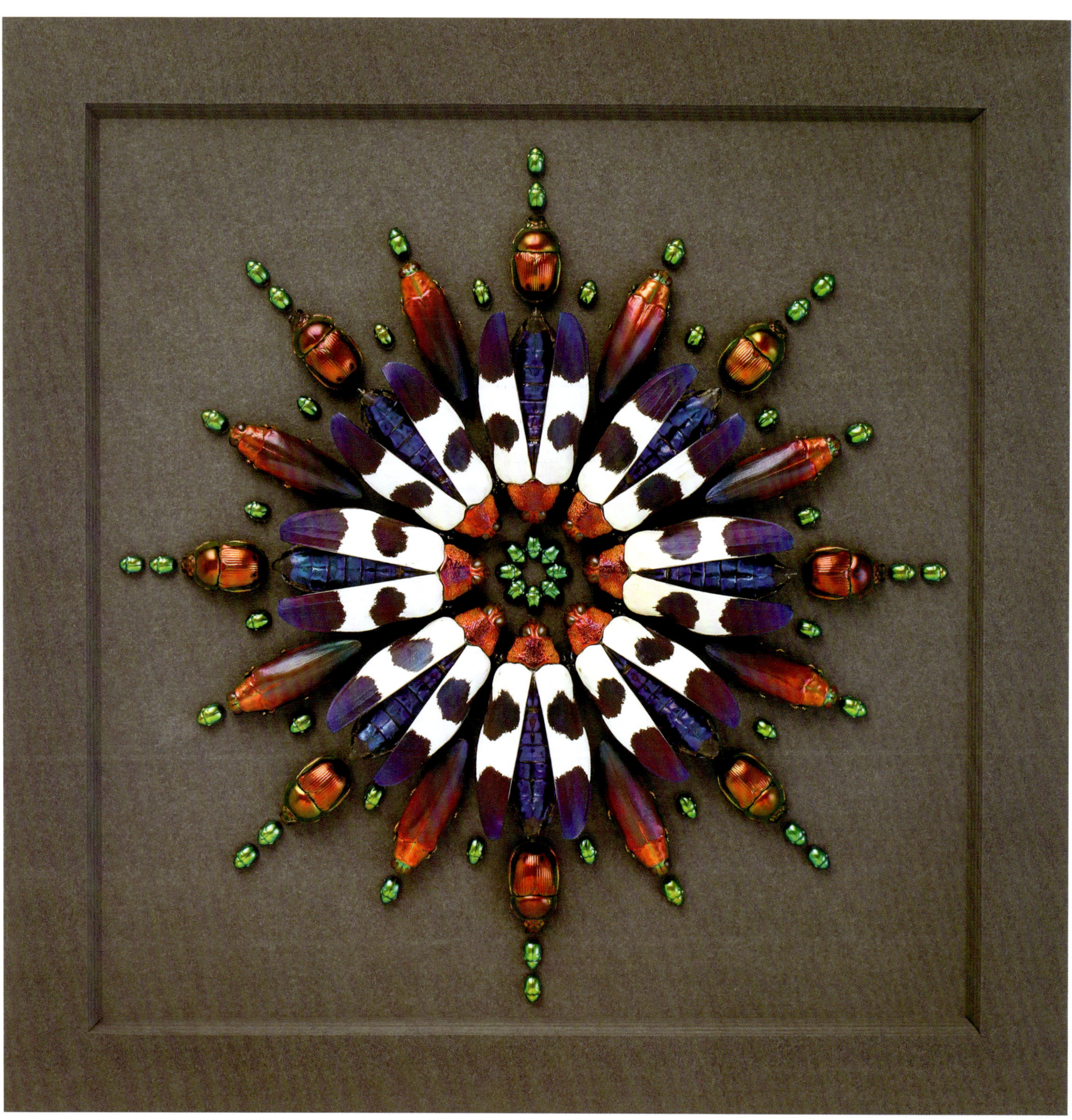

Buqueti Prism

Indonesia, Thailand, Japan

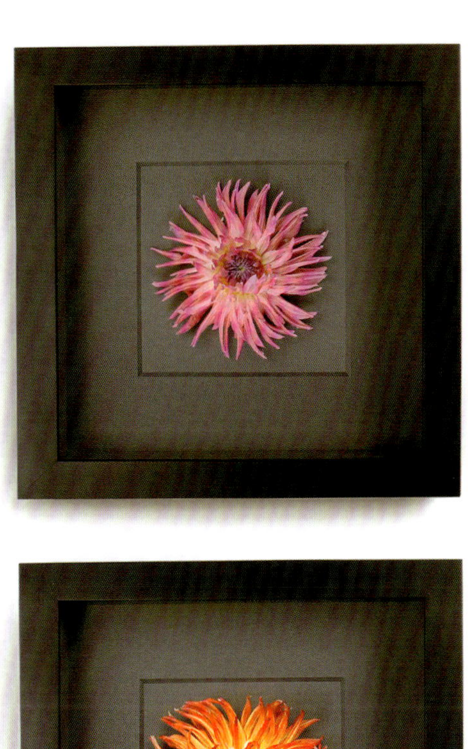
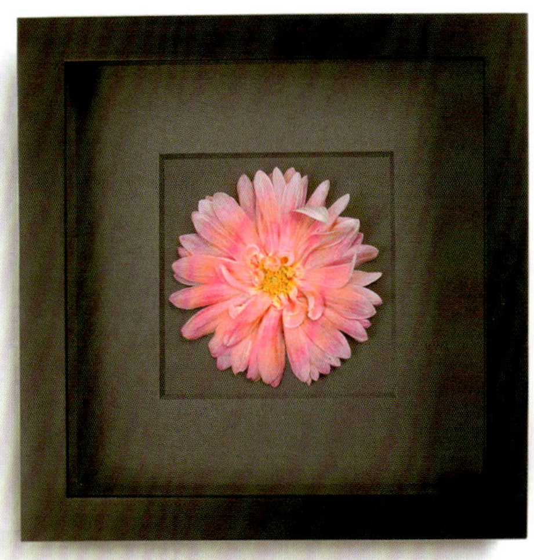
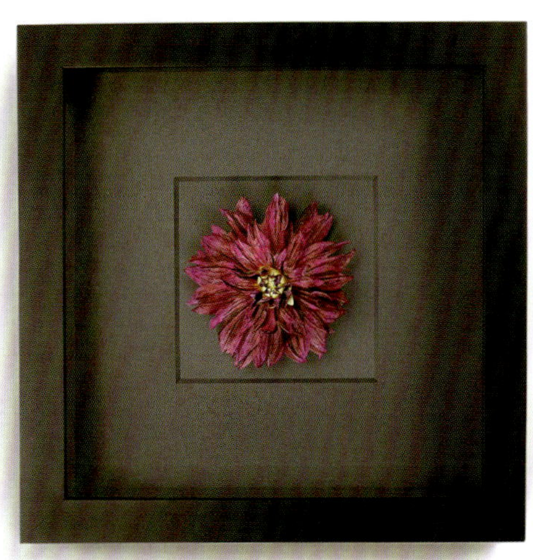
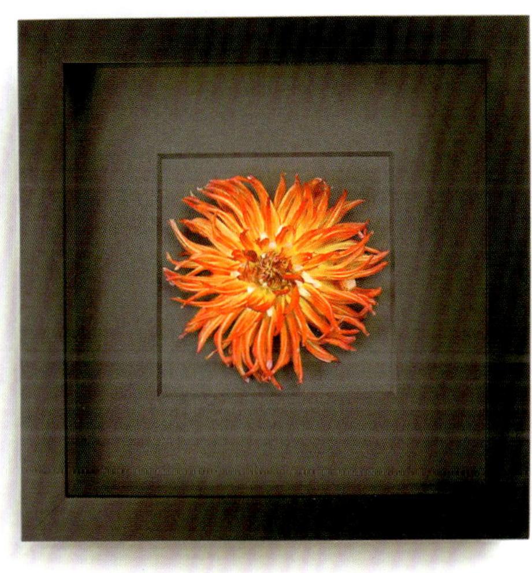
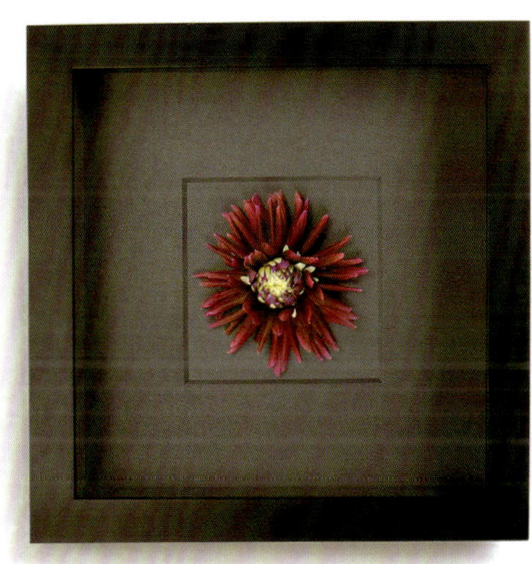
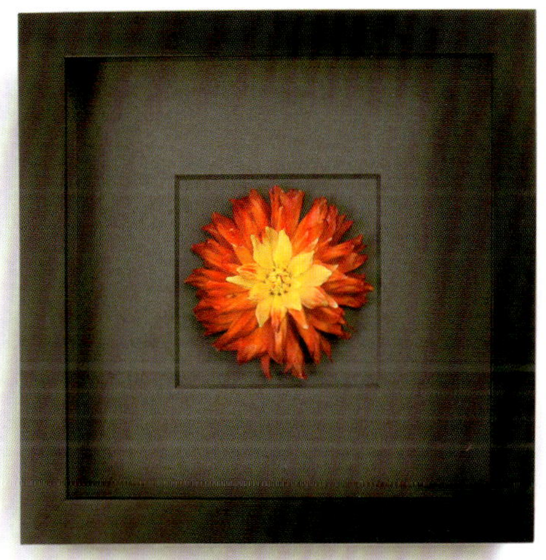
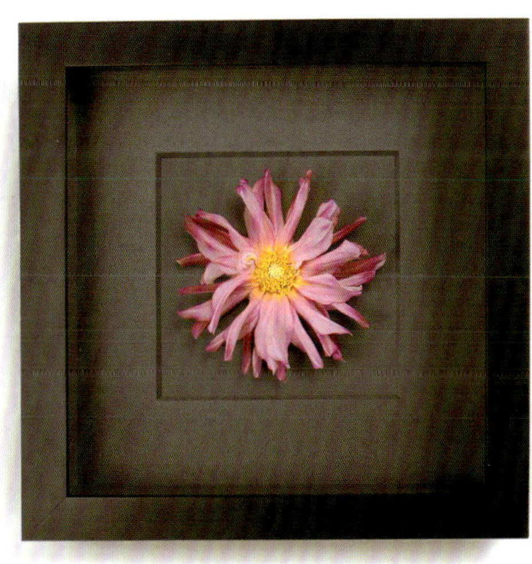
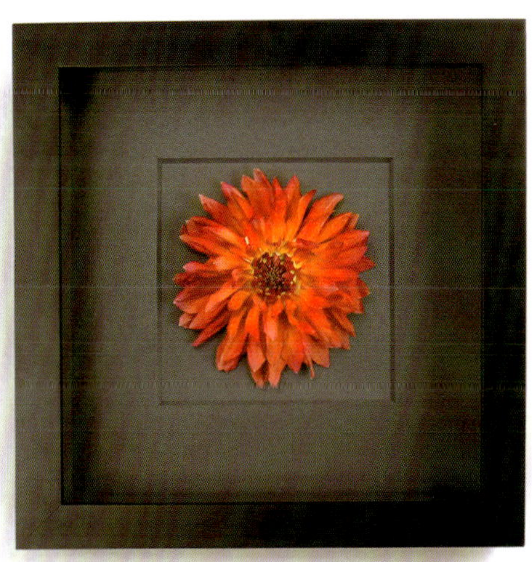
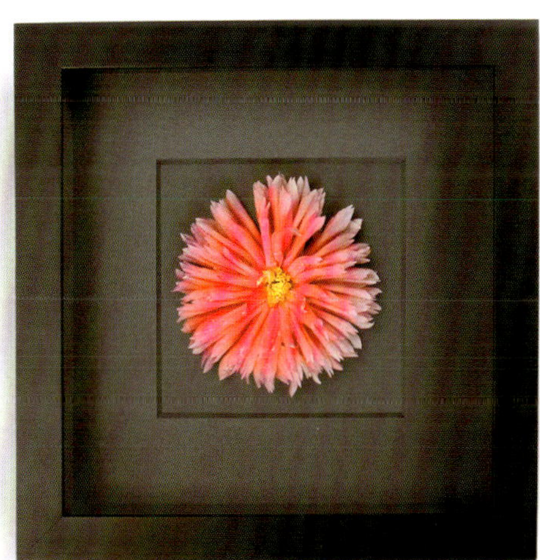

Preserved Dahlias

United States

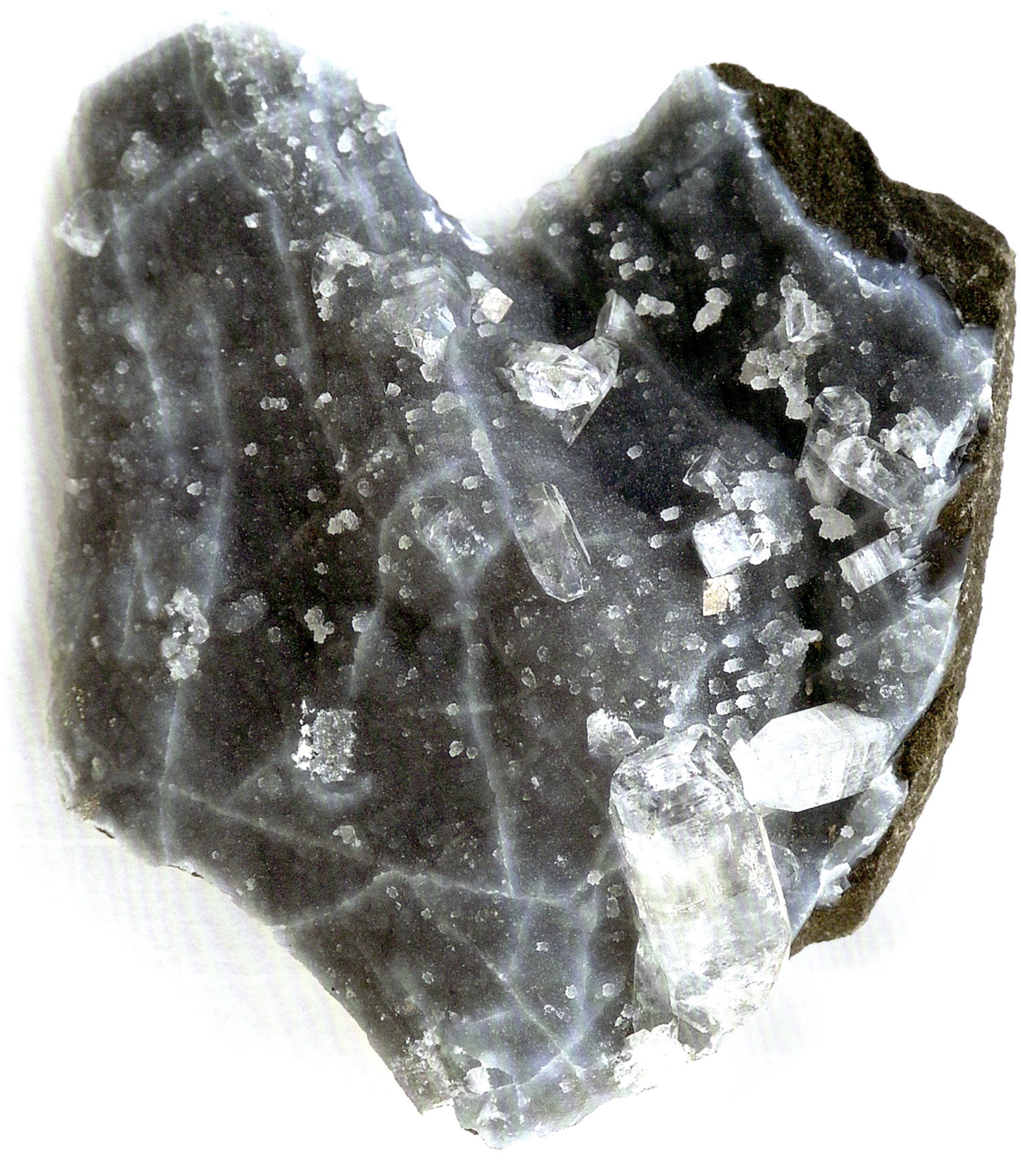

Apophyllite on Chalcedony

India

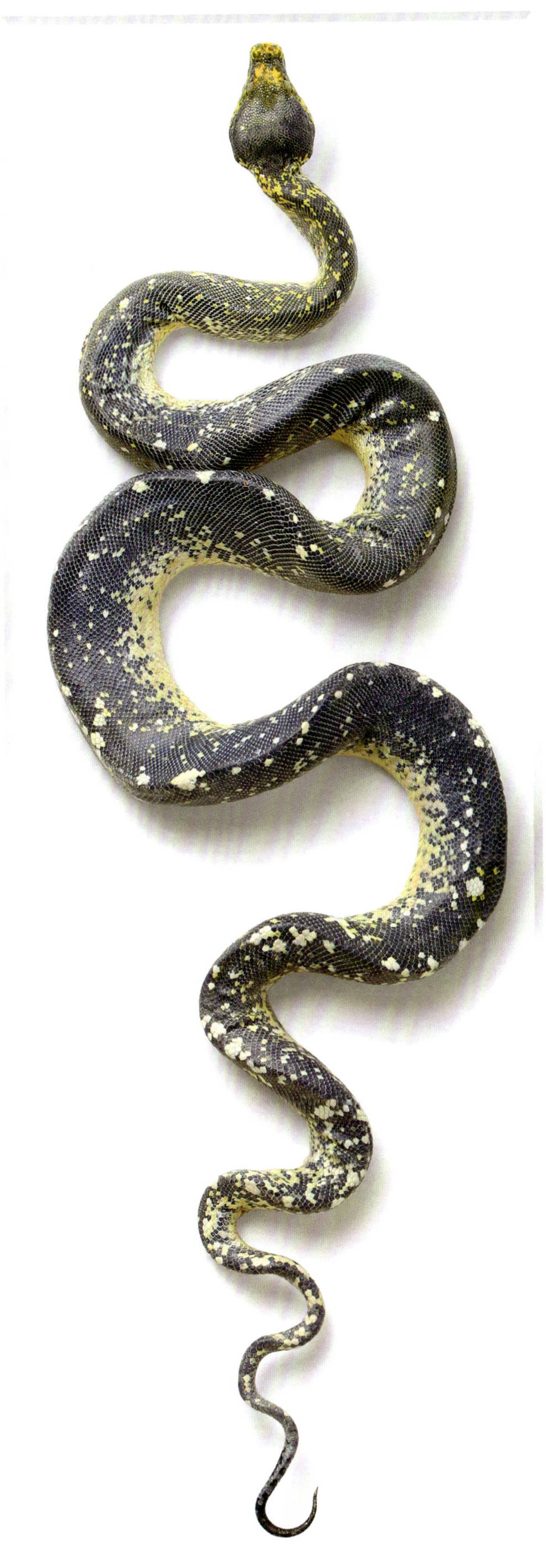

Green Tree Python, Blue Phase

Australia

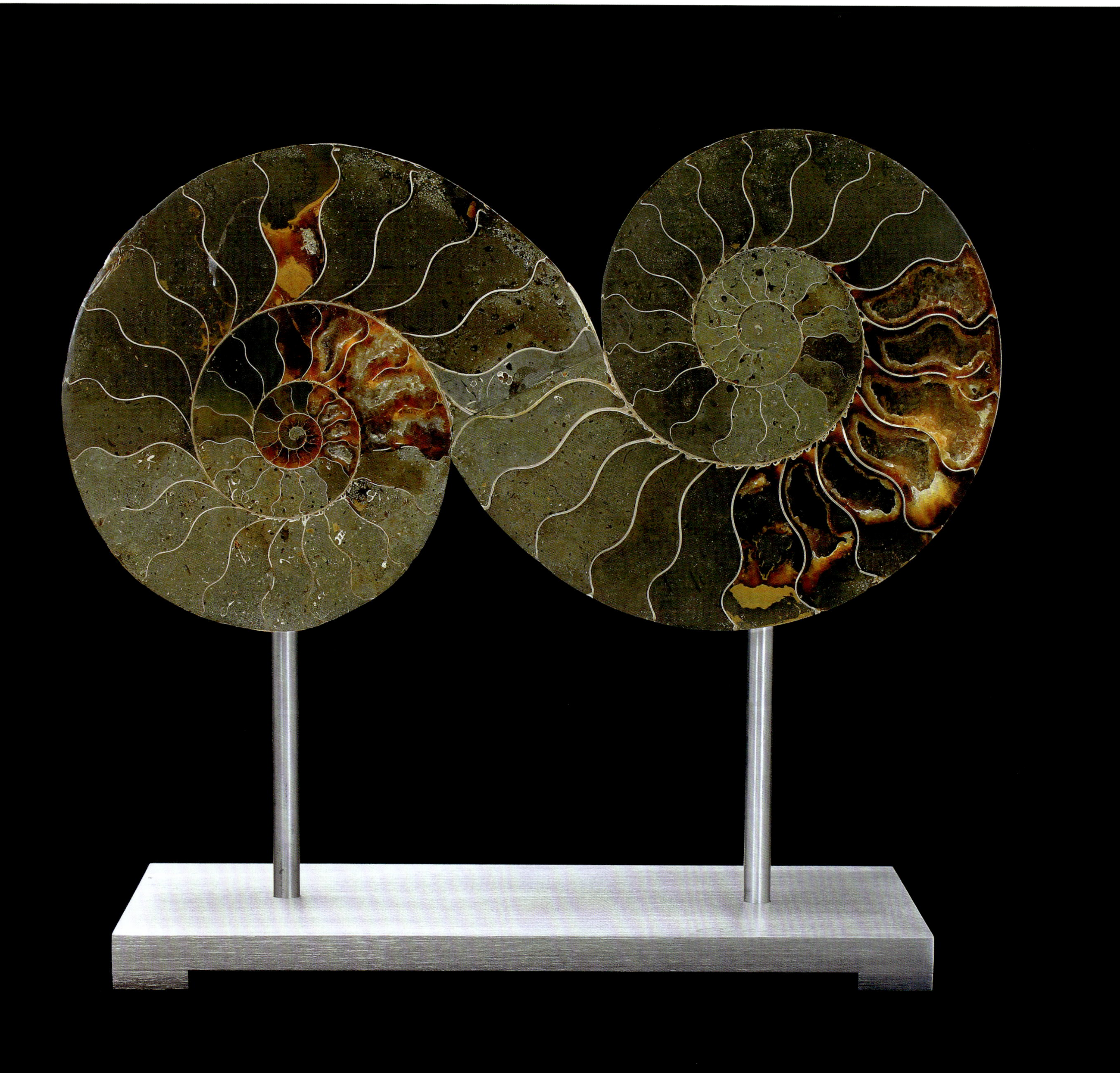

Cretaceous Ammonite Pedestal

Madagascar

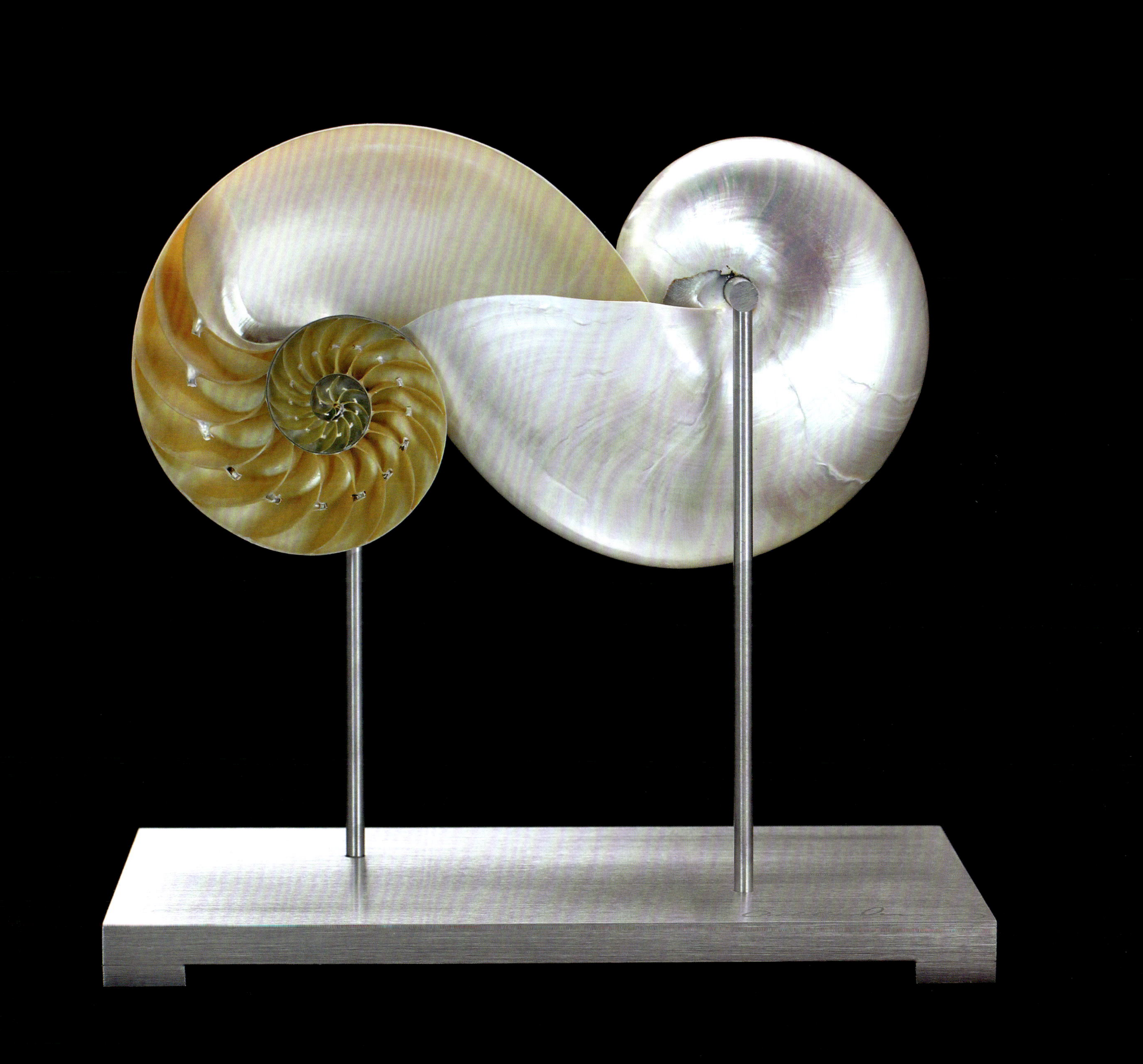

Nautilus Pedestal

Philippines

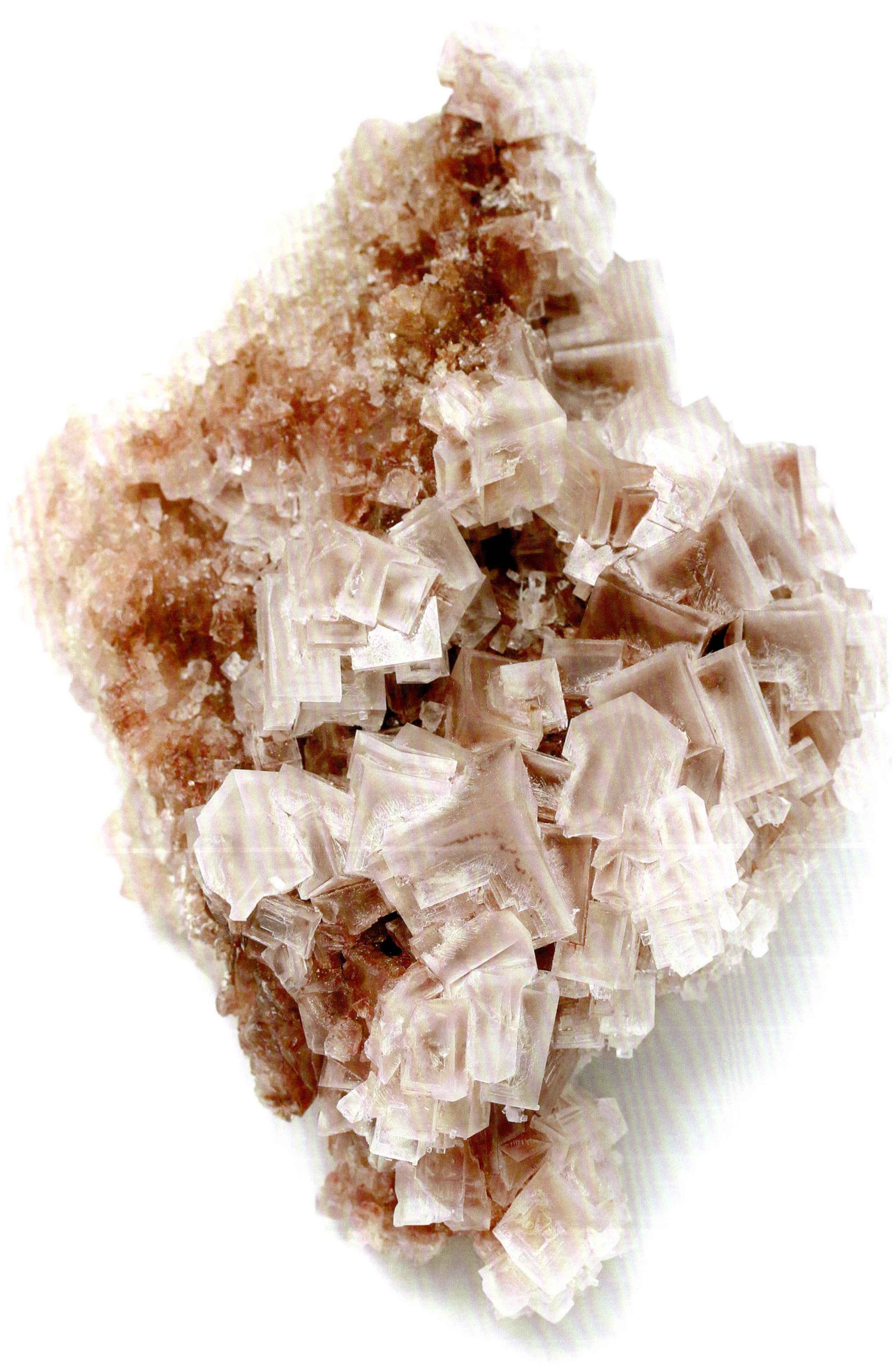

Halite

Mexico

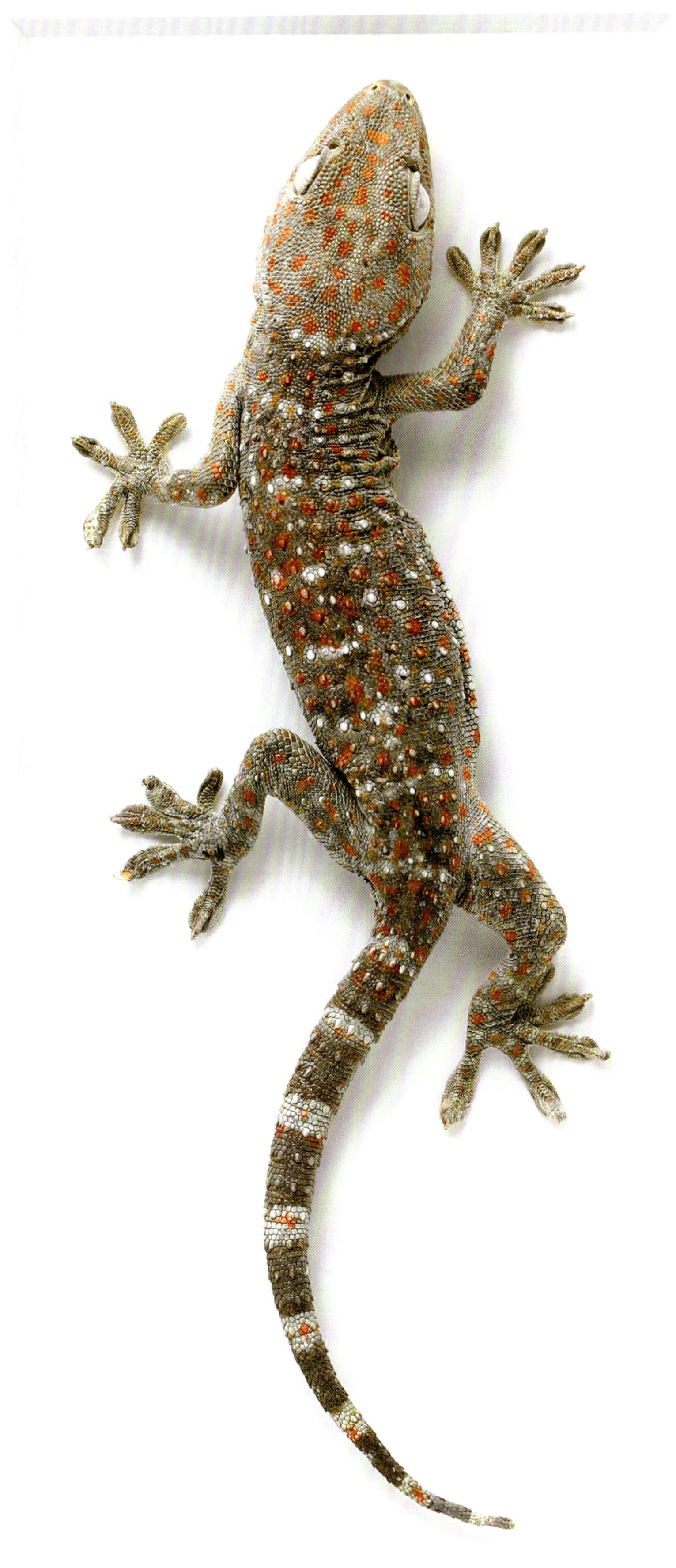

Tokay Gecko

New Guinea

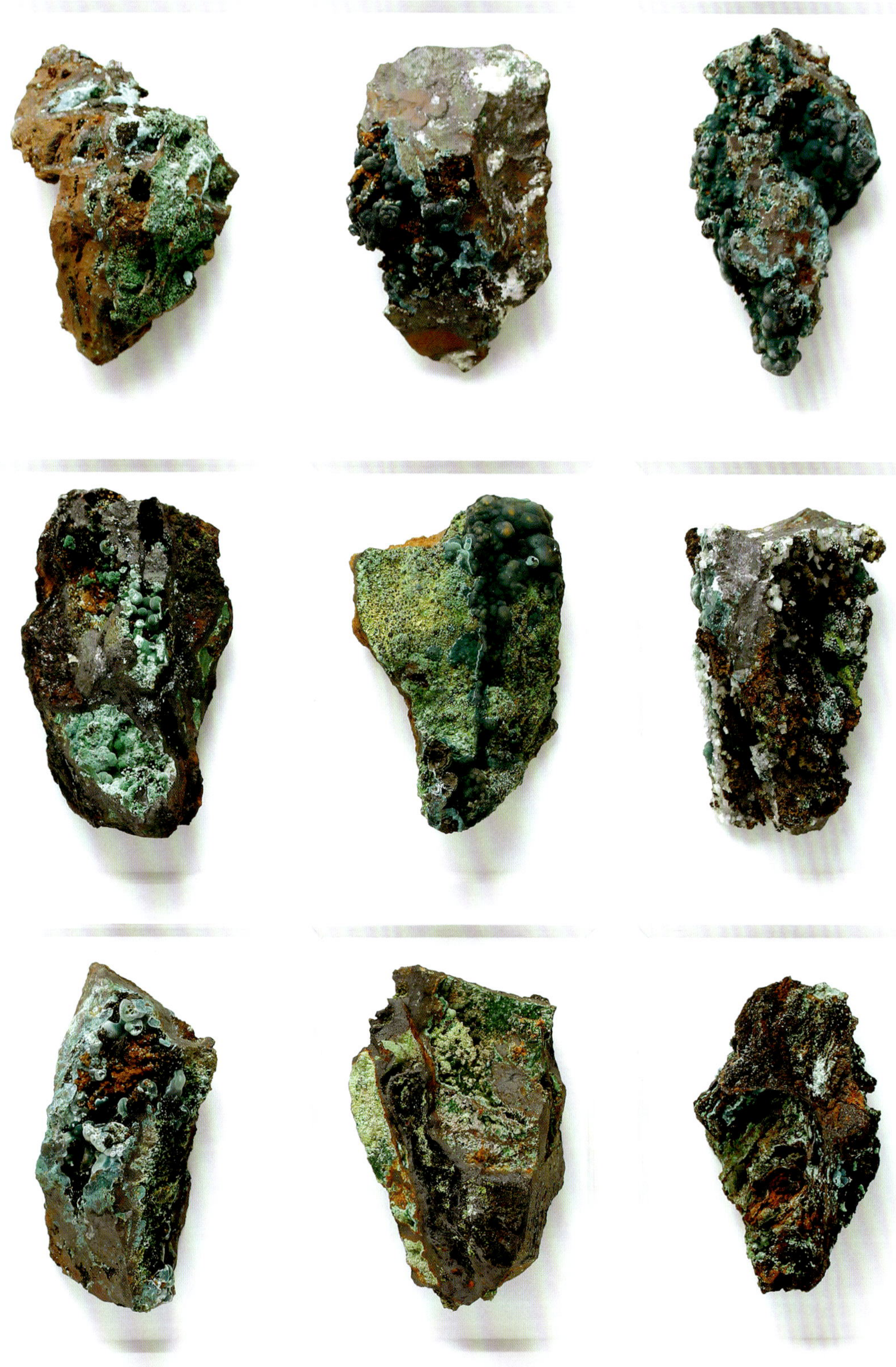

Rosasite

Mexico

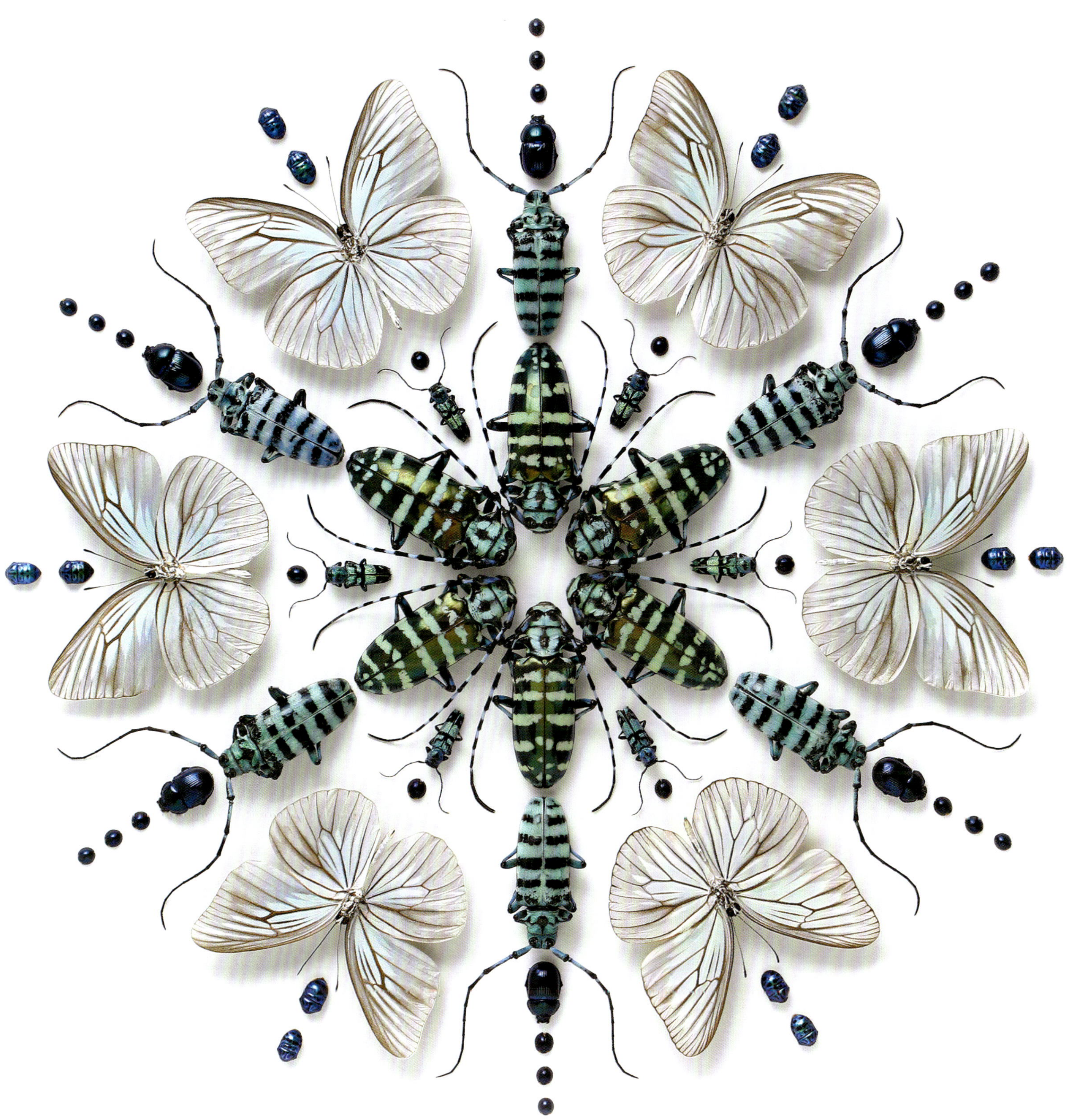

Elegans Prism

Malaysia, Indonesia, Japan

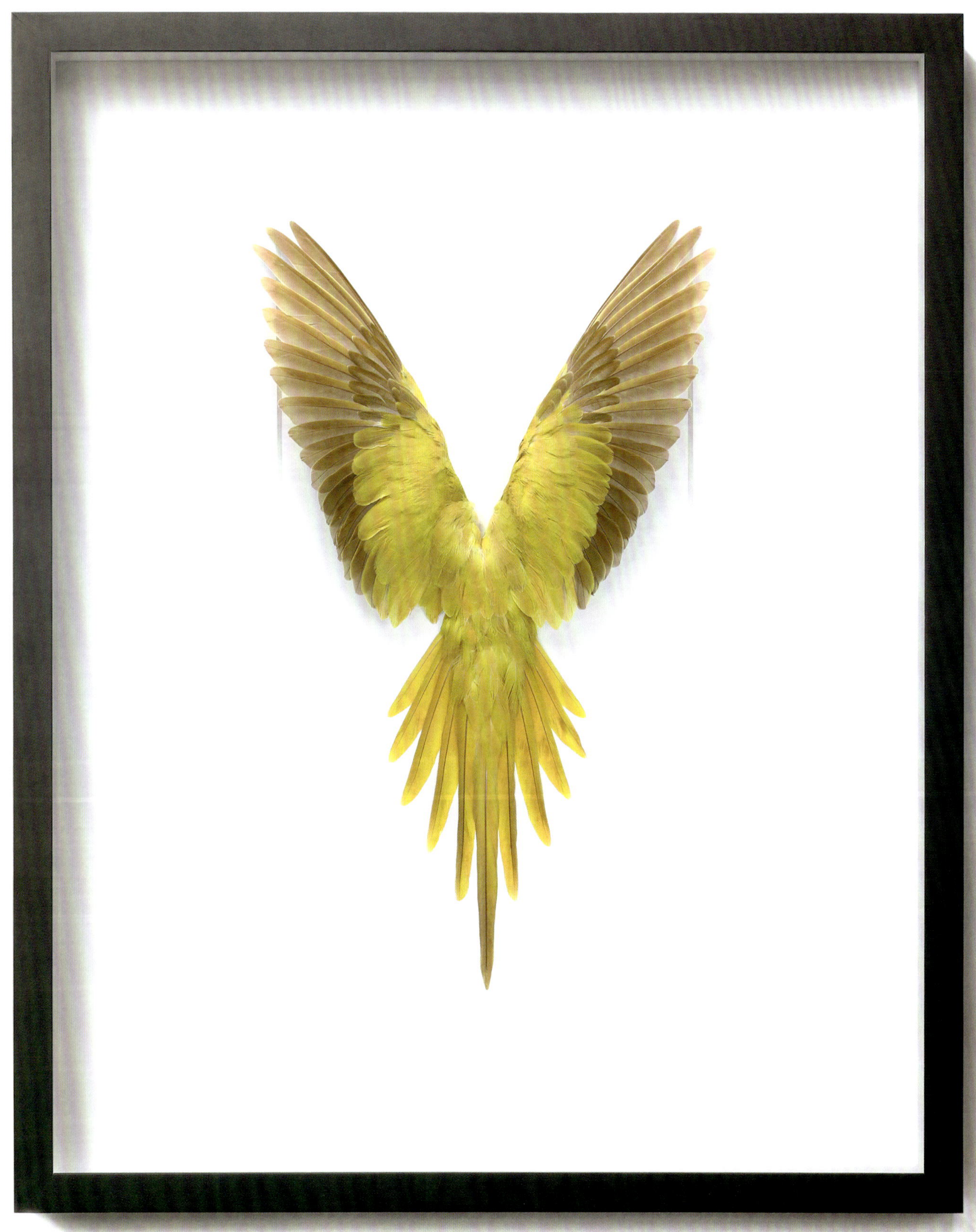

Golden Olive Ring-Necked Parrot

India

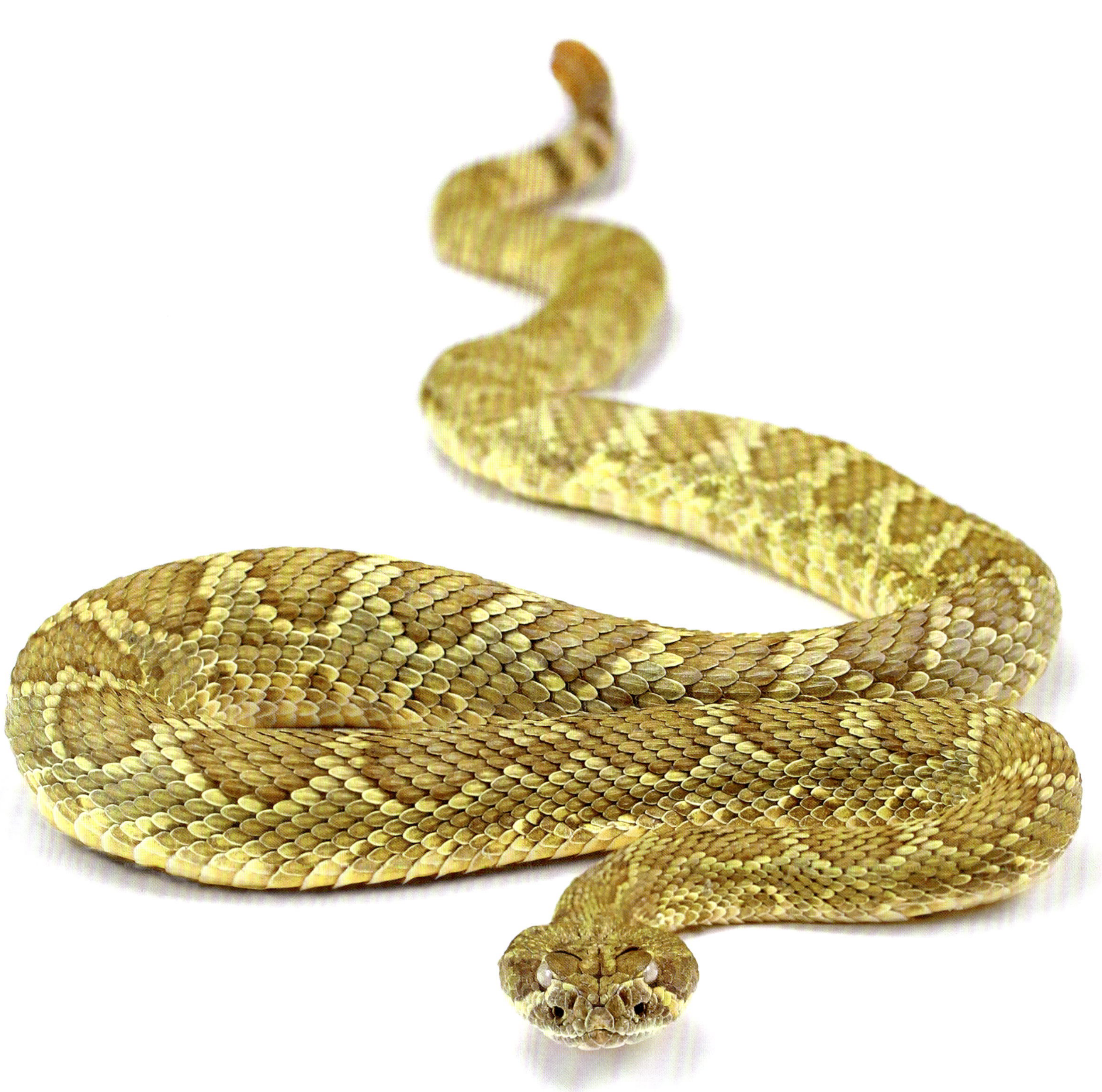

Pacific Rattlesnake

Western United States

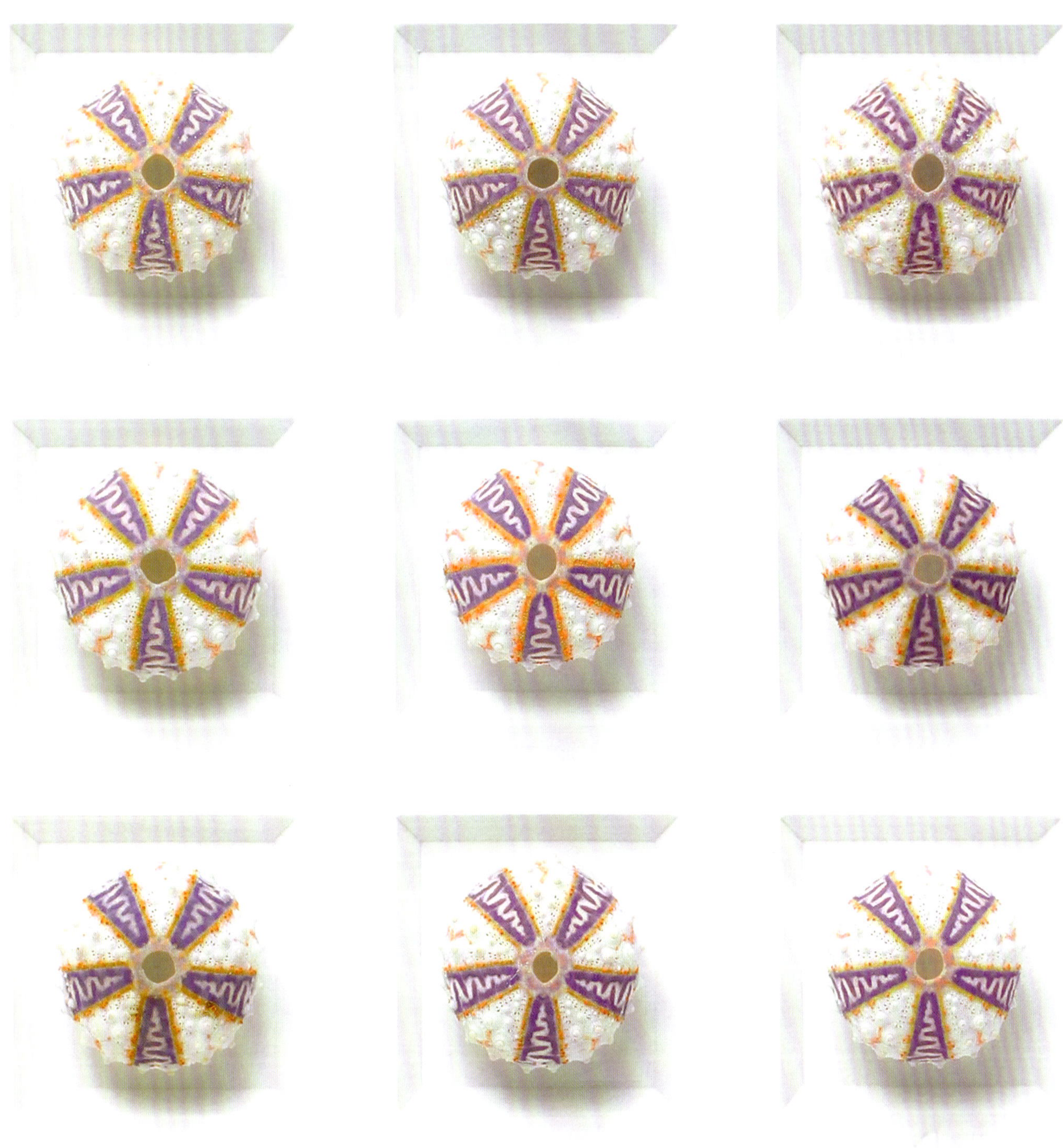

Exquisite Urchins

New Caledonia

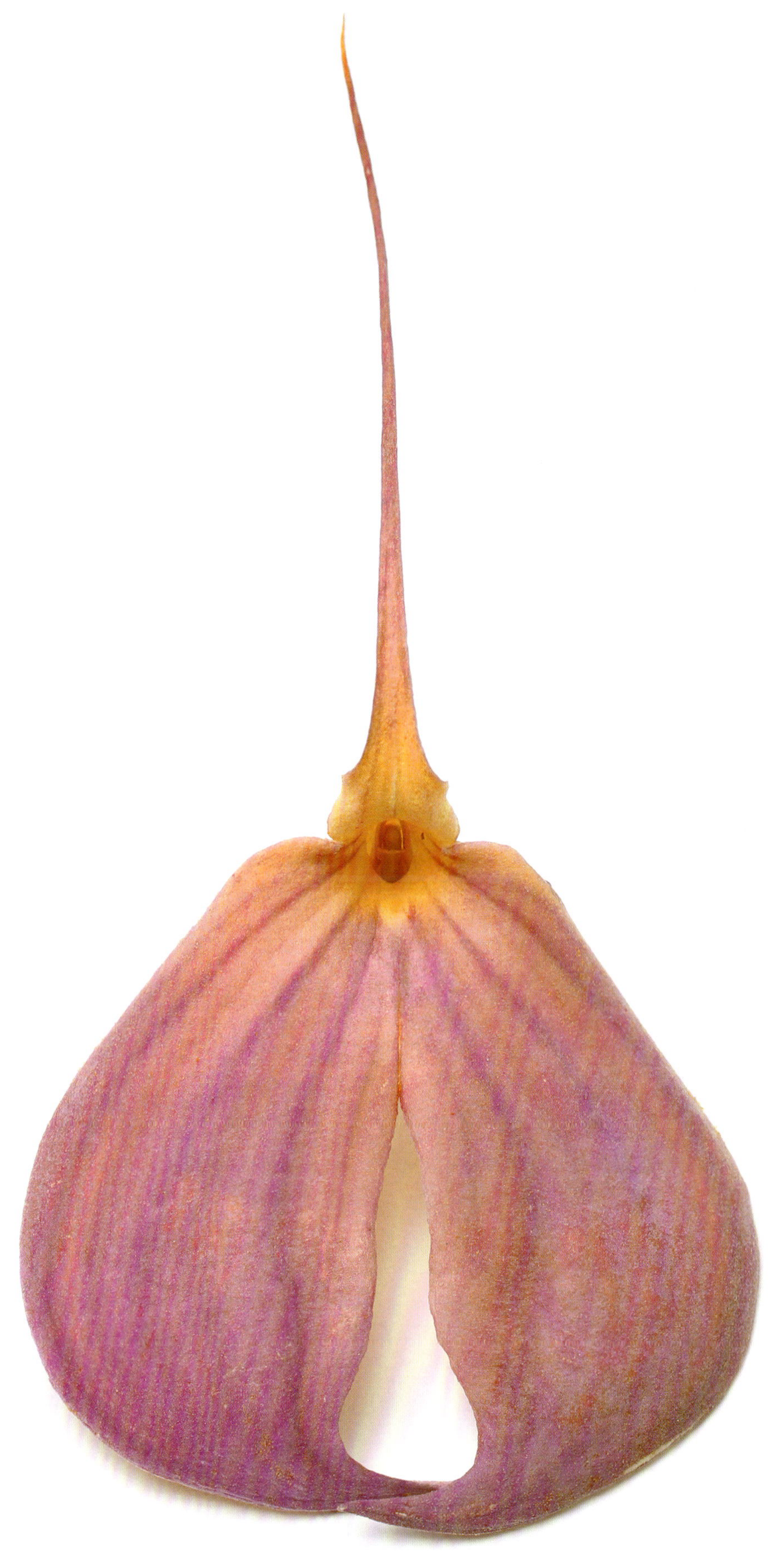

Dracula Orchid Bloom

Ecuador

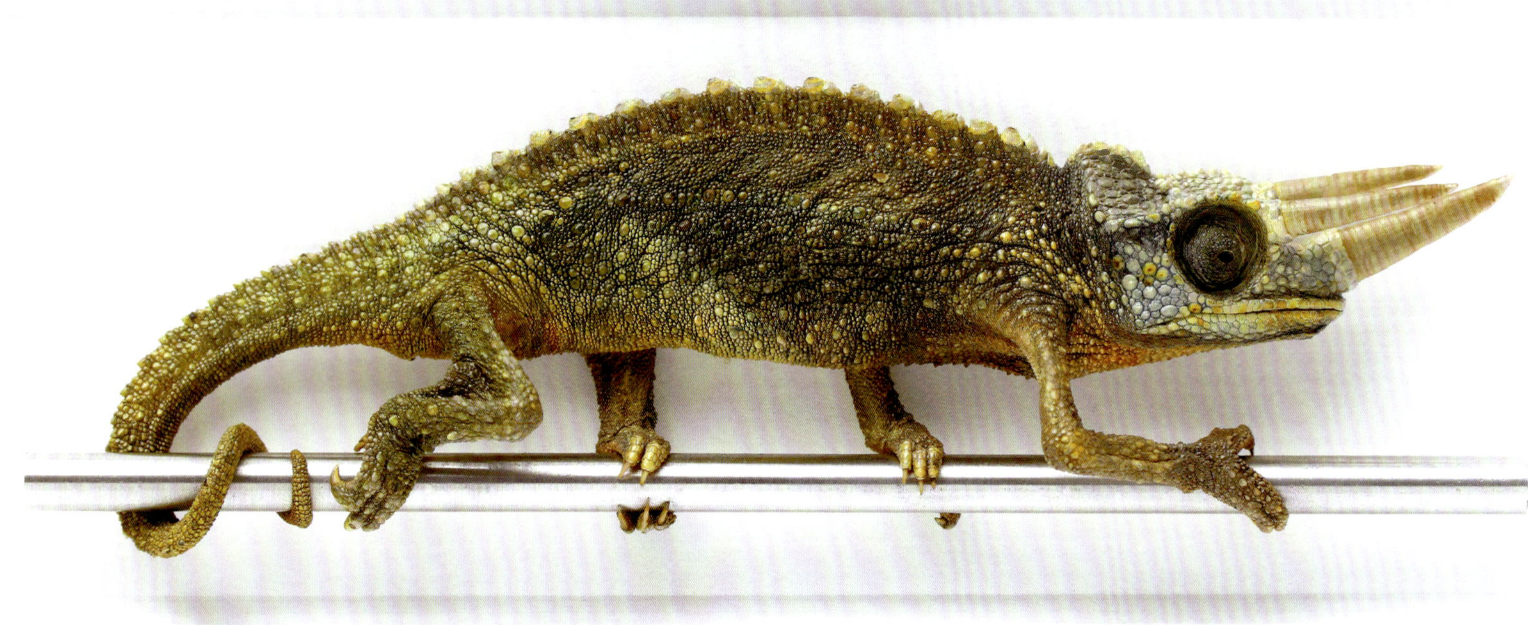

Jackson's Chameleon

Kenya

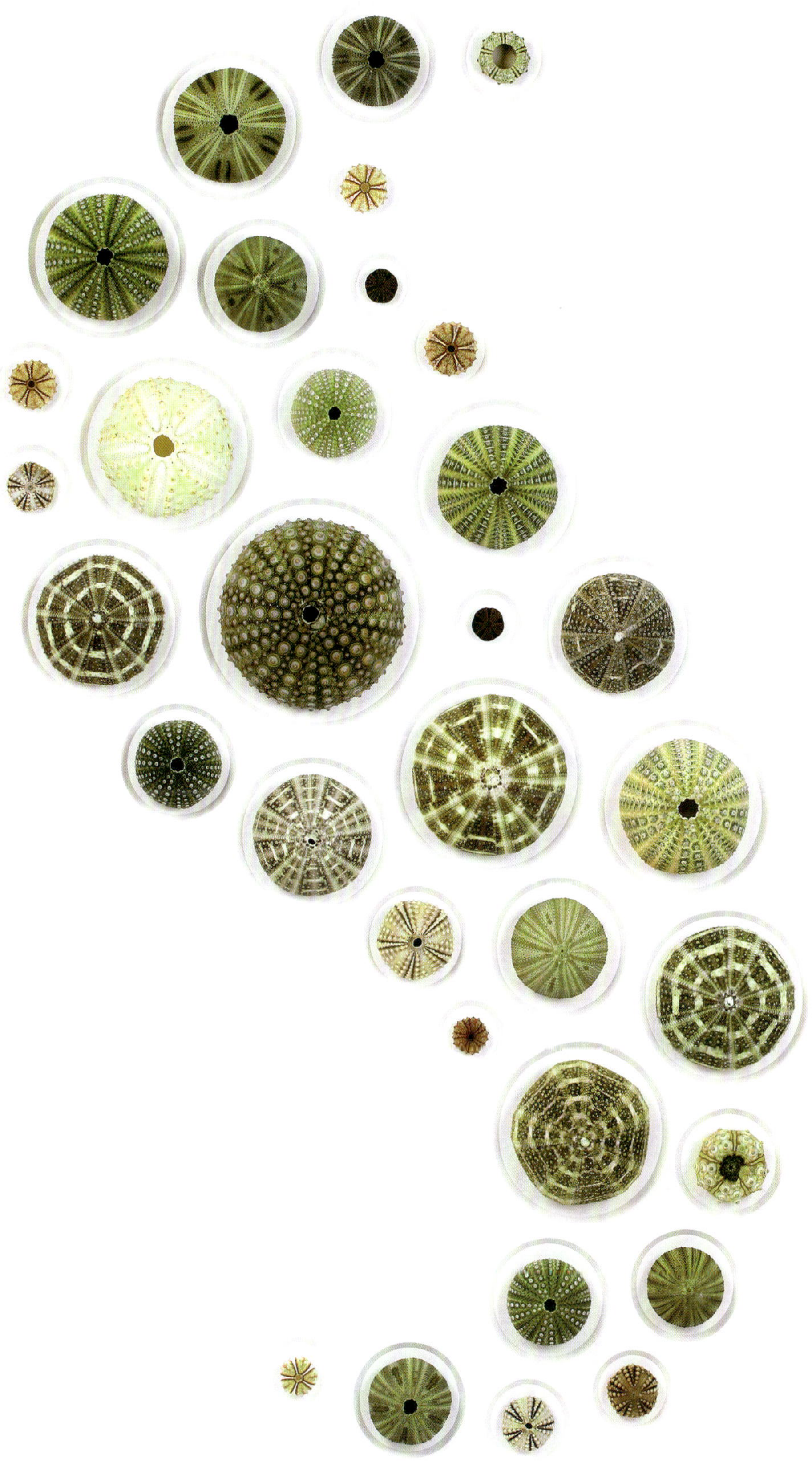

Urchin Spheres

Thailand, Philippines, United States, Mexico

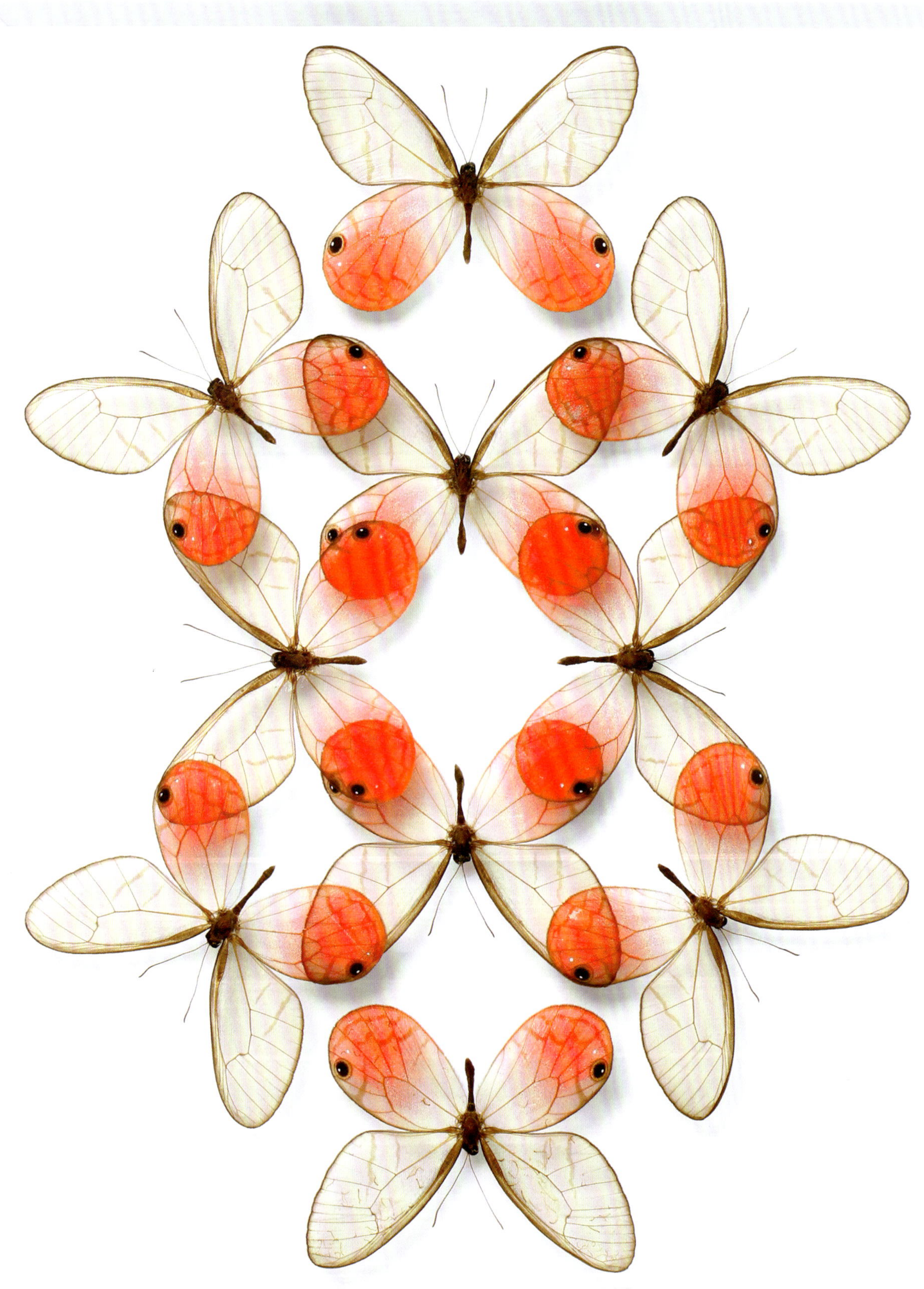

Cytheras

Peru

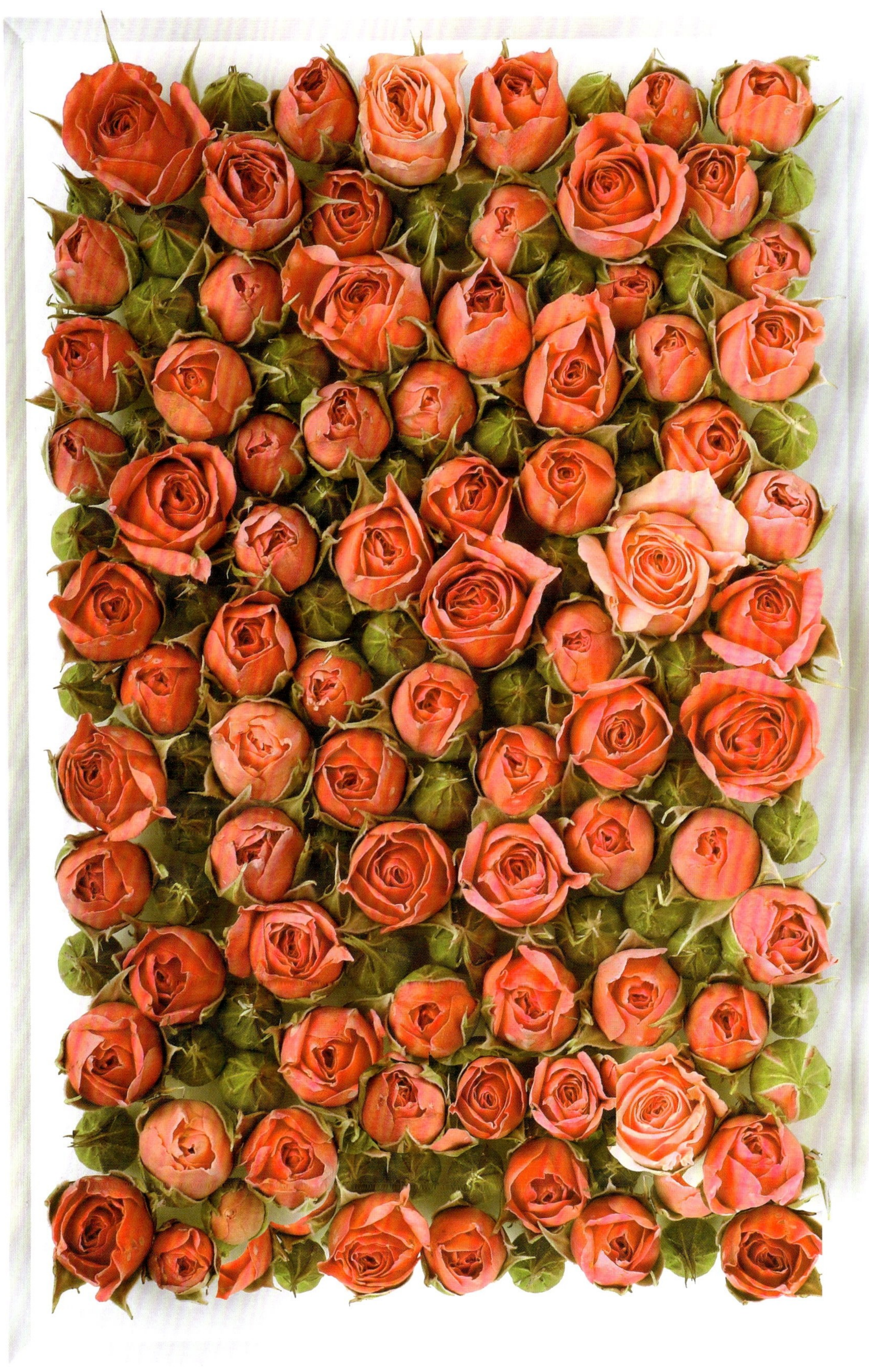

Spray Roses

Ecuador

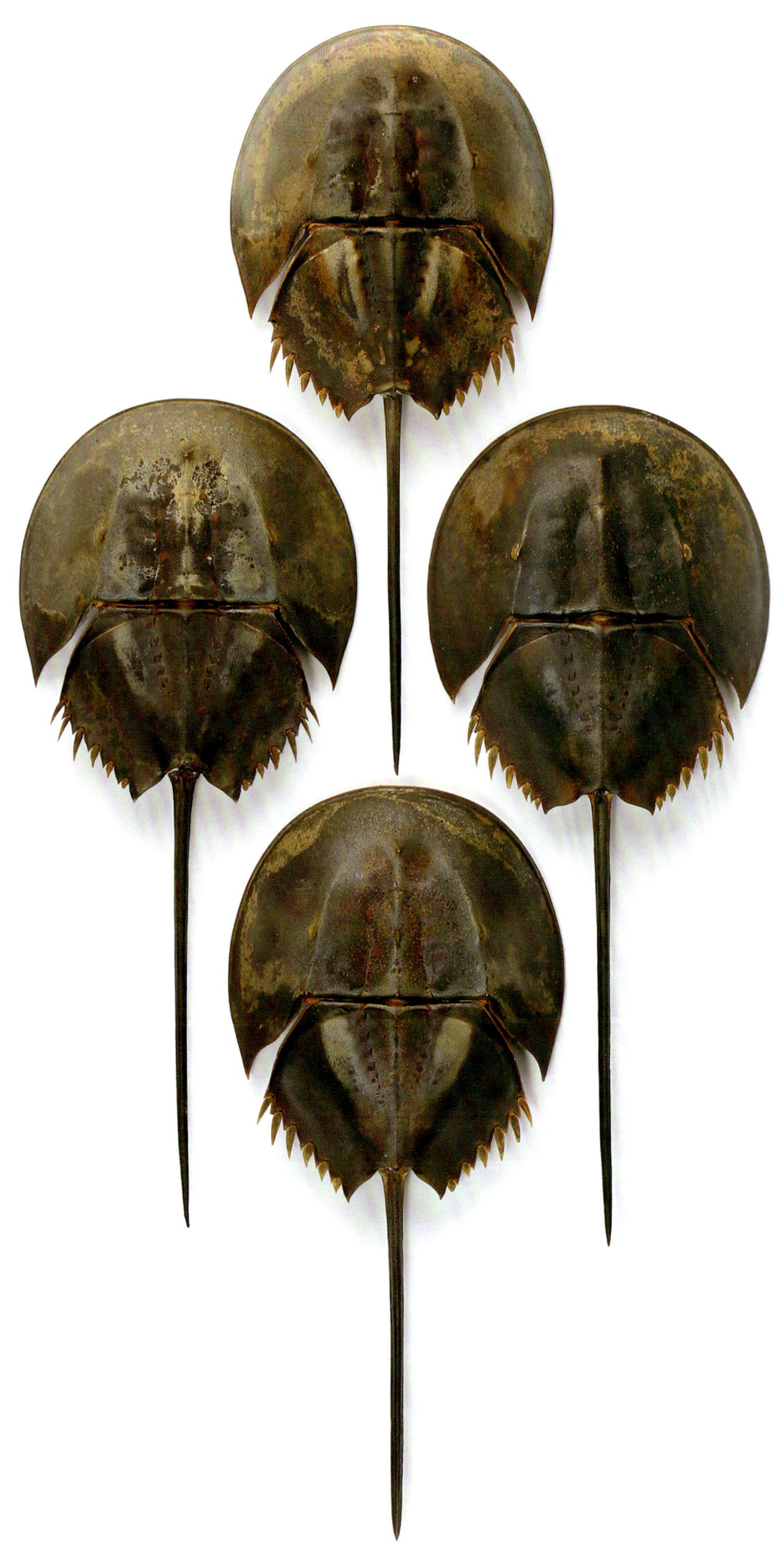

Horseshoe Crab Formation

Philippines

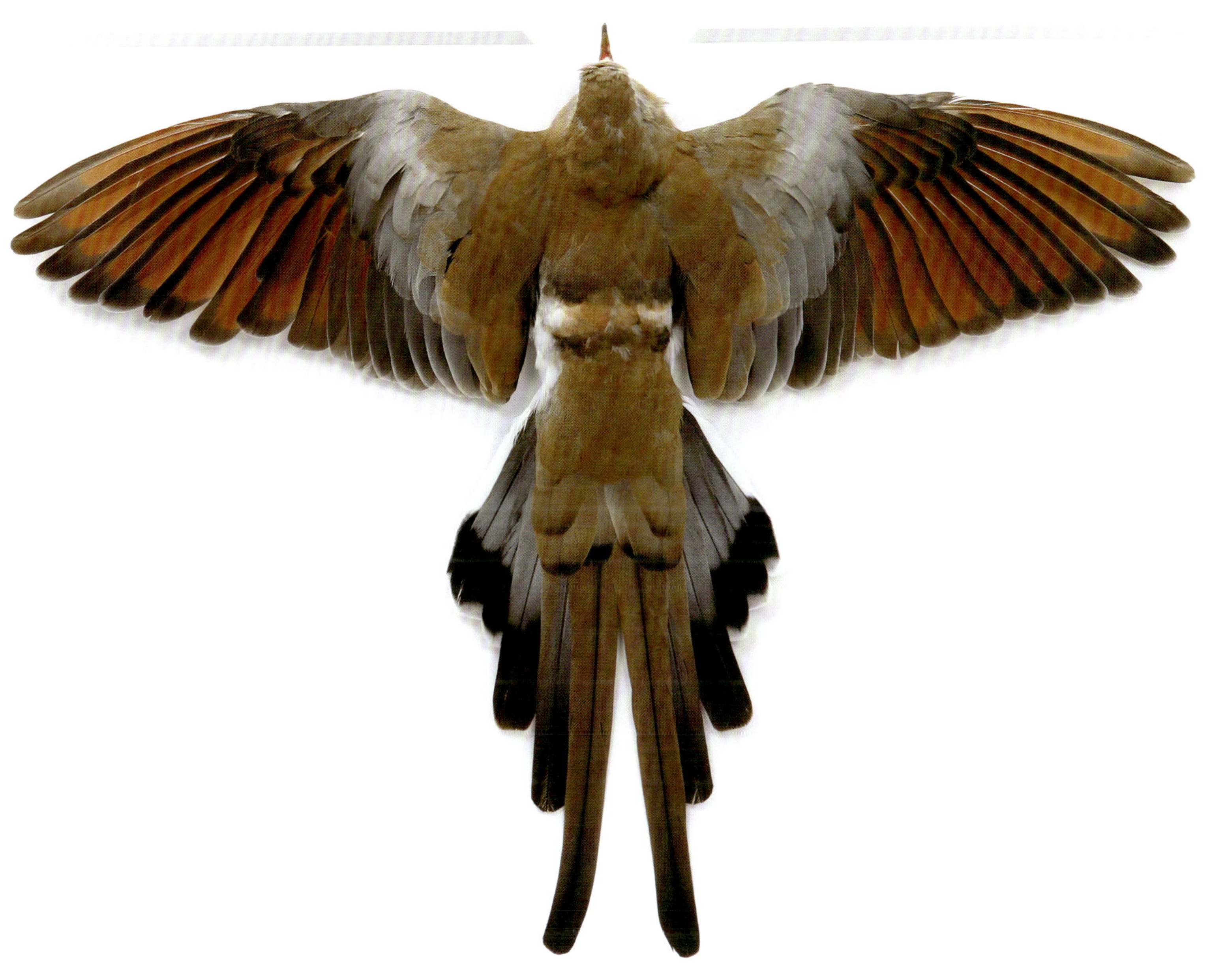

Cape Dove

Egypt

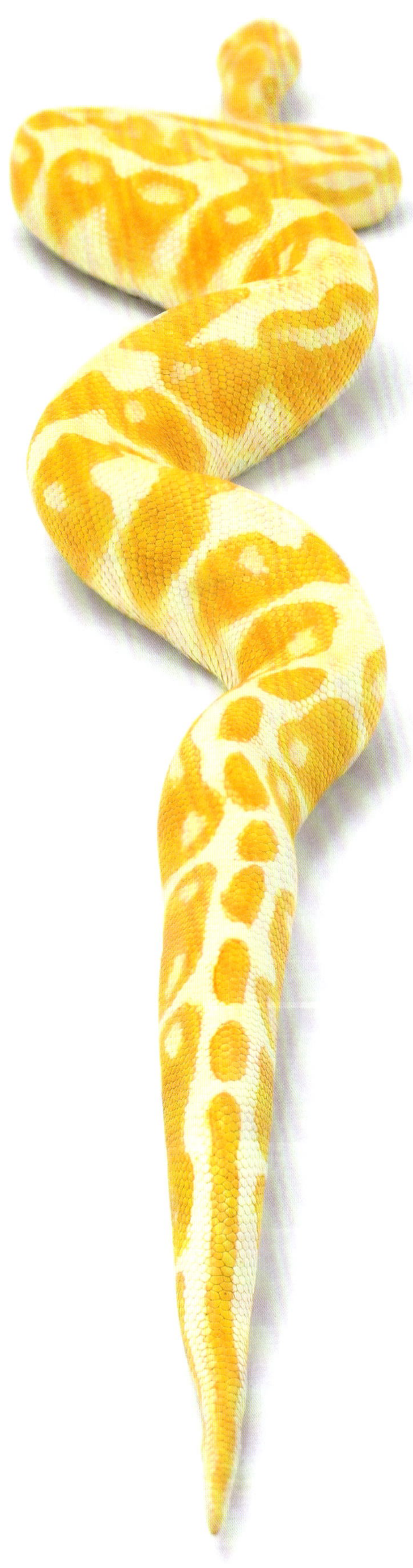

Amelanistic Burmese Python

Vietnam

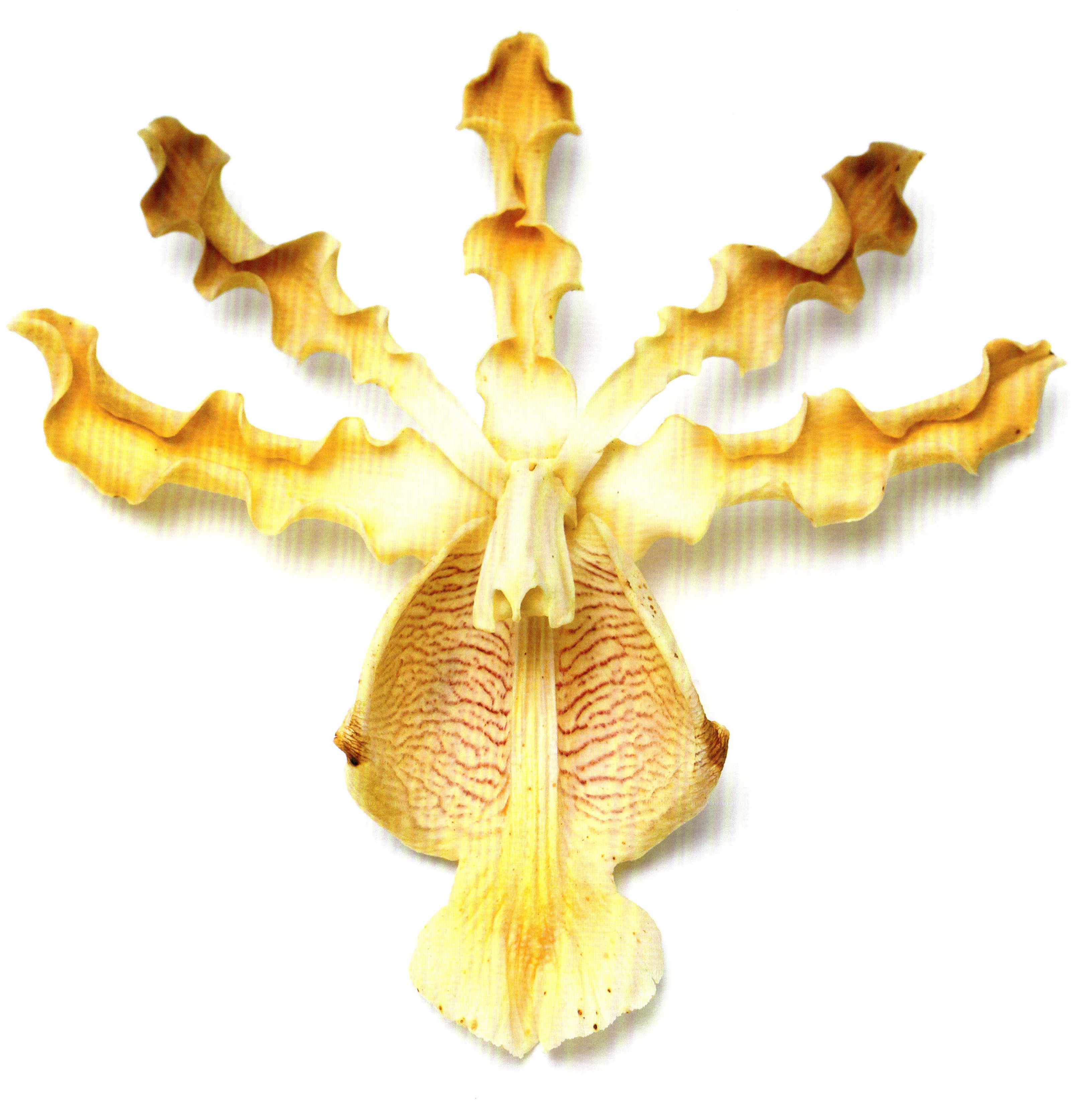

Preserved Ant-Loving Orchid

Venezuela

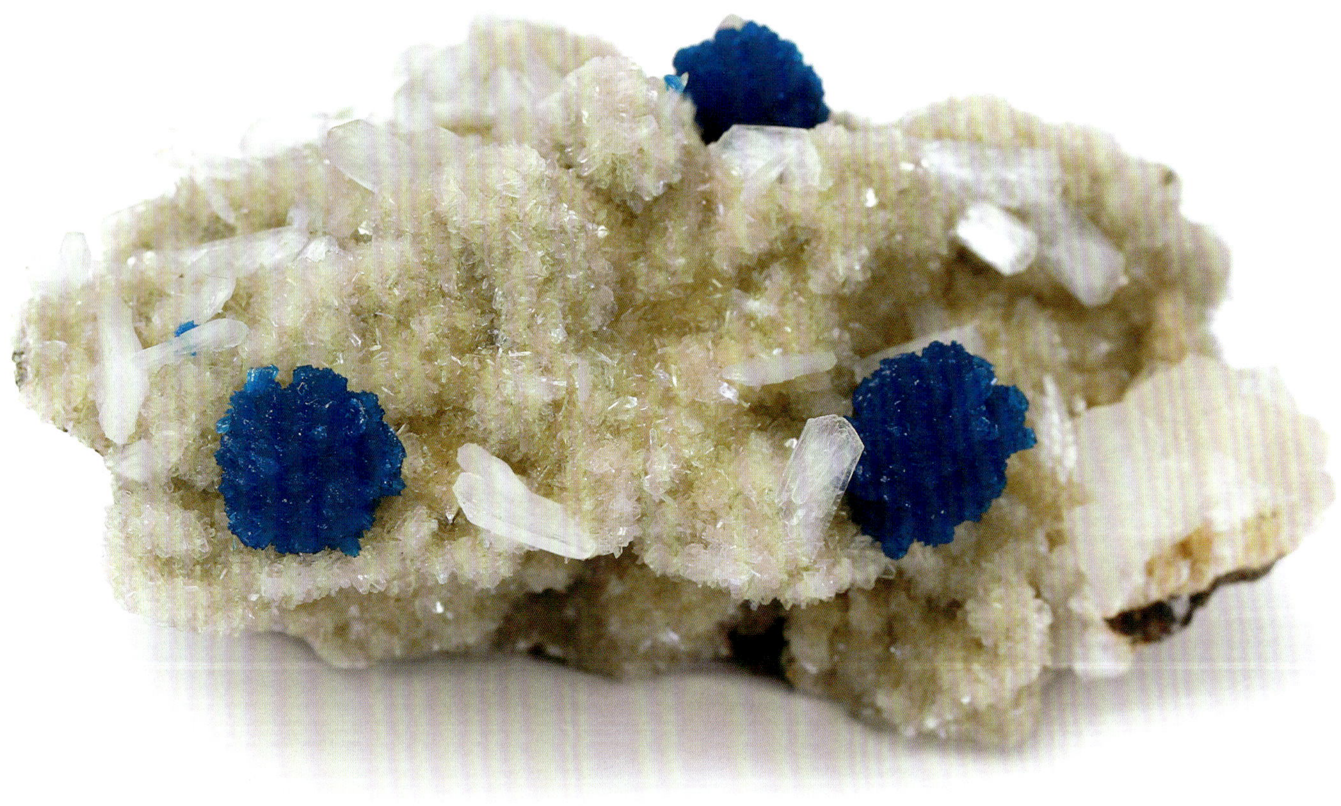

Cavansite and Stilbite on Heulandite

India

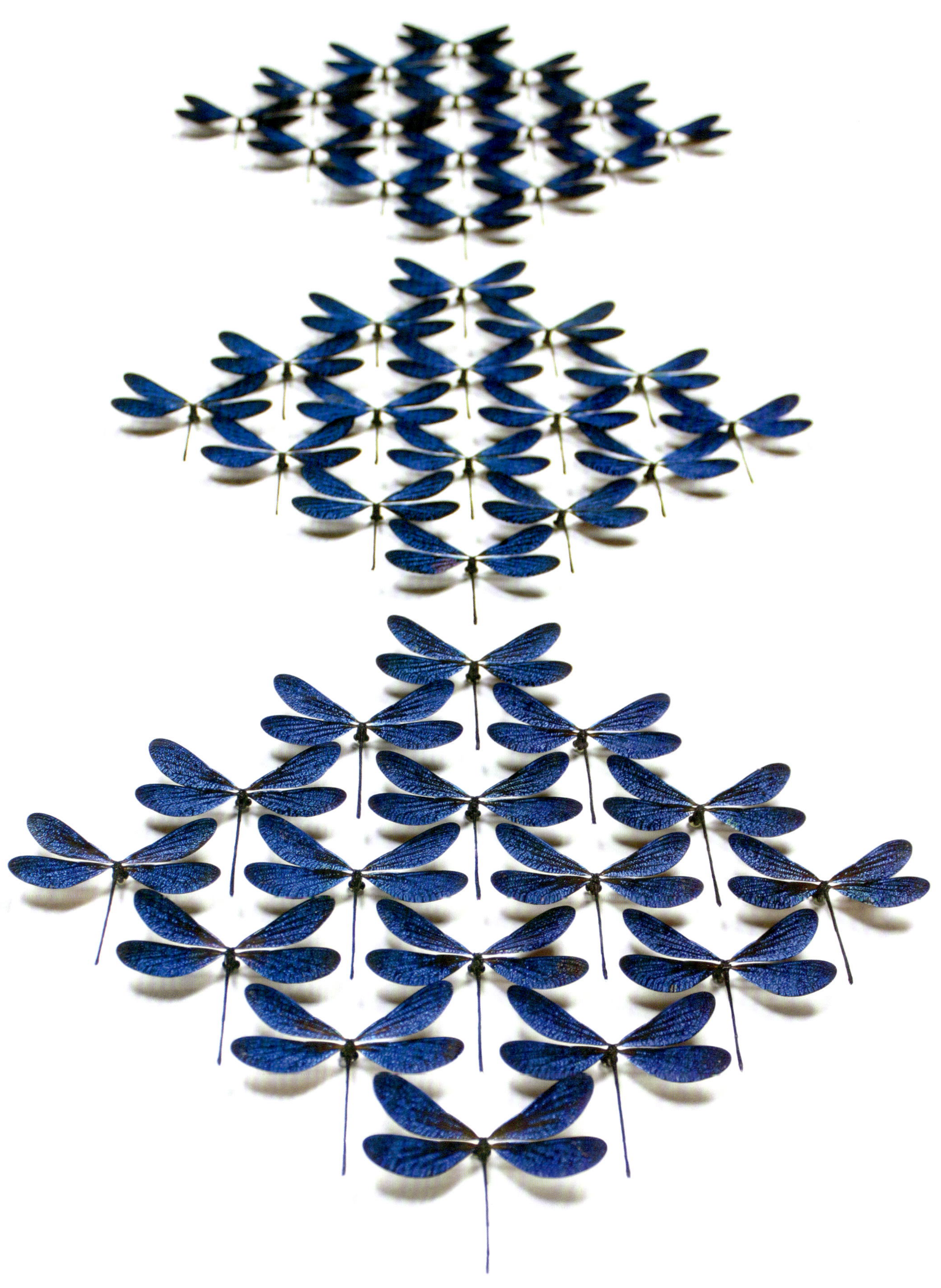

Damselfly Diamonds

Philippines

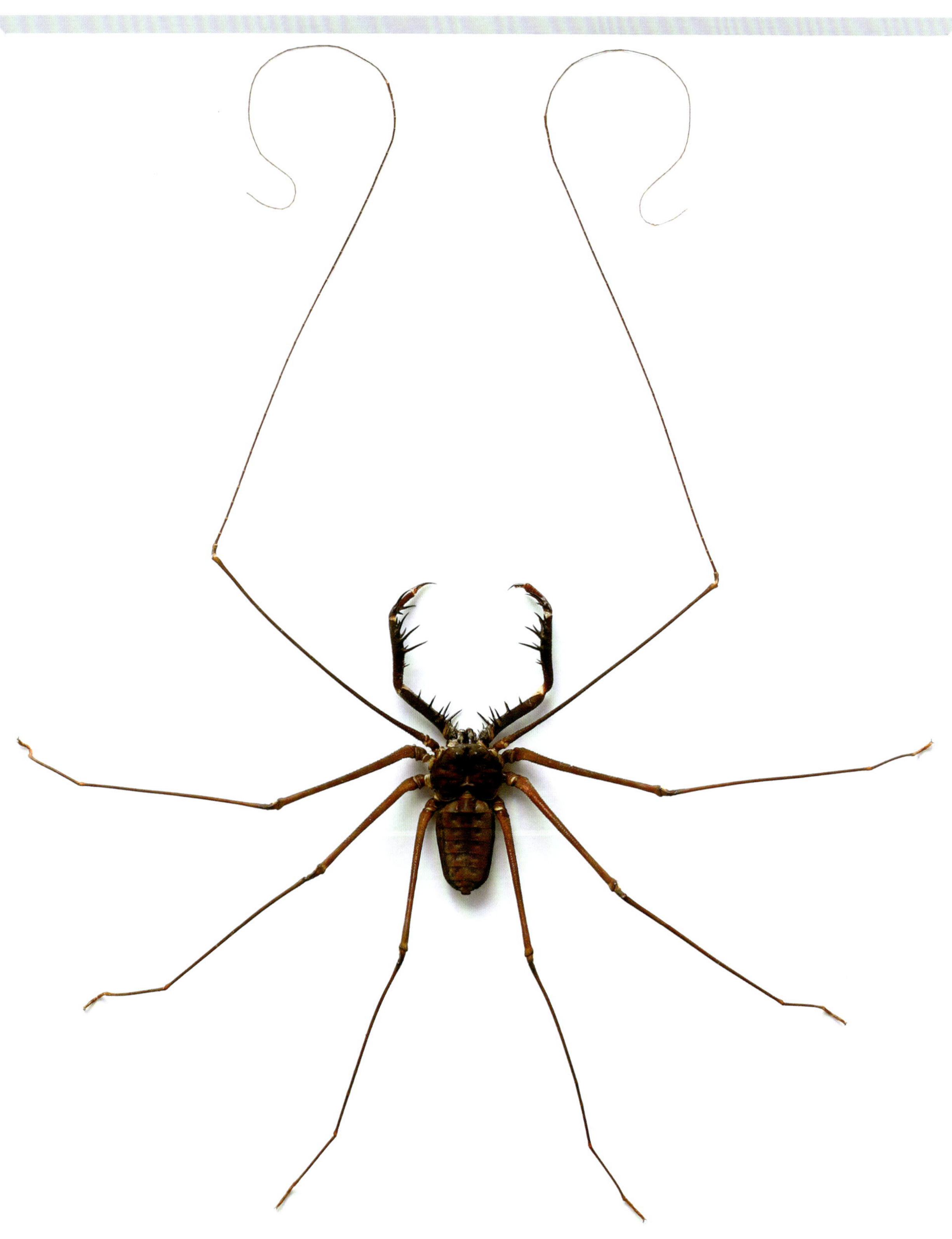

Whip Scorpion

Peru

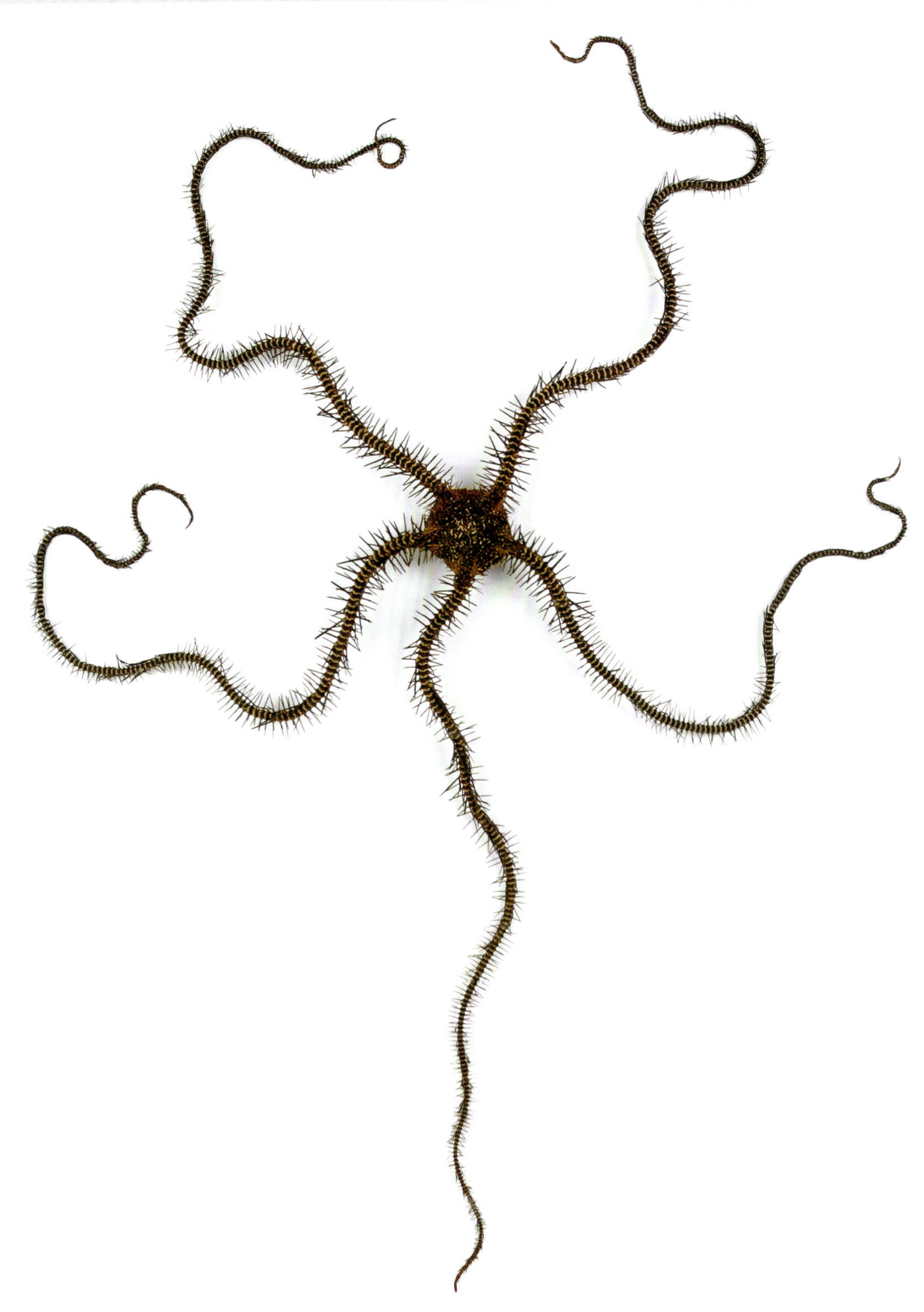

Serpent Star

Borneo

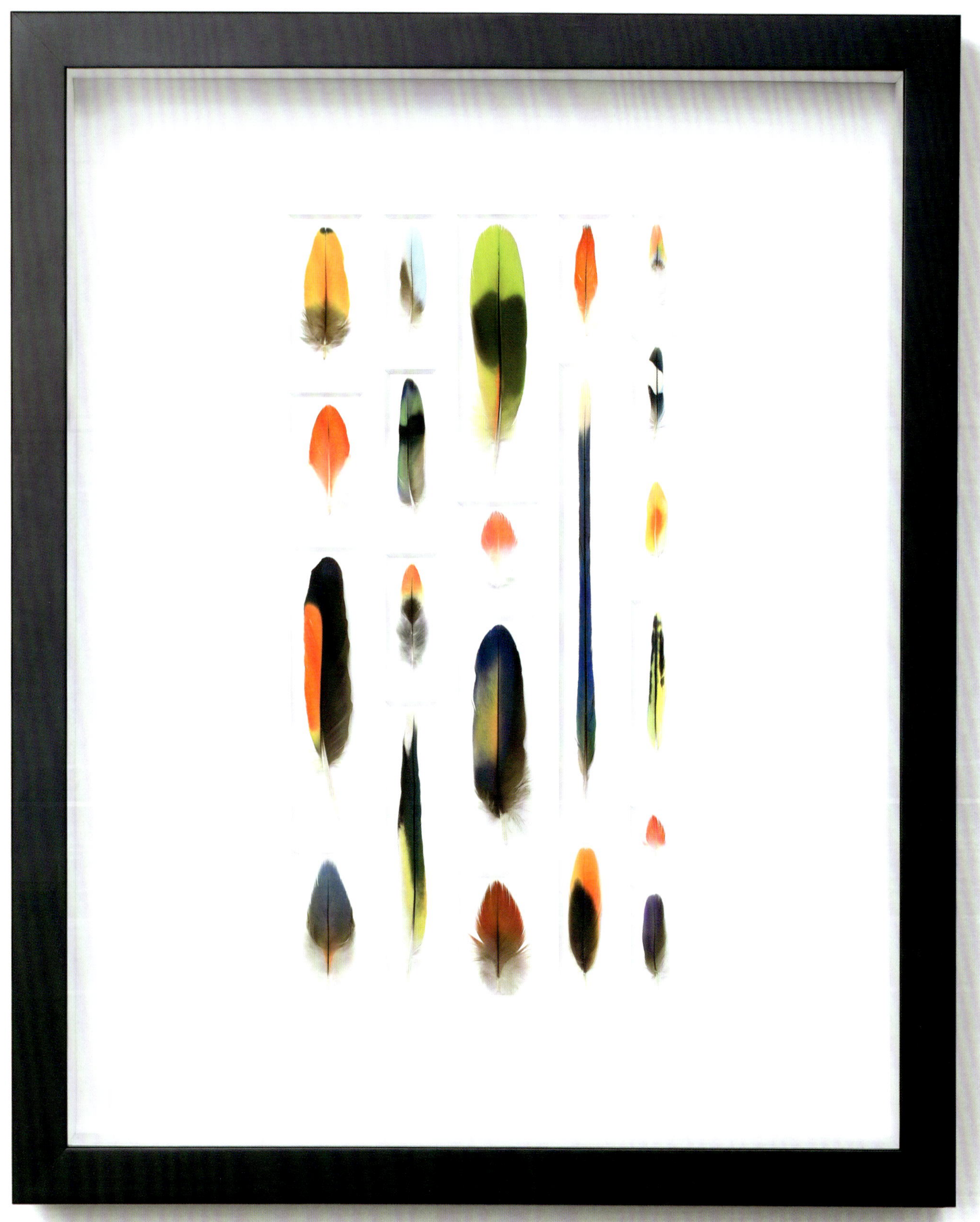

Feather Mosaic

Worldwide

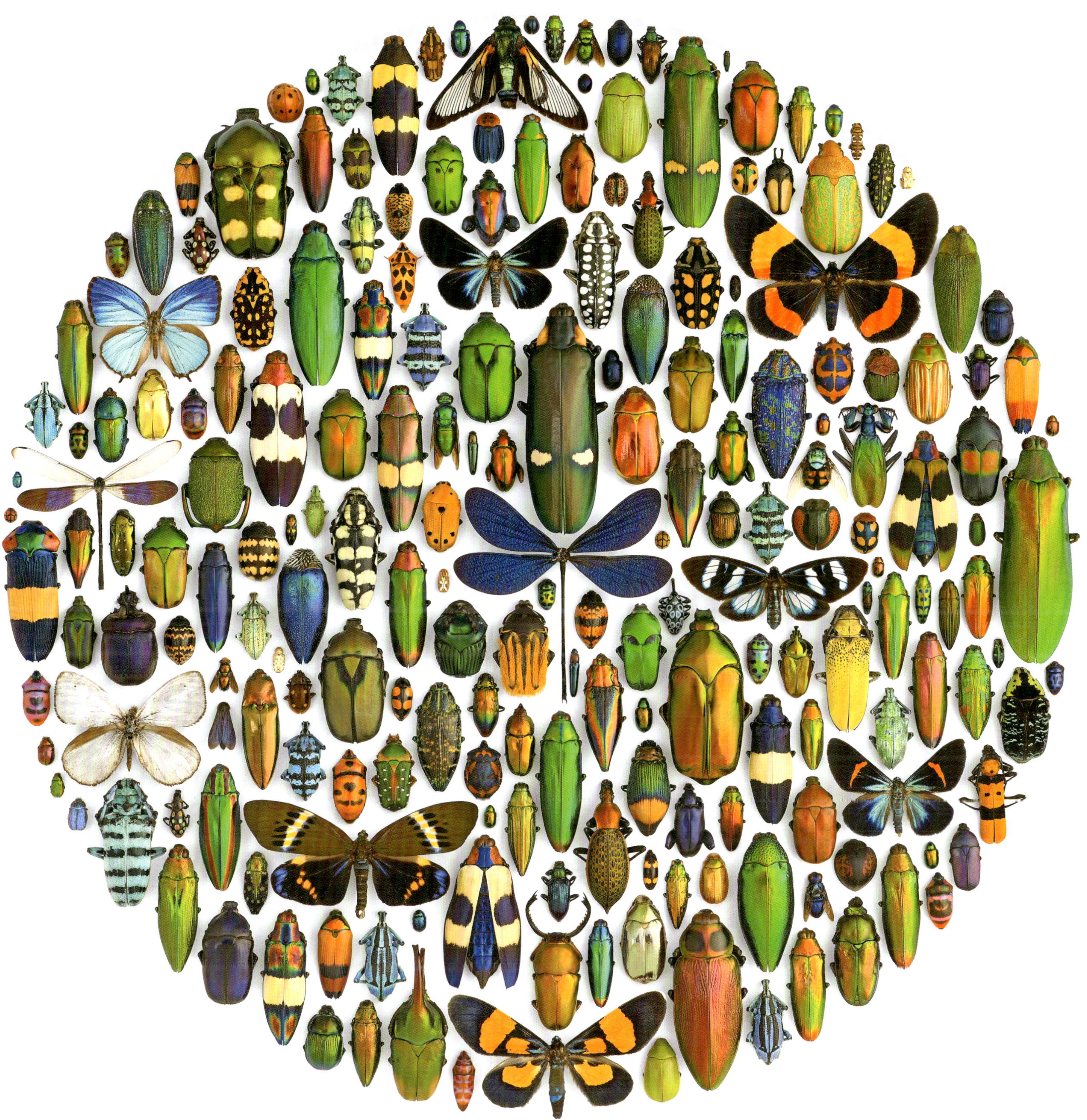

Limited Aesthetica

Worldwide

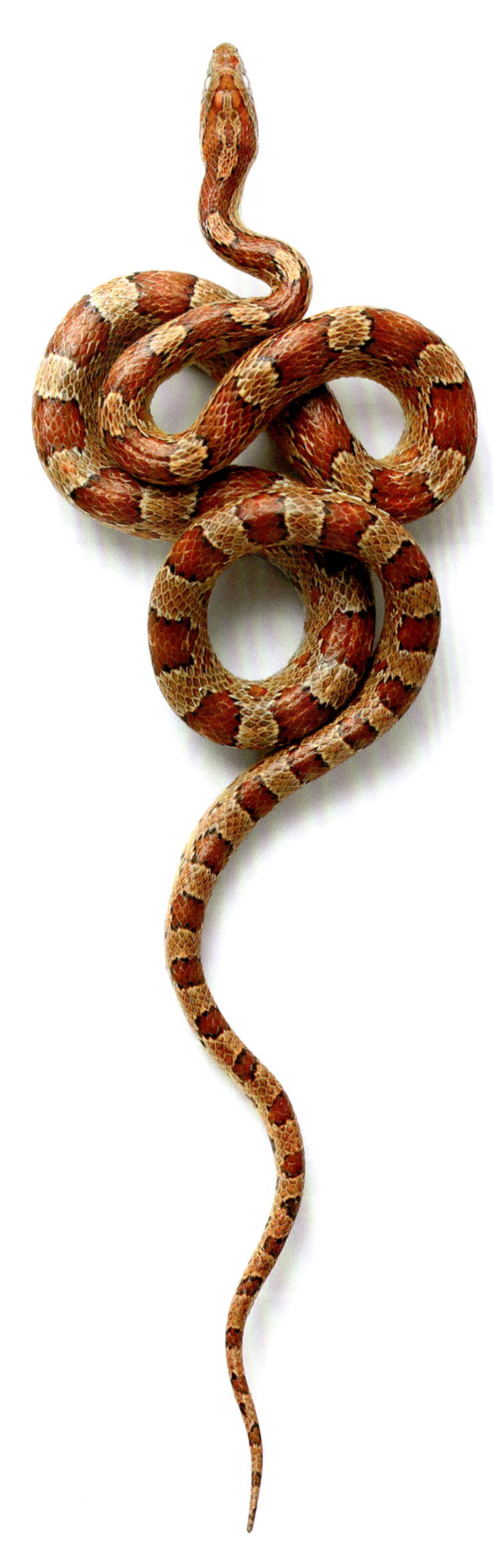

Corn Snake

United States

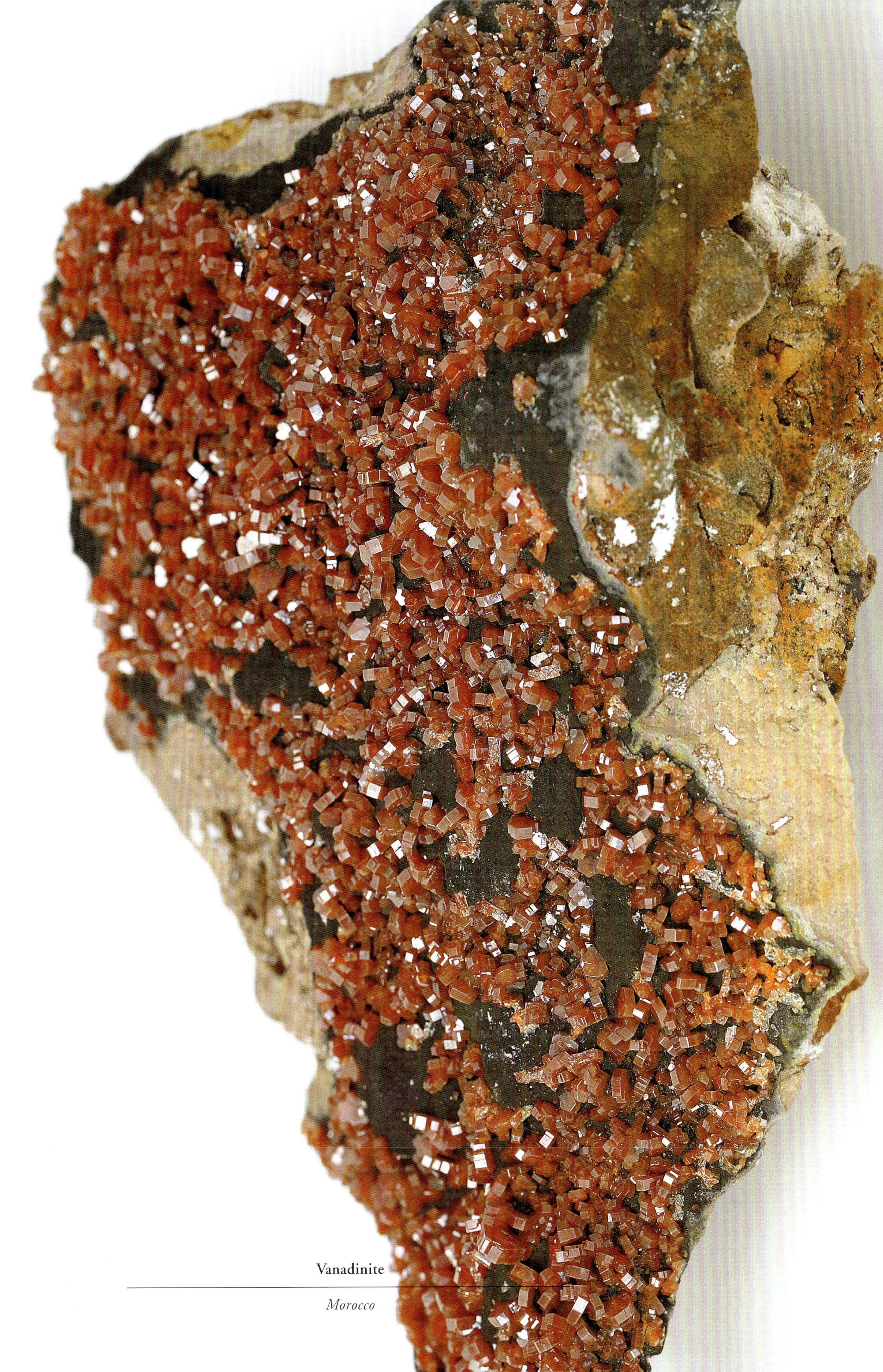

Vanadinite

Morocco

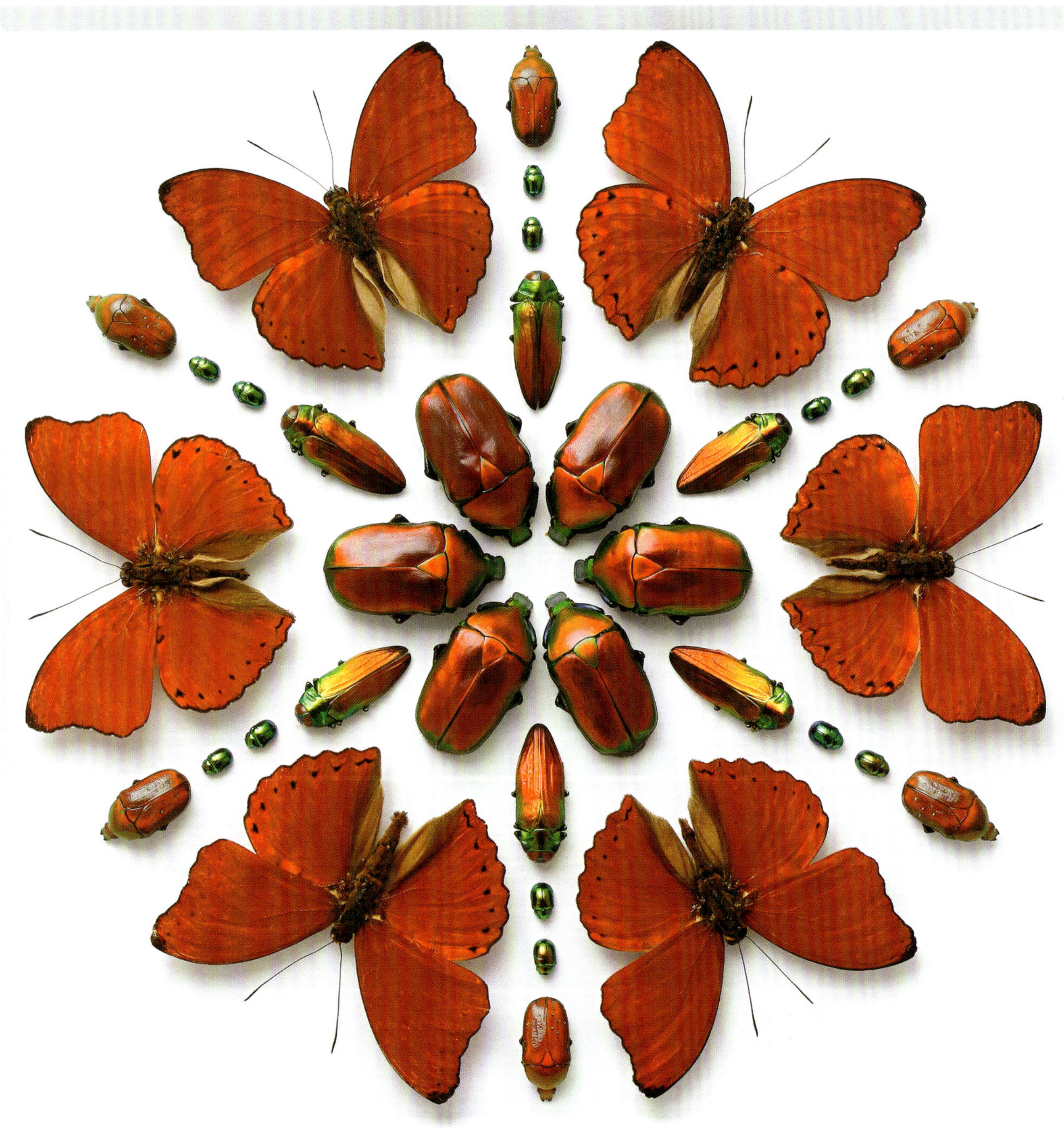

Sangaris Prism

Thailand, Indonesia, Central African Republic, Cameroon

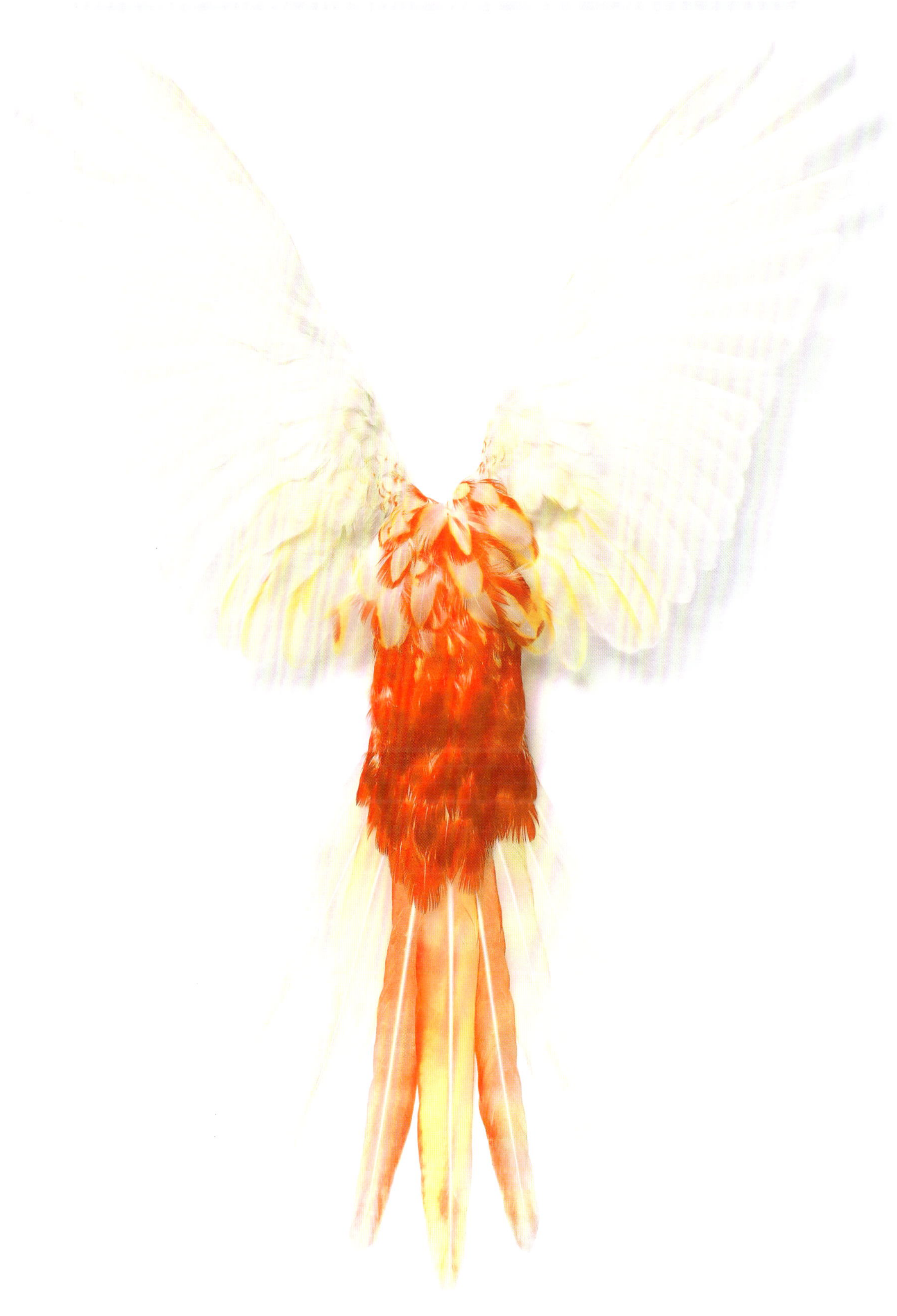

Rubino Eastern Rosella

Australia

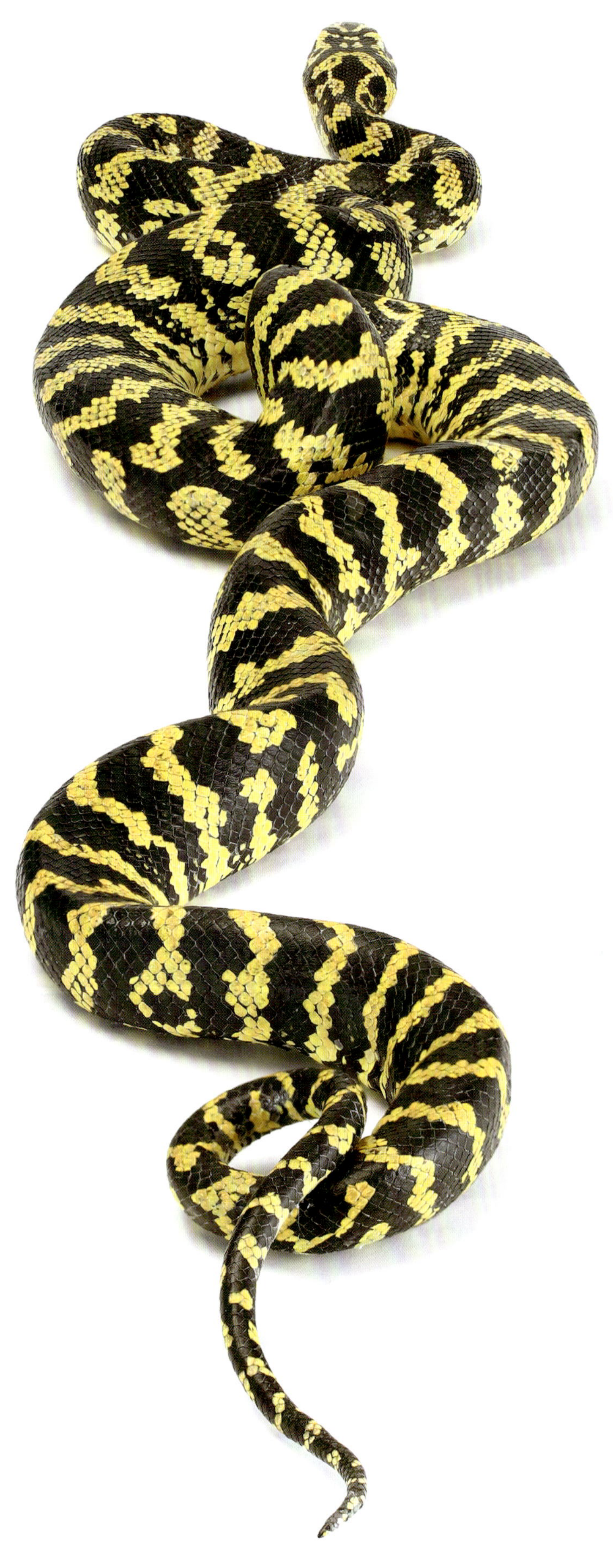

Carpet Python

Australia

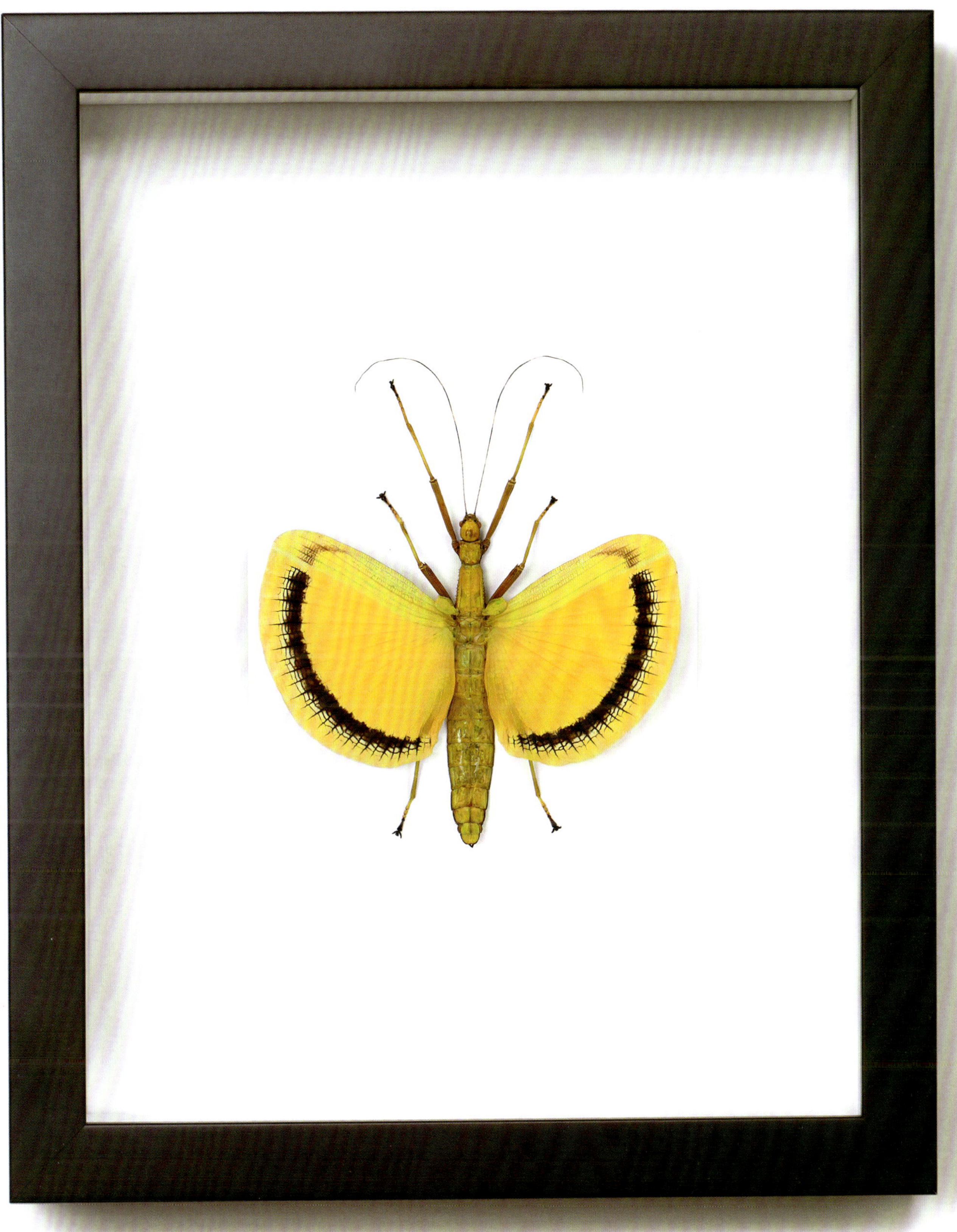

Sulphur Walking Stick

Malaysia

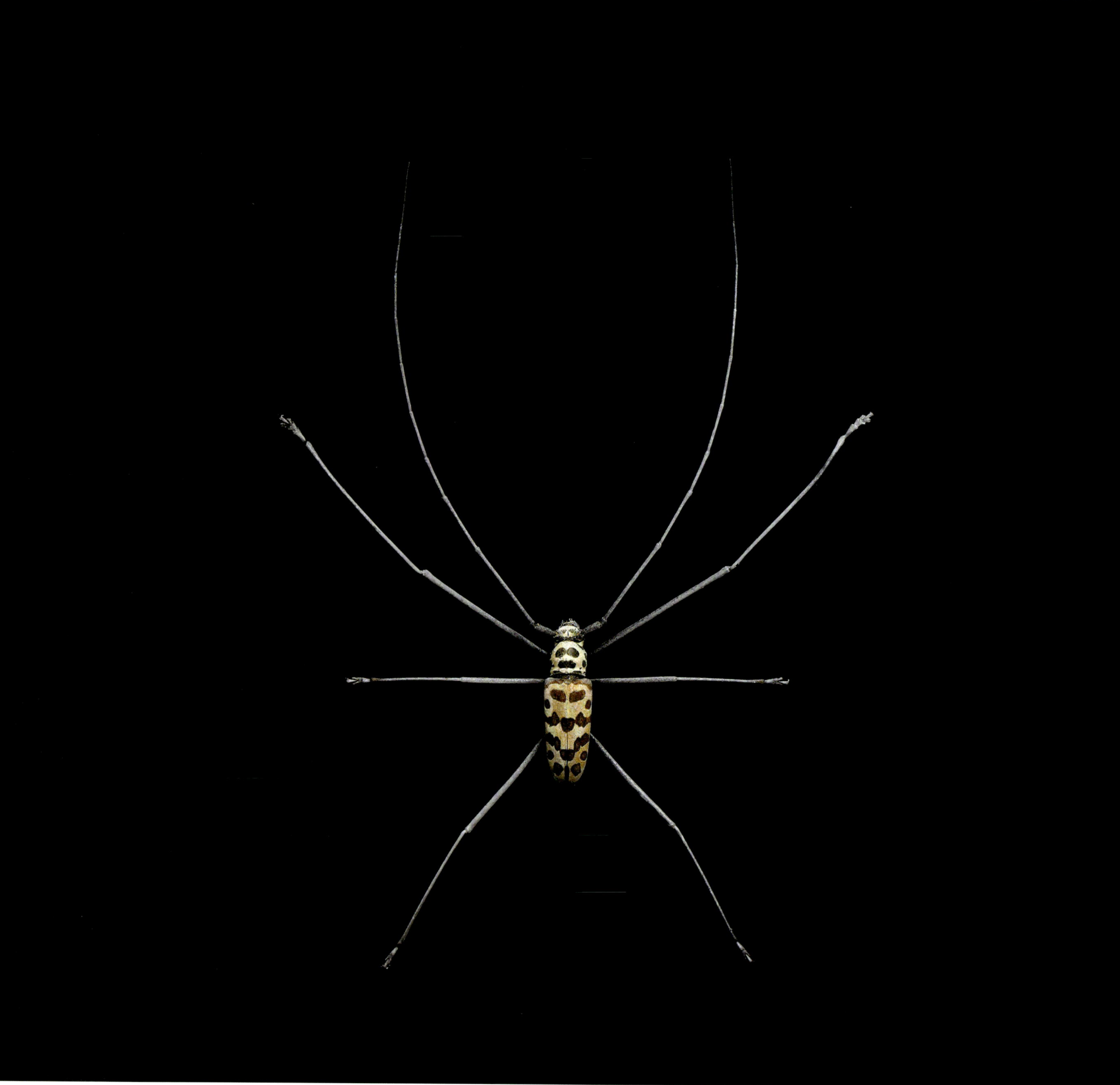

Long-Horned Borer

Thailand

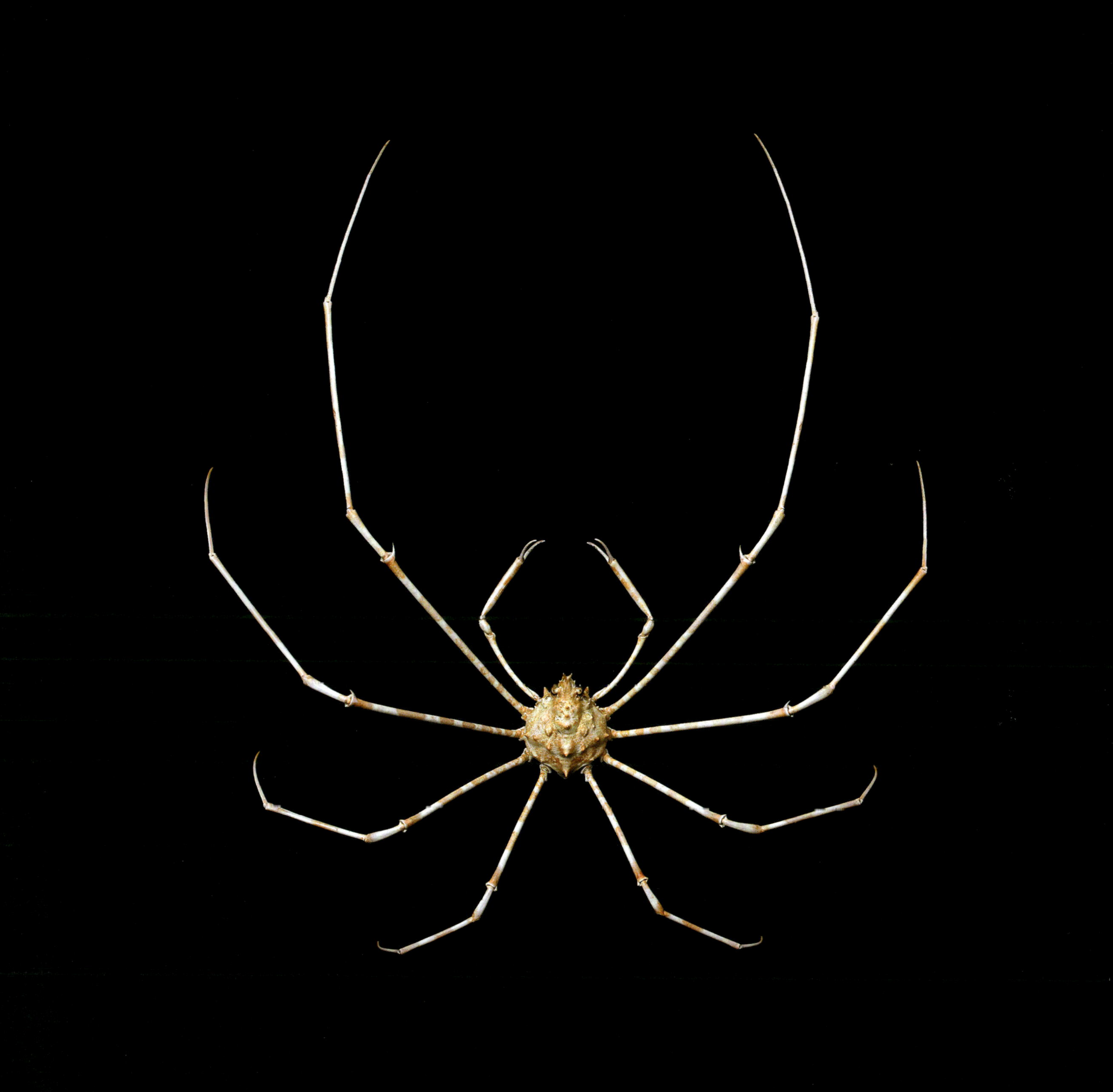

Attenuated Spider Crab

Philippines

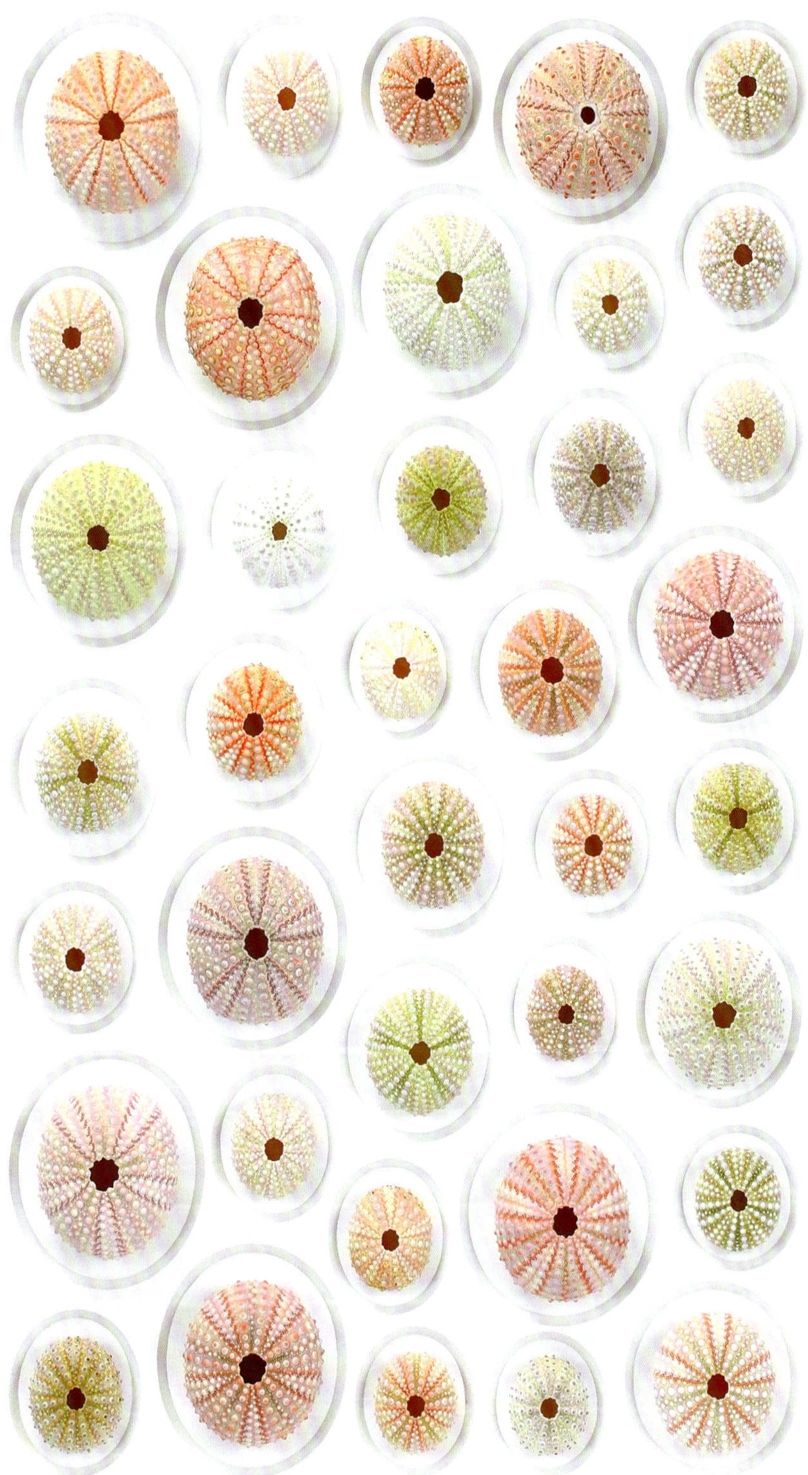

Pastel Urchin Mosaic

Philippines

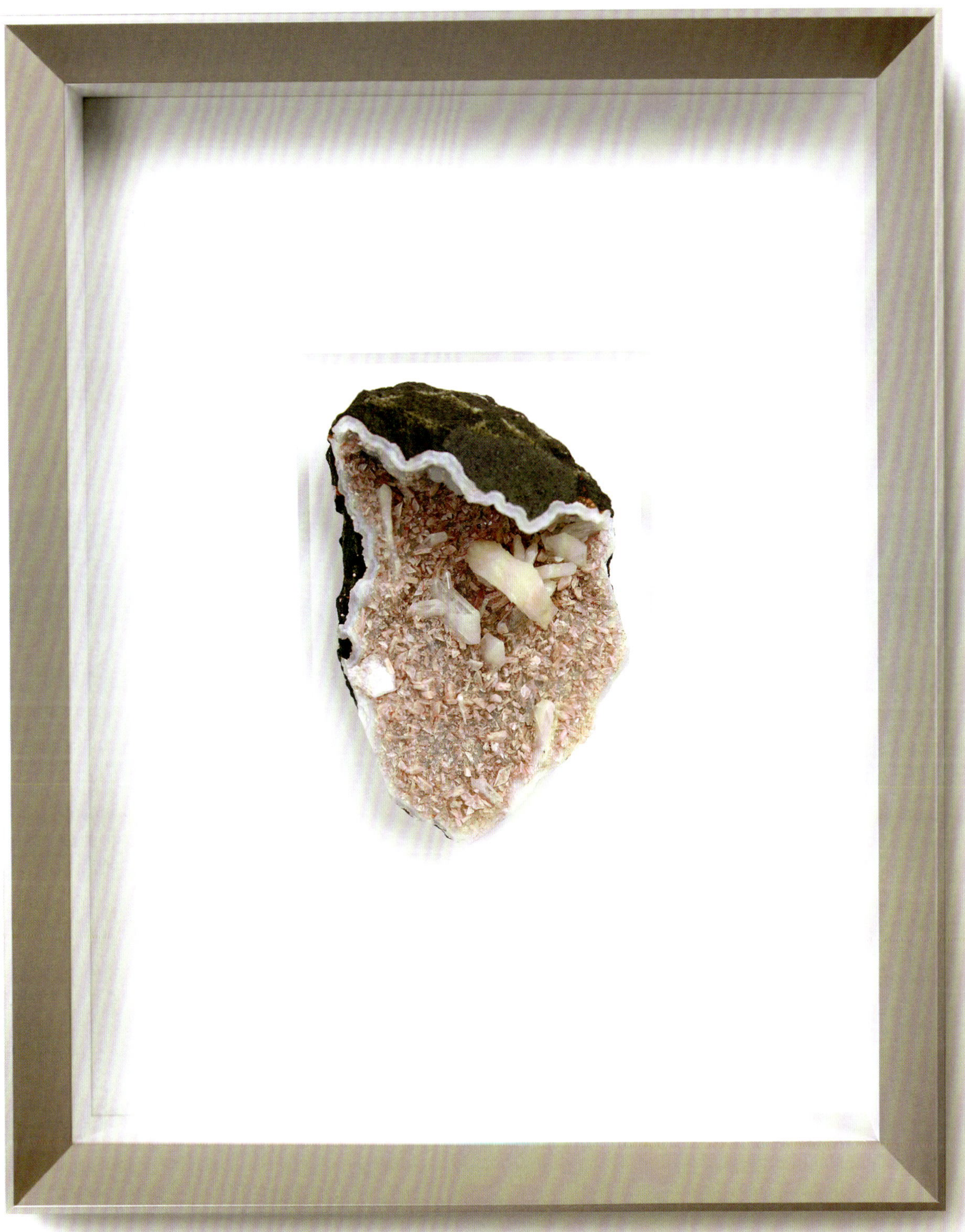

Heulandite and Stilbite

India

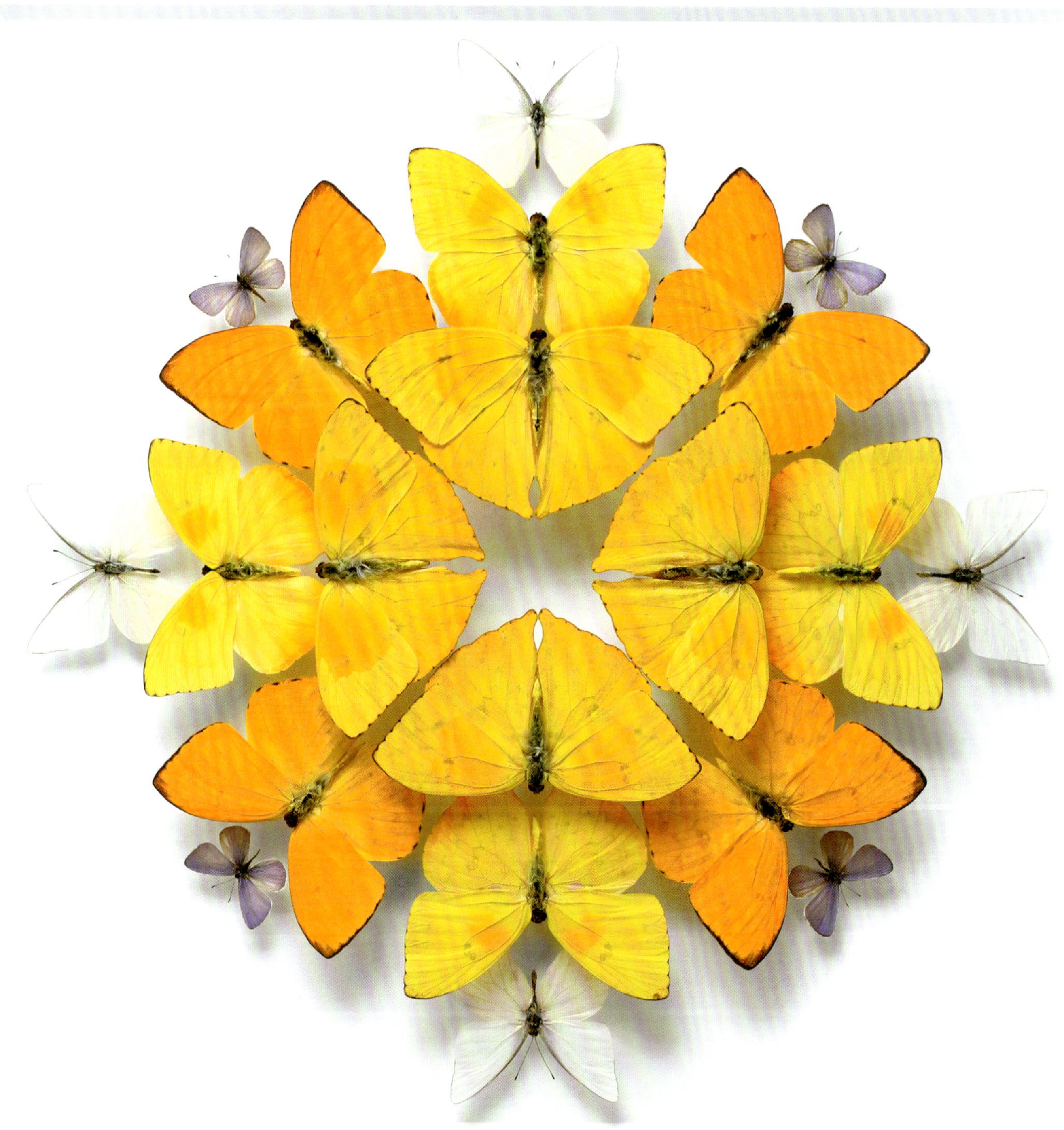

Solar Prism

Peru, Philippines, United States

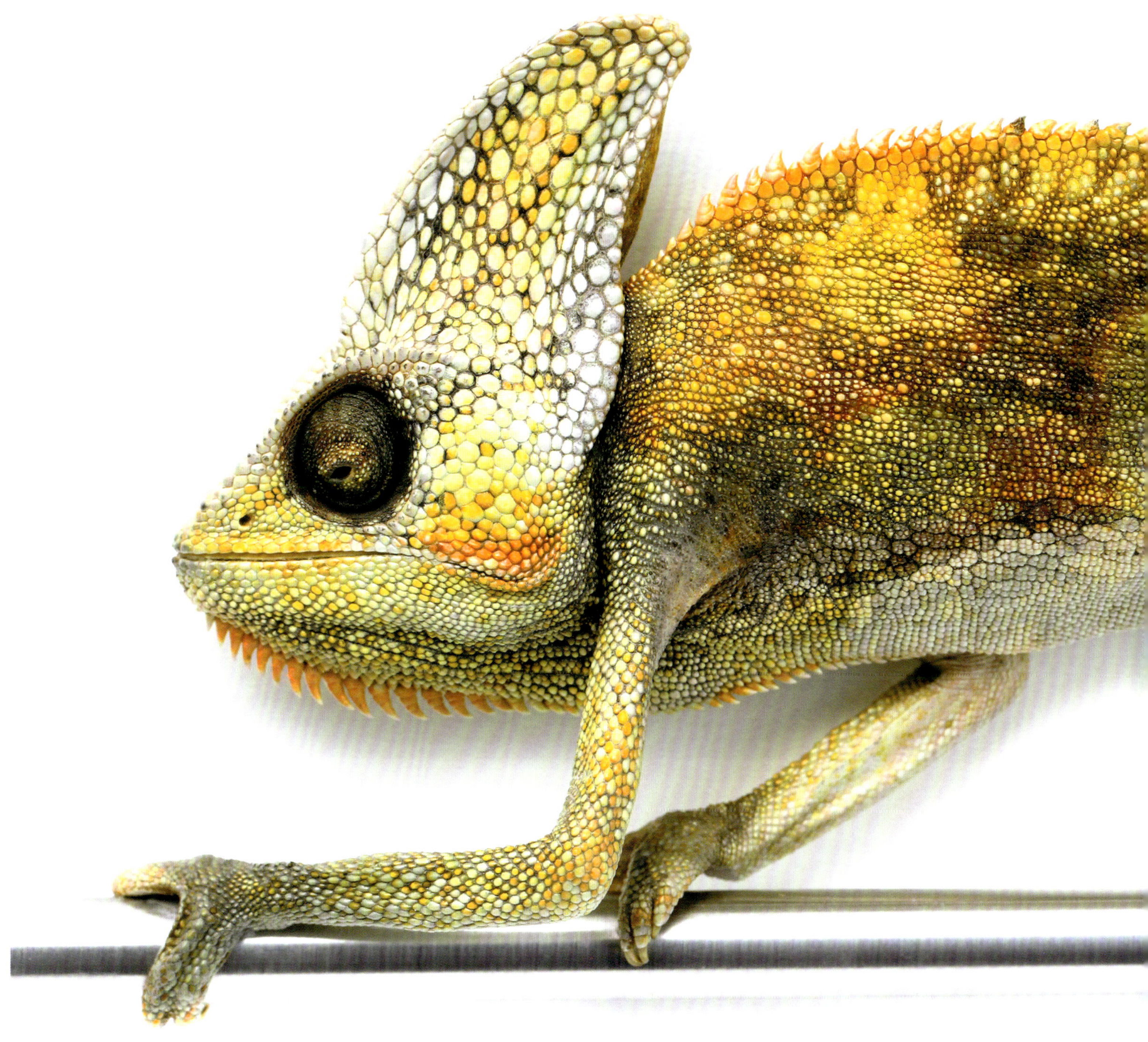

Veiled Chameleon

Madagascar

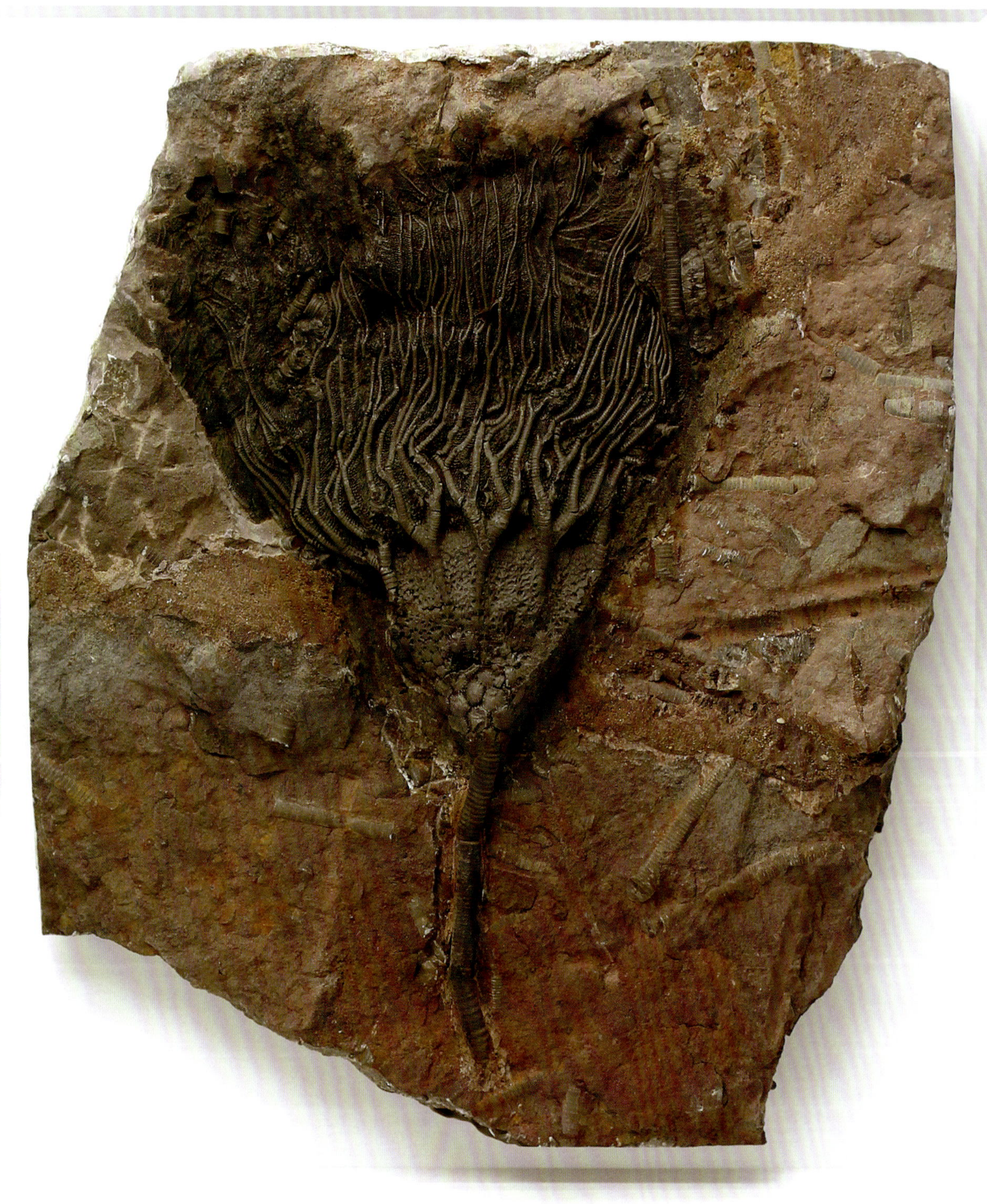

Silurian Crinoid Fossil

Morocco

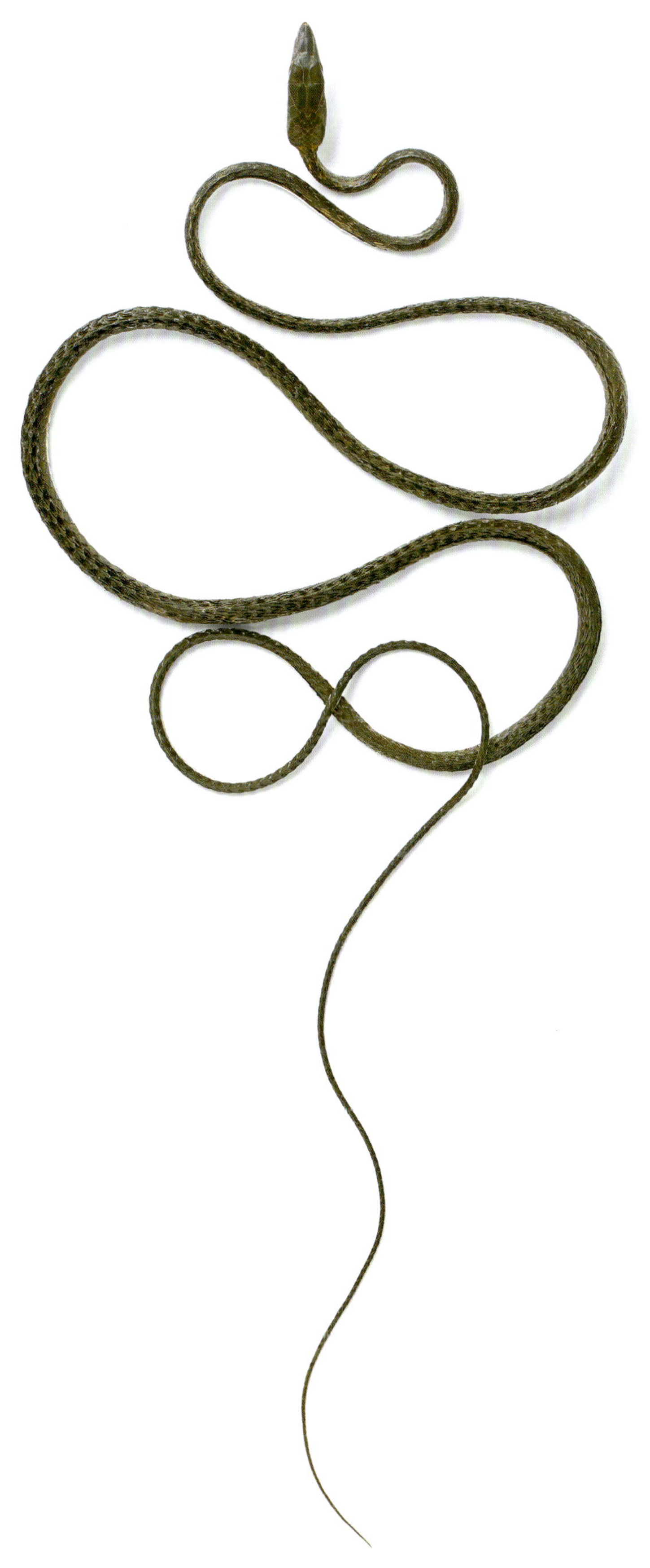

Vine Snake

Malaysia

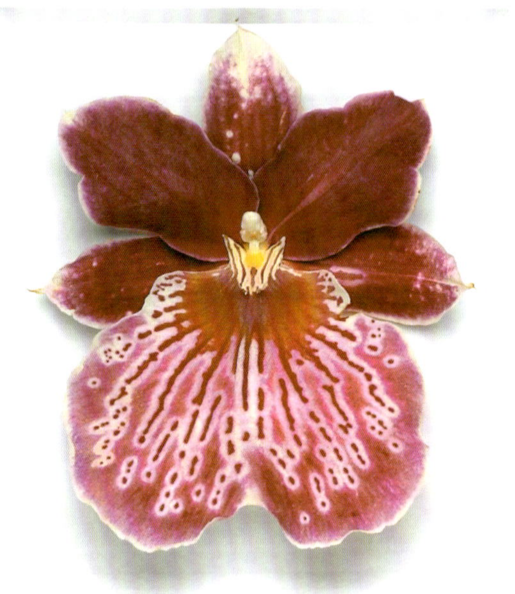

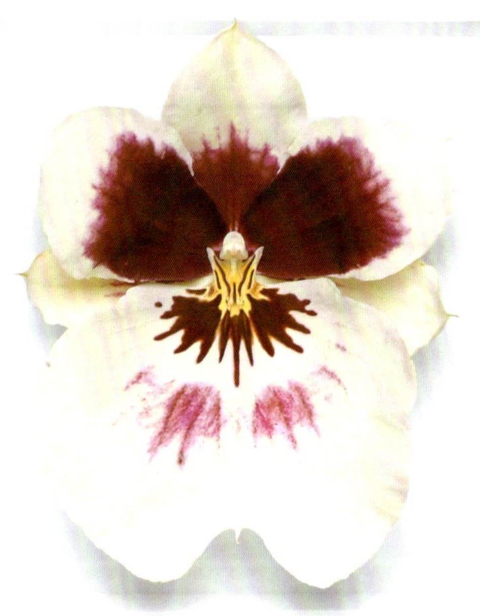

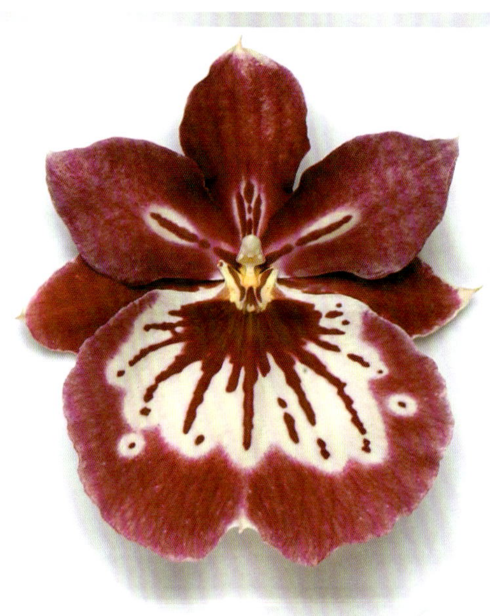

Preserved Pansy Orchids

Brazil

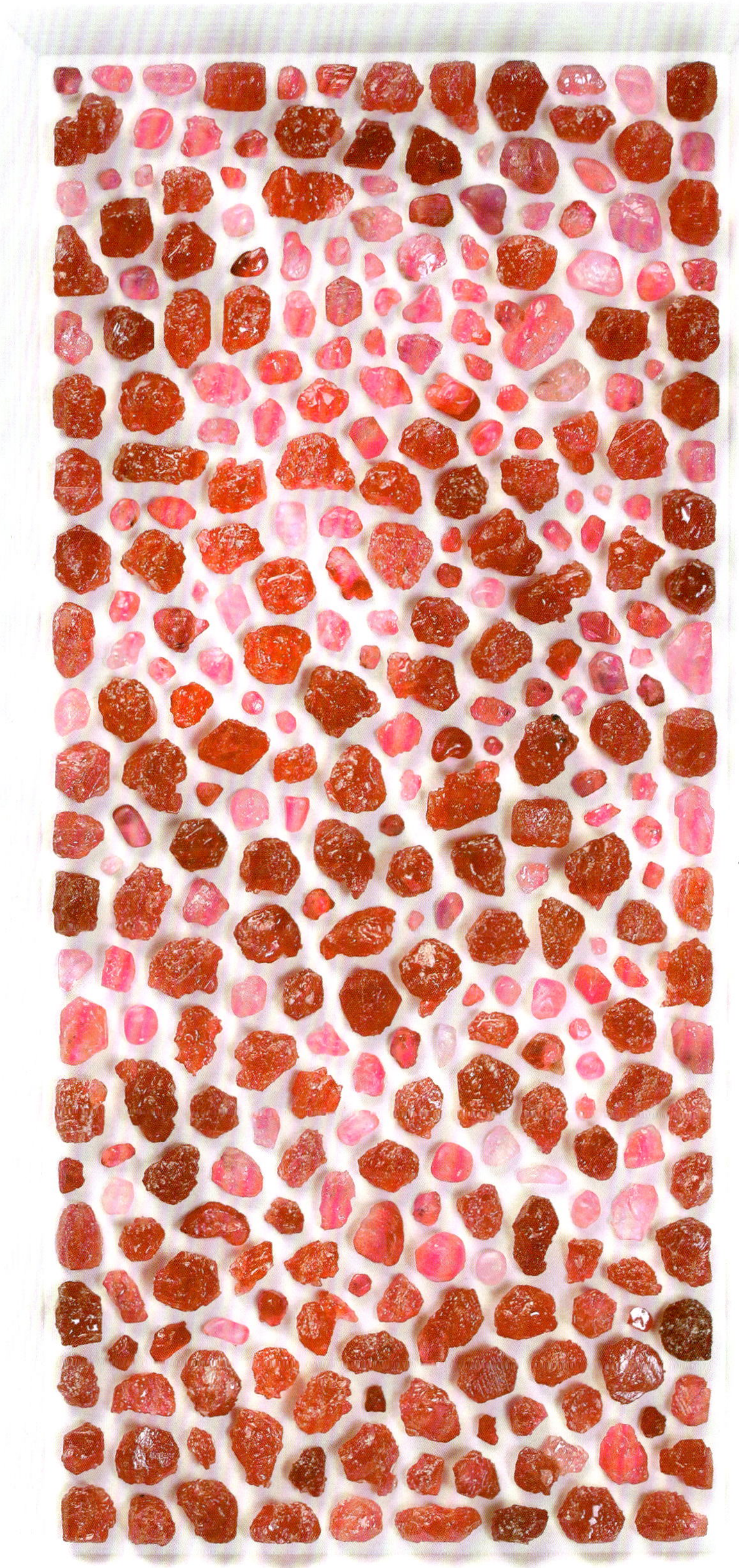

Rough Rubies

Madagascar

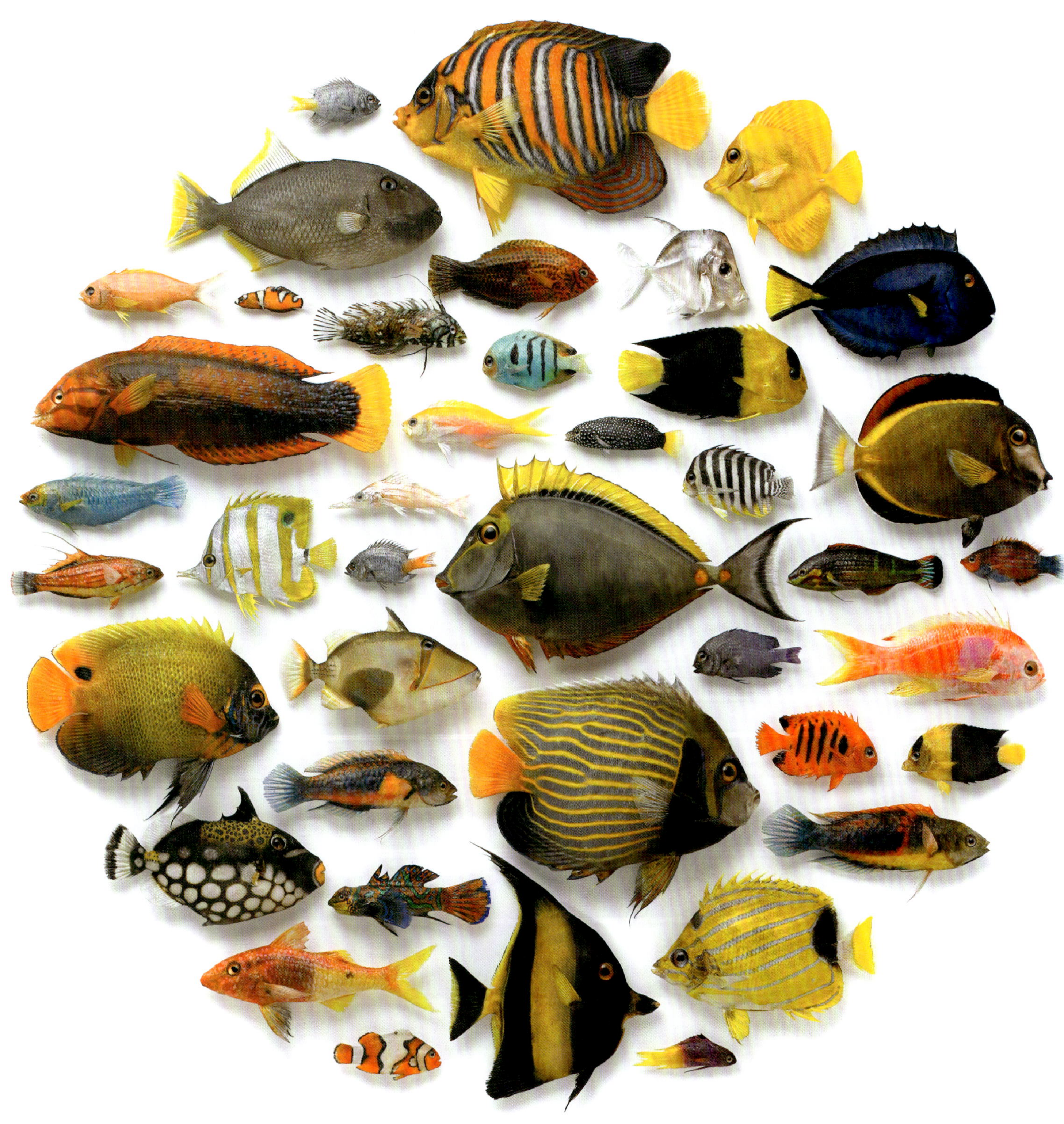

Tropical Fish Mosaic

Worldwide

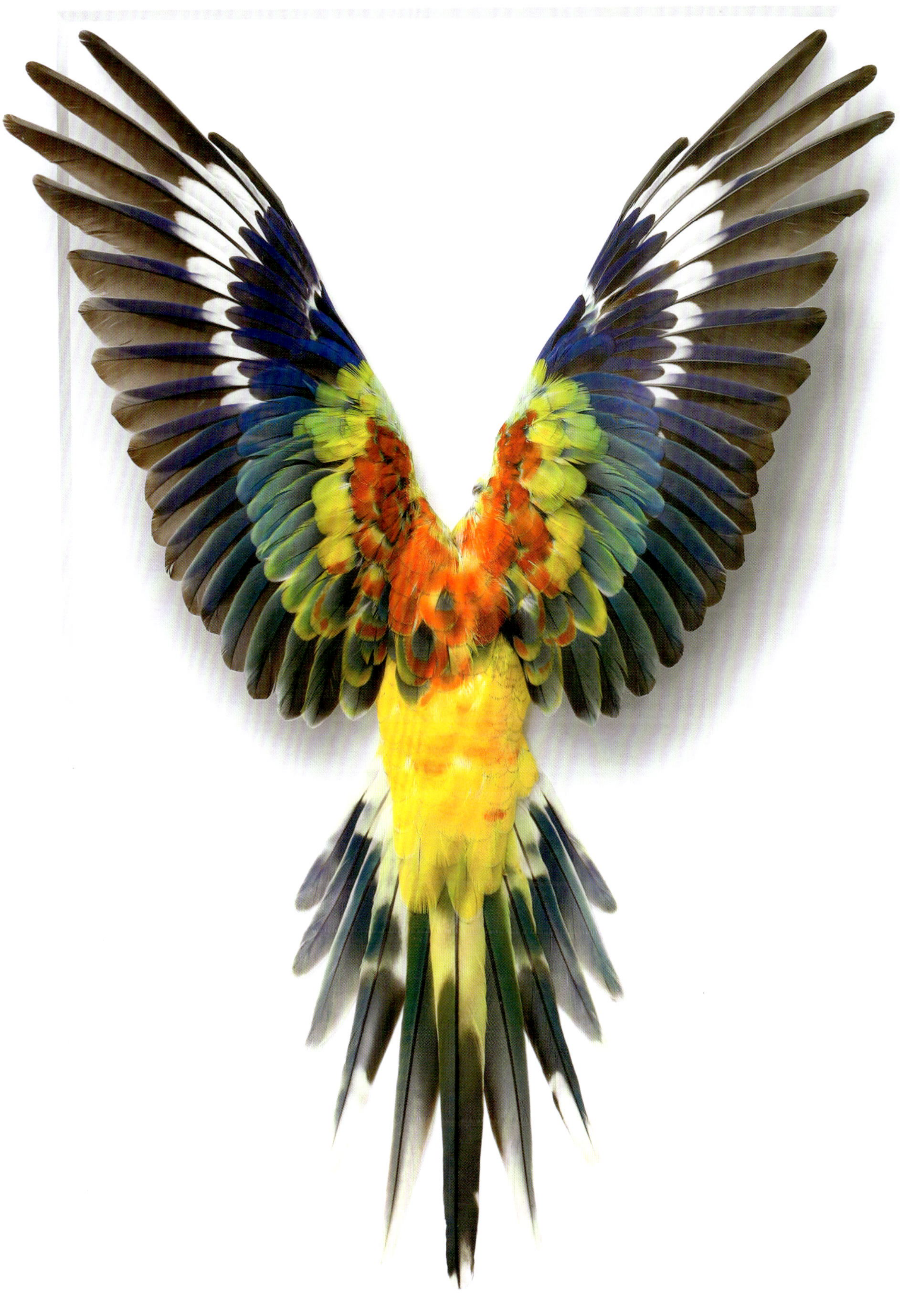

Pied Red-Rumped Parrot

Australia

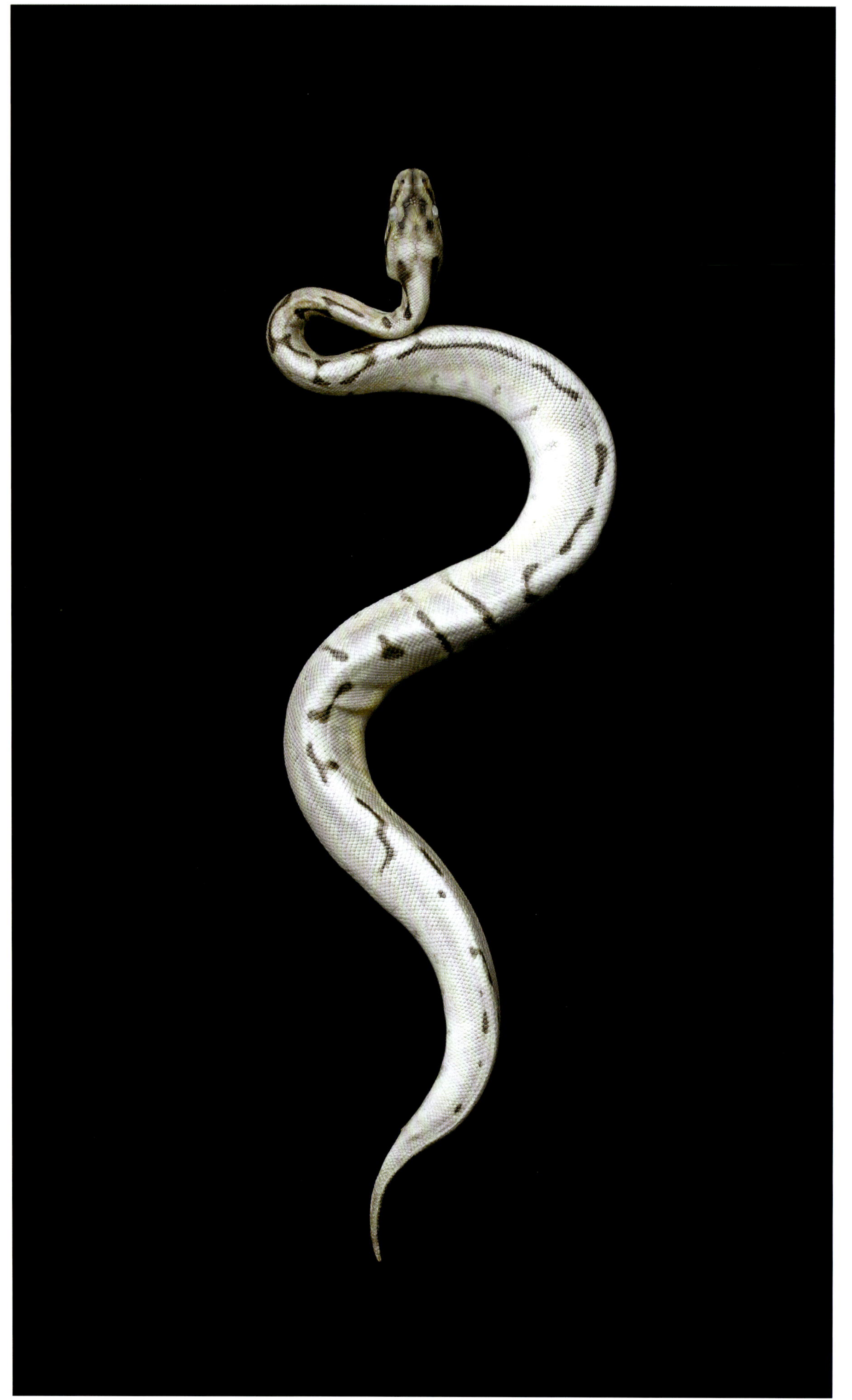

Royal Python, Color Mutation

Ghana

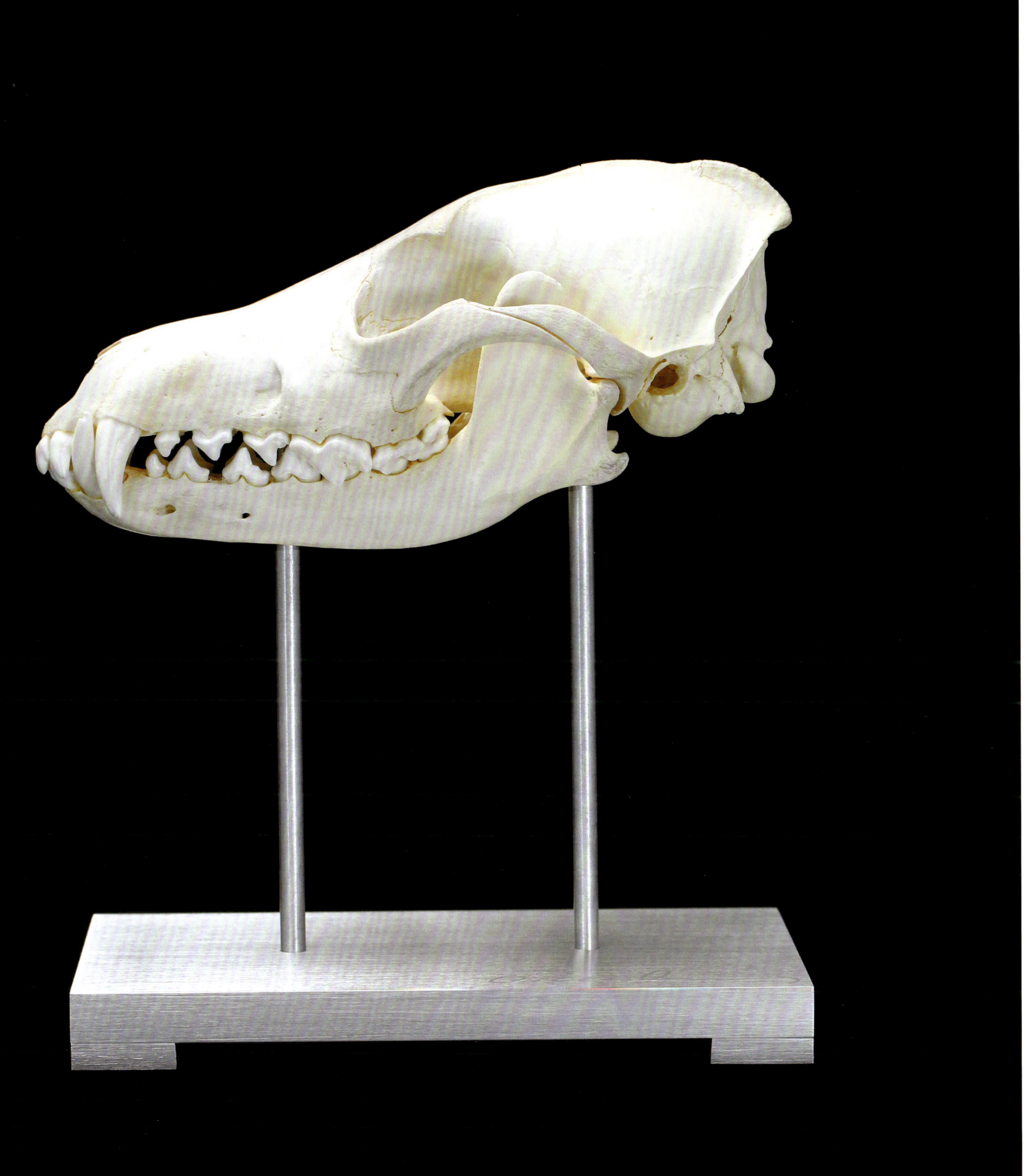

Coyote

United States

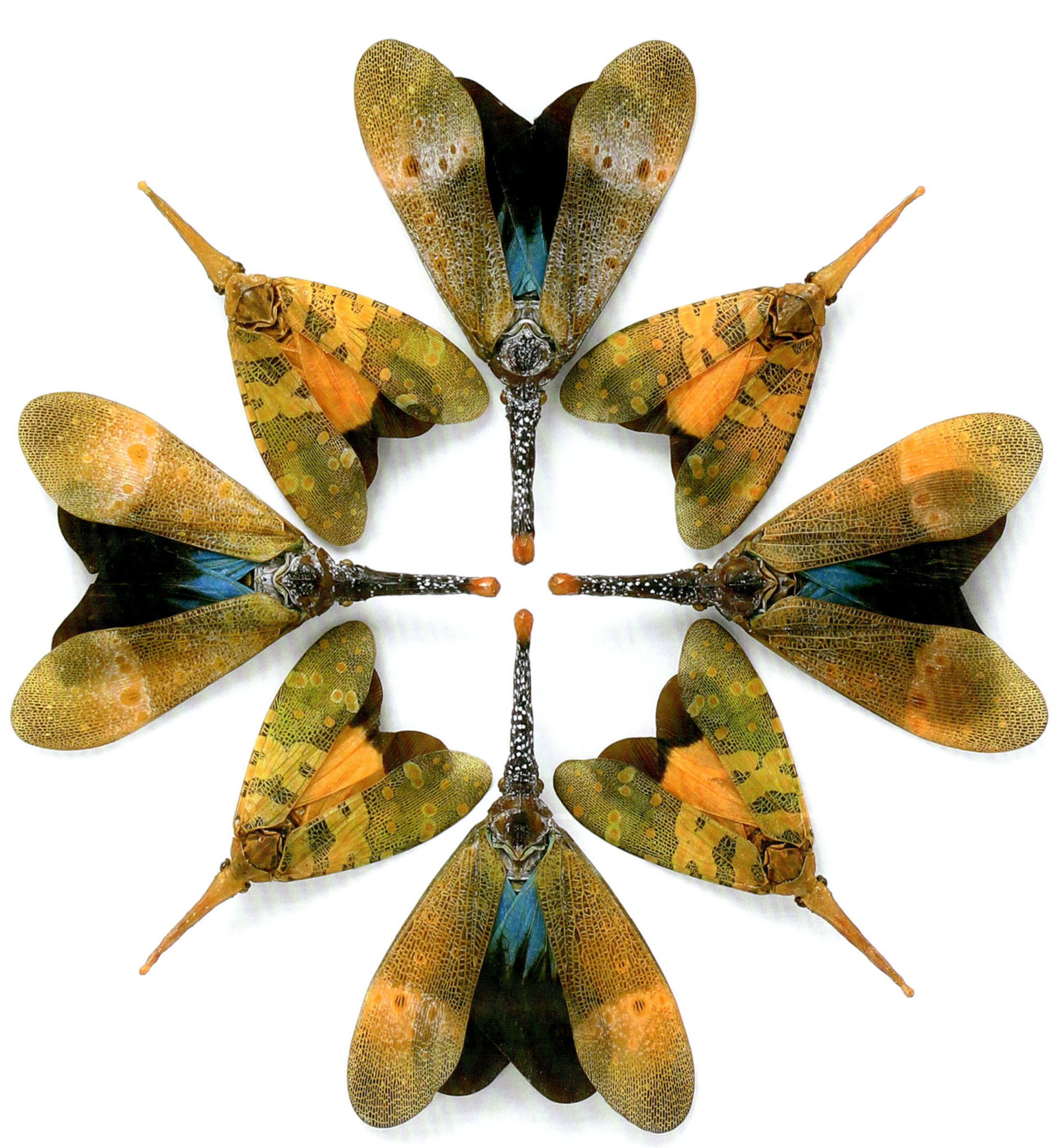

Lantern Fly Prism

Indonesia, Thailand

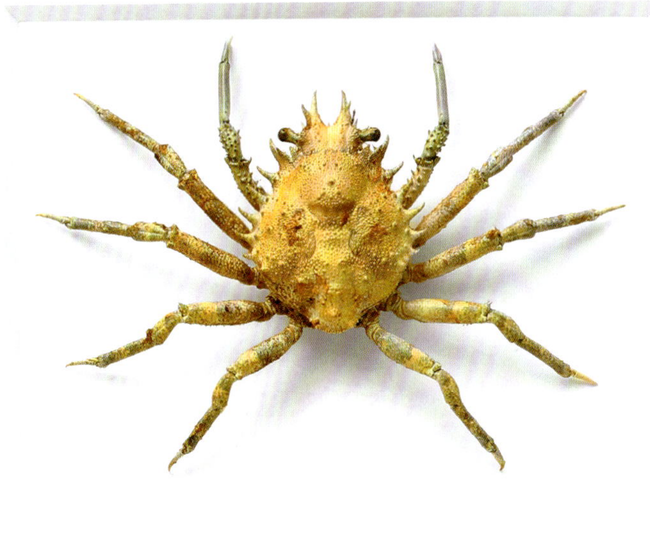

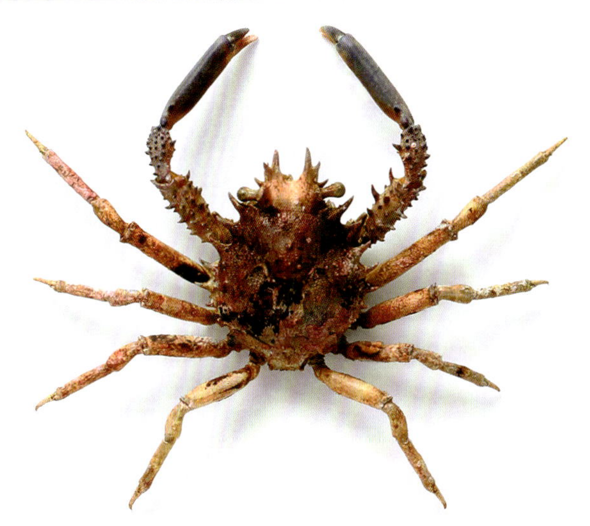

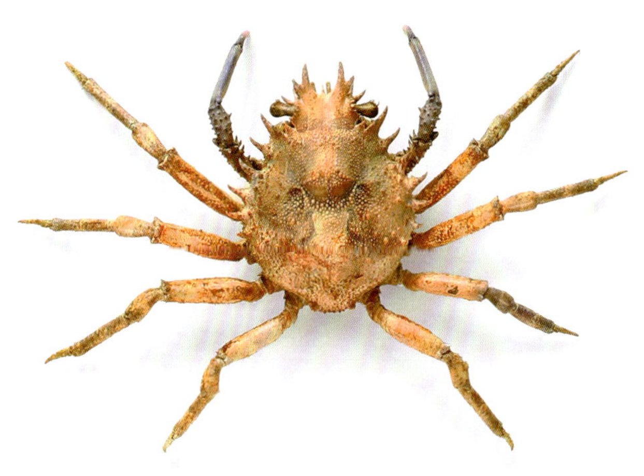

Armored Crab Color Forms

Philippines

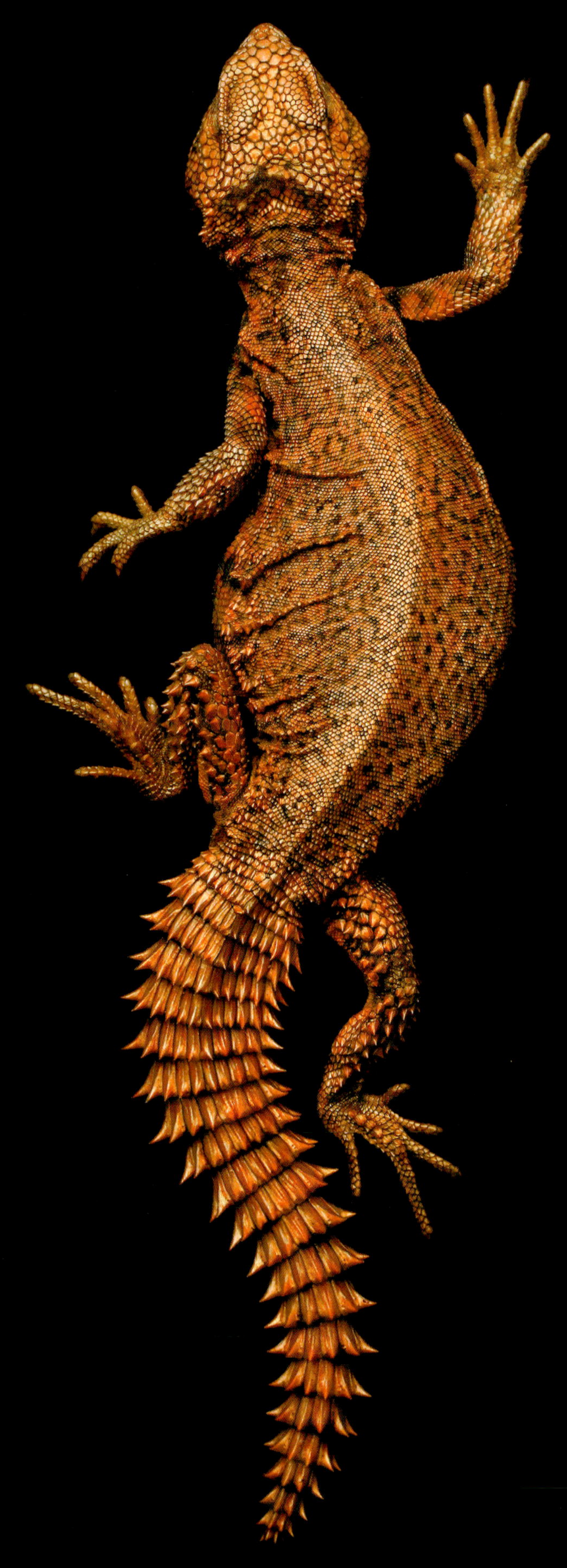

Saharan Uromastyx

Algeria

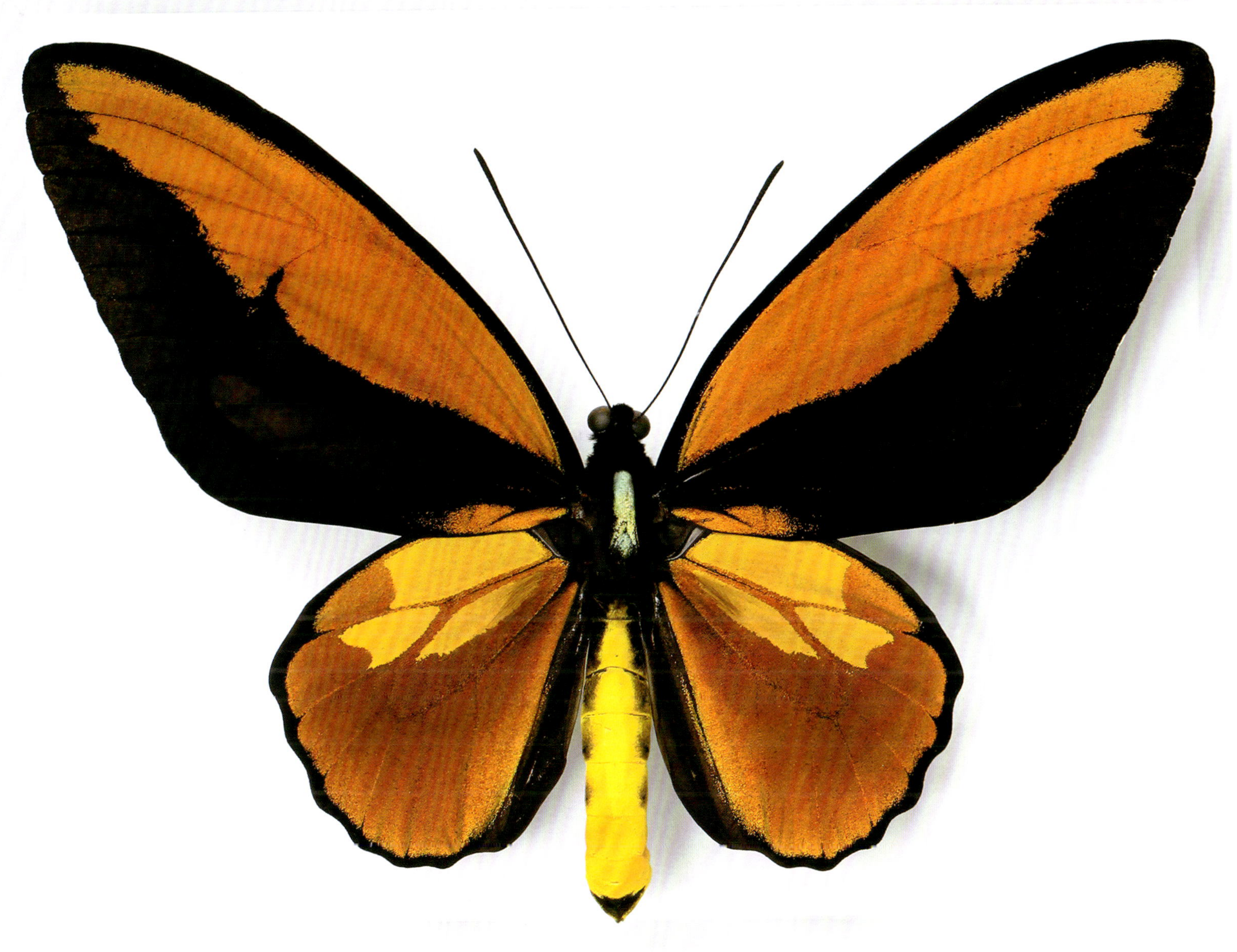

Fiery Birdwing Butterfly

Papua New Guinea

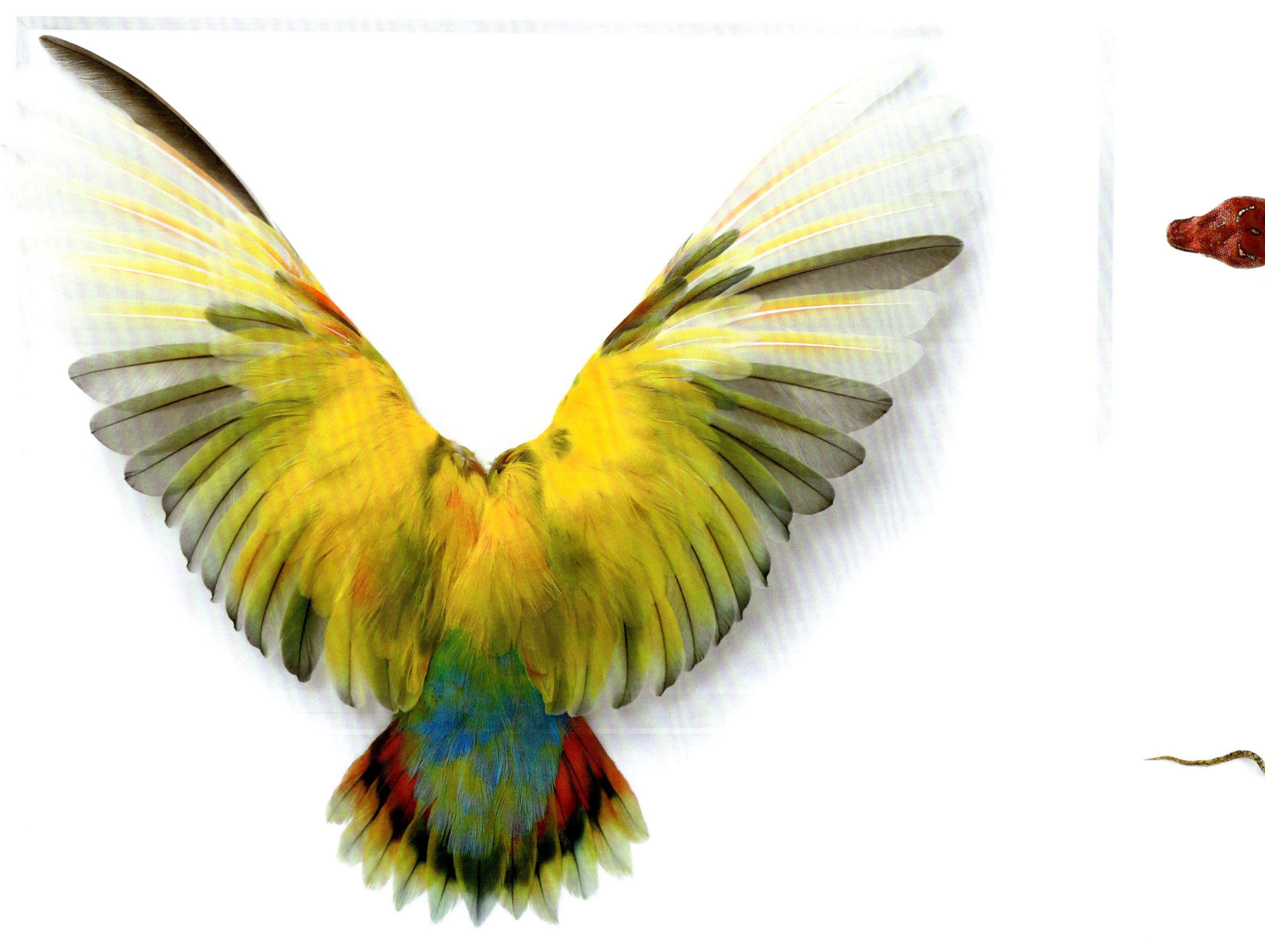

Pied Agapornis Parrot

Namibia

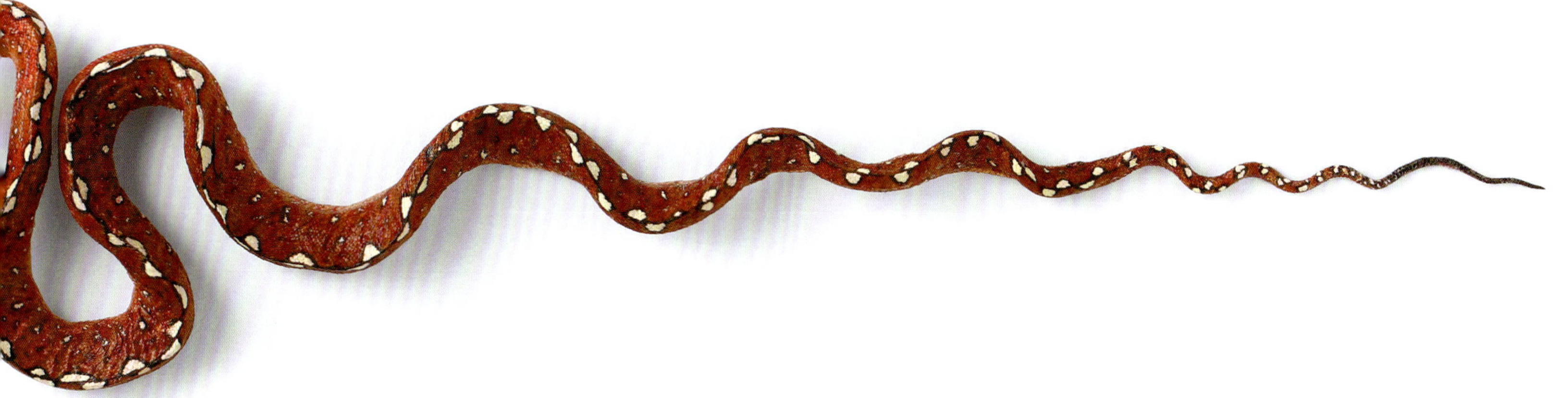

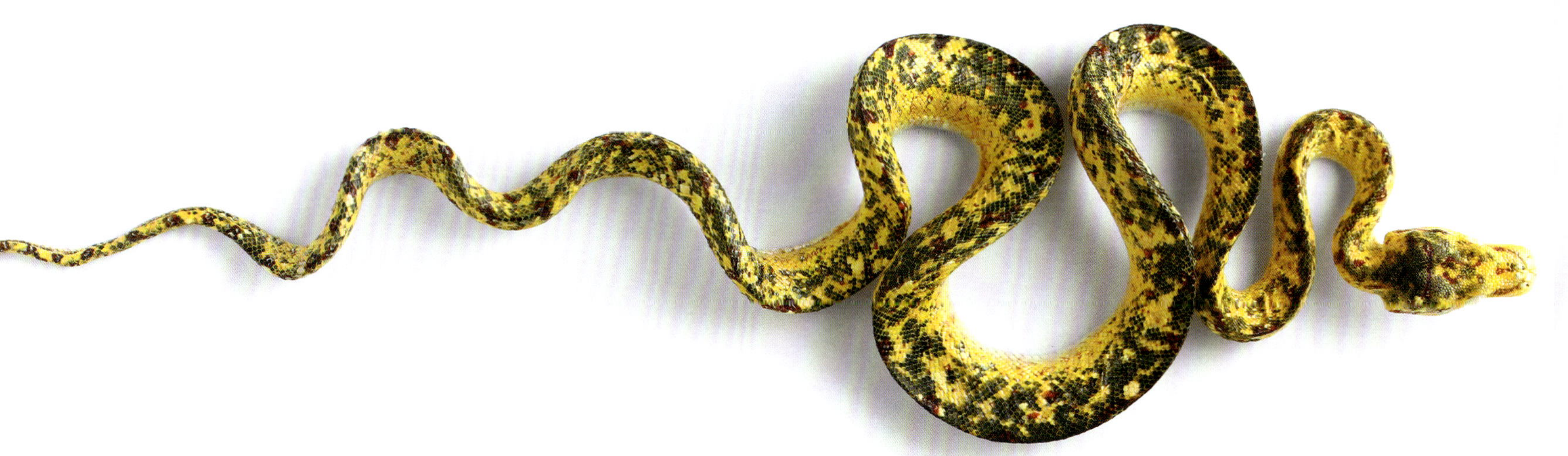

Green Tree Python Hatchlings

Australia

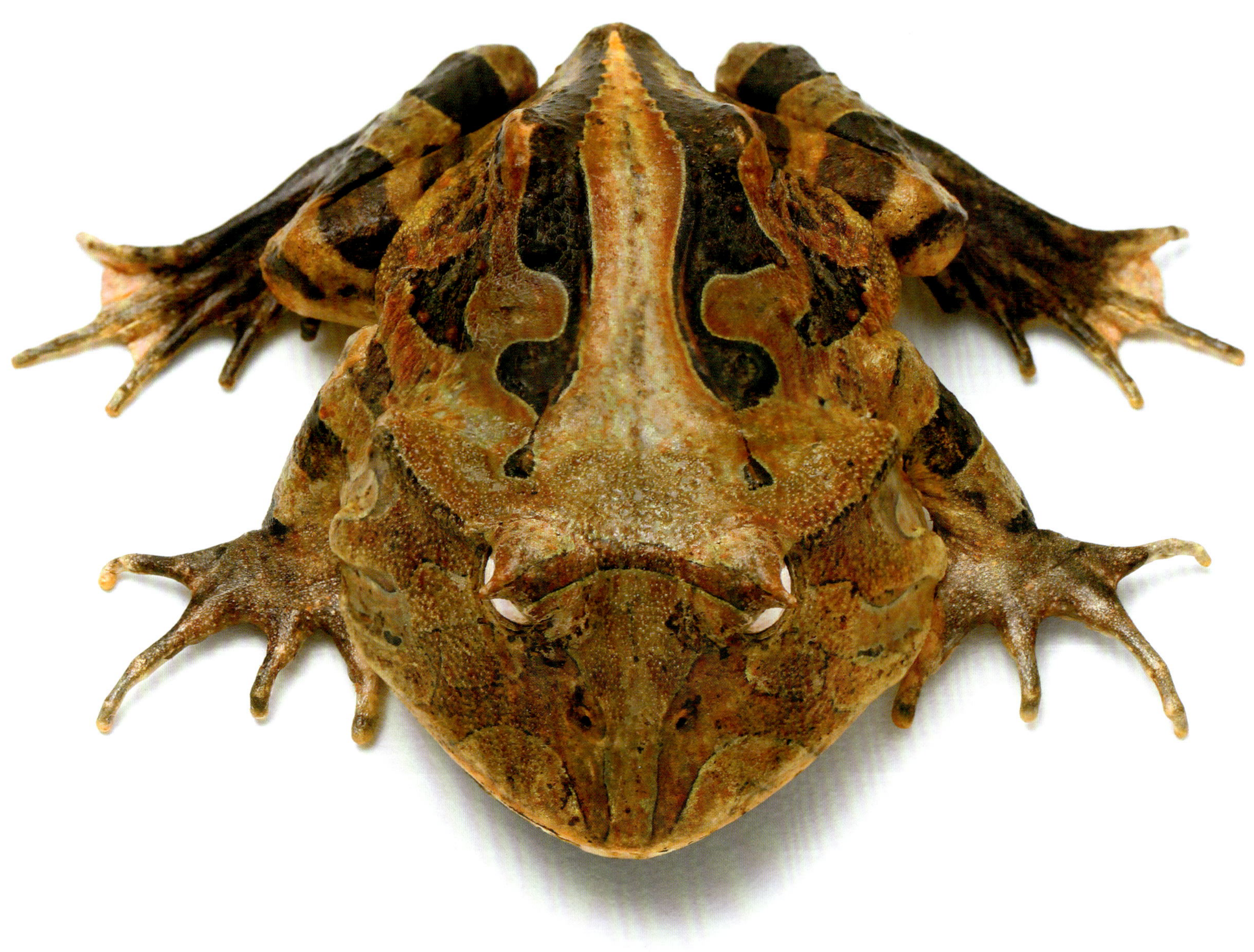

Amazonian Horned Frog

Suriname

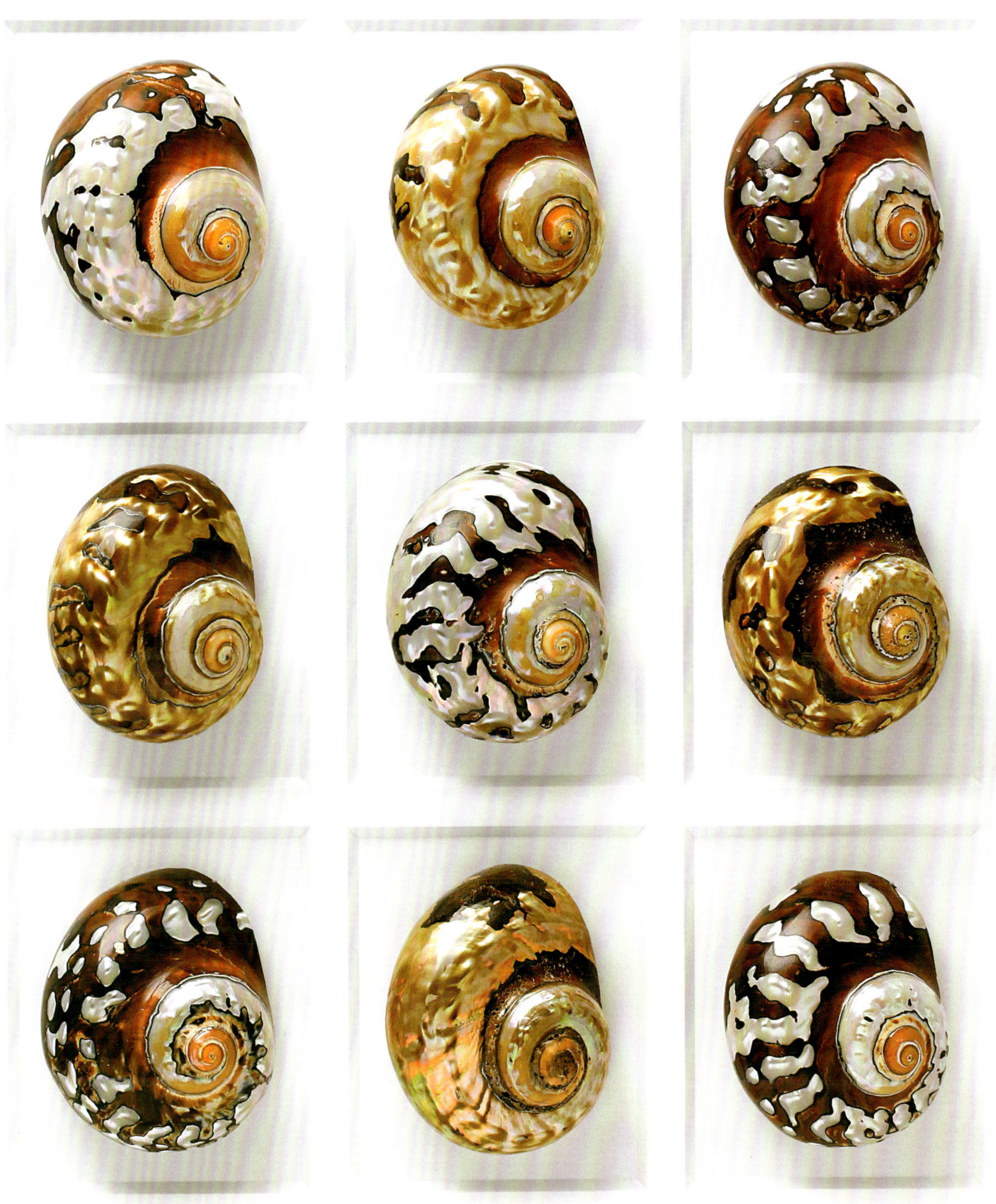

African Turbos

South Africa

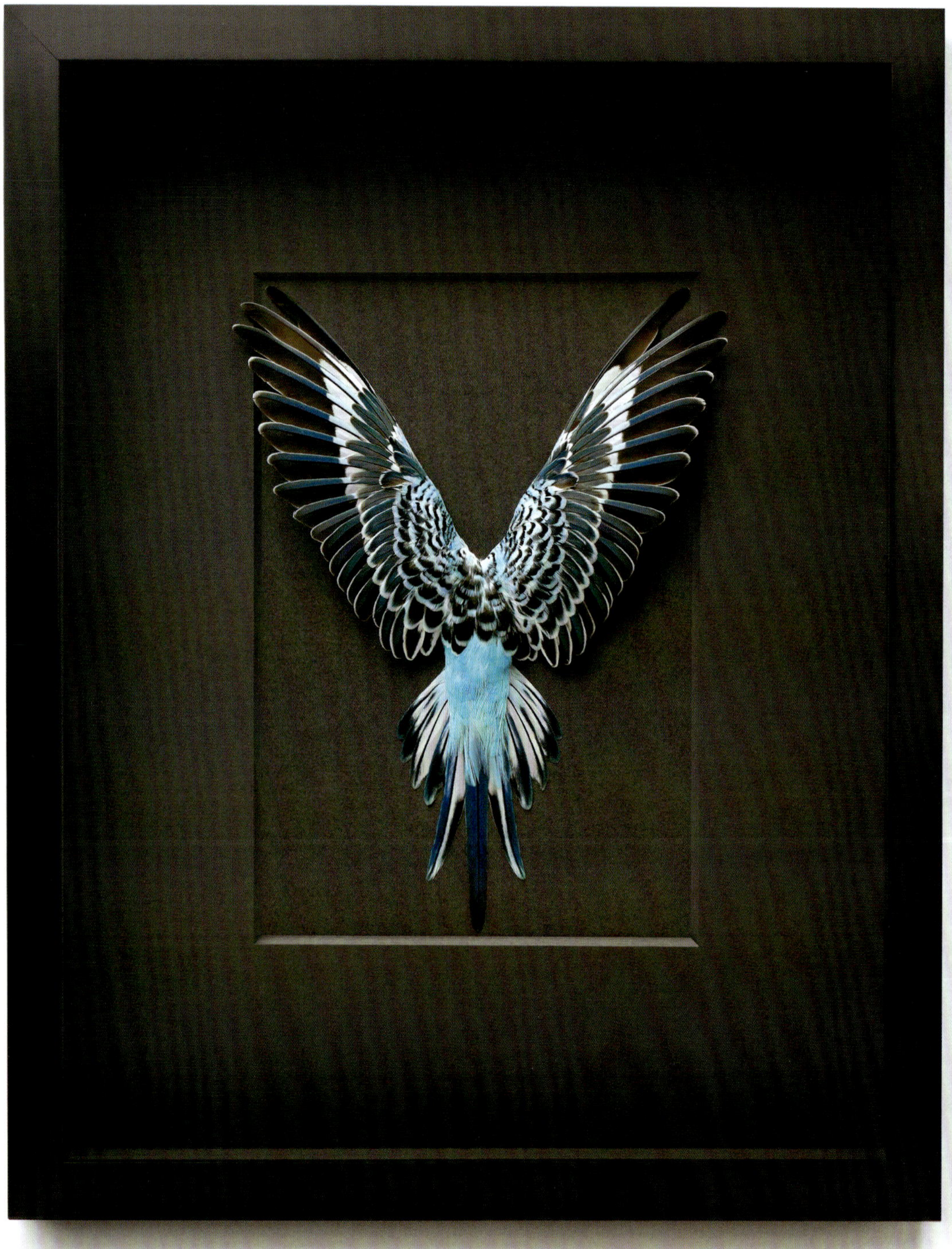

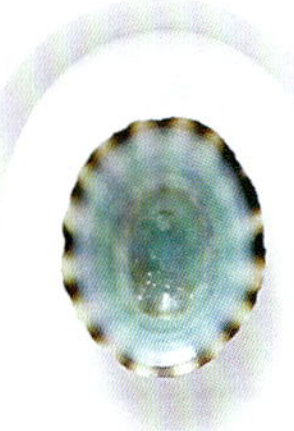

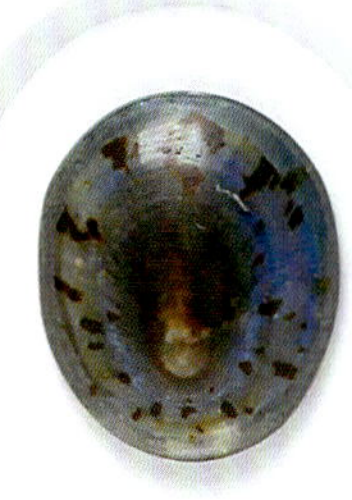

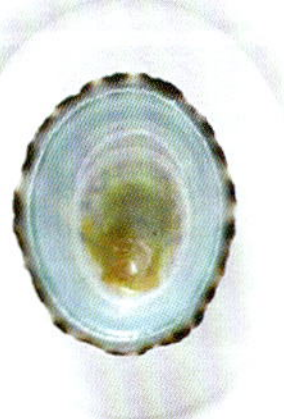

Australian Budgerigar

Australia

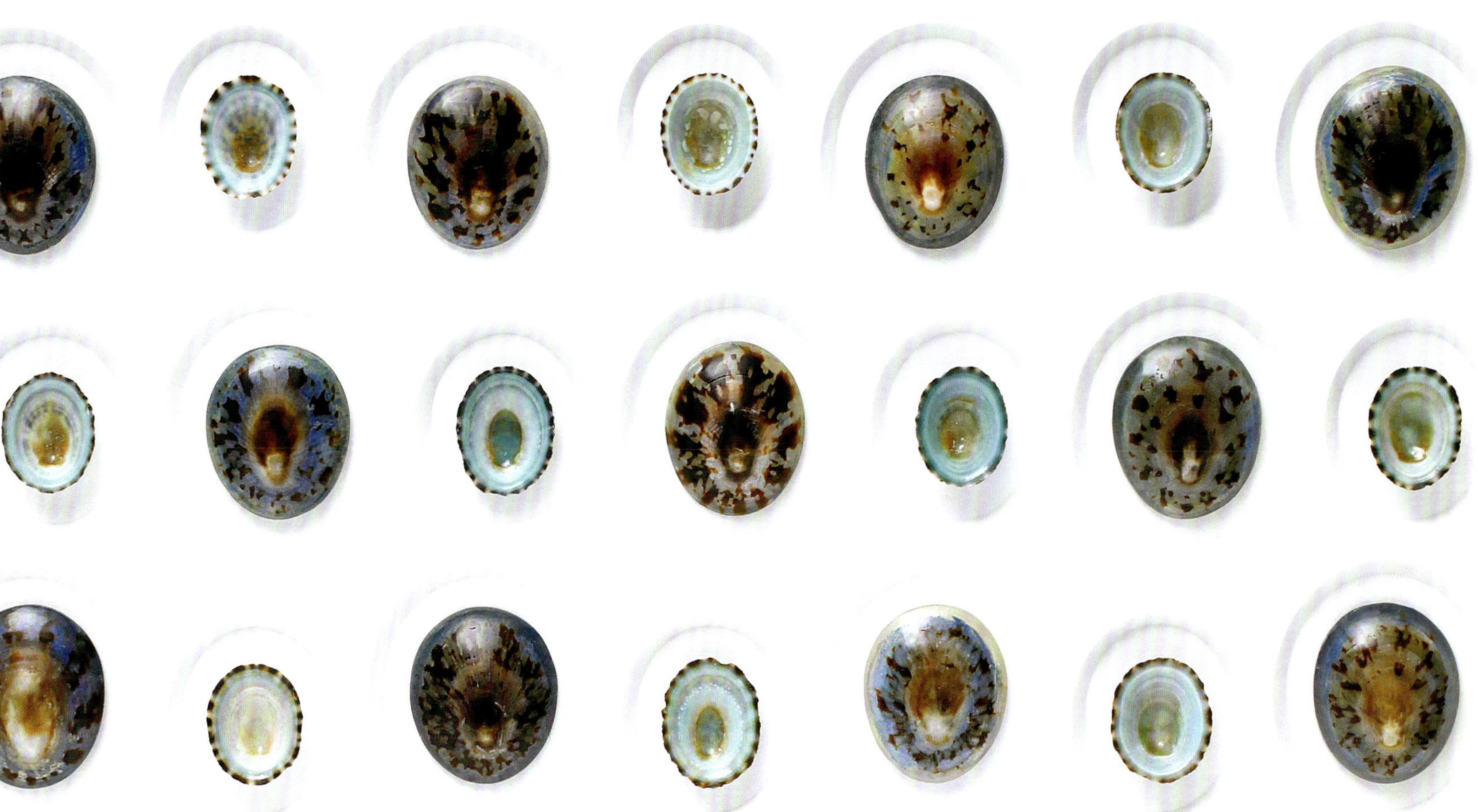

Limpets

Pacific Ocean

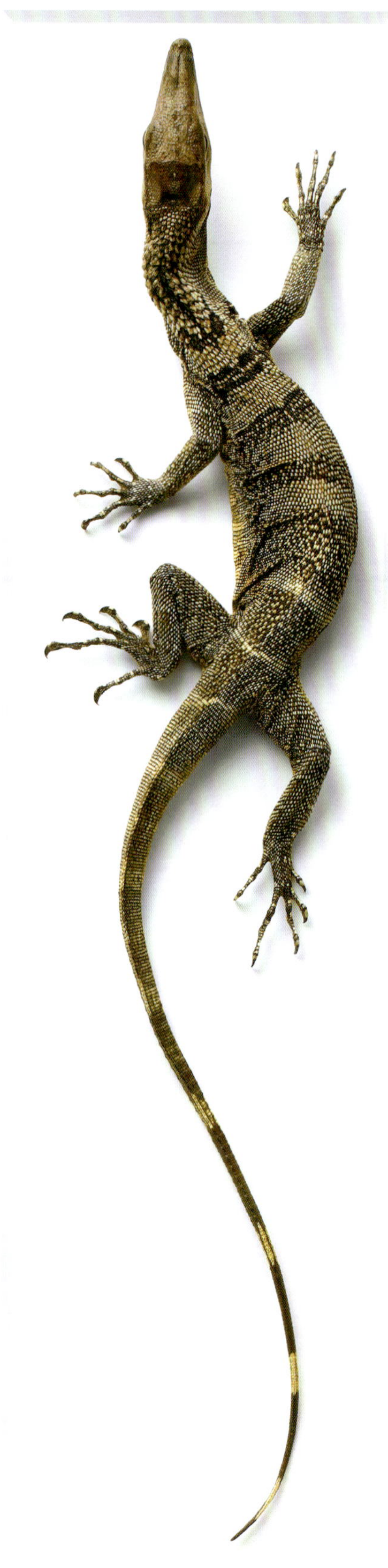

Black Roughneck Monitor

Myanmar

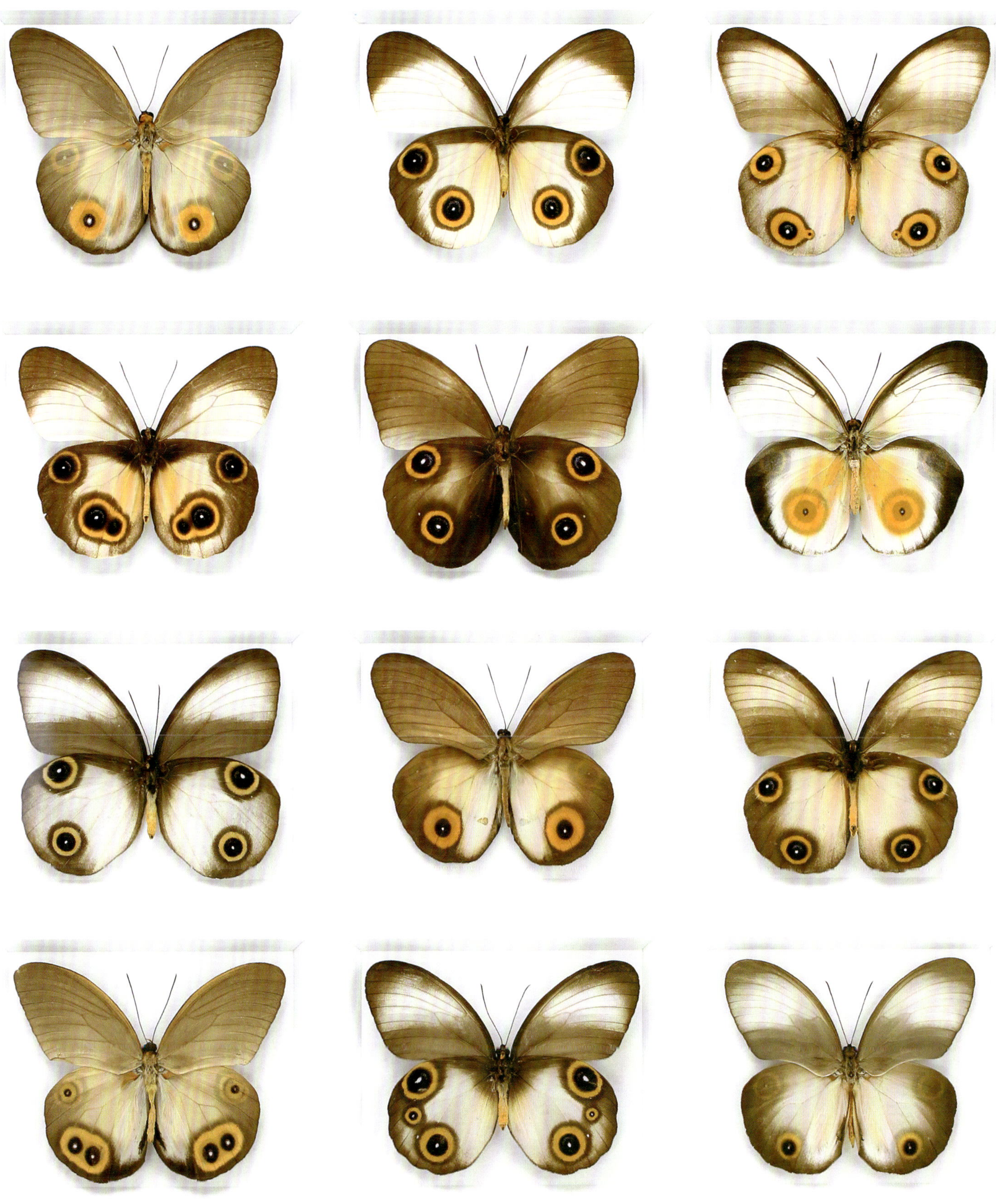

Taenaris Anthology

Indonesia, Papua New Guinea

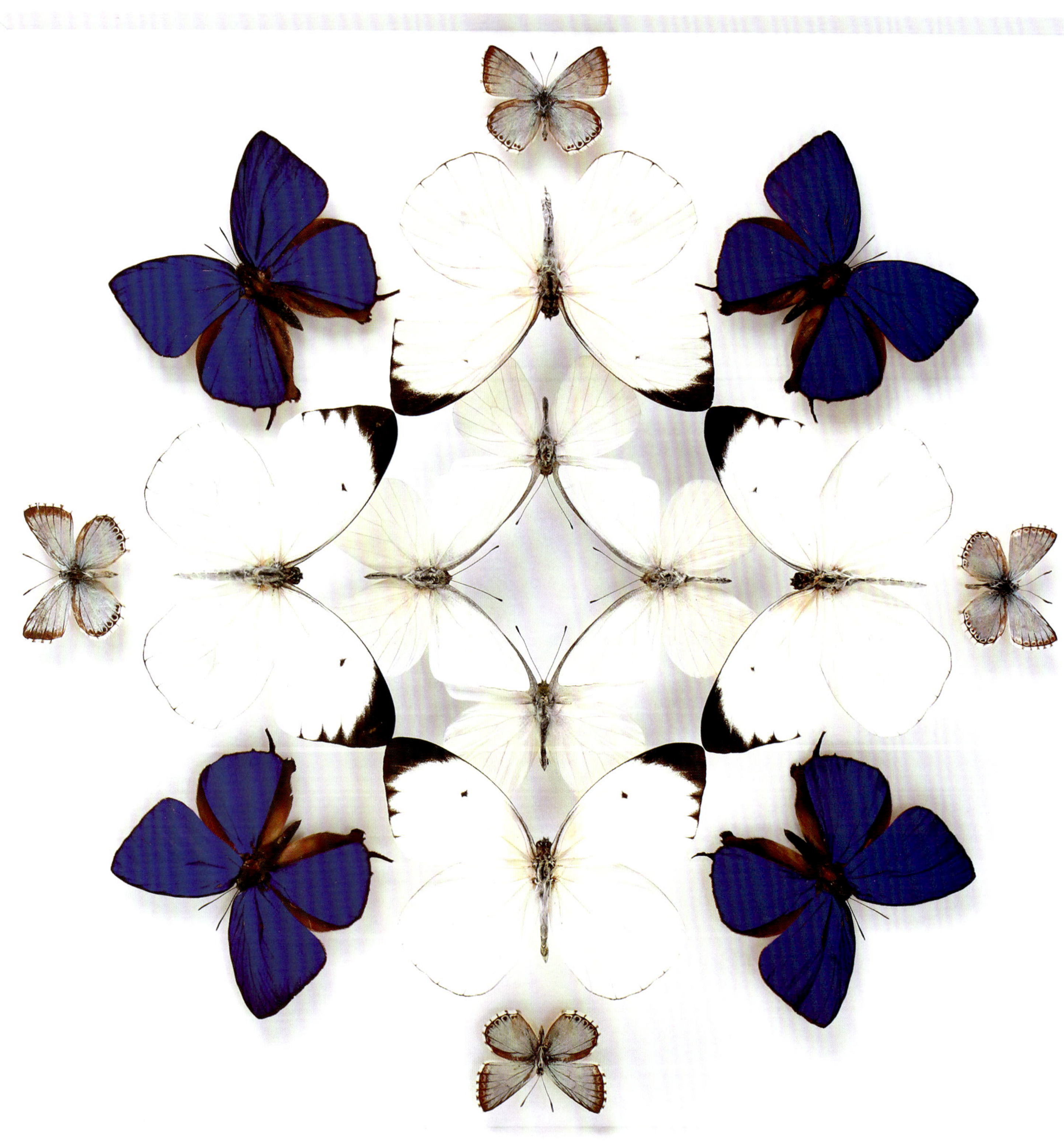

Inflorescence

Philippines, Peru, Indonesia, France

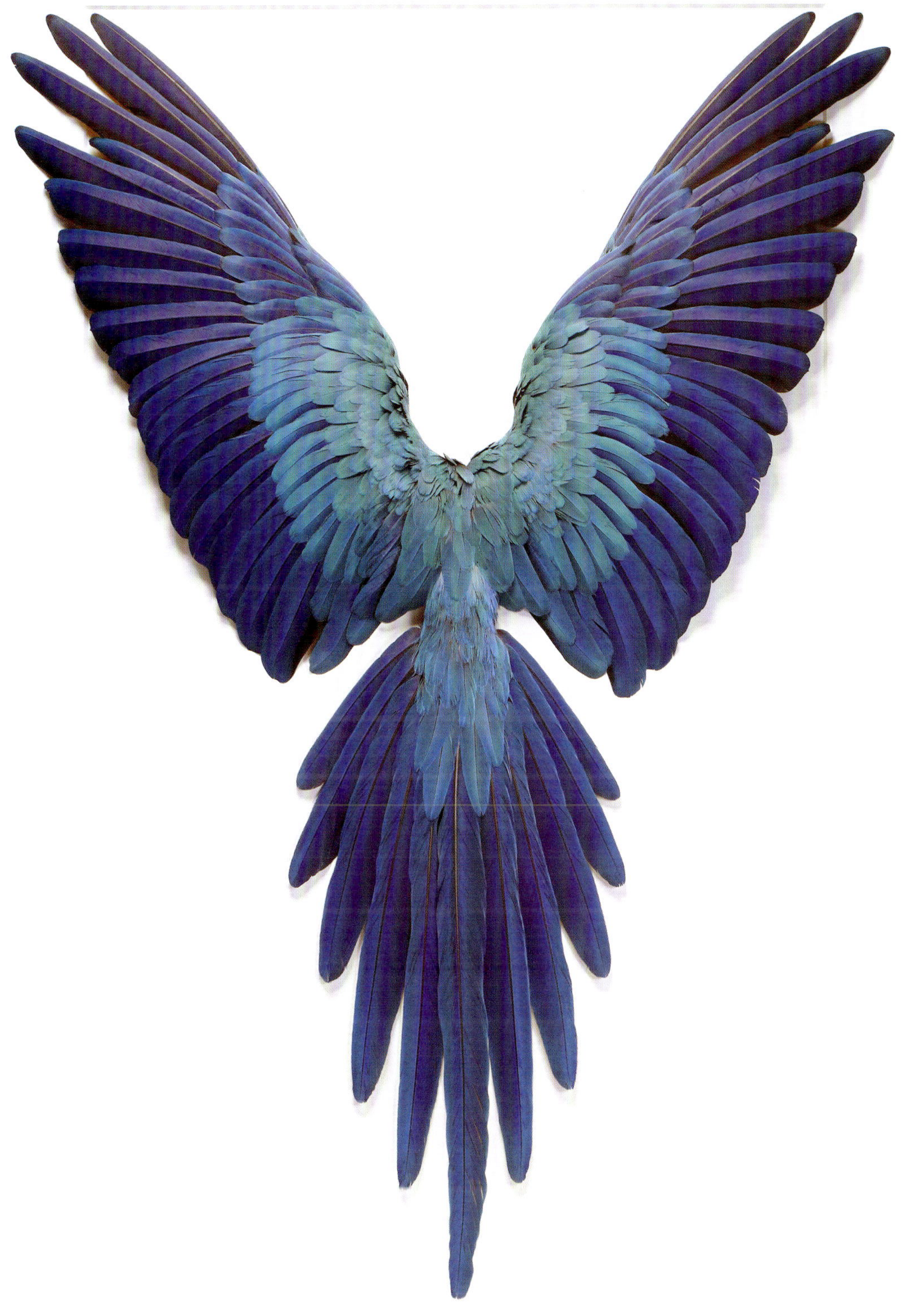

Blue and Gold Macaw

Bolivia

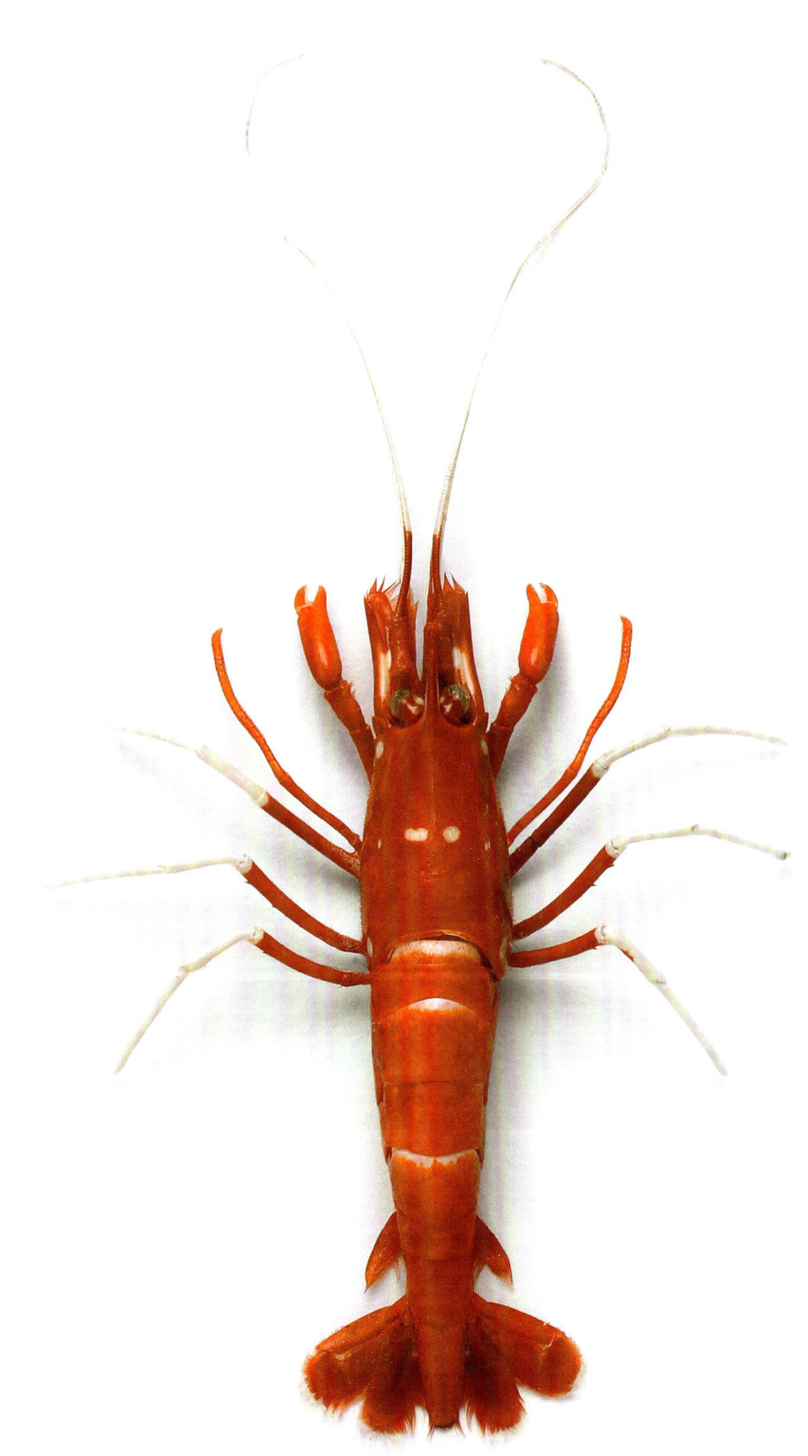

Fire Shrimp

Sri Lanka

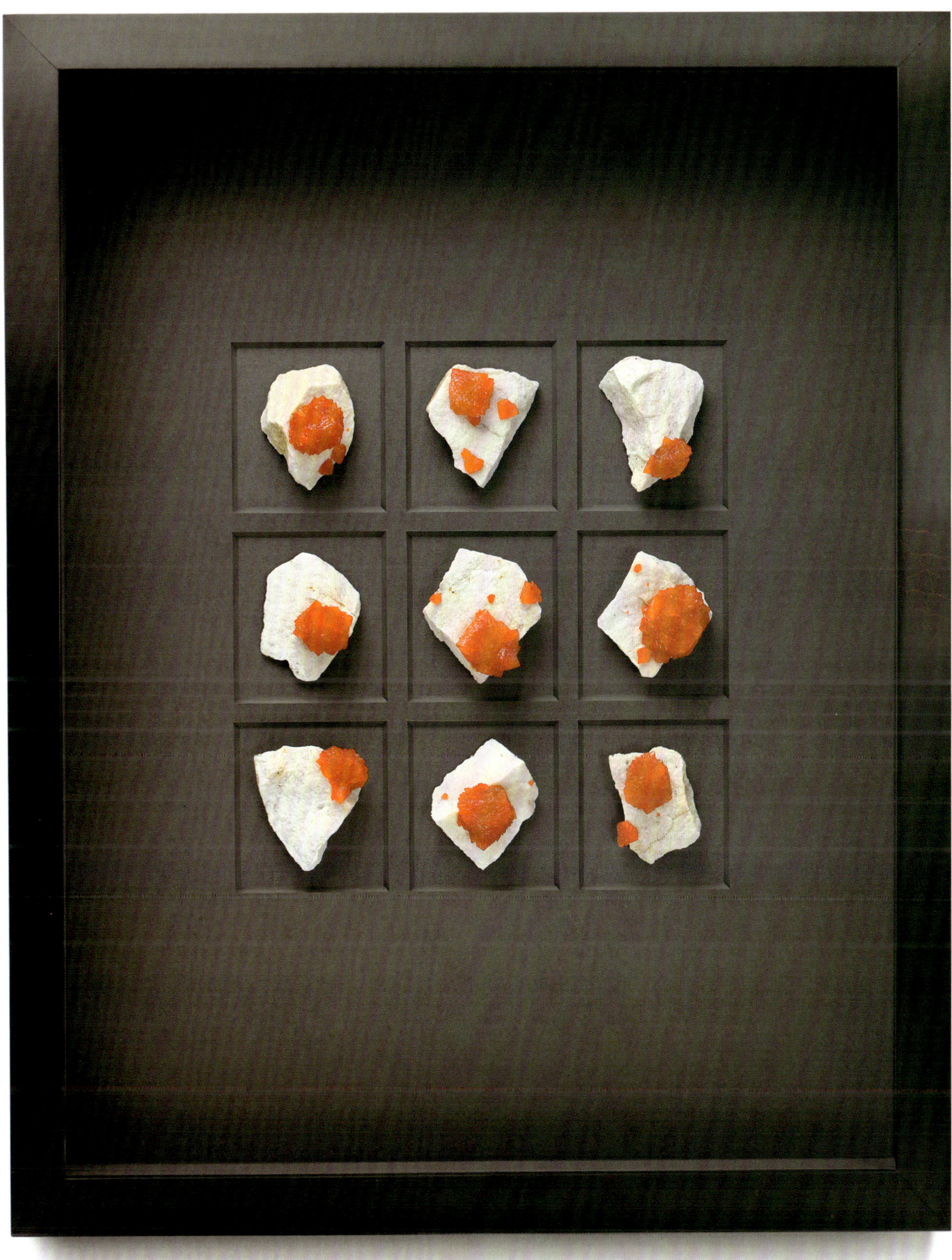

Accelerated Sulfate on Granite

Czech Republic

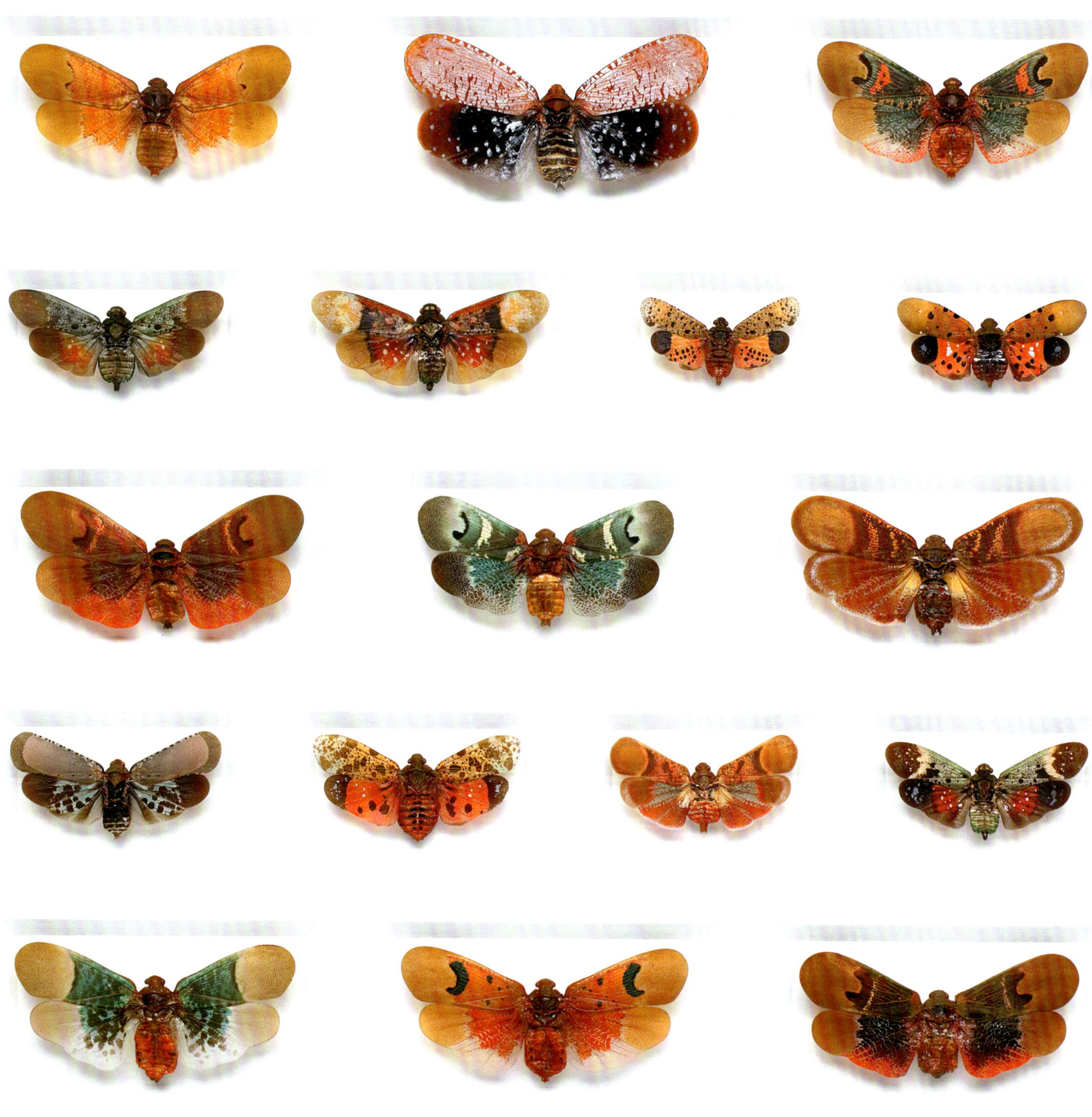

Planthopper Mosaic

Malaysia, Indonesia, Thailand

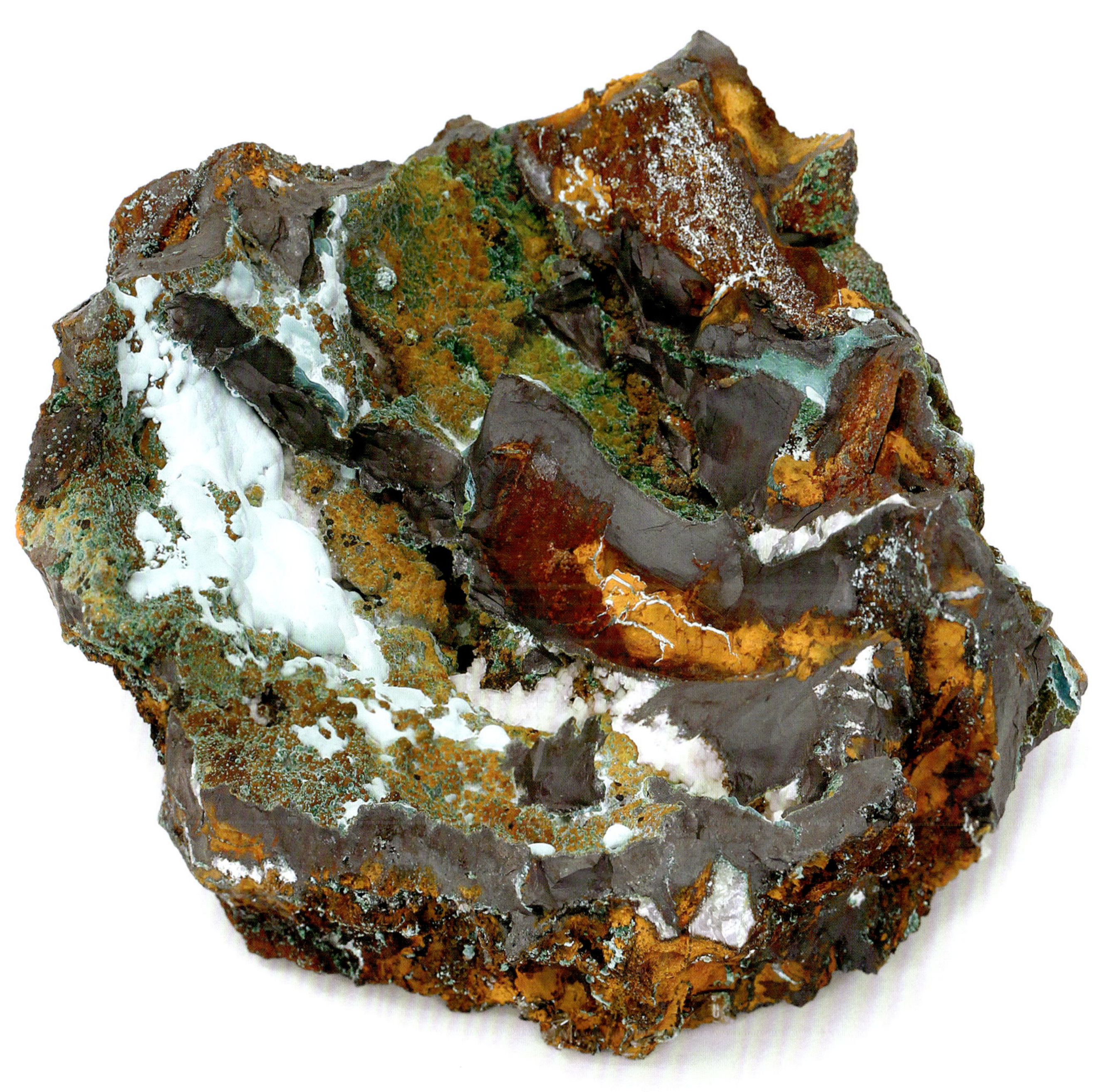

Rosasite

Mexico

Insects

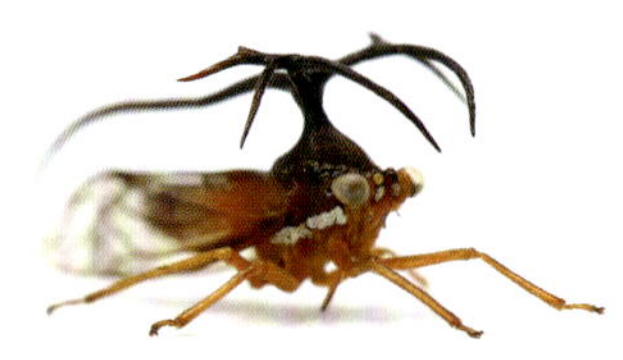

13. TREEHOPPER
(*Umbelligerus peruviensis*), Venezuela. One of the unquestionably bizarre denizens of the insect world. The exact purpose for the outrageous protrusions that treehoppers are famous for is unknown.

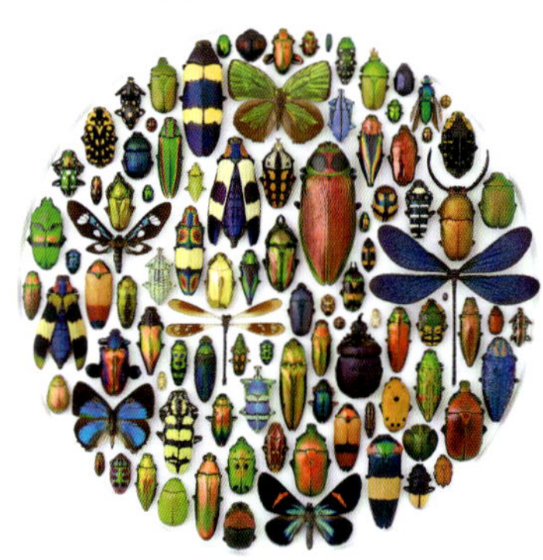

14–15. AESTHETICA SPHERE
(worldwide species). The latest iteration of my Mosaic series is more inclusive of all arthropods rather than focused solely on beetles. My only stipulation here is color: There must be a hue, sheen, texture, or pattern that merits inclusion into these elite groupings of the world's most elegant insects. Specimens from all six inhabited continents are used. Composition size, 20 x 24 in. (also in 16 x 20, 24 x 30).

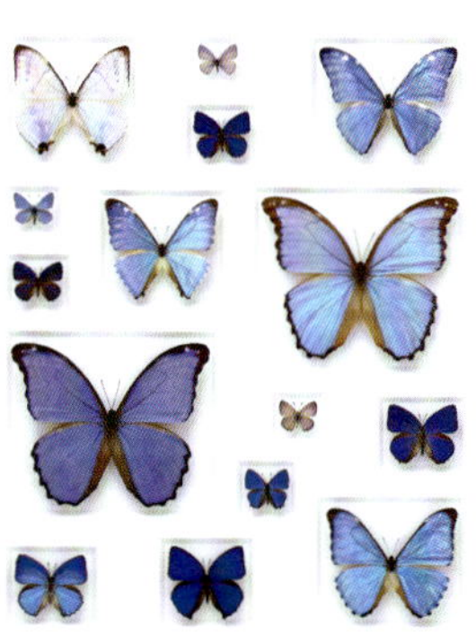

16–17. CERULEAN BUTTERFLIES
(*Morpho* and *Lycaenidae* spp.), Peru, Argentina, Brazil, Irian, Sulawesi, France. If it seems like I use a lot of morpho butterflies in my work, it is because they can scarcely be improved upon as a palette of luminescent color, except when I needed to add a touch of order. Here, I've combined the striking luminescence of the morpho family with the rich hues of the Lycaenidae butterflies. Composition size, 24 x 30 in.

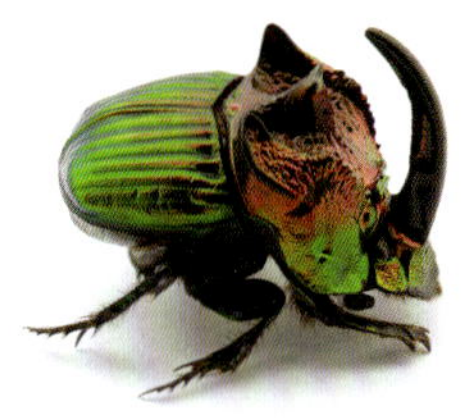

18. RAINBOW DUNG BEETLE
(*Phanaeus tridens*), United States.

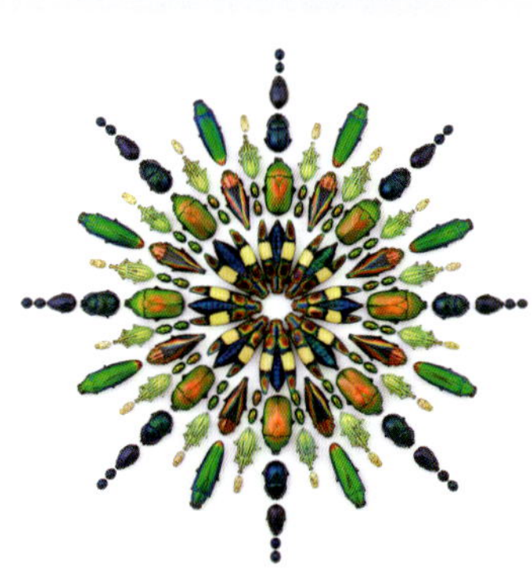

19. FULGENS PRISM.
Center out: Metallic Wood-Boring Beetles (*Chrysochroa fulgens*), Thailand; Leaf Beetles (*Chrysochus* sp.), Java; Metallic Wood-Boring Beetles (*Cyphogastra javanica*), Maluku Islands; Flower Beetles (*Torynorrhina* sp.), Laos; Lime Weevils (*Celebia arrigans*), Sulawesi; Metallic Wood-Boring Beetles (*Chrysochroa fulminans*), Java; Dung Beetles (*Geotrupes auratus*), Japan; Golden Chafers (*Rutelidae* sp.), Borneo; Shining Leaf Beetles (*Rutelidae* sp.), Thailand; Ladybird Beetles (*Coccinellidae* sp.), Java. Composition size, 20 x 24 in.

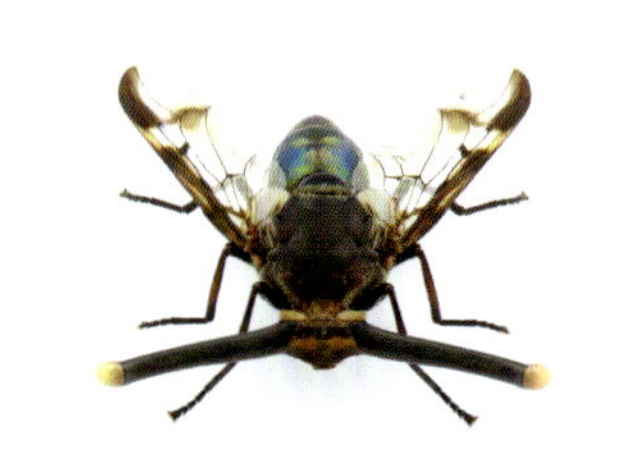

20–21. STALK-EYED FLY
(*Diopsidae* sp.), Indonesia.

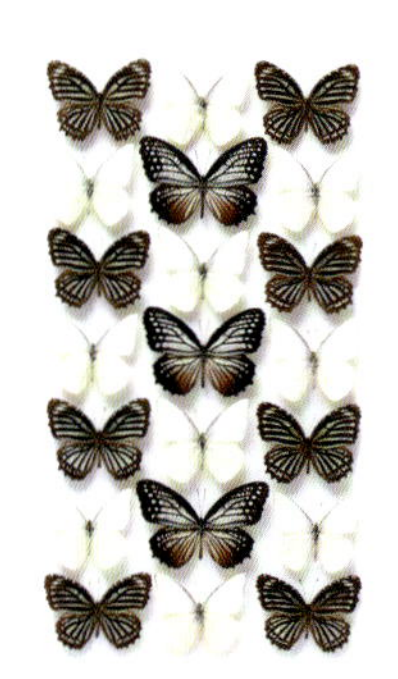

22. ELYMNIAS
(*Elymnias nesaea*), Bali; Common Albatross (*Appias albina*), Mindoro. Composition size, 20 x 24 in.

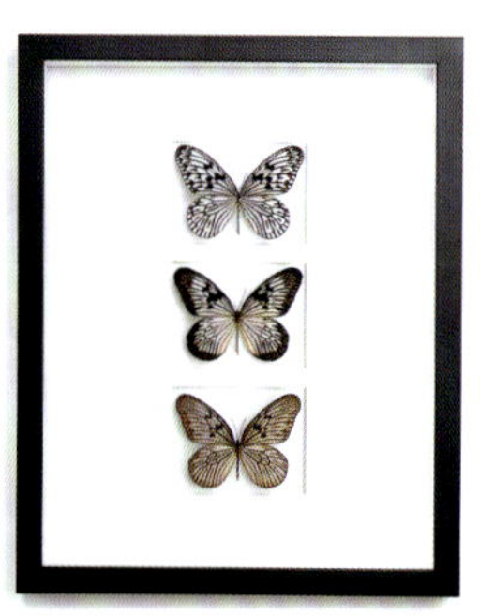

23.
RICE PAPER BUTTERFLY STUDY
Indonesian Rice Paper Butterflies (*Idea idea*, Seram; *Idea blanchardi munaensis*, Buton; *Idea blanchardi blanchardi*, Sulawesi).

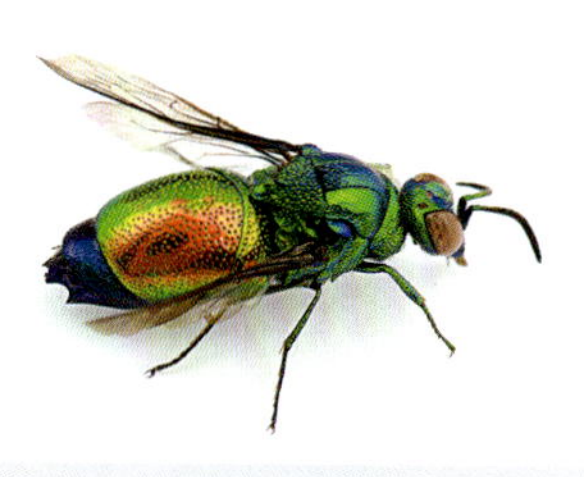

24. CUCKOO WASP
(*Stilbum cyanurum*), Cyprus. This brilliantly adorned wasp has an expansive range that extends through most of Africa, Europe, Asia, Australasia, and many Pacific islands.

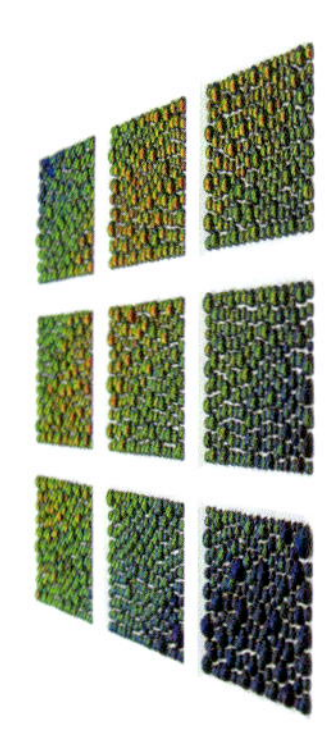

25.
CHRYSOMELID ARRAYAL NO. 1.
Leaf Beetles (*Chrysochus* sp., Java; *Chrysochus* sp., Peru). Ah, ambition. I had originally thought to do a long series of Chrysomelid Arrayal pieces. It only took the first three and a sprained eyeball to convince me otherwise. Composition size, 24 x 30 in.

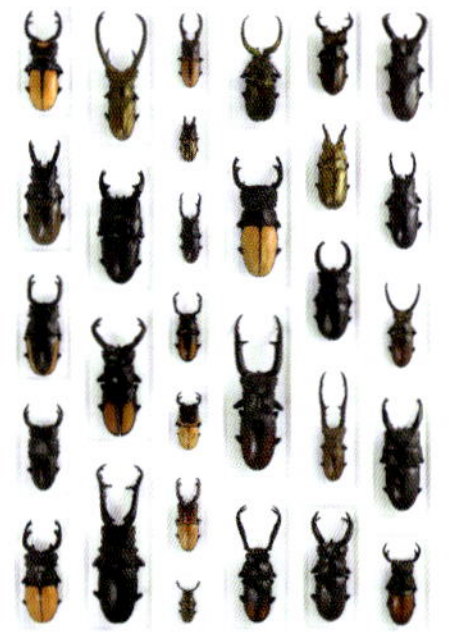

26.
LIMITED STAG BEETLE MOSAIC
(*Lucanidae* sp.), Indonesia, Thailand, Borneo, Chile. I generally feel that, due to my inauspicious early history with insects, I am able to gauge with a healthy degree of accuracy how well a particular piece will be received by my collectors. This piece proves how inaccurate I can be. I worked with my colleagues over several years putting together a remarkable collection of stag beetles from all over the world, to be sold in a limited series of one hundred. When it comes to stags, size truly matters, and included in these mosaics are some contenders for

world-record status. Truly a collector's piece. But to my amazement, there has been very little interest in this limited series. I cannot understand it. To me, the stately (albeit menacing), elaborate mandibles that are the defining characteristic of stag beetles are a proud homage to nature's mastery of industrial design. If there is a sexier manifestation of organic machinery in miniature in the natural world, I'm not aware of it. Composition size, 30 x 40 in.

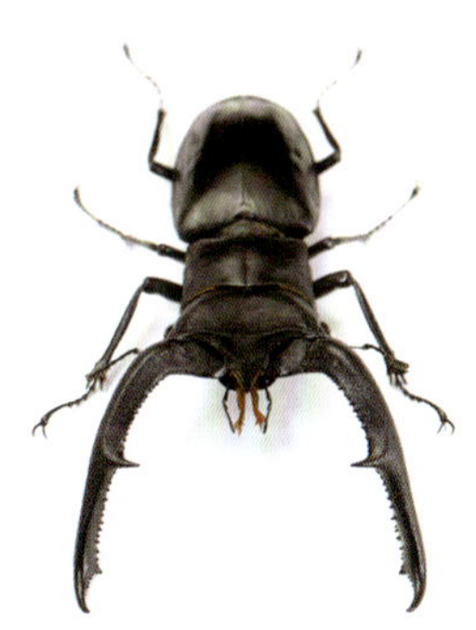

27. STAG BEETLE
(*Hexarthrius mandibularis*), Indonesia.

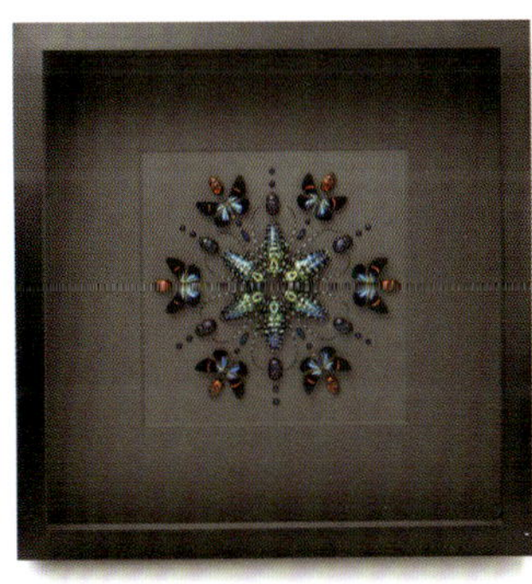

28. SOLLI PRISM.
Center out: Longhorn Beetles (*Calliplophora sollii*), Thailand; Bark Beetles (*Scolytinae* sp.), Cameroon; Dung Beetles (*Geotrupes auratus*), Japan; Ladybird Beetles (*Coccinellidae* sp.), Indonesia; Day-Flying Moths (*Milionia fulgida*), Bali. Composition size, 20 x 20 in.

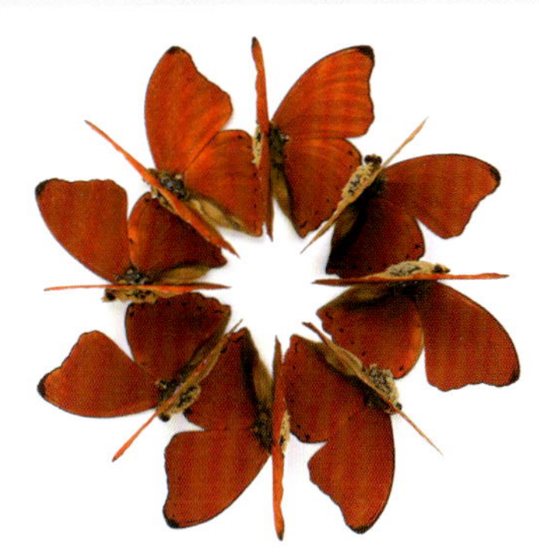

29. SANGARIS ELLIPSE
Red Gliders (*Cymothoe sangaris*), Central African Republic. A smaller yet bolder version of the popular Solar Ellipse. Composition size, 11 x 14 in.

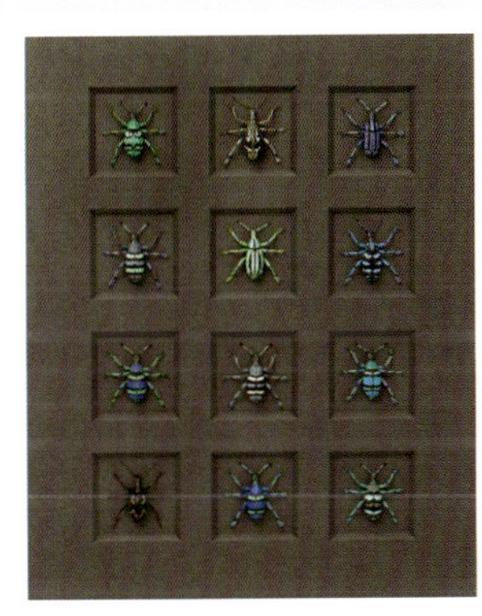

30. EUPHOLUS DEVIATION.
Painted Weevils (*Eupholus* sp.), Indonesia, Papua New Guinea. Composition size, 16 x 20 in.

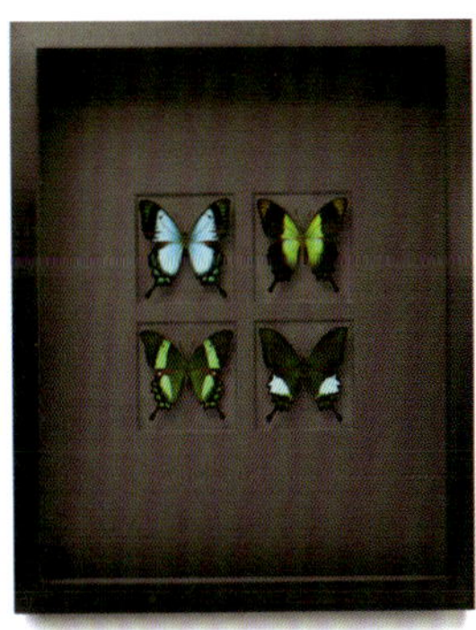

31. GLOSS SWALLOWTAILS.
Top to bottom, l. to r.: *Papilio lorquinianus*, Halmahera Island; *Papilio peranthus*, Sulawesi; *Papilio palinurus*, Malaysia; *Papilio karna*, Java. Composition size, 16 x 20 in.

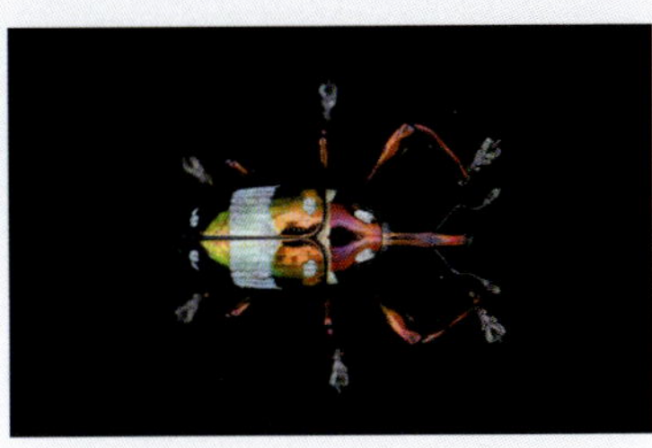

32. TROPICAL WEEVIL
(*Alcidodes* sp.), Philippines.

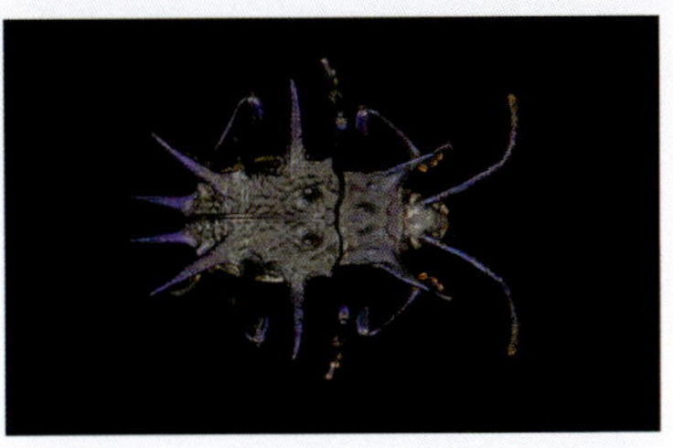

33. SPINY LEAF BEETLE
(*Dicladispa* sp.), Borneo.

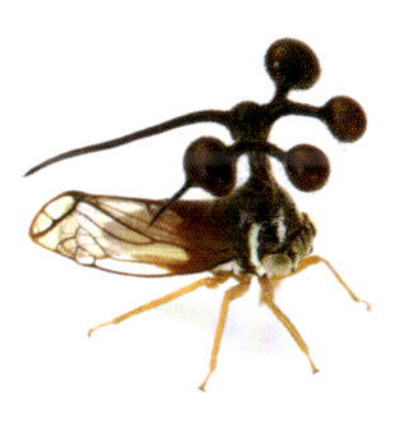

34.
GLOBE-BEARING TREEHOPPER
(*Bocydium globulare*), Brazil. The purpose for the ridiculously elaborate pronotal projections is unknown. It is a solitary species, apparently with good cause.

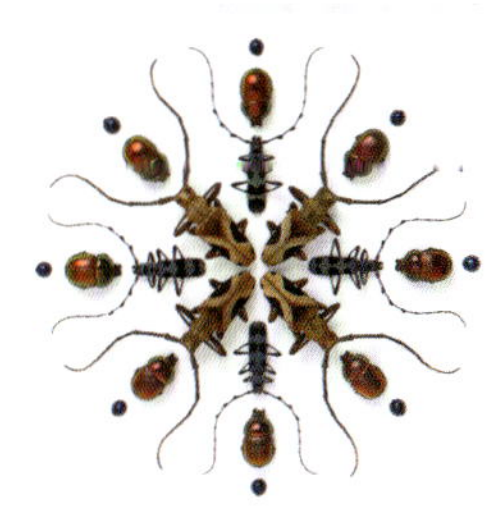

35. CRUCIFERA PRISM.
Center out: *Paraleprodera crucifera*, Thailand; *Rosalia alpina*, Slovenia; *Geotrupes auratus*, Japan; *Coccinellidae* sp., Indonesia. Composition size, 16 x 20 in.

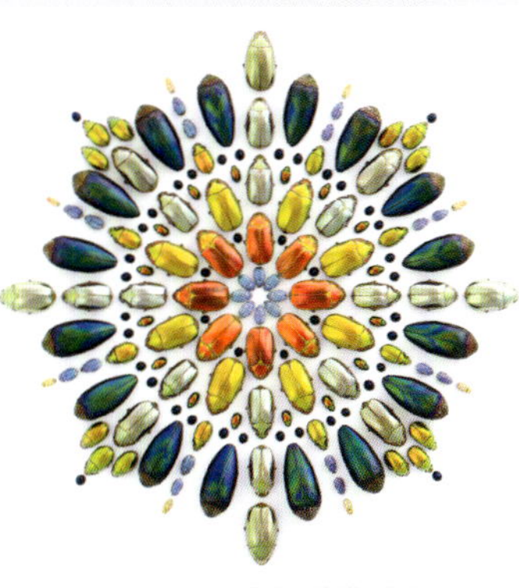

36–37. CHRYSINA PRISM.
Center out: Chafer Scarabs (*Hoplia coerulea*), France; Jewel Scarabs, Red Aberration (*Chrysina aurigans*), Costa Rica; Ladybird Beetles (*Coccinellidae* sp.), Indonesia; Jewel Scarabs, Normal Form (*Chrysina aurigans*), Costa Rica; Jewel Scarabs (*Chrysina strasseni*), Honduras; Leaf Beetles (*Chrysomelidae* sp.), Java; Jewel Scarabs (*Anoplognathus parvulus*), Australia; Metallic Wood-Boring Beetles (*Sternocera pulchra*), Tanzania; Jewel Scarabs (*Chrysina optima*), Costa Rica; Jewel Scarabs (*Chrysina batesi*), Costa Rica; Golden Chafer Scarabs (*Melolonthinae* sp.), Borneo. Australian and Central American jewel scarabs are quite literally worth their weight in gold. Though the inaccessibility of their habitat has left them largely undisturbed, the few enthusiasts knowledgeable enough, and insane enough, to attempt their capture without a helicopter must still rely on an unusual bit of fortune to not come away empty-handed. Here, I speak from sad and repeated experience. The rarity of some species in collections is only eclipsed by the color aberrations they occasionally manifest. Though normally silver or gold in color and polished, brushed, or chromed in texture, if temperature and humidity are precisely aligned, their natural hues can be even further tinted toward the extraordinary. I have spent the past decade and a half collecting such specimens. Composition size, 24 x 30 in.

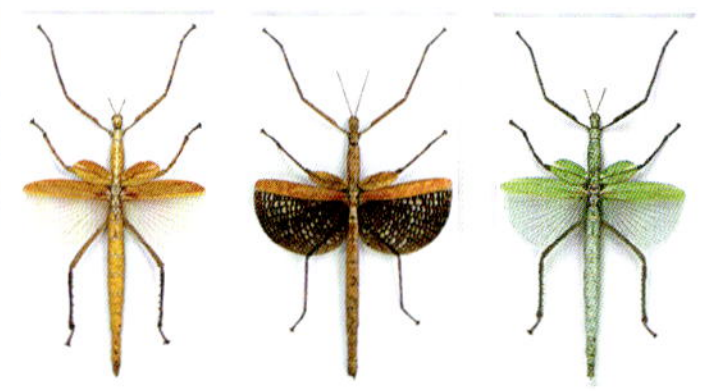

38–39. VERSI WALKING STICKS
(*Eurycnema versirubra*, orange and green forms, Java; *Anchiale maculata*, Halmahera Island). These female winged walking sticks are all much larger than their male counterparts. But unlike the males, they lack the ability to really fly. They will, however, glide from the treetops in an attempt to elude potential predators.

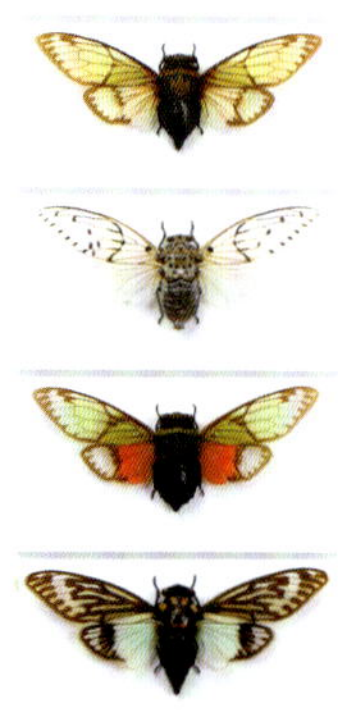

40. TROPICAL CICADAS
(*Salvazana mirabilis*, Thailand; *Ayuthia spectibilis*, Thailand; *Salvazana imperialis*, Thailand; *Distantalna splendida*, Thailand). The bane of nighttime insect collectors the world over—as well as any being with ears unfortunate enough to be in the vicinity of a mass emergence—cicadas are large, fast, and utterly erratic. Their behavior, especially around light traps, seems to indicate either drunkenness or profound stupidity, as they are as likely to fly into your eyes as into the nearby campfire. However, the occasional species exhibits subtle, elegant coloration that belies their often boorish behavior. Composition size, 16 x 20 in.

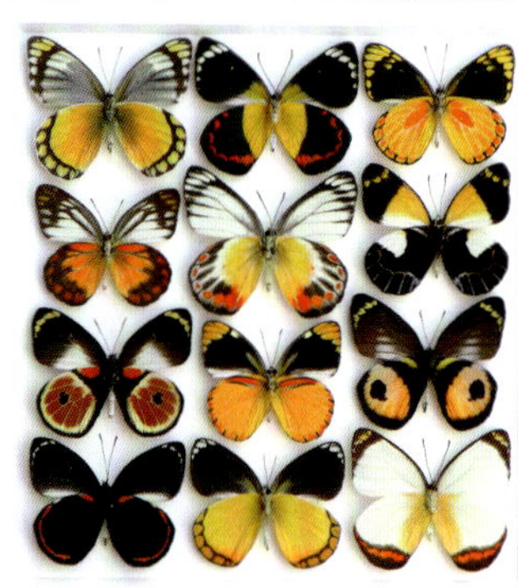

41. DELIAS
Indonesia and New Guinea. An almost ubiquitous genus of butterfly in Asia, delias are a particularly successful group, with species occurring in most Asian ecosystems up to ten thousand feet. Composition size, 16 x 20 in. (also in 20 x 24, 30 x 40).

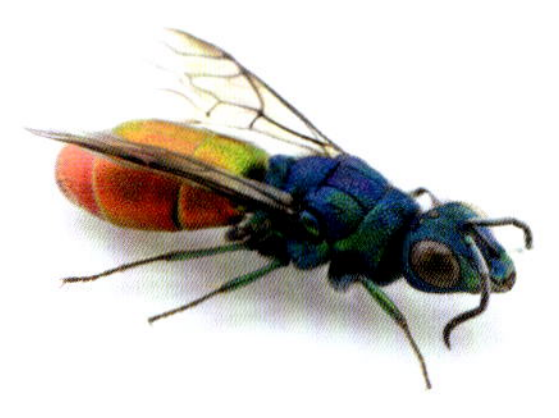

42–43. CUCKOO WASP
(*Chrysura refulgens*), Macedonia.

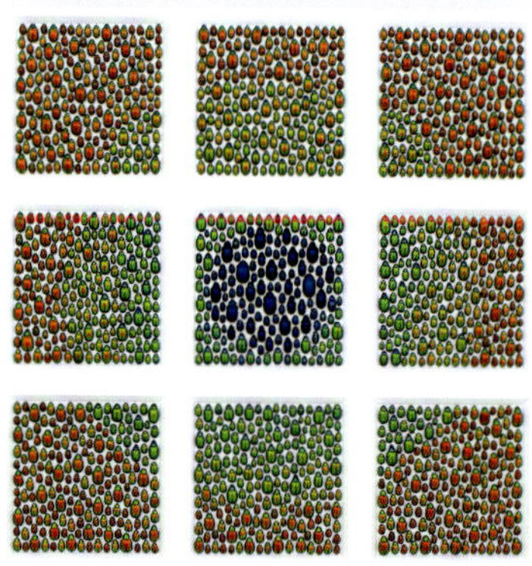

44–45. CHRYSOMELID ARRAYAL NO. 3
Chrysomelid Arrayal No. 2. *Chrysochus auratus*, Java; *Chrysochus* sp., Peru. *Chrysochus* beetles are common enough on several Indonesian islands when conditions are right and the host plant is plentiful. Working with this tiny, fragile insect is taxing, to say the least. After countless hours, my intended large run of Chrysomelid Arrayal pieces was necessarily cut short. Composition size, 24 x 30 in.

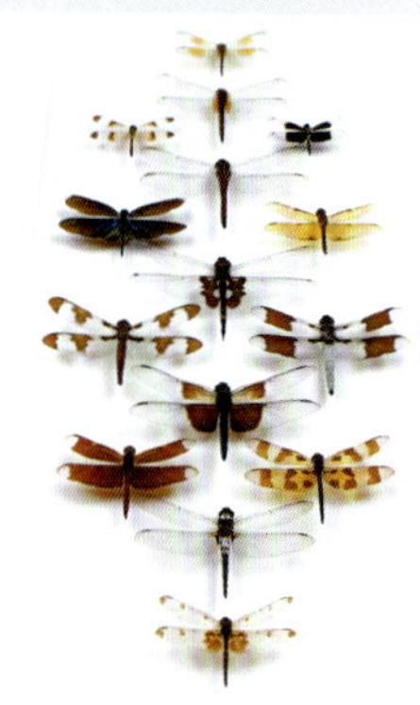

46. DRAGONFLY FORMATION
(*Anisoptera* sp.), Thailand, Malaysia, Indonesia, United States. Because the insect world is so vast, entomologists and enthusiasts necessarily choose only one or two areas to focus on. My area of expertise has always been tropical insect species because that is where I consistently find the most beautiful, brilliantly colored, and bizarre insects to work with. I am woefully uninformed when it comes to most species that are found in temperate climates. So when I set out to transition a bit from working with colorful damselflies (Zygoptera) to dragonflies (Anisoptera), I was surprised to find that nearly every specimen I netted in Latin America and Asia looked pretty much the same: brown body, clear wings. I found myself saying again and again, "I've seen prettier dragonflies around the pond in my home in Oregon!" I finally said it enough that I started looking at home and soon realized that the most attractive dragonflies in the world are, in fact, from North America. That's one in a row for the homeland. Composition size, 20 x 24 in.

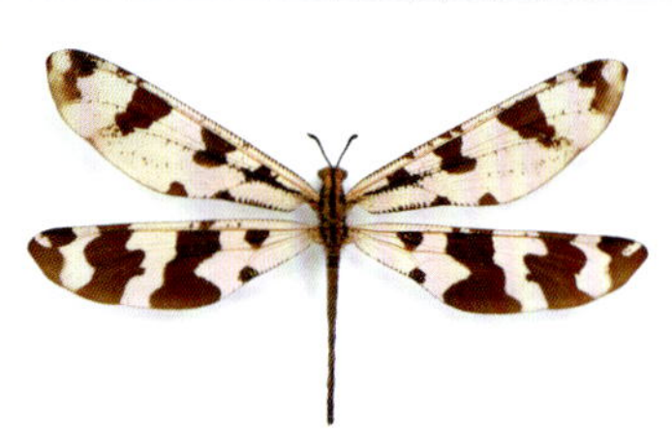

47. REGAL ANT LION
(*Palpares* sp.), Thailand. The radical transition an ant lion such as this makes—from vicious, repulsive grub to lithe, elegant adult—should give a measure of hope to us all.

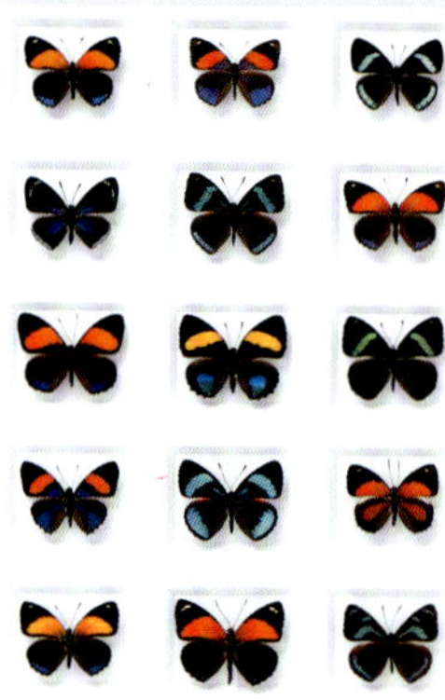

48. CALLICORE BUTTERFLIES
(*Callicore* sp.), Peru. The recto (top) side of *Callicore* butterflies is not what they are known for; it is the verso (bottom) side of their wings, which feature elaborate, intricate markings, some of which resemble numbers and letters. For this reason, they are commonly referred to as "eighty-eights." Composition size, 20 x 24 in.

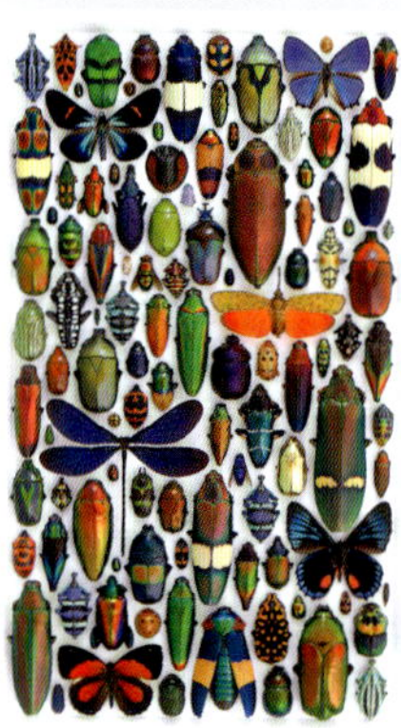

49. AESTHETICA MOSAIC
(worldwide species). My Aesthetica insect mosaics are available in several sizes, hence the dimensions at the end of each note to differentiate them. The insects they contain are collected on all six inhabited continents. Composition size, 24 x 30 in. (also in 16 x 20 and 20 x 24).

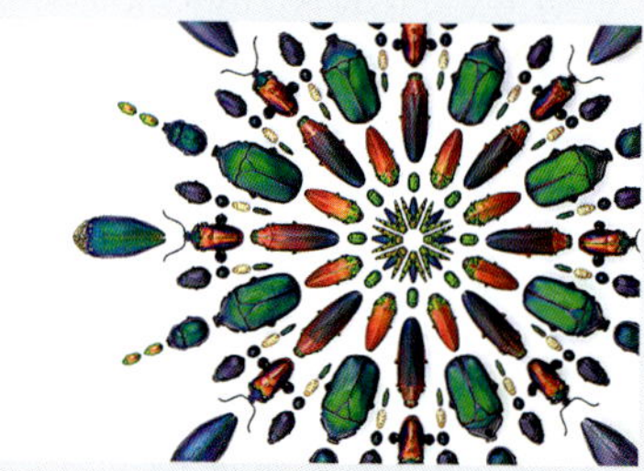

50–51. PRISM NO. 5.
Center out: Metallic Wood-Boring Beetles (*Obenbergerula bakeri*), Romblon

Island; Leaf Beetles (*Chrysochus* sp.), Java; Metallic Wood-Boring Beetles (*Belionota sumptuosa*), Morotai Island; Metallic Wood-Boring Beetles (*Chrysochroa fulminans nishiyamai*), Pulau Simuk Island; Flower Scarabs (*Torynorrhina flammea chicheryi*), Malaysia; Metallic Wood-Boring Beetles (*Agrilus acutus*), Java; Golden Chafer Scarabs (*Melolonthinae* sp.), Borneo; Rainbow Leaf Beetles (*Sagra buqueti*), Malaysia; Ladybird Beetles (*Coccinellidae* sp.), Indonesia; Shining Leaf Scarabs (*Rutelidae* sp.), Thailand; Dung Beetles (*Geotrupes auratus*), Japan; Metallic Wood-Boring Beetles (*Sternocera pulchra*), Tanzania; Leaf Beetles (*Chrysochus auratus*), Sulawesi. Composition size, 24 x 30 in.

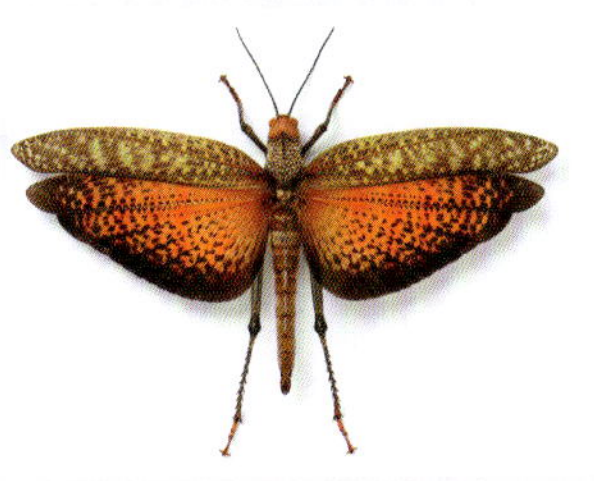

52. TROPICAL LOCUST
(*Tropidacris dux*), Guatemala. This is one of the largest grasshoppers in the world, although, thankfully, it is not known to swarm and is not considered an agricultural pest.

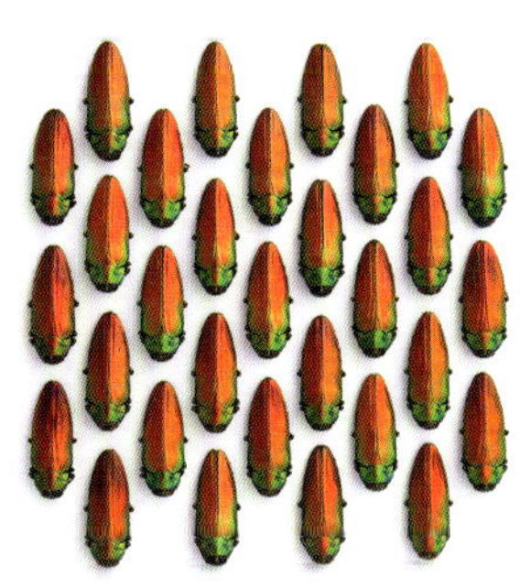

53. SUMPTUOSA
(*Belionota sumptuosa*), Morotai Island. Composition size, 16 x 20 in.

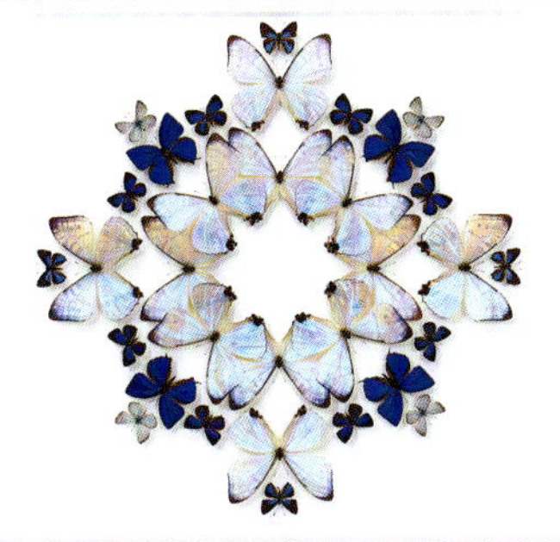

54. LUMENS PRISM.
Center out: *Morpho sulkowskyi*, Peru; *Arhopala hercules*, Sulawesi; *Arhopala admete*, Sorong; *Polyommatus icarus*, France; *Tajuria* sp., Indonesia. Composition size, 24 x 30 in.

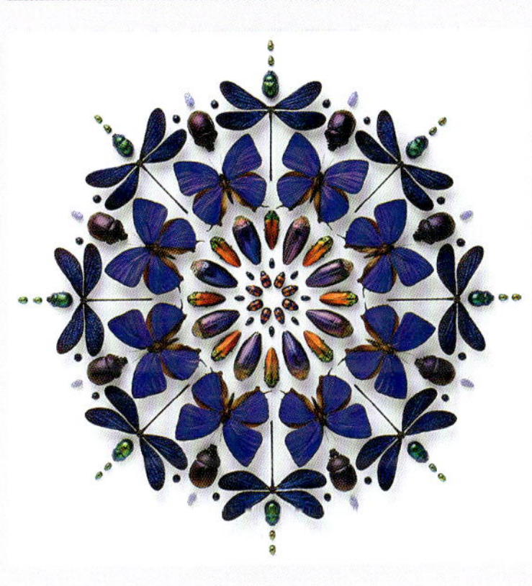

55. SUMPTUOSA PRISM.
Center out: *Chrysomelidae* sp., Laos; *Chrysomelidae* sp., Indonesia; *Sternocera pulchra*, Tanzania; *Belionota sumptuosa*, Indonesia; *Arhopala herculina*, Indonesia; *Euphaea laidlawi*, Philippines; *Enoplotrupes sharpi*, Thailand; *Coccinellidae* sp., Indonesia; *Geotrupes auratus*, Japan; *Hoplia coerulea*, France; *Chrysochus* sp., Indonesia. Composition size, 24 x 24 in.

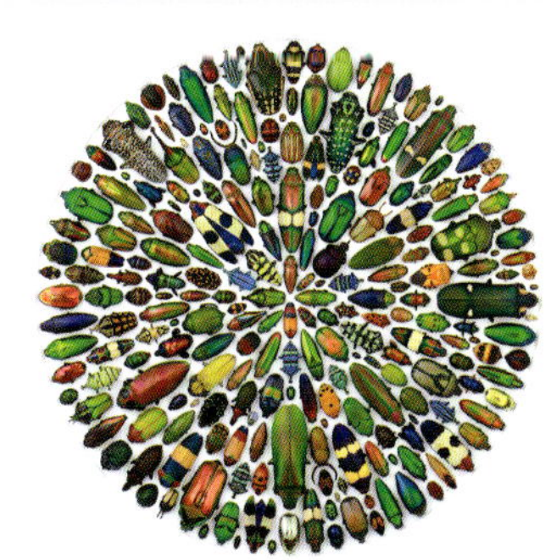

56. LIMITED MOSAIC PRISM
(worldwide species). A limited run of one hundred pieces comprise this kaleidoscopic series of worldwide Coleoptera. Composition size, 24 x 30 in.

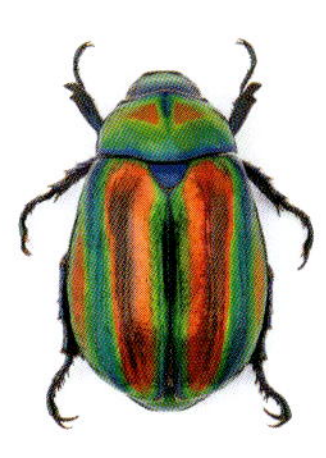

57. RAINBOW SCARAB
(*Anomala* sp.), Laos.

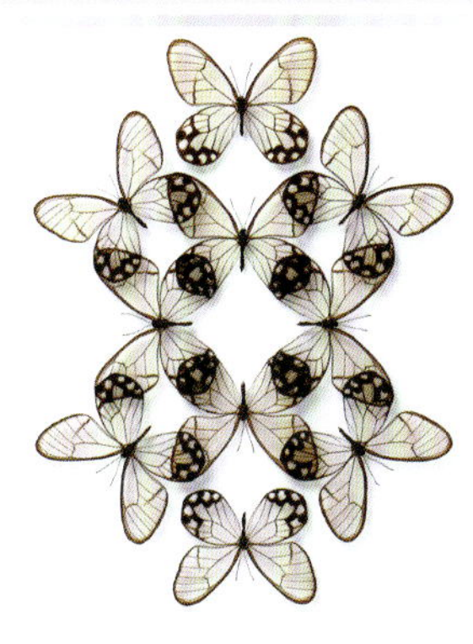

58. CLEARWING BUTTERFLIES
(*Haetera hypaesia*), Peru. Composition size, 16 x 20 in.

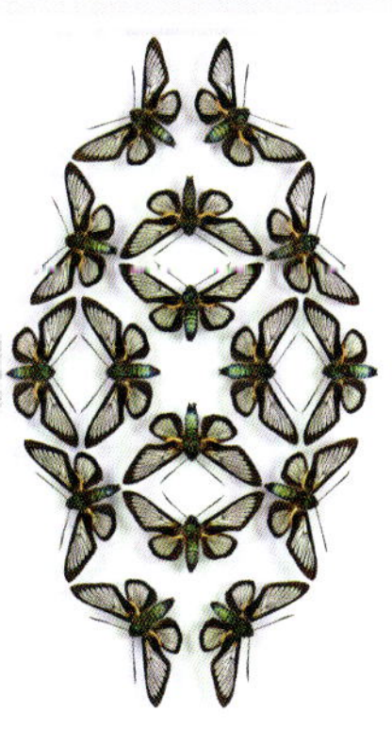

59. CLEARWING MOTHS
(*Cocytia durvillii*), Aru Islands. Composition size, 20 x 24 in.

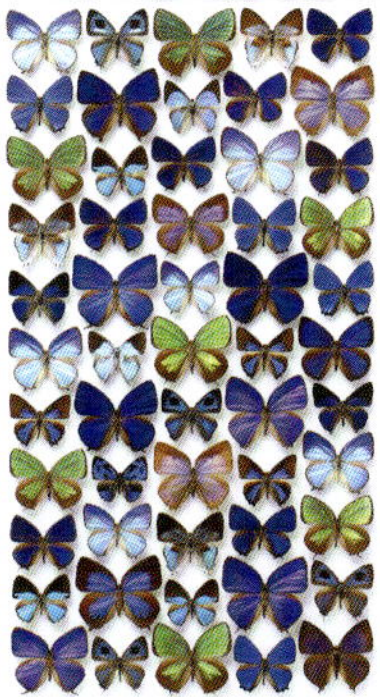

60.
LIMITED LYCAENIDAE MOSAIC
(*Lycaenidae* sp.), Southeast Asia. This was a difficult piece to make for several reasons. First, Lycaenidae butterflies do not swarm, so there is never a shortcut to finding one; each catch is serendipitous. Second, they are incredibly nimble fliers. I can't count the number of times I have examined my net for a hole because I could have sworn that I saw the butterfly actually enter the net midswipe only to watch it mockingly flit away. As if being difficult to find and nearly impossible to catch weren't enough, their rapid wing beat and competition among males damage their unusually fragile wing scales very early in their short adult lives. Therefore, catching a specimen that is sufficiently pristine for my work is rare. Finally, if one is captured, dispatched, field-dried, stored, shipped to the studio, and rehydrated without damage, chances are high that it will be rubbed or scratched beyond use when spread, pinned, dried, or handled during composition. A very limited piece indeed. Composition size, 24 x 30 in.

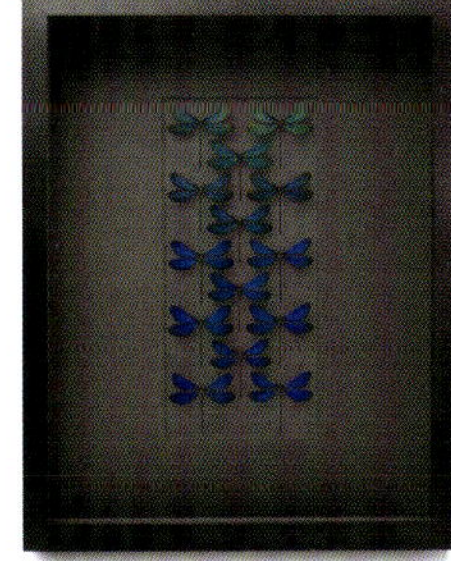

61. DAMSELFLY WASH
(*Euphaea laidlawi*), Philippines. Perhaps the most richly colored damselfly in the world is somewhat variable, but each hue, from oil-slick green to cobalt blue, is richer than the next. Composition size, 20 x 24 in. (also in 24 x 30).

Sea Creatures

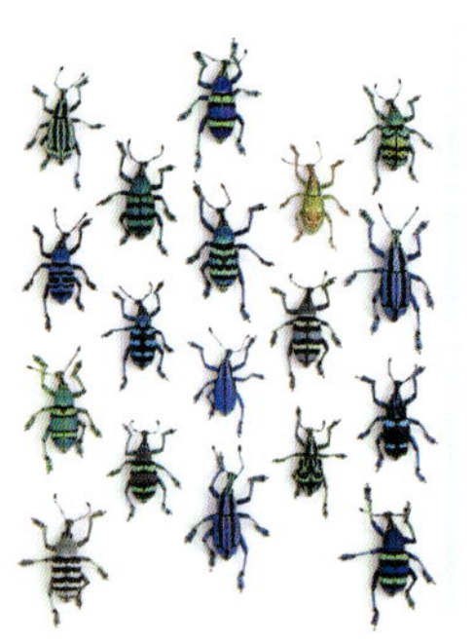

62. WALKING WEEVILS.
Painted Weevils (*Eupholus* and *Rhinoscapha* sp.), Indonesia, Papua New Guinea. This piece is the follow-up to the smaller 11 x 14 in. *Walking Weevils* featuring Ornate Weevils of the genus *Pachyrrhynchus* from the Philippines. Composition size, 16 x 20 in.

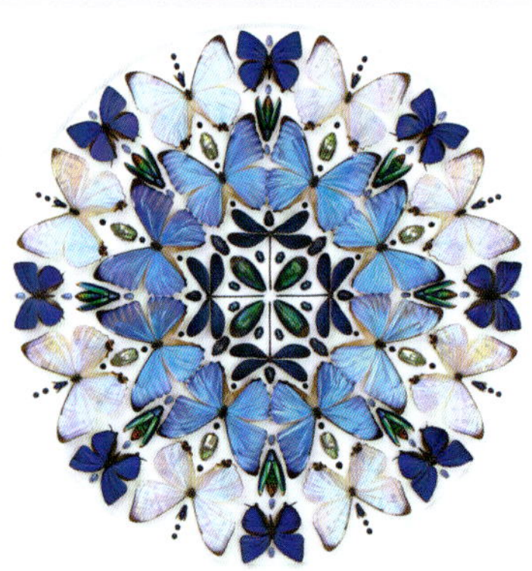

63.
LIMITED AESTHETICA PRISM.
Center out: Metallic Wood-Boring Beetles (*Sternocera pulchra*), Tanzania; Damselflies (*Euphaea laidlawi*), Philippines; Shield Bugs (*Scutelleridae* sp.), Java; Flower Beetles (*Chlorocara africana*), Tanzania; Shining Leaf Beetles (*Rutelidae* sp.), Thailand; Ladybird Beetles (*Coccinellidae* sp.), Indonesia; Morpho Butterflies (*Morpho aurora*), Peru; Jewel Scarabs (*Chrysina optima*), Costa Rica; Chafer Scarabs (*Hoplia coerulea*), France; Metallic Wood-Boring Beetles (*Chrysochroa fulminans cobaltina*), Philippines; Morpho Butterflies (*Morpho sulkowskyi*), Peru; Blue Butterflies (*Arhopala hercules*), Sulawesi; Cuckoo Wasps (*Chrysididae* sp.), Peru. Composition size, 30 x 40 in.

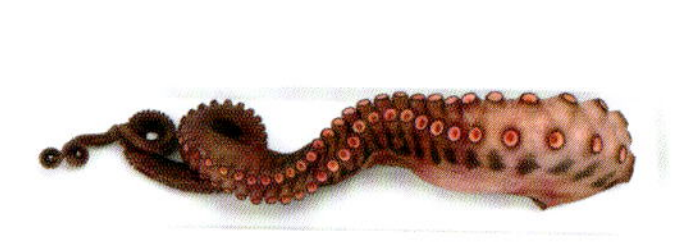

65. OCTOPUS TENTACLE
(*Octopus vulgaris*), Atlantic Ocean.

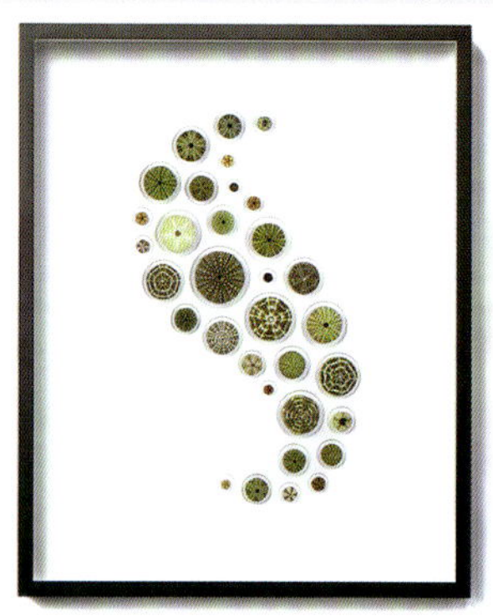

66–67. URCHIN SPHERES
(*Echinoidea* sp.), Thailand, Philippines, Mexico, United States. The shell of the sea urchin is called a "test." Composition size, 32 x 40 in.

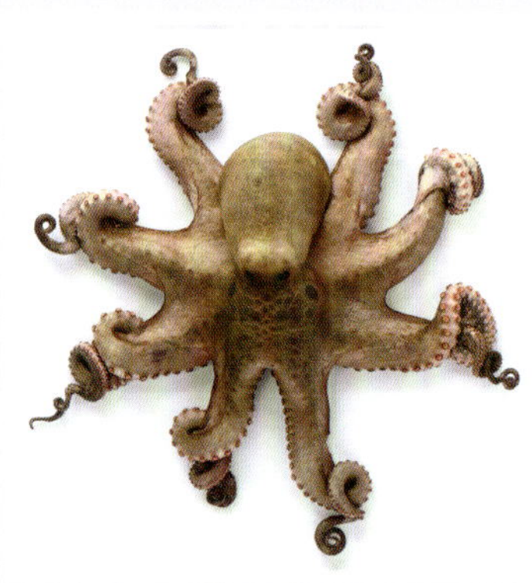

68. PRESERVED OCTOPUS
(*Octopus vulgaris*), Atlantic Ocean. Cephalopods are among the most difficult organisms to preserve well. The few successes I've had so far have been, unfortunately, quite serendipitous. However, when one is successfully preserved, there will be little to no deterioration over time, due to the scarcity of lipids in the muscle tissue.

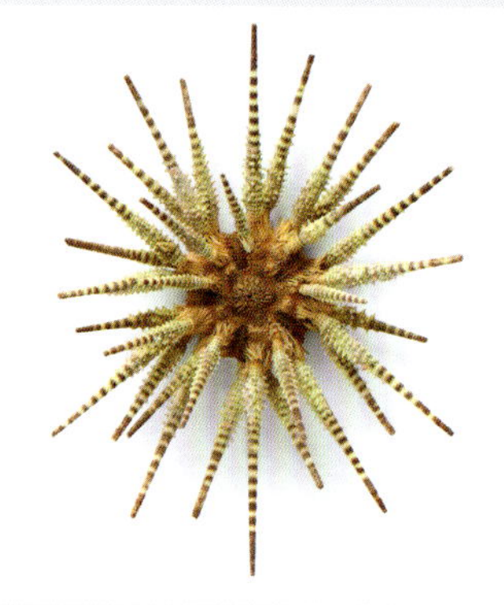

69. BARNACLED SEA URCHIN
(*Stylocidaris albidens*), Philippines.

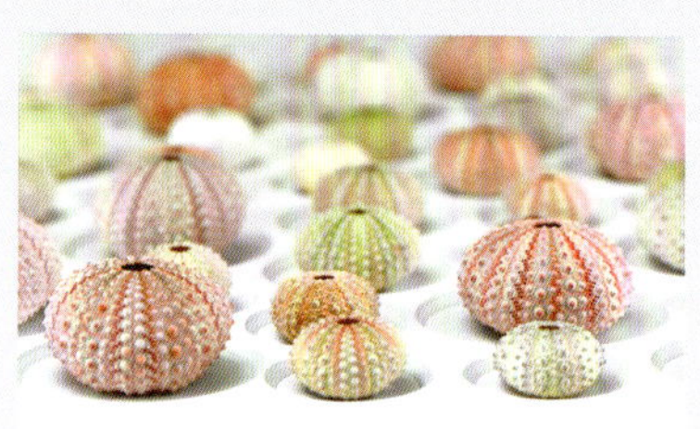

70–71. PASTEL URCHIN MOSAIC
(*Echinometra mathaei*), Philippines. A common rock-boring urchin with a massive range that covers nearly one half of the planet. Composition size, 24 x 30 in.

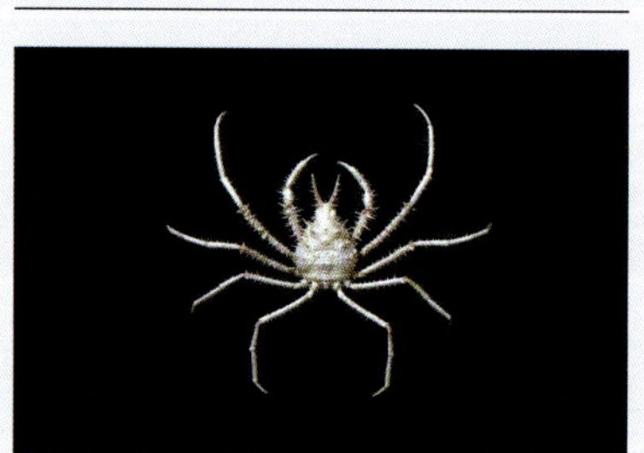

72. SPIDER CRAB
(*Pleistacantha cervicornis*), Philippines. 250 m.

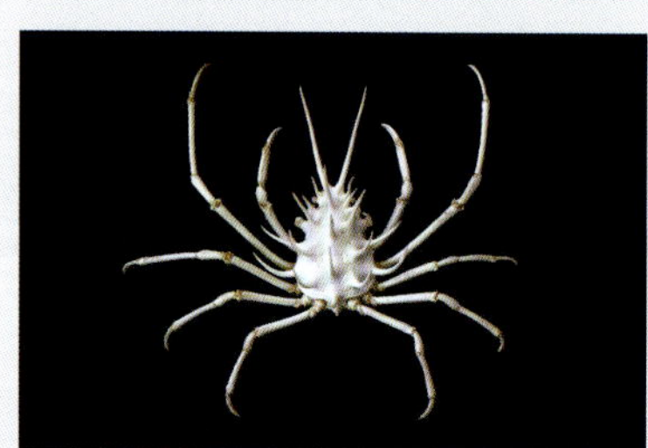

73. THORN CRAB
(*Naxioides teatui*), Philippines. 200 m.

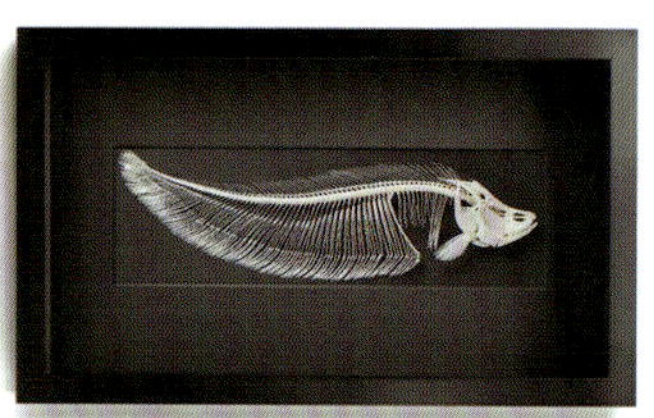

74. KNIFE FISH
(*Chitala* sp.), Thailand. This is an aggressive, carnivorous, freshwater species, originating in Indochina and Thailand, that has become invasive and damaging to indigenous populations of fish and amphibians in the Southern United States.

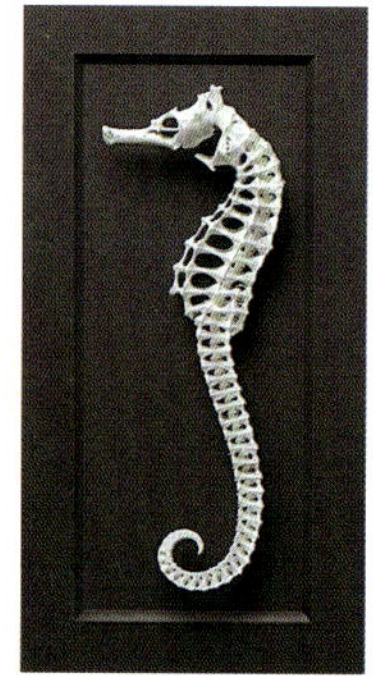

75. SEA HORSE SKELETON
(*Hippocampus* sp.), Philippines. Powder made from ground-up sea horses is a common ingredient in Chinese medicines used to treat impotence (unlike most Chinese medicines).

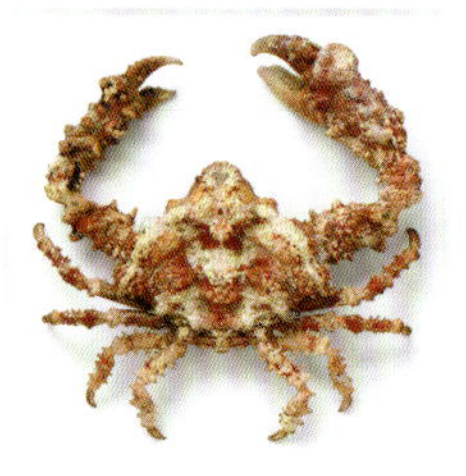

76. HORRID ELBOW CRAB
(*Daldorfia horrida*), Philippines. 15 m.

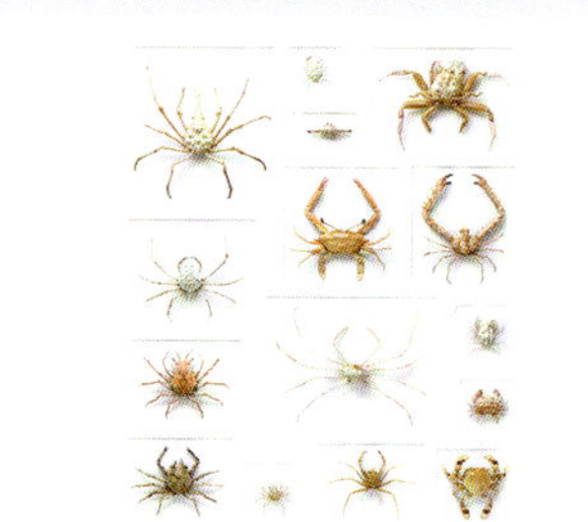

77. DECAPOD MOSAIC
(*Brachyura* sp.), Philippines. Composition size, 32 x 40 in.

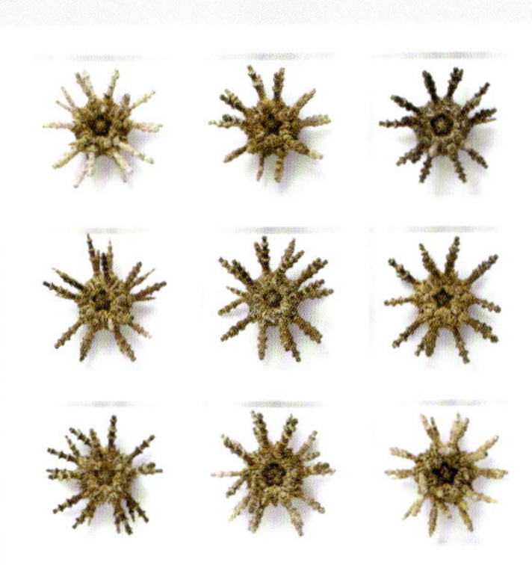

78. SPUTNIK URCHINS
(*Prionocidaris verticillata*), Philippines. Composition size, 16 x 20 in.

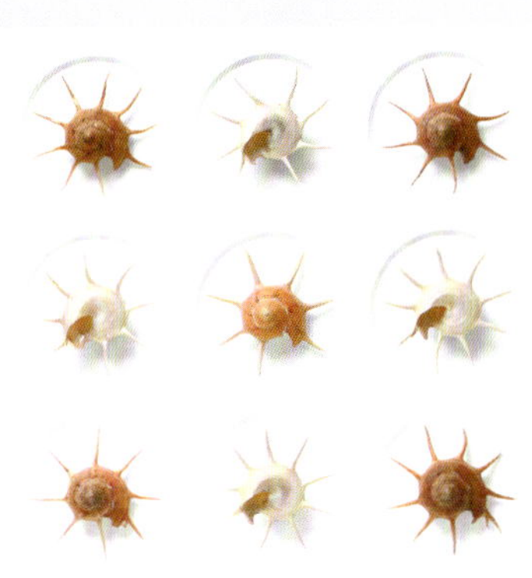

79. GILDED STARSHELLS
(*Guildfordia yoka*), Philippines. This gorgeous little species is what convinced me to start working with shells about ten years ago. Composition size, 16 x 20 in.

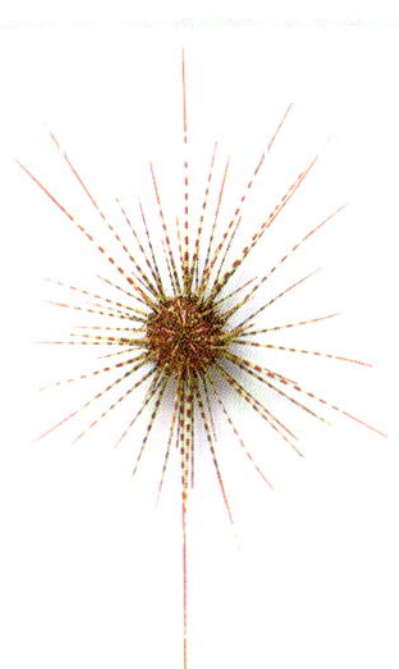

80. MAILLARDI URCHIN
(*Coelopleurus maillardi*), Philippines. The test of this intricate urchin is as singular when denuded as it is with its needlelike spines intact.

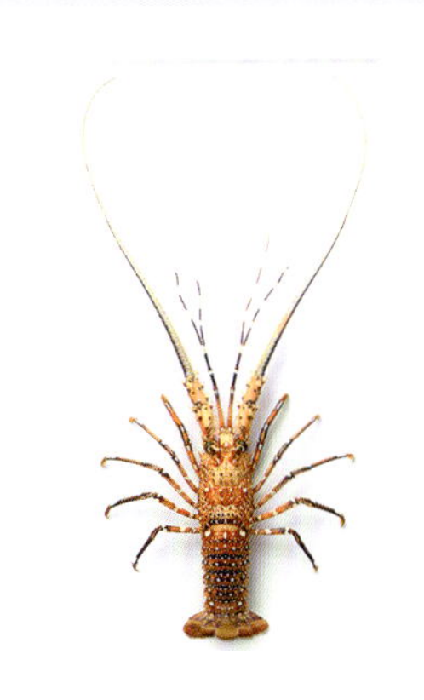

81. PAINTED LOBSTER
(*Panulirus* sp.), Indonesia.

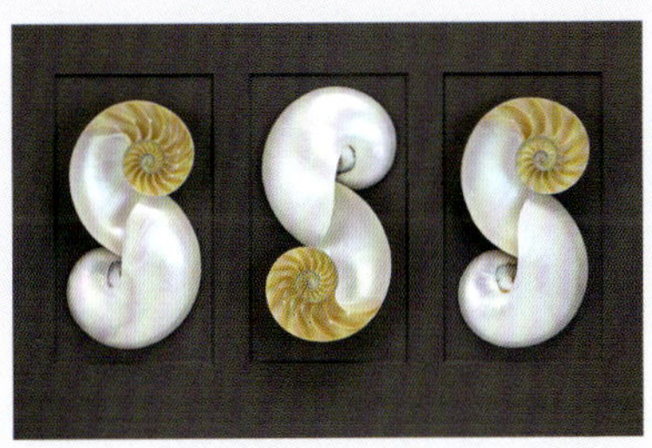

82. NAUTILUS TRIO
(*Nautilus pompilius*), Philippines. In the wild, this is probably the oddest of all cephalopods, with its more than ninety short, suckerless tentacles; oversize, primitive eyes; and ill-fitting fleshy sheath. The awkward undulations that slowly propel this species through the water only add to its otherworldly visage. However, the logarithmically proportioned chambers inside the nautilus's protective shell have been a vaunted epitome of the geometric spiral as it occurs in nature for centuries, and whether polished (as shown) or rough, the nautilus is among the most beautiful of mollusks. Composition size, 32 x 20 in.

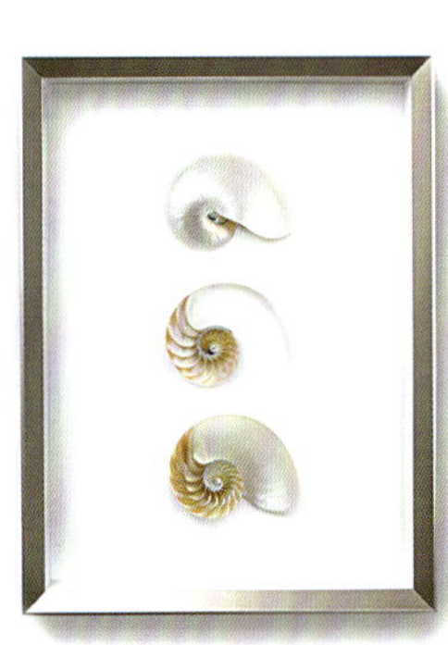

83. NAUTILUS TRIPTYCH
(*Nautilus pompilius*), Philippines. A tri-cut nautilus shell. Composition size, 18 x 24 in.

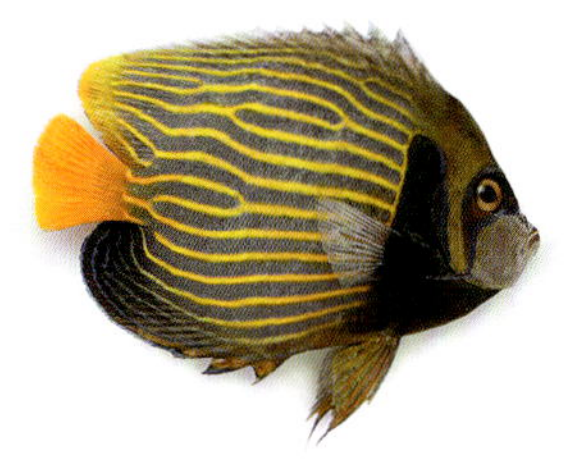

84. EMPEROR ANGELFISH
(*Pomacanthus imperator*), Red Sea. This gorgeous fish sports a radically different though equally intricate pattern for the first two to three years of its life until it transitions to the pattern seen here.

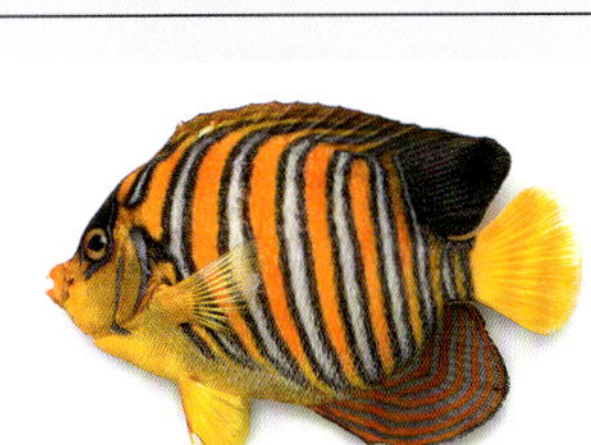

85. REGAL ANGELFISH
(*Pygoplites diacanthus*), Indian Ocean. Though perfectly preserved (if I do say so myself), the jury is still out on how colorfast the hues of dried tropical fish will be.

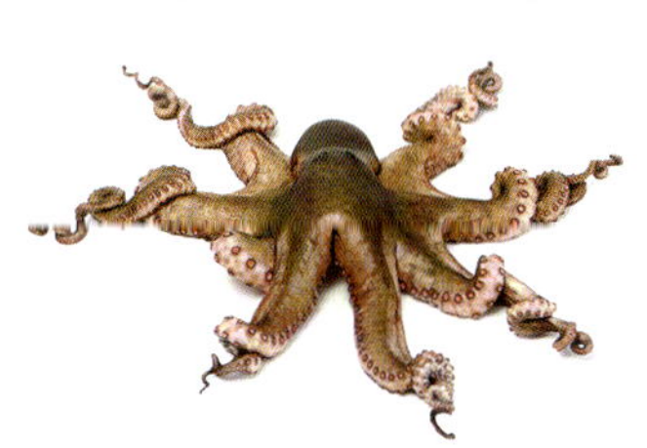

86–87. OCTOPUS
(*Octopus vulgaris*), Atlantic Ocean. The octopus is one of the most amazing and ironic of all creatures on earth. They are skeletonless, live very short lives, and are perhaps the most intelligent invertebrate in the world. They only breed once, and the experience is fatal to both sexes. Their ability to escape nearly any enclosure and to use tools and solve problems is legendary and astonishing. They are able to detach an apparently still-sentient limb in order to escape predation if their remarkable chromatophoric camouflage or the emptying of their ink sac does not do the trick. Most are poisonous, and one species is perhaps the most deadly toxic organism on earth. Truly, an animal replete with superlatives.

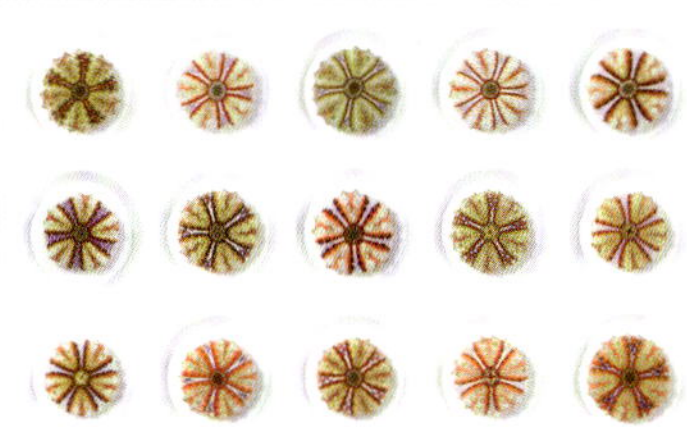

88–89. VARIEGATED URCHINS
(*Coelopleurus maillardi*), Philippines. The test of the long-spined Maillardi urchin is one of the most beautiful of any urchin species. I have seen thousands of specimens, and no two appear to be alike.

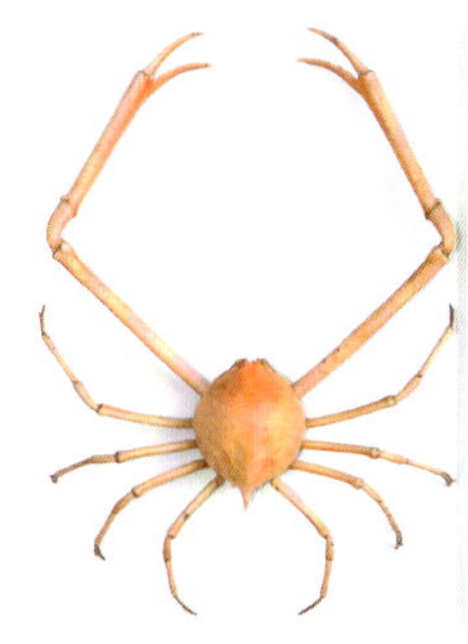

90. PEBBLE CRAB
(*Parilia major*), Philippines. 100 m.

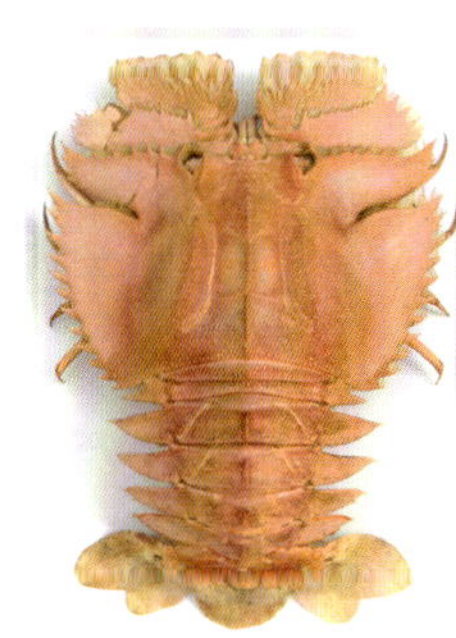

91. SLIPPER LOBSTER
(*Ibacus ciliatus*), Philippines. 125 m.

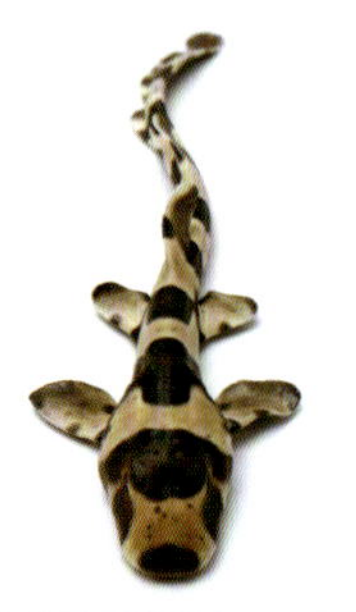

92. BANDED CAT SHARK
(*Chiloscyllium punctatum*), Japan. This is a smaller shark (1 meter long), and it is an opportunistic feeder, eating almost any fish, cephalopod, crustacean, or mollusk it can overpower.

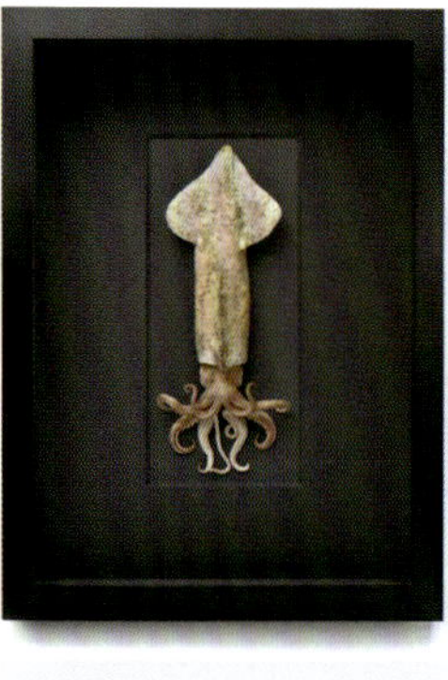

93. EUROPEAN SQUID
(*Loligo vulgaris*), Atlantic Ocean. One of the most widespread species of squid, and a popular food item in cultures around the world.

Reptiles

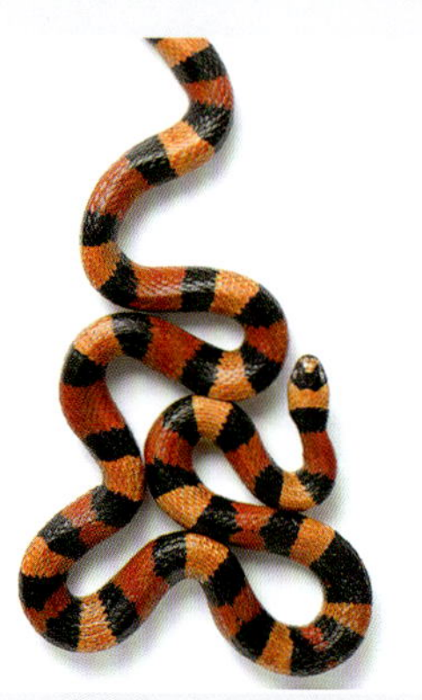

95.
APRICOT PUEBLAN MILK SNAKE
(*Lampropeltis triangulum campbelli*), Mexico.

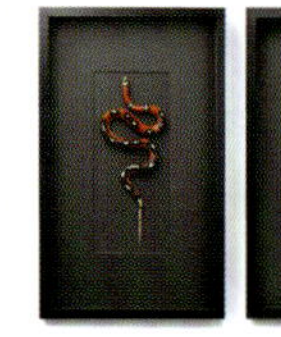
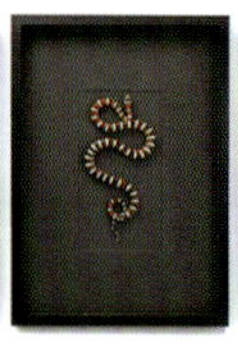

96–97. SPLOTCHED SINALOAN MILK SNAKE
(*Lampropeltis triangulum sinaloae*), Mexico; MOUNTAIN KING SNAKE (*Lampropeltis zonata*), Western United States and Mexico; GRAY-BANDED KING SNAKE (*Lampropeltis alterna*), Southern United States and Mexico.

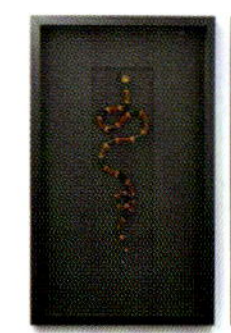
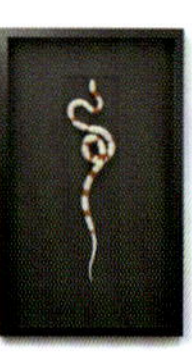
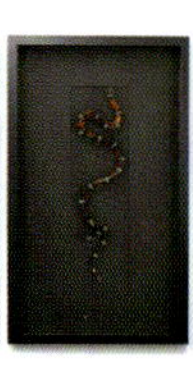

98. CORAL SNAKE
(*Micrurus fulvius*), Eastern United States; ALBINO NELSON'S MILK SNAKE (*Lampropeltis triangulum nelsoni*), Mexico; ABERRANT NELSON'S MILK SNAKE (*Lampropeltis triangulum nelsoni*), Mexico.

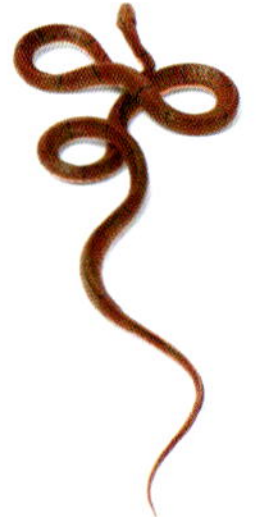

99. BAMBOO RAT SNAKE
(*Oreocryptophis porphyracea nigrofasciata*), Thailand.

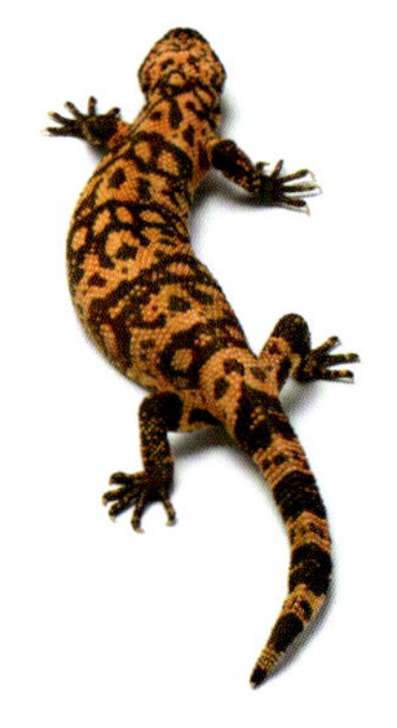

100. GILA MONSTER
(*Heloderma suspectum*), United States. One of only two venomous lizards in the world, Gila monsters are relatively rare in the wild and much more so in captivity.

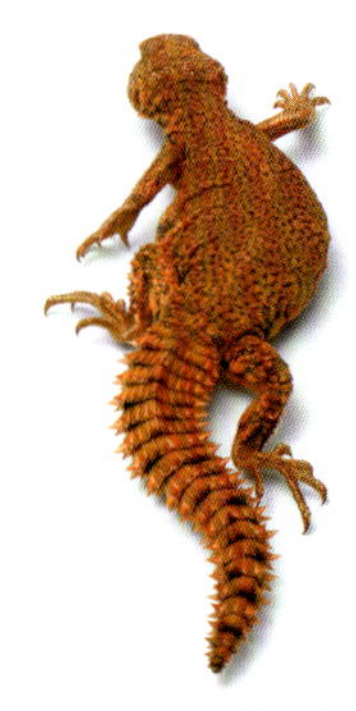

101. SAHARAN UROMASTYX
(*Uromastyx geyri*), Algeria. When I was a young herpetoculturist, the only *Uromastyx geyri* in captivity were drab, gray-brown, and ugly. (Sorry, *Uromastyx*, but it's true.) Little did I know that two other color forms of the species were abundant in different regions of their North African range—one neon yellow and one Day-Glo orange. Now I'm a huge fan.

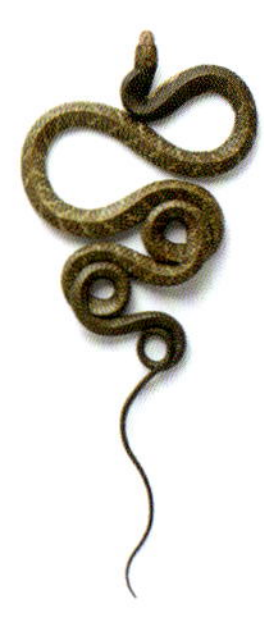

102. KING COBRA
(*Ophiophagus hannah*), Myanmar.

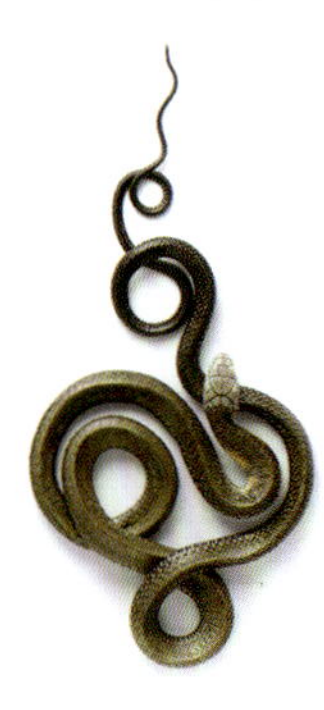

103. ASIAN COBRA
(*Naja naja*), Sri Lanka. There are increasingly few institutions or breeders raising venomous snakes in the United States. Those that remain are determined, highly skilled, and understandably defensive, as their trade either hangs by a legislative thread or has already been outlawed in their respective states. This is very unfortunate. Some of the most beautiful and captivating of all snakes are venomous, and though the dangers of working with them are obvious, tragic incidents are extremely rare. Like so many interests that are outside the mainstream, the husbandry of venomous reptiles appears to be in critical danger of extinction.

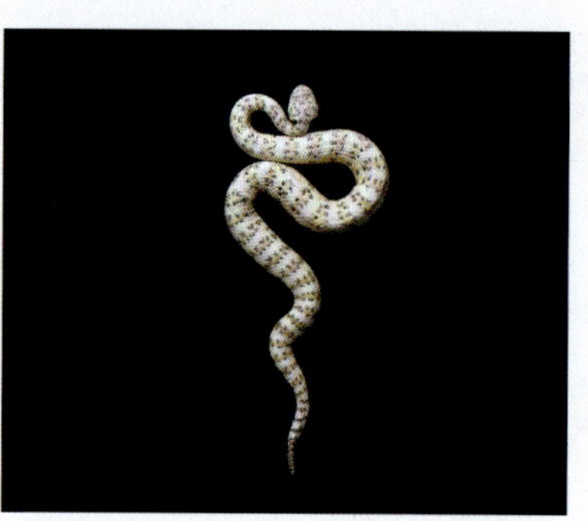

104. SPECKLED RATTLESNAKE
(*Crotalus mitchellii*), United States, Mexico. Like all reptiles I work with, this specimen was reclaimed after it died in captivity. I was thrilled when it arrived, as I was not familiar with this color form of *Crotalus mitchellii*. In my opinion, it is one of the most elegant rattlesnakes.

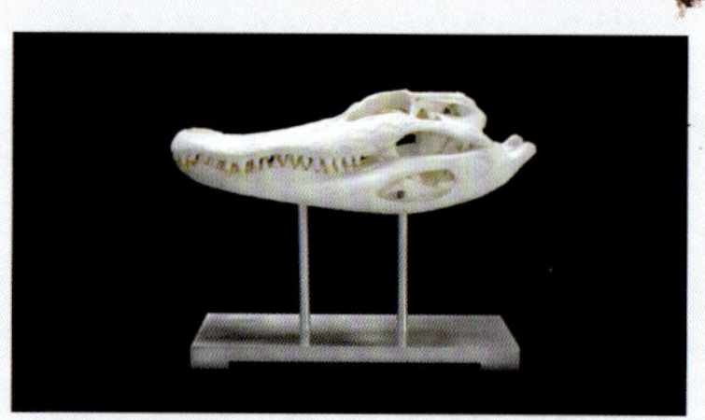

105. RECLAIMED AMERICAN ALLIGATOR
(*Alligator mississippiensis*), Southern United States. The largest species of reptile in the United States is endemic to the South. Though its status as a species was in doubt through the 1960s, conservation and breeding efforts resulted in a full recovery of the population, and alligators are now quite common in many parts of Louisiana, Georgia, Florida, and Alabama.

Tens of thousands of farmed alligators are harvested each year for their hides and meat, but very little use is made of the skeleton, which strikes me as a terrible waste of a fascinating artifact.

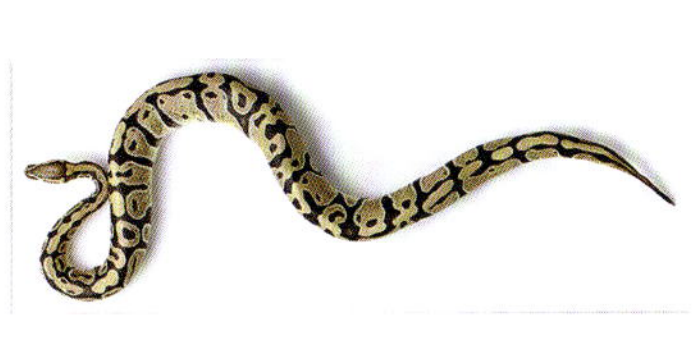

106–107.
ROYAL PYTHON, VANILLA FORM
(*Python regius*), Ghana. What used to be the most banal of all pet store fodder has become one of the most dynamic and exciting of all reptiles commonly kept in captivity. The royal, or ball, python has been selectively bred to such an extent that literally hundreds of different color forms now exist. Aside from being the quintessential animal for captivity due to its low maintenance and docile, sedentary nature, another bonus of a royal python color morph is that it is guaranteed to be captive-bred. In my mind, these features combine to make this python a near-perfect pet.

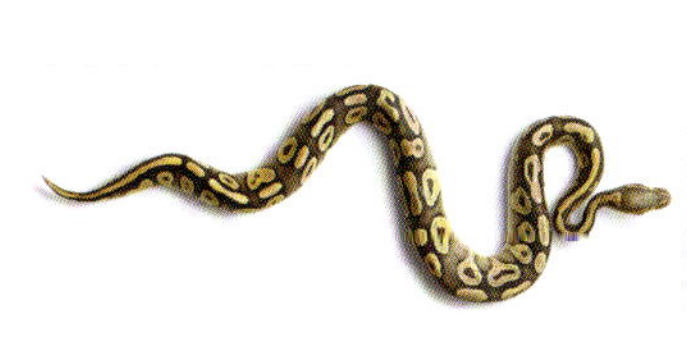

106–107.
ROYAL PYTHON, MOJAVE FORM
(*Python regius*), Ivory Coast.

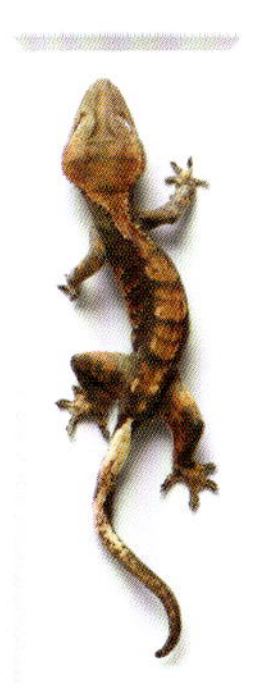

108. CRESTED GECKO
(*Correlophus ciliatus*), New Caledonia. Incredibly, this gecko species was thought to be extinct only twenty years ago. Then, a few breeding pairs were legally exported into Europe and the United States after they were rediscovered, in an attempt to establish a small population in captivity against the threat of extinction. Herpetoculturists quickly went to work, and within two decades, the crested gecko became one of the most widely bred species of gecko in captivity throughout the world. Though it is still rare in its tiny, endemic range in Southern New Caledonia, its perpetually healthy status as a species, at least in captivity, is virtually assured.

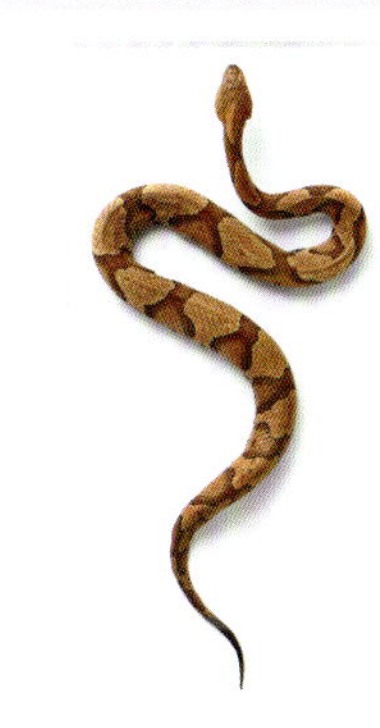

109. COPPERHEAD VIPER
(*Agkistrodon contortrix*), United States. Though it is quite common and one of the most beautiful of North American vipers, the copperhead is rarely bred in captivity. Consequently, this is the only specimen of the species I have ever had the opportunity to work on.

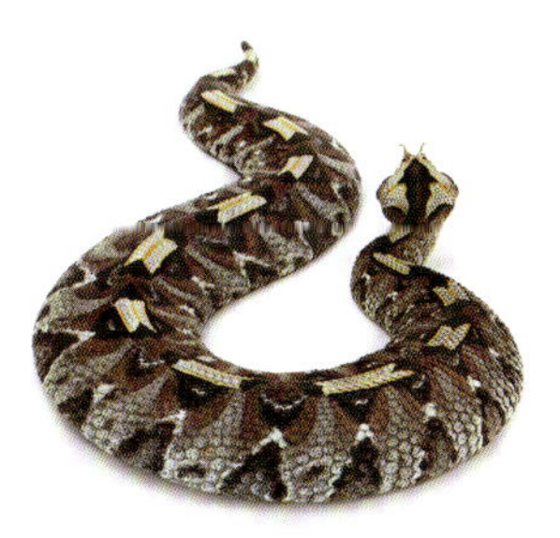

110–111. RHINOCEROS VIPER
(*Bitis nasicornis*), Central African Republic. Though this is thought to be one of the most deadly of African vipers due to its complicated cocktail of both neurotoxic and hemotoxic venom, it is also one of the more commonly kept species of venomous snakes. Of course, "common" here is a relative term, but the unusual morphology and astonishingly intricate markings of this species make it nearly irresistible to both institutions and individuals that venture to care for and breed venomous reptiles. Consequently, I have had the privilege of working on a number of specimens.

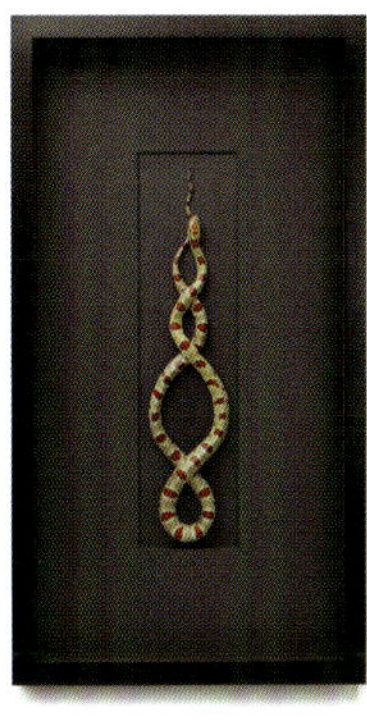

112.
KING/CORN SNAKE HYBRID
(*Lampropeltis mexicana thayeri* x *Pantherophis guttatus guttatus*), United States. A rare hybrid between a Nuevo Leon king snake and a corn snake.

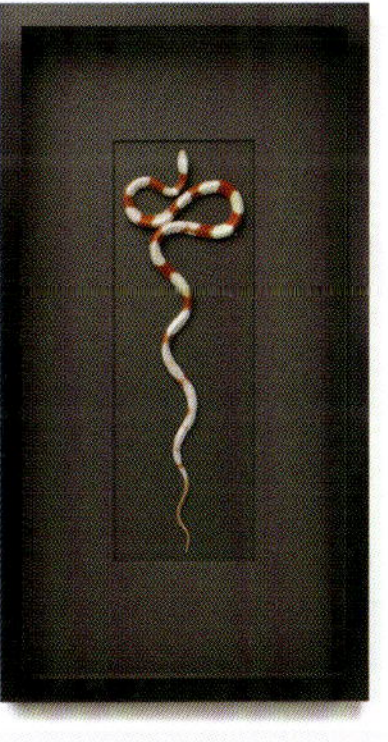

113. ALBINO NELSON'S MILK SNAKE
(*Lampropeltis triangulum nelsoni*), Mexico.

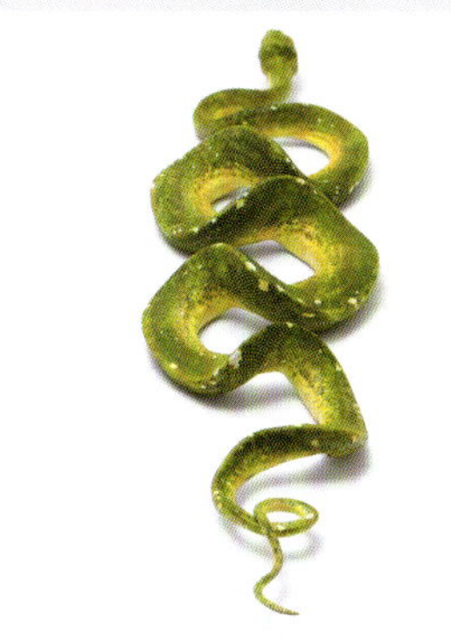

114. GREEN TREE PYTHON
(*Morelia viridis*), Australia. Due to highly successful breeding efforts in captivity, this species is one I have been fortunate to work with fairly consistently. However, because this snake is almost exclusively arboreal, it is nearly always wrapped around a branch or vine, with abdominal muscles constricted. When deceased, those perpetually contracted abdominals refuse to relax, greatly limiting my options for positioning the specimen in an elegantly serpentine shape. The unusual shape shown here reminds me of Kaa—the snake that seduces Mowgli in *The Jungle Book*.

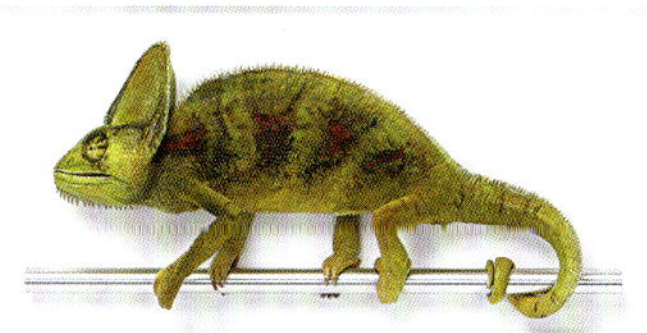

115. VEILED CHAMELEON
(*Chamaeleo calyptratus*), Madagascar. A perfect species for my work: It has brilliant, varied colors, is common in captivity, and is relatively short-lived, so mortalities are not infrequent. I love the juxtaposition of this wild, enigmatic animal with its sleek, machined perch.

Birds

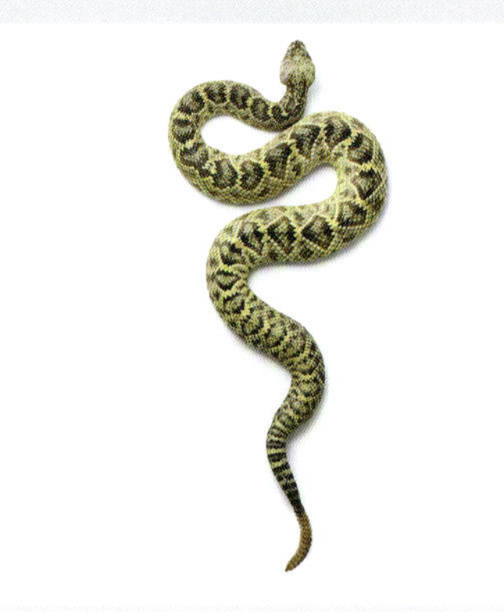

116–117. EASTERN DIAMONDBACK RATTLESNAKE
(*Crotalus adamantaeus*), United States. The largest and deadliest venomous snake in North America and the heaviest in the Western Hemisphere. Growing up to eight feet long, with fangs up to an inch, it is as formidable as it is beautiful.

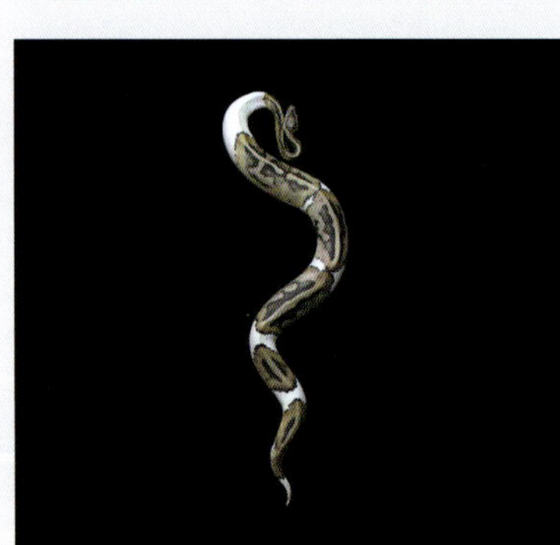

118. PIEBALD ROYAL PYTHON
(*Python regius*), Nigeria. Perhaps my favorite color morph in a species where the morphs are nearly endless. I love the piebalds because no two specimens are alike—the white blotches can take any shape and size.

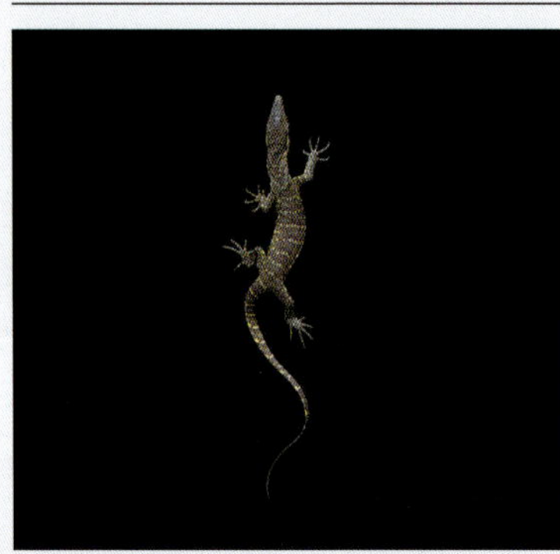

119. ASIAN WATER MONITOR
(*Varanus salvator*), Indonesia. Though I came into this world with a deep predisposition for reptiles, I confess that monitor lizards have always held the most vaunted place in my heart. From the moment I saw a black-and-white photograph of a Gould's monitor in a 1950s book of reptiles as a child, I was enamored of their dragonlike build; oversize, puppyish feet; and powerful, serpentine tail. They are the epitome of all that is wild and mysterious in the animal kingdom. I have successfully raised individuals of several species personally, many of which became dog-tame. A Dumeril's monitor I had in my twenties actually seemed to prefer following me around the yard to venturing out on his own. They are likely the most intelligent of reptiles and certainly among the most rewarding to interact with.

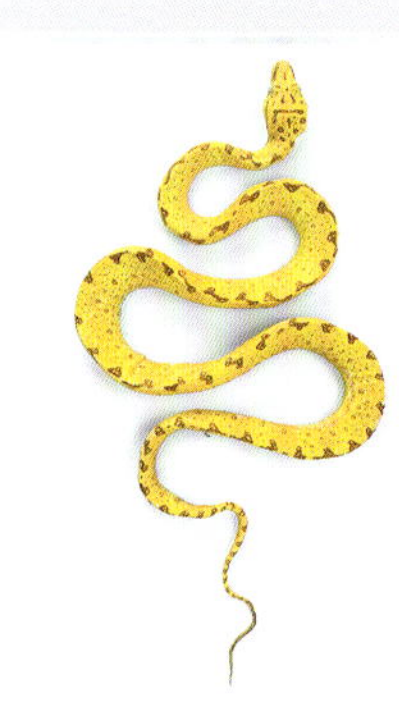

120. GREEN TREE PYTHON
(*Morelia viridis*), Australia. The young hatchlings of green tree pythons emerge from their eggs either lemon yellow, bloodred, bright orange, or deep maroon, each with distinctive, highly contrasting markings. They are luscious in the extreme.

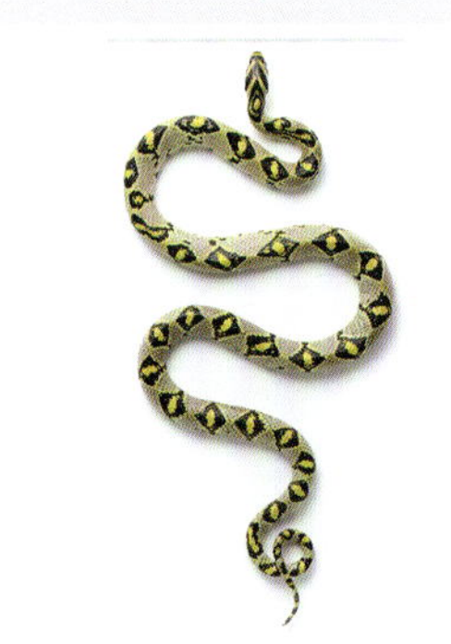

121. MANDARIN RAT SNAKE
(*Euprepiophis mandarinus*), China.

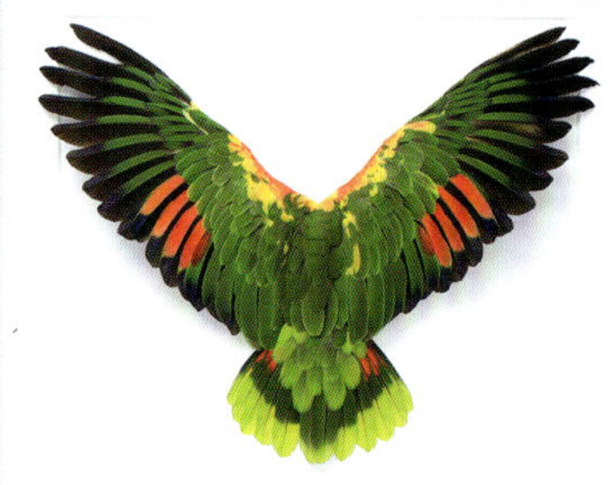

123. DOUBLE YELLOW-HEADED AMAZON
(*Amazona oratrix*), Guatemala. "Where is the head?" If I had a nickel for every time I was asked. There are reasons why I prepare many of the parrots as I do. Firstly, I love the presentation. I am not a taxidermist (as such). My objective is not to fill one's mind with picturesque scenes of animals scampering through idyllic settings; it is to shift the focus from the organism's life history to its design—skeletal structure, color, texture, or, in this case specifically, the relationships and placement of individual feathers and the colors and patterns formed thereby. And as color is a chief focus in my avian work, parrots and parakeets (hookbills) are central. But as my finished pieces are hermetically sealed wall art, the positioning of a hookbill on a mat is aesthetically problematic. Because of the position and shape of a parrot's bill, they appear to be always looking down while in flight, while softbills appear to be looking forward. This is just an illusion—the positioning of the eyes on the sides of their heads give both hookbills and softbills an extremely wide visual field. But as we humans associate a "nose" and mouth with a face, the hookbills appear to have belly flopped onto the mat, which I find distracting and a bit cartoonish. Consequently, I often prepare only the wings and tails of hookbills and do not use the body or head in the piece. This utilization of all the color and texture that I find remarkable about parrots, without the awkward story line that the body and head imply, is, in my view, an ideal solution.

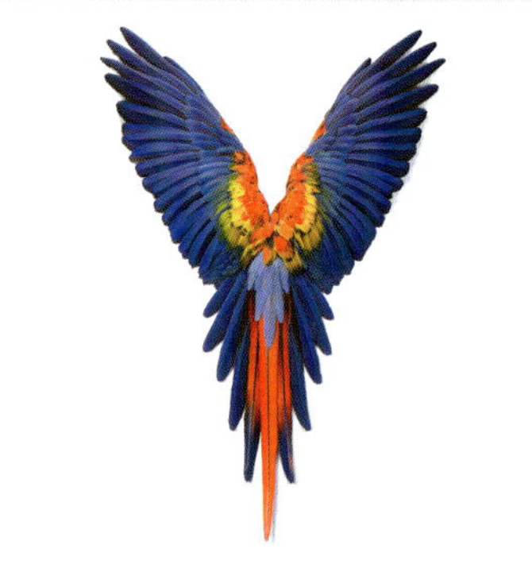

124. SCARLET MACAW
(*Ara macao*), Brazil. I was extremely fortunate that one of the organizations I work with in the United States stepped in to help with a macaw rescue. They had about thirty macaws that had passed in the preceding decades. This was the only intact scarlet. It is, in my opinion, the most incomparable bird on earth.

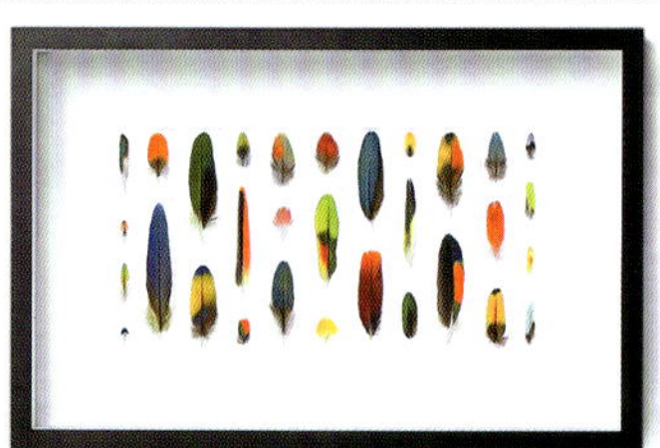

125. FEATHER MOSAIC
(worldwide species). It was only a few years ago that I was walking through my dad's aviaries when I happened to pick up the tail feather of a plum-headed parakeet. It was a work of art—even covered in poop. Previously, I had been quite strict about working with complete organisms. Work with animal parts, though sometimes masterful, has never captivated me. It is for this reason that I took so long to do anything with one of the most accessible, and beautiful, artifacts available to me. Composition size, 32 x 20 in.

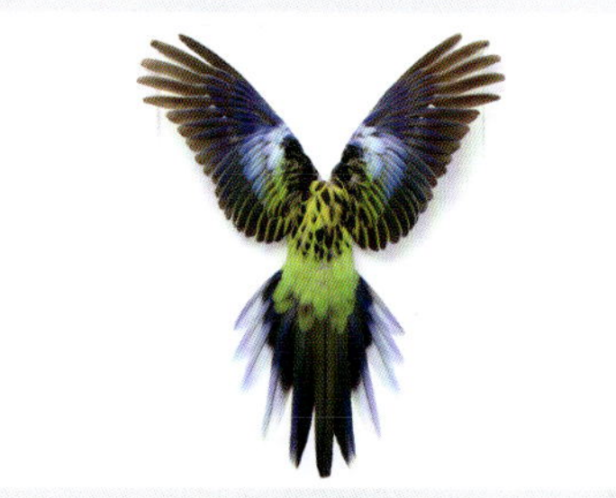

126. PALE-HEADED ROSELLA
(*Platycercus adscitus*), Australia.

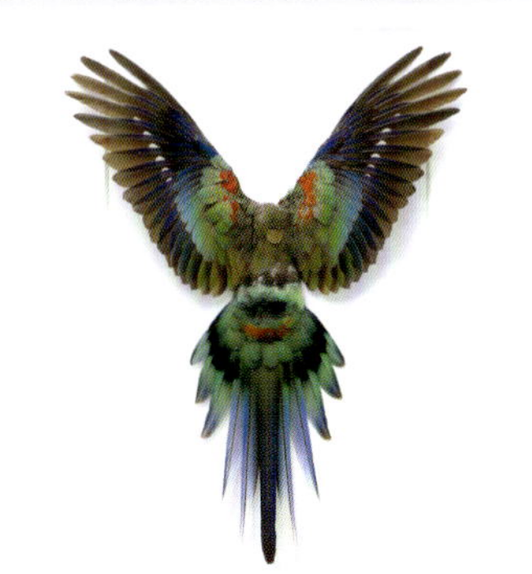

127. RED-RUMPED PARROT (*Psephotus haematonotus*), Australia.

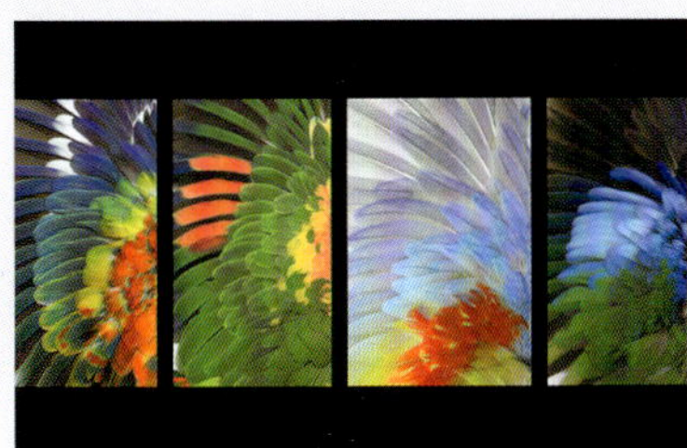

128–129. RED-RUMPED PARROT (*Psephotus haematonotus*), Australia; DOUBLE YELLOW-HEADED AMAZON (*Amazona oratrix*), Guatemala; TURQUOISINE GRASS PARAKEET (*Neophema pulchella*), Australia; SCARLET-CHESTED PARROT (*Neophema splendida*), Australia.

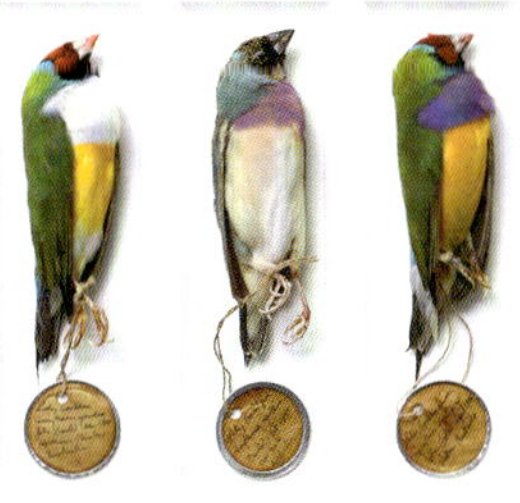

130. GOULDIAN FINCHES, Museum Collection (*Erythrura gouldiae*), Australia. This is another species that is in danger of extinction in its natural habitat, but it enjoys strong populations due to extensive breeding by institutions and private breeders in Australia, the United States, and Europe. Here, I chose to break from my established aesthetic and use a more traditional method of display. Avian specimens in the most renowned natural history museums are similarly prepared. Specimens are preserved and archived in a state that does nothing to try and mitigate the fact that the bird is dead. I find it oddly refreshing.

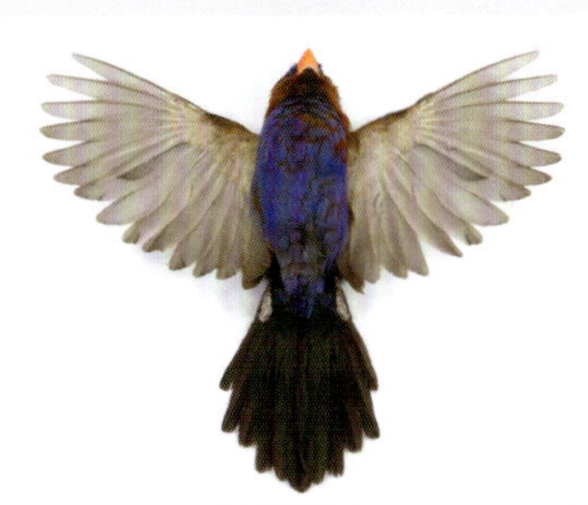

131. PURPLE GRENADIER FINCH (*Uraeginthus ianthinogaster*), Uganda.

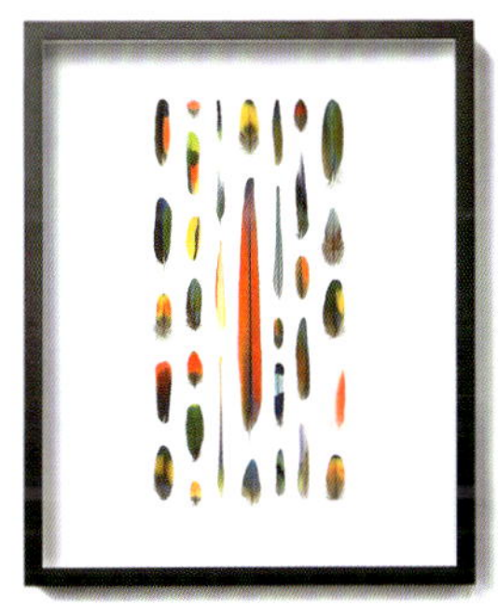

132. FEATHER MOSAIC (worldwide species). No, I don't color the feathers (or the birds, or the insects, or the minerals, or the shells). Trust me, if I could make my sourcing problems go away that easily. . . . Composition size, 32 x 40 in.

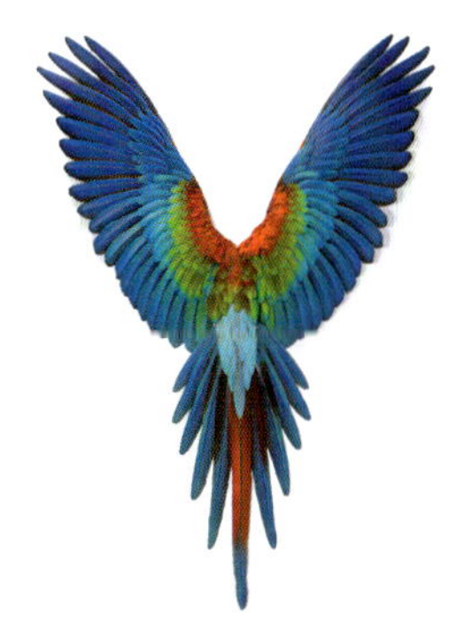

133. GREEN-WINGED MACAW (*Ara chloropterus*), Venezuela.

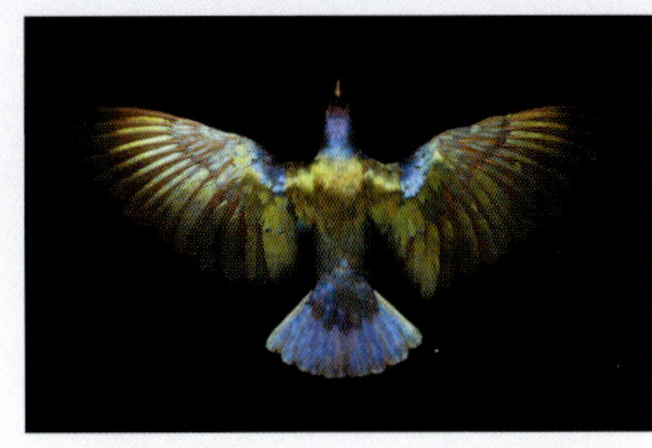

134–135. GREATER BLUE-EARED STARLING (*Lamprotornis chalybaeus*), Botswana. Unfortunately, I don't get to work with vibrantly colored, medium-size softbills very often. Apart from a few dove species, there is not an abundance of colorful softbills in captivity. This greater blue-eared starling is the antithesis of most of the birds I work with—very common in its native habitat and rare in captivity.

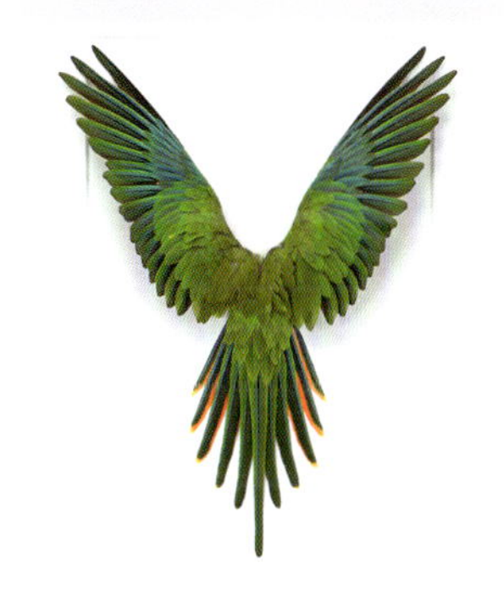

136–137. SUPERB PARROT (*Polytelis swainsonii*), Australia.

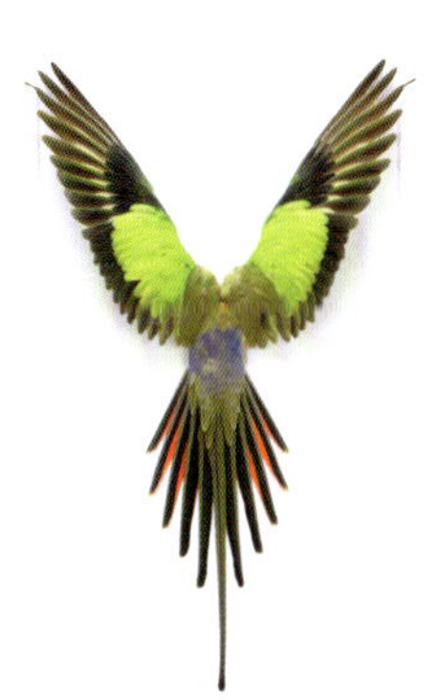

138. PRINCESS OF WALES PARAKEET (*Polytelis alexandrae*), Australia. One of the largest Australian parakeets and much prized in each of its color forms. The odd "spatula" projecting from each of the third wing feathers indicates that this specimen is male.

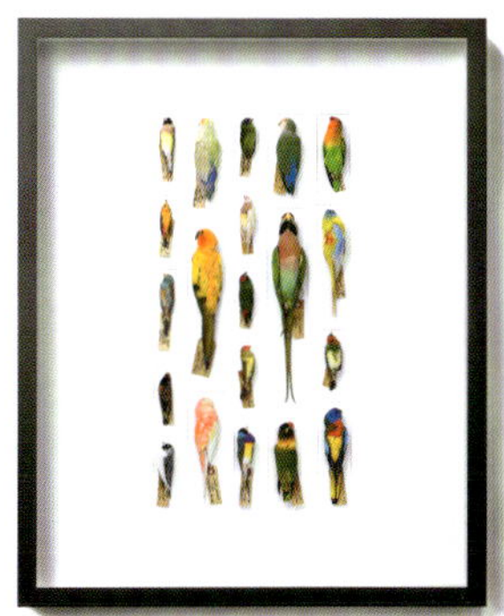

139. AVE MUSEUM COLLECTION (worldwide species). I created this piece at the request of the owner of one of my favorite stores in the world, Gold Bug in Pasadena. I had discussed the idea with Stacey on one of his trips to my studio, and after some nudging on his part, I finally completed the piece many months later and shipped it off. It was initially intended to join the already prodigious (and constantly revolving) collection that adorns the walls of his landmark store, but alas, it never made an appearance there. Once unpacked, it was immediately put back in its box and driven to his home. Thanks, Stacey, I'm honored. Composition size, 32 x 40 in.

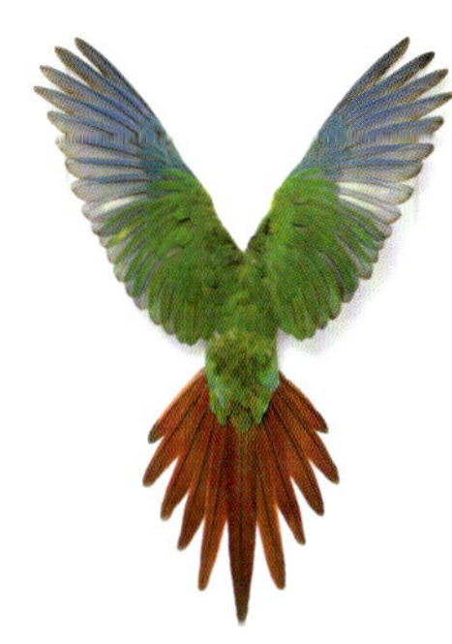

140. GREEN-CHEEKED CONURE (*Pyrrhura molinae*), Bolivia.

Minerals

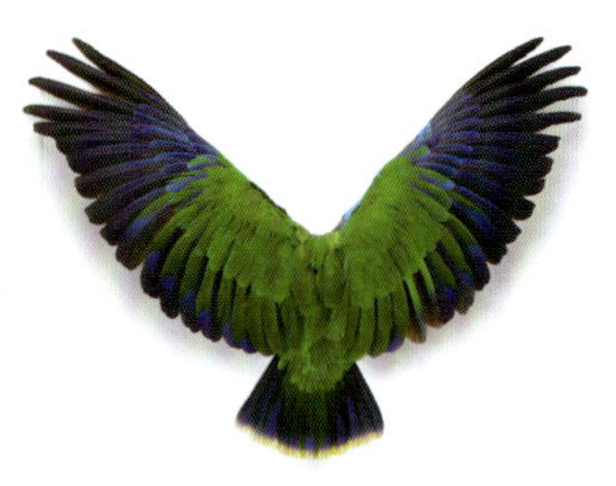

141. VOS ECLECTUS
(*Eclectus roratus*), New Guinea. A magnificent parrot, it is large and intelligent and displays some of the most marked sexual dimorphism to be found among parrots. The males are a brilliant emerald green with bright yellow and cobalt blue edging, while the females are bright red with mauve-blue wing edging. There has never been a more beautiful odd couple.

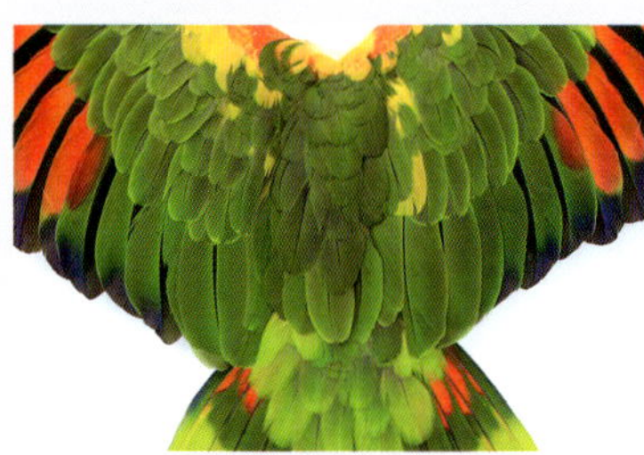

142–143. DOUBLE YELLOW-HEADED AMAZON
(*Amazona oratrix*), Guatemala (detail).

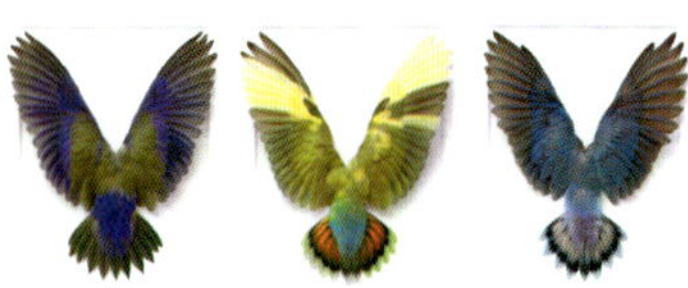

144–145. AGAPORNIS PARROT COLOR FORMS
(*Agapornis roseicollis*), Tanzania, Namibia.

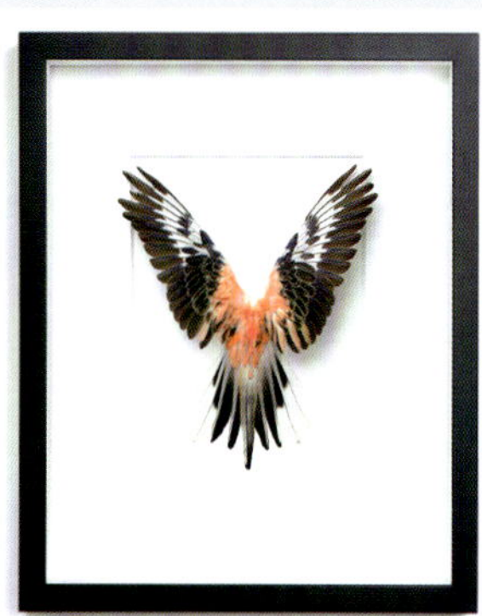

146. BOURKE'S PARAKEET
(*Neopsephotus bourkii*), Australia.

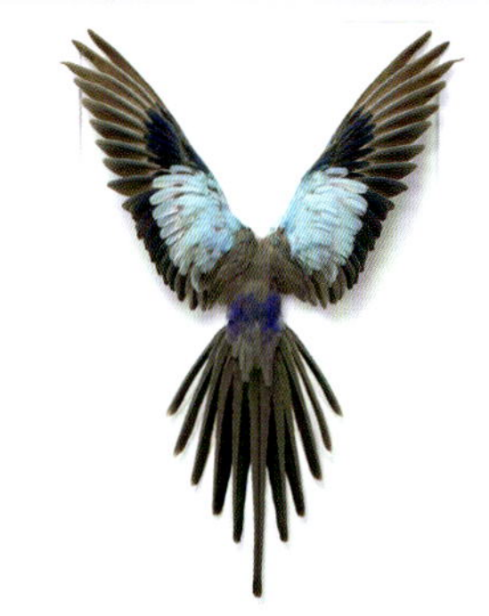

147.
PRINCESS OF WALES PARAKEET
(*Polytelis alexandrae*), Australia.

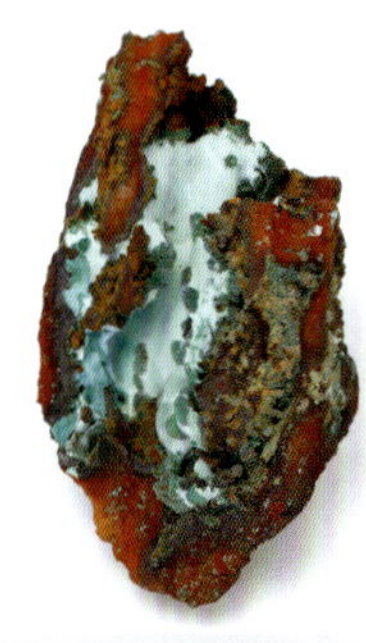

149. ROSASITE
Mexico. Rosasite is a gorgeous mineral often found in conjunction with limonite. The content of oxidized copper in the former and iron in the latter creates a striking marbling of greens and reds reminiscent of an alien ecosystem.

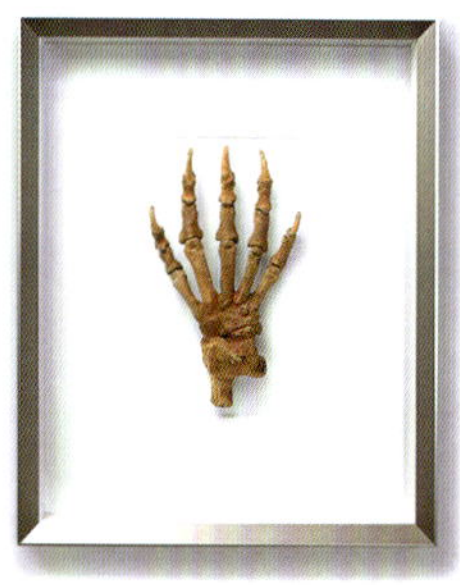

150.
PLEISTOCENE CAVE BEAR PAW
(*Ursus spelaeus*), Russia. About one hundred thousand years old.

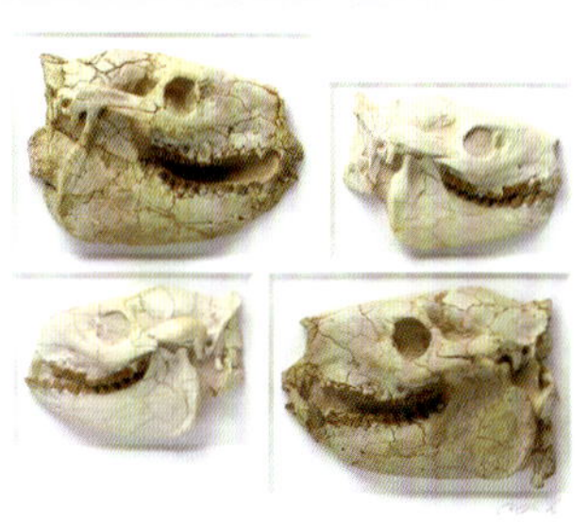

151.
MIOCENE OREODONT SKULLS
(*Merycoidodontoidea*), United States. The oreodonts became extinct about four million years ago. They were an odd amalgamation of mammals—a fang-toothed hog the size of a cow that lived like a hippo and preceded modern-day camels. Perhaps its ultimate demise was precipitated by an identity crisis? These fossils are about twenty million years old. Composition size, 20 x 24 in.

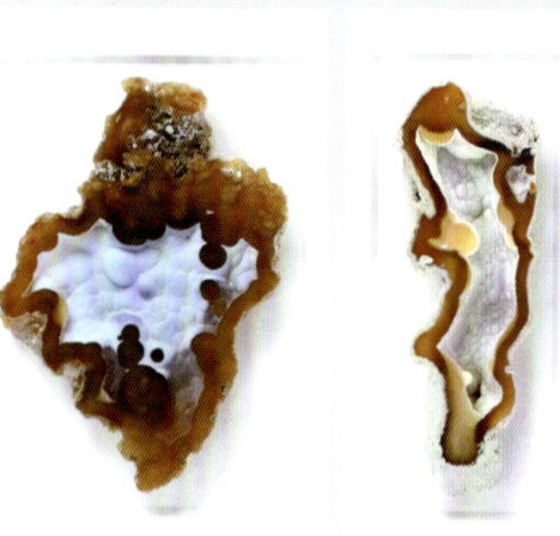

152–153. MIOCENE AGATIZED CORAL
United States. It takes about twenty million years for coral polyps to be replaced by silica, resulting in agatized coral. Of all agatized coral forms, those in Tampa Bay, Florida, are the most beautiful. The chalcedony that forms looks silky to slimy in texture and can be almost any color of the rainbow.

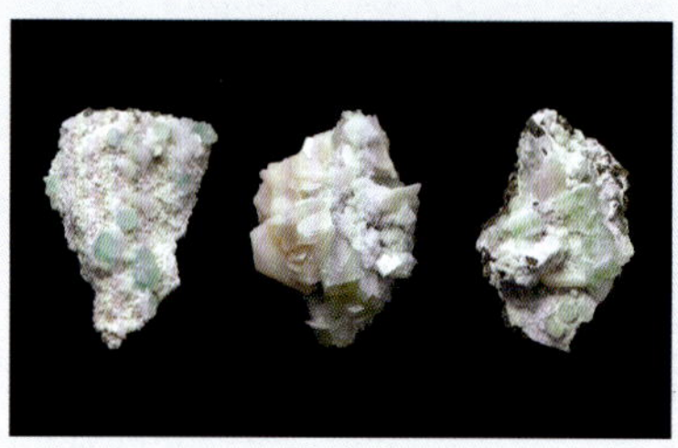

154–155. THREE INDIAN ZEOLITES
(Apophyllite and Stilbite on Heulandite, Apophyllite and Stilbite on Quartz, Apophyllite and Stilbite on Quartz), India.

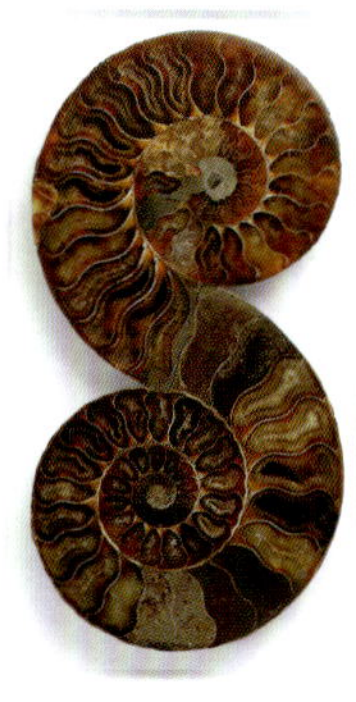

156.
CRETACEOUS AMMONITE DUO
(*Ammonoidea*), Madagascar. About one hundred million years old.

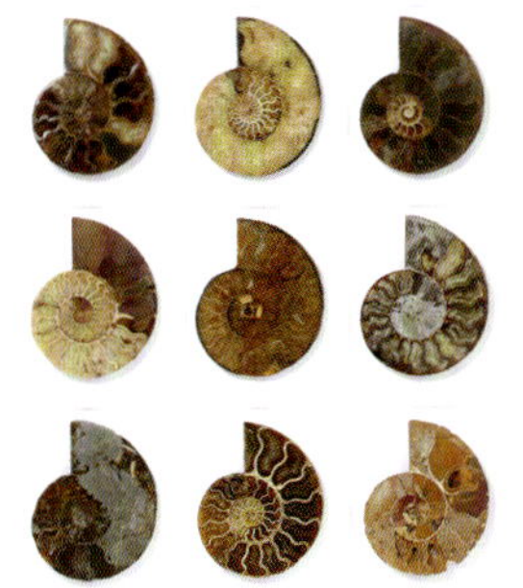

157.
CRETACEOUS AMMONITE STUDY
(*Ammonoidea*), Madagascar. Ammonites, an extinct ancestor of modern-day octopuses and squid, are a designer's wildest fantasy in the realm of fossils. Their size ranges from about an inch to more than four feet in diameter. Their colors can be as fiery as any opal or as muted as a river rock. When bisected, they show off their multicolored, agatized chambers and septa. These samples are about one hundred million years old. Composition size, 24 x 30 in. (also in 32 x 40).

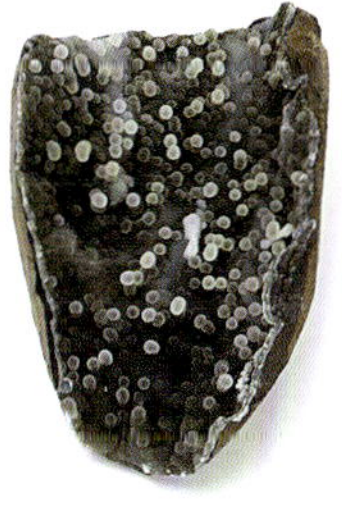

158–159. CHALCEDONY
India. Chalcedony is a silicate composition of quartz and moganite that takes many desirable forms. Agate, aventurine, carnelian, heliotrope, and onyx are all forms of chalcedony. But it is this silky, semitranslucent form I call "crushed ice chalcedony" that I am constantly in search of.

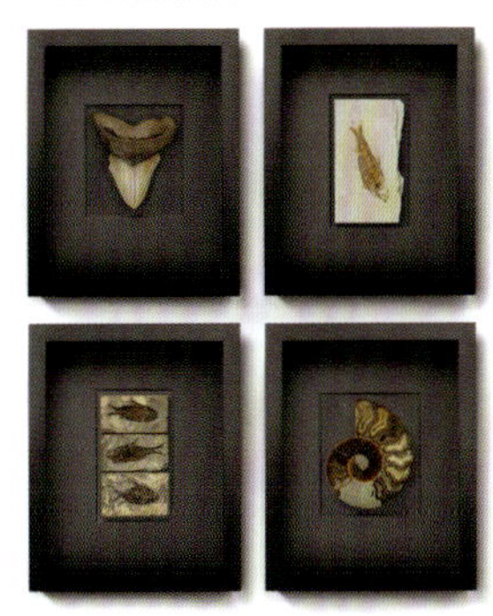

160. MEGALODON TOOTH
(*Carcharocles megalodon*), United States (Cenozoic, about ten million years ago); FOSSILIZED KNIGHTIA, United States (Eocene, about forty million years ago); JIANGHANICHTHYS, China (Eocene, about fifty million years ago); AMMONITE, Madagascar (Cretaceous, about one hundred million years ago).

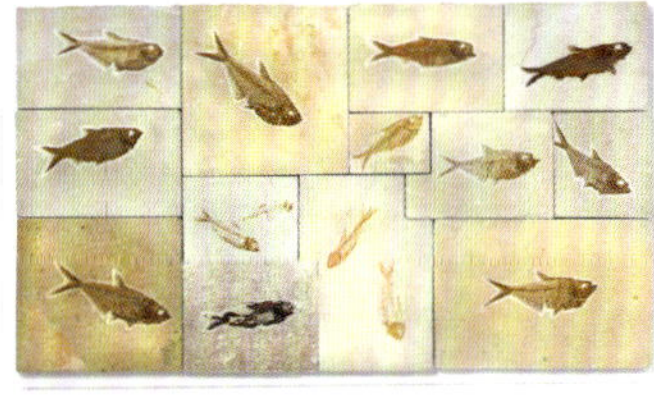

161.
EOCENE FOSSIL FISH MOSAIC
(*Knightia* and *Diplomystus* spp.) United States. The Wyoming badlands near Green River are home to one of the most massive and well-preserved prehistoric mass mortalities known in the world. Composition size, 40 x 30 in.

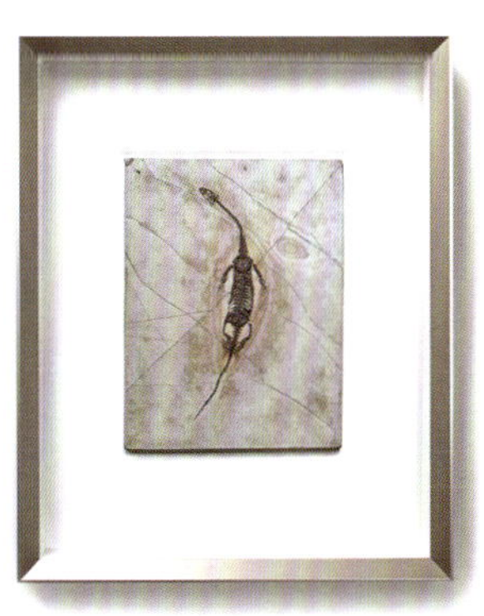

162–163. KEICHOUSAURUS
China. When I was first introduced to *Keichousaurus* many years ago, I could scarcely believe that two of my favorite things in the world, monitor lizards and dinosaurs, existed in a single package and were accessible to the common man. Unfortunately, in recent years, legislation and increasingly sophisticated forgeries have combined to taint the *Keichousaurus* experience, but they remain one of the most well-preserved and accessible of any fully articulated pre-dinosaur. These fossils are about two hundred million years old.

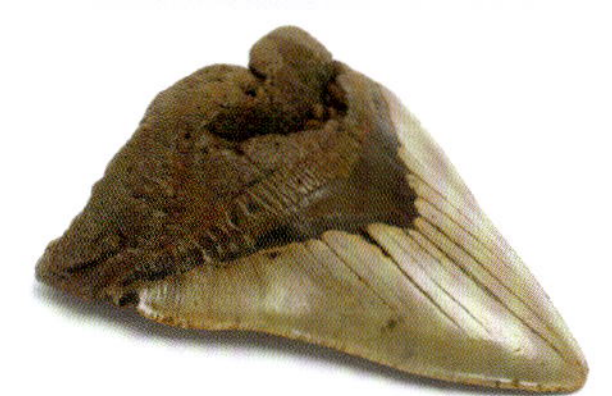

164. MEGALODON TOOTH
(*Carcharocles megalodon*), United States.

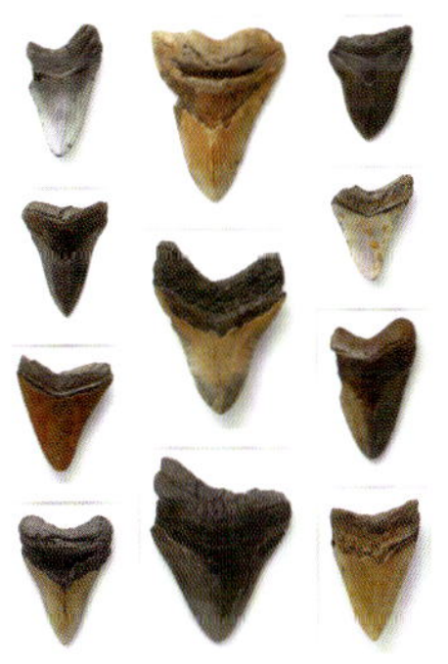

165.
MEGALODON TOOTH MOSAIC
(*Carcharocles megalodon*), United States. Megalodon is widely considered the largest predator that ever lived. It was essentially a sixty-foot-long great white shark that fed on whales. The most well-preserved fossilized megalodon teeth are found in rivers in North Carolina. These fossils are about five million years old.

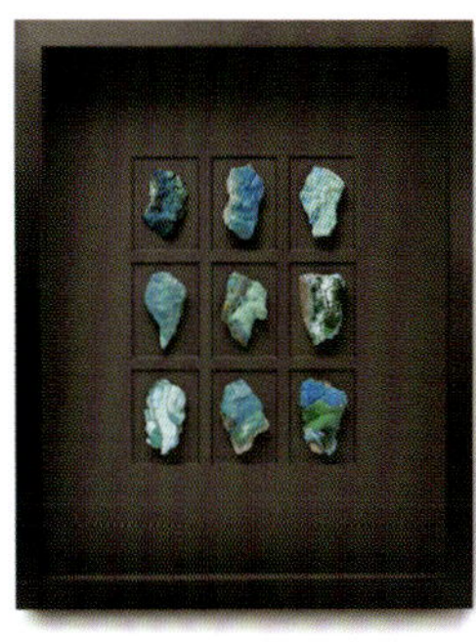

166. MALACHITE AND AZURITE
Democratic Republic of the Congo.

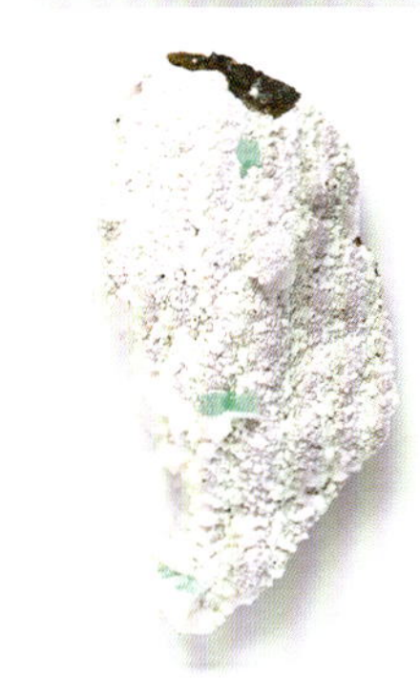

167.
HEULANDITE AND APOPHYLLITE
India.

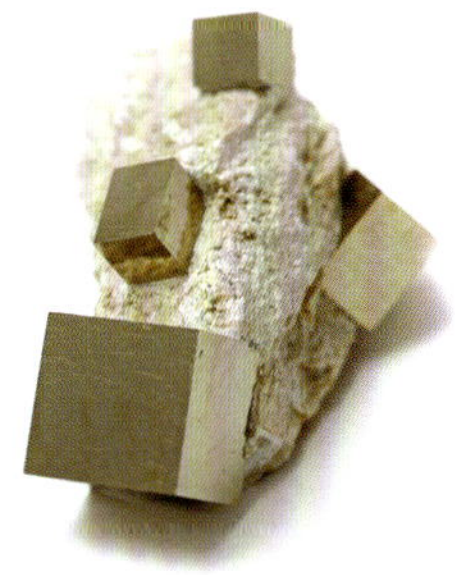

168–169. PYRITE, CUBE FORMATION
Spain. In 1960, Pedro Ansorena Garret discovered a cavity in the Alcarama Mountains near Navajún, Spain, that contained the most pristine specimens of naturally formed pyrite cubes in the world. As shown, they are uncut and unpolished. Composition size, 20 x 24 in. (also in 16 x 20).

Unity

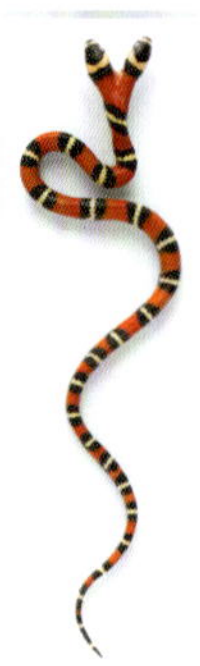

171. TWO-HEADED SCARLET KING SNAKE
(*Lampropeltis elapsoides*), United States. Though polycephalic snakes are indeed rare, snakes and turtles are the most likely organisms to be born with two heads. In the case of snakes, many survive into adulthood with both heads functioning normally, including feeding and directing the movements of the snake.

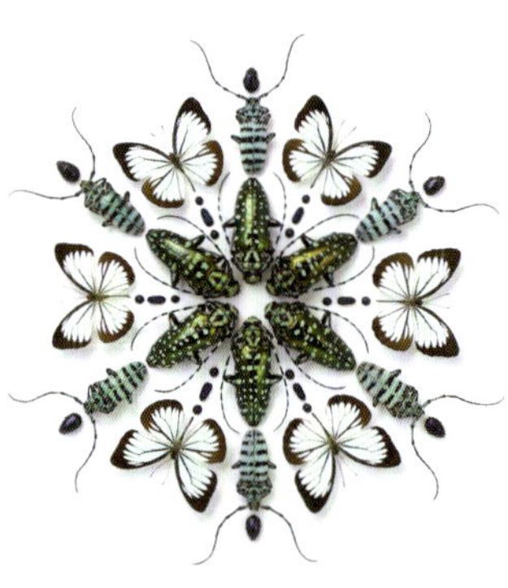

172. ELEGANS PRISM.
Center out: *Calliplophora sollii*, Thailand; *Coccinellidae* sp., Indonesia; *Scolytinae* sp., Cameroon; *Pareronia valeria*, Indonesia; *Anoplophora longehisuta*, Malaysia; *Rutelinae* sp., Thailand. Composition size, 20 x 20 in.

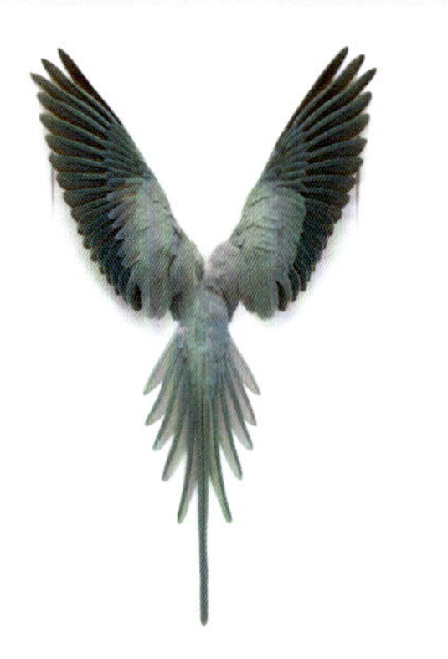

173. INDIAN RING-NECKED PARROT, BLUE FORM
(*Psittacula krameri*), Myanmar.

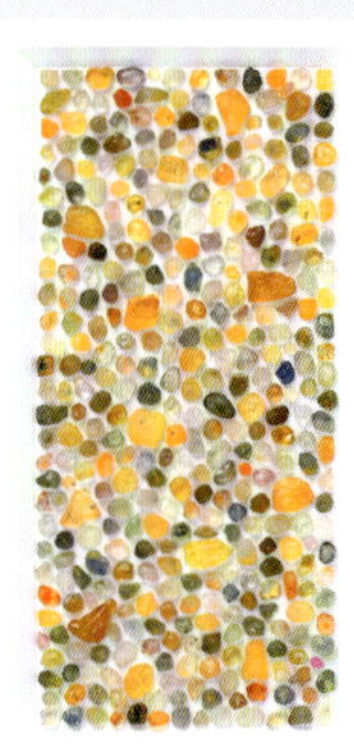

174. ROUGH SAPPHIRES
Madagascar. As my motive from the very beginning has been to bring to light and increase appreciation for those natural artifacts that are most obscure or undervalued, I have always avoided precious gemstones. However, a short foray into rough sapphires, rubies, and diamonds about eight years ago served to increase my understanding and regard for these most highly valued of natural artifacts. They were then abandoned. This collection weighs 190 carats. Composition size, 16 x 20 in.

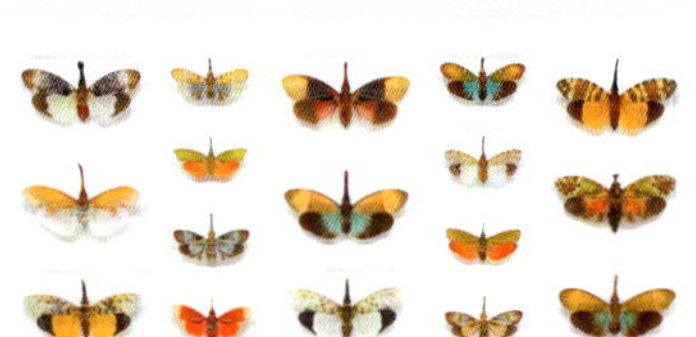

175. LANTERN FLY MOSAIC
(*Fulgoridae* of the genera *Fulgora*, *Pyrops*, and *Phrictus*), Thailand, Indonesia, Malaysia, Peru. Composition size, 30 x 24 in.

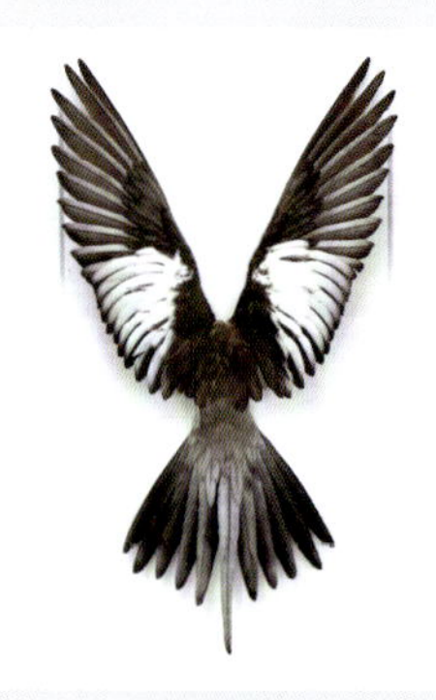

176. BLACK QUARRION
(*Nymphicus hollandicus*), Australia.

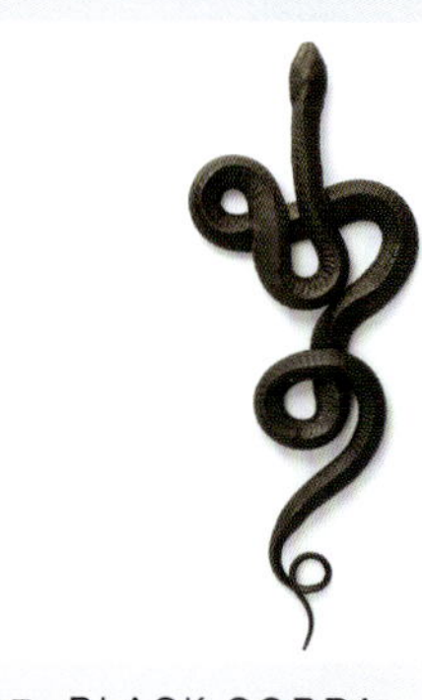

177. BLACK COBRA
(*Naja naja*), Pakistan.

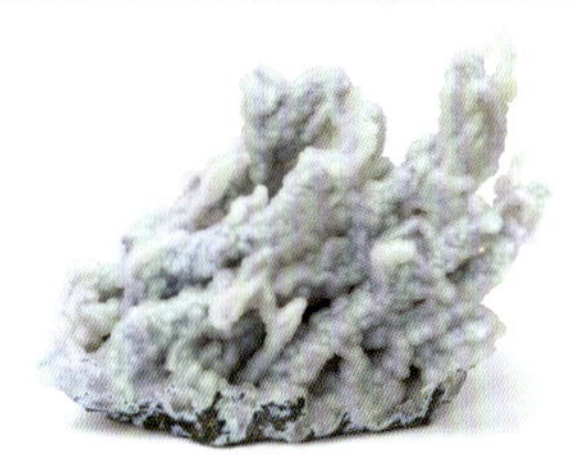

178. BLUE CHALCEDONY
India.

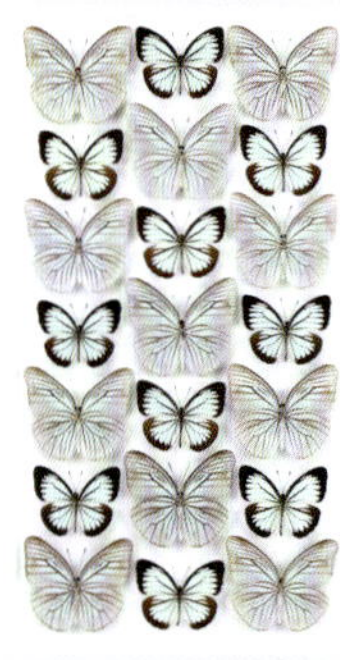

179. SILVER CELESTINA. COMMON WANDERERS
(*Pareronia valeria* and *tritaea*), Malaysia and Indonesia. Composition size, 24 x 30 in.

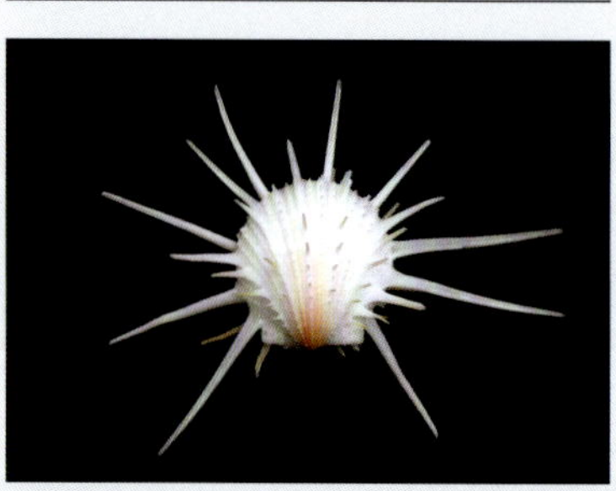

180. IMPERIAL SPINY OYSTER
(*Spondylus imperialis*), Philippines.

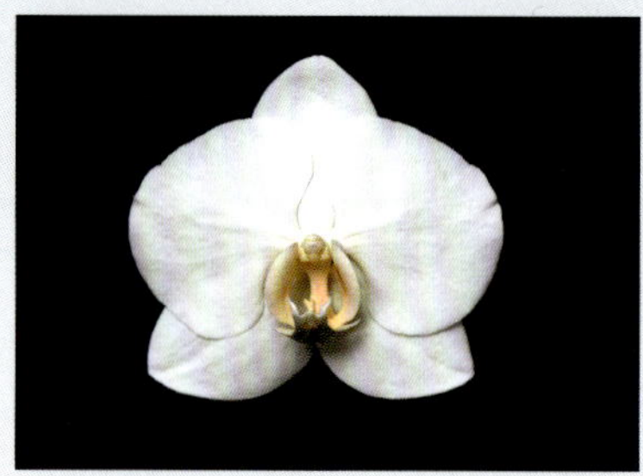

181.
PRESERVED PHALAENOPSIS
Borneo. *Phalaenopsis* orchids present a particular difficulty in preservation. Whereas most orchids respond relatively well to freeze-drying, I had very little luck with *Phalaenopsis*. I experimented with a series of chemical baths, various drying mediums, and heat, and eventually my results produced some remarkably well-preserved blooms. This specimen was five years old when photographed.

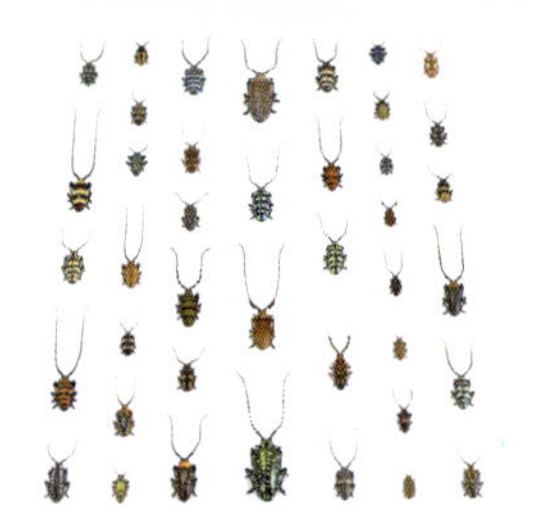

182.
LIMITED LONGHORN MOSAIC
(*Cerambycidae* sp.), Asia and Africa. Composition size, 32 x 40 in.

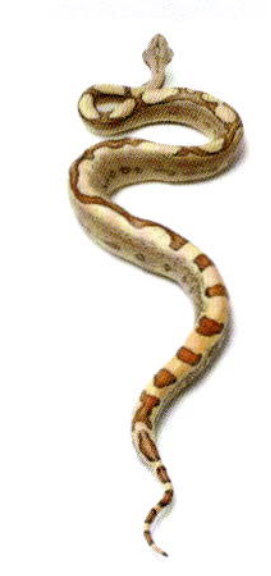

183. RED-TAILED BOA
(*Boa constrictor*), Suriname.

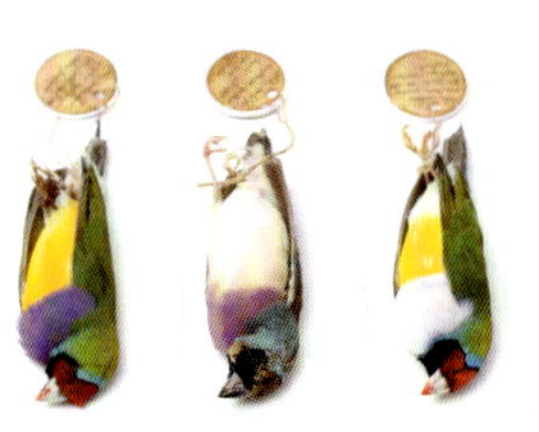

184. GOULDIAN FINCHES
(*Erythrura gouldiae*), Australia. Composition size, 11 x 14 in.

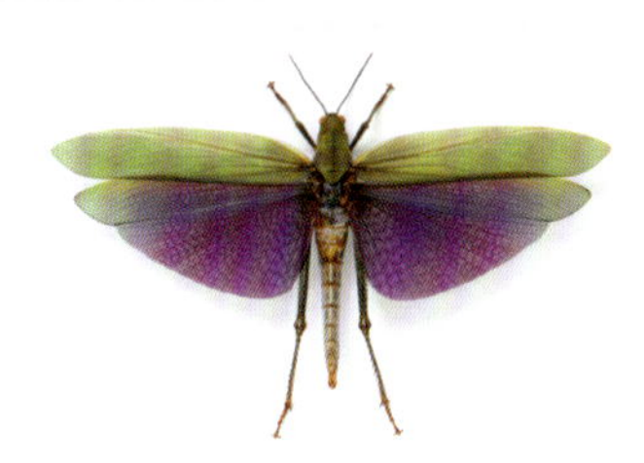

185. AMAZON GRASSHOPPER
(*Titanacris albipes*), Ecuador. Perhaps the most strikingly colored grasshopper in the world, this is a rarely encountered species with a small, localized range in Northwestern South America. They are not known to swarm and are therefore not considered a pest of economic importance.

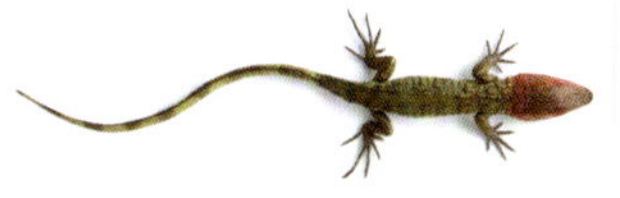

186. CAIMAN LIZARD
(*Dracaena guianensis*), Colombia. Though not a terribly uncommon species in the wild, Caiman lizards are rarely seen in captivity. Their extreme enclosure requirements, particularly powerful bite, and problematic diet (they feed almost exclusively on snails) make them unsuitable for all but the most well-equipped institutions.

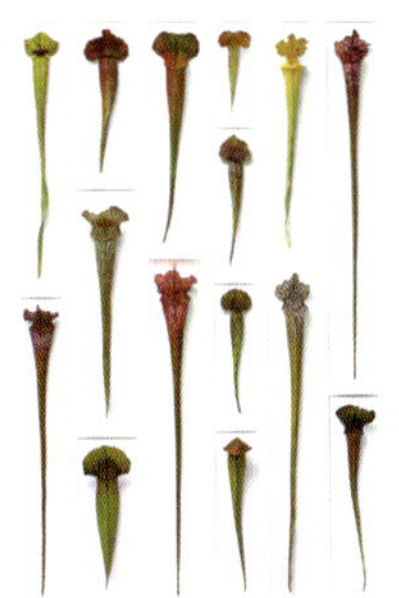

187. PITCHER PLANT MOSAIC
(*Sarracenia* sp.), United States. *Sarracenia* is a genus of carnivorous pitcher plants inhabiting swamps and wetlands in the Eastern United States. Much of the soil in their habitat is nutrient-poor, so *Sarracenia* require a little "something extra" in their diet. Insects are lured to the slippery edge of the pitcher by sweet-smelling nectar; then, when they fall inside, downward-growing hairs prevent them from crawling out. Digestive enzymes extract nutrients from the tissues of the trapped insects. Most *Sarracenia* are protected federally and internationally, so our pitchers come from a conservatory and nursery in Pennsylvania. The leaves (pitchers) are trimmed twice a year, and it does not harm the plant. Composition size, 32 x 40 in.

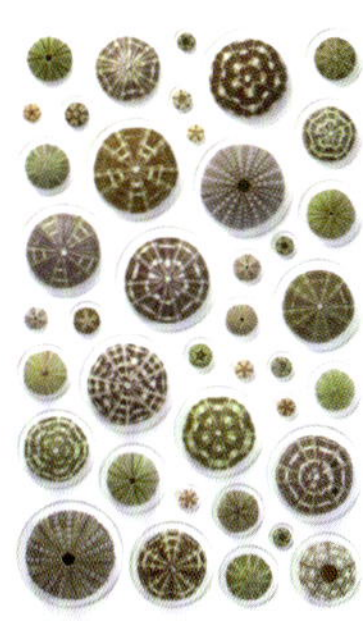

188. URCHIN SPHERES MOSAIC
(*Echinoidea* sp.), Philippines, Thailand, Mexico, United States. The sea urchin test reveals a five-fold symmetry not easily recognizable before its spines are removed. This pentamerism is a subtle design element that adds a degree of angularity to an otherwise globular composition. Composition size, 32 x 40 in.

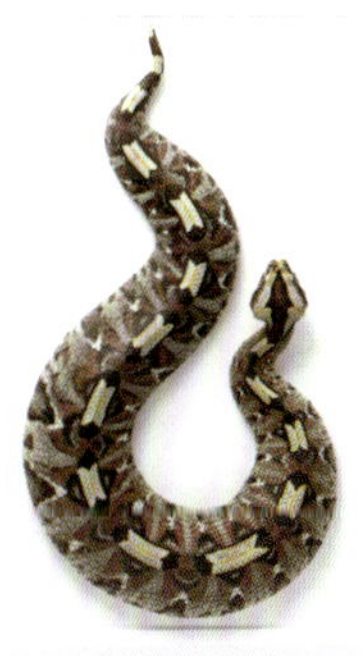

189. RHINOCEROS VIPER
(*Bitis nasicornis*), Central African Republic.

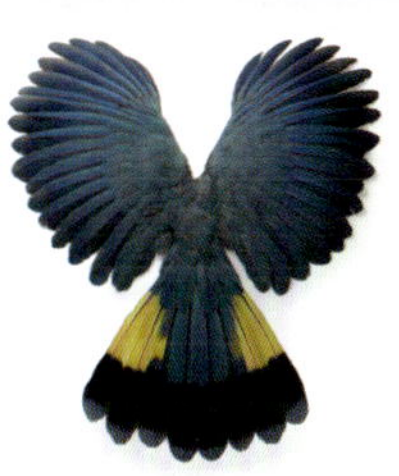

190. GREAT BLUE TURACO
(*Corythaeola cristata*), Democratic Republic of the Congo. The largest species in the entire order of Cuculiformes, *Corythaeola cristata* is extremely rare in captivity outside of the African continent, though it is eaten there with some regularity.

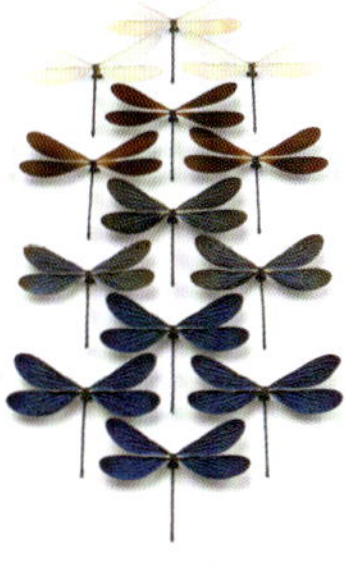

191. DAMSELFLY WASH.
Top to bottom: *Neurobasis chinensis* (female), Malaysia; *Vestalis luctuosa*, Indonesia; *Euphaea laidlawi*, Philippines. Composition size, 16 x 20 in.

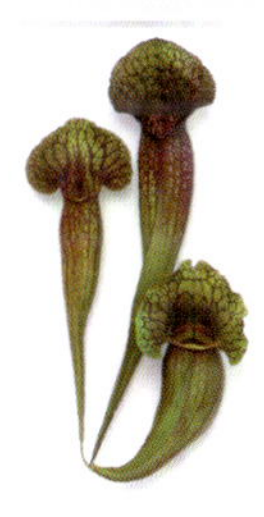

192. CARNIVOROUS PITCHER PLANT CLUSTER
(*Sarracenia* sp.), United States. Composition size, 16 x 20 in.

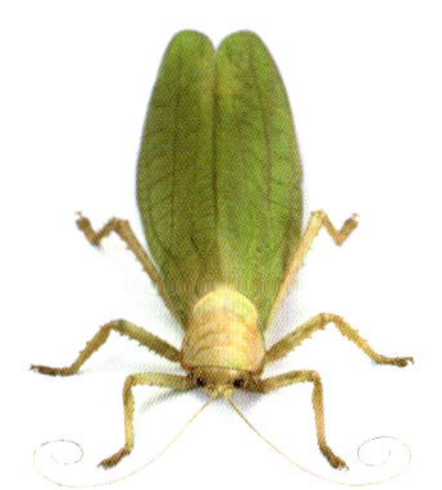

193. LEAF MIMIC KATYDID
(*Pseudophyllus hercules*), Thailand.

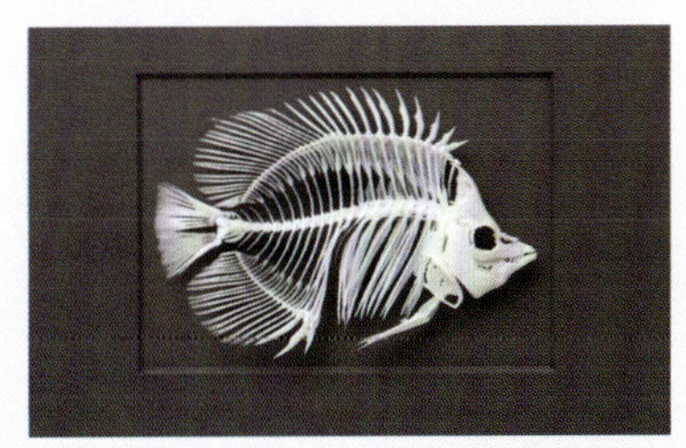

194. BUTTERFLY FISH
(*Chaetodon* sp.), Hawaii.

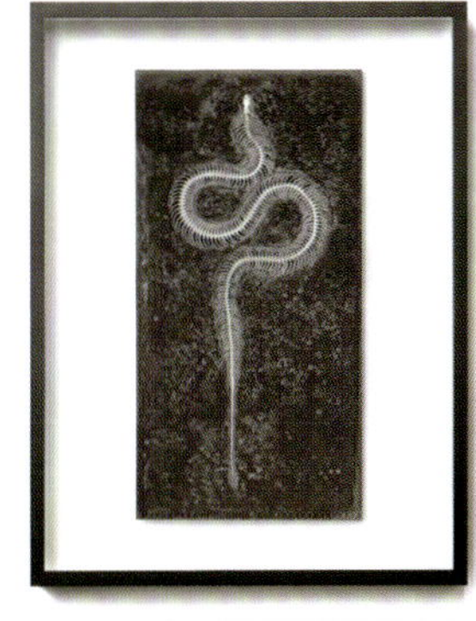

195. COBRA NEOFOSSIL
(*Naja* sp.), Malaysia. To create NeoFossils, I prepared vertebrate skeletons, then embedded them into faux rock. They appear to be impossibly immaculate fossils. Composition size, 32 x 40 in.

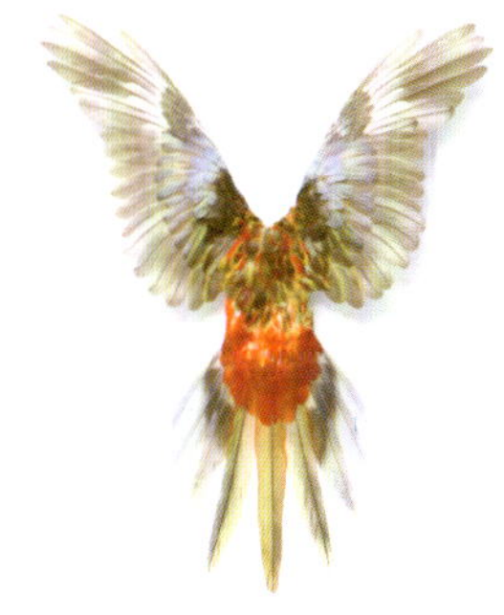

196.
OPALINE EASTERN ROSELLA
(*Platycercus eximius*), Australia.

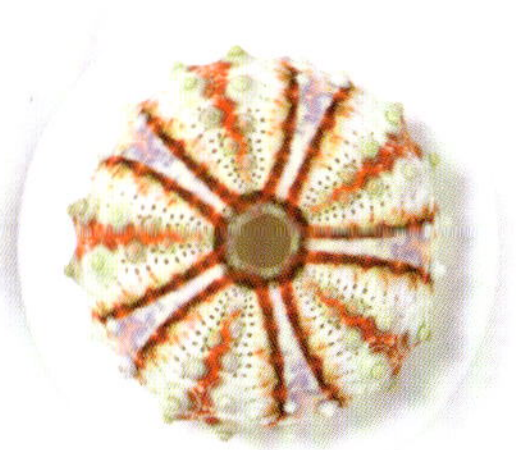

197. VARIEGATED URCHIN TEST. MAILLARDI URCHIN
(*Coelopleurus maillardi*), Philippines. This species of deep-sea urchin (up to 140 meters) has long, thin spines that are striped red and yellow. When the spines are removed, a gorgeous multicolored test is revealed.

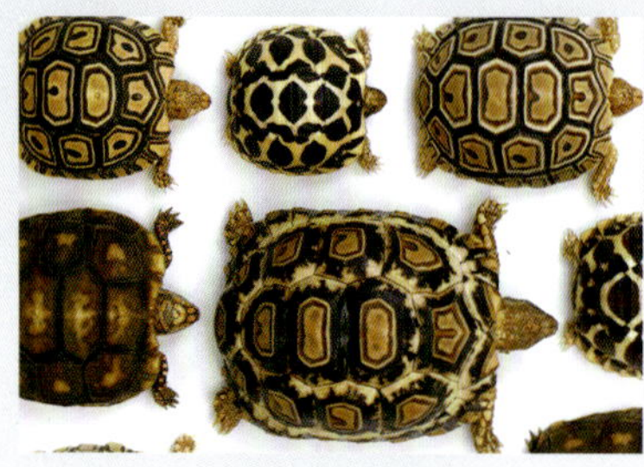

198. TORTOISE MOSAIC.
Leopard Tortoise (*Pardalis pardalis*), Africa; Red-Footed Tortoise (*Geochelone carbonaria*), Venezuela; Star Tortoise (*Geochelone elegans*), India. Composition size, 30 x 12 in.

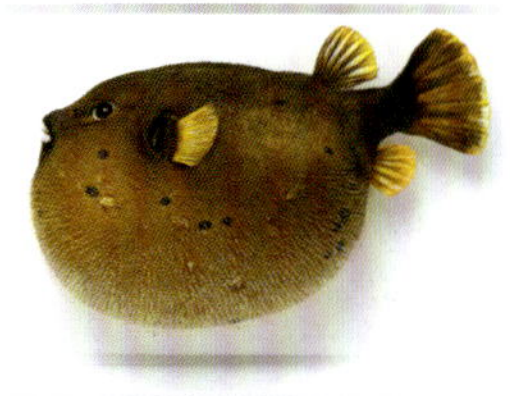

199. PUFFER FISH
(*Arothron* sp.), Indonesia. Puffer fish of the family Tetraodontidae claim the second most lethal venom of any vertebrate in the world. Yet people in some cultures still can't resist eating them, which is only possible if the fish is filleted with absolute precision. There's no shame in opting for a can of tuna.

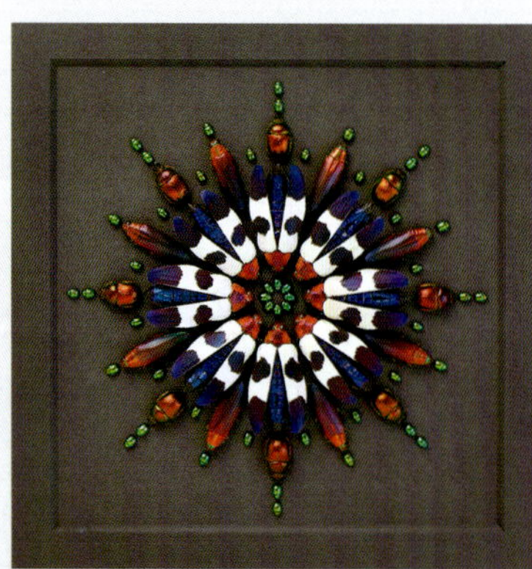

200. BUQUETI PRISM.
Center out: *Chrysochus* sp., Indonesia; *Chrysochroa buqueti rugicollis*, Thailand; *Chrysochroa fulminans nishiyamai*, Indonesia; *Geotrupes auratus*, Japan. Composition size, 16 x 20 in.

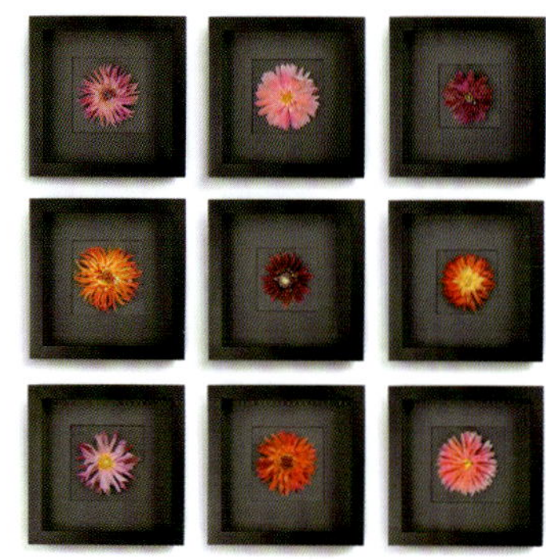

201. PRESERVED DAHLIAS
United States. Living in the verdant Willamette Valley, as I do, it is easy to be inspired by flowers. Every year our local farmers cultivate thousands of acres of tulips, dahlias, roses, irises, daffodils, and rhododendrons—the list goes on and on. So it seemed only natural to learn and perfect methods of bloom preservation. For dahlias, freeze-drying works best, and most species and cultivars respond well to it—initially. Unfortunately, many have not proven to last indefinitely, even in my hermetically sealed frames, so my work with them has necessarily been limited.

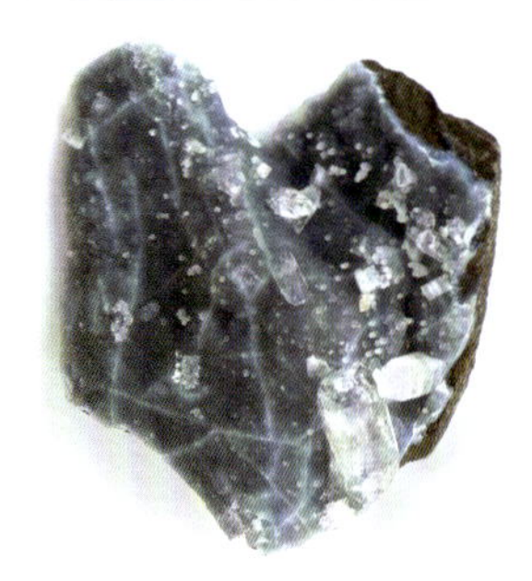

202.
APOPHYLLITE ON CHALCEDONY
India.

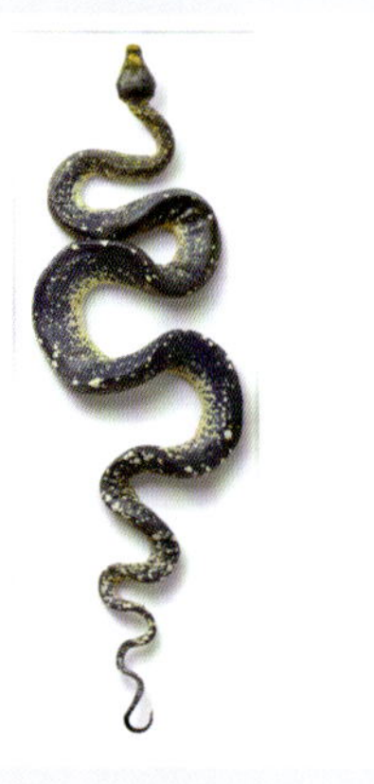

203. GREEN TREE PYTHON, BLUE PHASE
(*Morelia viridis*), Australia. Gravid females are known to turn deeper shades of blue with each clutch, though they usually return to their original green coloration once the clutch has been laid. There is also a very rare "super blue" form, which this specimen is believed to be.

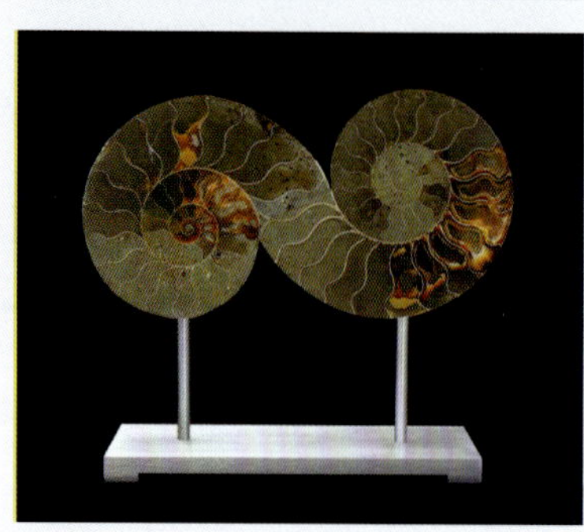

204. CRETACEOUS AMMONITE PEDESTAL
(*Ammonoidea*), Madagascar.

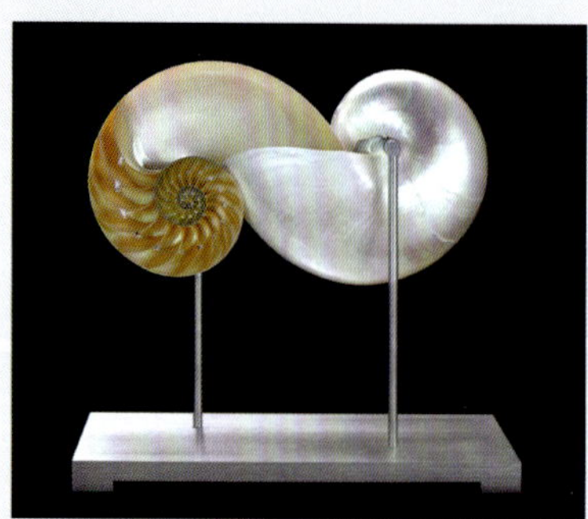

205. NAUTILUS PEDESTAL
(*Nautilus pompilius*), Philippines.

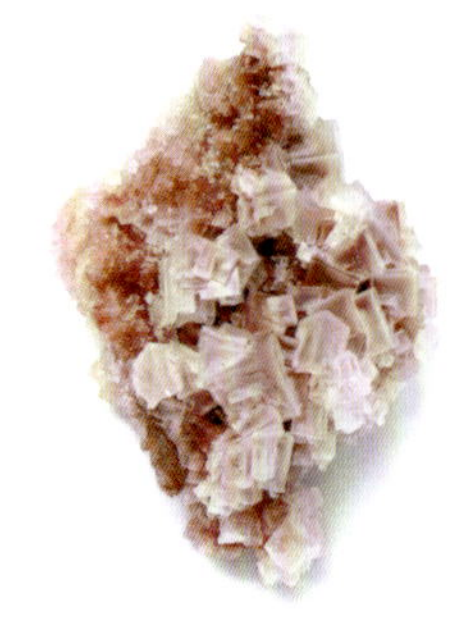

206. HALITE
Mexico. Halite is just a slightly sexier name for rock salt. It has one of the most isometric habits of all crystals, making it particularly geometric, architectural, and desirable. Unfortunately, it is also very unstable—prone to crumbling or melting if humidity levels are not precisely maintained. I am working on some methods of stabilizing this gorgeous manifestation of the world's most ubiquitous spice and hope to be able to work with it more in the future.

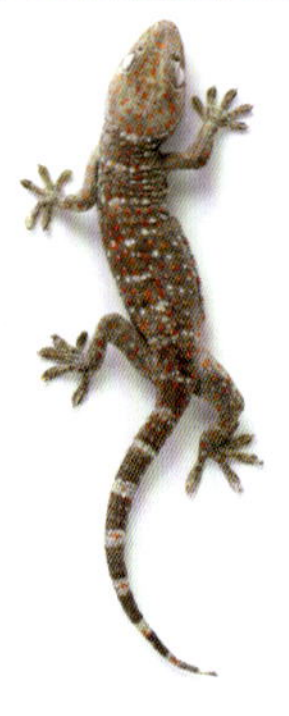

207. TOKAY GECKO
(*Gekko gecko*), New Guinea. Large, loud, and cantankerous, this species is the reason geckos are called "geckos." The word is supposed to be a transliteration of their vociferous call (though their call doesn't sound like "gecko" to me—more like the chirping of an enraged tree frog). They're beautiful lizards, but they belie the placid reputation geckos have earned. Their powerful, aggressive bite should be enough to earn them their own genus.

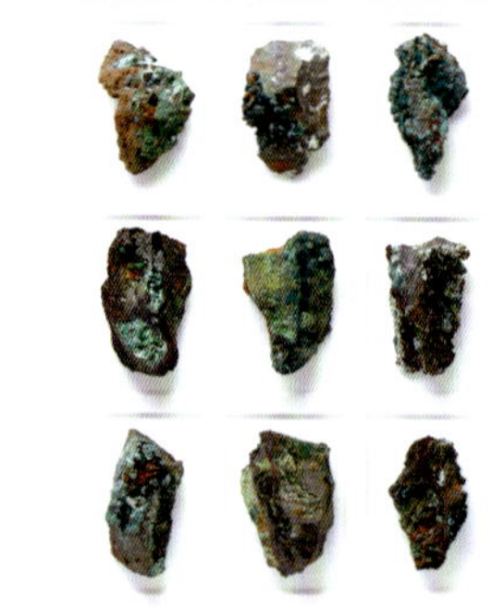

208. ROSASITE
Mexico.

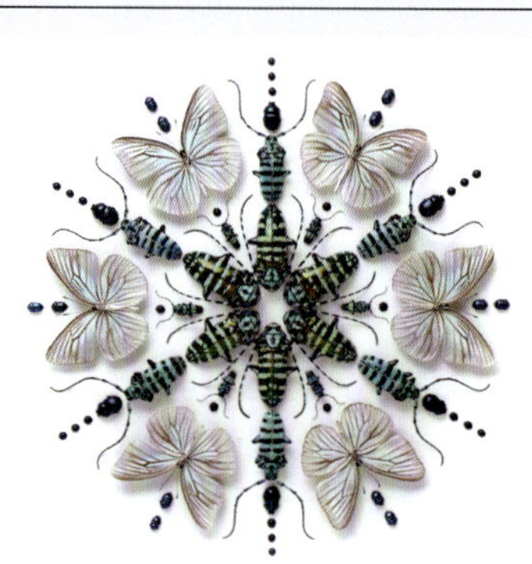

209. ELEGANS PRISM.
Center out: *Calloplophora graafi*, Malaysia; *Glenea celestis*, Indonesia; *Coccinellidae* sp., Indonesia; *Anoplophora longehisuta*, Malaysia; *Pareronia tritaea*, Indonesia; *Geotrupes auratus*, Japan; *Scutelleridae* sp., Indonesia. Composition size, 24 x 24 in.

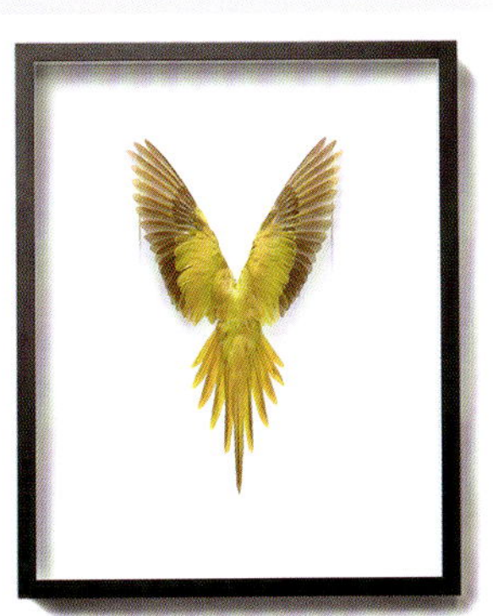

210. GOLDEN OLIVE RING-NECKED PARROT
(*Psittacula krameri*), India. A rare color form. Species are naturally lime green, with the only common mutation being blue.

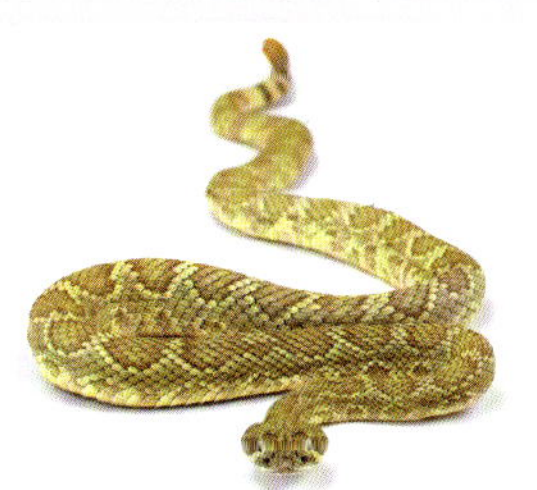

211. PACIFIC RATTLESNAKE
(*Crotalus oreganus*), Western United States. Though this is a local species, like all reptiles I work with, it was reclaimed from an institution. In this case, a venomous reptile museum.

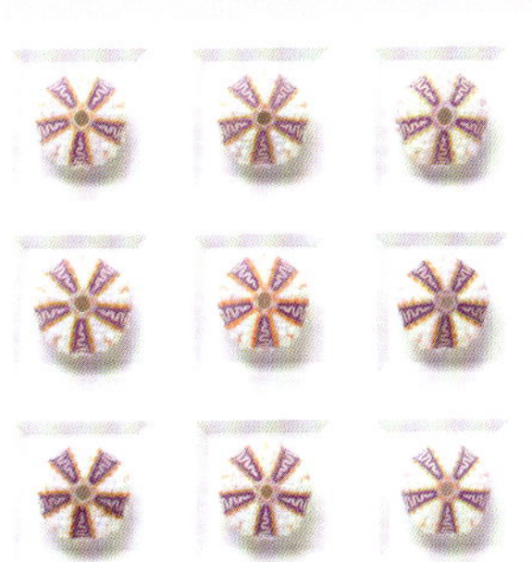

212. EXQUISITE URCHINS
(*Coelopleurus exquisitus*), New Caledonia. Because these urchins live at a depth of more than 1,700 feet, it is as difficult to collect them as it is to believe their colors and pattern are completely natural. This is a newly discovered species, identified in 2006.

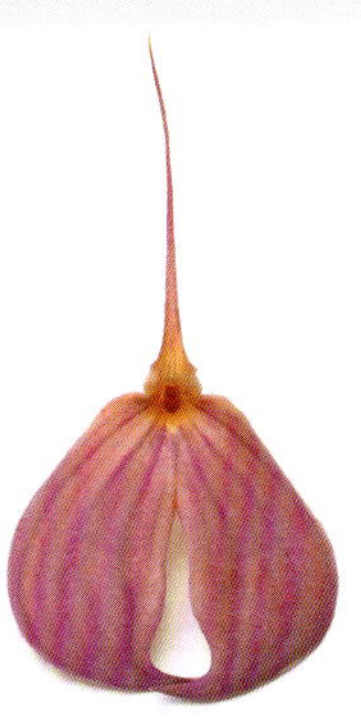

213. DRACULA ORCHID BLOOM
(*Masdevallia* sp.), Ecuador. A species of orchid that preserves remarkably well with my special recipe of chemical baths, silica, and heat. This specimen had been dry for about five years when I photographed it.

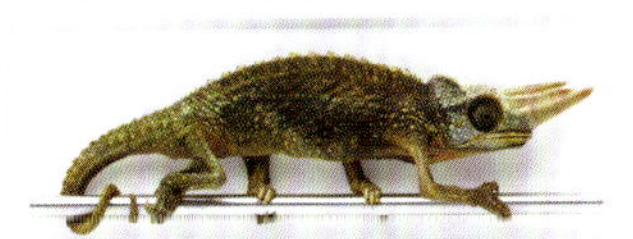

214. JACKSON'S CHAMELEON
(*Trioceros jacksonii*), Kenya.

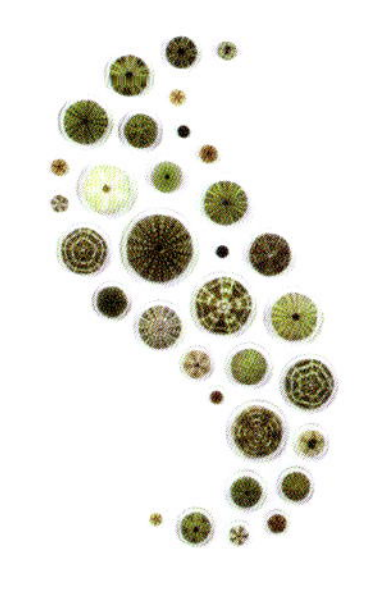

215. URCHIN SPHERES
(*Echinoidea* sp.), Thailand, Philippines, United States, Mexico. Composition size, 32 x 40 in.

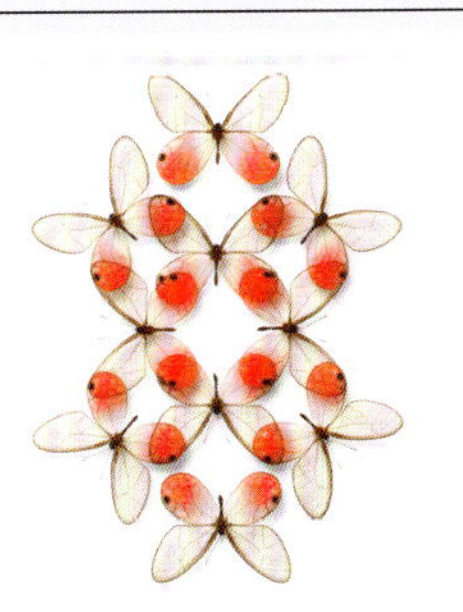

216. CYTHERAS
(*Cithaerias pyropina*), Peru. Composition size, 16 x 20 in. (also in 20 x 24).

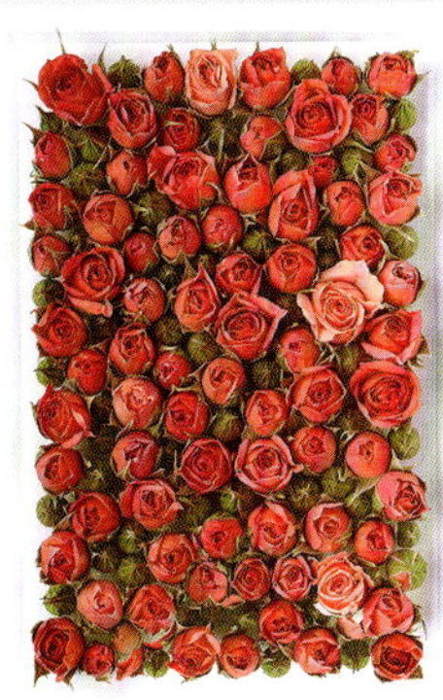

217. SPRAY ROSES
(*Rosa* spp.), Ecuador. It may seem that a piece comprised of preserved blooms from the most familiar flower on earth would be out of place in a book highlighting rare and exotic natural artifacts. And it is. But I find these tightly packed spray rosebuds timelessly enchanting nonetheless.

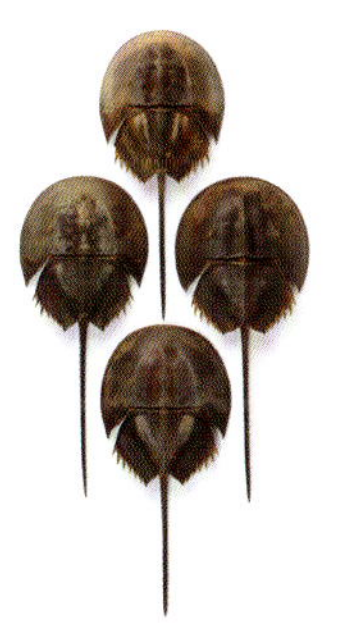

218. HORSESHOE CRAB FORMATION
(*Tachypleus tridentatus*), Philippines. Composition size, 24 x 30 in.

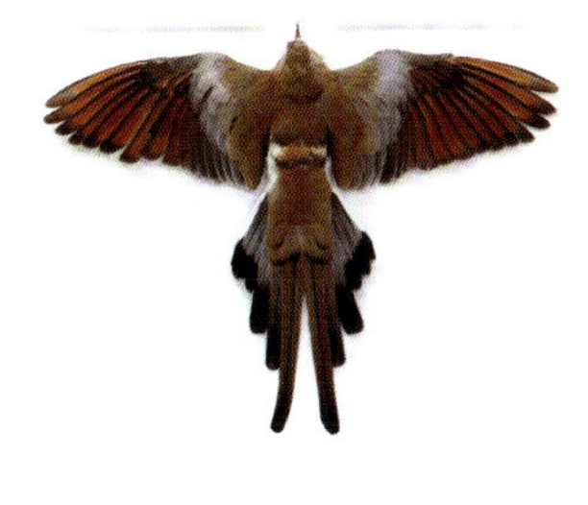

219. CAPE DOVE
(*Oena capensis capensis*), Egypt.

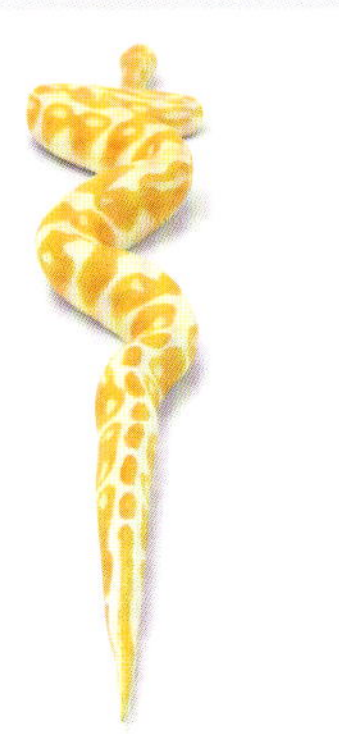

220. AMELANISTIC BURMESE PYTHON
(*Python bivittatus*), Vietnam. Burmese pythons have received a lot of bad press lately and will likely be completely outlawed in the United States by the time this book goes to print. This is unfortunate (and completely due to the irresponsibility of disillusioned pet owners in the South, where feral populations have become entrenched and invasive). However, they are still incredibly beautiful and one of the largest snakes in the world. Among captive-bred populations, amelanistic specimens are nearly as common as normal color forms. This is all due to a single specimen that was imported from Thailand in 1983 and successfully bred.

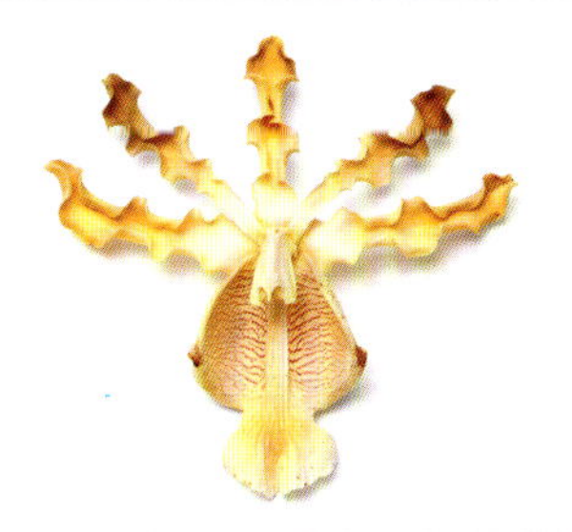

221. PRESERVED ANT-LOVING ORCHID
(*Myrmecophila christinae*), Venezuela. Another bloom that was photographed five years after it was preserved. It lightened a bit in color but, apart from that, has remained perfectly intact—this despite having sat around in my studio unprotected until now.

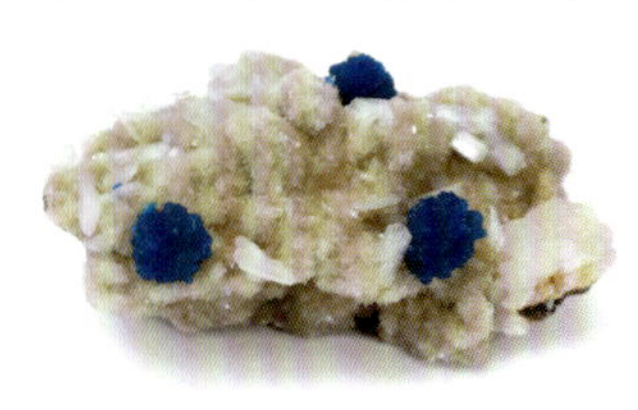

222. CAVANSITE AND STILBITE ON HEULANDITE
India. I've been very fortunate to work closely with what I would call the "royal family" of specimen miners in India. Their diligence, expertise, and knowledge of mineralogy is unparalleled. In a mutually beneficial arrangement, they follow road crews and major construction projects throughout their country, and when excavators stumble into a pocket of crystal, they rush in and remove it for them. They are responsible for salvaging some of the most spectacular specimens that have emerged over the past two decades.

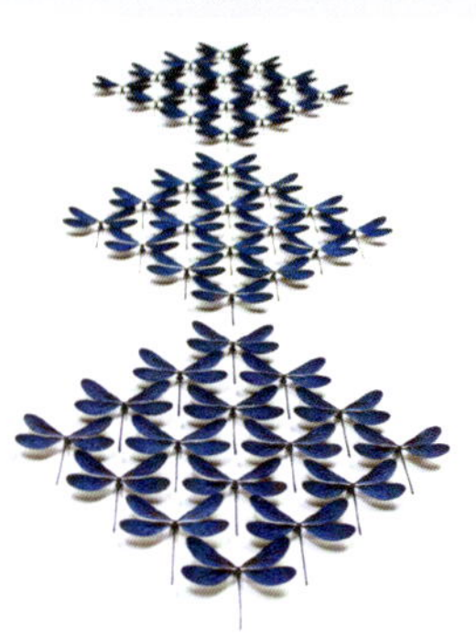

223. DAMSELFLY DIAMONDS
(*Euphaea laidlawi*), Philippines. Composition size, 30 x 40 in.

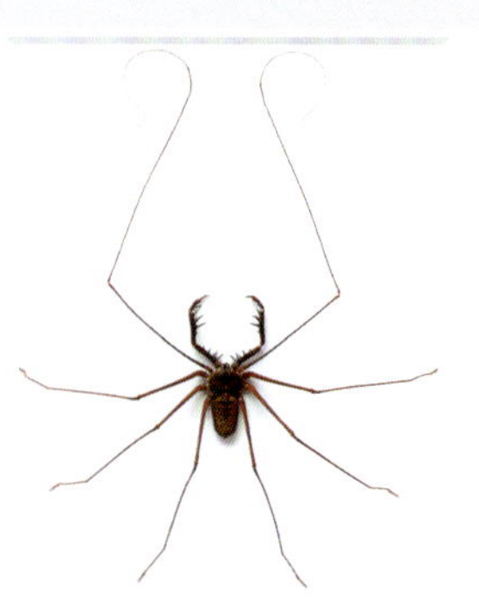

224. WHIP SCORPION
(*Phryna grossetaitai*), Peru. I'm a completely recovered bug-phobe, but this species still scares the crap out of me. Though entirely harmless, they are huge and fast and only dwell in dark, cramped places where you least want to be surprised by them. Though they've been offered to me by my catchers in Peru for years, I had no interest in working with them. Then I met the guy who won the first season of *Fear Factor* by eating one alive. I decided that anyone that (insert your own adjective here: courageous, off-kilter, insane) deserved to have a visceral souvenir of his televised trauma. After preparing the first specimen, I was pleasantly surprised to find that with strict symmetry and just the right amount of flourish, even a creature as terrifying as a whip scorpion can be imbued with a degree of sophistication, however minute.

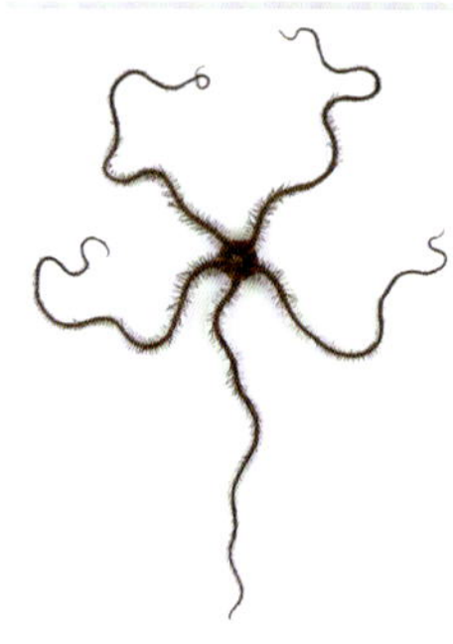

225. SERPENT STAR
(*Ophiomastix janualis*), Borneo. A very common species in the reefs near Kota Kinabalu in East Malaysia. Some nights, the sea is literally crawling with them at five to ten meters.

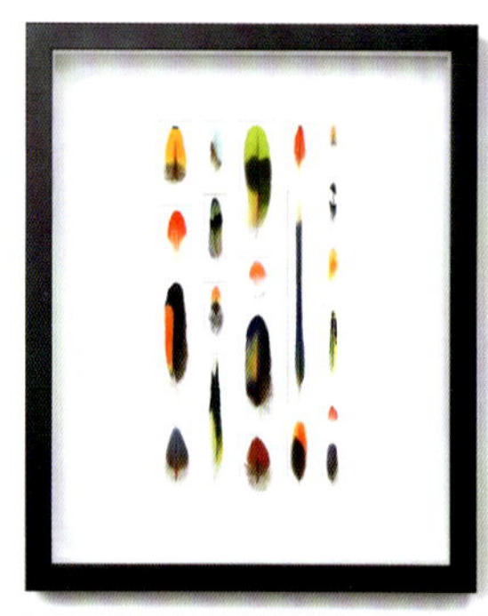

226. FEATHER MOSAIC
(worldwide species). My feather mosaics are available in several sizes. The feathers are all naturally shed and gathered from aviaries all over the United States. Composition size, 20 x 24 in.

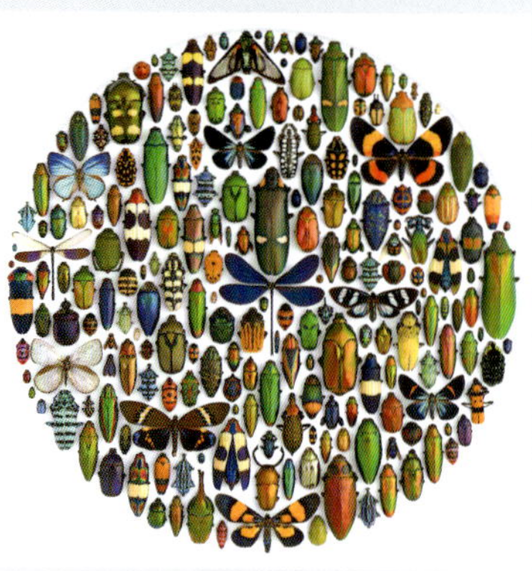

227. LIMITED AESTHETICA
(worldwide species). If I have a most-prized insect piece thus far, it is likely the Limited Aesthetica. Whereas my Coleoptera mosaics are comprised of the most colorful beetles and bugs in the world, Aesthetica takes the variety a step further by incorporating some of the most striking butterflies, bees, wasps, flies, day-flying moths, and even the world's only metallic mantis into one crisp design. Composition size, 24 x 30 in.

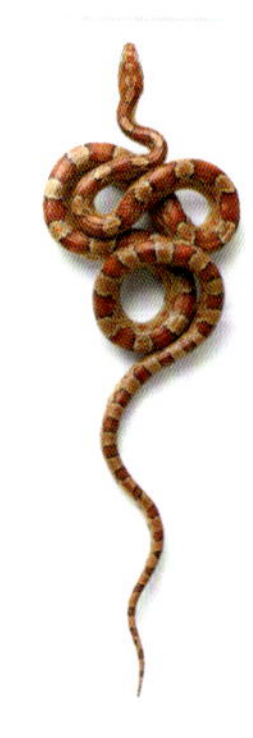

228. CORN SNAKE
(*Pantherophis guttatus*), United States. Even with more than fifty different engineered color morphs available, the original wild-type corn snake is still one of the most attractive.

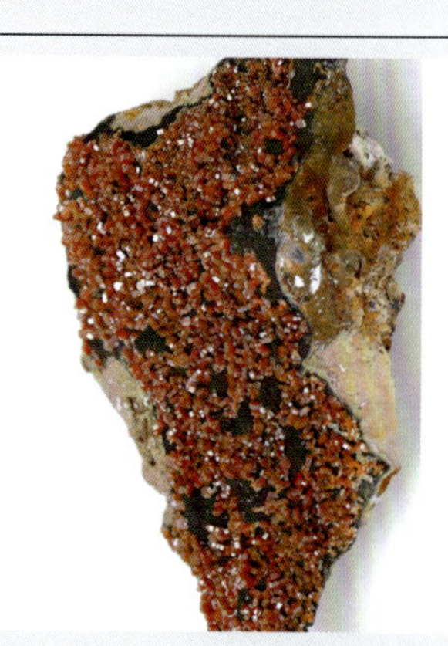

229. VANADINITE
Morocco. A moderately rare mineral, similar in nature to apatite.

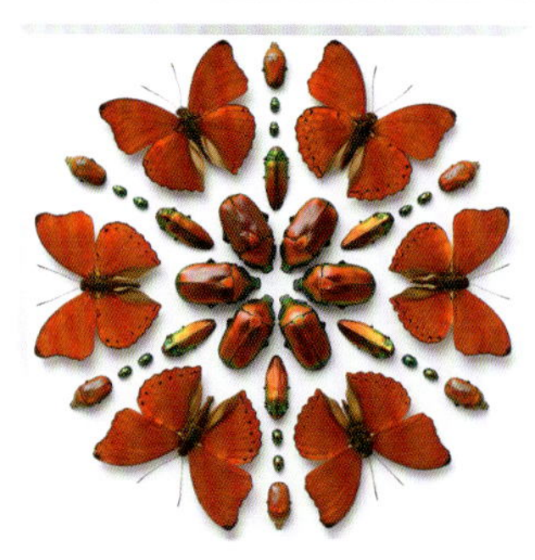

230. SANGARIS PRISM.
Center out: Flower Beetle (*Torynorrhina flammea*), Thailand; Jewel Beetle (*Belionota sumptuosa*), Indonesia; Red Glider (*Cymothoe sangaris*), Central African Republic; Leaf Beetle (*Chrysomelidae* sp.), Indonesia; Flower Beetle (*Dymusia variabilis*), Cameroon. Composition size, 16 x 20 in.

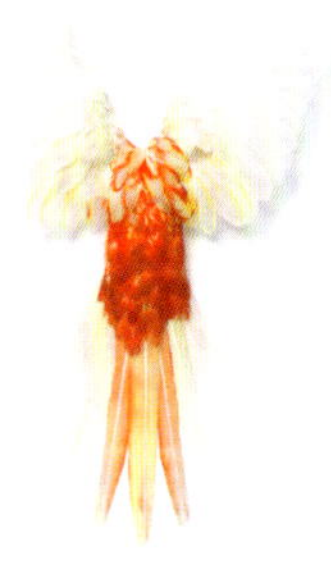

231.
RUBINO EASTERN ROSELLA
(*Platycercus eximius*), Australia.

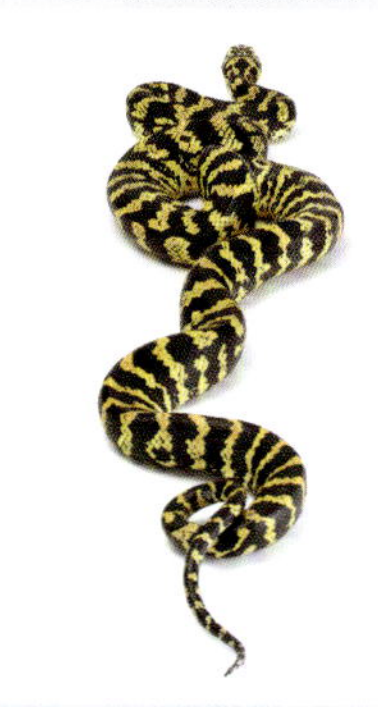

232. CARPET PYTHON
(*Morelia spilota cheynei*), Australia. A gorgeous, if somewhat cantankerous, species. As with other arboreal

pythons, its long teeth help it bite quickly through bird feathers and bat fur as it plucks its prey out of the sky.

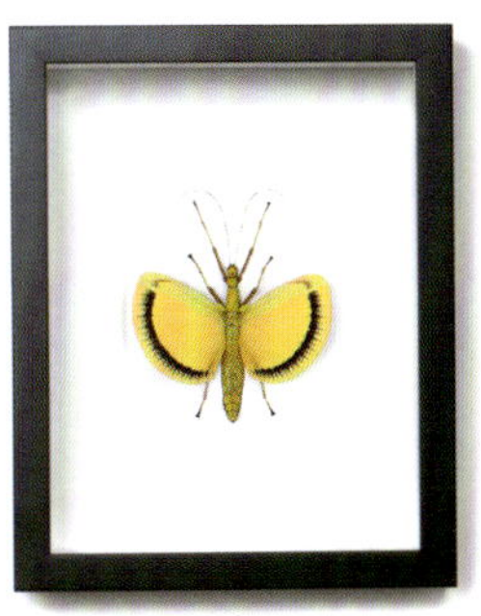

233. SULPHUR WALKING STICK
(*Tagesoidea nigrofasciata*), Malaysia.

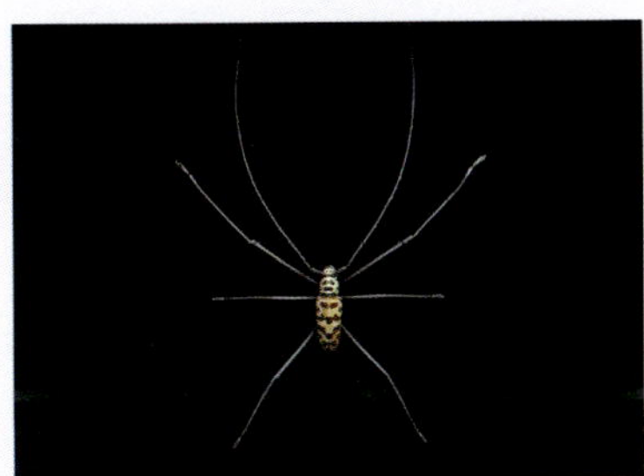

234. LONG-HORNED BORER
(*Gerania bosci*). An odd little long-horn beetle that is commonly seen flying around gardens and flowers on sunny mornings in Northern Thailand.

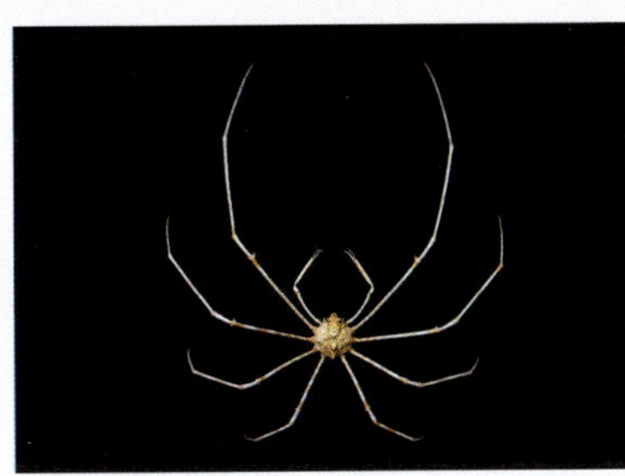

235. ATTENUATED SPIDER CRAB (*Phalangipus hystrix*), Philippines. A spectacular though delicate little scavenger that seems to have little in the way of preferences. It can be found at shallow or profound depths, in cold or warm waters throughout Asia. Though its body is only a little more than an inch wide, its leg span can reach more than one foot.

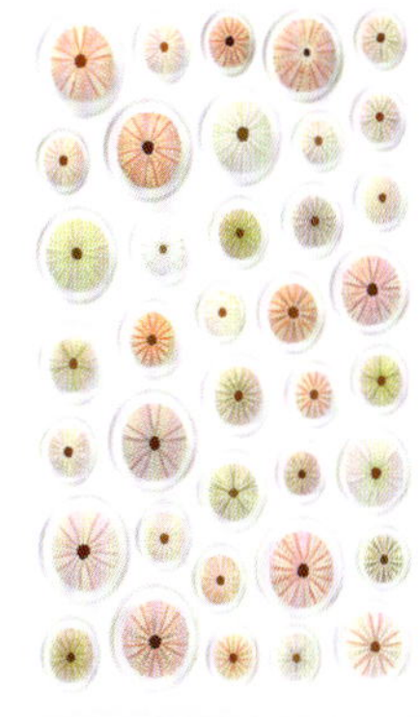

236. PASTEL URCHIN MOSAIC.
Burrowing Urchin (*Echinometra mathaei*), Philippines. Incredibly, this entire mosaic is comprised of the naturally colored test of only a single species. It is a designer's dream, common in seas from Africa to Hawaii, with a wide variety of sizes and pastel colors and a pleasing, simple shape.

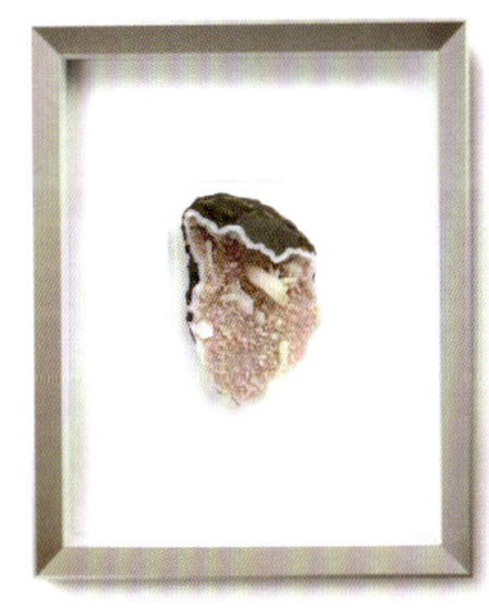

237. HEULANDITE AND STILBITE
India.

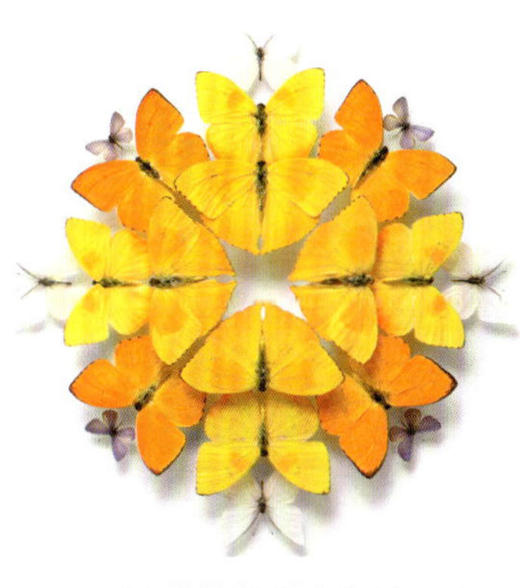

238. SOLAR PRISM.
Center out: Tailed Sulphur (*Phoebis rurina*), Peru; Apricot Sulphur (*Phoebis argante*), Peru; Orange Barred Sulphur (*Phoebis philea*), Peru; Common Albatross (*Appias albina*), Philippines; Spring Azure (*Celastrina ladon*), United States. Composition size, 24 x 24 in.

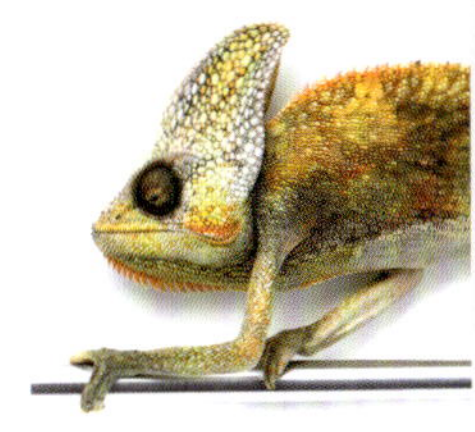

239. VEILED CHAMELEON
(*Chamaeleo calyptratus*), Madagascar. I have been amazed by the coloration of some chameleon species after they are preserved. Along with some pre- and post-treatments, their preparation involves freeze-drying them for about eight weeks. By the time I am finished, they are set to endure for life, but as colors can morph or fade with time in any substance, depending on the source and intensity of the light they are subject to, I can never guarantee unchanging color. With some of the chameleons, however, I've actually noted true morphing, almost as if the chromatophores are still active and metachrosis is actually taking place. This seems impossible, especially in an organism where such camouflage is instigated hormonally or neurologically, but I don't know how else to explain a complete change in color palette. Certainly a phenomenon worthy of further study.

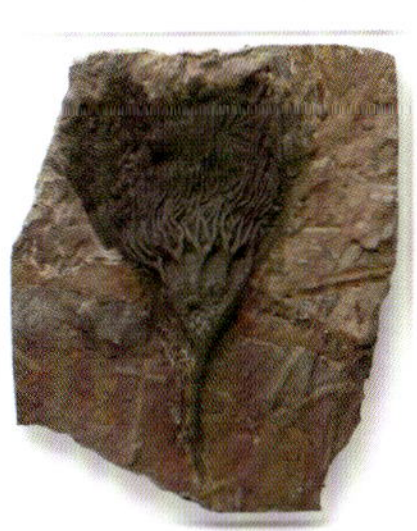

240. SILURIAN CRINOID FOSSIL
(*Scyphocrinites* sp.), Morocco. A now extinct marine mammal related to modern-day feather stars. This fossil is about 425 million years old.

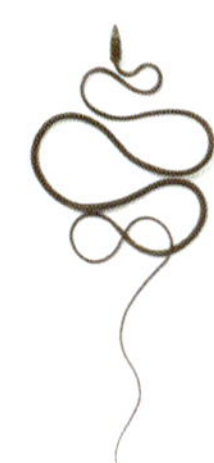

241. VINE SNAKE
(*Ahaetulla mycterizans*), Malaysia. A truly hypnotic snake. The vine snake is virtually weightless and can extend the majority of its body horizontally while gripping its perch with a strongly prehensile tail. Mildly venomous and feeding strictly on lizards and frogs, they're not well suited as pets, but few creatures are more fascinating to observe in the wild.

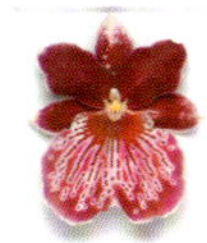
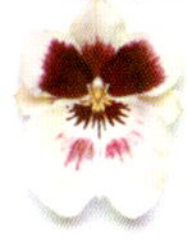
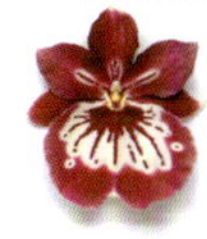

242.
PRESERVED PANSY ORCHIDS
(*Miltonia* sp.), Brazil. "Preserved" here is a bit redundant, since every organism in this book is preserved, but some of the pansy orchid blooms I've dried have resulted in such immaculate specimens that even I could not tell them from fresh blooms without handling them. They've also been quite durable, with some varieties remaining virtually unchanged for five years or more. Incredibly, many have retained their magnificent scent that long as well.

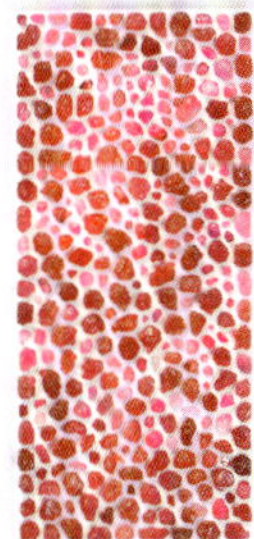

243. ROUGH RUBIES
Madagascar. The third-hardest mineral on earth and one of four gemstones considered to be precious, rubies are actually sapphires that happen to be red to pink. The deeper the red, the more precious the gemstone. These weigh 180 carats. Composition size, 16 x 20 in.

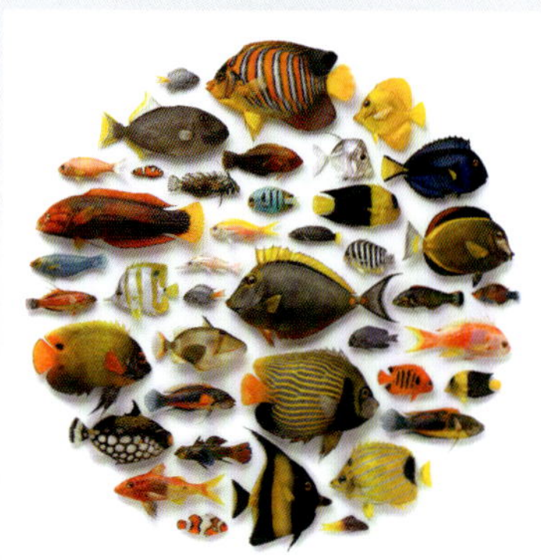

244. TROPICAL FISH MOSAIC (worldwide species). In my quest to reclaim and salvage every exotic organism I can, I've recently begun working with aquariums and other fish-centric facilities. When a specimen dies, it is frozen and shipped to me in Oregon, where my team and I get to work on the preservation process. The problem with preserving fish is that they almost invariably lose their color, and quite quickly. As a large mosaic of pallid, pasty organisms is not exactly what I'm shooting for, we've been experimenting with some unusual chemicals that show promise in being able to "set" the colors in tropical fish so that they will be relatively permanent. It is a work in progress but shows excellent signs of success. This piece is the inaugural composition created with the very first specimens I've successfully preserved. As is the case with most of my initial stabs, I may not be able to look at it by the time this book is in print, but for the time being, I'm quite proud of it. Composition size, 32 x 40 in.

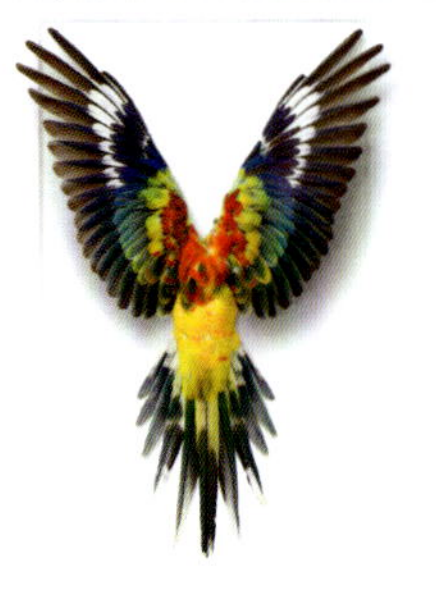

245. PIED RED-RUMPED PARROT (*Psephotus haematonotus*), Australia. Aside from a scarlet macaw, this is likely the most beautiful specimen I have ever had the privilege of working on. It came to me from a highly renowned facility in Southern California, and its loss must have been acutely felt. Because of their dozens of beautiful color mutations, red-rumped parrots have become a personal favorite.

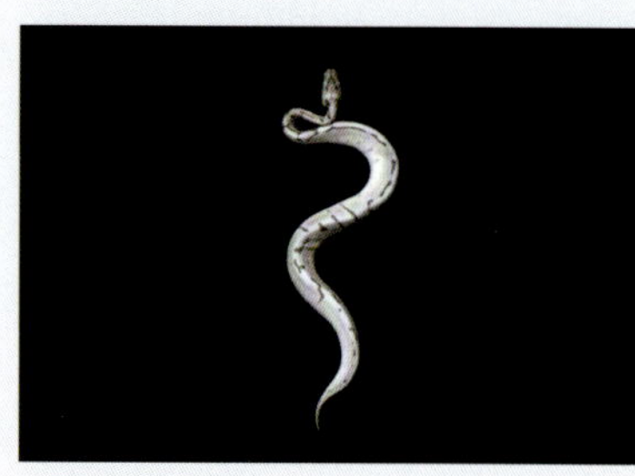

246. ROYAL PYTHON Color Mutation (*Python regius*), Ghana. An odd color morph—not exactly leucistic or albino. The closest standard color form is the fire bee.

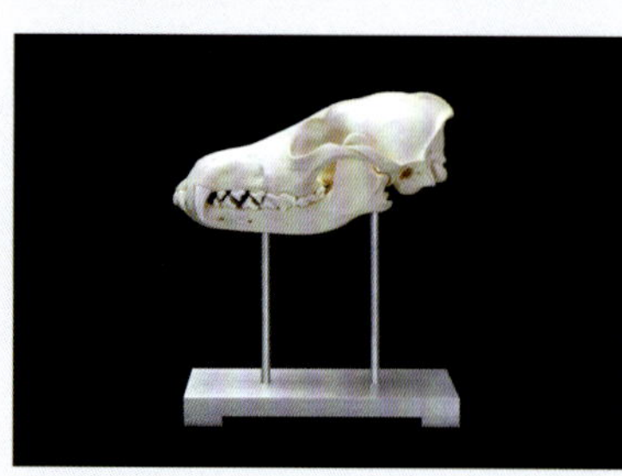

247. COYOTE (*Canis latrans*), United States. An incredibly adaptive canine with a massive range from Alaska to Panama, the coyote has actually increased in numbers with the encroachment of humans into its territory. Coyotes have shown a singular ability to adapt to changes in their environment and seem to be nearly as comfortable in urban settings as they are in the wild. They are the most prevalent predator of livestock in North America, and ranchers are constantly battling coyotes for the protection of their animals. The United States government kills about ninety thousand coyotes a year. Consequently, I have no shortage of reclamation opportunities.

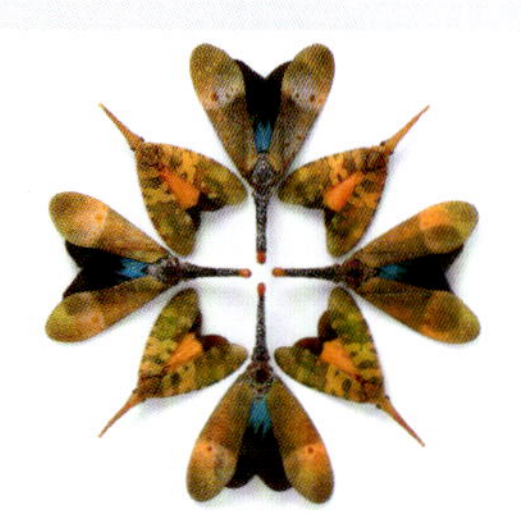

248. LANTERN FLY PRISM (*Pyrops* sp.), Indonesia and Thailand.

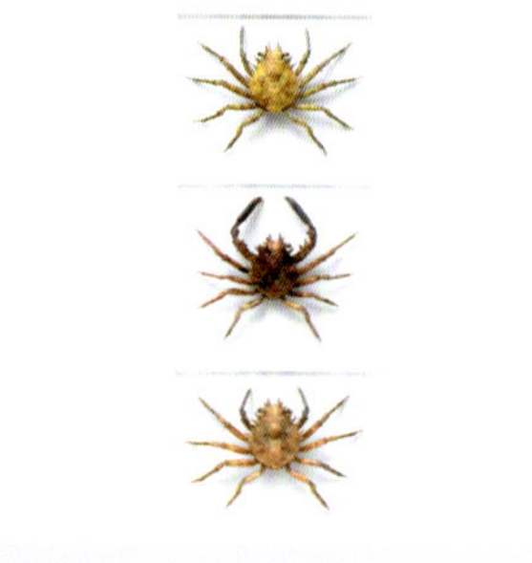

249. ARMORED CRAB COLOR FORMS (*Schizophrys aspera*), Philippines.

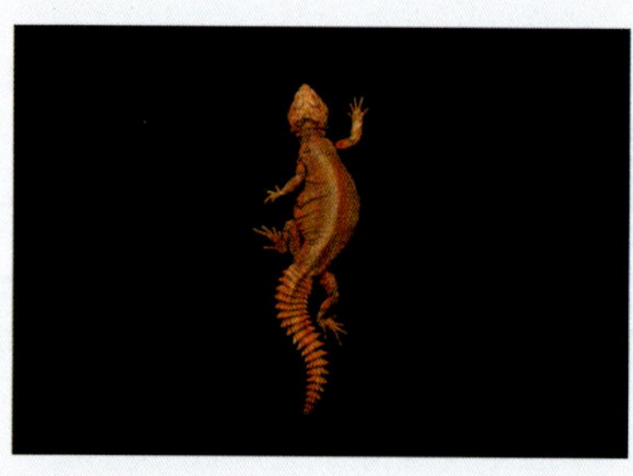

250. SAHARAN UROMASTYX (*Uromastyx geyri*), Algeria.

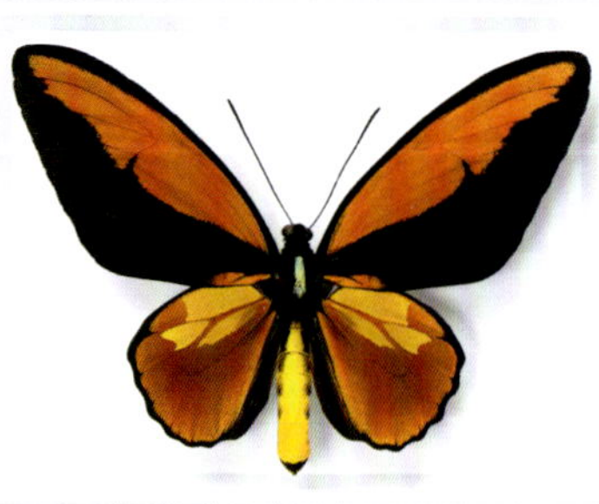

251. FIERY BIRDWING BUTTERFLY (*Ornithoptera croesus*), Papua New Guinea.

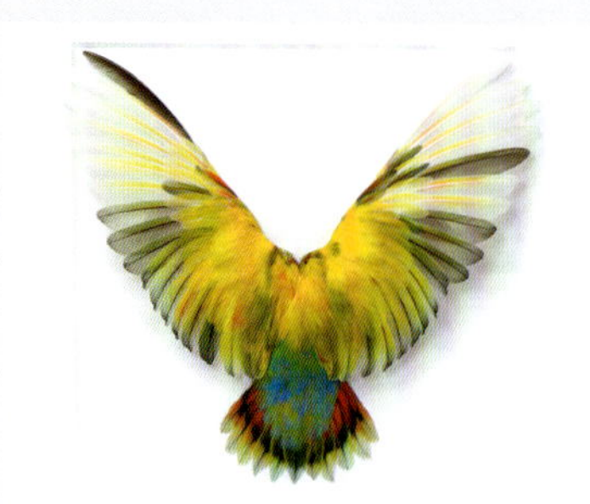

252. PIED AGAPORNIS PARROT (*Agapornis roseicollis*), Namibia. Known as lovebirds in the pet trade, Agapornis parrots are loud, social, chattering birds whose common name arose from the way they appear to snuggle together when sleeping.

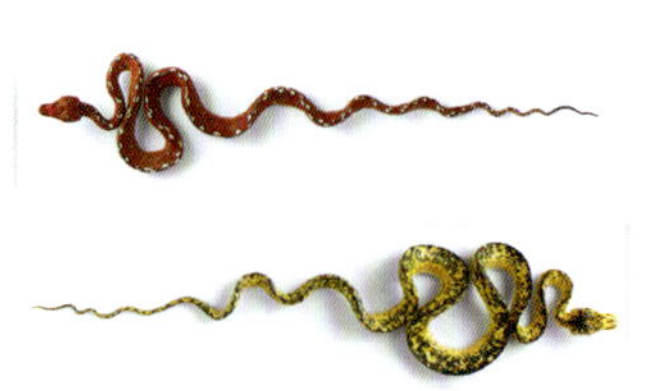

253. GREEN TREE PYTHON HATCHLINGS (*Morelia viridis*), Australia.

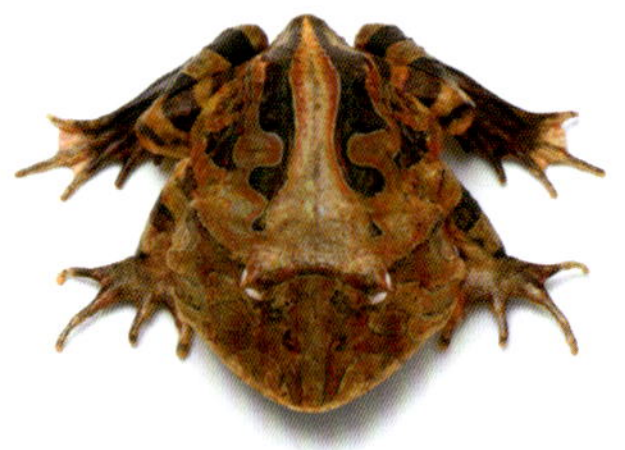

254. AMAZONIAN HORNED FROG (*Ceratophrys cornuta*), Suriname. This is one of my first attempts to reclaim an amphibian. I've been shocked to discover how common ranidaphobia (fear of frogs) is. I can't count the number of times I've been at a show with walls covered in monstrous beetles, headless birds, and deadly snakes only to have a timid soul approach me while furtively glancing over his shoulder, urgently whispering, "you don't have any frogs in here, do you?" It always struck me as most bizarre—why would anyone be afraid of a frog? Then I met the Amazonian horned frog and started to wonder if this is what has caused all the fuss. They're aggressive, omnivorous eaters that pounce on anything that will fit into their enormous mouths. Lizards, snakes, large insects, rodents—nothing is safe from the voracious horned frog. And though they are harmless to humans, perhaps just imagining being swallowed by a slippery amphibian without any teeth (to speak of) is enough to put some off frogs forever.

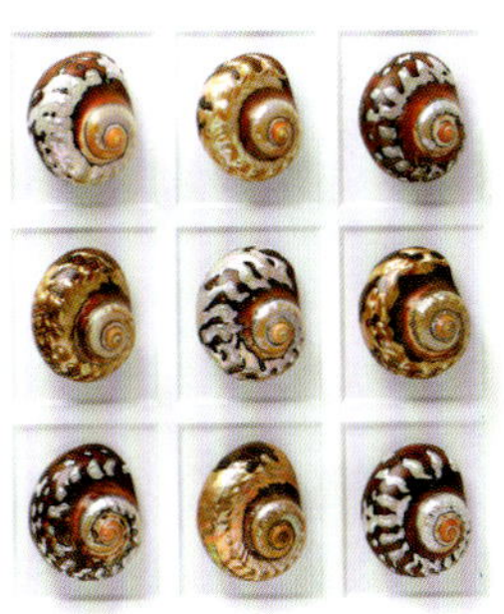

255. AFRICAN TURBOS
(*Turbo sarmaticus*), South Africa. One look at the genus of this behemoth snail will reveal a rare instance of taxonomic irony. I'm not sure how this one snuck past the governing board, but hats off to you, taxonomist with a sense of humor!

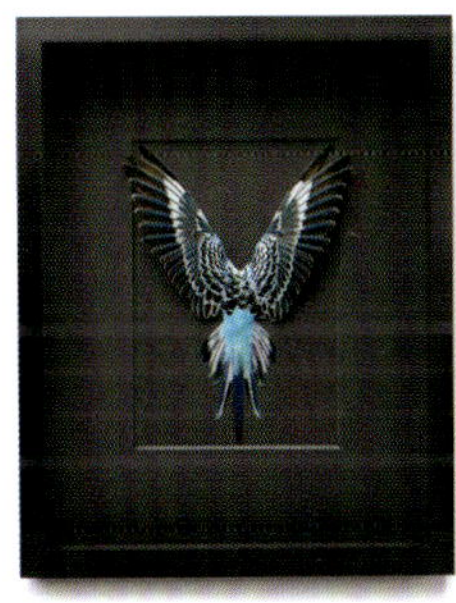

256. AUSTRALIAN BUDGERIGAR
(*Melopsittacus undulatus*), Australia. The budgerigar, or shell parakeet, is the most commonly kept pet in the world excepting dogs and cats. Though wild specimens that are not primarily lime green are quite rare, in captivity they have been selectively bred to exhibit shades of blue, yellow, green, gray, violet, and white in a nearly infinite combination of patterns. They are affectionate, intelligent birds and are able to mimic human speech with incredible accuracy.

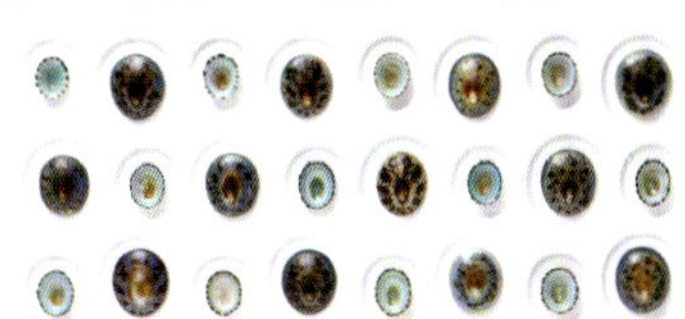

257. LIMPETS
(*Patellogastropoda* sp.), Pacific Ocean. Limpets are mobile, patelliform gastropods that are most known for their ability to cling with incredible strength to the hard intertidal surfaces where they feed. Using the suction of their powerful foot as well as adhesive mucus to virtually meld them to the surface of rock, they are nearly impossible to remove when clamped down.

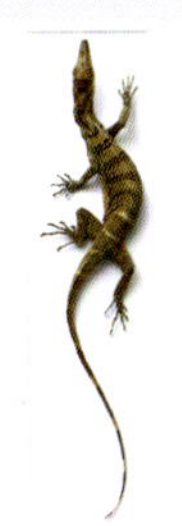

258.
BLACK ROUGHNECK MONITOR
(*Varanus rudicollis*), Myanmar. A personal favorite, black roughnecks are active, intelligent, strongly arboreal lizards that can reach five feet in length. The markings exhibited by juveniles like the one shown are less visible in the darker-colored adults.

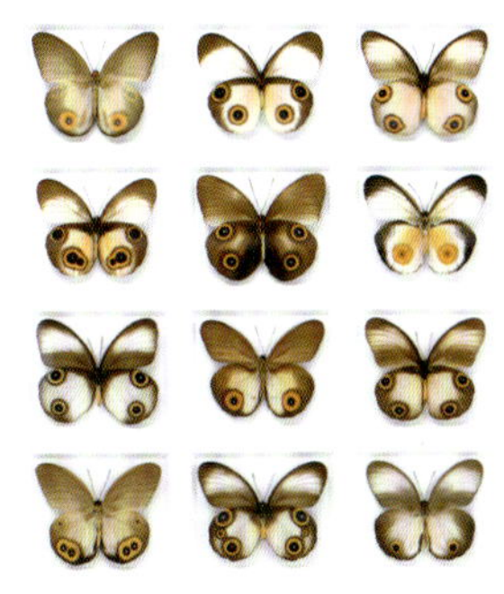

259. TAENARIS ANTHOLOGY
(*Taenaris* sp.), Indonesia, Papua New Guinea.

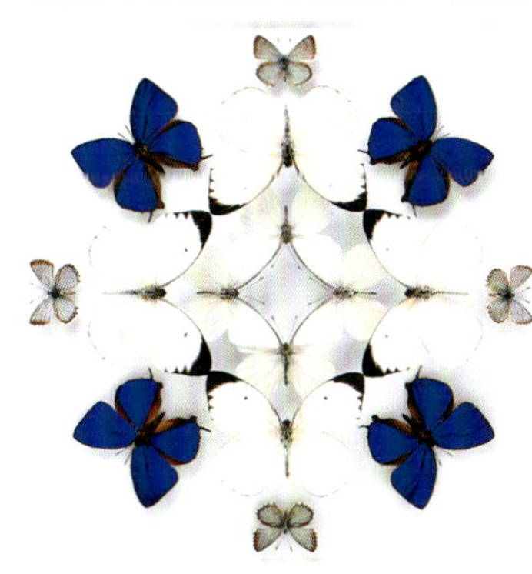

260. INFLORESCENCE,
Philippines, Peru, Indonesia, France.

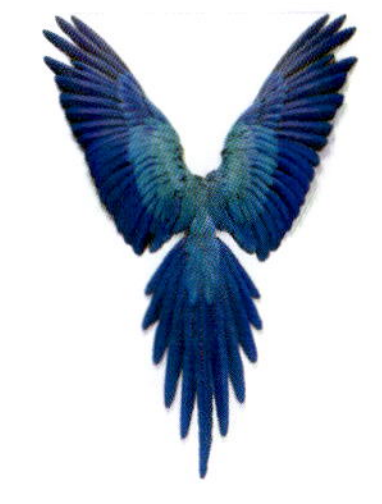

261. BLUE AND GOLD MACAW
(*Ara ararauna*), Bolivia. Blue and gold macaws are large, powerful, intelligent birds that are popular pets because of their tendency to bond strongly with their owners, sharing living spaces, meals, and many daily activities. They are incredibly long lived, so I am rarely presented with expired specimens with which to work.

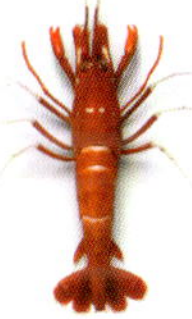

262. FIRE SHRIMP
(*Lysmata debelius*), Sri Lanka. A shy scavenger that is popular among saltwater aquarists for both its intense color and its habit of cleaning fellow tank mates of loose scales and parasites.

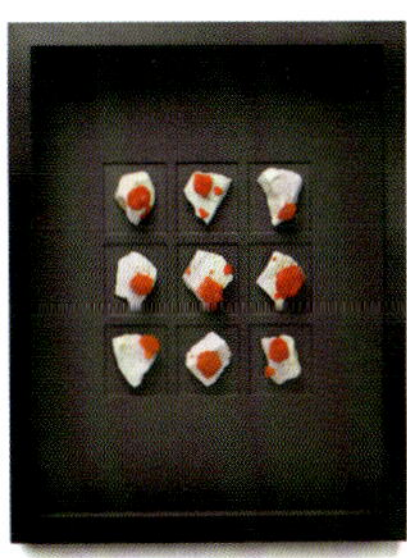

263. ACCELERATED SULFATE ON GRANITE
Czech Repulic. While every other specimen of animal, plant, and mineral in this book is completely natural, this calcite is "accelerated," or lab-grown, on granite by an associate of mine in the Czech Republic. Though I work exclusively with natural artifacts, I thought that the inclusion in this book of a single gorgeous artifact that did receive a bit of human assistance might be forgiven. Just this once.

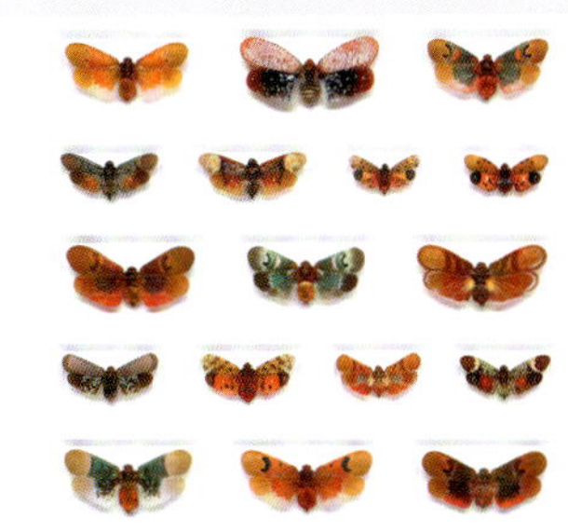

264. PLANTHOPPER MOSAIC
(*Scamandra* sp., *Aphaena* sp., *Kalidasa* sp., *Penthicodes* sp.), Malaysia, Indonesia, Thailand. People often ask me what these insects are and how the colors could be real. I can answer the first question thusly: They're actually true bugs of the order Hemiptera. Most people think that "bug" is just a colloquial term referring to all creepy crawlies, but it actually refers to insects that, among other things, do not have chewing mouthparts but instead a rigid proboscis with which they pierce the outer wall of plants (or, in some cases, other arthropods) and draw out fluids. As to their luscious coloration . . . well, you'd have to ask The Designer about that.

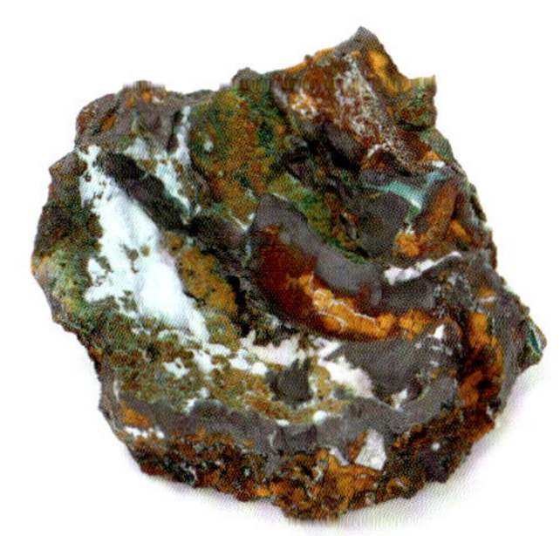

265. ROSASITE
Mexico.

INDEX

No artist, designer, photographer, or mortician does it on his own. I have been blessed to be surrounded by talented, devoted people who work tirelessly to help make what I do possible. Though by mentioning any by name I risk depriving other deserving souls of merited public thanks, this book could not have come to fruition without the following:

Dennon Ng has devoted more than a decade to running our studio in Kuala Lumpur with more efficiency and success than I would have thought possible. His preternatural steadfastness and fidelity are a constant inspiration to me. Our diligent KL team lead by Atlas, Nor, Diana, Low, and Zin Zin is nothing short of miraculous. Carrie Winkler is my stateside studio manager and personal assistant, without whom more things would fall apart than I can bear to think about. I am ever grateful for her long hours and prodigious natural gifts. The inestimable Seth Reed works closely with me in development and has been indispensable in cracking the code to some of our most puzzling processes. My talented and dedicated stateside team of artists, framers, and studio staff is incomparable. I am grateful to all of my associates out in the field—individuals as well as organizations. The hours they have spent researching, exploring, discovering, cataloging, raising, or otherwise caring for and studying an unimaginable host of organisms is what makes my joyful work possible. Thanks to Eric Himmel, Sebit Min, Anet Sirna-Bruder, and Michael Clark at Abrams. Melanie Tomanov and Susan Grode are world-class IP and copyright attorneys who have guided my various endeavors and have generously given of their time. I owe them both (again). The fetching Mrs. Marley almost singlehandedly runs our most important lab where she cultures the four most raucous and delightful organisms on earth. I will love her forever for it. And finally, to The Man to whom all of these masterful organisms and artifacts belong. I can't imagine how You designed it all, but I know it must have been a blast.

—Christopher Marley

All photographs by Christopher Marley, with the exception of those on pages 217 and 227, which are by Lynn Howlett

For more information on Christopher's three-dimensional work, please visit *www.pheromonedesign.com*

Designer: **Sebit Min**
Production Manager: **Anet Sirna-Bruder**

Library of Congress Control Number: 2014942732

ISBN: 978-1-4197-1561-7

Printed and bound in China
12 11 10 9

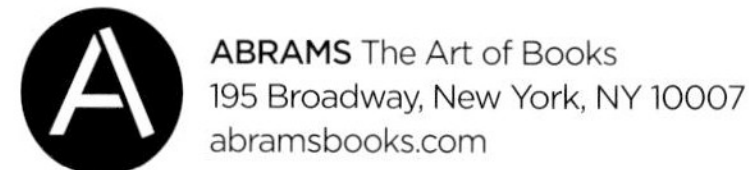

ABRAMS The Art of Books
195 Broadway, New York, NY 10007
abramsbooks.com